W9-CRL-856

Great Britain and
Ireland

Great Britain and Ireland

A Phaidon Cultural Guide

With over 500 color illustrations
and 12 pages of maps

PRENTICE-HALL, INC.
Englewood Cliffs
New Jersey 07632

Editor: Franz N. Mehling

Contributors: Mary L. James, Gernot Kachel, Maria Linhart, Dr Dieter Maier, Michael Raeburn, Gerhard Rebhan

Photographs: Gunda Amberg, Automobile Association (Basingstoke), British Tourist Board, Werner Grabinger, Ernst Höhne, Irish Tourist Board, Lore Nedoschil, Dr Herbert Neumaier, Northern Ireland Tourist Board (Belfast), Bernhard Rauscher, Susanne Ritter

Maps: Huber & Oberländer, Munich

Ground-plans: Herstellung + Grafik, Lidl

Library of Congress Cataloging in Publication Data

Knaurs Kulturführer in Farbe: Grossbritannien &
   Irland. English.
   Great Britain and Ireland, a Phaidon cultural guide.

   Translation of: Knaurs Kulturführer in Farbe:
Grossbritannien & Irland.

   Includes index.
   1. Great Britain — Description and travel —
1971 –   — Guide-books.   2. Ireland — Description
and travel — 1981–   —Guide-books.   I. James, Mary L.
II. Title.
DA650.K513   1985   914.1′04858   84-26618
ISBN 0-13-363755-7

This book is available at a special discount when ordered in bulk quantities. Contact Prentice-Hall, Inc., General Publishing Division, Special Sales, Englewood Cliffs, N.J. 07632.

This edition published in the United States and Canada 1985 by Prentice-Hall, Inc., Englewood Cliffs, New Jersey 07632

Originally published as *Knaurs Kulturführer in Farbe: Grossbritannien und Irland*
© Droemersche Verlagsanstalt Th. Knaur Nachf. Munich/Zurich 1983
Translation © Phaidon Press Limited, Oxford, 1985

ISBN 0-13-363755-7

Translated and edited by Babel Translations, London
Typeset by Electronic Village Limited, Richmond, Surrey
Printed in Spain by H. Fournier, S.A.–Vitoria

Cover illustration: Wells Cathedral, detail of inverted arches
(photo: Woodmansterne Limited, Watford)

Preface

This book is a guide to the most interesting places in Great Britain and Ireland, ranging from prehistoric remains (Stonehenge) via Roman constructions (Hadrian's Wall), magnificent Romanesque and Gothic churches and cathedrals (Durham, Salisbury, Canterbury), mighty and defiant castles, fortifications and palaces to romantic, intimate or imposing town and country houses. Also mentioned are the exhibits in museums, which include art and archaeological treasures not only from local areas but from all over the world.

As with the other guides in this series, the entries are arranged in alphabetical order for easy reference. There are over 500 illustrations in colour, showing excavation sites, churches, palaces, castles, museums and art treasures, and including ground-plans of many famous buildings.

The heading to each entry gives the town in bold type and, immediately below, the county and country and a reference to the map section (pp. 322–33), giving page number and grid reference. (Since each map covers two pages and the system of grid squares runs across both pages, only even-numbered page numbers are given.)

Within each entry the sights are identified in bold type and generally appear in the following order: sacred buildings, secular buildings, particularly significant objects of interest, theatres, museums, less significant objects of interest (under the heading **Also worth seeing**) and places of interest in the immediate vicinity (**Environs**). Larger cities are provided with a brief introductory text, which summarizes the city's cultural development and its importance. These introductions refer also to well-known people who were born in the city or who lived there.

At the end of the book there is an index of towns, castles, houses and churches included in the Environs sections.

The publishers would be grateful for notification of any errors or omissions.

Aberdeen
Grampian/Scotland   p.325□I 6

Herring, granite and oil provided the economic base on which Scotland's third largest city was built and they have also made the city a busy industrial area. The town, a Royal Burgh since 1179, was burned to the ground by the Edward III, the English king, in 1337. After reconstruction it emerged as two cities — *Old Aberdeen* at the mouth of the river Don, containing the episcopal residence, and *New Aberdeen*, at the mouth of the Dee around the docks. In 1498, New Aberdeen became the burgh of Barony, and it was not until 1891 that the two were re-united.

St.Machar's Cathedral: This cathedral was founded as far back as 1136, although the granite construction we see today was

Aberdeen, St.Machar's Cathedral

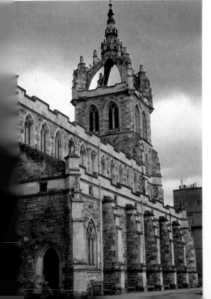

Aberdeen, King's College

Aberdeen, Provost Skene's House

to a large extent completed in the 15C under Bishop Leighton. Where variegated sandstone is visible, for example in a crossing pillar, in parts of the transept and by one of the windows in the S. aisle, there is evidence of the earlier construction. In 1540 the wooden ceiling, elaborately covered with the crests and emblems of European kings and bishops, was added. During the Reformation the cathedral's chancel was completely removed; additionally Cromwell ordered the destruction of the bishop's residence, which was built next to the church and out of whose stone he built a garrison. In 1688 the central tower along with part of the transept collapsed.

King's College: The college chapel, erected 1500–5, survived the Reformation and has remained more or less unchanged up to the present day. The *tower*, topped by an open crown, was built in 1525. It is the only medieval Scottish church still to have the original *choir screen*; oak *choir stalls* are by a Flemish artist. The *glass windows* are also most interesting.

The Church of St. Nicholas: Since the Reformation this 12C church has been divided into two. The crypt, which dates from around 1420, has original 15C woodcarving, in spite of having been used as a witches' prison in the 17C, and later as a plumber's workshop and a soup kitchen.

Provost Skene's House: Built *c.* 1545, this is a fine example of an old Town House. 1676–85 it was the residence of Mayor Sir George Skene. The House boasts painted ceilings and fine stucco work, and contains an exhibition of local history.

Museums: *Aberdeen Art Gallery and Museum*: A collection of local exhibits, a sculpture section and a painting gallery with pictures by Raeburn, Turner and Wilkie. *Anthropology Museum* (Marischal College): Egyptian and Chinese antiquities as well as exhibits relating to Scotland's history. Since their discovery in 1958 the silver Celtic treasures from the Shetland Isles have been housed here.

Also worth seeing: E. of the Town House stands the *City Cross*, erected in 1686. It was originally financed by 100 pounds taken out of the wine budget of the Merchants' Guild. The medieval *Brig o'Dee* is 394 ft. long, has seven arches and is decorated with coats-of-arms. The single-arched brick *Brig o'Balgownie* has a 62 ft. span over a ravine, and, dating back to 1320, is Scotland's oldest stone bridge. It was built by Bishop Cheyne.

Environs: Dyce(6 m. N.): The ruins of the Old Church are nowhere near as interesting as the two Symbol Stones in the churchyard, on which are carved Pictish symbols, such as a Celtic cross.

Abergavenny
Gwent/Wales   p.332☐H 14

St. Mary's Church: Today the parish church, it was founded in 1100 as a Benedictine monastery. However, the original church was frequently destroyed and rebuilt (in the 14&19C). Notable features include the 14C *choir stalls* with their fine misericords, and the carved oak Tree of Jesse (also 14C), and some old *tombs* in the Herbert and Lewis Chapels (13–17C, alabaster sculptures).

Castle: Hamelin de Ballon (the Norman

Abergavenny, St. Mary's Church

founder of the monastery) ordered the building of Abergavenny's first castle around 1100, since when it has undergone many alterations. Today it houses a small *local history museum*, with documents detailing the history of the town and surrounding area,

Environs: Bettws-Newydd (about 6 m. SE): The village church has a fine 15C carved choir screen. On the way out of the village is a 17C *house* set in a park.
Usk (12 m. SE): In this small town on the river of the same name is *St. Mary's Church*, which used to be part of a Benedictine monastery. It has a beautiful 15C choir-screen. The 12C Norman *castle* is privately owned and not open to the public.
Llanvaplay (about 5 m. E.): about 2 m. N. of the village, whose Rural Craft Mu-

seum has a fascinating collection of old farming and household implements, are the interesting ruins of *White Castle*. It was originally built by the Normans around 1100, like the neighbouring castles of Skenfrith (see Monmouth) and Grosmont, and its remains are most impressive. After crossing the moat, the visitor passes through a gatehouse into the Outer Bailey, which is surrounded by 13C walls. Through a further gatehouse is the Inner Bailey, with walls and towers dating back to the 12 or 13C. This is also moated and has a square keep against the curtain wall. This in turn was defended by the moat and outer hornwork.

Raglan (about 9 m. SE): Close by the village lie the imposing ruins of Raglan Castle, which is largely still intact. The shape we see today dates back to the period 1430–1610, and has, as well as the defensive buildings, a large amount of late Gothic ornament (coats-of-arms, gargoyles etc.). The hexagonal Norman keep, with its fine prospect, is known as the 'Yellow Tower of Gwent'; behind it is the main building, the Great Hall, with splendid

Aberystwyth, Castle

arched windows, and the gatehouse with well-preserved battlements. Under the late 15C lords the castle became a centre of Welsh poetry and song with regular meetings of bards ('bardic kings'). The *parish church* in Raglan, which dates back to Norman times, has a choir which has been displaced to the S. (as a symbol of Christ on the cross) and a 'poor wall' on the N. side (for the sick to lean against).

Aberystwyth
Dyfed/Wales   p.328 □ G 13

A well-known seaside resort situated at the mouths of the rivers Ystwyth (Aberystwyth is Welsh for 'mouth of Ystwyth') and Rheidol. With its population of around 13,000, it is the intellectual centre of mid-Wales. This characteristically Victorian town became, along with Cardiff and Bangor, one of the campuses of the *National University of Wales*, which was founded in 1872, and the site of the important *National Library of Wales*. This was founded in 1907 and is situated in Machynlleth St.; it contains over one million volumes, including valuable manuscripts and first editions of Old-Welsh documents (such as the 'Black Book of Carmarthen', the oldest Welsh manuscript, dating back to 1105, and the first printed Welsh language text, from 1546).

Castle: The castle was built in 1277, and often destroyed and rebuilt until its eventual total destruction in 1648. The remains of the concentric castle are on the S. shore, and the castle grounds are open to the public.

Also worth seeing: The *Ceredigion Museum*, in Vulcan St., is devoted to city and local history; as is the 'Aberystwyth Yesterday' exhibition in Upper Great Darkgate St.

It is also worth visiting the *Great Hall Gallery* in the University, which has exhibitions of paintings, prints and ceramics.

Environs: Aberaeron ('mouth of the Aeron', about 14 m. SW): Close to this small coastal town, in the tower of *Aberarth Church* (2 m. NE) stand three original Celtic gravestones from the 9 or 10C (Llandewi or St.David's Church). Other points of interest include the ruins of the 13C *Cadwgan Castle*.

Devil's Bridge (about 10 m. E.): This lies in the attractive countryside around the Mynach Gorge and the Rheidol Falls; it is the terminus of the narrow-gauge railway from Aberystwyth, opened in 1902. It consists of three bridges built one on top of the other, of which the oldest (Devil's Bridge) was built by monks from Strata Florida (q.v.) in the 12C. The bridge above it was built in 1753, and the top one, an iron bridge, in 1901.

Llanbadarn Fawr (1 m. E.): In the suburbs, which are older than the city, stands the Early English *St. Paternus,* an early-13C church and a memorial to the works of Bishop Paternus, a 6C saint. The S. transept has two Celtic crosses, from around 750; the larger is one of the most beautiful in Wales and is covered with decorative figures of men and birds. Nearby (about 2.5 m. SE) is *Nanteos,* an 18C house with fine furniture and paintings from the same period.

Llynwernog (about 11 m. E., near Ponterwyd): An interesting *mining museum,* well worth a visit.

Pen-Dinas (about 2 m. S.): On the hill lie the scant remains of a prehistoric *stone circle.*

Talybont (about 7 m. N.): Behind the village, and E. of Tre-Taliesin, is a hill with the remains of an old Celtic burial-mound. This is where Taliesin, the most famous Old Welsh bard (Wales's 'Homer'), is buried.

Ysbyty Cynfin (10 m. E.): The churchyard wall incorporates five Bronze Age *menhirs,* relics of an old pagan place of religion; two menhirs still function as the gateposts at the entrance to the graveyard. Nearby is the attractive *Parson's Bridge,* which spans a deep ravine.

Llanbadarn Fawr (Aberystwyth), St. Paternus

Abingdon, St.Helen's Church

Abingdon

Oxfordshire/England   p.332☐I 15

Formerly the county town of Berkshire, it owed its wealth to the wool trade. Many 15&16C buildings have survived.

Abbey: The once-mighty Benedictine abbey was founded in 675 and dissolved in 1538. Little is left of the huge complex. The oldest building is the square, stone *Checker House,* the 13C treasury and administrative centre of the abbey. It has a vaulted cellar and unusual gabled chimney-piece. The *Long Gallery* dates from around 1500, the *abbey gate* some 50 years earlier.

Church of St.Helen: The fine steeple of this late 13C church is visible from afar.

One surprising feature which is apparent on closer inspection is that the church is wider than it is long; the two aisles, which date from the 15&16C, are responsible for this. The oldest surviving part is the *Lady Chapel*, with its fine panelling, which was painted in 1390 and depicts the Tree of Jesse. There is also some noteworthy *wooden carving*, including the pulpit (1636) and the organ case (1725). Various *tombs* date back to the 15C; the *stained glass* was renewed in the 19C.

County Hall: This two-storey building, resting on powerful arcades, was built under the supervision of Sir Christopher Wren in 1677–82. Today, it houses the *town museum* and the *county archives*. Exhibits from the old Benedictine abbey, as well as weapons and uniforms from the 16C, can be viewed.

Environs: Dorchester-on-Thames, (8 m. E.): This site was originally a Roman camp, later a Saxon settlement and, in 634–705 the seat of the Bishop of Wessex. Its eventful history continued between 869 and 1072, when it was the seat of the Bishop of Mercia. Eventually in 1140, an Augustinian priory was founded. The older parts of the *Abbey Church of St.Peter and St.Paul* almost date back to this time. The W. part of the choir and the nave are from around 1180; the early Gothic aisle of the choir and the nave from 1280–1320. Especially interesting are the choir arcades. The Gothic E. end has three exceptional windows, beautifully decorated with tracery and carvings, and stained glass that dates back to the church's foundation. In the N. aisle is the famous Jesse window. A small, triangular window on the S. side depicts scenes from the life of St.Birinus, the apostle of Wessex. The leaden font from 1175 is decorated with the figures of the apostles. There are a number of other interesting sculptures, some of which date back to the 13C.

Adare
Limerick/Ireland   p.326☐B 13

This small Irish town just outside Limerick, called 'Ireland's most beautiful village'
by the Earl of Dunraven in the 19C, has
a number of interesting sights, such as the
ruins of *Desmond's Castle*, whose well-
preserved keep was built in the 13C by the
FitzGeralds. Nearby is *Adare Manor*, a
Tudor Revival mansion belonging to the
Earl of Dunraven, which contains some interesting paintings, including works by
Canaletto, Ruysdael and Reynolds. The
neighbouring *Franciscan Friary* was built
by the Earl of Kildare *c.* 1454 and restored
in 1875. The most interesting parts are the
cruciform ruins of the church with its fine
windows, the FitzGerald grave niches, the
high tower, the richly-ornamented cloisters
and other buildings (refectory and dormitory). In the N. of the castle is the small
Nicholas Chapel (13–16C). The 19C *Catholic parish church* was built on the site of
the ruins of the Trinitarian *White Abbey*
(built 1230–70). The *Protestant Church* was
built in 1807 on the site of the Augustinian *Black Abbey* of 1315 (extended in the
15C).
As Lutheran refugees from the Pfalz settled W. of Adare in the 18C the name Pfalz
is still associated with the area, which also
has some German surnames.

Environs: Garranboy Castle (*c.* 3 m.
SW): 15C cstle ruins with a fine keep.
Newcastle West (*c.* 12 m. SW): This
agricultural centre, with some 2,500 inhabitants, is the site of the ruined *Castle
Desmond*, a 15C building with two well-
preserved banqueting halls (Desmond's
Hall), which have been recently restored.
Rathkeale (7 m. SW): Near the village is
the recently-restored *Castle Matrix* (15C)
where, at the instigation of Sir Walter
Raleigh, Europe's first potatoes were
planted *c.* 1598.

Abingdon, St. Nicholas

Alfriston
East Sussex/England   p.332☐K 16

This small village is picturesquely situated
in the heart of the Sussex Downs on the
river Cuckmere.

St. Andrew's: A tiny church dwarfed by
its tall shingle tower, it dates from the 14C,
when it was built on the site of a Saxon
burial mound. The interior displays attractive contemporary furnishings.

Parsonage: This charming half-timbered
house dates back to the 14C and is one of
the few parsonages to have survived from
before the Reformation.

Star Inn: A half-timbered inn from the
13C, and probably Alfriston's most
remarkable building.

Also worth seeing: An excavated Saxon burial mound nearby.

Environs: Arlington (*c.* 1 m. NE): The small church of *St.Pancras* includes Saxon and Norman elements and fragments of old wall paintings.

Berwick (0.5 m. NE:) The church of *St. Michael and All Saints*, with its Saxon font, was originally constructed in the 12C; the wall paintings were painted in 1942 by Duncan Grant and Vanessa Bell (Virginia Woolf's sister).

Bishopstone (2 m. S.): *St.Andrew's church* has Saxon and Norman elements, including an original Saxon sundial on the S. tower. Inside there is a fine 12C coffin lid.

Charleston Manor (*c.* 1 m. SE): A country house recorded in the Domesday Book; 18C additions.

Wilmington (*c.* 2 m. NE): Former *Benedictine Abbey*; today a *museum of agricultural life*. Nearby is the *Wilmington Long Man*, a huge man carved in the chalk by unknown hands (it has probably undergone alteration).

Alnwick
Northumberland/England   p.324□I 9

Alnwick Castle: Since 1309 this has been the residence of the Dukes of Northumberland (a family who found immortality through Lord Henry Percy, Shakespeare's 'Hotspur of the North' in 'Henry IV'). The oldest parts of the heavily-fortified castle are the 12C walls, which were strengthened in the early 14C by the first Lord Percy at the same time as the towers were erected. Around 1400, the main outer gates surmounted by a huge gate tower were built; this gave access to the *Bailey* (the castle's outer courtyard). The inner castle is entered through a 14C gateway. In the 18C there was much restoration and in the 19C the interior was altered by Italian artists (in particular the state rooms). Features include 17C *French furniture*; a *weapon collection* (some fine medieval pieces); *porcelain collection*; *art gallery*, (with impressive works by Titian, Tintoretto, Canaletto, van Dyck and others); and an outstanding *library* (illumi-

Wilmington (Alfriston), Wilmington Long Man

nated prayerbooks, and many first or early editions). The *Postern Tower* (14C, E. of the keep) has an archaeological collection with pre-Roman and Roman exhibits. Gardens by Capability Brown.

Also worth seeing: *St.Michael's* (in the NW of the town): A parish church dating back to the 14–15C; *Hotspur Gate*, to the S., the last relic of the medieval walls, was built *c.* 1450; *Percy Tenantry Column* (also known as 'Farmer's Folly'), a memorial erected by the tenants of the then Duke of Northumberland in 1816; the *market place* has remained practically unchanged over the last 200 years; 18C *Town Hall* and 'Northumberland Hall' (1826, classical; now a municipal building).

Environs: Brinkburn Priory (*c.* 12 m. SW): Originally established by Augustinian monks, only the well-maintained 12C church is still standing.

Callaly Castle (*c.* 10 m. W.): A *manor house* dating back to the 15C; extended in the 17–18C.

Chillingham (*c.* 12 m. NW): This is the site of the original 14C family seat of the Grey family (the family of the famous statesman Earl Grey). A splendid park contains a free-range herd of wild cattle. The *village church* contains the beautifully decorated gravestone of Sir Ralph Grey, who died in 1443.

Craster (*c.* 6 m. NE): A village with an attractive harbour and a medieval *tower*; 1.5 m. along the coast is *Dunstanburgh Castle*, which occupies a commanding position on a cliff overlooking the sea; it was begun in 1313 by the Duke of Lancaster to protect the small harbour, and it was extended in the late 14C. The entry to the open bailey is through a huge gateway with a tower; the curtain wall is defended by towers.

Howick (about 4 m. NE up the coast): The *church* has a memorial to the second Earl Grey, who initiated the English Parliamentary reform of 1832; he lived in *Howick Hall*, which was built in 1782 and has a fine, extensive park.

Hulne Park (directly N. of the town; vehicles are not allowed, but permission to walk through the grounds is obtainable from the Estate Office at Alnwick Castle):

Alnwick, Alnwick Castle

At the entrance stands a 14C gatehouse, the only remains of Alnwick priory, founded in 1147. 1.5 m. further on are the 13C remains of *Hume Abbey,* the oldest Carmelite priory in England. There is a fine view from the Brizlee Tower (1781).

Old Bewick (about 10 m. NW): An Iron Age *hill-fort.*

Warkworth (about 6 m. SE, on the sea): *Warkworth Castle* is highly recommended: the seat of the Percy family since 1332 (Shakespeare mentions it in 'Henry IV'), the bulk of the castle is 13C; note especially the gatehouse, the Great Hall and the Lion Tower of 1480. A 14C sandstone *hermitage* (14C) which is accessible by boat from the castle. Also worth seeing are the *church* (12–14C, tower from about 1200) and the fortified bridge over the River Coquet (14C).

Alton
Hampshire/England　　　　　　p.332☐I 15

A small market town in E. Hampshire, lying on an old pilgrimage route. The poet Edmund Spenser lived in a house dating from 1590, near the market square.

St.Lawrence's: This church is 13–15C, with a Norman crossing and Saxon font. A 15C painting on one of the columns depicts Henry VI. In 1643 members of the Parliamentary party shot the south portal to pieces and killed a Royalist in the pulpit.

Curtis Museum: Exhibits of local historical significance, including crafts, furniture from old farmhouses, porcelain, ceramics, glassware and a doll collection.

Jane Austen's Home (Chawton): Jane Austen lived here in 1809 – 17, during which time she wrote 'Emma' and 'Persuasion'. Today the house is a *museum* dedicated to her.

Anglesey
Gwynedd/Wales　　　　　　p.328☐F 12

This quiet island of rich pastures fringed by coastal cliffs and sandy bays is separated from the mainland of the NW of Wales by the Menai Straits, which are some 14 miles long and no more than 2 miles wide. Referred to in ancient times as Mona (this is what Tacitus calls it), it was a stronghold of the Celtic druids and its numerous prehistoric burial-mounds (cromlechs) suggest how important it must have been to the Celts. It was conquered by the Roman commander Agricola in about AD 78. The medieval historian Giraldus Cambrensis called it 'Mona, mother of Wales' and praised it for its richness in grain. The name 'Anglesey' is of later origin, dating from Norman times.

Menai Bridge: This village is opposite the mainland town of Bangor, and takes its name from the bridge of the same name over the Menai Straits. The *Menai Suspension Bridge,* 1,060 ft. long, was erected in 1826 and widened in 1939. A mile to the W., the *Britannia Tubular Bridge*, which carries the railway, is 1,841 ft. long and was constructed in 1850 by the son of the railway pioneer, George Stephenson. In the village there is an interesting *Museum of Childhood* containing dolls, toys, etc.

Environs: A little over a mile to the W. is the village which boasts the world's longest place-name: 'Llanfairpwllgwyngyllgogerychwyrndrobwllllantysiliogogogoch', usually shortened to Llanfairpwllgwyngyll or even Llanfair PG.

The impressive megalithic burial mound at *Bryn-Celli-Ddu* dates from the 2–3C BC. Inside the huge hill four burial chambers have been found, marked by stone circles. Next to the village of *Bryn-Siencyn* (about 7 m. SW) lie the scant remains of the Celtic fort of Caer Leb (about AD 300, and the

Anglesey, megalithic burial site of Bryn-Celli-Ddu

Neolithic Bodowyr burial-chamber, with a capstone and three supports.

Beaumaris (about 2,000 inhabitants): This small bathing and sailing resort lies at the N. end of the Menai Straits. The Norman French name means 'beautiful marsh'. To the N. are the well-preserved remains of *Beaumaris Castle*, which was built by King Edward I in about 1295. The square castle is surrounded by a low octagonal wall with towers; the huge *gate-house*, with the state apartments, is particularly impressive. The Great Hall is on the upper floor of the N. gatehouse, and in the central tower is the attractive chapel. The moat is connected to the sea by a channel. Also worth seeing is the *parish church*, with its 14C nave and 16C sanctuary (traceried window, sedilia, choir stalls). The *County Hall* (Court House), which contains the old prison, dates back to 1614.

Environs: The interesting ruins of *Penmon Priory* lie 5 m. NE. The monastery was founded in the 6C; 13C sections such as the aisle, refectory, dormitory, calefactory and kitchen are still preserved. The nave of the *priory church* is 12C, as is the S. transept; the presbytery and sanctuary are 13C and the N. transept was added in the 19C.
Nearby are the remains of the 6&7C *St. Seiriol's Well*, an old *dovecote* from around 1600, and a fine 10C Celtic cross depicting the Temptation of St. Anthony.

Amlwch (about 2,900 inhabitants): A small harbour and resort in the N. of the island (about 18 m. NW of the Menai

Bridge), it has been known for its copper mines since Roman times.

Environs: In the nearby village of Llaneilian is an interesting 15C church with a remarkable rood screen and pews. The parish church at *Llanfechell* dates from the 12–14C and has a 12C Norman font, a gravestone from around 1300 in the gatehouse and a 16C tower.

Holyhead (Caer Gybi): This lively little town with an important ferry connection to Ireland (Dun Laoghaire) is the capital of Anglesey. It in fact stands on the small *Holy Island,* which is separated from the main island of Anglesey by a narrow channel which partially dries up at low tide. There are still remains of a small Roman fort (Caer Cybi), including part of the round towers. The cruciform Perpendicular parish church at *St.Cybi* is also worth seeing.

Environs: To the W. and S. of Holyhead are impressive prehistoric stone crosses and burial chambers.
Caer y Twr above Holyhead is an Iron-Age hill fort.
Around *Cytiaur Gwyddelod* to the W. are traces of a pre-Christian stone hut village. At *Penrhosfeilw* to the SW are two Bronze-Age standing stones.
By *Trefignath* to the S. are the remains of a Neolithic burial mound.

Aberffraw: Near this small coastal village in the W. of the island is the interesting prehistoric burial chamber of *Barclodiady-gawres.* Inside the mound, which is 100 ft. across, there was a passageway which led to the central chamber. Five of the megaliths which are still standing bear ritual linear markings.

Environs: The neighbouring village of *Llangadwaladr* (2 m. E.) has a remarkable early Perpendicular church with old windows and a 7C stone commemorating Cadfan, a prince.

Antonine Wall
Strathclyde-Central/Scotland   p.324□G 8

This defensive wall was erected by the Romans under Antonius Pius Caesar, and ran from Bridgeness in the Firth of Forth, just E. of Borrowstounness, over to Old Kilpatrick on the Clyde. The Antonine Wall was built as a result of the Roman Emperor's decision to abandon Hadrian's Wall, which had been built only ten years earlier, in favour of a more advanced line of defence, because the Romans had conquered S. Scotland in the meantime.
The earth wall, with ditches and forts two miles apart, was built by the 2nd, 6th and 20th legions under the command of Quintus Lollius Urbicus, the Roman Governor of Britain. On the N. side of the wall was a deep ditch, on the S. side a military causeway. By the end of the 2C, the wall had served its purpose and was abandoned. Inscriptions, carvings, distance markers and other markings are on display in the National Museum of Antiquities in Edinburgh and the Hunterian Museum in Glasgow.
The best-preserved sections of the Antonine Wall are in the area of Rough Castle around Bonnybridge and NW of Glasgow, close to Bearsden.

Antrim
Antrim/Northern Ireland   p.326□E 10

The capital of the county of the same name (with around 8,000 inhabitants) is situated on the NE of Lough Neagh, which at 17

Beaumaris (Anglesey), view t

by 11 miles is the largest lake in the British Isles. It is the site of one of the finest *round towers* in Ireland, which is 89 ft. high and has reliefs on the door and a conical roof (restored). The ruins of *Antrim Castle*, with their fortified *Gatehouse*, date from 1662. The castle was extended in 1816 and seriously damaged by fire in 1922. The beautiful 17C French gardens are also worth a visit.

Environs: Randalstown (about 3 m. NW): Outside the town are the ruins of *Shane's Castle*, which was restored by John Nash in 1812 only to be burnt down again in 1816.

Templepatrick (about 4 m. SE): *Castle Upton*, built in 1619, was the seat of the Upton family (the Viscounts of Templeton). In the garden of the now-ruined castle, which was altered by R.Adam in 1788, is the remarkable *Upton Mausoleum* of 1783. Some 2 m. NW is the prehistoric burial site at *Browndod; c.* 2 m. S. is *Lyles Hill*, where a number of prehistoric finds have been made.

Antrim, Sixmile Water

Aran Islands
Galway/Ireland   p.326☐B 12

The Atlantic Aran Islands, at the mouth of Galway Bay, have sparse vegetation but a dense population (*c.* 2,000), and a rich tradition of *pre-Christian* history and culture.

History: The islands played a significant role in early- and pre-Celtic (Bronze and Iron Age) times, as the surviving *ring forts* and *cliff forts* bear witness. The Celtic or Gaelic element has been preserved in unusually pure form. Many *monasteries* and *churches* were built after the introduction of Christianity in the 5C. After the Viking invasion the islands remained under the control of the Celtic O'Briens (11–16C) until annexed by England in 1587 for use as a military base.

Inishmore: This, the largest island, lies in the NW of the group and is 9 m. long and 1.5 m. wide. *Kilronan,* the harbour, on Killeany Bay in the NE, is the departure-point for Galway.

In the SE, by the village of Killeany, lie the remains of the small church of St. Benan (Temple Benan), an 11C building with a round tower, a 15C Franciscan monastery with a Celtic cross and the 16C Arkin Castle; there are also remains of the cliff-fortress of Doocaher (Dubh Cathair = 'Black Fort').

In the centre of the island (2.5 m. NW) is the famous stone-ring of *Dun Oghil.* This prehistoric fort has two concentric stone walls and stands in a remarkably good state of preservation on the highest point of the island.

Nearby *St. Kieran's Church* (13C) with some early Christian crosses and the small, simple 11C church of St. Sorney (Templesoorney).

Near the adjacent village of *Cowrath* there

is a graveyard with a small chapel and some early gravestones (12–15C).

Kilmurvy (*c.* 6 m. NW): The site of the remains of the pre-Romanesque 'Temple McDuagh', with choir and an E. window from the 15C and the remains of the Temple Naneeve and the Tober Mac-Donagh font with its Celtic cross.

Behind Kilmurvy, on a 300-ft. cliff on the S. coast, lie the imposing ruins of the prehistoric cliff-fort of *Dun Aengus.* The stone fort, which is one of the finest pre-Christian monuments in Europe, has a three semicircular limestone walls, facing the sea. In front of the middle wall a trench is defended by pointed stones.

Next to the nearby village of *Onaght* (to the NW) is a large and partially restored ringfort, Dun Onaght, with steps in the inside wall. A short distance away is a group of ruined monasteries — the 'Seven Churches'—which date back to the 13–15C.

Inishmaan ('Inish' is the Gaelic for 'island'): The smaller nearby island, just over a mile S., has a number of prehistoric remains, the most notable of which are the oval stone fort of *Dun Copor* with outworks, an outer and inner ward with the remains of some huts and a Bronze-Age burial chamber. Nearby is the ruined 15C church of *Templemurry.*

Inisheer: The smallest of the Aran Islands, it lies in the SE and has a prehistoric fortress (Creggankeel) with the 15C remains of *O'Brien Castle* in the inner circle. Also of interest are the 11C remains of the small Romanesque *Kilgobnet oratory.*

Arbroath
Tayside/Scotland   p.324□H 7

In 1320 the Declaration of Arbroath was signed in this small town on the E. coast. The Declaration was the Scottish response to a Papal Bull of Excommunication from Pope John XXII which, delivered at the instigation of King Edward III of England,

Arbroath, Abbey

Arbroath, Abbey, church vaulting

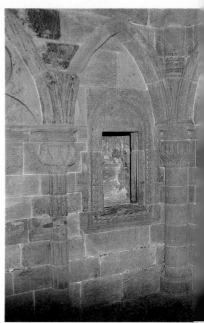

Sacristy

excommunicated Scotland. In the Declaration Scotland claimed independence and confirmed Robert the Bruce as King.

Abbey: The abbey was founded in 1178 by William the Lion in his role as Prior of the Cluniac House. In 1233 it became an abbey with the coming of the Tironensian monks from Kelso. During the Reformation the Abbey's possessions were seized, and it fell into a decline, eventually being used as a quarry. The ruins of the massive *W. Tower* remain, along with parts of the *S. aisle*. The *S. transept,* the *choir* and the *sacristy*.

The *Abbot's House,* which has a fine 13C kitchen, today houses a *Museum*.

The huge *rose-window* at the S. end of the transept was lit in the Middle Ages and used as a guiding light for ships.

Environs: Brechin (7 m. N.): *Round tower*, standing 87 ft and dating from the 10–11C, With the exception of a similar tower in Abernethy, it is the only example of an Irish tower in Scotland. A defensive tower and observation post, it was part of the church, following the Irish pattern.

Edzell(11 m. N.): One of Scotland's most beautiful *baroque gardens*, and a fine testimony to the Lindsays of Glenesk's love of horticulture. It was designed in 1602 and has many allegorical features after the French style. The oldest parts of the castle date back to 1500, and are built in red sandstone (with console decorations).

Montrose (6 m. N.): Each evening at 10 in the old church the huge *bell of St.Peter,* which was cast in Rotterdam in 1676, is still rung to signal the curfew. The *castle,* which goes back to the 10C, was King Ed-

Armagh, view of town

ward I's residence in 1296. One year later it was razed to the ground by Scottish nationalists under William Wallace.

Armagh
Armagh/N.Ireland   p.326□E 10

The capital of the county of the same name, the town has a total of around 12,000 inhabitants. It is the seat of both a Catholic and a Protestant archbishop, hence its importance as a religious centre.

History: Between 400 BC and AD 333, Armagh was the seat of the Celtic kings of Ulster. The old Gaelic place name 'Ard Macha' (which means 'Macha's Hill') refers to the legendary High Queen Macha.

The Celtic fort lay on the neighbouring hill of *Navan Fort* (a little over a mile W.), in Gaelic 'Eamhain Macha' or Emania.

This is the site of the remains of a huge *circular wall* with inner ditches and a mound.

The early Christian significance of Armagh stems from St.Patrick, who founded a church and monastery here in 445; this became an important *mission school*. Since then the town has been ravaged and plundered several times, and few buildings remain from the early period.

St.Patrick's Cathedral: The large building we see today was erected by L.Cottingham in 1834 and has few original medieval components. It does, however, stand on the site of the church founded by St.Patrick in 445. The 17&18C *tombs* inside are worth seeing, as is the slightly damaged *high cross*. On the outside of the transept there is a plaque dedicated to the Celtic king, Brian Boru, who died here in 1014.

Also worth seeing: The Catholic *St. Patrick's Cathedral* was built in neo-Gothic style in 1840 – 73, with magnificent Italianate decoration. The ruins of the *Franciscan monastery church* go back to 1264. The main street, the *Mall*, or boulevard, has some beautiful Georgian buildings from the 18&19C (the Royal School of 1774, the Court House of 1809, the Market House of 1742–1815). The *County Museum* in Mall Street has exhibitions of archaeology and local history.

Environs: Caledon (*c.* 9 m. W.): Next to the village is the beautiful 17C mansion, *Caledon House*, built in Georgian and Regency styles. Nearby are the remains of the 12C *Tynan Abbey* and the *high crosses of Tynan* (in a neighbouring village to the S.), which are 12C and ornamented with Biblical scenes.

Arran (I)
Strathclyde/Scotland   p.326□ F 9

In contrast to the rest of the Hebrides, Arran offers a wide range of scenery, with mountains up to 2,952 ft. high and scenery reminiscent of the Highlands.

Brodick Castle: The seat of the Dukes of Hamilton dating back to the 14C. It was extended by Oliver Cromwell in 1652, and further additions, including a tower, followed in 1844. The house contains an interesting collection of silver and porcelain, as well as numerous hunting trophies. The grounds include a garden laid out in 1710 in French style, and an English one (1923).

Also worth seeing: The S. half of the island has a large number of Neolithic sites. *Cairn Baan*, in the Kilmory area, is a remarkable passage tomb; to the W. is a burial chamber called *Torrylin Cairn*, also Neolithic in origin; when it was opened, eight skeletons, part of a clay pot and some

Arundel, Castle

flint tools were found. The *Standing Stones of Machrie Moor* are the remains of no less than five Bronze-Age stone circles, with menhirs up to 14 ft. 9 in. high. The *Stone Circle of Auchagallon* marks the spot of a Bronze-Age tomb, with 15 stones arranged in a circle.

Arundel
W.Sussex/England   p.332☐K 16

Arundel, a small town with attractive red brick houses, is picturesquely situated in the Arun valley.

Castle: Dominating the town, the castle lies in the middle of a large park, which also contains *Swanbourne Lake* and has been the property of the Dukes of Norfolk for the last 500 years. Work on it was begun under Edward the Confessor (1003–66), and the *keep* and *drawbridge* are from this time. In the 17C the castle was razed by Cromwell's troops. The present structure, often likened to Windsor Castle, is 19C in origin, although a considerable part of the interior dates back to the 15C. The art collection is of unusual interest, containing works by Gainsborough, van Dyck and Hans Holbein the younger.

St. Nicholas: This was built by Richard Fitzalan I in the 14C. The choir, known as the *Fitzalan Chapel,* has been in the possession of the family since 1880 and contains numerous *memorials* of the Fitzalans and Howards, who are better known as the Dukes of Norfolk. The old *altars* and the *E. window* are worth special attention.

Our Lady and St. Philip Neri: This church was built in 1863 in neo-Gothic style; it has a small tower and especially fine windows.

Environs: Amberley (5 m. NE.): An old village with thatched houses. At the end of the main street is the 12&13C *Church of St. Michael,* with a Norman font and choir vaulting. The S. aisle and tower are in the Early English style and the S. porch is late Gothic. The 17C *castle* of the Bishop of Chichester is unfortunately in ruins.

Bignor(7 m. N.): The *Roman villa* is worth seeing, especially for its impressive mosaics and the *museum,* with many archaeological finds on display.
Harrow Hill (just over 2 m. NW): This is the site of a Neolithic *flint-mine.*
Parham (6 m. NE): The Elizabethan *manor house*, set in a beautiful park, dates from 1577 and contains an impressive art collection. *St. Peter's Chapel*, restored in Gothic style in the 19C, has a 14C font.

Ashbourne
Derbyshire/England   p.328☐I 13

This old market town is known for its traditional football match, held every Shrove

Arundel, castle, keep

Tuesday, when all the inhabitants turn the entire town into a football pitch and play, without fixed rules, with the goals about 3 miles apart.

St.Oswald's: Built in the 13&14C in the Gothic style on the site of an earlier Saxon/Norman church; it has a cruciform plan and a 230 ft. high 14C tower over the crossing. Note the 13C font, the early stained-glass windows and the tomb of Penelope Boothby (a masterpiece by the sculptor Thomas Banks).

Also worth seeing: The *main street*, with its row of old houses, and the *Grammar School* (parts of the building are Tudor).

Environs: Cromford (*c.* 10 m. NE): The 15C *Cromford Bridge* spans the River Derwent; it has round arches on one side and pointed ones on the other. S. of the bridge are the remains of an old *fisherman's shrine*, with the inscription 'piscatoribus sacrum'. Also of interest is *Cromford Old Mill*, where, in 1771, Richard Arkwright (see

Preston) first used water to power a cotton-mill.
Fenny Bentley (*c.* 2.5 m. N.): The site of the Gothic church of *St.Edmund*, whose interior is notable for its early 16C choir screen.
Ilam (about 4 m. NW): The graveyard contains two fine Saxon *stone crosses*; in the church is a tomb by Sir Francis Chantrey.
Tissington (about 5 m. NW): Noteworthy for a Romanesque church porch and for *Tissington Hall* (1609), which is Jacobean.
Wirksworth (*c.* 8 m. NE): *St. Mary's church* has a 13C tower; the interior contains an interesting sculpted Saxon sarcophagus with New Testament scenes and a Romanesque font.

Ashford
Kent/England   p.332 □ L 15

With the introduction of the railway this small village became an important junction

Ashbourne, St. Oswald, tomb of Sir John Cokayne

and developed into a flourishing town, which is best known today for its cattle-market today.

Environs: Charing (5 m. NW): A typical small Kentish town with attractive houses and the remains of a 14C archbishop's *palace*.

Godinton Park (1.5 m. W.): This *gabled house* has impressive furnishings, a porcelain collection and 18&19C gardens.

Mersham (about 5 m. SE): The church of *St. John the Baptist* is Norman with fine windows (some of which are 14C) and the 18C tomb of Sir Wyndham Knatchbull by William Tyler.

Yardhurst (3 m. SW): Has a 15C *house*, which has been recently restored.

Ashby de la Zouch
Leicestershire/England   p.328☐ 13

St. Helen's: Built in the 15C, and extended at the end of the 19C. Of interest inside are the tombs (especially that of the second Earl of Huntingdon, who died in 1561, with two recumbent alabaster figures, and the tomb of the ninth Earl, which was designed by William Kent and decorated by Joseph Pickford and Michel Rysbrack) and an altar panel dating from 1679.

Also worth seeing: The ruins of the *castle* dating from the reign of Edward IV (1461–83) and in which Mary Queen of Scots lived for a time. The town itself has a row of Tudor half-timbered houses (15&16C).

Environs: Appleby Magna (about 5 m. SW): The church of *St. Michael* is 14C and has splendid Gothic windows; inside are remains of the original stained glass. It was restored in the 19C, when the stucco ceiling, pews and gallery were added.

Breedon-on-the-Hill (about 6 m. N.): The church of *St. Mary and St. Hardulph* was built on the site of a Saxon monastery of 885 (later destroyed by the Danes); the

Ashbourne, St. Oswald, tomb of Penelope Boothby

Athy, White Castle

present church is mainly Romanesque, with a few additions. In the S. aisle there are fragments of the original pre-Romanesque church.

Castle Donington (about 9 m. NE): *Donington Park Racing Car Museum*, has racing cars dating back to 1911.

Donington-le-Heath (about 5 m. E.): A restored 13C *manor house*, with some exquisite old furniture.

Kegworth (about 10 m. NE): The church of *St. Anthony*, early 14C, has some fine pieces of medieval stained glass.

Measham (about 3 m. SW): The *Midland Motor Museum* has an interesting exhibition of the history of the motor car.

Moat House (about 5 m. SW): The remains of a fortified 14C *manor house*. Only a wall and a well remain from the original structure; 15C stone gatehouse.

Staunton Harold (about 4 m. NE): The church, which dates from 1563, is one of the few to have been built during the Protectorate of Oliver Cromwell; interior furnishings have survived from that time almost unaltered. Staunton Hall, an 18C Georgian manor house—Palladian façade —is also worth a visit.

Askeaton

Limerick/Ireland   p.330□B 13

The remains of *Desmond Castle* lie on an island in the river Deel. The fine *Banqueting Hall* (the Great Hall), dating from 1550 and with tracery around the windows; and the *castle tower*, complete with windows and fireplace, have survived. This was the seat of the famous Earls of Desmond, the FitzGeralds. There are also remains of the

Avebury, avenue of standing stones

church which was part of a *Franciscan monastery* built by the Desmonds around 1420; it has a fine arcade, which survives along with some carved windows and *cloisters* with a statue of St. Francis.

Environs: Ballylongford (about 23 m. W.): The ruins of *Carrigafoyle Castle*, built by the O'Connors of Kerry around 1350, include a tower which has a fine view over the Shannon estuary.
Glin (about 15 m. W.): Near the coastal village on the estuary of the river Shannon lie the ruins of *Glin Castle*. It was built around 1300 by the FitzGeralds, the Knights of Glin, and rebuilt in 1800 in neo-Gothic style.
Scattery Island (an island in the Shannon opposite Ballylongford): Interesting remains of six churches from the 12–15C. There are also of some fragments of

Romanesque sculpture and Ireland's tallest *Round Tower*, about 118 ft. high. In the 6C the Celtic saint Senan founded a monastery here.

Athy
Kildare/Ireland   p.326☐D 12

This small country town of around 4,000 inhabitants is the site of the ruins of *White Castle*, by the bridge over the Barrow. Built by the Earl of Kildare in 1575, it was destroyed in 1649. Also of interest are the *Law Courts* and the *Market House*, both of which are Georgian and date from around 1800. The modern *Dominican church* (1965) with beautiful windows and a fine Stations of the Cross, is a good example of contemporary religious architecture.

Environs: Woodstock Castle (*c.* 1 m. N.): Remains of a 15C castle (destroyed in 1649).

Avebury
Wiltshire/England   p.332□I 15

Nowhere else in England can so many varied and impressive examples of prehistoric remains be seen in such a small area. The traces which archaeologists have revealed around the village date back to the 4th millennium BC.

Stone Circle: This circle of standing stones which dates back at least 4,000 years, is very much more significant than its better-known counterpart at Stonehenge. It has a circumference of about a mile, and was surrounded by an earth wall 16 ft 6 in. high and a ditch 33 ft. deep. The huge stone circle within this enclosure consisted of over 700 giant uncut stones: once there were also two smaller circles in the centre, made of smaller stones. At least 200 pairs of monoliths flank the two mile ritual route to what is known as the *sanctuary*. Lava stones have been found from this smaller circle and they have been shown to have come from the Eifel.

Silbury Hill: 131 ft. high and at least 590 ft. across, this artificial earth mound, also called 'the largest pyramid in Europe', is unique in terms of European prehistoric remains. It seems certain that the hill was built simultaneously on three levels at around 3,000 BC. The purpose of the hill, which must have had some 700 men working on it for at least 10 years, is still unknown.

West Kennet Barrow: Very close to the mysterious Silbury Hill lies the largest and most beautiful Neolithic burial chamber in the whole of England. The barrow,

Avebury, Silbury Hill

some 360 ft. long and built of limestone, is surrounded by a ditch, which contained pottery dating from between 3,000 and 1,600 BC (now housed in the museum at Devizes, see below).

Windmill Hill: This hill, NW of Avebury, is one of the oldest known Neolithic sites. Since pottery from all over the SW has been found here, it seems reasonable to assume that it was some sort of religious centre, probably used for sacrifices. As the remains go back to about 3,100 BC, the hill has given its name to the first agricultural society—the Windmill Hill Culture.

Alexander Keiller Museum: Named after its founder, it opened in 1938 and displays the most interesting finds from Avebury and Windmill Hill. It is here that

all the important discoveries about Avebury's local remains are documented.

Environs: Devizes (9 m. SW.): The *Museum of the Wiltshire Archaeological and Natural History Society* contains many significant finds from the Neolithic, Bronze and Iron Ages and Roman times, offering a fascinating picture of life in the W. of England in early times. The *Wiltshire Regimental Museum* displays the history of the county regiment since 1756.

Aylesbury
Buckinghamshire/England   p.332☐K 14

The county town of Buckinghamshire, it has developed into a busy industrial area. However, the old centre, around what used to be the market square, is still well preserved. The statue of John Hampden in the market place stands as a memorial to the fact that in 1635 he refused to pay a tax imposed by Charles I.

St.Mary's: A cruciform church with 13C origins and 15C additions. Unfortunately, Sir Gilbert Scott's restoration of 1860 was so extensive that little of the old work remains. Some of the Victorian *stained-glass windows* are interesting, as is late-12C *font*, finely decorated with tendril patterns.

County Museum: The county museum occupies the old elementary school, a 15C building rebuilt in 1730. Exhibits cover local archaeology and natural history and include a *Rural Life Gallery*.

Environs: Boarstall Tower (about 15 m.

W.): Only a 14C moated *gatehouse*, rebuilt in the 16&/17C, survives from what used to be a manor house.

Claydon House (12 m. NW): The seat of the Verney family dates back to the 16C and was enlarged by the second Earl Verney in the middle of the 18C. Under the supervision of Sir Thomas Robinson the reception rooms were decorated in rococo style, and the neo-Gothic rooms on the first floor were added; work which took over 30 years. The stucco and panelling were finished with painstaking care and the Earl's passion for China can be seen in his own China Room. The present S. front is 19C.

Long Crendon (about 8 m. SW): A half-timbered 14C *courthouse*.

Thame (10 m. SW): The cruciform church of *St. Mary the Virgin* is early Gothic and has a particularly impressive tower over the crossing. The windows, rood screen and portals are a mixture of high and early Gothic, and the font is late Norman. There are many interesting tombs, especially that of Lord Williams of Thame (1559), opposite the altar.

Waddesdon Manor (5 m. W.): This *manor house* was built 1880–9 in the style of the French Renaissance by Baron Ferdinand de Rothschild. It contains valuable 18C furniture and Gobelin tapestries, Sèvres porcelain and paintings including works by Rubens, Reynolds and Gainsborough; there is also a fine collection of weapons.

B

Ballina
Mayo/Ireland   p.326☐B 10

This small fishing village with a population of *c.* 6,000 lies at the mouth of the river Moy in Killala Bay. In the graveyard next to the Catholic church are the remains of an *Augustinian monastery* dating from 1427 and including a W. portal decorated with figures. To the S. a *burial chamber* from pre-

Bellavary (Ballina), Ballylahan Castle

historic times has three supporting stones and a cap stone.

Environs: Bellavary (*c.* 17 m. S.): To the N. of the village lie the ruins of *Strade Friary*, an old Dominican monastery from the 13C; magnificently decorated tombs in the chancel. Further N. are the remains of Ballyahan Castle (13C), while to the W. is the well-preserved *Turlough Round Tower*, near to which is a 13–14C Gothic church (restored). Beautiful *Meelick Round Tower* lies *c.* 2 m. E. of Bellavary; old Irish gravestone.
 Errew Abbey: On the W. bank of Lough Conn, in the shadow of the Nephin hill (a conical hill 2,648 ft. high), there is a *ruined monastery* which dates back to 1413 with a 13C church. Nearby a small square oratory known as Temple-nagal-liagh-doo ('church of the black nuns'), is all that remains of a 6C nunnery.
Killala (*c.* 8 m. N.): The *parish church* (restored) dates back to 1670 and includes a Gothic S. portal. Nearby a *round tower* from the 12C and some 82 ft. high has been restored. St.Patrick founded a *monastery* here for Bishop Muiredagh in the 5C.
Moyne Friary (*c.* 7.5 m. N.): This well-preserved Franciscan friary dates back to 1460. There is a fine monastery church

with a square central tower, an interesting cloister (Cloister Garth) and remains of other monastery buildings.

Rathfran Friary (c. 10.5 m. N.): Towards Rathlackan lie the remains of a *Dominican friary* (1294), with church and cloisters. To the N. there are the remains of a megalithic burial chamber, some *stone circles* and a celebrated 5C *Ogham stone*.

Rosserk Abbey (c. 3 m. N.): The remains of this *Franciscan abbey*, dating back to 1441, have been well preserved. Of especial interest are the *church*, with its fine portal and windows, the cloister and the high round tower.

Ballinasloe
Galway/Ireland   p.326□ C 12

A rural town with some 5,000 inhabitants, Ballinasloe lies on the *Grand Canal* which crosses Ireland from E. to W. It has attractive 18&19C town houses. In October of each year there is a horse and cattle market and a folk festival.

Environs: Clonfert (c. 9 m. SE): Here, in 560, St.Brendan the famous Irish navigator founded a monastery, of which nothing remains. Clonfert, the name of the village, is also a reference to St.Brendan's tomb (Clonfert means burial meadow). St.Brendan claimed he was the first to cross the Atlantic and look for the 'promised land of the saints'. Some of *St.Brendan's Cathedral* (12–15C) has survived, including the 13C chancel and the 15C bell tower. The *W. portal*, one of the finest examples of Irish Romanesque, has arches on columns and a triangular gable covered with relief carving, (triangular subdivisions and faces). The Gothic *E. window* is also of interest, as are the *chancel arches*, *font* and gravestones.

Clontuskert Abbey (c. 3 m. S.): The ruins of this *Augustinian friary* date back

to the 12&13C; there is a fine 15C *W. portal.*

Eyrecourt (c. 12.5 m. S.): There is a 17C *castle* in the village. Nearby there are the remains of the Franciscan *Meelick Friary*, which lies on the river Shannon. The monastery church with its gateway is still intact.

Kilconnell Friary (c. 8 m. W.): One of Ireland's best-preserved *Franciscan monasteries*. It was built in 1353 on the site of a church founded by St.Connal in the 6C (Kilconnal means 'church of St. Connal'). The ruins of the church are impressive and include a fine *tower, portal* and rich decoration around the windows (15C); *tomb niches* in the church's N. wall are also worth seeing. There are also remains of other monastic buildings including the cloister.

Banbury
Oxfordshire/England   p.332□ I 14

This old town, which grew up around the wool industry, saw heavy fighting in the Civil War, as a result of which the castle was finally destroyed in 1648. Some houses still standing date from the 16–17C. Puritans destroyed *Banbury Cross* in 1602, but it was replaced in neo-Gothic style in 1858. The large *parish church* was built by the Cockerell brothers 1790–1822, the previous one having been blown up by the people of the town.

Environs: Bloxham (c. 4 m. S.): The *Church of Our Lady* has a 14C tower decorated with smaller turrets and an octagonal spire. It was restored in 1866 by George Edmund Street. The E. window is by Morris and Edward Burne-Jones.

Broughton Castle (2.5 m. SW): Originally a 13C castle, it was extended by the Elizabethans. The building, which is the seat of the Lords Saye and Sele, assumed its present form 1554–99. On display in the house is a china collection.

Clonfert (Ballinasloe), St.Brendan's Cathedral

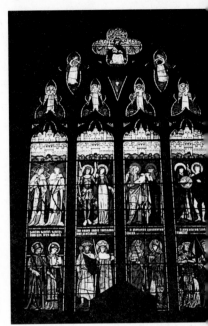

△ *Bloxham (Banbury) E. window*

Canons Ashby (*c.* 19 m. NE): The 13C church exterior is very beautiful. There are remains of a 13C monastery chapel. The fine *manor house* dates from the 16–18C, and was the family seat of the poet John Dryden. Earlier, the poet Edmund Spenser was a frequent guest in the house, whose gardens are also very fine.

Sulgrave Manor (12.5 m. NE): This manor first appears in the Domesday Book of 1086, when it belonged to a Northampton priory. In 1539 Henry VIII sold it to Lawrence Washington who, in 1560, built the house we see today. Partly renovated and restored 1920–30, it now serves as the Washington Museum. The house's coat-of-arms was the model for the American flag.

Wroxton Abbey (*c.* 3 m. W.): For centuries this Jacobean house was the seat of the North family. It was built in 1618 by Wil-

liam Pope on a site where there are remains of a 13C Augustinian priory.

Banff
Grampian/Scotland   p.324□H 6

This harbour at the mouth of the Deveron has been a Royal Burgh since 1372, but this former privileged position is reflected in only a handful of 17C houses. The Biggar Fountain in Low Street occupies the site of the gallows on which James Macpherson was hung.

Duff House: In 1730 William Adam started work on a baroque castle (modelled on the Villa Borghese in Rome) for the Whig MP William Duff. However, the three-storey construction, with central projection, pediment, Corinthian pilasters and an Attic storey, was never completed. After 13 years of building, the costs became too high for the owner, and two wing pavilions, which were to have been attached to the main building by curved colonnades, remained unbuilt.

Environs: Craigston Castle (5 m. SE): Built 1604–7, it is the seat of the Urquhart family. The two wings containing the living quarters have an E-shaped plan and are joined under the base of the gable by arches and a balcony. There are consoles for corner towers, but not the corner towers themselves. Inside the house there is some fine woodcarving on the walls and ceilings. **Turriff** (7.5 m. S.): Apart from the *church* with its 16C chancel, the most interesting building in the area is *Delgatie Castle*. This five-storey tower house is largely 15C, but has 12C elements. The seat of the Hay clan, it contains interesting paintings and weapons. The wooden ceilings of 1590 are especially lavish.

Bangor
Gwynedd/Wales   p.328□ G 12

This bustling little town of *c.* 17,000 inhabitants, is situated on the NE of the Menai Straits between North Wales and the island of Anglesey and it has become a favourite holiday spot. Like Cardiff and Aberystwyth it has one of the campuses of the National University of Wales, which was founded in 1872. The present buildings date back to 1911; there are *c.* 3,000 students.

Cathedral: Dedicated to Bishop Deiniol (*c.* 546), it occupies the site of a former monastery, which dates from 525 and of which no trace remains. It was 1120 before a cathedral was first built here. Razed by fire and rebuilt several times, it now

manifests different styles. The last rebuilding occurred in 1870. N. and S. external walls are 14C in origin, as are the portals; the W. tower is 16C. The sanctuary has a walled-up Norman window. Behind the S. portal there is a 15C *font*; the S. transept houses two remarkable *crucifixes* (14–15C). The large Perpendicular window in the sanctuary (E. and S. wall) dates from 1500. A small *museum* in the N. aisle contains a carved oak figure of Christ, 14C floor tiles, misericords and other carved figures which are 16C.

Museum of Welsh Antiquities: Welsh furniture (17–19C) and costumes, as well as documents relating to local history; there are also finds from prehistoric, Celtic and Roman times.

Also worth seeing: *Garth Pier* (the departure point for steamships to the Isle of Man and Puffin Island) extends about 1600 ft. into the sea and affords a fine view. It has to withstand powerful tides of up to 20 ft.

Environs: Bethesda (*c.* 5 m. SE): Above this slate-mining town with a biblical name (it was previously called Glanogwen) lies the *Ogwen Valley*. Llyn-Ogwen, a lake some 12.5 m. SE into which the River Ogwen drains in numerous waterfalls, is surrounded from N. and S. by imposing mountains over 3,000 ft. high. The highest peak, Carnedd Llywelyn, is *c.* 3,480 ft. high, only *c.* 70 ft. lower than Snowdon, which lies *c.* 6 m SW.
Menai Bridge (*c.* 2 m. SW): The Menai Suspension Bridge links the Welsh mainland with Anglesey. When it was built in 1826 it was the longest suspension bridge in Britain. It was restored and considerably widened in 1939. Trains cross on the nearby *Britannia Tubular Bridge*, built in 1850 by Robert Stephenson, the son of George Stephenson, who invented the locomotive.
Penrhyn Castle (*c.* 1 m. NE): A 19C

Bantry, Bantry House

house with a collection of more than 1,000 dolls from all over the world.

Bantry
Cork/Ireland   p.330☐B 14

This small fishing village lies on one of the most beautiful bays in Ireland, Bantry Bay, which is 4 m. wide and has a mild climate in which exotic plants flourish. In 1689 and again in 1796 French troops—sent in support of Irish rebels—beached here.

Bantry House: Built in 1740 in Georgian style, it overlooks the bay. It was restored in the 19C by Lord Bantry, who filled the house with an interesting collection of paintings and furniture. The Italianate *castle garden* is also impressive.

Environs: Ardgroom (*c.* 25 m. W.): The site of one of Ireland's tallest *Ogham Stones*, which is 17 ft. high and dates from the 5–6C.

Baltimore (*c.* 12.5 m. SE): An attractive fishing village founded in 1608. The remains of a 16C *castle*, have been converted into a sailing school.

Castletown Bearhaven (*c.* 19 m. W.): The village sits spectacularly on the cliffs of the *Beara peninsula*. Next to the village and between the Kenmare River and Bantry Bay lie the 15–16C ruins of *Dunboy Castle*.

Clear Island (*c.* 15.5 m. S.): An interesting island with a tradition-conscious, Gaelic-speaking population. The *lighthouse*, in the S. on *Cape Clear* (Ireland's southernmost point), has a spectacular view).

Garinish Island (*c.* 7.5 m. NW): In 1910,

on this rocky island off Glengariff, the enchanting 'Italian Garden' was constructed. G.B.Shaw wrote 'St.Joan' here.

Sherkin Island (*c.* 13 m. S.): This island, which lies off Baltimore, has the remains of a 15C *Franciscan priory* with a central tower.

Barnard Castle
Durham/England   p.328□I 10

Barnard Castle: Built by the Norman Guy de Bailleul in the 11C on a steep slope above the River Tees, a site of strategic importance. The fortifications were extended 1112–32 by his nephew, Bernard Baliol, who gave his name to the castle. In 1569 Barnard Castle was besieged and conquered during the course of the northern barons' resistance to Cromwell; therefter it fell into decline. Remains of the inner moat in front of the castle are still visible, as are the round three-storey *keep* and the 14C *Great Hall.*

Bowes Museum (accessible via Newgate):

Built 1869–74 by John Bowes in the style of a French château to house art in his family's possession. The centrepiece of the collection is the *painting gallery*, with many masterpieces by Spanish (Goya, El Greco's famous 'St. Peter'), French (Boucher, Courbet and others) and Italian (Sassetta, Tiepolo) painters. Of especial interest are the *porcelain and ceramics collections* (including examples of Sèvres, Meissen and Delft pieces), 17–18C English and French *furniture*, and an interesting *toy collection* with old dolls and dolls' houses. There are also collections of costumes (16–18C), manuscripts (some of which are medieval), woodwork and sculpture, jewellery, wall hangings, clocks and tobacco jars.

Also worth seeing: The medieval *bridge* over the river Tees and the main street, with its picturesque old houses.

Environs: Bowes (*c.* 4 m. SW): Once a Roman military base; remains of a Norman *castle* have survived (part of the keep).
Egglestone Abbey (*c.* 1 m. SE): The re-

Barnard Castle, ruins

Barnard Castle, Bowes Museum

mains of a *Premonstratensian Abbey*, including part of the church with an Early English chancel (13C) and part of the nave (12–15C).

Raby Castle (*c.* 5 m. NE): Originally built in the 14C, it was restored in 1765 and extended in the mid 19C. The interior is remarkable for the *Great Hall*, which is 148 ft. long and has an old stone minstrels' gallery on the W. side. An art gallery includes some fine Dutch masterpieces, as well as collections of furniture and porcelain.

Romaldkirk (*c.* 5 m. NW): The church of *St.Romald*, built in the 12C, was much restored in the 13–15C when a Perpendicular tower was added. The interior includes a beautiful old vaulted roof, the figure of a knight (1304), a Romanesque font and an 18C pulpit.

Staindrop (*c.* 5 m. NE, S.of Raby Castle): The old church of *St.Mary*, Anglo-Saxon in origin, has a Norman W. tower and some 13C rebuilding in the Early English transept. The interior is notable for its tombs, which date from the 13C (the Earls of Westmorland) to the 19C (the most recent is that of the Duchess of Cleveland, which dates from 1859). The font and the choir stalls (both Perpendicular), and the 19C stained-glass windows, are also worth seeing.

Barnsley

South Yorkshire/England   p.328☐I 12

Mentioned in the 'Domesday Book' as *Berneslai*, which means 'field of Bern', Barnsley has been a coal-mining town since early times and became known as a glass-blowing centre in the early 17C—both of these professions are depicted in the city's coat-of-arms. A market town since 1249, in 1850 it was connected to the railway network by Joseph Locke, a native of Barnsley and a colleague of George Stephenson.

Church of St.Mary: Built in the 15C in Perpendicular style (the castellated tower is original), it was much altered later. The interior includes some original furnishings.

Town Hall (Church Street): Completed in

1933, this four-storey building has a clock tower some 150 ft. high. The exterior is clad in light Portland stone, in strong contrast to the surrounding buildings, which have been darkened by the coal dust in the air.

Also worth seeing: The *Cooper Art Gallery* in Church Street, housed in the old grammar school, has an interesting collection of English paintings and drawings.

Environs: Cawthorne (*c.* 5 m. W.): *Cannon Hall* is a 17C manor house which was altered in the 18C by John Carr of York; it now houses a fine *museum* with exhibitions of paintings, furniture and objets d'art. The *village church* is also interesting, having a beautiful pulpit decorated with pictures in the Pre-Raphaelite style, and a small *museum* devoted to the writer and painter John Ruskin.

Monk Bretton Priory (*c.* 2 m. NE): The remains of a *Cluniac Abbey*, originally founded in 1153, include the 15C church and gatehouse and a 13C guesthouse.

Silkstone (*c.* 4 m. W.): The 14–15C Perpendicular *All Saints' Church* was built on the site of an earlier building; the most interesting aspect of the interior is the tomb of Sir Thomas Wentworth, made in 1675 by the London sculptor Jasper Latham.

Worsbrough (*c.* 2.5 m. S.): *Worsbrough Mill Museum* is dedicated to the history of technology and contains working machinery; of especial interest is a restored 17C water mill.

Barnstaple
Devon/England   p.332□F 15

This small town at the mouth of the river Taw has been a port since Norman times; there has been a bridge over the Taw since 1273. Barnstaple's merchants and ship owners procured five warships for the struggle against the Spanish Armada. John Gay was born here in 1685, and in 1728 he wrote the 'Beggar's Opera' (which 200 years later became the model for Bertold Brecht's 'Threepenny Opera').

St.Anne's Chapel: The upper section of the building dates from 1450, but the crypt-like lower part, which is very much older and originally served as a charnel-house. After 1685 the house became a meeting place for the Huguenots, and from the beginning of the 18C it housed a primary school which John Gay himself attended. Today the rooms have been converted into a *museum* devoted to John Gay.

Environs: Atherington (*c.* 9 m. S.): The church of *St.Mary* is Gothic and dates back to around 1200. The large W. tower was restored in 1884. The mighty barrel vaulting and the Tudor windows are very impressive, as is the rood screen, which is unique of its kind in Devon. Some of the bronze plaques are 15C.

Braunton (*c.* 4.5 m. NW): The church of *St.Brannock* was begun in Norman times, but the greater part is 13C. The base of the S. tower is Norman; the rest is 16C. 15C barrel vaulting in the nave. The most interesting feature is the pews which are among the finest in Devon: the chestnut wood is carved with stars and figures, the latter including the Celtic missionary St. Brannock, who is shown riding on a cow.

Horwood (*c.* 5.5 m. SW): The church of *St.Michael* has a low W. tower with twin spires; N. transept only. Inside: a square Norman font and the remains of some 15C stained-glass windows, 16C carved pews and a pulpit dating from 1635.

Ilfracombe (12.5 m. N.): The chapel of *St. Nicholas* dates from the 14C. It is recorded that from 1522 a window on the N. side served as a beacon. After the Reformation the chapel was converted into a

Ilfracombe (Barnstaple), harbour

house and a light-chamber was installed in the W. gable. Of the many such chambers installed in churches and houses up and down the coast, this is one of the only ones to have survived.

Barton-upon-Humber
Humberside/England   p.328□K 12

Church of **St. Peter:** One of the oldest Anglo-Saxon churches in England, it was founded in 669 during a mission by St. Chad. The W. part of the church and the tower are original; nave and choir stalls were modified in the Gothic style of the 14C. The richly-decorated *E. window* is of particular interest.

Church of **St.Mary**: Largely Romanesque,

but later rebuilt and modified in Decorated and Perpendicular styles. The interior includes the highly decorated late Gothic *choir screen* from the 15C and a 15C *gravestone* of Simon Seman, a Hull wine merchant.

Environs: Appleby (*c.* 6 m. SW): The church of *St.Bartholomew* was almost completely rebuilt in the 19C; a Romanesque font has survived. The 19C windows are also of interest.
Bigby (*c.* 9.5 m. S.): *All Saints' Church* is Early English; inside there is a fine madonna from around 1300.
Bottesford (*c.* 11 m. W): The church of *St.Peter's Chains* has beautiful lancet windows and a 15C Sanctus bell which was only rediscovered in the last century.
Broughton (*c.* 10 m. SW): The church of *St.Mary* is largely Romanesque, but the W.

tower is Anglo-Saxon and has fine small staircase turrets. The interior contains some interesting 14C tombs.

Cadney (*c.* 11 m. S.): *All Saints' Church* is mostly early Gothic from the 13C with Romanesque elements. Interesting features include the Romanesque font and the late Gothic E. window.

Goxhill (*c.* 5 m. E.): The site of the remains of a building locally referred to as *Goxhill Priory*; it is probably the former seat of the Despenser family. A fine late Gothic window has survived, as has a spiral staircase and also some arches on the N. and S. sides.

Normanby Hall (*c.* 9 m. SW): This *manor house* was designed in the 19C by Sir Robert Smirke, the architect of the British Museum. The interior is exquisitely furnished in Regency style and includes life-size figures in costumes of the period. **Thornton Abbey** (*c.* 6 m. SE): The remains of an *Augustinian monastery* originally founded in 1139. The most interesting part is the fortress-like gatehouse, built half in natural stone and half in brick.

Basing
Hampshire/England   p.332☐I 15

This small town in the Loddon valley has many old brick houses. On a nearby hill the earth walls of a Norman *fortress* can be seen.

Basing House Ruins: The site of a Saxon fortress, later a Norman castle and eventually in 1530 a fortified castle, which was besieged by Cromwell for three years, before eventually being taken and destroyed in 1645. Since then, excavations have confirmed earlier occupation and finds include ceramics from the Iron Age, Roman coins and 13C bricks alongside numerous relics from the Civil War. The finds are currently on exhibition in Hampshire County Museum.

Church of St.Mary: This huge Gothic church was seriously damaged in the Civil War; rather careless attempts at restoration in the second half of the 17C made the extensive alterations of 1874 necessary. The church has 15&16C *tombs*.

Environs: Basingstoke (2.5 m. SW): The *Willis Museum* has an exhibition of local history and archaeology, as well as a collection of clocks and watches.

Odiham (*c.* 6 m. E.): The ruins of the *castle* are Norman in origin. Here Simon de Montfort held Prince Edward prisoner, and the Scottish king David Bruce was also held captive until ransomed for 100,000 gold pieces in 1357. *All Saints Church* is 13C in origin but extensively restored in the 19C; the pulpit is early 17C, and the two superb stained-glass windows in the chancel are by Patrick Reyntiens.

Silchester (*c.* 11 m. N.): Once the local Roman capital of *Calleva Atrebatum*, it is the most completely excavated Roman town in England. The foundations, however, were exposed for scientific analysis and not preserved for posterity—everything was covered over and given up to agriculture. The most important finds, on show in the *Calleva Museum*, include a bronze eagle, urns, vases and inscriptions. The exhibition also includes models of Roman buildings. The church of *St.Mary* has an early-16C choir screen, a 15C font and a pulpit from 1639.

The Vyne (*c.* 3 m. N.): This Tudor *country house* dates from 1500–20 and was built by Lord Sandys, Henry VIII's chancellor. It takes its name from a vineyard which the Romans are said to have cultivated on the same spot. The chapel and the large panelled gallery are original. In 1654 Chaloner Chute, the speaker of the House of Commons, commissioned the rebuild-

Basing, old brick house ▷

ing of the house, adding a classical portico designed by John Webb. Around 1760 John Chute restored the staircase and some of the rooms; the stained-glass windows in the chapel date from *c.* 1700.

Bath
Avon/England   p.332□H 15

England's only hot mineral springs (49 degrees C). According to legend, they were recognized as having healing properties when the king's swineherd Bladud, the father of King Lear, cured his leprosy by bathing in them. It can, however, be proved that the Romans used the springs, since they began to build *Aquae Sulis* in AD 54. In 577 it was taken by the Saxons, who renamed it *Akemanceaster*. 1090–1294 the city, well-fortified by this time, was the residence of the Bishop of Wells. Its prime was in the 18C, when it became a spa with a reputation for quality and distinction. The two John Woods, father and son, designed and built an entire new city in

Bath, Abbey Church, façade

Georgian style. This has been extensively maintained and today over 4,000 buildings are protected by preservation orders.

Roman Baths: By the time of the governorship of Agricola (78–84) there was already an active social life revolving around the baths. The Romans' predilection for them led to the mineral springs being supplemented by a sophisticated network which included not only warm baths, but also cold baths and specially heated rest rooms. To keep the system going they used lead water-pipes and underground heating (hypocaust). In the 2C the main bath, an 82 ft. x 39 ft. pool in a 115 ft. x 66 ft. pillared hall, was built. Next to the bath there was a Temple to Minerva, part of which was excavated in the 18C, when impressive fragments of a bronze head of Minerva, votive offerings and part of the altar were uncovered. A head of Medusa was also found. All in all, the Roman baths, which were visited by Trajan and Hadrian, form one of the most impressive monuments which the Romans left in Britain.

Abbey Church: In 676 this became the site of a nunnery, but King Edgar (crowned here in 973) made it a Benedictine Abbey. In 1107 John de Villula turned it into the seat of a Norman bishop, but this fell into decline when the bishop resumed the former seat of Wells in 1244. In 1499 a new building was begun under the supervision of Bishop Oliver King, but its completion was prevented by the dissolution of the monasteries. Eventually this, the last of the great pre-Reformation churches was consecrated in 1616. It became known as the 'lantern of the west' due to its huge *windows*, particularly in the clerestory, which flood the church with light. A most impressive feature is the *fan vaulting* by Robert and William Vertue, which is amongst the finest in England. It was originally only built over the choir but Scott extended it over the main nave in a style faithful to the original. The aisles of the late Gothic church contain over 600 *memorial plaques*, and a wide range of other commemorative items. The *W. front*, with its massive oak (1617) and depicts angels climbing up and down ladders from heaven—a dream of the founding bishop.

Museums: The *Roman Bath Museum*, to the N. of the main spring, contains all the notable excavated Roman relics. The *Victoria Art Gallery and Museum* has collections of glass and ceramics, together with a coin collection and some geological exhibits. The *Museum of Costume* contains the world's largest collection of costumes, from 1580 to the present day, and includes baby clothes, footwear and undergarments. The *Holburne of Menstrie Art Museum* consists largely of Lord Holburne's art collection, which was donated to the city by his sister in 1882. It includes Dutch, Flemish and German work dating from the 15C, as well as paintings by Gainsborough and Ramsay.

Also worth seeing: There are many exceptionally fine buildings in Bath, but the following are worth a special mention. *The Circus*, designed by John Wood the elder and completed by his son in 1758, is the perfect example of a circus of houses. The house fronts, with pairs of Tuscan, Ionic and Corinthian pillars, look, in the words of a contemporary commentator, 'like Vespasian's amphitheatre turned outside in'. The imposing *Royal Crescent* — 30 houses arranged in a 600 ft. semicircle with more than 100 Ionic pillars. This row of supremely elegant terraced houses was built in 1767–74. *Pulteney Bridge* (1770) is by Robert Adam and spans the Avon on three arches. It looks like a delicate house which has become a little too wide.

Environs: Claverton Manor (3 m. E.): This *manor house*, built in classical Grecian style in 1820, houses an *American Museum*. Its rooms contain original American furniture from the 17–19C, and an exhibition of American crafts and Indian art. **Dyrham Park** (about 8 m. N.): A fine manor house, attractively set in a park, it was built in 1692–1702 on the site of an

Bath, Abbey Church, fan vaulting

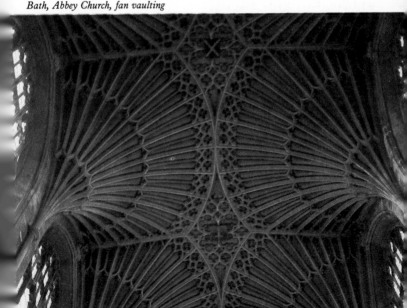

earlier country house. William Talman was responsible for the E. front and the baroque, Italianate orangery. The interior contains collections of Delftware, Flemish wall hangings and paintings by Dutch masters.

Prior Park (2.5 m. SE): Ralph Allan's *country seat* was designed by John Wood the elder and begun in 1735. Originally it served as a meeting place for eminent writers, but since 1830 it has been a boarding school. The park has a Palladian bridge, which dates from 1750.

Beaulieu
Hampshire/England   p.332☐ I 16

This small village is attractively situated at the southern edge of the New Forest, a large area of woodland which has always been of interest to the rulers of England. William the Conqueror was concerned to protect his hunting grounds and threatened severe punishment for poachers: however, in the 18C the principal intention was to protect the forest oaks from shipbuilders and smelters. Even today the 155 sq. miles of forest are still Crown property and are one of the most beautiful areas of England.

Beaulieu Abbey: Originally a Cistercian abbey, it was founded by King John in 1204. After the Reformation the Early English refectory was converted into the parish church, which has impressive *lancet windows*. The *pulpit*, which is built into the wall and adorned by a 13C arch, is of special interest. The abbey itself has disappeared with the exception of some ruins and a piece of the S. wall. The original abbey gatehouse has been converted into *Palace House*, the country seat of the current owner of Beaulieu Abbey, Lord Montagu. To enhance his property, he built an overhead railway through his grounds and opened *Lord Montagu's National Motor*

Museum, which contains over 200 vintage sports cars.

Environs: Bucklers Hard (2.5 m. S.): The site of a *model village* dating from 1724, when the second Lord Montagu tried to set up a sugar factory. When that failed, he established a branch of the royal dockyard at Portsmouth. In 1749, Henry Adam began building the ships that were to form Nelson's fleet out of New Forest oak, consuming some 2,000 trees for a ship of the line, and the techniques involved are graphically illustrated in the *Maritime Museum*.

Lyndhurst (10 m. NW): The *Church of St.Michael* was built in 1858–70. The interior features slender pillars of Purbeck marble with ornamented capitals, and a pre-Raphaelite E. window of the New Jerusalem, designed by Edward Burne-Jones in 1862 and made by William Morris in 1864. The fresco of the 'Wise and Foolish Virgins' on the E. wall is by Lord Leighton. Eventually completed in 1864, it was the first wall painting to be added to an English church since the Reformation.

Beccles
Suffolk/England   p.338☐ M 13

This old town on the River Waveney was seriously damaged by no fewer than four major fires in the 16&17C, which completely destroyed the old building; today its charm lies in some fine Georgian brick houses. Chateaubriand lived here in exile in 1794–7.

Environs: Barsham (2.5 m. W.): The *Church of the Holy Trinity* is Norman, but has since been enlarged. It has a round W. tower and a decorated W. front. One of the two fonts is Norman, the other Gothic. All the wood, including the pulpit, is Jaco-

Beaulieu, Abbey, altar wall

bean; the E. window, by C.E. Kempe, is 19C.

Bungay (7.5 m. W.): Here, too, most of the houses built before 1688 were destroyed by fire. There are remains of the *Norman castle* which Hugh Bigod, the Earl of Norfolk, began in 1165. In 1294 a gatehouse with two towers was added, but at the end of the 14C the whole castle fell into disrepair. The *Church of the Holy Trinity* is essentially Norman, although its round tower is probably Saxon. The church has subsequently undergone many alterations, the last being in 1926, when the sanctuary was replaced. The church contains 16&17C carvings, and a tomb by Thomas Scheemacher (1774).

Mutford (9 m. E.): The *Church of St. Andrew* is also Norman in origin; the impressive round W. tower is from this period, as are some fine arches. The carved font, which dates from 1380, is interesting, as is a fresco of St. Christopher.

Bedford
Bedfordshire/England   p.332□K 14

Now the county town of Bedfordshire, it was a Saxon stronghold as far back as 915. Taken by the Danes in 1010, in 1166 Henry II granted it a charter. It later achieved notoriety through John Bunyan (1628–88), whose religious views led to his imprisonment here for 12 years, during which time he wrote 'Pilgrim's Progress'. His *statue*, by Joseph Boehm, stands near the Church of St. Peter.

County Museum: The exhibits are devoted to the history of the town and county; the archaeological finds go back to the Iron Age, and Roman and Saxon items are well represented.

Cecil Higgins Art Gallery: The museum contains a number of individual exhibitions, including a display of coloured drawings from the 17C to the present day; prints from Dürer to the present and a collection of sculptures. There is also a series of continental porcelain, glass and furniture.

Environs: Ampthill (10 m. S.): The *Church of St.Andrew* is 14C in origin with a 15C tower. It contains the tomb of Richard Nicholls (1624–72), who fought the Dutch in America and ended up as the first governor of New York. On his tomb is the cannon-ball which killed him in the Battle of Solebay. *Katherine's Cross* was erected in 1773 in memory of Catharine of Aragon, the wife of Henry VIII. It marks the site of Ampthill Castle, where Catharine lived in 1531-3. The cross was set up by James Essex and has an inscription by Horace Walpole.

Elstow (*c.* 2 m. S.): The church of *St.Mary and St.Helen* goes back to a Norman monastery church built around 1100. The W. front was extended in the 13C. The E. part was destroyed in the 16C; the nave, with its fine Norman arches, and the N. portal have survived. In the 19C both the church and its detached tower were restored, great respect being paid to the church's ancient form and contents. 16C tombs.

Felmersham (8 m. NW): The W. front of the 13C church of *St.Mary the Virgin* is a fine example of Early English style. The roof was restored in the 15C, when the aisle walls were extended upwards to accommodate a clerestory. From the same time dates the rood screen we see today, which is in keeping with the massive pillars of the crossing.

Marston Moretaine (*c.* 9 m. SW): The church of *St.Mary the Virgin* was begun in 1340 and altered in 1445. The W. tower is massive. Inside, the bosses are sumptuously decorated. In 1969 a large fresco of the Last Judgement was uncovered on the wall over the triumphal arch. Dating from the early 16C, it shows the resurrection of

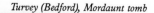

Turvey (Bedford), Mordaunt tomb

the dead and their despatch to heaven or Hell, with Christ sitting in judgement.

Old Warden (7.5 m. SE): The 12C church of *St. Leonard* houses the tomb of Sir Samuel Ongley, which was carved by Peter Scheemaker and Laurent Delvaux in the 18C. It shows an idealized figure clad in Roman style, which appealed to contemporary taste. The original sketches for the work are in the Victoria and Albert Museum in London. The *Shuttleworth Collection* includes an exhibition of old aeroplanes, the showpiece of which is a Blériot monoplane from 1909. Many of the exhibits are still airworthy and flown from time to time. As well as old planes, the collection includes cars, bicycles and devices connected with flying.

Turvey (*c.* 9 m. W.): The church of *All Saints* was originally Saxon, but was restored and extended in the 14&15C, further 19C restoration is by Gilbert Scott. The font is 12C in origin, and there is an early-14C fresco of the Crucifixion. Tombs of members of the Mordaunt family date from the 15&16C.

Belfast

Antrim / Northern Ireland   p.326 □ E 10

Belfast (lit. 'Sand Ford'), the capital of the Province of Northern Ireland, has over 400,000 inhabitants. As well as having an important harbour and world-famous shipyards, it is a large industrial centre. The economic development of the city, which as recently as the 18C was still a small village in the shadow of the port of Carrickfergus, is largely due to its advantageous position at the point where the river Lagan flows into Belfast Lough.

History: Scarcely anything remains of the original settlement and early medieval castle which was destroyed in 1177. The town's fortunes, which first began to flourish with a charter from James I in about 1613, grew the arrival of the French Huguenots around 1685, under whom the linen trade expanded. Since the 'Act of Union' of 1800, which officially linked it to England, Belfast has grown into an industrial centre with fine 19C buildings. It has been

Elstow (Bedford), church portal

Church tower

the capital of the six counties of Northern Ireland (Antrim, Armagh, Derry, Down, Fermanagh, Tyrone) since 1920, and the question of its, and the province's, independence from Great Britain has led to the bloody conflict of recent years.

City Hall (Donegall Square): The magnificent city hall, built by B.Thomas in 1900, takes the form of a *domed palace* with four towers in neo-Renaissance style. Its height of nearly 200 ft., is the main feature of the city's skyline. Inside there are: the huge *reception hall* with a marble staircase and paintings illustrating the city's history; the *council chambers;* the *great hall. Statues* in front of the building depict Queen Victoria and famous citizens. To the W. of the building is the impressive *war memorial* in the *Garden of Rememberance*; on the E. there is a memorial to the British luxury liner, the 'Titanic', which was built in a Belfast yard in 1912.

St.Anne's Cathedral (Donegall St.): The Anglican Church of Ireland was begun by Thomas Drew in 1898 in the neo-Romanesque basilican style. The three *W. portals* have impressive arches and carvings. The marbled *nave,* which is some 90 ft. wide, is magnificent, especially the *arches,* which have carvings, including carved heads of Irish princes. The *Chapel of the Holy Spirit* in the NW is fine; as is the *baptistery* and the fine *mosaic roof.* The *tomb* of Lord Carson, the leader of the Unionists, who died in 1935, is in the nave.

Ulster Museum (in the Botanical Gardens): Interesting old Celtic finds (*c.* 200 BC), early Christian and medieval times, including swords, harps, coins, medallions, uniforms, household implements and jewellery. Also of interest are the *gold and silver treasures* from Girona, recovered in 1968 from a Spanish galleon which sunk off the Giant's Causeway (see Coleraine) in 1588. The *art gallery* has European paintings from the 17&18C (including Breughel, Jordaens, Turner and Gainsborough), modern British and Irish painters, as well as glass, silver and ceramics. Sections devoted to geology, natural history and industrial development are also worth seeing.

Also worth seeing: *St.Patrick's Church* in Donegall St.(Catholic) was built at the end of the 19C and contains a pre-Raphaelite triptych. *St.Malachy's Catholic Church* in Alfred St.was built in 1848 in Tudor style with Renaissance elements. The church of *St.George* in the High St. dates from 1816 and has a classical Corinthian portal. Also of note is the oval *Presbyterian (Unitarian) Church* (1783) and the *Assembly Buildings* with their crenellated *bell tower.* Secular buildings of note include the classical *Royal Courts of Justice* in May St. (1929); *Prince Albert Memorial* (19C) in Queen's Square which is leaning as a result of subsidence; *Linenhall Library* (1788), which has an exhibition documenting the history of the linen trade; the impressive *Custom House* from 1855 and the *Clifton House,* which is Georgian and dates from 1774. The new *castle* (on Cave Hill), built in 1870 in Scottish baronial style, was the prime minister's seat. *Parliament House,* the seat of the Northern Irish parliament, is located in the suburb of Stormont. This neoclassical building dating from 1928 was a present from Great Britian. *Queen's University,* in University Road, was founded in 1845 as Queen's College and became an independent university in 1909. The oldest buildings are brick and were built in Tudor style in 1845-94; the central tower is very fine. The university has an interesting *historical museum.*

Belfast, City Hall

Belfast, Queen Elizabeth II and Queen's Bridge

Environs: Cultra Manor (*c.* 7.5 m. NE on Belfast Lough): The extensive castle park has an interesting open-air museum, the *Ulster Folk Museum*. This is composed of reconstructed 'cottages', workshops, watermills, forges, weaving mills and farmsteads, which illustrate the lifestyle and crafts of the past. The *castle* houses an exhibition of household tools and implements, as well as Irish paintings; also a *transport museum*.

Berkeley

Gloucestershire/England   p.332□H 15

This small town, only a few miles from the E. bank of the river Severn, has many old houses. The church and castle in particular make Berkeley well worth a visit.

Church of St.Mary the Virgin: Dating from Norman times—although only the S. portal and font survive from the original construction; all the rest of the church is Gothic. The interior contains a splendid stone *rood screen* and many fine tombs of the Lords of Berkeley. Some frescos have survived, including a *Last Judgement*.

Berkeley Castle: The seat of the Lords of Berkeley. The round keep dates from 1153 and by 1160 dungeon, battlements, ramparts and burial vaults had also been completed. The Great Hall, kitchens and the gatehouse were added around 1340. Edward II was murdered here in 1327 and the room in which the murder took place has been preserved in its 14C state. In fact, the whole building is in remarkably good condition and contains paintings, furniture and other articles, many of which are of ex-

Berkeley, Berkeley Castle

ceptional quality. The most precious piece is a 15C carving of a *Madonna and child* by a French master; the Madonna looks thoughtfully at the Child, who has a globe in its hand.

Environs: Frampton-on-Severn (*c.* 9 m. NE): The church of *St.Mary* was originally Norman, although only the font has survived from this time. The church visible today is Gothic and has a finely-proportioned W. tower. The pulpit dates from 1622; the oldest tomb is 14C.
Leonard Stanley (*c.* 9.5 m. NE): The surprisingly large cruciform church of *St. Leonard* was built in the 12C and was originally the church of an Augustinian priory. The Gothic parts are not as interesting as the remains of the Norman building, which has fine arches and portals. The Augustinian priory has not survived.

Woodchester (10 m. E.): The *Roman villa* is one of the largest known in Britain. First excavated in the 19C, it has now largely been levelled again.

Berwick-upon-Tweed
Northumberland/England   p.324□I 8

This town at the mouth of the river Tweed has *c.* 11,000 inhabitants today. Founded in about 870, it was originally Scottish. During the extended frontier battles between the Scottish and the English it frequently saw fierce fighting; from 1147–82 it changed hands 13 times before being finally won by the English.

The Ramparts (also known as the

'Elizabethan Wall') were built 1558–69 inside the original 13C city wall by order of Elizabeth I as a defensive bulwark against the Scots. There are four bastions (Meg's Mount Bastion, Cumberland Bastion, Brass Bastion and Windmill Bastion), with walls over 10ft. thick, which were specially constructed to withstand cannon bombardment. The old gates which still exist are Cow Port Gate (NE), Ness Gate (S.), Shore Gate (SW) and Scotsgate (NW).

Also worth seeing: The parish church of the *Holy Trinity*, which was built in 1652 by the London architect John Young in English classical style (English baroque), is one of only two churches to have been built during the Republic under Cromwell. The church has fine Venetian windows. The *Town Hall* is 18C in origin. The remains of the old *castle*, behind the railway station in the NW, include the remains of fortifications E. of the 'bell tower'. *Berwick Bridge*, opened in 1634, has five arches and is built in red sandstone. The *Royal Border Bridge*, a railway bridge built by Robert Stephenson in 1847 and opened

by Queen Victoria in 1850, has 28 arches and stands some 130 ft. above the water. The *Museum and Art Gallery* has Daubigny's 'Cap Gris Nez' and Degas' pastel 'Russian Dancer'; the 'Berwick Room' contains 16C tempera wall paintings from the 'Old Bridge Tavern'.

Environs: Akeld (*c.* 15 m. S.): The outer circular wall with three entrances and the foundations of about 130 huts have survived from the large Iron Age hill fort of *Yeavering Bell.*
Bamburgh (*c.* 15 m. SE): In the 6–8C this was the capital of Northumbria. It was previously a Roman settlement. *Bamburgh Castle*, built by the Normans (the keep is original 12C), was a royal fortification until the 15C. It was restored 1894–1903. Inside there are collections of weapons and armour. The church of *St. Aidan* is also interesting. Dating from the 13C, it has no side aisles; there is a fine crypt under the chancel.
Doddington Moor (*c.* 12.5 m. S.): There are remains of stone huts from the Bronze Age hill fort of *Dod Law.*

Bamburgh (Berwick-upon-Tweed), Bamburgh Castle

Flodden Field (*c.* 10 m. SW): A *memorial* to the battle of 1513 commemorates the death of King James IV of Scotland, who was killed in battle by the English.

Holy Island (*c.* 10 m. SE): *Lindisfarne Priory* was founded in 635 by St.Aidan and sacked by the Vikings and the Danes; it was taken over by the Benedictines in 1081. The ruins of the 12C priory survive, as do those of the fortified monastery from the 13–14C. Opposite is *Lindisfarne Castle*, which was built in 1549 with spoils from the priory. Sacked in the Civil War, it was restored in 1900.

Kirknewton (about 15 m. SW): The church of *St.Gregory* contains a primitive 12C relief of the 'Adoration of the Magi'; the transept and chancel vaulting springs from floor level.

Norham (*c.* 7.5 m. SW): Fine partially Romanesque *church* and a large *castle*, which since 1121 has been the border fortress of the Bishop of Durham. 12C parts of the castle have survived, along with 16C rebuilding.

Roughtinglinn (*c.* 7.5 m S.): An Iron Age *hill fortress* with surrounding wall. To the

E. there is a rock face with *Bronze Age drawings*.

Beverley
Humberside/England   p.328□K 11

Minster/Church of St.John the Evangelist: One of England's most important Gothic churches. It was founded as a priory in *c.* 700 by Bishop John of York, who died in 721 and was canonised in 1037 (his tomb is in the nave). The building was badly damaged several times (in 866 by the Danes, in 1188 by fire); in 1220 work began on the building we see today, which was eventually completed in 1400. It was restored by Sir Gilbert Scott (1866–80). Despite the slow pace of construction the building has maintained reasonable stylistic unity. Choir and transept are Early English, the nave is partly Decorated and partly Perpendicular; W. front and towers are Perpendicular.
Exterior: The church is 361 ft. long and 180 ft. wide at the transept; the W. towers

Holy Island (Berwick-upon-Tweed), Lindisfarne Priory, ruins

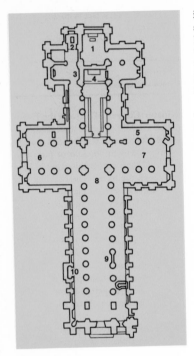

Beverley Minster 1 Lady Chapel **2** Percy Chapel with the tomb of the 5th Earl of Northumberland (d.1489) **3** Percy Tomb (Tomb of Lady Percy, d.1365) **4** altar **5** War Memorial Chapel **6** N. transept **7** S. transept **8** tomb of Bishop John of York (d.721) **9** Maiden Tomb **10** N. porch

are 177 ft. high. The *W. front* is one of the most splendid in Europe, especially the window and its ornate canopy; the towers have buttresses with niches for statues. Fonts in the *transept* are pure Early English.

Interior: The oak choir screen dates from 1880; the fine late-Gothic choir stalls are from 1520. The Fridstool, on the right of the altar is 9C and guaranteed freedom from pursuit to lawbreakers. To the left of the altar is the magnificent *Tomb of Lady Percy*, who died in 1365; this high Gothic monument is one of the finest of its kind

in Europe. Bishop John's tomb (mentioned above) is also worth seeing, as is the Romanesque font (with Renaissance lid). The E. window has medieval stained glass. The *Percy Chapel* contains the tomb of the Fifth Earl of Northumberland who died in 1489.

Church of St.Mary: Originally built as the church of the guilds and free citizens in the 12C, and then considerably altered. Little remains of the original Romanesque, except for the wreath cornices on the buttresses, the interior arches in the S. porch and the geometrical embellishments over the arches in the N. transept. In 1520 the crossing tower collapsed during rebuilding, which caused a shift of balance. The most interesting parts of the interior are the 15C choir stalls and *Michael's Chapel* in the E. part of the N. aisle, above which is a small *museum* with an old pillory and some valuable church treasures, including two 16C chalices. The parish library, which is 17C with fine 15C work in oak is in the S. transept.

Also worth seeing: The *Guild Hall* of 1832 has fine stucco. *North Bar* is the only one of the five original city gates to have survived. The *Market Cross* dates from 1714.

Environs: Dalton Holme (*c. 5 m. NW*): The Victorian Gothic church of St.Mary was built by John Loughborough Pearson and has a fine high tower.
Goodmanham (*c. 9 m. NW*): *All Hallows' Church* was probably built in the 7C on the site of a pagan temple. The Romanesque portals are impressive and there are fine Romanesque chancel arches and a late Gothic font.
Hornsea (*c. 11.5 m. NE*): Mentioned in the Domesday Book in the 11C. The Perpendicular church dates from 1430 and was restored in 1868 by Sir Gilbert Scott.
Lockington (*c. 5.5 m. NW*): The church

Beverley, Minster

Throne

of *St. Mary the Virgin* was originally Romanesque, but later rebuilt; the portal is original. 17C pulpit and some fine old stained-glass windows.

North Newbald (*c.* 7.5 m. SW); The church of *St. Nicholas* is Romanesque, with a nave and no aisles. The portals, Romanesque windows and 12C font are all worth seeing.

Bexhill

East Sussex/England   p.332□L 16

This sleepy coastal village is largely inhabited by retired people.

De la Warr Pavilion: This broad-fronted white building with balconies facing seawards is Bexhill's main attraction. It was built in 1936 by the German Bauhaus architect Erich Mendelsohn. The beautifully-decorated *banqueting room* is the main in of the interior. The *museum* has an exhibition of local history.

Environs: Ashburnham (*c.* 6 m. N.): *St.Peter's Church* is a Perpendicular building, which was restored in the 17C. It has original furnishings, two tombs of members of the local nobility and an interesting painting of the Ten Commandments.
Herstmonceux Castle (*c.* 6 m. NW): This *country seat* was built in *c.* 1440 by the then Chancellor of the Exchequer; it later fell into disrepair. Since 1949 the restored building has housed a *royal observatory* (not open to the public).
Penhurst (7 m. N.): *St.Michael's Church*, a perfectly preserved Perpendicular building, has a roof built in three different styles.

Herstmonceux Castle (Bexhill)   *Penhurst (Bexhill), St. Michael's Church* ▷

The setting is picturesque, near an Elizabethan *country house* and numerous *farmsteads*.

Birmingham
West Midlands/England   p.328☐I 13

Although it only began to flourish with the onset of the industrial revolution, Birmingham was known as a centre for metalwork as early as the first half of the 16C. It supported the Parliamentarians in the Civil War, when over 15,000 swords were produced; it was, nevertheless, occupied by Prince Rupert. Thanks to the wealth of ore and coal in the surrounding area, Birmingham developed rapidly into an area with the highest concentration of factories in England. Anything that could be made of metal was produced here, including over 800,000 guns, rifles and pistols for the American Civil War. Naturally enough, the spread of factories left little room for old buildings, and the most interesting sights are all relatively modern.

St. Martin's Church: Although built on the site of a 14C church, the building we see today dates from 1873. It contains *tombs* of members of the De Bermingham family.

Church of St. Philip: Begun in 1711 under the supervision of Thomas Archer; who had studied in Rome and attempted to transpose his ideas of Roman baroque into an English industrial context. The church was eventually completed in 1719; the baroque W. tower in 1725. The stained-glass windows are by Burne-Jones and date

from 1884–5. In 1905 this parish church attained the rank of a cathedral.

Cathedral of St.Chad: Started in 1839, this was the first Roman Catholic cathedral to be built in England since the Reformation. It was designed under the supervision of Augustus Pugin, who attempted to realize his interpretation of medieval architecture in its construction.

Aston Hall: Built 1618–35 in Jacobean style, it is one of the city's few old buildings. It was built for Sir Thomas Holte, who played host to Charles I in 1642. The estate was later seized by the Parliamentarians. The house is of interest for its *staircase* and its balustrade, the long *gallery* and fine *stucco ceilings*. Pictures and furniture are Jacobean and Victorian.

Town Hall (Victoria Square): Begun in 1832 by J.Hansom and E.Welch and modelled on a classical temple with 40 Corinthian columns. In 1846 Mendelssohn's 'Elijah' received its first performance here. Statues of Queen Victoria and James Watt are by Alexander Monro and date from 1899.

Museums: The *City Museum and Art Gallery* houses one of England's finest art collections outside London. It is famous above all for its Pre-Raphaelite paintings and drawings, as well as sculptures by Rodin and Henry Moore. As well as the art collection there are displays of clothing and fashion accessories from the 17C and a collection of silver from the 17–19C. The Archaeological Museum is a separate department and has finds dating back to the Stone Age. It is of especial interest because its exhibits come from all over the world and include, for example, such things as the reconstruction of a tomb from Jericho (1800 BC). The *Barber Institute* consists largely of Lady Barber's private collection, a small but exceptionally fine art collection ranging from the early Renaissance to the early 20C and including Rubens, Gainsborough and Degas. The *Museum of Science and Industry* documents the city's industrial development. Inside what used to be a factory, exhibits

Birmingham, Town Hall

include old water-powered machinery, gas-powered machines, steam engines and electrical appliances; the transport department contains old carriages, cars, motorcycles and bicycles. The *Geology Museum* contains minerals, fossils and precious stones from all over the world.

Environs: Dudley (*c.* 9 m. W.): The church of *St. Thomas the Apostle* was built by W.Brooks in neo-Gothic style in 1817 –19. The stained-glass window in the E. wall depicts the Ascension and is the work of Joseph Backler from 1821. *Dudley Castle* is a ruined fortress from the 13C, which was extended in the 16C. The most impressive exhibits in the *Central Museum* are geological, especially those relating to fossils and formations found in coal seams. **Walsall** (*c.* 12 m. NW): England's only *lock museum*. Walsall was the centre of the lock and key industry in Queen Elizabeth I's time, and a collection of locks going back to the 16C was assembled here, including English locks and those from all over the world. The *Museum and Art Gallery* contains the Garman-Ryan collection

donated by Lady Epstein in 1973. As well as work by Jacob Epstein there are paintings and drawings by over 100 artists.
West Bromwich (*c.* 9 m. NW): *Oak House,* a half-timbered house dating from *c.* 1500, has a Jacobean wing from 1635. The most interesting part is the tower with an openwork lantern, which is the only domestic example of its kind in England. The interior is notable for its carved panelling and Jacobean furnishings.

Bishop Auckland
Durham / England   p.328 □ I 10

Church of St. Andrew (in the SE of the town): Built in the late 13C in Early English style; it has a W. tower and a fine S. *portal.* Inside an Anglo-Saxon *stone cross* from Northumbria, dates from *c.* 800 and is ornately engraved with an image of Christ with other Biblical figures and saints. There is also the *figure of a knight* in recumbent position with legs crossed, which is carved in oak and dates from 1340.

Birmingham, Museum, C.Clay clock

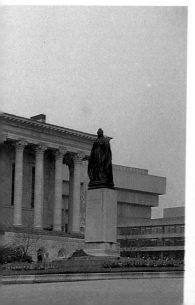

Bishop Auckland, Church of St. Andrew

Auckland Castle: The country seat of the Bishop of Durham since the 12C. The building we see today is mostly 16–18C. It has a well-preserved medieval chapel (12–13C).

Environs: Escomb (*c.* 2.5 m. W.): The church of *St. John the Evangelist* is one of England's oldest existing churches. It was probably built in the 7C with spoils from the Roman settlement of Vinovia at Binchester, N. of Bishop Auckland. The antique building material is clearly visible because of the careful way it was handled. The church has an early Christian ground plan, with a nave with no aisles, a chancel but no transept. The windows are original. **Sedgefield** (*c.* 8 m. E.): The church of *St. Edmund*, originally Early English and then Decorated, has a Perpendicular W. tower. Inside there is an ornate choir screen and choir stalls, both from 1670, a fine marble font and an 18C organ.

Bishop's Stortford
Hertfortshire/England   p.332 ☐ K 14

This old town on the Stort was the birthplace of Cecil Rhodes (1853–1902). His house, the old vicarage, is now a museum devoted to him.

Church of St. Michael: This is 15C in origin; the impressive *W. tower* was built in 1812. The 12C *font* is carved from Purbeck marble, and the ornate *choir screen* is 15C, as are the choir stalls with their finely carved misericords. The pulpit dates from 1658.

Environs: Hatfield Broad Oak (*c.* 6 m. SE): The church of *St.Mary the Virgin* was originally part of a small friary founded by Aubrey de Vere in 1135 (of which only the nave remains). The W. tower and S. portal were added in the 15C, as was the choir screen. The church also contains numerous tombs.

Much Hadham (*c.* 5 m. SW): This town, the country seat of the Bishop of London for over 900 years, has fine 16&17C houses which make it well worth a visit. The church of *St.Andrew* is 12C in origin, although most of the building dates from the 13 - 14C. There are fragments of 15C stained glass as well as more recent glasswork (19C).

Sawbridgeworth (5 m. S.): The church of *Great St.Mary's* is largely 14C. The oldest element is the octagonal font, which dates from 1400. The pulpit is from 1632, the large E. window was replaced by Hardmanin 1864. The church has many tombs dating back to the 16C.

Blackpool
Lancashire/England   p.328☐H 11

England's largest and most popular seaside resort, it is almost exclusively geared to holidaymakers; 153,200 inhabitants cater for 8.5 million visitors each year. The most striking sight is the *observation tower* some 568 ft. high, which was modelled on the Eiffel Tower when built in 1889-95. The tower-building contains a zoo, an aquarium and England's largest dance hall. The *Grundy Art Gallery* in Queen's Street has an interesting collection of 19&20C paintings and drawings. The only electric tramway in England runs from Blackpool to Fleetwood (*c.* 7 m.).

Environs: Lytham St.Anne's (to the S.): One of the area's last surviving *windmills* is in the E. of the town.

Poulton-le-Fylde (*c.* 3 m. N.): The church of *St.Chad* was originally built in the 15C in Perpendicular style; the tower was rebuilt 1751-3. The church contains some fine old coats-of-arms and the remains of the Hesketh family pews from the 17C. The pulpit is 19C.

Blair Castle
Tayside/Scotland   p.324☐G 7

The façade of this much-visited castle tells little of its chequered history. The watchtower, *Cumming's Tower*, dates from 1269. The Lords of Atholl were able to hold on to their family seat through the centuries and even, by means of skilful family politics and temporizing, steadily increase their prestige. In 1703 they received the title of Duke, and in 1845 Queen Victoria granted the Duke of Atholl the right to maintain a private army. The Atholl highlanders, archers, bagpipers and drummers, still parade in the green tartan of the Murray clan from time to time.

The castle visible today was the work of the Victorian architect David Bryce in 1868 and it is in keeping with his contemporaries' taste for the picturesque. The step gables, corner turrrets and crenellations imitate the style of the 17C. About 25 rooms open to the public are crammed with a mixture of valuables and curios; paintings of assorted value vie with damask wallpaper, four-poster beds, Chippendale furniture, Sèvres porcelain, valuable Gobelin tapestries and velvet coverings. There are also many personal possessions, including old documents, and keepsakes such as dog collars.

Also worth seeing: The *Meal and Flour Mill* was formerly a corn mill in which cereal used to be ground. It has been reconstructed so that the process not only functions again, but can be clearly observed.

Blackpool, sea front

Visitors can try traditional Scottish oat bread and biscuits.

Blandford Forum
Dorset/England   p.332☐H 16

This town on the river Stour was damaged by an extensive fire in 1731, which has meant that with the exception of a few houses, the town is mostly Georgian.

Church of St. Peter and St. Paul: This Georgian church was built in 1748 to the designs of John Bastard. It is built in ash-lar stone and has a square tower with a dome. The interior is dominated by massive Ionic columns. In 1895 it was separated along the line between the nave and the small chancel; the apse was put on rollers and moved away from the nave. A new sanctuary was built in the gap and the old apse re-attached.

Environs: Milton Abbas (*c.* 6 m. SW): The *model village* dates from 1786 when Lord Milton, owner of Milton Abbey, decided that his view should no longer be interrupted by the village which had grown up around the abbey. Over 100 houses were pulled down and new ones built just over a mile away; the village school was transferred to Blandford Forum. The first design of the new village was overseen by Capability Brown, although the actual plans were by William Chambers.
Milton Abbey (*c.* 7.5 m. SW): The *abbey*, founded by Athelstan in 938, was dissolved by Henry VIII and eventually sold. Lord Milton bought it in 1752, and commissioned first John Vardy, then William

Blair Castle, castle

Chambers (1771) and James Wyatt (1774) to convert it into a castle. The abbot's old hall (from 1498) was integrated into the scheme. The adjacent *abbey church* was rebuilt in the 14–15C but never completed; the chancel, transept and central tower (100 ft.) are the only elements which were finished. There is a fine altar screen from 1492 and a 15C wooden tabernacle. The aisle houses the marble tomb of Lord and Lady Milton, made by Agostino Carlini in 1776 to the designs of Robert Adam.

Blenheim Palace
Oxfordshire/England p.332☐I 14

The palace was built as a reward for John Churchill, the first Duke of Marlborough, after his victory over the combined French and Bavarian troops at Blenheim on the Danube. Designed by Sir John Vanbrugh and built 1705–22, it is a baroque building of two storeys, constructed around three sides of a huge courtyard. The middle section has a portico supported on Corinthian columns. The interior decoration is the work of many leading artists of the day: the *frescos* in the Great Hall are by Sir James Thornhill and Louis Laguerre; the *carving* is by Grinling Gibbons; Marlborough's tomb in the chapel is by Michael Rysbrack; and the *State Rooms* have fine paintings, tapestries and other furnishings.

The extensive *gardens* have been redesigned several times. The original park was designed by Henry Wise, gardener to Queen Anne, but his work was hardly finished before Capability Brown was called in to match the design of the park to the recently altered tastes. Parts of the gardens were altered more recently (1925–32) by Achille Duchêne, who redesigned them in the style of the great French garden designer André Le Nôtre.

Blickling Hall
Norfolk/England   p.328□L 13

This Jacobean brick house was built by Robert Lyminge for Sir Henry Hobart 1619–25. The main building is elongated with towers at each end and extended wings; the courtyard thus formed was closed by Thomas Ivory 1765–70. A 17C staircase, decorated with figures and stucco, leads to the reception rooms. The *gallery* is at least 130 ft. long and has a remarkably fine stucco ceiling.
The house contains a number of valuable furnishings, tapestries and paintings.

Environs: Aylsham (1.5 m. S.): Attractive houses from the 17&18C, including *Aylsham Old Hall* (1689) and the Old Bank House (1710). There is also an interesting early Perpendicular *church*.
  Cawston (*c.* 5 m. SW): Attractive Perpendicular *church* with an impressive tower and a ceiling decorated with angels.
Feldbrigg House (*c.* 7.5 m. N.): The *country seat* of the Wyndham family, it dates from 1624; the W. wing was added in 1686. The park contains an interesting *church*, with tombs from the 14–17C.
Reepham (*c.* 9 m. SW): The church of *St.Mary* dates back to the 13C and was extended in the 14C. It has a square Norman font and a grave slab from 1391. There is also the tomb of Sir Roger de Kerdiston, who died in 1337.
Salle (*c.* 9 m. NW): The 15C church of *St. Peter and St. Paul* has a well-proportioned tower and N and S. porches of two storeys. The carved choir stalls with fine misericords are also 15C, as is the

pulpit. Some original stained-glass windows have survived and there are a number of tombs, including one with a swathed skeleton from 1454.

Bodmin
Cornwall/England   p.330□F 16

The county town of Cornwall, Bodmin lies on the SW edge of Bodmin Moor. In fact, it is not as isolated as it used to be, when the saying went: 'Into Bodmin and out of the world'.

Church of St.Petroc: This, the largest parish church in the county, is predominantly 15C. However, the lower part of the *tower* and the unusual *font*, are 12C Norman. The huge stone, which is supported by 4 columns with angels' heads at the corners, attempts a complete symbolic interpretation of life: the tree of life growing undisturbed among the untamed fury of witches, dragons and snakes, continues to branch out to infinity. The *shrine of St.Petroc* (*c.* 1170) is also worth seeing, as is the *tomb figure* of Prior Vyvyan (d.1533).

Environs: Lanhydrock House (*c.* 2 m. S.): This house, picturesquely situated over the Fowey, was built in Jacobean style in 1642 by Lord Robartes. The gatehouse and N. wing still stand, but the rest was rebuilt in Victorian style after a fire in 1881. The picture gallery in the N. wing is almost 130 ft. long, and its ceiling is highly decorated with stucco and scenes from the Old Testament. The geometrically-designed garden dates from 1857 and is decorated with bronze amphorae from Castle Bagatelle, which are the work of Louis Ballin, purveyor to the court of Louis XIV.
St.Neot (10 m. E.): The church of *St.Neot*

Llanhydrock House, Bodmin ▷

was consecrated to a Celtic monk who found himself here as a wandering missionary. It is famous for its stained-glass windows, which date back to 1480. The four oldest windows depict Adam and Eve in Paradise, the rescue of Noah, St. George and the Dragon, and the Creation. Local skill was used and thus it is a fascinating example of 15-16C glass work.

St. Winnow (*c.* 9 m. SE): The church of *St. Wynnocus* lies on the bank of the Fowey and is Celtic in origin. Two windows still have the original 16C stained glass; the ornate ends of the pews and the pulpit are also 16C.

Wadebridge (*c.* 6 m. NW): The *bridge*, which has 17 arches dates from 1470; it was financed by the wool trade, and its pillars stand on bales of wool to stop them sinking into the soft ground. It is the oldest bridge in Great Britain still in use as part of a main street.

Bolton
Greater Manchester/England   p.328□H 12

This town of some 160,000 inhabitants was formerly known as Bolton-le-Moore. Until the 18C it was a centre of the wool industry and after that it became an important cotton centre. In the history of the Industrial Revolution, it is known as the home town and industrial base of Richard Arkwright (1732-92), who invented the cotton spinner in 1769, and of Samuel Crompton (1753-1827), who invented an improved automatic version, the 'Spinning Mule'.

Textile Machine Museum: This houses a collection of machines demonstrating the development of the textile industry in Lancashire. The main exhibits are the originals of three machines which revolutionized the cotton business in the late 18C: the 'Spinning Jenny' (invented in 1764 by the weaver James Hargreave, it is a mechanical spinning-wheel with multiple reels); the spinning machine patented by Richard Arkwright in 1769 (the 'Water Frame', which was improved so much in 1772 and 1775 that production was increased some 200 fold); and Samuel Crompton's 'Spinning Mule'.

Museum and Art Gallery: The Natural History section of the museum has a unique collection of British birds. The local history section displays a further selection of exhibits related to the history of the cotton industry. The Egyptology section is also interesting. There is a painting gallery which contains Italian masters from the 16C and some 18-19C English watercolours.

Environs: Bury (*c.* 6 m. E.): The home town of Robert Peel, the founder of the British police force, (policemen are still known as 'Bobbies' after him). John Kay (who invented the 'Flying Shuttle', a mechanical weaving loom, in 1733) was also born here. The *Wrigley Collection* in the City Museum is interesting and has work by 19C English painters such as Turner and Constable, and an impressive collection of sculpture. The *Lancashire Fusiliers Museum* has memorabilia of the division which guarded Napoleon on St. Helena until 1821.

Chorley (*c.* 10 m. NW): The Elizabethan manor house, *Astley Hall*, was built in 1666. Inside, the Great Hall has a small art gallery, the Long Gallery has a fine old gaming table, and the Drawing Room has a highly ornate ceiling. There are also many of the original furnishings.

Deane (*c.* .5 m. W.): The church of *St. Mary* was built in Perpendicular style with a Decorated W. tower; the ceiling of the nave, which is continuous with that of the chancel, was restored in the 19C along with other parts of the 1510 building.

Ecclestone (*c.* 12.5 m. NW): The 14C

Bolton, Abbey, portal

Museum

church of *St.Mary* has a Perpendicular S. aisle; the interior contains a fine 15C gravestone.

Hall i' th' Wood (NE edge of the town): This half-timbered *manor house* dates from 1483; an Elizabethan stone wing was added in 1591, and the house was restored and extended in 1648. Here Samuel Crompton designed his spinning-machine. It now houses a museum of local history.

Hindley (*c.* 4 m. SW): The church of *All Saints*, rebuilt in 1766 in classical style, is a brick building with attractive windows and fine carvings inside.

Rivington (*c.* 9 m. NW): An interesting 16–17C *church*. The attractive *Lever-Park* contains artificial castle ruins and an Italianate garden.

Rochdale (*c.* 11 m. E): In 1844 the world's first co-operative society was formed here —the original store in Toad Lane has been preserved. Other points of interest include the town church of *St.Chad*, the *Town Hall* and the *museum*, which houses a collection of paintings.

Smithills Hall (*c.* 2.5 m. NW): A 14C *manor house* in extensive grounds. The house has Tudor additions from the 15–16C. Fine furniture from the 17C.

Turton Tower (*c.* 4 m. N.): A 12C structure which was rebuilt in the 16C; *Ashworth Museum*, housed inside a 15C tower, has an interesting weapon collection.

Bolton Abbey
North Yorkshire/England   p.328□I 11

Priory Church: The priory was founded in the 12C by Augustinian canons; during the course of the Reformation in the 16C

Bolton Abbey, ruins and river

it was dissolved by Henry VIII and sold to the Earl of Cumberland. It then fell into disrepair. The nave of the ruins was restored in 1864.

Structure of the church: The total length is *c.* 85 ft., and it has a cruciform ground plan. The nave was built in Early English style and the aisle added in the early 13C has fine Decorated windows. The chancel, which is now ruined, was originally late Romanesque; along with the S. transept it was renovated in the 14C. There is a Perpendicular tower in front of the church's W. front, which was begun in 1520 by the priory's last abbot, Richard Moone; it was never completed owing to the Dissolution.

Interior points of interest: The W. wall of the nave includes 4 support stones which, until the 19C restoration, supported the vaulted roof. By the organ is an intricate depiction of the 'Agnus Dei'. A fine old altar table (by the sacristy door) has five crosses on the top and in the middle of the front to symbolize the five wounds of Christ; the hollow in the middle was originally a reliquary.

East of the church is the river Wharfe, which can be crossed at low tide by 57 *stepping-stones*. The date of origin of the stones is unknown; they were formerly used in place of a bridge by the villagers on the E. bank.

To the W. of the church is *Bolton Hall*, which was formerly the abbey gatehouse.

Environs: Barden Tower (*c.* 2 m. NW): The relic of a *castle* (which formerly had six towers) in the domain of Skipton Cas-

Boston, St. Botolph

tle. Lord Clifford, a former owner, became known as 'the Butcher' during the Wars of the Roses because of his brutal methods. The chapel nearby is in a similar state of disrepair.

Burnsall (*c.* 5 m. NW): The *church* contains a fine old font with pagan symbols; some interesting old Scandinavian gravestones are also decorated with pagan inscriptions.

Boston
Lincolnshire/England   p.328 □ K 13

A monastery was founded here *c.* 650. In the 14C Boston, the most important of the English textile ports, had strong connections with the Hanseatic league. In 1620 the 'Mayflower' sailed from here on the Pilgrim Fathers' famous voyage to America; Puritans who emigrated at that time founded Boston in Massachusetts, USA.

Church of St. Botolph: Building began *c.* 1310 and continued in Decorated and Perpendicular styles. One of England's largest parish churches, it was restored in the 19&20C with funds from the citizens of Boston Massachusetts. The tower known as *Boston Stump* (*c.* 300 ft. high, completed in 1460 and with an octagonal lantern) is one of the town's distinguishing features.

The interior includes interesting *pews* and some impressive *tombs* of rich medieval merchants (including a tomb from 1340 of a merchant from Hanse). 17C *pulpit* is 17C, an 18C wrought-iron *parclose* and 19C *stained glass*.

Guildhall (South Street): Built *c.* 1450, this brick building has interesting windows in five sections. In 1607 the Pilgrim Fathers were tried in the Guildhall; some of them were also imprisoned here. Today it houses the *City Museum*, which contains interesting exhibits relating to local history, and an art collection.

Fydell House (next to the Guildhall): Built in 1726 in Georgian style, it has remained unaltered since that time and is one of the town's most interesting buildings. The façade is clearly laid out with six pilasters, above which there is lavish timber-work and a balustrade; the portal is flanked by Doric pillars. Inside: a fine staircase, rococo decorations and unusually fine stucco work.

Also worth seeing: The church of *St. Nicholas* has a late Gothic tower and, inside, a fine Renaissance pulpit. The *parish church* of Skirbeck (a district of the town) is 13C. *Shodfriars Hall* in South Street, is a 16C timber house (19C restoration). In Spain Lane there are ruins of a 13C *Dominican monastery. Custom House* dates from 1725. *Hussey Tower*, in Skirbeck Road, has a staircase tower and fine vaulting.

Environs: Ewerby (*c.* 12.5 m. W.): The church of *St. Andrew* is in Decorated style; the interior includes an interesting font which is partly Romanesque.
Freiston (*c.* 3 m. E.): The church of *St. James* remains from a monastery founded in the 12C; some of the original Romanesque elements have survived; inside there is a late Gothic font.
Friskney (*c.* 11 m. NE): Romanesque *church* with interesting 14C frescos.
Heckington (*c.* 11.5 m. W.): The church of *St. Andrew*, built in Decorated style in the 14C, has remained almost unchanged. The interior is interesting, especially the ornamented E. window.
Howell (*c.* 12 m. NW): The church of *St. Oswald*, which is partly late Romanesque transitional and partly Decorated, contains the remains of medieval stained glass and a 14C font.
Kirton (*c.* 4 m. S.): 14C Gothic *church*.

Boston, St. Botolph, choir stalls

What is the W. tower today was formerly the crossing tower until the 19C.
Old Leake (*c.* 6 m. NE): Interesting late Gothic *church*, with an octagonal tower.
Sibsey (*c.* 4.5 m. N.): The church of *St. Margaret* is partly Romanesque. The W. tower is Gothic and the S. vestibule dates from 1699.
Sleaford (*c.* 15 m. W.): The 12C church of *St.Denis* has beautiful windows and interesting tombs. Other things of interest include the public buildings in the town centre (the *Sessions House* from 1831, the *Union* from 1838 and the *Corn Exchange* from 1857).
Tattershall (*c.* 10 m. NW): Interesting remains of a *castle* dating from 1231. It is fine example of a medieval brick building and a keep over 100 ft. high has survived. The church of the *Holy Trinity*, near the castle, was rebuilt in the 15C. The interior contains an interesting choir screen and remains of the original stained glass in the E. window.
Wrangle (*c.* 7.5 m. NE): The E. window of the *church* has fine 14C stained glass.

Boyle
Roscommon/Ireland   p.326□C 11

This small town of some 1,700 inhabitants is located by Lough Key on the Shannon.

Boyle Abbey is the remains of what was formerly one of the most interesting Cistercian monasteries. Founded in 1161 (from Mellifont), it became the religious centre of the Irish kingdom of Connaught. The *abbey church* lacks a roof, but is otherwise well preserved and has a 13C nave, chancel, transept and low crossing tower. Two E. portals and a W. gate have survived from the collapsed cloisters. The *monastery buildings* around the cloisters (refectory, kitchens) are 16&17C.

Environs: Ballindon Friary (*c.* 9 m. N.): To the N. of Lough Arrow lie the remains of a *Dominican monastery* from 1507; fine central tower and bell tower. Nearby are the remains of the Megalithic burial site, *Heapstone Cairn*; a further prehistoric burial mound can be seen to the W. of the

Boyle, Boyle Abbey

Bradford, Cathedral, W. window

lough. The Megalithic cemetery at *Carrowkeel* provides more evidence of the significance of the area in early times.

Ballinafad (5 m. NW): This point, on the S. tip of Lough Arrow, has the remains of a *castle* (c. 1590; massive corner towers). It was also the site of the prehistoric battlefield, *Northern Moytura* (to the SE), where the Celtic invaders 'Tuatha Dé Dana' (people of the goddess Dana/Diana) fought the inhabitants of Fir Bolgs in *c.* 1300 BC.

Ballymote Castle (*c.* 11.5 m. NW): The imposing *castle* ruins (including huge towers) date from the early 14C, when it was the strongest fortress in Connaught and subject to frequent changes of ownership. Little is left of the adjacent 14C *Franciscan monastery*, where the celebrated *Book of Ballymote* was written in 1390. (The book is now in Dublin).

Bradford is the centre of the English wool and worsted industry. In the 19C during the course of the Industrial Revolution Bradford changed from a peaceful country town into an industrial city and the buildings erected at this time have given the town its character. At the vanguard of industrial progress, Bradford played a leading role in social development during the 19C; education of workers' children was pioneered here, and Richard Oastler, a local man, was to promulgate the first Factory Act.

Cathedral: As St.Peter's church, it was the city's parish church until 1920, when it became the cathedral. 15C in origin, it was extended 1954–65. The interior includes fine old *stained-glass windows*, an interesting *oak ceiling* in the nave, a highly decorated *episcopal throne* and a 15C *font*.

City Hall: Completed in 1873, the façade is decorated with statues of English sovereigns. The tower (some 200 ft. high) has a fine *carillon*.

Bolling Hall (Bolling Hall Road, in the S. of the city): A late medieval manor house which has been much modernized over the centuries. The massive entrance tower served to defend the house during the 15C. Today it is a *museum*, with collections of old furniture, ceramics, costumes etc. from the 15–18C.

Industrial Museum (Moorside Road, Eccleshill): Housed in a disused textile factory, it gives a comprehensive view of the development of the wool trade and transport in Bradford. Most of the originl machinery is still in working order.

City Art Gallery and Museum (Lister Park): Housed in Cartwright Hall, which

Bradford, Cathedral, font

is baroque. The *gallery* has Chinese vases and a collection of paintings. The *city museum* has sections devoted to geology, natural history and archaeology.

Also worth seeing: The *Wool Exchange*, near Market Street, which was once the centre of the international wool trade. *Apperley Bridge* is a fine 16C road bridge on the A658.

Environs: Bingley (*c.* 6 m. N.): Fine 18C *main street*.

Haworth (*c.* 12.5 m. NW): Home of the famous Brontë sisters, Charlotte, Emily and Anne, who attained world-wide fame with their novels. The former *rectory*, where they lived 1820–61, is now a *Brontë Museum*, with manuscripts and personal memorabilia.

Ilkley (*c.* 12.5 m. N.): In 1843 hydrotherapy was administered here for the first time in England (the Ben Rhydding Hydro has survived in poor condition). The church of *All Saints'* is interesting, being constructed on Roman foundations. The W. wall has two Roman altars (possibly originally from a temple to Hercules), which were at one time built into the inner wall of the tower. The N. aisle contains a fine pew from 1633. The park opposite the church of St. Margaret has three *cup and ring stones*, into which regular recurring rough figures have been incized. The origin and significance of these prehistoric monuments have not yet been satisfactorily explained. Other points of interest include the *Manor House Museum and Art Gallery* (Castle Yard), which is on the site of an old Roman fortification and includes interesting archaeological finds from Ilkley and the surrounding area.

Keighley (*c.* 10 m. NW); The interesting *museum* has reconstructions of local craftsmen's workshops. Less than a mile across the Aire lies *East Riddlesden Hall*, a well preserved 17C manor house with a medieval tithe barn. *Cliffe Castle* nearby is a 19C Victorian building which houses an interesting *local museum*.

Shipley (*c.* 3 m. N.): The model village of *Saltaire* was built in Italianate style in 1853 by the textile magnate Sir Titus Salt, who wanted to ensure that his workers had an acceptable standard of living. The village was built around the largest industrialized textile complex of the time and included some 800 homes, school, hospital, library, public baths and other public institutions. The Congregational church contains the tomb of the town's founder.

Tong (*c.* 4 m. SE): *Tong Hall*, built in 1702, today houses an interesting *museum* (beautiful chimney-piece). The *church* contains a heated private box pew belonging to the Tempest family, the owners of Tong Hall.

Bradford-on-Avon

Wiltshire/England   p.332□H 15

According to William of Malmesbury in 'Gesta Regum Anglorum' Abbot Aldhelm, a celebrated late 7C teacher and monk, founded a small church by the broad ford of the Avon. It is possible that his church might be the small church now dedicated to St.Lawrence.

Church of St.Lawrence: Built in *c.* 700 with a second storey added in *c.* 1000, the nave is 25 ft. long. The church is among the very few unaltered Anglo-Saxon churches in England, escaping change because for nearly 1300 years until the 19C, no one realized its original function. It served as a gardener's lodge, a charnel house and a school, and there was never any cause to alter the somewhat irregular masonry. Thus the narrow and dispropor-

tionately high *nave* and the square *chancel* with two angels over the arches were maintained almost intact (when the second storey was added *c.*1000, a surrounding blind arcade with small flat pilasters was also added). The *portals* on both sides of the nave are unchanged, being very narrow with simple undecorated round arches; two tiny windows on the S. of the nave and chancel also remain unchanged.

Church of the Holy Trinity: This 12C parish church betrays clear traces of the original construction, especially around the sanctuary windows. The nave has Gothic additions from the early 14C, and the W. tower with its squat spire is 15C. The church has an interesting medieval *fresco* of the Virgin, and two paintings depicting God the Father.

The finest item in the church's treasury is the first English *Bible* to be used in a church; dating from 1572, it is a reprint of the 1568 Episcopal Bible.

Environs: Corsham (*c.* 12 m. N.) : The Saxon church of *St. Bartholomew* was extended in the 12C. It was completely rebuilt by G.E.Street, who also took down the original tower and built a new one. *Corsham Court*, an Elizabethan manor house with Georgian additions, dates in its present form from 1840. It is well worth a visit, as it houses the *Methuen Collection*, the finest art collection in Wiltshire, which includes furniture by Adam and Chippendale, paintings by Fra Filippo Lippi, Tintoretto, Rubens, Van Dyck and many others. The park is Capability Brown's design.

Great Chalfield (*c.* 3 m. NE): The church of *All Saints* from the 15C, is adjacent to the manor house of the same name. The former has frescos depicting the life of St.Catherine. The pulpit is in three sections and dates from the 17C. The *manor house*, built by Thomas Tropnell in 1480, is a fine example of domestic Gothic architecture. It now belongs to the National Trust, which ensures that it remains unaltered.

Lacock (10 m. NE): A very fine village, now owned by the National Trust, its houses date from Medieval times up to the beginning of the 19C. The *Church of St. Cyriac* has a cruciform ground plan and was built in the late 14/early 15C. A chapel on the NE side dates from 1430 and has interesting vaulting; it houses the original tomb of Sir William Sharington from the mid 16C. *Lacock Abbey* was founded as an Augustinian nunnery by the widow of William Longespées in 1229. In 1540, after the Reformation, it was taken over by Sir William Sharington, and the 13&15C nunnery building was converted into a Tudor country house. In 1755 the huge medieval hall which was originally used by the abbess became one of the first rooms in England to be renovated in Gothic Revival style. It was here, in 1839, that Fox Talbot invented negative photography. His oldest negative dates from August 1835 and is on display in the Science Museum in London.

Westwood Manor (2.5 m. SW): 15C *manor house* with alterations from 1610 and 16&17C extensions. There are late Gothic and Jacobean windows. The valuable furniture is of especial interest.

Braemar
Grampian/Scotland   p.324□H 7

This village on the upper reaches of the Dee was a centre for sport long before the present day. In the 11C King Malcolm III regularly called his clans together to compete amongst themselves, in order that he could establish who were the best warriors. Such were the roots of the present-day's *Braemar Gathering*, which is regularly attended by the Royal family. Fontane maintained that 'the blue flower of Scotland' was to be found here, and R.L.Stevenson wrote 'Treasure Island' here.

Castle: Built in 1628 as the Earl of Mar's hunting lodge, it was, however, destroyed only thirty years later by the Jacobite John Farquharson, the 'Black Colonel'. In 1748

Bradford-on-Avon, St. Lawrence

Church of the Holy Trinity

it was converted into an English garrison for Hanoverian troops and a castellated defensive wall was built in accordance with the contemporary European practice; the original corner towers with conical roofs were replaced by crenellated passages. However, English occupation was only temporary and the castle can be said to have belonged to the Farquharson family since 1733. The castle has interesting barrel vaults, an underground dungeon and a staircase tower.

Environs: Balmoral Castle (*c.* 9 m. E): This small castle changed hands many times before Queen Victoria made it her summer residence. Built by the Gordons in 1484, it was bought by the Farquharsons in 1662 and sold to the Lords of Fife in in 1798. The Royal Family rented it in 1848, and a legacy enabled Queen Victoria to buy it four years later. Prince Albert then designed a new building with the help of Aberdeen architect William Smith; this building, with its icing-sugar decoration, can be considered as epitomizing the architecture of the Victorian Age. It was completed in 1855 at which time the previous building was pulled down. Only the park is open to the public (when the Royal Family are not in residence).

Brecon/Aberhonddu
Powys/Wales   p.332□G 14

This attractive small town of some 6,000 inhabitants is situated at the point where the river Honddu flows into the Usk River. (Honddu=mouth). The town and the castle are both Norman and date from the 11C.
There are a few remnants of the Norman *castle* and the old *town fortifications*.

Cathedral: This cruciform building, once the *priory church of St. John's*, was built *c.* 1100 by the Normans; the font and parts of the walls date from this time. The sanctuary and transept are Early English and date from the 13C; the old nave and side chapels were restored in Decorated style in the 14C. Other points of interest include a Norman stone candelabrum for oil lamps, a number of tombs, an ornamental candlestick from 1722 and glass cabinets containing old Bibles.

St. Mary's Church (town centre): This church still has a few *Norman pillars*, a 14C *font* and a 16C *tower*.

Brecknock Museum: This has a fine collection of archaeological and geological finds, including early Christian pieces and objects of local interest.

Environs: Brecon Gaer (2.5 m. NW): Remains of an old Roman fortification with surrounding earth wall and ditches. The site was founded *c.* 75AD and eventually abandoned in the 4C. Parts of the walls and gates are well preserved (the main gate was in the W, with smaller ones in the S, E and N sides); there are remnants of small watchtowers). It was closely connected with the Roman fortification at Caerleon (see Newport).

Hay-on-Wye (*c.* 19 m. NE): This small town on the banks of the Wye has the remains of a 13C *castle* and *gateway* but today it is known for its antiquarian bookshops. The remains of *Painscastle* nearby are interesting. Only the earthworks (walls, ditches, etc.) of this once-massive Norman castle are still in good condition.

Heol Senni (*c.* 11 m. SW): The attractive *Brecon Beacons National Park* contains the Bronze Age *Menhir Maen Llia*, a stone which is 12 ft. high and nearly 3 ft. thick. Nearby are the interesting natural caves of *Porthyr-Ogof* in the Mellte Valley.

Talgarth (*c.* 9 m. NE): The village con-

Balmoral Castle (Braemar) ▷

Llantwit Major (Bridgend), New Church

Celtic cross

tains a 14C *tower and an old bridge*. There are scanty remains of the nearby 11C Norman *Bronnlys Castle* (tower, sections of wall, etc.).

Bridgend/Pen-y-Bont
Mid Glamorgan/Wales   p.332□G 15

This industrial town at the mouth of the Ogmore River (*c.* 40 m. W. of Cardiff) has a few remains of the 12C Norman *New Castle*, including a fine gatehouse. The northern suburb of *Coity* contains the interesting ruins of *Coity Castle*. The remains of the round tower (keep) are 12C, the walls and citadel are 12–14C. The E. suburb of *Coychurch* contains a well-preserved Decorated *church* (early/high Gothic).

Environs: Cowbridge (*c.* 6 m. SE): This small provincial town includes the remains of the 14C medieval *town fortifications* with a well-preserved *mill gate* (Port Mellin), near Church Street.

Ewenny (*c.* 2 m. S.): This is the site of the interesting remains of the early medieval *Ewenny Priory*, which was Benedictine. This strong fortified monastery was founded by the Normans in 1115 under the supervision of William de Londres, and, along with the neighbouring castles of Ogmore, Bridgend and Coity, it formed a strong defensive square against the aggressive Welsh. The sombre Norman building style remains largely unchanged, apart from damage on the N and W sides. The S. transept contains tombs of the de Londres family and others.

Llantwit Major (*c.* 9 m. SE): A medieval village on the S. coast where the Celtic

Llantwit Major (Bridgend), church

monk Illtyd founded a monastery in the 5C. Famous for its grammar school and workshops (no traces of which survive).

The *monastery church* (parish church) is interesting as it is divided into two sections by a central tower in transitional style. The W. section (for the congregation), known as the 'Old Church', is of Norman origin. The SW portal (gateway) and the stone altar are also Norman. The chancel, which underwent major renovation in the 15C, has Perpendicular windows. In the W. part of the church there is a row of Celtic crosses, with inscriptions, dating from *c.* 800. Along with a decorated half column from the 10 – 11C they are probably products of the monastery workshop.

The E. part (New Church) is a 13C addition which functioned as the monastery church; it contains some interesting 13–14C wall paintings, including a St. Christopher (*c.* 1400) and female saints (*c.* 1300). The finest part is a 13C 'Jesse niche', now rather faded, depicting the Tree of Jesse (the branches of the tree supporting Jesus grow out of the sleeping Jesse). The font and the stone sanctuary are also of interest.

Ogmore Castle (*c.* 3 m. NW): An interesting castle built to protect the crossing over the river Ogmore. The original 12C earth walls and ditches are well-preserved, as is the three-storey *keep* from the 13C.

St. Donat's Castle (*c.* 12.5 m. S.): This restored and modernized castle from the (14–16C) lies right on the coast and just some 2.5 m. from Llantwit Major. It was the residence of the American newspaper magnate W.R. Hearst who died in 1951.

Bridlington
Humberside/England   p.328☐K 11

Priory Church of St.Mary (Old Town):
Now the town's parish church, it was originally attached to a monastery (founded in
1113 by the Norman Walter de Gaunt for
Augustinian canons. The monastery was
dissolved in 1539 during the course of the
Reformation, and the church—with the exception of the nave—was torn down. It was
restored under Sir Gilbert Scott 1850–80,
when the two W. towers were completed.
The W. front includes a fine, highly decorated Perpendicular *window* and the E. end
has a *Jesse window* with 30 sections; there
is an exceptional Early English window in
the nave. On the N. side of the nave are the
remains of 12C cloister arcades. Inside, the
nave is supported by 10 arches (with interesting bundles of columns); the three
last bays form the present chancel. The
gravestone of the monastery's founder,
Walter de Gaunt, is at the W. end.

The Bayle (near the church of St.Mary):
This is the gatehouse of an old monastery
dating from 1388. Partly brick, it was extensively rebuilt in the 17C and now only
the spiral staircase is original. After the dissolution of the monasteries, it served as
school and a prison, and since 1631 has
also been the seat of 'Lord Feoffe', the
former organ of the town's autonomy
which still exists. The Bayle now houses
the *Museum of Antiquities*, which contains
objects of local historical significance,
paintings and drawings, a collection of
dolls' house furniture and a collection of
old tools.

Sewerby Hall (NE of the town centre):
Built *c.* 1720 in Georgian style and extended in the first half of the 19C. It has
served as a *museum* since 1936. The archaeological section has Bronze Age finds,
including stone axes and flints. A small art

gallery has works by local artists; the Amy
Johnson Room' is devoted to memorabilia
of the famous aviator.

Environs: Bainton (*c.* 15 m. SW): The
church of *St.Andrew* is 14C. Around the
outside there are numerous animal figures
and human grotesques; the interior contains a fine Romanesque font.
Barmston (*c.* 7 m. S): The late Gothic
church of *All Saints* is 15C; the interior
contains an unusual Romanesque font.
Boynton (*c.* 3 m. W.): The church of *St.
Andrew* was completely rebuilt by John
Carr of York in 1768; the tower, however,
is 15C. *Boynton Hall*, a Tudor manor
house from 1550, is also worth seeing.
Burton Agnes (*c.* 6 m. SW): The church
of *St.Martin* was originally Romanesque
and has a fine Romanesque font. *Burton
Agnes Hall* is also interesting. Built 1598
–1610 in Elizabethan style, it was extended
by Inigo Jones in 1628. It houses a valuable collection of the work of French Impressionists, period furniture and Chinese
porcelain.
Carnaby (*c.* 2.5 m. SW): The *church* has
a fine 11C Romanesque window.
Flamborough (*c.* 5 m. NE): The church
of *St. Oswald* is basically 13C, although
some of the structure is older still. The
chancel wall is interesting, as is the medieval window in the N. aisle which was only
discovered in 1969. The *Danish Tower*,
along with the remains of a 14C fortification, are also worth seeing. To the W. of
the village is *Danes' Dyke*, a fortification
running N-S, whose origin has not been
fully explained, but which is thought may
possibly be prehistoric.
Great Driffield (*c.* 12 m. SW): A fine
early Romanesque *church* with a Perpendicular tower.
Rudstone (*c.* 6 m. W.): A fine Gothic
church with a Romanesque tower; the interior contains an ornate 12C font.
Skipsea (*c.* 10.5 m. S.): The *church* was
built in 1196 from which time parts of the

Llantwit Major (Bridgend), gravestone

original Early English building have survived.

Sledmere (*c.* 15 m. W.): The Georgian manor house, *Sledmere Hall*, was built in 1787. The library, which is 100 ft. long has period furniture and fine porcelain and paintings.

Weaverthorpe (*c.* 12.5 m. W.): The Romanesque church of *St.Andrew* was restored in 1872. Inside there is a Romanesque font.

Brighton
East Sussex / England   p.332 □ K 16

The former fishing village of Brighthelmstone came to public attention in 1750 when Dr.Richard Russell wrote a book about the healing effect of salt water and sea air. In 1782 the Prince of Wales, later King George IV, took up residence here, and Brighton became one of the most elegant and celebrated bathing resorts in the country.

Royal Pavilion: The pride of the city, it was built by John Nash in 1811 in pseudo-Indian style. This fairytale palace is decorated with onion domes, tent-roofs over the side pavilions, crenellations, minarets and latticed balconies. A royal residence until 1845, it is said that Queen Victoria loathed it. Today it houses collections and large exhibitions.

The *interior* decoration is Chinese, and the furniture, some of which was very costly, was taken to Windsor and Buckingham Palace (although most of it has now been restored to its original place.

There are 23 state rooms in the Royal Pavilion, of which the following are the most interesting: the *Banqueting Room* has a palm-like ceiling, a chandelier decorated with dragons and walls covered with attractive wall paintings; the *Music Room*; the *Kitchen*, which has old copper pots and pans, and the *Royal Private Library*.

Parish church of St. Peter: Built in Gothic style by Sir Charles Barry in 1825. The chancel was added 1896–1902.

Museums: Brighton has a number of museums and stages many exhibitions to delight the visitor.

Museum and Art Gallery: This has exhibitions of folklore, archaeology and botany and collections of musical instruments, furniture, porcelain and paintings.

Booth Museum: Houses an extensive collection of British birds.

Aquarium: At the foot of the cliff, it has many species of fish, which can be seen in their natural environment.

Also worth seeing: *Preston Manor*, a late-18C manor house, houses collections of furniture, paintings and silverware from all over Europe. **The Dome**, the main concert venue, and the old *Corn Exchange*. The old fishing village is brought to mind with *The Lanes*, which have been converted from attractive little 17C fishing cottages into shops (predominantly selling antiques). Most of the other town houses are Regency or Victorian in style and have beautiful windows and balconies. The impressive *rockery* is the largest in the world.

Environs: Danny (*c.* 3 m. NW): This village contains a late-Elizabethan *house* (16C).

Falmer (*c.* 1 m. E): The *University of Sussex*, was built by Sir Basil Spence in 1961.

Hollingbury (*c.* 5 m. N.): Remains of an Iron Age *fort*.

Hove: Like Brighton, to which it is attached, Hove is a well-known coastal resort. The *museum* is interesting in that it exhibits the most important periods of British art in the context of contemporary design and furnishings. *All Saints Church* is 19C and has a fine carved high altar.

Brighton, Royal Pavilion

Brighton, Royal Pavilion

Shoreham-by-Sea (*c.* 3 m. SW): The *Marlipins Museum*, which is housed in a 12–14C house, is dedicated to seafaring, nd includes model ships, maps, nautical equipment and paintings on the theme of sailing.

Bristol

Avon/England   p.322☐H 15

This busy industrial town and trading centre at the mouth of the Avon was founded by the Saxons and has been known as a port since early times because it could be reached up the Avon on a flood tide. For this reason, the old castle belonging to Robert, Earl of Gloucester, which stood at the confluence of the Avon and the Frome, was converted into a fortress in 1126. In 1497 John Cabot sailed from Bristol to the American mainland, and his son Sebastian explored the E. coast from Newfoundland to Florida the following year. The city was claimed by both parties during the Civil War, until finally, in 1655, Cromwell ordered the destruction of the castle. How-ever, this had little effect on the flourishing trade with America (most of the English ships which took slaves to America and returned with sugar, rum or tobacco were based in Bristol). The prosperity of the city at the time is most clearly displayed in its splendid religious buildings.

Cathedral: Founded by Robert Fitzhardinge for Augustinian canons in 1148. Only the *chapterhouse* has survived from the original Norman construction; the oldest part of the church itself is the *old Lady Chapel* from 1215, on to which the chancel and the N. transept were built. The chancel itself dates from 1298–1363; the transept was rebuilt in 1465. At the time of the dissolution of the monasteries, the new nave was only half finished and further building was out of the question. Work did not continue until 1868, when G.E.Street took on the job. In fact the old sections were maintained and the new ones completed as a result of the former abbey church being designated to be the cathedral church of the see of Bristol created by Henry VIII in 1542.

Immediately before the entrance is the *hall choir*, which at the time of its construction was unique. The spatial effect is no longer given by the dynamic rise from the aisles to the centre, but by the rise of the arches to the vaulting, which opens the central space in both directions. Instead of triforium and clerestory there is an integrated space, defined by bundles of columns which join directly to the ceiling. Together with England's first liernes they form continuous *stellar vaulting*, which is no longer limited by the girder arches of the truss. The chancel, basically early Gothic, represents the first attempt in Europe to move from a basilican to a hall church. The *choir stalls*, added by Abbot Elyot, date from 1515–26; the organ case and the ornamental pipes are from 1685. The E. Lady Chapel, built at the same time as the chancel, has a fine *E. window*, which still has some original pieces from 1340. On the S. side of the chancel is the old monastery *sacristy* (1306–10), which has a flat, early Gothic stone ceiling. The *Berkeley Chapel*, attached on the E. side, displays fine decorations on the arches of the entrance. The *old Lady Chapel* (*c.* 1215) is attached to the N. side of the chancel; it has been maintained in Early English style and has finely decorated arcades with grotesque sculptures. The Norman *chapterhouse* is attached to the S. transept and dates from around 1160; it is decorated with geometrical zig-zag patterns.

Church of St. Mary Redcliffe: In 1574, Queen Elizabeth I called this 'the most famous parish church in England'—an epithet not lightly bestowed. The building is high Gothic from 1330–75, and was built to replace an older 12C building. The lower part of the tower is mid-13C; the Gothic spire early-14C. The finest external feature is undoubtedly the late-13C *N. portal*, which is divided into three sections, the arches of which are each broken down into rows of ogee arches with almost orien-

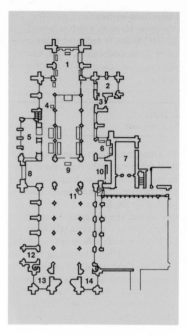

Bristol Cathedral 1 Lady Chapel **2** Berkeley Chapel **3** sacristy (1306–10) **4** pulpit **5** old Lady Chapel (1215) **6** Newton Chapel **7** chapterhouse (*c.* 1160) **8** N. transept **9** altar **10** S. transept **11** pulpit **12** N. portal **13** NW tower **14** SW tower

tal decorations. The *interior* is high Gothic at its most splendid. The large windows of the clerestory make the building (260 ft. long) light and airy, and emphasize the structure of the slim bundles of pillars uninterrupted by capitals. The *net vaulting* has delicate bosses and more than 1,000 gilded keystones at its peak. The *American Chapel* under the tower contains a polychrome wooden figure of Queen Elizabeth I from 1574, in whose hands are a globe and sceptre. The church also contains a number of gravestones and memorial plaques.

Church of St. Mark: This church, also

Bristol, cathedral tower

known as the *Lord Mayor's chapel*, was founded by Maurice de Gaunt in 1230. It was originally the chapel attached to Gaunt's Hospital but, in 1541 after the hospital was closed down, it was taken over by the town. It was used by the Huguenots 1687–1722, but since that time it has belonged to the town again. The original building dates from the 13C, but there have been numerous alterations so that now only the walls of the nave and the transept arches are from the original construction. The sanctuary and tower are late-15C, the roof over the nave was restored in the 16C, and the *stained glass*, which includes some impressive pieces, is French/Flemish work from the 16–17C. The church houses many tombs, some of which date back to the 13C.

Museums: The *City Art Gallery* was donated by Sir W.H.Wills and contains fine paintings, sculptures, ceramics, glass and textiles.

The *City Museum* houses archaeological, geological and natural history exhibits.

Clifton Suspension Bridge: England's finest 19C suspension bridge, it was erected 1831–64 by the engineering genius Isambard Kingdom Brunel, who built the Great Western Railway between London and Bristol. The total length of the bridge is some 1,350 ft., with a span of 700 ft. between the two pylons; traffic crosses some 250 ft. above the Avon. Brunel used parts of the old Hungerford Bridge in London in the construction.

Environs: Almondsbury (*c.* 6 m. N.): According to legend, the Anglo-Saxon king Almond is buried here. The church of

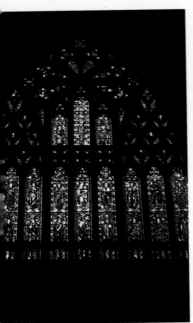

Bristol, Lady Chapel, E. window

St.Mary has Norman remains and an Early English sanctuary. There is a double tomb with figures from the 16C.
Clevedon Court (*c.* 14 m. SW): 12C *manor house* with extensions and alterations in a range of later styles. Since 1709 it has been the seat of the Elton family. It houses collections of paintings, pottery and porcelain and there is an exhibition of the history of the railway, as well as an exceptional display of Naisea glass and other glass curiosities. The 19C satirist Thackeray wrote much of his novel 'Vanity Fair' and his novella 'Henry Esmond' here; a Thackeray room has memorabilia of the writer. The terraced garden was designed in the 18C.
Dodington House (*c.* 9 m. NE): This house was originally Elizabethan and has been the seat of the Codrington family since 1578. The house visible today was

commissioned by Christopher Codrington and built in Regency style by James Wyatt 1769–1813. Its W. front is dominated by a portico supported by six mighty Corinthian columns and extending over both storeys. The entrance hall is decorated in white, red and black with brass inlay work, and the staircase, which is open to both floors, is separated into half sections. It is framed by arcades on the ground floor, and a gallery and balcony on the floor above. The wrought-iron bannisters, which are probably Italian from around 1760, were installed in 1808, having come from the demolished Fonthill Abbey. The house is furnished in Regency style and houses a *coach museum*. The gardens dating from 1764 are by Capability Brown. Two attractive lakes on different levels are linked by means of a waterfall.
Severn Bridge (*c.* 14 m. N.): This suspension bridge was finished in 1966 and has a span of *c.* 3,250 ft. between its two 400 ft. pylons. Each of the two cables carry about 7,000 tons.

Buckingham
Buckinghamshire/England   p.332☐I 14

This pleasant old town grew up around the market place and the Georgian town hall. The prison, near the market place, was built in the style of a small castle in 1758.

Chantry Chapel: Originally part of a Norman church, of which only the portal survives. The remains of the old church were replaced by the new chapel in 1475.

Environs: Chetwode (*c.* 8 m. SW): The church of *St. Mary and St. Nicholas* was originally the sanctuary of an old monastery church built around 1250. The E. end is interesting having fine lancet windows (the original 13–14C stained glass has been replaced by Victorian replicas). The pis-

Bristol, cathedral, nave

cina and sedilia have tooth-shaped decorations.

Chicheley (*c.* 9 m. NE): The church of *St.Lawrence* is 14C (nave and N. aisle); 15C tower. An interesting pulpit dates from 1708.

Gayhurst (*c.* 10 m. NE): The church of *St.Peter* was built in 1728 on the site of an older church; interesting W. tower. Inside there are fine wood carvings; the monument to Sir Nathan Wright and his son is decorated with two standing figures in clothing of the period.

Hillesden (2.5 m. S.): The late-Gothic church of *All Saints* has a well-proportioned W. tower with fine crenellations. A row of stone angels holding scrolls decorate the underside of the sanctuary roof.

Perhaps the most interesting piece is the celebrated stained-glass window depicting scenes from the life of St.Nicholas. In eight sections, it dates from the 16C and shows clear Flemish influence.

The church also has many tombs, including one in marble for A.Denton and his wife which was carved by Sir Henry Cheere in 1733.

Burford
Oxfordshire/England   p.332☐I 14

This small town on the Windrush was once the centre of the wool industry in the Cotswolds. As well as the old *bridge* over the Windrush, a number of old wool traders' *houses* are still standing.

Church of St.John the Baptist: This dates back to Norman times, and has a central tower decorated with a fine spire; most of the structure we see today is early and mid Gothic. There are an impressive number of *memorial chapels* and numerous *tombs*, including those of Speaker Lenthall and John Falkner.

Tolsey Museum: The 16C former *customs house* now houses an exhibition of local history, documenting development from Norman times to the present day.

Environs: Great Barrington (2.5 m. W.): The church of *St. Mary the Virgin* dates back to Norman times, although most of the structure visible today is early and mid Gothic. The triumphal arch is entirely Norman; the vaulting in the nave is 15C. Two interesting children's tombs are the work of Christopher Cass and date from 1711 and 1720.

Minster Lovell (*c.* 6 m. E.): The cruciform church of *St. Kenelm* (15C) has a central tower which is unusual in that the dimensions of the tower do not correspond to those of the church itself. Because the tower is thinner, its pillars cut into the nave

at the crossing. There are interesting 15C glass windows, a Gothic font and a few fine wood carvings. The alabaster tomb of Lord Lovell, the church's founder, is from 1430. *Minster Lovell Hall*, the old manor house of the Lords of Lovell, was destroyed *c.* 1750. Francis Lovell made the mistake of becoming too closely involved with Richard III and, after Richard's defeat, Henry VII refused to pardon him and he had to hide away at his country seat. It was not until rebuilding in 1708, over 200 years later, that his skeleton was found in its hiding place. The remains of the main hall are all that has survived.

Northleach (11 m. W.): The church of *St. Peter and St. Paul* is predominantly 15C. It would seem that its architect was more concerned with impressing through size than beauty, although the S. entrance with vaulted ceiling is pleasing. The clerestory over the triumphal arches is by John Fortey. The stone pulpit is Gothic and the font, which is also 15C, is decorated with reliefs of faces.

Witney (10 m. E.): A small town known for its blankets. It is situated on the Win-

Burford, St. John the Baptist, W. portal (l.), view (r.)

drush and still has some old 18C factory buildings. The *Butter Cross* in the market place dates from 1683. *Blanket Hall*, a wool exchange and meeting place for buyers, was built in 1721. The church of *St.Mary the Virgin* dates back to Norman times, although the present building is predominantly early and mid Gothic. The early-Gothic N. window is interesting; there are some 14–15C tombs.

Burnley
Lancashire/England   p.328☐H 11

Towneley Hall (in the SE of the town): This fortified manor house was the seat of the Towneley family from the 13C until 1902. The building visible today was originally 14C, although it has been rebuilt on many subsequent occasions (especially the 16, 17&19C). The entrance hall is early-18C in English baroque style; two rooms are in Regency style of the early 19C; the Long Gallery is in Elizabethan style and the chapel is 16C. The interior contains some fine old furniture (Tudor and Jaco-

bean), interesting paintings and stucco. It also houses two modern art collections. In summer the exhibitions are changed regularly. The house's former brewery is now a local museum, which includes some interesting examples of local crafts.

Also worth seeing: The church of *St. Peter* has the remains of some old crosses.

Environs: Accrington (*c*. 5 m. SW): The *Haworth Art Gallery* is housed in a neo-Renaissance building commissioned by the textile magnate William Haworth in 1909. The interior has some fine stucco and panelling. Exhibits include an exceptionally fine collection of Tiffany glass by the American L.C.Tiffany (1848–1933).
Bacup (*c*. 5 m. S.): The *Bacup Natural History Society's Museum* is housed in an old 18C inn and includes displays of natural history, local archaeology and past local culture.
Clitheroe (*c*. 7 m. NW): A market town since the 12C. The *ruined castle* (Norman in origin) houses a small *museum* with some interesting fossils.

Burford, St.John the Baptist, carving on tomb

much related to local history. The display of the clogmaker's skills is interesting, as are the scores, and instruments of 'The Larks of Dean', a well-known group of 18C musicians.

Slaidburn (*c.* 16 m. NW): There is a *church* with a well-preserved 17C Jacobean rood screen.

Whalley (*c.* 7 m. NW): The site of the remains of *Whalley Abbey*, which was built by Cistercian monks in 1296 (the cloisters are among those parts which have survived best). The church of *St. Mary and All Saints*, originally Norman/Romanesque, was rebuilt in Gothic style from the 13–15C. Old choirstalls came from the abbey church; the fine organ dates from 1729. In the *graveyard* nearby there are pre-Romanesque crosses.

Bury St.Edmunds, St.Mary

Colne (*c.* 5 m. NE): The church of *St. Bartholomew*, which was completed by 1122, was altered in the 15C in Perpendicular style. Inside there are some fine 18C tombs of the Emmot family (by Sir Thomas Taylor). Other things of interest include the *British in India Museum*, which documents some 150 years of British rule in India. On display are old photographs, uniforms, coins, illustrations and models, as well as a costume, which formerly belonged to an Afghan princess and was presented to Queen Victoria.

Gawthorpe Hall (*c.* 3 m. W.): The seat of the Shuttleworth family since 1330. The *castle*, built in Jacobean style, houses a *museum* of textiles and early European furniture.

Rawenstall (*c.* 6 m. S.): *Rossendale Museum* is housed in the former residence of a 19C industrialist. Its exhibits include

Bury St. Edmunds
Suffolk/England   p.328□L 14

This county town was known to the Saxons as Beodericsworth. Its motto 'Sacrarium Regis, Cunabula Legis' details the crucial points of its history: it was the burial site of King Edmund, who was later canonised, and in 1214 the lords swore on the high altar of the monastery church to force King John to sign the Magna Carta. The shrine of King Edmund became a pilgrimage destination, and a monastery was built around it. Abbot Baldwin was able to prevent the destruction of the monastery during the Norman conquest, since he was a Frenchman himself. In 1121 Abbot Anselm was appointed, and under his supervision the monastery developed one of the most celebrated writing-rooms of the time, whose valuable illustrated manuscripts can now be found in the world's most prestigious museums. The famous *Bury Bible* is now housed in Corpus Christi College in Cambridge. In 1327 the townspeople and monks quarelled so fiercely that the

Bury St. Edmunds, abbey gate-tower

Cathedral of St. James

monks destroyed the parish church and the townsfolk the abbey church.

Abbey: The first monastery was founded in 636, and in 1032 King Canute elevated it to the rank of an abbey. In the second half of the 11C, Abbot Baldwin converted it into a large, fortified square structure with no less than five mighty *gate-towers*. In the first half of the 16C the abbey of St. Edmundsbury was one of the most famous and wealthy in the whole of England. Only parts of the west façade and the remains of the east section still stand from the massive old abbey church. The abbey's overall groundplan can still be easily recognised, but none of the buildings are still there except for two of the gate-towers. The older of the two is 12C, a fine example of early Norman architecture. The more recent one was renovated in the mid-14C after its destruction by the townspeople in 1347.

Cathedral of St. James: The church is near the Norman gate-tower; it was begun in 1438 and elevated to the rank of cathedral in 1914. Only the walls of the nave are 15C; the windows and roof were restored in the 19C. The sanctuary was extended by G. Scott and renovated by S. Dykes-Bower.

Church of St. Mary: This large 15C church has a fine dragon-beam ceiling, decorated with angels, over the nave, and barrel-vaulting over the chancel. It also has a number of *tombs*, some of which date back to the 15C. In the NE corner of the sanctuary is the tomb of Mary Tudor (1496–1533), sister of Henry VIII and the Queen of France.

Moyses Hall Museum: The house, which used to belong to a Jewish trader, was built in the 12C; it is the *oldest residential house* in East Anglia and now houses a museum. The exhibits include a monks' chronicle from the 13C, and a range of pieces from prehistoric to medieval times. The most interesting are from a Bronze Age find in Isleham, Cambridgeshire in 1959, whose treasures are among the most significant of their time so far found in Great Britain. The decorations on the numerous tools found there show parallels with similar finds in the Upper Rhine area, Western France and Hungary.

Suffolk Regiment Museum: This is a museun dedicated to the history of the regiment of the county of Suffolk.

Environs: Bardwell (9 m. NE): The *Church of St. Peter and St. Paul* dates back to the 15C, but was renovated and extended in the 16C. The south portal is still standing from 1430, and the dragon-beam ceiling was originally decorated with angels, but little of the decorative work remains. There are also a few fragments of 15C stained glass.

Hawstead (5 m. S.): The *Church of All Saints* dates back to Norman times, and has a highly decorated Gothic west tower. The nave has a dragon-beam ceiling decorated with angels, highly ornamented pews and a 16C pulpit. The choir screen is 15C, and there are a number of tombs, some of which date back to the 13C.

Hessett (6 m. NE): The *Church of St. Ethelbert* is 14C in origin, with a west tower from the 15C. The pews, choir screen and font are also 15C, and there are 14/15C frescos depicting the Seven Deadly Sins, St. Barbara and St. Christopher. The sacristy was built in the 14C and was once the cell of a hermitage, which is why it still has its own altar.

Ickworth House (4 m. SW): Frederick August Hervey, the Fourth Earl of Bristol

and the Bishop of Derry, commissioned this unusual house in 1792 to house and display his collection of art and paintings. It was begun in 1794 with the two side-wings, according to plans by the Irish architect Francis Sandys, and after the bishop's death in 1803 the Marquis of Bristol completed it in 1830. Today it houses some valuable furniture, an impressive collection of silver, a painting collection and a varied selection of art pieces. The gardens were designed by Capability Brown.

Stowlangtoft (9 m. SE): The *Church of St. George* is Gothic, and is celebrated for its wood-carvings. The sides of the pews in the nave are as highly-decorated as the choirstalls, and the misericords are exceptionally fine. The Passion scenes on the altar were carved by Flemish masters in the 15C, and the font is 14C in origin. There are some fragments of a fresco of St. Christopher which may be 15C.

West Stow Hall (8 m. NW): The *manor house* was built in 1520 by Sir John Crofts, who was Maty Tudor's marshall. One of the rooms contains an Elizabethan fresco, which depicts the four ages of man.

Buxton
Derbyshire/England   p.328☐I 12

Buxton was already known in Roman times as a place of hot springs, but in the 19C it became a much-sought-after spa, as the radioactivity in its springs was believed to have power against gout and rheumatism. The atmosphere of *Lower Buxton*, the elegant bathing quarter, is dominated by the Victorian buildings.

The Crescent: This was built from 1780–84 at the instigation of the Duke of Devonshire on the site of an old Roman hot bath. It is a semi-circular Palladian-

Bury St. Edmunds, water spout

influenced late Renaissance structure. Opposite, at the foot of the 'slopes' of *St.Ann's Well*, are the oldest and best-known of the town's hot springs. The *Old Hall* (1600) was extended in 1670.

Museum: This houses collections of local town history, local geology (includes some interesting minerals), and a small art collection with paintings, prints, ceramics and glass-work.

Also worth seeing: The parish church of *St. John the Baptist* dates from 1811. The *Devonshire Hospital* was built as a riding-school in the 18C. *Poole's Cavern*, a chalk cave with stalactites and stalagmites has a small geological museum near the entrance. *Solomon's Temple* (S. of the city centre), a round tower on a prehistoric burial mound known as 'Grin Low', was erected

in 1896 to the memory of Solomon Mycock, who two years previously had given permission for scientific excavation of the mound, which was on his land.

Environs: Arbor Low (*c.* 9 m. SE): This *arrangement of stone crosses*, dating from the early Stone Age or Bronze Age (some 1700 BC), originally consisted of *c.* 50 free-standing stones, 2–3m high, and surrounded by a wall and a ditch. Nearby there is a Bronze Age burial mound.

Bakewell (*c.* 10 m. SE): The church of *All Saints* is Norman in origin but has since been altered. There is a fine Romanesque W. portal; the nave is early Gothic. Inside there are interesting tombs. The 13C *bridge* over the Wye is also worth seeing (being one of the oldest bridges in England), as is the *Old House*, a 16C house with original furnishings (now a museum).

Castleton (*c.* 9 m. NE): The church of *St.Edmund*, originally Norman, was later rebuilt. Inside there are Romanesque chancel arches, 17C stucco and a fine old font. The ruins of *Peveril Castle* are also interesting. Built in the 11C, it was one of the first Norman castles to be built in stone. The keep dates from 1176. To the NW is *Mam Tor*, an Iron Age hill fortress. There are also Bronze Age burial mounds in the area.

Chapel-en-le-Frith (*c.* 5 m. N.): The church of *St.Thomas à Becket* was already standing in 1225; the building visible today is late-14C. The font is late Gothic. Remains of the old church are still visible in the chancel.

Eyam (10 m. NE): The pre-Romanesque church has an Anglo-Saxon font in the sacristy; Romanesque remains include two pillars on the N. side. In the churchyard there is an Anglo-Saxon cross some 10 ft. tall. The village became famous in 1665 when a large proportion of the inhabitants died of the plague; the rector persuaded the villagers not to leave the village and thus the spread of the plague was checked.

Haddon Hall (*c.* 12 m. SE): This *manor house* dates back to Norman times, although most of what we see today is 14–16C. The banqueting hall, dining room, chapel and Long Gallery (*c.* 100 ft.) are all interesting.

Hope (*c.* 9 m. N.): The late-Gothic *church* from the 15C has part of an Anglo-Saxon cross near the S. porch; there are also a Romanesque font and a fine oak pulpit.

Taddington (*c.* 6 m. E.): The 14C *church* has been restored. There is an old stone lectern and, in the churchyard, the remains of an old Anglo-Saxon cross. Near the village is *Five Wells Tumulus*, a prehistoric burial ground.

Tideswell (*c.* 6m. NE): The church of *St. John the Baptist*, known as the 'Cathedral of the Peak', was built in the 14C and has remained largely unaltered. The font and the choir screen are from the original construction; there are some interesting 14/15C tombs.

Youlgreave (*c.* 12 m. SE): The church of *All Saints* has a Romanesque nave and a late-Gothic W. tower. The font is Romanesque and there is a stained-glass window by Sir Edward Burne-Jones.

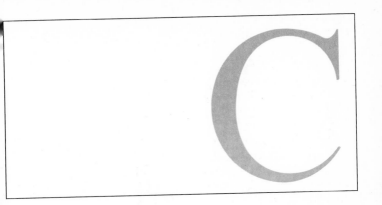

Caernarfon
Gwynedd/Wales   p.328□F 12

This charming little ancient town (pop. *c.* 10,000) is on the SW of the Menai Straits, a sea channel about a mile wide between the mainland of NW Wales and the island of Anglesey (q.v.). The town has an eventful history. The son of Edward I of England (later King Edward II) was born here in 1284; he was later proclaimed 'Prince of Wales' by agreement. This tradition by which the heir to the throne of England is first crowned Prince of Wales has been retained and indeed Prince Charles was invested as Prince of Wales in 1969.

Caernarfon Castle: In the S. of the town where the river Seiont flows into the Menai Straits. It is one of the best-preserved and most impressive medieval fortresses in Europe and is protected by the sea, the river and a moat. The building was completed 1283–1327 (under Edward I) and stands on the site of an earlier wooden Norman

Caernarfon Castle 1 King's Gate **2** kitchen **3** Well Tower **4** inner ward **5** Eagle Tower **6** town walls **7** Queen's Tower housing the museum of the Royal Welsh Fusiliers **8** Knight's hall **9** Chamberlain Tower **10** Black Tower **11** Cistern Tower **12** Queen's Gate **13** NE tower **14** Granary Tower **15** outer ward

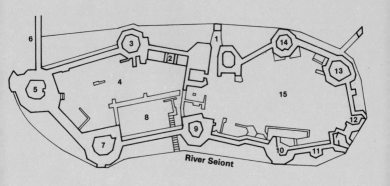

castle with ramparts. To enter the castle you cross the moat in the N. and pass through the *King's Gate* which has a statue of Edward II. The *gateway* has openings for the portcullis, machicolations (holes for pitch) and arrow slits as far as the *gatehouse*. You then enter the *lower or inner castle courtyard*. Here there are the foundation walls of the *kitchen, well tower* and battlemented sentry walkway as far as the *Eagle Tower*, where medieval armour is on display. The *town wall* leading northwards also began here. Then follows the *Queen's Tower* to the E., which today houses the *Museum of the Royal Welch Fusiliers*. There are also the foundation walls of the former *Great Hall* with a sally port towards the river. From the *Chamberlain Tower* (opposite the main entrance; open to visitors) 3 *sentry walks* lead E. over the Black Tower to the Cistern Tower. The *Queen's Gate* in the SE is the second castle gate and originally led to a drawbridge over the river Seiont. The *NE Tower* has an exhibition of Prince Charles's Investiture (1 July 1969). The *Granary Tower* then follows to the NW.

Caernarfon, Caernarfon Castle

St.Mary's Church: This much restored 14C church is in the NW of the old town, close to the bend in the town wall. The old *rampart tower* is at the same time the bell tower and the sacristy (installed in 1740). The Early English *arcades* between the aisles of the church are interesting and have good carvings of heads in the arch spandrels.

Also worth seeing: The *town walls*, which in parts have survived well. They are closely related to the castle (see plan) and are reinforced by defensive towers. There are 2 large *town gates* at the W. and E. ends of the High Street. At the E. end is the impressive *Porth Mawr* or Great Gate, which has been subject to several conversions and was the Town Hall for a time (damaged in 1963). The streets of the

old town are planned in the following way: the High Street has an E-W axis, there are three streets on a N-S axis and a passage around the wall. In the SE of the town, towards Beddgelert, there are the interesting excavated remains of *Fort Segontium*, the most northerly Roman fortification (AD 78–385) in Wales. The *archaeological museum* near the fort has good finds from the Roman and Celtic periods. On *Twt Hill* (just outside the town, at Twt Hill West), there are traces of a primitive *Celtic settlement* (rocky ditch). In the suburb of *Llanbeblig*, near the Roman fort in the SE, there is a 13C *church* with funerary monuments.

Environs: Beddgelert (about 12.5 m. SE): A delightfully located holiday village in the S. of Snowdonia. Nearby, at *Dinas Emrys* and close to the lake, *Llyn Dinas*, there are earthworks and some remains of

an early Celtic refuge from the 5C; the site is associated with the wizard Merlin. A scenic tour through the peaks can also be made from Beddgelert.

Llanberis (c. 7.5 m. to the SE): Located between two lakes. From here there are excursions into the nearby *Snowdon National Park*. You can travel to *Snowdon's summit* (at 3,560 ft. it is Wales's highest mountain) on the only rack-and-pinion railway in Great Britain. The track is c. 5 m. long and dates from 1896. There are magnificent views from the train. On the smaller lake (Llyn Peris) there are the remains of *Dolbadarn Castle*, with a circular keep. Built in the 12–13C under Llewelyn the Great, it provided protection against Norman raids and defended the Llanberis pass.

Nant Peris (Old Llanberis, c. 9 m. to the SE): A picturesque village. Part of the church of *St. Peris* dates back to the 6C.

Caerphilly/Caerffili
Mid Glamorgan/Wales   p.332☐G 15

A small town some 8 m. N. of Cardiff which has given its name to a fine white cheese.

Caerphilly Castle: A well-preserved castle standing in marshy countryside. It is the largest fortification in Wales and is said to be the second largest in England and Wales after Windsor Castle. Edward I, who conquered Wales, had it built in c. 1270 to a concentric ground plan, which made it easy to defend on all sides. It has several *sally ports* and *sally gates* and instead of a keep, one of the *gatehouses* was enlarged into a last refuge (with portcullises). You enter the castle through the outer *castle gate*. There are a *castle moat, dungeon* and

Cambridge, King's College, The Backs

water mill. You then pass over a bridge and through the second castle gate into the *castle courtyard*. Here are the *Great Hall* the *E. Gatehouse* which functions as the keep and more *sally ports*, which lead to the outside front courtyard in the W. The W. gatehouse leads to the *outwork*, a small island in the marshy sea. The castle began to decay in the 14C. One of its towers was blown up by Cromwell's soldiers and since then, known as the *Leaning Tower*, it has been Caerphilly's landmark. (The 79 ft. high tower has 10 ft. deviation from the vertical.)

Environs: Castle Coch (some 4 km. to the S.): Built and decorated throughout in fairy-tale style by William Burges in the 19C. Inside there are paintings on the walls and ceilings (birds, monkeys, butterflies, scenes from Aesop's Fables, heraldic mo-

tifs). There are also ruins of a 13C castle with a triangular ground plan which previously occupied the site.

Cahir

Tipperary/Ireland   p.330□C 13

A town with 2,000 inhabitants on the river Suir. The imposing, well-preserved *Cahir Castle* (Gaelic 'cahir' = fortification) stands on a rock on the river. The castle was built by the Butler family in the 15–16C and is one of the largest castles in Ireland. Restoration work was carried out in 1840 & 1964. At the edge of the town there are ruins of *Cahir Abbey*, an Augustinian house founded in 1220. The neo-Gothic Protestant *cathedral* was built by the famous architect John Nash in 1817.

Cambridge, Queens' College

Environs: Mitchelstown (*c.* 16 km. SW): A dairy town, with *c.* 3,000 inhabitants; it received a large-scale conversion frfrom Kingston, the landlord in the 18C. The *castle*, built in Tudor style in 1823, was much damaged by a fire in 1922. Nearby are the interesting *Mitchelstown Caves*, which have stalagmites and served as a refuge in the Munster rebellion of 1601.

Cambridge
Cambridgeshire/England   p.328□K 14

The settlement on the bridge across the Cam, originally called the Granta, already existed at the time of the Romans. Its name was formed from the previous Grantebrycge via Cantebrigge to the modern Cambridge, which then in turn gave the river its name. From an early stage the importance of the settlement was associated with the reputation of an educatiional establishment: in the early 12C there was a monastery school, which Henry III praised in 1231. The oldest college, *Peterhouse*, was founded in 1284 by Hugh of Balsham, Bishop of Ely. There was a setback in 1381, when friction between the university and the town became so great that the various colleges already in existence were plundered and many of their writings destroyed. However, the *university* itself survived the attack. It reached a high point in 1510 when it obtained the teaching services of Erasmus of Rotterdam, the most important humanist of that period. Even the Reformation, which greatly harmed the other universities, left only slight traces here. No subsequent event has had any lasting impact on the continuous development of the university, and today there are 23 colleges. Thus the charm of the city lies in the fact that its growth as a small town continued undisturbed for about a millennium, old houses and little alleyways surviving with minimal alteration.

Church of the Holy Sepulchre: One of the four round Norman churches still surviving in England, it dates from 1130. The chancel was added in the 14C and vaulted with oak in the 15C. The church was restored in 1842 with regrettably little skill.

Peterhouse: Founded in 1284, this is the oldest college in the University. The hall still contains sections of the original buildings dating from the end of the 13C. The *chapel* built 1628–32 is worth seeing; the E. window has the original glazing. The altar is adorned by a 15C carved Pietà.

King's College: Founded by Henry VI in 1441. The late Gothic *chapel* on the N. side of the large courtyard was begun under Henry VI in 1446 and completed under Henry VIII in 1515. It is regarded as

the university's 'crowning glory' and is furnished accordingly. The 25 superb *stained-glass windows* all date from the 16C, except for one window at the W. end which is the work of Clayton and Bell. The breathtakingly beautiful *fan vaulting* complements the windows, *choir stalls* and the carved *wooden organ case* (1536). The altar has a painting of the Adoration of the Magi by Rubens. Most of the furnishings of the side chapels date from the time of the first phase of building: the vault of the chapel in the NE corner was completed before 1461; the *War Memorial Chapel* in the SE corner still has its Flemish glazing dating from 1530. The *Fellows' Building* was built by Gibbs from 1724 onwards in classical style.

Queens' College: Founded in 1448 by Andrew Dokett and refounded by Margaret of Anjou, Henry VI's wife. Its buildings and courtyards are among the most picturesque in the city. The buildings around the first courtyard date from the 15C. The large hall, with its painted ceiling, was restored in 1732. The *President's*

King's College, gateway

King's College

Lodge on the N. side of Cloister Court was built in 1537 and contains a splendid 16C wooden panelled gallery. By the Pump Court is *Erasmus Tower*, where Erasmus lived when he was teaching Greek in the college (1510–13).

Jesus College: Founded in 1496 by John Alcock, Bishop of Ely, on the site of the Benedictine nunnery of St. Radegunde, which he dissolved. Without any great effort the Bishop thus obtained all the buildings required to operate a college. The convent church served thereafter as college chapel, the rector took on the abbess's house and the refectory became the dining hall; the only residential building needed an additional storey. Consequently sufficient funds remained for the Bishop to build a splendid *gatehouse*—probably intended to honour him rather than to be of use to the college. The oldest part of the complex is the cruciform *monastery church*, which was built *c.* 1200. Thanks to Bishop Alcock, it survived practically unaltered; only the W. part of the nave was separated off and integrated into the rector's house.

The carefully restored *chapel* has Norman parts, especially in the N. transept but the overall impression is Early English. The *stained glass windows* are by Pugin and Hardman, Madox Brown, Burne-Jones and Morris. On the E. side of the early 16C *Cloister Court* the chapterhouse of 1210 has an outstandingly finely carved portal.

St. John's College: Founded by Lady Margaret Beaufort, who was the Countess of Richmond and Derby and Henry VII's mother, to replace the 13C Hospital of St. John. The foundress herself died in 1509 and thus did not live to see the college open to students but her adviser, Bishop John Fisher, continued the work and the college opened in 1511. The splendid entrance is impressive; the three-storeyed *gatehouse*, by the royal architect William Swayne, is decorated with all Lady Margaret's and Henry VII's heraldic insignia. The sculpture of St. John in a niche above the symbols of royal power dates from 1662 and replaces the original figure, which was removed in the Civil War. The college *chapel* is by Sir George Gilbert

Scott 1864–9. The large *hall* has a fine dragon-beam ceiling, good panelling and numerous portraits. The *Combination Room* is also worth seeing, with its outstanding panelling, stuccoed ceiling and interesting portraits. The *Second Court*, 1598–1602, is a good example of Elizabethan brick architecture and is probably the finest courtyard in the university.

Trinity College: The largest college in the University. It was founded in 1546 by Henry VIII and incorporated the *King's Hall*, founded by Edward II in 1317 and *Michaelhouse*, founded by Harvey de Stanton in 1323. The large *gatehouse* was begun in 1518 and is decorated on the outside with a statue of Henry VIII and on the inside with sculptures of James I, Anne of Denmark and Charles I. The *Great Court* has a fountain built by order of Thomas Nevile, Rector from 1593–1615 and thereafter Archbishop of Canterbury. On its N. side is the *chapel*, built in the Tudor style and completed in 1561; partially refurnished in the 18C. Statues of Newton, Bacon, Barrow, Macaulay, Whewell and

Tennyson can be seen in the antechapel. The W. side is taken up by the hall which was completed in 1605; inside there are various portraits, including one by Reynolds. The *library* was built 1676–95 in classical style to designs by Sir Christopher Wren. The figures on the balustrade are the work of C.G.Cibber (1681). Numerous busts of famous members of the college are to be seen inside. These are by Louis Roubiliac, Michael Rysbrack, Peter Scheemakers and John Bacon the Elder. Bookcases and shelves are richly decorated with carvings by Grinling Gibbons. Famous manuscripts are on display in glass cases.

University Library: One of the largest libraries in the country. It has some 15,000 manuscripts and much early printed material. The treasures include the first book ever printed in English, the first dated Mainz Bible (1463), as well as numerous precious codices dating back to the 6C.

Fitzwilliam Museum: Founded in 1816 by the 7th Viscount Fitzwilliam of Merrion. He donated to the university not only

Queens' College Cambridge

the sum of 100,000 pounds but also his own library, his collection of 144 paintings and 130 medieval manuscripts as well as other works of art. From 1837–47 George Basevi and C.R.Cockerell built a classical building to accommodate the collection. E.M.Barry built the present entrance hall in 1875. The collections comprise exhibits from the ancient world (Egypt, Greece and Rome), medieval manuscripts and codices, paintings, drawings and printed materials from all periods, coins, medals and other works of art.

New Museum: In fact a group of several museums and a new central library.
The most interesting individual collections are the *Archaeological and Ethnological Museum*, the *Geological Museum* and the *Museum of the History of Science*.

Environs: Anglesey Abbey (some 6 m. E.): The luxuriant garden of this 17C house has the remains of a 13C *Augustinian abbey* (including the crypt). The house itself has an art collection belonging to Lord Fairhaven.

Madingley (4 m. NW): The *church of St.Mary Magdalen* has a tower with a fine spire at the W. end and in the main dates from 13&14C. Fragments of the 15&16C stained-glass windows also survive. The 17C communion rail comes from Cambridge. The church contains numerous tomb monuments, mainly to the Cotton family; the finest of these was the work of Edward Stanton in *c.* 1710. *Madingley Hall* is an Elizabethan mansion where Edward VII lived during his student days. Today it is part of Cambridge University.

Trumpington (3 m. S.): The 14C cruciform *church of St.Mary and St.Michael* is impressive for its beautiful arches and fine clerestory windows. The famous *memorial plaque* to Sir Roger de Trumpington, dating from 1289, is worth seeing; it is thought to be the second oldest in England. The *war memorial cross* by Eric Gill dates from 1921.

Wimpole Hall (about 9 m. SW): This splendid *mansion* dating from 1638 has 18C additions and alterations. It once belonged to the daughter of Rudyard Kipling. Inside there are numerous

Queens' College, Friar's Court

mementoes of the author's life and work. The drive up to the house is framed by magnificent elms.

Canterbury
Kent/England   p.332□L 15

This appealing S. English cathedral city can look back upon a history of over 2,000 years. There was already a Belgic settlement here before Caesar's legions conquered the area in 54 BC and founded the settlement of *Durovernum*. The town was given the name *Cantwarabyrig* during the Anglo-Saxon period. It was here in AD 597 that St.Augustine, who converted England to Christianity, founded the forerunner of the present cathedral. Since the 7C Canterbury Cathedral has been the mother of English churches; its Archbishop is the spiritual head of the established Church of England.

Both city and cathedral suffered considerable devastation during the Danish raids (10–11C), in the English Civil War and also during World War 2. The story of Thomas Becket (1118–1170) is indissolubly linked to the city's history. He was Lord Chancellor and friend to King Henry II, who made him Archbishop in the hope that he could increase royal influence on the church. However, once Becket had been consecrated he uncompromisingly sided with the church, aroused the King's anger and was murdered in the cathedral in 1170. The Pope canonized him in 1173.

St.Thomas à Becket's tomb, which occupied the site of his murder—until it was destroyed by order of Henry VIII in 1538 —became the destination of numerous pilgrims. The *Canterbury Tales* by Geoffrey Chaucer are a loosely connected series of stories told by such pilgrims on their way to Canterbury. The story of Becket has provided several writers with inspiration

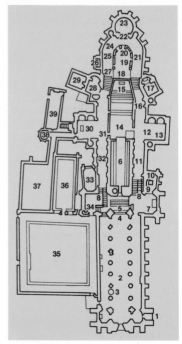

Canterbury Cathedral 1 S. porch **2** nave **3** font **4** nave altar **5** Bell Harry Lantern (splendid fan vaulting) **6** choir (one of the longest and most impressive in the city's late Gothic style) **7** SW transept **8** staircase to crypt **9** Warrior's Chapel (with numerous tombs, including that of Lady Holland, who died in 1439 and is lying between her two husbands) **10** tomb of Stephen Langton **11** S. ambulatory **12** SE transept with St.John's altar **13** Bossanyi window (completed 1960) **14** presbytery **15** high altar **16** Pilgrims' Stairs **17** St.Anselm's Chapel with 12C fresco (Paulus of Malta) **18** Trinity Chapel (with splendid stained-glass windows) **19** Tomb of Edward, the Black Prince (d.1376), with bronze sculpture **20** tomb of Coligny **21** tomb of Hubert Walter **22** Becket's Crown **23** St.Augustine's Chair **24** tomb of Dean Wotton **25** tomb of King Henry VI (d.1471) and Queen Joan of Navarre, with splendid alabaster figures **26** Chapel of Edward the Confessor **27** Becket Window (12C) **28** St.Andrew's Chapel **29** treasury **30** NE aisle with altars of St.Martin and St.Stephen **31** tomb of Archbishop Chichele (whose body can be seen inside the sarcophagus wrapped in a cloth) **32** N. ambulatory **33** Dean's or Lady Chapel **34** NW transept (in which Thomas à Becket was murdered; there is a bust and a memorial plaque) **35** cloister (vaulting with keystones bearing coats-of-arms) **36** chapter-house **37** main library **38** water tower **39** Howley Library

e.g. Tennyson (1884), T.S.Eliot (1935) and Jean Anouilh (1959).

Cathedral: Nothing has survived of the church founded by St.Augustine in 597. The present structure was built in the 12–14C in English late Gothic style. The exterior is articulated by pinnacles and flying buttresses and is overlooked by the central tower, *Bell Harry*, which rises between the chancel and the nave and was rebuilt by John Wastell in the 17C. Its shape conforms with that of the two lower W. towers. In the E. the flat *Becket's Crown* is of comparatively simple design. The chancel, which was built by William of Sens after a fire in 1174, is taller than the nave built by Henry Yvele in 1374. The visitor passes through the S. portal into the *nave,* where the tall, slender pillars direct the gaze upwards towards the magnificent vault. Most conspicuous is the large *W. window,* which has both old and modern sections. A richly decorated *dividing wall,* with statues of bishops and saints, marks the transition to the tall, majestic *chancel.* The *crypt* is the largest and probably also the finest in all of England. The main room is the *Lady Chapel,* whose splendid internal walls were added by order of Edward the Black Prince, who wanted to be buried here. Elizabeth I opened the chapel he founded *(The Black Prince's Chantry)* to Huguenots as an oratory. Its Norman simplicity has survived to the present day. The capitals of the columns in the *Chapel of St. Gabriel* are decorated with animal heads and figures; 12C wall frescos. The two Romanesque *Chapels of St.Mary Magdalene and St.Nicholas* are also worth mentioning, as is another *Lady Chapel* in the E. Next to the cathedral are the 12C *monastery buildings.* These had a water supply system which was most advanced for the time. Today the water tower still stands. The *Christchurch Gateway,* a richly-equipped twin-towered building from the 16C in English late Gothic style, leads from the cathedral precinct into the town.

Other churches:
St.Dunstan's: 11C; restored in the 19C. It was here than Henry II left his clothes when he went to the cathedral in 1174 to do penance, in a manner prescribed by the Church, for Becket's death.

St. George's: Christopher Marlowe (1564–93) was baptized here. The church was destroyed in World War 2 and only the tower survived.

St.Martin's (about half a mile to the E.): A little church with a medieval tower. It is said to have been built at the time of St.Augustine and is thought to be the oldest Christian church in England.

St.Mildred's: Built in the 13C on foundations of a later date.

St.Peter's: 13C; it has splendid windows.

St. Augustine's College: St. Augustine built an abbey on this site, the ruins of

Canterbury, Canterbury Cathedral

which can still be seen today. Fydon's Gate, the entrance gate, is especially noteworthy. The modern buildings of Christ Church College adjoin the site.

Archiepiscopal Palace: Rebuilt in *c* 1900.

Grey Friars: Originally 13C, it was restored in 1920; some old features remain.

Poor Priests' Hospital: 14C building. Today it contains the regimental museum of the Buffs (East Kent Regiment).

St. Thomas's or Eastbridge Hospital: A late medieval building (restored) with a fine crypt.

The Weavers: A group of charming half-timbered Tudor houses formerly inhabited by Huguenots. Looms and weaving are exhibited on the first floor and bear witness to the skill with which the Huguenots plied their trade.

City walls: Of the walls built on Roman foundations in the 13–14C there are only scant remains. There were originally 7 gates but today only the *Westgate* at the entrance to St. Peter's Street survives. This gate was used as a prison; today it houses the *West Gate Museum* of local history.

Also worth seeing: *Dane John Gardens* with a monument to Christopher Marlowe. The *Marlowe Theatre* in Castle Street with an imitation Tudor façade. Ruins of the Roman castle. *Roman Pavement* (Longmarket) with the remains of Roman mosaics. The *University of Kent*, where the old college building tradition was converted into modern architectural terms. The *Royal Museum and Art Gallery*, with excavation finds and paintings.

Environs: Adisham (3 m. SE): *Holy Innocents Church*, a small Norman church (not open to visitors).
  Barfreston (5 m. SE): *St. Nicholas*, a small Norman village church with especially rich and interesting carving from the late 12C; the S. portal is particularly fine with Christ in Glory in the tympanum.

Chilham (Canterbury), Chilham Castle

Chilham (5 m. SW): Charmingly located village with an early-16C *castle* and a *Battle of Britain Museum.*

Julieberrie's Grave (4 m. SW): A grave from the Neolithic period.

Patrixbourne (2 m. SE): *St. Mary's Church* is a pretty little church with a Norman portal. There is a depiction of Christ in the tympanum; pretty 17C *glass windows.*

Reculver (9 m. N.): Ruins of the 17C *church of St.Mary.* Only remnants of walls survive from the *Roman fort,* the oldest in the country.

Cardiff/Caerdydd
South Glamorgan/Wales   p.332□G 15

A city on the broad Severn estuary which extends into the Bristol Channel. It experienced a tremendous upswing in importance during the increasing industrialization of the last 150 years. The capital of Wales since 1955, it is both the cultural centre (with a university) and the economic centre of the principality.

History: A *Roman fort* was founded here in the 1C AD, on the ramparts of which the Norman count Robert FitzHamon built the first castle in c. 1090. The charter of the city was granted in 1147. As a result firstly of the construction in 1794 of the canal leading into the coalmining area of Merthyr Tydfil (the economic centre at that time), and secondly of the enormous harbour and docks, which were built around 1830 for shipping coal, the population rose from 1,000 inhabitants in c. 1800 to the present figure of about 300,000. The foundation of the *National Museum of Wales* in 1907 and of the Welsh *University of Wales* in 1893 helped Cardiff become a cultural centre.

Cardiff Castle: *Earthworks* and considerable *sections of wall* survive from the former Roman fort, including the interesting 4C *N. gate* (lower layers of stone). In c. 1090, the Normans built a small *castle* with a keep. The castle was later enlarged and then destroyed. Some of the present buildings, especially the state rooms in Pre-Raphaelite style, date from the reconstruction and restoration work of the 19C.

Llandaff Cathedral (in the suburb of Llandaff): The first church is said to have been founded in the 6C by the Celtic St. Dyfrig. The present building in the Norman and Early English styles dates from 1107 and was completed in late Gothic in the 15C. The ancient *W. front* is flanked by two towers, the *NW tower* of 1495 and the *SW tower,* which was rebuilt in 1869. The interior, restored in the 18–19C, has fine Norman *arched portals* leading into the Lady Chapel and the David Chapel at the *S. portal.* The Celtic *wooden cross* in the right aisle dates from the pre-Norman period. Impressive features include: 14C –16C *sculptures of recumbent figures;* the *Kings' gallery* with its sculptures of the

Cardiff, Cardiff Castle

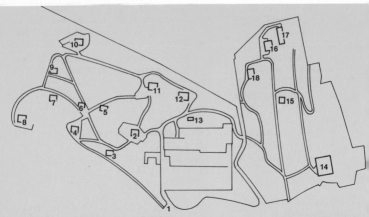

Cardiff, Welsh Folk Museum 1 entrance **2** Kennixton farmhouse (1630, restored in the 18C) from the Gower peninsula **3** model of an old water-mill for grain **4** Uschaf farmhouse from the 15C **5** Caernarfonshire cottage of 1762 **6** customs house from Aberystwyth, 1771 (fully furnished) **7** round house from Denbigh, 1726 with cockfight arena **8** 18C tannery from Rhayader **9** 18C smithy from Monmouthshire **10** 16C farmhouse from Radnorshire with old implements **11** 16C Montgomeryshire farmhouse with interesting 17C furnishings **12** 18C Unitarian chapel (Chapel Penrhiw) from Carmarthenshire **13** old gipsy wagon from Carmarthenshire **14** 17C castle with furnishings and museum buildings (documents, musical instruments etc.) **15** old dovecote **16** water-powered tweed mill from Brecknockshire (c. 1760, modernized in the 19C) **17** reconstruction of a Chepstow boat- and nethouse (with fishing equipment) **18** 16C Flintshire barn

heads of English monarchs (from the 19–20C); and the modern aluminium *figure of Christ* on the organ casing (by J.Epstein). The church was greatly damaged during the war in 1941, and was re-consecrated in 1960.

National Museum of Wales (Civic Centre, near the castle): This museum has valuable early Christian monuments, particularly *Celtic stone crosses* and archaeological finds from prehistoric *megalithic tombs* (including gold jewellery, pottery and tools from Llyn Fawr and Llyn Cerrig). There are also exhibits from the Welsh Middle Ages and an exhibition of old Welsh handicrafts and the development of industry (e.g. a model of a coal mine).

The *picture gallery* has valuable works, mainly by Welsh artists, but also by Rembrandt, Botticelli and the Impressionists (Degas, Manet, Monet, Renoir, Cézanne and others). The insignia of the investiture of the Prince of Wales (crown, ring, sceptre, etc.) are also preserved here.

Also worth seeing: The impressive *Civic Centre,* with a number of monumental public buildings. Built in Cathay's Park (city centre, near the castle) at about the turn of the century. It includes the neo-baroque *City Hall* (1904) with bell-tower, cupola and crowning Welsh dragon. The marble hall and stairwell are decorated with figures from Welsh history. The Civic Centre also includes the *University,* the *Law Courts,* and the famous *National Museum of Wales*, which dates from 1907.

Environs: Penarth (about 5 m. S.): Good paintings and prints by English and Welsh

Cardiff, Catholic Mathew tomb

artists are on show in the *Turner House Gallery.*

St. Fagans (some 4 m. to the W): village containing the *Welsh Folk Museum*, an excellent branch of the National Museum of Wales, housed since 1948 in the 16C Elizabethan *St. Fagan's Castle* with its fine park. Its numerous *peasants' and craftsmen's houses,* which have been moved here and rebuilt, give a vivid impression of Welsh life and domestic circumstances of past centuries. The old utensils and furnishings have been collected from all parts of Wales.

St. Nicholas (about 5 m. SW): A small town. Nearby there is the impressive megalithic burial chamber (cromlech) of *Tinkinswood.* A family grave for some 50 people, it dates from the middle of the 3rd millennium and was excavated in 1914. The enormous covering stone of the ob-

long burial hill measures *c.* 26 ft. x 16 ft. x 3 ft. and weighs *c.* 40 tons. The entrance in the E. has a front courtyard and 5 surviving supporting stones. Near to St. Nicholas (about 3 km. W.) is the *Dolmen of St. Lythan,* related to the megalithic grave of Tinkinswood. Three supporting stones and the covering stone have survived.

Cardigan/Aberteifi
Dyfed/Wales   p.330☐F 14

This lively little town (about 4,000 inhabitants) lies on the wide curve of Cardigan bay, where the River Teifi (Welsh: Aber-Teifi = mouth of the Teifi) flows into the sea. Of the 13C *castle,* only 2 round towers near the bridge survive. There are also some remains of walls from the medieval *town fortifications.* The *Teifi bridge* dates from the 17C.

Environs: Cenarth (about 7 m. SE): A village with a fine three-arched *bridge* (1800). Nearby on the *Cenarth Falls*, which have numerous cataracts, is the oldest *water mill* in Wales (18C).

Cilgerran (about 4 m. SE): Near the village there are the remains of a *castle* (1270) on a cliff in beautiful surroundings. 2 massive cylindrical towers and the remains of a gatehouse survive. An ancient Celtic tombstone with an inscription in Latin and Ogham can be seen in the nearby *churchyard.*

Llanarth (some 19 m. NE): The village church has a 13C *font* and a Celtic *tombstone* with an Ogham inscription.

Llandyssul (about 17 m. to the SE): A Norman *church tower* (parish church) and a 6C ancient Celtic *tombstone* with a Latin inscription have survived.

Llechryd (3 m. SE): This village has a picturesque 16C *bridge* across the Teifi.

Newcastle Emlyn (about 11 m. SE): A pretty little market town with the scant remains of a 13C *castle* and a good view from the castle hill.

St. Dogmaels (1 m. W. across the Teifi bridge): The ruins of a 12C *Benedictine monastery* with a monastery church (sculptures and inscriptions) survive here; other remains of buildings from the 13–16C.

Carlisle
Cumbria/England   p.328□H 10

Cathedral: Building began in 1092 on a church for an Augustine monastery dedicated to the Virgin Mary; completed in 1123. In 1133, under Henry I, it was made the cathedral of the newly founded diocese of Carlisle; additions and alterations in the 14–15C. Partly destroyed in the 17C in the Civil War. Its long period of construction gave the church many architectural styles (Norman Romanesque, Early English, Decorated and Perpendicular). The church's main features are to be seen in the *chancel,* which was finished in 1362 in Decorated style: the richly decorated *E. window,* completed in 1380, is c. 62 ft. tall and c. 33 ft. wide, with a depiction of the Last Judgement; the *choir stalls* built c 1400 have paintings from the lives of saints; there is a magnificent tunnel-vaulted *roof.* The nave was shortened from 1645 onwards (today it is the regimental chapel) and has fine Early English *pillars* with splendid capitals on which the months of the year are shown. The *pulpit* dating from 1599 (until 1964 it was in a church in Bedfordshire), and the *Renaissance chancel wall* (1542), are also worth seeing. Sir Walter Scott was married here in 1797.

Castle: Built by the Norman king William II (William Rufus) in c. 1092 and subsequently extended. From the beginning it was an important border fortress in the English-Scottish border wars. Mary Stuart was imprisoned here in 1568. It was captured by Parliamentary troops in the Civil War after a siege and was partly destroyed in the early 19C. The 14C *main gate, Queen Mary's Tower* and the massive Romanesque *castle keep* survive from the original building. The *King's Own Royal Border Regiment Museum* is housed in the castle and contains mementoes and documents concerning the history of the border troops.

Also worth seeing: *Church of St. Cuthbert* (SW of the cathedral), built in 1778 on the site of a 7C Anglo-Saxon church (inside is a fine 14C window). Opposite is an old *tithe barn* of 1490 (today the parish hall). The *market-place,* with the old market cross dating from 1682, the Town Hall of 1717, and the Guild Hall (also called Rednesshall) of 1377 which is the meeting place of the eight tradesmen's guilds resident in Carlisle. *Tullie House Museum* (Castle Street), the city museum is housed in a mansion built in the 17C Jacobean Renaissance style; the most interesting exhibits are the Roman excavation finds (for about 3 centuries, this town was the most northerly town in the Roman Empire). The old *city wall* is also worth seeing, especially in the W. of the city, where there is also a secret gate, or sallyport.

Environs: Armathwaite (about 9 m. SE): Notable *chapel* (dedicated to Christ and Mary); restored in the 17C. The fine E. window by Morris & Co. dates from 1914.
Brampton (about 9 m. NE): Church of *St.Martin* with fine windows by Sir Edward Burne-Jones.
Burgh-by-Sands (about 5 m. NW): An old fortified *church* on a Roman substructure. N. of the village is a *monument* to Edward I (1307).
Holme Cultram Abbey (about 15 m. W.): Remains of a *Cistercian abbey* of 1135; Romanesque W. portal in a 16C porch; the

17C E. window is in the very latest Perpendicular style.
Warwick Bridge: (about 4 m. E): The church of *St. Leonard* has a fine Romanesque apse and chancel arches in the same style.
Wetheral (about 3 m. SE): With the Gothic church of the *Holy Trinity* (inside is a notable tomb monument to Mrs. Howard from Corby by Joseph Nollekens) and the 17C *Corby Castle.*

Carlow
Carlow/Ireland   p.330☐D 13

The county town, it lies on the river Barrow and is today a lively trading and industrial town of about 10,000 inhabitants.

Carlow Castle: In *c.* 1180 the Anglo-Normans built a *river fortification*, which was further enlarged 1207–13. Today, the W. wall of the *main tower* (castle keep) and 2 corner towers survive. In 1798 it was the

Carlisle, Carlisle Castle

Carlow, law court

scene of a bloody battle between rebellious nationalists and English troops.

Also worth seeing: The Catholic *cathedral* was built *c.* 1820 in neo-Gothic style. It contains a fine *marble monument* to Bishop James Doyle, who fought for the emancipation of the Catholics (19C). The imposing *law court* was built in neoclassical (Ionic) style in 1830.

Environs: Browne's Hill (2 m. E.): Has the remains of an immense primitive *dolmen* with a covering stone weighing some 100 tons.
Killeshin (3 m. W.): Romanesque *chapel* with a fine 11–12C portal.
Leighlinbridge (7 m. S.): A 14C *tower* is all that survives of the *Black Castle.*
Muine Bheag (some 10 m. SE): Nearby is the interesting early 14C ruin of *Bally-*

moon Castle. The rectangular castle courtyard, with walls, remains of buildings and remains of defensive towers, has survived. The doorhouse with watchtower was in the W.
Old Leighlin (about 8 m. S.): The Protestant *Cathedral of St.Laserian,* with a central tower and N. chapel, dates from the 13C (enlarged 16C); noteworthy 13C font and 16C tombstones.
Tullow (about 7 m. SE): There is an old *Celtic cross* in the former abbey graveyard.

Carmarthen/Caerfyrddin
Dyfed/Wales   p.332☐F 14

An old county town with a population of 13,000 people. It lies near to the mouth of the river Towy (Welsh: Afon Tywi) and was

Carmarthen, view over town

formerly an important seaport—the river is still tidal here, some 16 m. from the sea).

History: No traces have survived of the Roman *Caer Moridunum*. According to Celtic folklore, the legendary *wizard Merlin* from King Arthur's Court had his home here (*c.* AD 500)—the Welsh place name means 'Merlin's Town'. Around 1100 the Norman conquerors enlarged the town into a fortification.

Castle: Originally Norman but considerably altered in the 14C, especially the gatehouse. For a long time it served as the county prison. Only scant remains survive today.

St.Peter's Church: This beautiful parish church with its magnificent *defensive tower* dates mainly from the 13C. It has a *Roman altar* and various interesting *tombs*, including that of Rhys ap Thomas from the 12C, and that of Sir Richard Steele.

Also worth seeing: The fine *Guild Hall* of 1766. The town has various *statues* of victorious generals and national heroes. No traces have survived of the Norman *monastery* (*c.* 1105). The most ancient Cymric manuscript, the famous 'Black Book of Carmarthen', was written in the monastery (today it is in the National Library in Aberystwyth). At the edge of the town, towards Brecon, are the remains of an ancient *oak tree,* known as Merlin's Enchanted Oak.

Environs: Laugharne (about 16 m. SW): A town with a uniform and unpretentious 18C townscape and a *Town Hall* (converted) dating from 1746, which has old documents. *St.Martin's Church* dates from the 14C but was restored in the 15C & 19C (old stone cross). The 12C *castle* of Laugharne was converted in about 1300; two of its towers were included in the later residence dating from 1582. The present gatehouse is medieval; the residential house next to it is Georgian (18–19C). The famous Welsh poet Dylan Thomas (1914–53) is buried in the *graveyard*. He spent much time during the last years of his life with his family in Laugharne.

Llansteffan (about 12 m. SW): This pretty coastal village on the mouth of the Towy has an impressive *ruined castle*. The originally Norman structure of wood and associated earthworks was destroyed in the 13C and rebuilt in its present form with a massive gatehouse.

In the vicinity of Llansteffan, particularly in the rather isolated landscape around *Llan-y-bri,* there are several small medieval *chapels* with old tombs and churchyards.

St.Clears (about 12 m. SW): A little old town with the earthworks of an old Norman castle and a Norman *church,* which has a finely carved chancel arch (formerly a Cluniac church).

Carndonagh
Donegal / Ireland   p.326☐ D 9

A little town with 1,000 inhabitants in the N. of the peninsula of Inishowen (river island). It is the site of the notable early Christian *St.Patrick cross* (Donagh Cross) from the 7C. This was one of the first crosses to be decorated with reliefs and is a predecessor to the later High Crosses. It is a guilloche (interlaced) cross and has a figure of Christ with outstretched hands. Next to it are two *carved slabs* decorated with reliefs of David and the Crucifixion. Nearby, the Protestant *Church* has a fine 15C portal.

Environs: Carrowmore (about 9 m. E.): Near the village there are 2 fine *High Crosses* with reliefs of angels; *tombstones* are all that remain of a former monastery. Nearby (to the N., towards Culdaff), the 17C *Clonca Church* stands on the site of a former monastery of St.Buodan from the 8C. The beautiful medieval *tombstone* in the NE of the church bears an ancient Gaelic inscription. Beside the church is an interesting *High Cross* with Biblical reliefs (Feeding of the Five Thousand).

Greencastle (about 17 m. SE): This town lies on the mouth of the sea inlet of Lough Foyle with the nearby vantage point of *Inishowen Head*. The ruined *castle* dates from 1305 and has an oblong ground plan with strong rampart walls, a large rectangular central tower and a gatehouse with a tower. Built by Richard Burgh, the 'Red Earl of Ulster', it guarded the mouth of the inlet.

Carrickfergus
Antrim / Northern Ireland   p.326☐ E 10

A seaport on Belfast Lough, a sea inlet. It was important before the rise of Belfast and played an important part in the Anglo-Norman invasion in the 12C. Its name means 'Rock of Fergus' and refers to the legend of the Scottish King Fergus, who is said to have drowned here *c.* 320.

Carrickfergus Castle: This strategic maritime fortress was built *c.* 1180 by John de Courcy, the Norman conqueror of Ulster. King John captured it in 1210 without capturing any land at the same time; it remained an English garrison until 1928. The *gatehouse* is flanked by 2 crescent-shaped *towers;* next to it is the 16C *granary*. Between the outer and inner courtyards is the massive square *keep,* which has 5 storeys and walls *c.* 9 ft. thick. This early-13C citadel is 89 ft. tall, and today it houses a *museum of local history and culture*. The

Carrick-on-Suir, view over town

Norman *Hall of Fergus* is on the 3rd floor. There is a splendid view from the roof. A *well*, 39 ft. deep and a *castle dungeon* may also be seen.

Also worth seeing: The parish church of *St.Nicholas* with some Romanesque parts and, in the N. transept, the fine *tomb* of the Chichester family; the S. windows in the 16C Flemish style are also noteworthy. The church was rebuilt in *c.* 1604. In the N., a 17C *town gate* survives from the old *town fortifications*.

Environs: Ballygalley (about 19 m. N): The castle was enlarged in *c.* 1625; the central keep dates from the 16C.
Glenarm (about 25 km. N.): The 17C *castle* of the Earl of Antrim; near the churchyard are the remains of a 15C *Franciscan monastery*.

Island Magee (about 7 m. NE): A peninsula steeped in legend with basalt cliffs 253 ft. high known as the *Gobbins*; also caves and prehistoric *dolmens*. **Larne** (about 14 m. N.): Modern copy of a *round tower* (by the harbour). Also the remains of the *Olderfleet Castle* from the 13–14C with its three-storeyed defensive tower.

Carrick-on-Suir
Tipperary/Ireland   p.330□D 13

A town of about 5,000 inhabitants, charmingly located on the river Suir. It was founded in the 13–14C by the Butler family, who were the Earls of Ormonde.

Ormonde Castle: This well-preserved castle was built by Edmund Butler in 1309

Carrick-on-Suir, Ormonde Castle

and considerably enlarged in the Elizabethan style in the 16C. Anne Boleyn (1507–36) of the house of Ormonde is said to have been born here. The rooms have fine *stucco* and *fireplaces.* The 15C *castle keep* has also survived.

Also worth seeing: The Catholic *parish church* on the other side of the river. The church has the remains of a 14C *Franciscan monastery*—tower and N. wall.

Environs: Ahenny (about 7 m. N): With two very beautiful 8C *wooden crosses,* the shafts and wheels of which are decorated with geometric patterns (spirals and guilloches). The pedestals have carved figures. Nearby are the 3 so-called *Kilkieran Crosses* (10C), of which the decorated W. cross is particularly beautiful.
Castletown House (2 m. N.): This lovely

building was built for the Archbishop of Cashel in *c.* 1170.

Cartmel
Cumbria / England   p.328 □ H 11

Priory church of St.Mary: An existing building was rebuilt from 1188 onwards by William Marshall, Earl of Pembroke and Baron Cartmel for Augustinian canons; a long period of construction lasted into the 15C. However, the priory was dissolved in 1537 in the course of the Reformation and subsequently fell into decay. Restoration work began in the early 17C under George Preston of Holker and the interior furnishings were restored in Renaissance style. *Exterior:* The chancel and transepts are transitional between Norman and Roman-

Cartmel, Priory Church of St. Mary

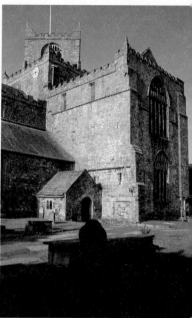

Nave

esque; the nave is in 15C Perpendicular style (late Gothic); the lower section of the crossing tower is Norman-Romanesque, while the diagonally added upper storey is 15C.

Interior: Cruciform ground plan. The main entrance to the nave is through the fine S. portal. The chancel, which is the oldest part of the church, is entered through a splendidly-worked Renaissance chancel wall, which is 17C and was possibly the work of a Flemish craftsman. Features worth seeing in the chancel itself are the round arches opening into the side chapels, the Decorated windows in the S. aisle (this aisle was for a long time used as a parish church), and the choir stalls. The E. window was inserted in the 15C, replacing the old Norman windows (which went to the church of St. Martin in Windermere). Other items of interest are the

sedilia (priests' seats built into the S. chancel wall) and the 14C Harrington tomb monument, opposite which is the even older tomb of William Walton, Prior of Cartmel.

Also worth seeing: The *gatehouse* of the 14C monastery. The 18C *market cross*.

Environs: Holker Hall (about 1 m. W.): Formerly seat of the Dukes of Devonshire. Built in the 17C and restored in 1873 after a fire. Inside there are fine wood carvings by local artists and fine period furniture.

Cashel
Tipperary/Ireland   p.330☐C 13

The *limestone rock* of the legend-wreathed

Cashel (Castle) is about 330 ft. high and stands in the middle of the Tipperary plain. At an early date (4C) it became the fortified centre of the Celtic kings of Munster. It was here in c. 450 that St. Patrick converted King Aenghus. From then on, many kings of Cashel were simultaneously bishops (prince bishops). The famous High King Brian Boru, who in c. 1010 repulsed the Scandinavian aggressors at the battle of Clontarf near Dublin, resided here in about 1000. The castle rock was entirely handed over to the power of the clergy in about 1100. The bishops, particularly Cormac MacCarthy in the 12C, enlarged Cashel into the citadel of the Irish Catholic faith. The spendour of the ecclesiastical fortress did not fade until the 18C, when the buildings fell into disrepair. The Catholic diocesan seat was transferred to Thurles (q.v.); today Cashel is the seat of a Protestant bishop.

Cormac's Chapel: The *church,* built in c. 1134 by Prince Bishop Cormac MacCarthy, is regarded as one of the finest examples of the Irish Romanesque. It is built of red sandstone with a tall, stone-roofed *nave* and fine arches with columns, including *chancel arches.* The splendidly designed round-arched *N. gate* with a triangular gable (front section of portal) and the *S. gate* (today the entrance), which is also elaborate, are particularly well worth seeing. The inside of the church is decorated with numerous *stone carvings* (sculptures, ornaments, etc.). The *MacCarthy sarcophagus* (12C), with rich, Scandinavian relief work, can be found in the chapel. The two square *side towers* have German Romanesque elements—Bishop Cormac obtained advice on their design from specialists working for the Irish abbot Dionysius of Regensburg.

Cathedral: A large, cruciform Gothic church built in the 13C, some 100 years after Cormac's Chapel. It consists of the *nave* and *chancel,* a N. and S. *transept* (c. 1260) and a massive 14C *crossing tower.* Inside are fine *peaked-arched vaults, sculptures* and *tomb monuments* (15–16C). The 11C *round tower,* which stands 105 ft. tall by the N. transept, is probably the oldest surviv-

Cashel, Cormac's chapel

ing building on the 'Rock of Cashel'. The cathedral was burnt down by the Earl of Kildare in 1495. In 1749 Archbishop Price ordered the cathedral roof to be removed. He was said to be too lazy to climb up the hill to the cathedral, and the building of a new one in the lower town began in 1763.

Also worth seeing: The *castle* to the W. of the cathedral was built by Archbishop O'Hedigan in the 15C on top of parts of an older building (with passages leading to the church). At the entrance to the 'Irish acropolis' is the 15C *Hall of the Vicar's Choral,* a residence for the clergy. Next to it is *St. Patrick's Cross* (11–12C), which has fine reliefs of Christ and St. Patrick. The *cross pedestal* also has good ornaments and reliefs (Lamb of God), and is said to have been the font of the first Christian Celtic king from 450. It was later used as a coronation stone. At the bottom of the castle rock (in the W.) are the remains of the Cistercian *Hore Abbey,* which was founded in 1272 and is the daughter monastery of Mellifont, Drogheda (q.v.). The 13C cruciform church ruin (one nave, two aisles),

rood screen, 15C central tower, chapterhouse and sacristy have survived. In the town there are remains of the *Dominican Friary* (1243), the Georgian *archiepiscopal palace* dating from 1730 (today it is a hotel) and the new (Georgian) Protestant *cathedral* of 1750–80 with a spire dating from 1812. A defensive tower survives from the 15C *Quinke's Castle* (Main Street).

Environs: Athassel Abbey (about 5 m. SW): The remains of this interesting Augustinian monastery date from the 12&13C. It was one of the largest medieval monasteries in Ireland. The *church* has two transepts, a crossing tower and a smaller NW tower. The fine Gothic W. portal is worth seeing, as is the 13C tomb monument with equestrian figures in the S. of the chancel.

Castle Acre
Norfolk/England   p.328 □ L 13

A little town on the Nar, which is un-

Castle Acre, Priory, W. façade

Castle Acre, Church of St. James

Gothic pulpit

usually rich in the remains of ecclesiastical and secular buildings. There was a settlement here in Roman times, when *Peddar's Way*, an important Roman road, led past the settlement. A 5C Saxon *graveyard* has been excavated.

Priory: In 1090 William de Warenne, the 2nd Earl of Surrey, founded a Cluniac priory, of which some impressive remains have survived. Most interesting are the remains of the *W. façade*, which has beautiful 12C arches. The prior's *house* and *chapel* were restored in the Renaissance and are both also worth seeing—the walls are 14C and the chapel's wooden ceiling is *c.* 1500. The *gatehouse* dates from the 16C.

Castle: This Norman castle stands on ramparts which are probably Roman. The castle itself, also built by William de

Warenne, is late 11C. It fell into disrepair in the 14C and was used by the village people as a stone quarry. Only the 13C *gatehouse*, with its two round arches, has survived.

Church of St. James: The parish church dating back to the 13C. It stands between the castle and the monastery. Its present form derives largely from the 14C and 15C. There is a lovely Gothic *pulpit*, which has painted panels, and a very fine *chancel railing*, which is also painted and dates from *c.* 1400. The Gothic *font* has a tall superstructure on which some painting has survived. The choir stalls have good misericords.

Environs: Narborough (5 m. W): The *Church of All Saints* is Norman but was later converted and enlarged. The remains of the 15C stained-glass windows and also numerous tomb monuments dating from the early 14C and dedicated to the members of the Spelman family have survived. Especially pleasing is the monument to Clement Spelman, who died in 1672. It shows him standing on the tomb wearing the clothes of the period. He had left instructions that the monument should take this form and also that he should be buried in a standing position underneath his figure to prevent anyone from walking about on top of him.

Oxburgh Hall (12 m. SW): Work on this fortified *mansion* was begun by Edmund Bedingfield in 1482. The house is surrounded by a rampart and has an oversize gatehouse thought to be the largest 15C brick gatehouse in the whole of England. The building is still in the possession of the founder's family. It contains furnishings from the time of the building's origin. The *Bedingfield Chapel* in the nearby parish church contains two early-16C terracotta tomb monuments to members of the founder's family.

Swaffham (5 m. S.): This little town has numerous fine houses from the Georgian period. The splendid *rotunda*, crowned by a figure of Ceres, was built by the Earl of Oxford in 1783. The 15C *Church of St. Peter and St. Paul* has a pleasing clerestory. Its nave is decorated by an outstandingly well-designed double dragon-beam ceiling adorned with angels.

Moone (Castledermot), High Cross

Castledermot
Kildare/Ireland   p.326☐D 13

This little town in the county of Kildare has numerous documents from the early Christian period. It was here, in *c.* 812, that the Celtic Saint Dermot founded a fortified *monastery* (Castledermot = 'Dermot's Castle'), from which a 10C *round tower*, and also a Romanesque *church portal* survive.

Celtic High Crosses: The two surviving 9C High Crosses, with their beautiful reliefs of biblical scenes, are worth seeing. The *South Cross:* Arrest of Christ, Crucifixion, Isaac, Adam and Eve, Daniel in the Lions' Den. *North Cross:* Adam and Eve, Isaac, Daniel, Massacre of the Innocents (W. side); Feeding of the Five Thousand (S. side).

Also worth seeing: At the S. end of the village there are the ruins of a *Franciscan monastery* dating from 1300. In the N. is a 15C *Pigeon's Tower* on the site of a 13C monastery of St. John.

Environs: Baltinglass (about 9 m. NE): Interesting remains of the Cistercian *Baltinglass Abbey* founded in 1148. The nave and chancel, both 12C, have survived, as have parts of the transepts and parts of the monastery buildings. On the hill in the village there are the remains of a *megalithic tomb*.

Moone (about 5 m. N.): The famous early Christian *Celtic cross* (a High Cross) dates from the 8–9C. It is a granite cross on a pyramidal pedestal and is some 18 ft. tall, with a long shaft and rather small cross. The stone panels include reliefs of the 12 Apostles, the Feeding of the Five Thousand, and the Flight into Egypt. Nearby are the remnants of a 13C *Franciscan monastery*, which was probably an early Celtic Columban monastery.

Castle Douglas
Dunfries and Galloway/Scotland   p.328☐G 10

A little town formerly called *Causewayend*, then *Carlingwark* and finally Castle Douglas in 1789.

Threave Castle: The Douglas clan's fortress was built by Archibald Earl of Douglas from 1369–90. The 4-storeyed tower building, the last Douglas fortress, was captured by James II in 1455 in a battle with the clan. James's success only came after he employed the 'Mons Meg' cannon, which today once again stands on the castle rock in Edinburgh. In 1640 the Covenanters wreaked havoc in the restored castle and destroyed its interior.

Threave Gardens: The park around the Victorian Threave House is famous for its rhododendrons. There are also peat, rock and water gardens. Towards the River Dee is a wildfowl preserve for water birds.

Environs: Cardoness Castle (14 m. SW, in Gatehouse of Fleet): The ruins of the four-storeyed tower from the 15C, with cellar vaults, spiral staircase, stone benches and carefully worked fireplaces, have survived. The tower gives an outstanding view across Fleet Bay.

Dundrennan (16 m. S.): The *Cistercian abbey* founded here in 1142 is one of the most important monasteries in Scotland. Unfortunately, little of it survives except

Castle Howard, view

for some remains of the late Romanesque chapterhouse and the early Gothic transept (both 13C).

Kirkcudbright (12 m. SW): This town has a picturesque little harbour and the ruins of *MacLellan's Castle*, built in 1582. The *Town Hall* is 16C and the nearby *market cross* dates from 1610. A comprehensive collection of the pictures of E.A.Hornel is to be seen in *Broughton House*. The *Stewartry Museum* is Galloway's museum of local history and culture.

gatehouse has survived; there are only remains of the church.

Malton (about 6 m. NE): The site of a Roman *fortification* (excavation finds in the local museum). The two churches of *St. Michael* and *St.Leonard* are worth seeing; both have Norman-Romanesque features.

Old Malton (about 7 m. NE, part of Malton): The *parish church* is worth seeing as it integrates the remains of a Gilbertine priory (including one of the two original W. towers) founded *c.* 1150.

Castle Howard
North Yorkshire/England   p.328□I 11

One of the finest palaces in England. Begun in 1701 for the 3rd Earl of Carlisle, it is one of the most important of John Vanbrugh's designs, although incomplete when he died in 1726 (Nicholas Hawksmoor, a pupil of Christopher Wren, assisted). Apart from the main building, Vanbrugh was also responsible for the 'Temple of the 4 Winds' — with ancient marble statues inside—in the castle park. The pyramid and the family mausoleum, which has a peristyle and is near the temple, are by Hawksmoor. The stables were built by John Carr of York 1781-4 and now house a collection of costumes.
The interior: The Great Hall is 82 ft. high and has a baroque dome and spacious main staircase. The Long Gallery is over 160 ft. in length. The chapel has a copy of a picture by Holbein on the ceiling. Notable *furnishings* include ⎯⎯⎯⎯⎯⎯⎯⎯⎯⎯⎯⎯ of antiques, 18C tapestries, and paintings by great European artists (including the English painters Gainsborough, Reynolds and Romney, and Italian artists such as Paolo Veronese).

Environs: Kirkham Priory (about 3 m. S.): Remains of a 13-14C *House of Augustinian Canons.* The fine 14C Decorated

Cavan
Cavan/Ireland   p.326□D 11

This quiet little country town has some 3,000 inhabitants and is on the SE of *Lough Oughter,* where there are remains of the 14–15C medieval *tower* of Clough Oughter, the half-devastated round tower of *Drumlane* from the 13C and a ruined church). Cavan itself has a modern *episcopal cathedral,* built in 1942, and a Protestant *parish church* from 1810.

Castle Howard, fountains

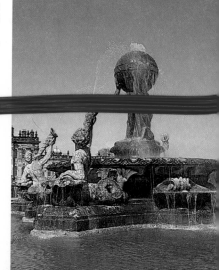

Environs: Clones (about 12 m. NE): This border town contains a 12C *ruined church* which is all that remains of a monastery founded by St. Tighernach in the 6C; next to it is a *round tower*. There is also *St. Tighernach's Shrine* (a stone sarcophagus) and an interesting 10–11C *High Cross*, which has been reconstructed and has fine biblical reliefs.

Cootehill (about 12 m. NE): Here, in the SE, are the splendid remains of the prehistoric burial ground of *Cohaw Court-Cairn*, with 5 burial chambers and a stone rampart. Nearby: the pretty villa, *Bellamont Forest*, built by Thomas Coote (cf. the town's name), has a Doric portico (1730); the curious *Dartrey Mausoleum* is by J.Wyatt (1770).

Kilmore (about 4 m. SW, at the S. end of Lough Oughter): A fine 12C *Romanesque portal* has been built into the modern *Cathedral of St. Feidhlimidh.*

Monaghan (about 27 m. NE): This county town has some interesting 18–19C buildings, including the *Market House* of 1791 and the neo-Gothic Catholic *Cathedral of St. Macartan*, 1861 – 92 by J.J.McCarthy.

Chelmsford
Essex/England   p.332□L 15

This, the county town of Essex, became a diocesan seat in 1914 and consequently the parish church was raised to the rank of cathedral.

Cathedral: The old parish church of St. Mary was completed in 1424 but only the W. tower dates from this time—the church having collapsed almost entirely in 1800 after which it was rebuilt. Some fine details of the present church are the *S. entrance* and the *spire*, completed in 1749. A peculiarly shaped arch from the early 15C survives in the N. wall of the chancel. The

oldest tomb monuments, the Mildmay Monuments, date from the 2nd half of the 16C. The furnishings all date from the 19C.

Museum: Contains exhibits from all periods, including numerous finds from Roman times. There is also the Tunstill Collection of English drinking glasses.

Environs: Ingatestone (7 m. SW): *Ingatestone Hall* was built in 1540 for Sir William Petre, a minister of State. Since 1953, the N. wing has housed the *archive of the county of Essex*, with over 3 million documents, manuscripts, prints and old photographs. The main building has furniture from the 18C & early 19C; the garden room has panelling and Tudor furniture.

Margaretting (4 m. SW): The Gothic *church of St.Margaret* dates from the mid 15C; the octagonal font is of the same date. The stained glass of the E. window, with the remains of a large Tree of Jesse, is worth seeing. The middle section, depicting King David playing a harp and King Solomon holding a church, is particularly beautiful. Unusually for a window of this date, white is among the colours used.

Rivenhall (16 m. NE): The *church of St. Mary and All Saints* stands on the site of a Roman church and, by good fortune, possesses what are probably the finest early stained-glass windows in the whole county. In 1839 the vicar acquired 12C stained glass in France, which he installed in his church. 17C tomb monuments.

Cheltenham
Gloucestershire/England   p.332□H 14

A city on the W. edge of the Cotswold Hills dating from Anglo-Saxon times. It was at its zenith in the 18C after the healing

Cheltenham, Church of St. Mary

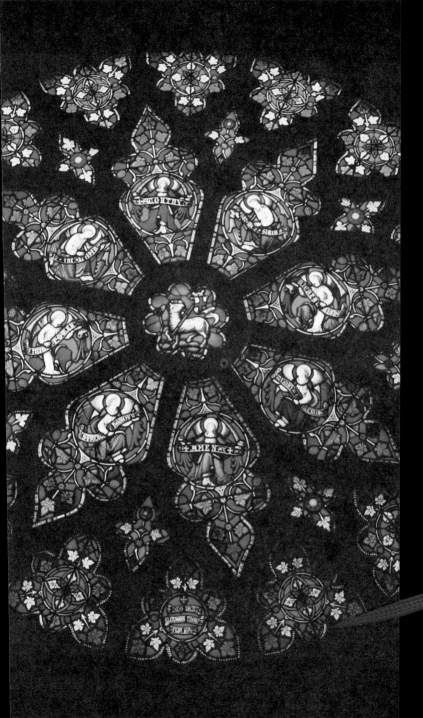

properties of its saline springs had been discovered in 1718. The numerous 18&19C buildings date from the time of the town's expansion into a spa after the medicinal baths had finally achieved renown as a result of George III's visit to the town in 1788.

Church of St. Mary: Norman, restored in modern times. The tower is transitional between Romanesque and early Gothic; the N. entrance hall is late Gothic. The oldest memorial tablet on the N. side of the sanctuary dates from 1513.

Museum and Art Gallery: The *town museum* contains Chinese porcelain, English ceramics and archaeological, geological and natural-history exhibits from the surrounding area. The *art gallery* houses mainly Dutch paintings.

Environs: Bishop's Cleeve (4 m. N.): The cruciform *church of St. Michael and All Angels* is Norman. Its W. façade, decorated with turrets and an excellent Norman portal, is especially impressive. The two-storeyed entrance hall on the S. side is also worth mentioning. The massive central tower was restored around 1700; the gallery is Jacobean. The church contains several tomb monuments, including that to Richard de la Bere and his wife (1636).
Hailes (9 km. NE): *Hailes Abbey* was a Cistercian monastery founded in 1246 and famous for its relic of Holy Blood. The founder of the monastery was Richard, Earl of Cornwall. A small museum has exhibits concerning the history of the abbey. The *parish church* was begun in 1140. It contains frescos from c. 1300 of St. Cecilia and other Saints along with heraldic decorations.
Winchcombe (7 m. NE): The Gothic *church of St. Peter*, built 1456–74 is typical of the wool churches of the Cotswolds. Of interest are the skilfully-carved gargoyles on the outside and the 16C altar inside. *Sudeley Castle* was built in the 12C and restored in c. 1450. One of Charles I's headquarters during the Civil War, it was captured in 1644. The chapel, built in c. 1450, contains the tomb of Catherine Parr, the 6th wife of Henry VIII. After his death in 1547, she married her lover Lord Seymour of Sudeley but died a year later. The castle was restored in the 19C. It houses mementoes of Catherine Parr, valuable furniture and paintings by Rubens, Turner and van Dyck.

Chepstow/Cas Gwent
Gwent/Wales   p.332□H 15

A town on the border of Wales, where the river Wye flows into the Severn estuary. It was founded by William FitzOsbern, Earl of Hereford in c. 1067. Today it is still English in character rather than Welsh.

Chepstow Castle: Dominating the town's landscape is the magnificent ruined Norman castle, built by William FitzOsbern in c. 1070 and considerably enlarged in the 13C. The visitor passes through the *gatehouse* and enters the lower castle courtyard (13C). The central courtyard was part of the original Norman complex and leads to the *keep*, the main section of every Norman castle. The keep occupies the narrowest limestone rock and has wall reinforcements in the E. and S. The entrance with its Norman *portal* and staircase (2nd floor) was in the SE; the *knights' room* with sleeping niches was also here. Redesigned with dividing arcades in the 13C; the present entrance is later. Behind the keep is the Norman *upper courtyard*, which was connected to the central courtyard by a covered *passage*. The *bailey* by the upper courtyard has Crusader battlements and dates from the 13C.

Tintern Abbey (Chepstow), porta

Tintern Abbey 1 outer gate **2** cloister **3** monastery church **4** Norman portal **5** library **6** sacristy **7** chapterhouse **8** inner gate **9** prior's residence **10** Prior's Hall **11** Novitiates' Room **12** Monks' Room **13** refectory **14** kitchen **15** lay refectory

St. Mary's Church: An interesting church, which belonged to a Benedictine monastery founded by FitzOsbern in about 1070. The *W. portal* is early Norman; *archivolts* on columns are decorated with chevrons and diamonds typical of the period. The *round arches* and *grotesque animal heads* from the old *sacristy* are also worth seeing. The inside of the church was much altered in 1891.

Town fortification: The 14C *W. gate* is well preserved but parts of the older *town wall* (13C) still survive. This wall ran from the harbour to the castle.

Museum: (Bridge Street): A small but interesting collection devoted to local history.

Environs: Caerwent (about 5 m. SW): The well-preserved Roman *town walls* are worth seeing. The civilian Roman settlement of *Venta Silurum* did not have a fort. It was named after the Celtic tribe of the Silures. Founded in AD 75, it was surrounded by a massive stone wall 1 m. long in *c.* AD 200; this was reinforced by bastions in the 4C. Today the *main street* follows the Roman E-W axis; baths, a temple, the forum, shops and taverns lay along this street, but no remains have survived. The side streets had a chessboard-like arrangement. Some Roman finds may be seen at the entrance to the *parish church of St. Stephen.* (There are more finds in the museums in Newport and Cardiff.) After

Chelmsford, Cathedral, view

Carving on exterior

the departure of the Romans in the 4–5C, the settlement fell into ruin.

Caldicot (about 7 km. SW): This village has an interesting *ruined Norman castle* from the 12C. The castle keep (today housing a small museum) and the remains of the W. gate date from the original building; the S. gate with today's entrance is 14C. Popular medieval banquets are held every evening in the summer months in the castle, part of which has been well restored.

Tintern Abbey (5 km. N.): The splendid ruins of the old *Cistercian monastery*, which was founded in 1131, are located in peaceful countryside in the valley of the river Wye; they were the inspiration for the poem by Wordsworth which bears their name. After Henry VIII dissolved the monasteries in Wales, the abbey went to ruin. However, the surviving remains of

the building give a very good impression of the lay-out of the large monastery, which had quarters for both monks and lay brothers. The traveller passes from the *outer palatorium* (the porch) to the NW entrance of the former *monastery church*, built 1270–1301 in high Gothic style. Its lead roof was removed and melted down in 1536. The church still has rich decoration and good window tracery. The E. window is some 62 ft. tall. Coming from the *cloister*, the monks entered the church through a fine Norman *portal* in the N. Next to this are the *library, sacristy* and *chapterhouse* (8 stumps of columns survive). After the *inner palatorium* there follow the *novices' room* with the latrine and in the E., the rooms for old and sick monks; adjoining this to the NE are the remains of the *abbot's residence* and the *abbot's hall*. To the N. of the *cloister* are the heated *warming*

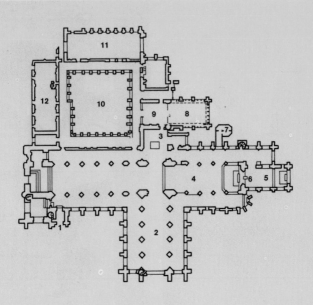

Chester Cathedral 1 SW porch **2** S. transept **3** N. transept **4** choir **5** Lady Chapel **6** shrine of St. Werburgh **7** sacristy **8** chapterhouse **9** vestibule **10** monastery **11** refectory **12** Norman crypt

house, the *refectory* with its fine windows, the *kitchen* and next to these, the *lay brothers' refectory*.

Finds and documents from the old monastery are on display in an impressive *museum*.

The remains of old monastery walls with a *water-gate* (by the guest-house) are to be found nearby.

Chester

Cheshire/England   p.328□H 12

This city on the lower reaches of the Dee

has both Roman and Anglo-Saxon ramparts and walls and has the best-preserved old town in the whole of Great Britain. The headquarters of the famous 20th Roman legion, the 'Valeria Victrix', was in this old quarter. The Roman *Castra Devana* was called *Caerleon* by the Welsh, and *Legaceaster* by the Anglo-Saxons. After the Roman withdrawal *c.* 380, the Anglo-Saxons and the Danes fought over the town, and Ethelred of Mercia rebuilt it in 908. William the Conqueror did not reach it until 1070.

In 1237 under Henry III the earldom of Chester joined the Crown, the last of the Norman territories to do so. Henry VII finally gave the county a charter in 1506 and Chester became a diocesan seat in 1541.

Castra Devana: In part the medieval city wall followed the line of the ramparts

Chester, Cathedral

around the Roman camp. The main products of the Romans enthusiasm for building—apart from the extensive remains of walls in the old part of the city (not a few houses have Roman foundations)—are the remains of towers, the remains of water pipes and heating installations, stumps of columns, and the amphitheatre. Roman influence is most visible in the SE corner of the medieval city wall. Apart from the remains of the corner tower built AD 74–96, the amphitheatre, which was excavated from 1929 onwards, can also be seen. This was built in *c.* AD 100 and at the present time is the largest individual Roman building in Great Britain. It is 341 ft. long, 312 ft. wide, contains an arena 213 ft. long and 180 ft. wide and was able to accommodate some 9,000 spectators. A earlier building in wood from *c.* AD 77 was discovered under the stones.

The *Grosvenor Museum* provides excellent documentation of the Roman way of life and work in the military camp, with finds from excavations on show.

City wall: Built with four unequal sides with an overall length of some 2 m. surrounding the old core of the city. It is made of red sandstone and its height ranges from 13 ft. to 33 ft. On the N. and E. sides the wall in the main follows the rampart of the Roman camp. The medieval wall had towers and gates added to it at different periods. For example, the massive tower at the NW corner of the wall was built by John de Helpstone in 1322, while the tower at the NE corner, now known as Phoenix Tower, was given its present appearance after reconstruction work in 1658—an exhibition devoted to the Civil War is now housed here.

Chester, Cathedral, portal

Cathedral: This building in red sandstone replaces a predecessor which was built in *c*. 700 and dedicated to St. Werburgh. Hugh Lupus, the 2nd Norman Earl of Chester, working in co-operation with St.Anselm, added a Benedictine abbey to the church. The oldest sections of the Norman church *(N. side)* were built at this time. The *E. section,* with the *Lady Chapel,* followed in 1250–75. The *chancel* was built at the turn of the 14C under the supervision of Richard of Chester, Edward I's military architect. The arches of the S. transept and the S. arches of the nave were in place by the mid 14C. The rest of the building was completed in the late 15C. The abbey was dissolved in 1540 and a year later the church was elevated to the status of the cathedral of the new diocese of Chester. While the exterior is not particularly convincing, owing to its diversity of

styles, the interior is certainly worth seeing. The chief item is the Norman section on the N. side of the aisle and in the N. transept. The passage leading to the monastery buildings behind was built in *c*. 1100. The entrance to the N. transept, above which is the stone gallery housing the organ, also comes from the Norman church; windows and roof are Gothic. The *S. transept,* begun in the 14C and completed in the 15C, has its own aisles, and is larger than the chancel and almost as large as the nave. Until 1881 it was used as the parish church of St.Oswald. Its large S. window was built by Blomfield in 1887. The Gothic *chancel* built in the 13&14C is distinguished by a magnificent triforium and by the choir stalls of *c*. 1390. The wrought-iron gates of the two side aisles of the chancel were made on a Spanish model *c*. 1560. The shrine of St.Werburgh, built *c*. 1330 and reconstructed from fragments, is today in the Lady Chapel behind the high altar.

The monastery buildings are astonishingly well preserved. The *chapterhouse* with its vestibule was built in the 13C. It is interesting to note that the vestibule's vault was designed without any change in the capitals. On the W. side of the monastery complex a large Norman *crypt* with 2 vaulted aisles has survived. It was probably originally used as a cellar. The 12C *chapel of St.Anselm* is also very well worth a visit. Its stucco ceiling dates from the 17C. The monks' lectern, with the stairs built into the wall, is in the Early English *refectory.* Apart from a similar arrangement in Beaulieu, this is the only example of such a lectern in England.

St.John's Church: This large Norman church close to the Dee dates from 1075. For some 10 years it was the cathedral of the diocese of Mercia, before the diocesan seat was moved to Coventry. A section of the *nave* is all that survives — the tower rebuilt in 1523 fell down 50 years later and

Chester, Cathedral, arcade supporting organ

Ceiling

pulled down the whole W. section of the church with it. Impressive features inside are the massive early Norman *columns* and *arches,* probably built about 1095. However, the *triforium* with its 4 arches and also the *side aisles* already show transitional style and were probably built *c.* 1200. The *Warburton Chapel* houses a baroque monument to Lady Warburton by E.Pierce. He executed it after 1693, using the motif of a skeleton holding its own shroud, which follows a French model.

Also worth seeing: Apart from the various towers in the walls the old part of the city also has numerous *medieval buildings* and 17C *town houses*. The *Cheshire Military Museum* at the S. corner of the city wall occupies the site of a castle built *c.* 1069. Henry III had a fortress built here,

but this was torn down in 1789. The military museum contains mementoes of the Cheshire regiments.

Chesterfield
Derbyshire/England   p.328☐I 12

Church of St. Mary and All Saints: Built *c.* 1350 towards the end of the Decorated phase of English Gothic. The crooked spire, the town's landmark, is over 230 ft. tall and is made of wood covered with lead. Over the centuries it has deviated some 10 ft. from the vertical and simultaneously turned around its own axis. The main things of interest inside the church are the tomb monuments to the Foljambe family, who were Earls of Liverpool.

Also worth seeing: The *church of the Holy Trinity* with the tomb of George Stephenson, the famous English railway pioneer (1781–1848; builder of the first serviceable locomotive). *Revolution House Museum* (in Old Whittington, N. of the town) is housed in the former Cock and Pynet Inn, where those conspiring to depose King James II met in 1688. (interesting memorabilia).

Environs: Ashover (about 6 m. S.): The church of *All Saints* is 14–15C Gothic. Inside there is a beautiful Romanesque font; the fine chancel wall dates from *c.* 1500.

Ault Hucknell (about 7 m. SE): The church of *St.John the Baptist* was originally Romanesque and may even be Anglo-Saxon. Inside is the tomb of Thomas Hobbes (1588–1679), the famous English political theorist, author of 'The Leviathan' and supporter of absolutism.

Beeley (about 7 m. SW): The *village church* has a fine Romanesque portal, which probably came from a previous building.

Birchover (about 11 m. SW): The *Heathcote Museum* has Bronze Age finds from the neighbourhood, including the finds from Stanton Moor (see below).

Bolsover (about 6 m. E.): There was a *castle* here in the 11C at time of William the Conqueror. It was rebuilt in the early 17C under Sir Charles Cavendish; classical additions date from *c.* 1660.

Chatsworth House (about 7 m. W.): One of the most interesting *houses* in England. It was built for the first Duke of Devonshire in 1687–1707 in classical style (a mixture of Renaissance and baroque) and was restored in the 18&19C. The inside is very interesting. Apart from the contemporary furnishings there are a picture collection with Flemish and English works, valuable furniture and a library with first editions and other early printed works. There is also a splendid park.

Eckington (about 6 m. NE): The church of *St.Peter and St.Paul* is Gothic and dates from the 13C–15C; the S. aisle was restored in Georgian style in the 18C and the chancel is 19C neo-Gothic.

Edensor (about 8 m. W.): The *church*, designed by Sir Gilbert Scott, incorporates

Chester, old town houses

Chichester, Cathedral

parts of a previous Romanesque building, including the portico, some columns, arches and window ornaments.

Hardwick Hall (some 7 m. SE): A *mansion* built 1591–7 in Tudor style, with 4 corner towers and large windows across the entire front. Inside there are fine pieces of furniture, tapestries and good paintings.

Hathersage (about 11 m. NW): Fine Gothic *church* with a three-storeyed tower and an octagonal spire. Near the church is the reputed *birthplace of Little John*, follower of Robin Hood.

Matlock (about 9 m. SW): *Rutland Cavern* was used by the Romans for lead mining in the 1–2C AD. *Willersley Castle,* built by Sir Richard Arkwright in 1788, is also worth seeing.

Stanton Moor (about 11 m. SW): An extensive Bronze Age *cult site*. To the N. is the stone circle known as Nine Ladies, immediately next to which and standing alone is the 'King Stone'; to the W. of this are the standing stones of 'Doll Tor'. There are also over 70 Bronze Age burial mounds.

Teversal (about 8 m. SE): The church of *St. Catherine* was originally Romanesque but restored much later. Fine Romanesque portal. 17C interior furnishings.

Chichester
West Sussex   p.332☐K 16

A city founded by the Romans, which is clear from the plan of the town, whose 4 straight streets meet in the main square. In the 5C it was taken over by the Saxons. Its present name is derived from that of the Saxon leader Cissa.

Cathedral: The present building was begun by the Norman bishop Ralph in 1080 and extensively restored in 1187 after a fire. The free-standing *bell tower*, the only one of its kind in England, was added in the 15C. It is a well-proportioned building dominated by its 19C central tower with a spire, which is visible from afar. The *interior* is also an English rarity in that the nave is flanked by double aisles. The windows are of a more recent date as the old ones fell prey to Cromwell's soldiers. It is

Chichester, Bishop's Palace

likely that the two 12C *stone panels* in the S. aisle with reliefs of the legend of Lazarus both come from the same workshop; they are probably the country's most impressive monument to Romanesque stonemasonry.

Also worth seeing: The *war memorial* to the Royal Sussex Regiment in the S. aisle chapel; the *monument* to the poet William Collins under the NW tower, and the 14C *choir stalls*. The portraits of bishops in the N. transept and the pictures in the S. transept are both 16C.

Bishops' Palace: A 12C building with a medieval *kitchen* (13C), a 15C *dining-hall* with ceiling paintings by Bernardi and an Early English *chapel*. Fine inner courtyard.

St. Mary's Hospital: Since 1562 a home for poor women. The wood-panelled *refectory* and the 13C *chapel* are especially worth seeing.

Market Cross: This splendid cross was erected in the 15C and later altered. It is regarded as one of the finest in the whole country.

Also worth seeing: The 17C *city library* and the modern *County Hall*; the medieval *North Walls*, probably built on Roman foundations; and *Canon Gate*, which is probably 16C. Beautiful 18C houses are to be found in *St. Martin's Square* and in the area known as the *Pallants*.

Museums: The *Corps of Royal Military Police Museum* with military exhibits. The *District Museum* with collections of archaeological finds and exhibits relating to local history, as well as to the history of the Royal Sussex Regiment. The *Guildhall Museum* in the old Greyfriars Monastery in Priory Park, with Roman excavation finds.

Theatre: The famous festival is held annually at the Chichester Festival Theatre, which was built in 1962. Classical and modern plays are performed with an international cast.

Goodwood House (Chichester), view

Environs: Bosham: (4 m. W.): A fishing village with the church of the *Holy Trinity*, which is Saxon in origin and can be seen on the Bayeux tapestry. It has a Saxon chancel arch and tower; the E. window, with stained-glass fragments, dates from the 13C. In the chancel is the 13C tomb of a girl.

Bow Hill (4 m. NW): Bronze Age *burial mound,* neolithic *flint mines* and other pre-historic relics.

Boxgrove (4 m. NE): *Church of St.Mary and St.Blaise:* Remains of a 12C Norman monastery, with a late-13C chancel; the *De la Warr chapel* is a mixture of Gothic and Renaissance elements.

Cowdray Park (9 m. N.): Ruins of a 16C *country house* which belonged to the Earl of Southampton.

Fishbourne (2 m. W.): Remains of an enormous Roman *villa.*

Goodwood House (4 m. N.): Late Jacobean mansion, restored by James Wyatt in the late 18C. Today it has paintings by Canaletto, van Dyck and other artists.

South Harting (9 m. N.); The cruciform *church of St.Mary and St.Gabriel* is Saxon in origin but the existing building dates from the 14–16C. Especially noteworthy are the 13C font, the spiral staircase and some tomb monuments.

Trotton (11 m. N.): The 14C *church of St.George* has a modern mural painting of the Last Judgement and 2 tombstone slabs, to Lord Camoys (15C) and Lady Camoys (14C).

Uppark (7 m. NW): Splendidly located 17C *brick house* built by William Talman in the style of Wren and given a Georgian conversion in the 18C. Its original furnishings, some of them valuable and very tasteful, are still in the house.

Chipping Campden
Gloucestershire/England   p.332□ 14

Once the centre of the wool trade in the Cotswolds. Today numerous houses, originally built entirely of stone, still bear witness to the prosperity of the wool traders.

Church of St.James: A Gothic church,

Bosham (Chichester), view

Christchurch, Priory Church

which is mainly 15C with a well-proportioned *W. tower* from that time; the *chancel* is 14C. Inside there are a number of memorial tablets and tomb monuments, including that to William Grevil (d. 1401) with the beautiful inscription 'flos mercatorum tocius Anglie'. The *S. chapel* has tomb monuments to the families of Hicks and Noel, which are decorated with figures.

Woolstapler's Hall: A wool store built *c.* 1340. Today it houses a collection of varied antiquities.

Environs: Broadway (4 m. W.): A little town famous for its numerous Elizabethan stone houses. The *Lygon Arms*, formerly a manor house, was used as quarters by both Charles I and Cromwell.
Hidcote Manor Gardens (3 m. E.):

These gardens, which are unusual for the Cotswolds, were laid out from 1907 onwards when Lawrence Johnston, an American, bought the site and had a number of different gardens laid out. He counteracted the raw climate and cold winds by planting tall hedges to protect the exotic plants which came from all parts of the world.
Snowshill Manor (5 m. SW): This 16&17C *manor house* has an extensive collection of clocks, musical instruments, weapons, scientific implements and fire-fighting equipment.

Christchurch
Dorset/England   p.332☐I 16

An old harbour town between the mouths

Christchurch, Priory Church

Norman arches

of the Avon and the Stour. It was formerly called Twineham before being given the name of the old abbey church.

Priory Church: Augustinian monks built a monastery here in 1150 and enlarged the existing Norman church to the size it is today. (The church was originally founded in 1093 by Bishop Ralph Flambard of Durham.) Some 330 ft. long, it is the longest parish church in England. Its tower dates from the 15C and, *c.* 130 ft. tall, it offers a superb view of this part of the coast. Although the abbey was dissolved under Henry VIII and the Norman buildings were destroyed in the Civil War, the church itself survived undamaged and its external decorations are even today splendid. The turned and latticed columns support overlapping arches decorated with scale patterns and form a most impressive

example of Norman art. Inside, the most striking item is the *reredos* with a Tree of Jesse in the chancel. This early Gothic carving, dating from about 1350, continues upwards as far as the Gothic vault. The *nave* has very fine Norman architecture from *c.* 1100; the *triforium* is particularly fine. The *chancel* is mainly 15C and the *choir stalls* have misericords from the 13–15C. At the bottom of the W. tower there is a white marble monument of 1854 built in memory of Shelley, who drowned off the coast of Italy in 1822.

Red House Museum and Art Gallery: Accommodated in a house built in 1760 with local archaeological finds and geological and natural history exhibits.

Environs: Bournemouth (3 m. W.): This bathing resort is picturesquely located on Poole Bay. It is dominated by Victorian villas and there has been a visible effort to bring the style of the Riviera to the Channel coast. The *Rothesay Museum* has a collection of furniture, paintings and ceramics from the 16&17C and also exhibits from Africa, New Zealand and the Pacific. The *Russell-Cotes Museum and Art Gallery* contains a room in memory of the Shakespearean actor Henry Irving; it also has an interesting collection of paintings and drawings by R.Wilson and Morland and Victorians. Exhibits from Burma, China, India, Japan, Ceyon and Tibet are witness to Russell-Cotes's ties with East Asia.

Poole (6 m. W.): A town on a natural harbour, which was made use of as early as the Bronze Age. It is chiefly of interest for its museums. The *Guildhall Museum* displays 16C ceramics and glass. The *Scaplen's Court Museum,* housed in an old 14C merchant's house, is devoted to local history and archaeology. The showpiece of the collection is an Iron Age fishing boat, 33 ft. long, salvaged from the harbour mud in 1964. The *Maritime Museum* is devoted to the development of local navigation from the Middle Ages until today.

Wimbourne Minster (9 m. NW): The *church of St.Cuthberga* is surprisingly large. It has a cruciform ground plan, a central tower in transitional style and a Gothic tower on the W. side, which was completed in 1448. The E. window has the original 15C Flemish glass. The tomb monument to the Duke of Somerset and his wife, built in 1444, is also worth seeing, as is a 16C bell in the W. tower.

Cirencester

Gloucestershire/England   p.332☐H 15

This little market town on the Churn was formerly the Roman *Corinium Dobunorum*; it was also the Roman administrative centre for the SW of the country. In the 2C the town was already the second largest Roman settlement in Britain. The Anglo-Saxons then destroyed much left by the Romans. After the Normans assumed power, William FitzOsbern built a castle but this

Cirencester, St.John the Baptist

Church portal

was destroyed towards the end of the Middle Ages. The once flourishing abbey was dissolved in 1539.

Church of St. John the Baptist: Some 200 ft. long. Originally Norman, the present church dates mainly from the 14C, when rich wool merchants spared no expense to make their parish church the most beautiful Perpendicular church in the S. of England. It has a fine *W. tower* over 130 ft. tall and a three-storeyed *porch* with fan-vaulting. The interior is impressive for its tall *clerestory*, a splendid *window* above the chancel arch, and magnificent *stonemasonry*, apparent in all the decorative work. The *pulpit*, built in 1515, is one of the few to have survived from before the Reformation.

The fan-vaulting in *St. Catherine's Chapel* is also of outstanding quality. *Trinity Chapel*, built in 1430 has numerous memorial tablets. Several tomb monuments are to be seen in the *Lady Chapel*, including one dating from 1776 for Lord Bathurst and designed by Joseph Nollekens.

Corinium Museum: The museum deals with the Romans in Britain and has items excavated from the Roman settlement, including sculpture, mosaics, frescos, architectural fragments and everyday utensils.

Environs: Bibury (5 m. NE): The *Parish Church* was originally Anglo-Saxon but was subjected to Norman and Gothic alterations and restorations. It was renovated by Sir Gilbert Scott in the 19C. The casts of Anglo-Saxon tombstones are worth seeing. *Arlington Row* is a row of 17C stone houses on the banks of the Colne, which were formerly used for the wool trade. *Arlington Mill* dates from the 17C and today serves as a museum for Victorian art and clothing, and also craft exhibits.

Chedworth (6 m. N.): The *Roman Villa* is the best-preserved in Britain. Many of the original walls have survived and these were slightly raised and re-roofed wherever necessary, so that the visitor today gets a good impression of a complete house. The items excavated around the house have been collected in a small museum. The

Cirencester, St. John the Baptist

Old town house

church of St. Andrew is Norman, although its present form is mainly Gothic. Inside there are Norman arches in the N. aisle and a Norman font. The nave has a Gothic roof and the stone pulpit is 15C.

Daglingworth (2 m. NW): The *church of the Holy Rood* dates from Saxon times. Its W. tower was added in the 15C and the chancel was restored in the 19C. 3 Saxon reliefs of the Crucifixion and Christ and St. Peter were found in the 19C and can be seen in the nave.

Elkstone (about 9 m. NW): The Norman *church,* with its high Perpendicular tower, is one of the finest in the area. Fine pulpit inside.

Fairford (6 m. E.): The *church of St. Mary the Virgin* dates from the late 15C and has a central tower over the crossing. The parish church, formerly furnished by rich wool traders, is the only one in the whole of England in which all the old stained-glass windows have survived. The 28 windows date from 1495–1505 and show a strong Flemish influence. The motifs depicted range from the horned devil through the Old Testament prophets to the Last Judgement. Stylistic comparisons have shown that the windows may have been the work of Flemish glass painters employed by King Henry VII.

North Cerney (4 m. N.): The cruciform *church of All Saints* was originally Norman and has a 15C saddleback W. tower. 3 glass windows and the stone pulpit also date from the 15C. The S. outer wall of the transept has a grotesque sculpture of the head of a man with the body of a lion.

Oaksey (9 m. S.): The *church of All Saints* was begun in the 13C and given its present form in the 14&15C. The Gothic clerestory betrays the fact that side aisles were planned but only the S. aisle was executed. The choir screen and parts of the choir stalls date from the 15C. In 1933 medieval frescos were uncovered depicting Christ and St. Christopher. Some remains of 14C stained glass survive.

Rendcomb (5 m. N.): The late Gothic *church of St. Peter* dates from the early 16C and has a W. tower. It has a 16C screen and fragments of Renaissance glasswork sur-

Chedworth (Cirencester), Roman mosaic

vive. The glasswork in the E. window is 19C. The font is Norman and has carvings of 11 Apostles; Judas being absent.

Clonmacnoise
Offaly/Ireland   p.326□C 12

The extensive *monastery* was founded by the Celtic St.Kieran in 548. Today it is still one of the most interesting sacred sites in Ireland. The name of this secluded ruined town means meadow of the sons of Nós. The Celtic High Kings gave abundant gifts to the monastery. It was plundered and destroyed over 50 times (especially by the Vikings, Normans and English) and then rebuilt. In the Middle Ages the monastery was famous all over Europe as a centre of religion and art. It was finally abandoned from *c.* 1647 onwards. Valuable manuscripts were produced in the monastery including the Lebor na h-Uidre (Book of the Dun Cow, 12C), the Annals of Tighernach (11C) and the Chronicon Scotorum. The remains of the monastery town on the left shore of the Shannon today consist of nine *churches,* two *round towers,* five *High Crosses* and a graveyard with over 200 splendid old *tombstones* (8C–12C).

Cathedral: The single-aisled *Great Church* was built by Abbot Colman and High King Flann in *c.* 910. In the W. is a Romanesque *portal.* There is a tripartite *chancel* in the E. A *sacristy* was added in the S.

Temple Doolin (Doolin Church): One of the oldest churches (9C), restored by E.Dowling in *c.* 1689 (hence its name). The *Hurpain Church* (Temple Hurpan) was added in the E. in the 17C.

Temple Ri (Teampull Ri): The *King's*

Clonmacnoise, monastic settlement 1 car park and entrance **2** South Cross **3** Temple Doolin **4** Temple Hurpan **5** cathedral **6** sacristy **7** King Flann's Cross **8** O'Rourke Tower **9** North Cross **10** Temple Connor **11** Temple Finghin **12** Temple Kelly **13** Temple Kieran **14** Temple Ri

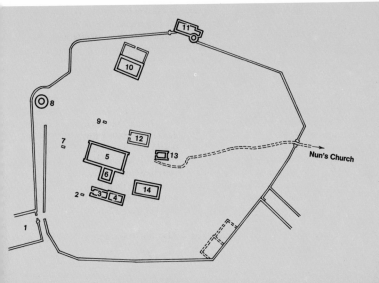

Nun's Church

Clonmacnoise, Nun's Church

Church (Gaelic Ri = Latin rex) was built in *c.* 1200; lancet-shaped *E. windows, W. gallery* and 16C *S. entrance.*

Temple Kieran (Kieran's Church): The smallest and oldest church, built *c.* 800 with the supposed *tomb* of St.Kieran, the monastery's founder, in the NE corner.

Temple Connor (in the NW): Built by King O'Connor in *c.* 1010; a *round-arched portal* survives in the W. The church has been restored for the Church of Ireland.

Temple Finghin: A rectangular church in the N. of the enclosure, with a 12C chancel, chancel arch). A *round tower* dating from 1124 is attached in the SE; 56 ft. tall, its *roof* has survived in good condition.

Nun's Church: This church stands about 1300 ft. E. of the graveyard. A fine Romanesque building, it dates from 1166 and was restored in the 19C. Chancel arch, W. portal with animal heads. The beautiful Dervorgilla, for whose sake the Anglo-Norman invasion was initiated, retreated hither *c.* 1170 to do penance as a nun. She is said to be buried in the church.

King Flann's Cross: A famous *High Cross* (*c.* 13 ft. tall including pedestal) to King Flann, the founder of the church. It dates from *c.* 913 (the time of Flann's death) and stands in the W. of the cathedral. It is also called 'The Cross of the Scriptures' owing to its splendid *relief decorations* with their Biblical scenes. An *inscription* reads: *'Abbot Colman erected this cross for King Flann'.*

Also worth seeing: Further *High Crosses*

in the NW (*North Cross,* 9C) and in the S. (*South Cross* with a relief of the Crucifixion, 9C). The famous 9–10C *Cross of Clonmacnoise* is today in the National Museum of Dublin. The round *O'Rourke's Tower* (in the W.) was a 10C watch tower and stronghold; it is now in a state of disrepair. A little out of the way, to the NW are the remains of the Norman *castle* dating from *c.* 1212 — gateway, castle courtyard and ruined tower.

Environs: Athlone (7 m. N.): This town of some 10,000 inhabitants to the S. of the charming Shannon lake of Lough Ree has the remains of a much-contested *Norman castle* (King John's Castle) built in 1210. The 13C keep and the 15C corner towers have survived; there are also alterations from the 17&19C.

Clonmel
Tipperary/Ireland   p.330 □ C 13

Clonmacnoise, High Cross

A little town of some 11,000 inhabitants in a beautiful location on the river Suir. It is the county town of Tipperary and a dairy centre. In Gaelic its name means honey meadow (mel = honey). It was the seat of the powerful Anglo-Norman Earls, the Butlers of Ormonde. The 'Irish revolution' of the adherents of 'Young Ireland' failed here in 1848.

Franciscan Church (Abbey Street): This church is a remnant of a monastery dating from 1269. The 13C *chancel,* 15C *central tower,* a medieval *font* and a 15C *tomb monument* to the Butler family have survived. The church was restored in 1886.

St. Mary's Church: The Protestant church of 1857 was built above a medieval church building of the same name. Structural elements from the 13–15C and 16–17C burial sites have survived. The oc-

tagonal *tower* and the beautiful *E. window* are worth seeing.

Also worth seeing: The *W. Gate* in the main street is all that has survived of the old *town fortifications.* The *Main Guard* dating from 1674 has the town's and the Earl's coats-of-arms. *The Tholsel* (Old Town Hall) was built in 1715; the new *Town Hall* contains documents etc. concerning the history of the town.

Environs: Ardfinnan (about 9 m. W.): Remains of a 13C *castle.*
Donaghmore (about 4 m. N.): Remains of a 13C *monastery,* and a fine chiselled 9C *High Cross.*
Fethard (about 9 m. N.): The Catholic church incorporates ruins of an *Augustinian priory* dating from *c.* 1300. The Protestant *parish church* has a nave, W. gate and

window, which date from the 14C. *Tower houses*, a *town gate* and parts of the *town wall* have also survived (15&16C).

Cockermouth
Cumbria/England   p.328☐G 10

Cockermouth is the home town of William Wordsworth (1770–1850), one of the finest of English Romantic poets. *Wordsworth House*, the house in which he was born (in Mainstreet) is open to visitors. It was built in 1745 and has some of the original furnishings, including stairwell, fireplace and panelling. There is also an exhibition of mementoes of the poet and his sister Dorothy. Other items worth seeing in the town are the *church of All Saints*, the *Old Hall*, and the ruined *castle*. Built in 1134, this castle was a refuge for the Scottish Mary Queen of Scots in the 16C; it was razed in 1648. A once-secret dungeon, accessible only by a portcullis, has survived.

Environs: Bridekirk (about 2 m. N.):

The town has a *church* with 2 Norman portals and a richly decorated 12C font.

Crosscanonby (about 7 m. NW): The church of *St. John the Evangelist* was originally Norman-Romanesque but later altered. Interesting Anglo-Saxon and early Romanesque details and 18C wood carvings.

Isel (about 3 m. NE): The 12C church of *St. Michael* is Norman. Inside there are the remains of Anglo-Saxon crosses from the 10C.

Maryport (about 6 m. NW): Built on the site of the Roman fort *Aluna* (with finds from Roman altars). The *Maritime Museum* is of interest. Apart from items of local history it also houses an interesting collection on maritime history).

Moorland Close (about 1 m. S.): Fletcher Christian, the leader of the mutiny on the Bounty, was born in 1764 in a simple house typical of this region.

Workington (about 7 m. W.): A few remains of the Roman fort of *Gabrosentium* can be seen here above the harbour. The church of *St. Michael* was restored in the late 19C; inside, a fine Romanesque arch

Clonmel, view of town

and the remains of Anglo-Saxon crosses from the 8C). *Workington Hall* was built in 1379 (Mary Queen of Scots stayed here in 1569). The *Helena Thompson Museum* of local history is also worth seeing.

Colchester
Essex/England   p.332☐L 14

This town on the S. side of the Colne was inhabited as early as the Bronze Age and is thus some 3,000 years old. Its strategically favourable location induced Cunobelin (Shakespeare's Cymbeline) to set up his capital town here. Claudius took over this residence in AD 44 and established *Colonia Camulodunum*, the first Roman colony in Britain. 17 years later, Boadicea, Queen of the Britons, tried in vain to drive the Romans out. The Romans were followed by the Saxons, who built *Colneceaster*. The Danes repeatedly plundered the settlement in the 9&10C, until in 1085 William the Conqueror built the castle, which at that time had Europe's largest keep. Interesting remains survive from the past.

City Walls: The Roman town wall consisted of a rectangle of walls extending almost 2 m. in length and in places over 19 ft. tall (remains of up to 10 ft. in height have survived on the E. side).

Castle: The Norman building was erected in the 2nd half of the 11C using Roman building materials. The enormous castle keep (165 ft. by 115 ft.) had walls 13 ft. thick; it lost its top storey in 1683. The castle was built above the Roman temple which Claudius built in AD 50. The remains of the castle are today used as a *museum* devoted to the Celtic and Roman periods. The Roman period is outstandingly well represented, with coins, ceramics, glass and jewellery, and also statues of bronze and stone. The collection is complemented by models of the Roman settlement.

Holly Trees: A Georgian house built in 1718. Today it houses a good collection of antiquities, old costumes and old jewellery.

Former church of All Saints: Today

Colchester, Town Hall

houses the town's *Museum of Natural History*, which is mainly devoted to geology and biology.

Minories: A Georgian house dating from 1776 with Georgian furniture, a collection of paintings and a collection of 18C clocks.

Environs: Copford (6 m. W.): The *church of the Holy Trinity* is undoubtedly one of the most impressive in the whole county. It was built in *c.* 1150 and the nave, altarpiece and apse survive from the original building; only the S. aisle was added later. The frescos with which the church was once painted throughout are also 12C. Today only parts remain and from these you may imagine the church's former beauty. **Dedham** (8 m. NE): The village featured in many of Constable's paintings. There are several fine houses, including some from the 16C and some which are Georgian. *Southfields,* the weavers' quarter, built around 1500, is also of interest. The painter Alfred Munnings lived and died in *Castle House.* Today the house is a memorial to the painter and contains many of his works.

Layer Marney (10 m. NE): The *church of St. Mary the Virgin* was rebuilt by the first Lord Marney in the early 16C. The church is particularly worth seeing for two fine tomb monuments. The older of these is typically English and has the alabaster figure of Sir William Marney in full knight's armour (15C). The more recent monument, in black marble, shows Henry, the first Lord Marney, under an enormous terracotta baldachino and is the work of Italian sculptors. *Layer Marney Towers* dates from the early 16C and was never completed. There is a conspicuous disproportion between the gatehouse, which is enormously high with 8 storeys, and the main house which gives the impression of being very small by comparison. This disproportion also indicates the transition between early castle architecture and residential house architecture. While the pretensions towards a castle-like structure were exaggerated to an absurd degree in the case of the gatehouse, the building intended to be actually lived in never passed

Colchester, Castle

beyond the rudimentary stage. All the decorations of the building of 1510–25 (built by order of the first two Lords Marney) show Early Renaissance features. There are fine terracotta decorations by Italian craftsmen.

Coleraine
Londonderry/Northern Ireland   p.324 □ E 9

A harbour town on the mouth of the river Bann with some 16,000 inhabitants. It is one of the oldest English settlements (from plantation times) and today is a university town (the University of Ulster). In the S. of the town is the Stone Age circular *Mountsandel Fort* on the river Bann.

Environs: Ballycastle (about 16 m. NE): This charming fishing port (with about 3,000 inhabitants) contains the scant remains of *Dunanymie Castle* (14–15C) and the nearby Franciscan *Bonamargy Friary* dating from 1500. The latter's crypt is the

mausoleum of the MacDonnel family, who founded the monastery. In about 1898 the Irish-Italian physicist Marconi built the first radio station communicating with the offshore *Rathlin Island* (which has traces of an 11C monastery).

Downhill Castle (about 7 m. NW): The Earl of Bristol (Bishop of Derry), who enjoyed travelling, ordered the castle to be enlarged *c.* 1770; the classical rotunda of the *Mussenden Temple* (*c.* 1783), standing at the edge of the cliff, also survives. (The numerous 'Bristol Hotels' all over the world were named after this Earl).

Dunluce Castle (about 12 m. NE): This imposing complex was built in *c.* 1300 by the Earl of Ulster, Richard de Burgh, on a rock just off the coast, which is linked to the mainland by a bridge; two massive *defensive towers* have survived. The later additions (towers and gable, gatehouse) are 16C. Buildings on the land side were erected after the collapse of the cliff in 1639. Nearby (some 2 m. NE) is the interesting volcanic basalt formation known as *Giant's Causeway*. The innumerable

Coleraine, town centre

Conwy, Conwy Castle

polygonal basalt columns resulted from the cooling of a volcanic flow.

Cong
Mayo/Ireland   p.326□B 11

A pretty town on a strip of land some 4 m. wide between the lakes Lough Corrib (in the S.) and Lough Mask (in the N.). The Gaelic word cong means isthmus. *Cong Abbey* was built in the 12C, on the site of an early monastery from the 6C, by the O'Conors, the kings of Connacht, for the Augustinians. Roderic O'Conor, the last Irish High King, died here in 1198. The Romanesque and early Gothic *ruined church, gatehouse* and *cloister* (dating from 1200 and restored in the 19C), have sur-

vived. The gold *Cong Cross* which dates from 1123 (now in the National Museum in Dublin) and a 14C *roadside cross* in the village square are splendid. *Ashford Castle,* built in the Victorian Gothic style in the 18C, stands at the edge of the town on the site of a former Norman castle.

Environs: Castle Kirk (some 9 m. W.): This massive *ruined castle* is in the NW bay of Lough Corrib, SE of Maam Bridge. It was built by the O'Conors in the mid 13C. The entire surrounding area, especially towards the W., has a delightful landscape, particularly the area called *Joyce's Country,* which is named after a 13C Gaelic family. The lakes and mountainous country of the province of *Connemara,* between Oughterard on Lough Corrib and Clifden on the Atlantic coast, are also beautiful. Prehistoric, early Christian and medieval

Conwy, St.Mary's

buildings are to be found everywhere here, but they are often in a sad state of repair. The inhabitants of the Gaeltacht are known for their traditional Gaelic way of life.

Inchagoill (about 5 m. SW): The remains of an early Christian *oratory* built of stones and mortar (*c.* 9C) and of a 12C Romanesque *church* with a beautifully decorated portal are to be found on the small island in Lough Corrib.

Inishmaine (about 4 m. N.): This little island in Lough Mask (Gaelic: Inish, Inch = island) has the remains of a 13C *Augustinian monastery*. Some parts of the cruciform church, which has good stonemasonry and an early Irish rectangular gate, have survived.

Ross Abbey (about 7 m. SE): This interesting, well-preserved *Franciscan monastery* near Headford was built in *c.* 1351 and enlarged in the 15C. The W. gate, E. window and Gothic round arches are notable features of the 14–15C *church*. The tower dates from 1498; parts of the monastery were inhabited until 1765.

Conwy
Gwynedd/Wales   p.328 □ G 12

This small town has some 10,000 inhabitants and is located on the wide tidal estuary of the river Conwy, where it flows into Conwy Bay. The town's medieval characteristics have survived well.

Conwy Castle: Started in 1283. Now an impressive castle ruin with walls up to 15 ft. thick, 8 drum towers at the corners, fir-

Conwy, St.Mary's, 15C font

ing slits but no gatehouse. The visitor passes through the narrow gateway into the *outer ward* (in the E. there is a second gateway across the outwork with its water gate). Here are the walls of the *Great Hall*, which measures 125 ft. x 39 ft. with one surviving stone arch of the former 8 which supported the roof; there are also the remains of the kitchen and a well shaft. The *inner ward* has the *King's Hall* and the *king's quarters*, the walls of the audience chamber, the *Queen's Tower* in the NE with a small chapel on the top storey, and the *king's tower* in the SE, with the castle dungeon. The adjoining *queen's garden* is a delightful little terrace above the river. King Edward I had this castle built in the 13C at the same time as the castles of Caernarvon, Criccieth and Harlech, at a time when medieval fortress architecture flourished.

Also worth seeing: The impressive *town wall* is even today over 1 m. long, has 21 semi-drum towers and dates from the same time as the castle (13C); a walk around the walls well repays the effort. Of the 3 original gates, the *Upper Gate* (Welsh: Port Uchaf), with its outworks, is striking. The town church of *St.Mary's* in the town centre has a fine 13C N. gate, 13C nave pillars, a font in the 14C S. transept and a good 15C rood screen. *Plas Mawr* (Great House) in the High Street was built around 1585 in typically Elizabethan style; it has 365 windows and 52 doors! Today it is the seat of the Royal Cambrian Academy of Art, which has a permanent exhibition. *Aberconwy House* (on the corner of the High Street and Castle Street) is a half-timbered building of *c.* 1500; today it has a display of antiquities. Near to Porth Isaf (= riverside gate) is *The Smallest House,* a small 18–19C fisherman's house measuring only 7 ft. x 10 ft. x 8 ft. The old medieval *privy houses* are also added to the town walls. The *village church* of Gyffin (a suburb to the S.) has a 13C portal and font, while the altar paintings and the roof date from the 15–16C.

Environs: Betws-y-Coed ('Chapel in the Wood'; about 16 m. S.): A holiday village surrounded by fine woods with beautiful walks. The four-arched *stone bridge* of Pont-y-Pair is 15C and there is an old *church* with a Norman font and good tomb sculptures. Telford's *Waterloo Bridge* in the S. dates from 1815. Nearby, at Ty Hyll, are the well-known *Swallow Falls.*
Caerhun (about 5 m. S.): Scant remains of the *Roman camp of Conovium* can be seen around the village church. This part of the Vale of Conwy is most delightful.
Llandudno (about 20,000 inhabitants; 4 m. N.): A popular seaside resort opposite Conwy on the spit of land between the steep cliffs of the Great Orme in the NW and the Little Orme in the NE. The church of *St.Tudno,* named after a 7C her-

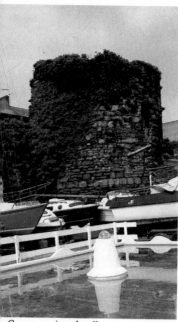

Conwy, section of wall

Corfe Castle, view

mit, is on the *Great Orme,* a steep headland some 680 ft. high and which merits a visit. The town is also named after him (Llandudno = town of Tudno). The church, which was restored in 1855 dates from the 15C and has fine wood carvings over the apse (which is in fact the N. wall of an older, 12C building). To the SW of this there are the scant remains of the medieval *Gogarth Abbey* (12–13C). Dolls from all over the world are on display in the *Llandudno Doll Museum.* The *Rapallo House* has an exhibition of paintings, old weapons and armour. In the S. of the town, by the wide river Conwy there are some remains of a *castle* destroyed as early as *c.* 1260.
Llanrwst (some 12 m. S. of Conwy): The parish church of *St. Gwyst* was built in the 15C in Perpendicular style; restored 17C. It has a fine rood screen and crucifix. The Gwydir Chapel dates from *c.* 1633 and has

fine decorations and monuments, including the reputed coffin of Llewelyn the Great (13C). Nearby, on the shore of the Conwy there is an old *courthouse* (Ty Hwnt y'r Bont) from the 15C. It has been the site of a modern eisteddfod (bards' congress for singing competitions). The fine three-arched *Conwy bridge* dates from 1636. The 15C *Gwydir Castle,* later restored several times, is on the opposite shore. Some 2 m. outside is the 15C church of *Llanrhychwyn,* with a 12C font.

Corfe Castle
Dorset/England   p.332 □ H 16

This ruined castle, in the middle of the Isle of Purbeck and visible from afar, is one of the most historic sites in England. The

Anglo-Saxons built a royal residence here and Elfrieda was ruler of the castle in 978. She ordered the murder of Edward the Martyr (King Edgar's son and her own son-in-law) to help her son Ethelred the Unready (978–1016) to the throne. William the Conqueror (1066–1087) expanded the castle by building a massive Norman keep. The fortress was not only the favourite residence of King John (1199 – 1216, who signed the Magna Carta) but also his treasury. The State prison and the crown jewels were both equally closely guarded. The complex was gradually expanded and secured with ramparts and bastions. In 1643, Lady Bankes defended the fortress for 6 weeks against 600 soldiers of the Parliamentary party. 3 years later the castle was destroyed after treachery on the part of its own garrison.

Cork
Cork / Ireland   p.330□C 14

This, the second largest town in the Republic of Ireland, has some 135,000 inhabitants and lies on the many-branched mouth of the river Lee. The Gaelic name Corcaigh means marshland.

History: In the 6–7C the Celtic St.Finbar founded a monastery in the SW of the town. Norwegian pirates settled here *c.* 846, and the Vikings *c.* 917 (simple fortifications). Cork became the main town of the MacCarthys, lords of Desmond in 1118, until it was captured by the Anglo-Normans in *c.* 1180. Nearly all the medieval buildings were destroyed in the course of the many battles and in 1690 the town walls and fortresses were also torn down. The civil war of 1920–2 resulted in more damage. The town largely gained its pres-

Cork, St. Finbar's Cathedral ▷

ent appearance from the 17&18C onwards, when Cork was developing into an important trading and manufacturing centre with a harbour. Since 1845 it has also been a university town and at the same time the seat of both Catholic and Protestant bishops.

St.Finbarr's Cathedral (on the Southern Channel): An imposing cathedral in French Gothic style by William Burges, built 1867–79 on the site of the former monastery of St.Finbarr. It has 3 towers (the middle one is some 260 ft. high), a chancel and apse, wall and floor mosaics, and a magnificent chime of bells.

St.Anne's Church (also known as Shandon Church): This Protestant church in Church Street (N. of the river Lee) was built 1722–1826 on the site of an previous church. Its red and white *tower* in sandstone and limestone makes it a town landmark. The bells were cast in 1750 and their chime is well known.

Also worth seeing: The Dominican church of *St.Mary* (by the river Quay) dating from 1839, with a miraculous 15C Flemish statue of the Madonna. The Catholic *St.Mary's Cathedral* (N. of the river Lee), with its Gothic tower and 9 bells, was built in 1808 on top of an older church; richly decorated neo-Gothic interior. The former *Custom House,* built in classical style 1814–18, stands where the tributaries of the Lee meet. The elegant *St. Patrick's Bridge* was built in 1859 and is regarded as the finest bridge in Cork. Nearby is the modern *opera house* completed in 1965. Near to St.Finbarr's Cathedral is the *Red Abbey Tower,* a remnant of an Augustinian monastery founded about 1300. The *Elizabeth Fort* (near Parliament Bridge) was built in 1603 and used as a prison in the 19C (the intermediate rampart from the 17C has survived). The *Court House* in Liberty Street is a classical court house with a Corinthian portico and an allegorical *bronze group* (Justice, Law, Charity). The Protestant *St. Peter's Church* (North Main Street) was built in 1785 on the site of a medieval church. Not far away is the *Mercy Hospi-*

Blarney Castle (Cork)

tal dating from 1763; there are fine stucco ceilings in the associated *Mansion House*. The church of *Holy Trinity* on the S. Channel with its pointed bell tower and beautiful glass windows was built in neo-Gothic style in 1832. The *Crawford School of Art* (on the Coal Quay) has a collection of copies of ancient Roman sculptures, casts of works by the Irish sculptor Hogan (1800–58) and good paintings by contemporary Irish painters.

Environs: Blarney Castle (6 m. NW): A charmingly located *castle*, which belonged to the MacCarthys. It has a massive *keep* (89 ft.) and corner towers dating from 1446. The legendary 'Blarney stone' is to be found just below the battlements; kissing it is supposed to bestow eloquence of speech.

Cloyne (about 16 m. SE): An old episcopal town stemming from a monastery founded by St. Colman in the 6C. The church, which was restored in 1856, dates from 1250 and has some medieval features. The S. transept has the grave of George Berkeley (1685–1753), the famous bishop

and philosopher; a *round tower* survives near the church.

Cobh (about 12 m. SE): Cork's harbour, from the 18&19C; also called 'Queenstown'. Hundreds of thousands of Irish emigrated to North America from here during the famine of 1845.

Kilcrea Friary (about 12 m. W.): A partially restored *Franciscan monastery* dating from 1465 with a well-preserved *tower church*.

Monkstown Castle (about 4 m. SE): This *fortress* dating from 1636, with 4 massive corner towers, is on the bay opposite Cobh.

Coventry
West Midlands/England   p.328☐I 13/14

A modern industrial city with an interesting history. Couentrey, as it was originally called, had a small monastery even in the Anglo-Saxon times; a Benedictine priory founded by Leofric, Earl of Mercia, was built here in 1043. The Benedictine church served as a cathedral for Coventry

Cobh (Cork), view of town

and Lichfield simultaneously from 1102-85. In the late 14C this town was one of the most important cities in the country after London, York and Bristol. Accordingly, the cathedral dedicated to St.Michael was built in an appropriately liberal style in the 14&15C. The priory was dissolved in 1539 but St.Michael's Cathedral was used as a parish church until 1918. From the 17C onwards, the town became more and more a centre of the English clothing industry, light engineering and heavy industry coming later. During the night of 14 November 1940, the city had to pay for its success in the armaments industry by receiving some of the severest German bombing experienced in Britain. The entire old part of the city, including the old cathedral, sank in ruins.

Old Cathedral: The cathedral completed in 1433 was a fine example of English Gothic. Its E. section, which was pentagonal, was unique, as was the large *W.tower* of 1394, which had an octagonal lantern, supported by slender arched buttresses, on a square base. The tower at a height of almost 330 ft. was thus one of the highest church towers in the country. The church itself was flattened by the bombs, leaving only parts of the surrounding walls intact, but the tower remained a standing memorial. Along with the remains of the surrounding walls, the tower was joined to the new building when the new cathedral was built in the 1950s.

New Cathedral: Built 1954–62 to plans by Sir Basil Spence. The building material was a reddish sandstone, which was worked in different layers and harmonizes well with the coloured window strips. Epstein's sculpture of St.Michael vanquishing the devil can be seen on an outside wall near the point where the old and new buildings meet. The bronze figures are some 26 ft. tall overall. The nave is some 300 ft. long and 90 ft. wide and has a chessboard-like

floor of black and white marble; the whole is dominated by an enormous *tapestry* above the altar. Some 85 ft. tall and 36 ft. wide, it is probably the largest wall tapestry in the world. Designed by Graham Sutherland and manufactured from Australian wool, it was made in 30,000 hours in Felletin in France. The tapestry shows Christ victorious, with a lone human figure between his feet. Four medallions represent the Evangelists. St.Michael vanquishing the devil appears again. The background is green.

Between the nave and aisles there are 2 rows with 7 concrete columns each; the columns end in ribs, which form a uniform diamond pattern as far as the chancel. The baptism chapel on the right side is impressive with its enormous *glass window* by John Piper and Patrick Reyntiens, which reaches from the floor to the ceiling. The window is composed of some 200 individual panels and symbolizes baptism; the light of the Holy Spirit illuminates the world and joins Heaven and earth. The windows of the aisle are so designed that they throw their light on to the altar and only gradually reveal themselves as you progress E. The 10 windows belong together in pairs, each pair having a dominant colour. The first pair is green and symbolizes the beginning, the second is red and symbolizes God's intervention into the world, the third has various colours and symbolizes human contradiction, the fourth is blue and purple and symbolizes maturity, and the fifth is in gold and silver, symbolizing redemption. These windows were designed by Lawrence Lee, Geoffrey Clarke and Keith New. The *Chapel of Christ in Gethsemane* contains a fine gold mosaic by Steven Sykes. It shows the angel appearing to Christ in the Garden of Gethsemane in preparation for the approaching Crucifixion.

Church of Holy Trinity: A Gothic church from the 15C&16C with a tower

Coventry, Old Cathedral with new roof

New Cathedral

N. window

nearly 265 ft. high. Its richly decorated 15C *pulpit,* and the *W. window* created by Hugh Easton in 1955, are both worth seeing.

St.Mary's Hall: This house, built for the merchants' guild in 1342 and enlarged in 1394, survived the bombing. The famous Coventry Gobelin, executed in Flanders in the early 16C, hangs in the Great Hall on the 1st floor. It was probably commissioned on the occasion of the visit of Henry VII and Elizabeth of York to Coventry in 1500. The 13C *Caesar's Tower* adjoins the S. side of the house. It was probably part of a castle destroyed by the Earls of Chester. Destroyed by the bombs, it was then reconstructed using the original materials. Mary Stuart was kept prisoner on the 2nd floor in 1569.

Herbert Art Gallery and Museum: Archaeological exhibits, including Anglo-Saxon finds from the excavations of the old city rampart. There are also cars, motorcyles and other machines dating from 1900 onwards.

Environs: Berkswell (3 m. W.): The late-12C *church of St.John the Baptist* is probably the most beautiful Norman church in the county. The crypt under the chancel is impressive, parts of it are probably Anglo-Saxon. Its octagonal ground- plan has not yet been clearly explained.

Craigievar Castle
Grampian/Scotland   p.324☐H 6

This, probably the most exotic and at the same time best-executed of all Scottish tower houses was built from 1610–26 by John Bell, the architect, for William Forbes, a merchant known as Danzig-Willie. Favourable circumstances ensured that neither the Civil War, the disturbances

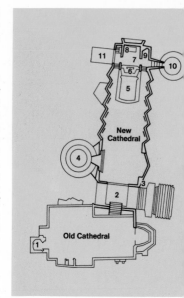

Coventry, Old and New Cathedral 1 W. tower of old cathedral **2** hall connecting Old and New Cathedrals **3** St. Michael triumphing over the Devil **4** Chapel of Unity **5** choir **6** high altar **7** Lady Chapel **8** tapestry over the altar **9** Chapel of Christ in Gethsemane **10** Chapel of Christ the Servant **11** refectory.

of Cromwell, nor the Jacobite revolts, caused any damage to the building. The castle is therefore one of the most important buildings in Scotland. The 5-storeyed residential tower, with its L-shaped ground-plan, has a total of 19 rooms which, though small, are agreeably and tastefully furnished.

The ground-plan and the narrow spiral staircases are of a sophisticated design, ensuring that possible intruders could always only advance one at a time and that the defenders always had a separate staircase by which to escape. The turrets, with their conical helm roofs, are rather amusing and give the impression of having been stuck on, although they were originally built as watch-towers at the corners of the once open parapet. The watch-towers gradually became roofed and the spaces between the towers were closed to yield additional living quarters. A necessary result of this was the frieze of corbel stones around the entire building, which softens its form.

Environs: Crathes Castle (16 m. SE): This castle is another Scottish rarity. In many respects it is similar to Craigievar Castle. Here too there are corner turrets with conical roofs, and also stepped gables, battlements, and decorated panels on the corbel stones. However, there are also differences. Crathes Castle is not only nearly half a century older, but also lacks the outer elegance. Building work began in 1553 by Alexander Burnet of Leys. The house was occupied in 1596 and the interior furnishings were completed in 1602. It was mainly for its sumptuous decoration and furnishing that the castle became famous. The *wooden ceilings* in the Chamber of the Nine Nobles and in the Chamber of the Nine Muses deserve special attention. These are painted with biblical and allegorical motifs and aphorisms. The gallery on the top storey has impressive and unique *oak panelling*. The *Horn of Leys*, in bejewelled ivory, is a particular treasure. Alexander Burnard is said to have received it from King Robert the Bruce in 1323. Since 1951 the castle has been in the care of the National Trust, which has also seen to it that the gardens surrounding the castle are once again flourishing in their former splendour.

Kildrummy Castle (9 m. NW): A ruin, which nevertheless is a good example of a medieval Scottish castle, because its architecture can still be clearly discerned. The surrounding wall, reinforced with towers at the corners and above the gateway, is particularly impressive. The complex was built 1214 – 49 by Gilbert de Moravia, the bishop of Caithness. The outwork and drawbridge are 14C. The castle was finally completed in the 16C. It was

the seat of the earls of Mar before being destroyed in 1717 in the Jacobite rebellions.

Crichton
Lothian/Scotland   p.324☐H 8

Crichton Castle: Picturesquely located on a gentle slope, it is a good example of the conversion of a 14C tower house into a palatial mansion (16C). The early tower house belonged to Sir William Crichton, James II's chancellor. The 5th Earl of Bothwell acquired the property *c.* 1585. He had visited Italy and was deeply impressed by the country's architecture. Thus, by 1591, the tower house had been converted into a complex with an inner courtyard, on the model of the palace in Ferrara.

The ruins of Crichton Castle survive up to the roof storey; there are splendid Renaissance arches in the N. wing. The façade itself has masonry hewn with facet-like surfaces.

Also worth seeing: In Crichton there is also an Iron Age *fort*. The ring wall encloses an oval 295 ft. long and almost 200 ft. wide. The *abbey church,* used as a parish church since 1449, has fine tunnel vaulting and a splendid tower.

Environs: Borthwick Castle (3 m. S.): Built in 1430 it is one of the largest Scottish tower houses. The 2-winged tower, about 115 ft. tall, has walls up to 13 ft. thick and withstood many sieges undamaged, even that undertaken by Cromwell in 1650. Mary Queen of Scots lived here after her marriage to Bothwell. When the rebellious lords encircled the castle, Mary Stuart was able to escape disguised as a page. During the last war, Borthwick Castle was used as Britain's main state archive. The castle has been preserved in such good condition that it is still inhabited today.

Crickhowell
Powys/Wales   p.332☐G 14

This small town of some 1,500 inhabitants is some 6 m. NW of Abergavenny in the charming valley of the river Usk, in the foothills of the Black Mountains. The ruins of the *castle* date from the 13C (destroyed in *c.* 1403). A fine 13C *bridge* with 13 arches, restored in 1808, leads over the Usk. The *parish church,* with a shingle-roofed tower, was built in the 14C Decorated style. Remains of the *town wall,* with the town gate, still survive.

Environs: Cwmyoy (8 m. NE): Medieval *village church* with leaning tower.
Llanthony (about 15 m. NE): The remains of the old *Llanthony Priory,* founded in *c.* 1108 and later inhabited by Augustinian monks, are worth seeing. Fine arches, parts of the window tracery, capitals, and a passage with a groin vault, all in the strict Norman style, survive. Not far from this, today's parish church of *St. David's,* also from the 13C, may be visited. The buildings of the later *Llanthony monastery,* an Anglican foundation from 1870, are also nearby, 3 m. NW of the old priory. The monastery building became an artist's residence; the neo-Gothic church with the tomb of Ignatius the founder is falling into disrepair.

Partrishow (Welsh: Merthyr Issui, about 6 m. NE): An interesting medieval *church* dedicated to the Celtic St. Issui. It was founded as early as the 11C; the parts visible today are 13C, with later alterations, the latest dating from 1908. The visitor passes through the 14C gatehouse with its holy-water stoup; the font is pre-Norman with an old inscription. There are good wall paintings with contemporary allegories on the W. wall and a richly decorated 15C carved rood screen on the chancel wall. There are also two old altars (13C altar slabs) in front of the screen. The chancel arch the roof of the nave (15C), the 14C belfry, and an old Welsh bible dating from 1620, are of interest.
Tretower (about 4 m. NW): Here there is a well-preserved fortified medieval man-

Crichton, Castle, N. wing

sion, *Tretower Court*. The gatehouse, hall and inner courtyard date from 14–15C. Nearby are the remains of a Norman *castle,* including a round tower.

Culross
Fife/Scotland   p.324□G 8

This delightful town on the N. shore of the inner Firth of Forth no longer gives the impression of having once been an important trading centre which in the late 16C was perfectly well able to compete with Glasgow. There were saltworks here and in particular an extensive coal mine with a system of tunnels which extended under the Firth of Forth. Sir George Bruce built a flood-proof hoisting shaft right through the water, so that the coal could be loaded on to the ships direct. Fortunately, however, the industrial age which then followed completely by-passed Culross, with the result that the hub of the little town from *c.*1600 remained intact. The local building tradition can be clearly seen in the town houses from the 16&17C belonging to the middle class—it is probably clearer here than anywhere else in Scotland. The individual rows and groups of houses are as well-proportioned as is each house in itself. The relationship of the small square windows to the picturesque doors, stepped gables, and turrets, is always harmonious in spite of all the variations. The National Trust has succeeded not only in preserving the ensemble in its former state, but in ensuring that the householders take equal pride in their own houses too. The idea of buying and restoring the houses on an individual basis has certainly been successful here. The following are the most important buildings:

Culross Palace: Begun in 1597 for Sir George Bruce, the great engineer; continuously enlarged up until 1611. Its particu-

lar charm derives from the fact that Scottish and Dutch elements of style have here found a blend of their own. The bipartite *windows* are typically Scottish, with leaded lights in the upper section and wooden shutters in the lower. The combination of painted timber ceilings and distemper walls is delightful.

The Town House: The town hall was built in 1626; the double staircase and clock tower date from 1783. The council chamber has a painted wooden ceiling. The ground floor was at one time used as a prison, as was the attic when necessary.

The Study: Built in *c.* 1600 and so-called because Bishop Leighton occasionally studied and meditated here. Today it houses the National Trust's information centre and a museum of local history and culture. The *Culross Room* has an exhibition illustrating local history of the past 3 centuries. The entire house is equipped with Scottish, English and Dutch furniture from the 17C. The panelling of Scottish oak, dating from *c.* 1633, is especially splendid.

Culross Abbey: A Cistercian abbey founded by the Earl of Fife around 1300. However, only scant remains have survived. The restored abbey chancel is today used as a parish church.

Environs: Dunimarle Castle (W. of Culross): Dates from the 19C and particularly interesting for its picture collection and park.

Culzean Castle
Strathclyde/Scotland   p.326□F 9

The castle is depicted on the Scottish five pound note and is an outstanding example of the splendid period of Scottish architecture in the 18C. Its origins lie in the 12C and, for some 600 years, it was nothing more than a tower-house with an L-shaped ground plan, which was owned by the Kennedy clan. In 1762 the tower house passed into the possession of the 19th Earl of Cassillis and 13 years later his brother commissioned Robert Adam to modernize and expand the house. For 15 years, 1777–92, work was carried out on the extensive rock castle immediately above the cliffs. The greatest architect of Scottish classicism was given a free rein and he built a castle with a medieval exterior, crenellated corner towers and side towers, windows with arrow slits and a continuous parapet as a conclusion to the roof. The external, almost martial plainness of the building is eliminated inside where drawing rooms have refined furnishings and an elegance no one would expect from the outside.

Adam dealt with every detail, from the shape of the rooms, their decoration, the furniture, down to the smallest detail of the fittings. The decorations impress by their

Crichton, Castle, detail

scarcely surpassable perfection, whether in the famous Oval *Staircase* with its two-storeyed colonnaded gallery or in the Round Drawing Room. The best example of the decoration of the drawing rooms is the latter, which demonstrates Adam's art particularly clearly. Garlands, urns, palmettes, friezes and sills have been brought into an ideal harmony, supported by soft colours such as pale pink, light blue or light green. The severe spatial form is broken up in this drawing room by apse-like niches. Floor lamps and wall lamps, tendrils, mirrors and, last but not least, the carpet, have all been designed to increase the overall effect. A W. wing was added to the house in 1879. The castle was transferred to the National Trust in 1945, but the top floor was retained as a National Guest Flat. General Eisenhower was the first tenant.

Environs: Crossraguel Abbey: Founded by Duncan, Earl of Carrick, it dates from the 2nd half of the 12C. Monks from Paisley took over the abbey in 1214 and enlarged it. During the monastery's heyday in the 14&15C, the abbot was also the secular ruler of the surrounding area, with separate currency and laws under the abbot's jurisdiction. The abbey was the last bulwark against the Reformation in the 16C. Not until 1592 did the last monks give way. The ruins of the abbey buildings date from the 15C. The size of the complex becomes especially clear from the Abbot's Tower in the E. and the enormous gatehouse in the W. The remains of the church foundations and sacristy foundations date in part from the 13C. The walls of the chancel, sacristy and chapterhouse, along with the vaults, are late Gothic. The use of simple rubble-stones and precisely hewn ashlars clearly shows the varying age of the ruins.

Maybole (3 m. E): The *castle* dates from the 17C. It was formerly the residence of the Earls of Cassillis, a branch of the

Kennedy clan. The restored tower house has very picturesque turrets. The collegiate church, founded in 1371, was later used by the Earls of Cassillis as a Kennedy burial site. However, only ruins survive. **Kirkoswald** (3 m. S.): *Souter Johnnie's Cottage*, the house of John Davidson the shoemaker, has been preserved in its original state. The shoemaker was an early friend of Robert Burns, who perpetuated him in Tam o'Shanter. The 18C house has been furnished as a museum. Both the shoemaker's way of life and contemporary mementoes of Burns are on display.

Crichton, Castle, detail

Darlington
Durham/England   p.328 □ I 10

St.Cuthbert: The town's parish church, built in 1190–1220 in Early English style. The tower over the crossing has a spire and dates from the 14C.

The beautiful *chancel wall* is a particularly fine feature of this cross-shaped church; the *font cover*, and the 19C stained-glass *windows*, which are the work of Clayton & Bell, are also worth seeing.

North Road Station Railway Museum: The museum stands on the site of the railway line opened by George Stephenson in 1825, which was the first to carry passengers (the 'Stockton & Darlington Railway'). Locomotive No. 1 of this line was formerly exhibited in the Bank Top Station, but is now on display here.

Environs: Croft (about 2 m. S.): *St.Peter's Church* was originally Norman, but was later much altered. Features worth seeing inside include the richly decorated sedilia (seats for priests, built into the S. wall of the chancel) and the remains of an Anglo-Saxon cross.

Gainford (about 7 m. W.): Beautifully restored 13C church.

Haughton-le-Skerne (about ½ m. N.): Except for the 19C transepts, the interesting *St.Andrew's Church* is Norman; there is a tower on the W. side of the church. Inside there are fine 17C furnishings, including the boxed pews, the pulpit and the covering over the font. Also note the Anglo-Saxon architectural fragments.

Hurworth (about 3 m. S.): A village built mainly in the 18C, it was the birthplace of the 18C mathematician William Emerson, who was born in the *Emerson Arms;* his tomb is in the village graveyard.

Piercebridge (about 5 m. W.): Built from the remains of a Roman *fort* which guarded the point where the Roman road from York to Corstopitum (today Corbridge) crossed the River Tees.

Stanwick (about 5 m. S.): One of the most interesting *hill forts* in the whole of England, built by the 'Brigantes' (a tribe of Britons). The first building (the so-called 'Tofts') dates from the early 1C BC and its only fortifications are a simple rampart and ditch; some 50 years later the fort was expanded on its N. side (a dry wall was employed here). The S. side of the building was extended in about AD 72. One of the reasons for building this fort was the internal disputes within the tribe over whether they should seek the support of Rome.

Dartford
Kent/England   p.332□K 15

Dartford is one of the busiest industrial towns in the region.

Parish Church of the Holy Trinity: Only the Norman tower still bears witness to the church's 11C origin. 11C wall paintings were uncovered during 19C restoration work.

Also worth seeing: The *Royal Victoria and Bull Hotel* reminds us of older and easier times; interesting exhibits of local history, from primitive times up to the present, are on display in the *Borough Museum*.

Environs: Gravesend (about 6.5 m. E.): *St. George's Church* (1731) was built by Charles Sloane in Georgian style in 1731; in the chancel is the *tomb of Pocahontas*, the American Indian wife of John Rolfe; she died here in 1616.
Lullingstone (5.5 m. S.): A *castle* from the early Tudor period, expanded by Queen Anne (1702–14) who is commemorated in the interesting Queen Anne Room.
Lullingstone Villa (4.5 m. S.), a well-preserved Roman villa with what might have been a Christian chapel.
Sutton-at-Hone (3 m. S.): *St. John's Jerusalem*, a 13C seat of the knights of the Order, with the chapel of the Order preserved in a 16C house. The large oak in the garden is said to be descended from the tree under which Napoleon died on St. Helena.

Dartmouth
Devon/England   p.332□G 17

In the Middle Ages, the entrance to this natural harbour on the Dart could be closed by means of an iron chain. Not only was it possible for ships to shelter here, but they could also hide. The 146 ships of the English, French, German and Flemish Crusaders assembled here in 1147, and Crusaders gathered here again in 1190,

Lullingstone Villa (Dartford), mosaic in Roman villa

whereas in the summer of 1944 over 400 Allied warships lay here waiting for D-Day. Between 1488 and 1502, fortifications were built on both sides of the narrow estuary mouth. Nine ships were placed here to await the Spanish Armada. In 1705, 60 years before James Watt, Thomas Newcomen from Dartmouth invented the atmospheric steam engine.

St.Savior: This Gothic church, altered in 1630, has a particularly splendid *choir screen*, built *c*. 1500 entirely of wood, with filigree tracery and leaf frieze. The stone *pulpit*, richly decorated with numerous sculptures, dates from about the same time. The *gallery* decorated with the merchants' arms was built in 1633. A *panel,* which shows John Hawley, the Mayor of Dartmouth, in full armour between his two wives, dates from 1408. The wrought-iron *ornaments* on the oak S. door (14C) are outstanding. They show two leopards guarding the tree of life.

Butterwalk: 11 granite columns support a carved half-timbered stucture built in 1535-40. The colonnades were damaged by bombs in 1943 and restored in 1954.

Town museum: This is in one of the merchants' houses on the Butterwalk. The house dates from the early 17C, and Charles II visited it in 1671. The collections are all connected with maritime history, and include numerous models of famous ships.

Environs: Torquay (12 m. N.): Built on seven hills above Torbay, Torquay is thought to be the site of one of the oldest human settlements in England. From 1823 onwards, Palaeolithic tools, and fossils of animals which became extinct long ago, have been excavated here in layers 10 ft. deep. This protected bay, with its mild climate, has always attracted artists and writers. Agatha Christie, the 'Queen of Crime', was born here in 1890. In 1971 she was made a DBE and when she died on 12 January 1976 her detective play 'The Mousetrap' had been performed 9, 611 times at the Ambassadors Theatre in London (now at St.Martin's Theatre). The total number of her books printed has probably reached 400 million copies by now. In the SW part of the town is *Torre Abbey,* the ruins of a Premonstratensian abbey founded in 1196. Some arches of the chapterhouse (*c.* 1200), and the gatehouse built in about 1320, survive from this abbey. The monastery barn, which also survives, was used as a prison for over 400 Spanish sailors after the destruction of the Armada. The 19C *Church of St.John* is the work of George Edmund Street and two large stained-glass windows to the W. and E. are by William Morris to designs by Burne-Jones. He also painted the two frescos on the N. and S. walls of the chancel, depicting the Holy Family and the Magi.

Totnes (11 m. NW): If the legend written down by Geoffrey of Monmouth in 1136 is to be believed, Brutus, the great grandson of Aeneas, landed here. He is said to have been the first king of Britain and to have given the country its name. However, what is certain is that the settlement was established as early as the Norman period and was protected in the Middle Ages by a rampart, a moat and four gatehouses. The E. gatehouse survives and has been restored. The *Church of St.Mary* was built in 1432 – 60 and has a well-proportioned W. tower. The church's finest feature is the stone choir screen (1460). The notable stone pulpit dates from the same period.

Denbigh/Dinbych
Clwyd/Wales   p.328□G 12

Castle: The castle, now ruined, was built under Edward I in *c.* 1282. Note the well-

Dartmouth, Church of St. Saviour, carved choir screen

Coats-of-arms

preserved polychrome stone *gatehouse,* with a statue of Edward I above the gate arch (octagonal towers).

Also worth seeing: The tower of the ruined church of *St.Hilary* (chapel) and the foundation of a large 16C church, never completed, are in the old part of town. The *Burgess Tower,* a former town gate, survives from the town's fortifications. The mother church of *St.Marcella* is about half a mile to the E., and has a 13C tower, a double nave and hammerbeam roofs (14C), a pulpit wall and an altar table (17C). Various interesting medieval tombs have also survived. Nearby are the ruins of *Denbigh Friary,* a Carmelite monastery dating from 1289 (the church is 14C).

Environs: Bodrhydan Hall (about 9 m. NW): A 17C country house with a collection of arms, paintings and antique furniture.
Efenechdyd (11 m. SE): An interesting medieval *village church* with a wooden font, old door knockers, and choir screen.
Llanrhaeadr (yn Cinmerch; about 2 m.

SE): The *church* has a fine medieval portal, woodwork (chancel roof), and graveyard gate; the double nave and the 'Jesse window' (1533) are also worth viewing.
Rhuddlan (about 8 m. NW): This town on the lower reaches of the Clwyd has an interesting, ruined 13C *castle.* King Edward I built it, along with Flint Castle, immediately after landing on Welsh soil in *c.* 1277. It has a square ground plan, a double wall, two gatehouses and six towers. The *parish church* with its tower (a landmark for the former harbour) and its double nave originally dates from the 15C.
Rhyl (about 11 m. NW): In this popular seaside resort, some scant remains of a medieval *castle* still survive.
Ruthin (about 8 m. SE): The town has some beautiful old half-timbered houses, including the *Old Court House* (Council House) dating from 1401 on the main square (restored). On the W. side of the square is Exmewe Hall in front of which is the block of stone, the *Maen Huail,* where, according to Arthurian legend, Huail was beheaded. *St.Peter's Church,* N. side of the main square, was built about 1310.

Rhuddlan (Denbigh), castle ruins

The spire is recent, and the old choir no longer survives. Note the fine carvings (panelled oak ceiling) of the roof of the N. aisle and the gates (13C). *Ruthin Castle*, 13C, is now a hotel where 'medieval banquets' are held.

St.Asaph (Llanelwy; about 6 m. N.): This small city of some 3,000 inhabitants has a notable late-13C Decorated Style *cathedral*. At 180 ft. in length and 69 ft. in width, it is regarded as the smallest cathedral in England and Wales. The tracery on the W. window is worth seeing. The tower, which can be climbed (good view), was restored in the 18C, as was the cathedral. In the S. transept (chapel) there is a good collection of old Bibles (Welsh and Greek), and in the N. aisle is a recumbent figure (*c.* 1293). Four angels beneath the roof over the crossing. Carved choir stalls (15C). In the churchyard is a small *museum* with exhibits including finds from the earlier Norman church. The *parish church* in the 15C Perpendicular Style, the old poorhouse called *The Barrow* dating from 1686, and the *Pont Dafydd Bridge* (1630) across the Clwyd, are also worth a visit.

Derby
Derbyshire/England   p.328☐I 13

Cathedral of All Saints (Iron Gate): Until 1927 it was the town's parish church, and since then it has been the seat of a bishop. The massive tower, some 215 ft. tall, survives from the previous medieval building which stood on the same site. This tower, the second tallest parish church tower in England, is in the Perpendicular Style. The church was torn down in the early 18C and rebuilt in neoclassical style by James Gibbs, a pupil of Fontana; it was not until 1725 that the building was finally completed by Francis Smith. Features of particular interest inside are the 18C *wrought-iron work* by the local artist Robert Bakewell, the *pulpit* and *choir stalls* dating from the 19C (the work of Temple Moore), and the *altar* by Sir Ninian Cimper. There are also some notable *tombs* (including that of Bess of Hardwick, Countess of Shrewsbury, who died in 1608) by well-known sculptors of the 17&18C (Roubiliac, Nollekens, Rysbrack and others).

Derby, All Saints' Cathedral

Wrought-iron screen

Derby Museum and Corporation Art Gallery: Collections on local and municipal history, the natural history of the region, and archaeology. Especially worth seeing is the *Prince Charlie Room* commemorating the visit of Bonnie Prince Charlie during the rebellion of 1745 (the original wood panelling from Exeter House in Derby, where the Prince lived, is outstanding). The technical department, with a working model of the Midland Railway, is also worth visiting. The art gallery includes some paintings and drawings by the local painter Joseph Wright (1734–97) which are worth seeing.

Old Silk Mill Industrial Museum: This museum is on the site of the oldest factory in England, founded in 1717. The foundation walls of the building still survive. There are some notable exhibits relating to the industrial history of Derbyshire, including a collection of aero engines built by Rolls-Royce, who have a factory in Derby. At the entrance is a magnificent wrought-iron gate by Robert Bakewell dating from 1728.

Also worth seeing: *St. Werburgh's church* with a notable wrought-iron font cover. The *Bridge Chapel of St. Mary* on the old bridge over the Derwent. The *County Hall* dating from 1660. The *Royal Crown Derby China Factory*, a famous factory with a museum.

Environs: Crich (about 12 m. N.): It has a unique *tram museum* (over 40 examples, built in all parts of the world between 1873 and 1953, all of which are in working order).

Dale Abbey: (about 5 m. E.): The 12C *All Saints' Church* is today part of a farmhouse. It was once the hospital chapel of Dale Abbey, which is in ruins today. Inside, the 17C decorations are worth seeing.

Foremark (about 7 m. S.): *St. Saviour's Church:* The exterior (1662) is a very late example of the Perpendicular Style. The interior decoration is in 17C Renaissance style; features of interest include the three-decker pulpit and the wrought-iron choir stalls, which are probably the work of Robert Bakewell of Derby.

Kedleston Hall (about 4 m. NW): This

Derby, All Saints' Cathedral, main portal

has been the seat of the Curzon family since the 12C. The present neoclassical building was begun in 1760 and is mainly by Robert Adam. The rooms worth looking at include the Great Hall, the dining room and the library. There is a fine art collection and some period furniture. Other features: the 'Indian Museum' and the old chapel (12C).

Melbourne (about 8 m. S.) The Romanesque church of *St. Michael-St. Mary* has a notable Romanesque window in the clerestory. *Melbourne Hall* (16–18C; inside there are important paintings and period furniture; a splendid park).

Radbourne (about 4 km. W.) *St. Andrew's Church* dates mainly from the 13/14C. The choir stalls are from Dale Abbey.

Repton (about 6 m. SW): *St. Wystan's Church* was built in Anglo-Saxon times; the chancel and crypt have survived from the original structure. The remainder of the church is in the Gothic style of the 13–15C. Also worth seeing is the *Repton School Museum*, which is housed in a medieval Augustinian monastery and contains exhibits devoted to local history.

Shardlow (about 6 m. SE): The *canal museum* in the 'Clock Warehouse' (warehouse and basin dating from 1780) is worth visiting.

Sudbury Hall (about 12 m. W.): With a *'Childhood Museum'* (fine toy collection).

Wingfield (14 m. NE): With a *house* which was used for a time as a prison for Mary Queen of Scots.

Dingle
Kerry/Ireland   p.330☐A 13

The fishing port of Dingle on the peninsula of the same name is the centre of the Gaelic-speaking area (Gaeltacht), with Gaelic summer schools. The entire peninsula is rich in *prehistoric* and *early Christian antiquities*.

Environs: Ballynagall (also known as Ballynana; about 13 m. NW): Near this town is the famous *Gallarus Oratory*. This early Christian house of prayer dating from the 7C is built of dry stones without mor-

Ballynagall (Dingle), early Christian oratory

tar, in the style of the prehistoric clochans (beehive-shaped stone huts). It has a rectangular base measuring about 22 ft. x 18 ft., and tapers towards its top in the form of an overturned boat. The dome is corbelled. The entrance to the building also narrows towards the top and has a lintel, and there is a single semicircular window. Nearby are the remnants of *Gallarus Castle* and some more *clochans* (restored), as well as the remains of *ring forts*.

Dunquin (15 m. W.): The former inhabitants of the island of *Great Blasket* live here, having been settled here in 1953. They are known for their patriarchal way of life which has remained unchanged since primeval times. From here a boat trip can be made to Great Blasket Island (today an uninhabited bird sanctuary).

Fahan (Glanfahan, about 10 m. W.): This is the site of the famous prehistoric castle of *Dun Beag*. Protected on the land side by a massive stone rampart up to 23 ft. in width, the castle stands on a tongue of land which slopes steeply down to the Atlantic. There is a fine view, especially from nearby Slea Head. A large number of primitive *clochans* may also be seen in this locality.

Kilmalkedar (about 14 m. NW): This town has a 12C Romanesque *ruined church* with fine arches and columns; to the left of the chancel there is an old *alphabet stone* (a tombstone from the 11/12C), and in the churchyard is an old *ogham stone* (5C). Apart from this there are some further *stones* and nearby some remains of *dolmens*. There is a fine view from nearby *Brandon Mountain* (3,127 ft.), the second highest mountain in Ireland. It is named after the legendary Celtic St. Brendan (about 483–576). The peak was formerly visited by pilgrims; hardly any traces of this have survived.

Ventry (a harbour; about 5 m. W.): Between this fishing village and *Slea Head* (about 11 m. W.) there are numerous primitive *clochans*. These small dwellings from the Bronze Age (later on, early Christian

houses of prayer were designed in the same manner) are built from dry stones piled on top of one another without mortar, using the principle of corbelling. There are some 400 such stone huts in this region, particularly in the vicinity of Fahan.

Dolgellau
Gwynedd/Wales   p.328□G 13

This little town, situated in charming surroundings at the mouth of the Afon Mawddach to the N. of the Cader Idris (2,923 ft.) massif, is notable for the solid appearance of its terraced houses built of grey natural stone. Beside the pulpit of the medieval *parish church*, rebuilt in 1716, is the tomb of the knight Meurig ap Ynyr Fychan (14C), with a recumbent figure.

Environs: Abergynolwyn (about 12 m. S.): Here there are the scant remains of the old Welsh castle of *Castell-Y-Bere* from the pre-Norman period. It was rebuilt under Edward I in *c.* 1270, but fell into ruin shortly thereafter, in about 1300.

Bala (19 m. NE, at the N. end of Lake Bala): This well-known holiday resort contains a few remnants of a 12C Norman *castle* ('Tomen' earthworks survive).

Cymer Abbey (about 2 m. N.): The remains of a *Cistercian abbey* (1200). The church has survived. It has three pointed arches on its E. side (*c.* 1220), a font with sedilia, and a tower (*c.* 1350). The foundations of the cloister also exist.

Llandderfel (about 20 m. NE): This town has a *church* dating from 1500, with fine grotesques and a carved 16C choir screen.

Llanegryn (about 8 m. SW): The *village church* has an embossed crucifix and a superbly carved choir screen (both 15C); there is also an early Norman *font*.

Llangower (16 m. NE, on the S. shore of

Tywyn (Dolgellau), St. Cadfan

Machynlleth (Dolgellau), Victorian clock-tower

Lake Bala): Here the visitor may see a *church* with an ancient bier.

Llanuwchllyn (on the S. shore of Lake Bala, 16 m. NE). Near this town, at *Caer Gai*, is a 17C *house* standing within the vestiges of a Roman *rampart*.

Machynlleth (about 19 m. S.): This town with its pretty Victorian *clock tower* came to prominence in the Middle Ages when Owen Glendower, a Welsh rebel active around the year 1400, assembled his 'parliament' here in 1403.

Tal-y-Llyn (about 8 m. S.): With a pretty mountain lake of the same name, this is the starting point for climbs to the peak of *Cader Idris* (2,923 ft.), a mountain which offers one of the most beautiful views in Wales. Its name means 'seat of Idris' and refers to Idris, the legendary Celtic astrologer.

Tywyn (also known as Towyn; about 9 m. SW): This coastal town contains the cruciform church of *St. Cadfan* with a 12C Norman nave (restored), a font and old tombs. The ancient *St. Cadfan's Stone*, which is 7 ft. high and has inscriptions in semi-uncials of the 7/8C on all four sides, is worth seeing. This is the first written document in the ancient Welsh language.

Doncaster
South Yorkshire/England   p.328□I 12

Founded as a castle in the 1C AD during the Roman conquest of Britain; later, when known as *Danum,* it was an important station on the Roman road from Lincoln to York and a centre of ceramics manufacture. Since 1776 the oldest horse race in England has been held here. This is the classic 'St. Leger', named after Colonel Anthony St.Leger, its originator.

Mansion House (High Street): This Georgian house was built by James Paine in 1745–8 as the Mayor's official residence. London and York are the only other places to have such buildings which were originally built for this purpose. Inside, note the splendid *Ball Room;* richly decorated ceiling, musicians' gallery, beautiful white marble chimney-pieces, fine paintings on the walls.

Museum and Art Gallery (Chequer Road): On the ground floor is an extensive collection devoted to the history of the town and the area. The art gallery on the 1st floor has a permanent exhibition of English artists of the 18–20C. The sculptures by Jacob Epstein and Henry Moore are especially worth viewing.

Also worth seeing: *Parish church of St. George* (St.Georgegate), built in the 19C on the site of a Romanesque church destroyed by fire. *Christ Church* (Thorne Road), with a fine octagonal tower and fine glass by Belgian artists. The *South Yorkshire Industrial Museum* (Cusworth Hall, on the N. edge of the town), with interesting exhibits relating to the region's industrial history.

Environs: Campsall (about 7 m. N.): The church of *St. Mary Magdalene* was originally Romanesque but was later altered. Inside, the chancel wall and a tomb built by John Flaxman in 1803 are worth seeing.

Conisbrough (about 5 m. SW): This town has a 12C *Norman castle,* the site of Sir Walter Scott's novel *Ivanhoe.* The surviving features include the cylindrical keep, some 100 ft. high (the walls are about 16 ft. thick and are reinforced on the outside by six tower-like projections; one of which contains the hexagonal chapel). The *town church* is also worth seeing. Although mostly Romanesque, there are some Anglo-Saxon fragments. Inside there is a Norman tomb chest depicting Adam and Eve and a scene from a knights' tournament.

Epworth (about 12 m. E.): With the *Old Rectory,* where John Wesley (1703–91), the founder of the Methodist movement, was born. The building was rebuilt in 1709 after being destroyed by arson.

Fishlake (about 9 m. NE): The Romanesque church of *St. Cuthbert* was later altered in the Gothic style. The richly decorated Romanesque S. portal is especially fine, and the features inside include a beautiful medieval font.

Hatfield (about 7 m. NE): A picturesque village in Hatfield Chase, a marshy area. It was not until the early 18C that it was drained by Cornelius Vermuyden, a Dutchman. Part of the *village church* is still 11C.

High Melton (about 5 m. W.): The church of *St. James* was originally Romanesque, being altered in the late Gothic period. Inside there are medieval stained-glass windows.

Maltby (about 7 m. S.): The W. tower is all that survives of the original Romanesque structure of *St. Bartholomew's Church.* The remainder was rebuilt in 1859. Inside there are fine stained-glass windows in the 'Hoyle Chapel'.

Roche Abbey (about 9 m. S.): The ruins of a *Cistercian abbey* founded in 1147. Surviving features include the Gothic transept of the abbey church, and the porter's lodge with its fine vaults.

Sprotbrough (about 2 m. W.): *St.Mary's Church* dates from the 12–15C. The tower is in the Decorated Style. Inside, objects of interest include the choir stalls and the chancel wall.

Tickhill (about 7 m. S.): The church of *St.Mary,* begun in the 13C, and not completed until the late Gothic period; inside are the remains of the medieval stained-glass windows.

Donegal, bay

Donegal
Donegal/Ireland   p.326□C 10

This, the county town of the county of the same name, has about 1,500 inhabitants and is situated on Donegal Bay, at the mouth of the river Eske.

The imposing ruins of *Donegal Castle* date from 1505 and were built on top of an older fortress ('Donegal' means 'river castle'). A Jacobean castle was added in about 1610 to the angular *keep*, built in the 16C.

The ruins of the Franciscan monastery of *Donegal Abbey*, built in 1475, are to be found on the edge of the town. The monastery and its cloister were almost completely destroyed by an explosion *c.* 1601.

The historical work 'Annals of the Four Masters' was written here in about 1632 (the book is now preserved in Dublin).

Environs: Glencolumbkille (about 19 m. NW): This fishing village with its steep cliffs possesses remains from the prehistoric and early Christian periods, including *megalithic tombs*, *ring forts* with *beehive huts*, *pillar stones* and a *high cross*. The Celtic St.Columba (5/6C) was active here. His alleged house *(St. Columba's House)*, *oratory*, *well* and *stone bed* (a slab of rock) are on display. Gaelic is still spoken in this tradition-conscious village with its 'Irish Folk Village'. It is the goal of a St.Columba pilgrimage, which takes place on 9 June each year. Nearby, some 4 m. S. of the village, are the impressive, precipitous cliffs of *Slieve League*, some 2,000 ft. in height.

Station Island (about 6 m. SE): *Lough Derg*, a secluded lake in which lies Station Island, is possibly the oldest pilgrimage site in Ireland. It is said that St.Patrick

Bere Regis (Dorchester), Church of St.John the Baptist

Bere Regis, Norman font

asted here in the 5C and thereby expelled the demons. *St. Patrick's Purgatory:* In 1931, an octagonal *basilica* and a pilgrims' hospice, both in the neo-Byzantine style, were built here for the numerous pilgrims, who can number up to 30,000. The time of the pilgrimage is from 1 June to 15 August. On the nearby *Saint's Island* are the ruins of a 12C monastery.

Dorchester
Dorset/England   p.332□H 16

The county town of Dorset dates back to Neolithic times. From AD 70 to 400 it was the Roman *Durnovaria,* whose ramparts became 'The Walks' in the 18C. There was a Saxon settlement here as early as about 660, and King Athelstan (925–39) established his mint here. The town was almost completely burnt down in 1613 and soon afterwards some Puritan emigrants, led by John White, left to found its namesake in Massachusetts. Judge Jeffreys' Bloody Assizes were held here in 1685. Over 300 of the town's citizens were executed.

Dorset County Museum: The exhibits here date back to the Iron Age. Numerous finds from Maiden Castle have brought the Neolithic period back to life. There is also an abundance of Roman finds, including a splendid mosaic from Hinton St. Mary depicting the head of Christ, and there are numerous *silver coins* in the treasure of over 22,000 coins. There is a separate department devoted to manuscripts, notebooks and letters by the writer Thomas Hardy (1840–1928).

Dorset Military Museum: The history of the army in Dorset from 1660 onwards is documented here by means of arms, uniforms, medals and pictures.

Environs: Athelhampton (6 m. NE): This 15C *house* was built as the country seat of a Lord Mayor of London and is one of the finest examples of secular Gothic architecture in Dorset. The roof of the great hall, the splendid wood panelling, the bay windows with the heraldic decoration on their glazing, and the large Tudor room, all go to prove that the splendours of Gothic architecture were not confined to churches.
Bere Regis (11 m. NE): The 12C *Church of St. John the Baptist* has a Gothic tower. The magnificent timber ceiling was donated by Cardinal Morton, the Archbishop of Canterbury, in about 1480. Its dragon beams end in almost life-size oak figures of the 12 Apostles in 15C dress. Also note the decorated Norman font and the 16C pews.
Cerne Abbas (12 m. N.): The *Church of St. Mary* has a W. tower and dates mainly

from the 15&16C. Some remains of frescos and stained-glass windows date back to the 14C. The stone choir screen is 15C, while the pulpit is from 1640. Beside the church are the ruins of a *Benedictine abbey* founded in 987. The figure of the *Cerne Giant* (a naked man swinging a club; 200 ft. from top to bottom) was drawn by cutting through the thin topsoil to the white rock below. It has not yet proved possible to date this figure, which can be seen shimmering among the grass from afar. It may be either a prehistoric Priapus or a Roman Hercules.
Maiden Castle (2 m. S.): It was in *c.* 3000 BC that the settlers of the Windmill Hill culture began to build this, the finest and most impressive prehistoric *fort* in England. It continued in use until the Romans under Vespasian (the future Emperor) arrived in AD 44. Oval in shape, it is 2,600 ft. long, has a four lines of ramparts and ditches, and its inner core is today still nearly 100 ft. higher than the surrounding land. The Neolithic tools and household objects found here may be seen in the Dorset County Museum.

Dornoch Firth
Highlands/Scotland   p.324 □ G 5

Until 1812 the firth, which extends deep inland, could only be crossed by ferry. Over 100 people lost their lives when the ferry was wrecked in 1809 and the decision was then taken to build the first bridge. In 1650, the Marquis of Montrose fought his last battle at the end of the firth before he fled to Ardvreck Castle and was betrayed to the Covenanters. A few miles above the old battlefield, there is a waterfall on the Shin where salmon can be seen leaping in summer.

Dunrobin Castle: This castle, to the S.

Bere Regis (Dorchester), ceiling

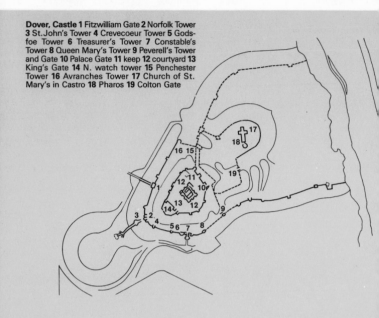

Dover, Castle 1 Fitzwilliam Gate **2** Norfolk Tower **3** St. John's Tower **4** Crevecoeur Tower **5** Godsfoe Tower **6** Treasurer's Tower **7** Constable's Tower **8** Queen Mary's Tower **9** Peverell's Tower and Gate **10** Palace Gate **11** keep **12** courtyard **13** King's Gate **14** N. watch tower **15** Penchester Tower **16** Avranches Tower **17** Church of St. Mary's in Castro **18** Pharos **19** Colton Gate

of Brora, was lived in by the Dukes of Sutherland until 1963. Its oldest sections date back to the late 13C. The tower was probably built about 1400. The 17C extensions and the new 19C buildings were burned down in 1915. The latter, which were originally built in 1835–50, were faithfully rebuilt from 1919 onwards. They had been designed by Sir Charles Barry, whose other works included the Houses of Parliament. In 1963, an attempt was made to enliven the castle by making it into a private school but this was a failure.

Dornoch: This little town was the Royal Burgh of the former county of Sutherland from 1628 onwards. What is probably the oldest golf course in Scotland is to be found here (documents exist proving that games were played here in the 17C), and the last burning of a supposed witch in Scotland

took place here in 1722. The small *cathedral* of the Bishops of Caithness was built from 1150 onwards on the remains of an older church. 16 Earls of Sutherland are buried at the church; there is an effigy of Sir Richard de Moravia, the brother of the founder of the House of Sutherland, slain by Danes in 1248.

Tain: The Gothic *collegiate church* was built in 1371, and the *town hall* with its peal of bells dates from the 17C. The oldest bell dates from 1630.

Dover
Kent/England   p.332 □ M 15

The first sight a traveller on a ferry catches of Dover, the largest of the Cinque ports,

Dover, Pharos, Castle

s of the *White Cliffs*, the famous chalk cliffs which rise steeply out of the sea. The own has seen numerous invaders: starting with Caesar's legions and followed by Angles, Saxons and Jutes. Two ships of the Armada were stranded near here, and the fortifications of the town and castle were later further strengthened to counter a Napoleonic invasion. Dover suffered heavy bombardment during both World Wars.

Castle: This fortress, high above the town, was formerly of great importance to the harbour. The walls were probably built along Saxon ditches. The *Pharos Lighthouse* survives from the Roman period, while the other walls and buildings date back to the 13&14C and were later rebuilt and extended several times.

St.Edmund's Chapel: This, the smallest chapel in England, was built in the 13C and briefly used as a smithy in the 16C.

Church of St.Mary-in-Castro: Heavily restored in the 19C, it has Norman origins. It stands in the castle grounds.

Parish Church of St.Mary: This, the oldest church in the town, retains many Norman features but was extensively rebuilt in the 19C

St.James's Church: This church was not rebuilt after being bombed in World War 2.

Maison Dieu House: Built in the Dutch style in the 17C, it today houses the town library.

Town Hall (Biggin Street): This was built in the 19C on the foundations of the 13C

Dover, Castle

Maison Dieu. The fine *windows* depict scenes from the town's history, and on the ground floor there is a museum of local history.

Roman Painted House: It probably once belonged to a Roman commander. Well-preserved paintings from the 2C still decorate the walls today.

Environs: Deal Castle: (7 m. NE): One of the many *forts* built by Henry VIII as a defence against a French invasion. It is in the form of a Tudor rose: six small, semi-circular bastions are grouped about a circular inner courtyard and are surrounded by six powerful outer bastions, also semi-circular, and a moat.
St. Margaret's at Cliffe (1.5 m. E.): A fine, Norman *church* having a fortified tower, a finely formed W. portal, and rich detailed decoration both inside and in th cloister.
Walmer Castle (6 m. NE): A *fort* buil by Henry VIII, like that of Deal. The com plex is arranged in the form of a four-lea clover around a two-storeyed central towe In the 18C it became the residence of th Lord Warden of the Cinque Ports. Amon those to hold this post were William Pit and the Duke of Wellington. The latte died here in 1852 and there is a small mu seum in memory of him.

Downpatrick
Down/Northern Ireland   p.326☐E 1

This, the main town of County Down, ha some 7,000 inhabitants and lies to the SW of Strangford Lough, an enclosed se lough. The name actually means 'Patrick' own' (the Gaelic 'dun' means 'town, fortress'). St. Patrick, who has never been canonised, is said to have landed here about 432 and to have worked as a missionary. The enormous earth mound known as the *Mound of Downpatrick* to the NE has been fortified since Celtic times and bears the Saint's name (three rings of ramparts). In 1176, the Anglo-Norman John de Courcy took the town and built fortifications (only traces remain) on Mount Downpatrick and in the town (a 12C *fortified tower* survives near the Protestant parish church).

St.Patrick's Cathedral: The new building dating from 1798–1812 retains parts of its 13C predecessor (apse, arches in the chancel). The *tomb* of St.Patrick, whose relics John de Courcy transferred here, are probably to be found under the *high altar*, where the Saint is said to have built his first church of stone. Other surviving features are an 11C Celtic *font,* a 10C *high cross,* a 17C monument to Edward Cromwell, a governor, and in the graveyard is a *monolith* with the inscription 'Patric' (said to be his tombstone).

The *Wells of Struell*, to the E., are connected with the Saint. There are wells, the remains of 17C *bath-houses* and a 17C *church.*

Environs: Ardglass (about 7 m. SE): The remains of the 16C *Jordan's Castle* are near the former port of Down, with towers and a storehouse. Not far off, above the sea, is the 15C former parish church — *Ardtole Church.*

Ballynoe (1 m. S.): Prehistoric *stone circle,* about 100 ft. in diameter.

Castlewellan (about 11 m. SW): Fine 18C buildings (*Market House* of 1764) and a 19C *castle* with a park. Nearby, to the SW, is the prehistoric stone fort of *Drumena,* and towards the NW is the beautiful megalithic *Legananny Dolmen* with its three uprights and single covering stone standing on the S. slope of Slieve Croob).

Dundrum (about 7 m. SW): Near this fishing village, on the bay of the same name, we find the imposing ruins of *Dundrum Castle.* This once strongly fortified building was erected *c.* 1240 by order of John de Courcy, and has a thick-walled keep (destroyed by Cromwell in 1652).

Inch Abbey (about 3 m. NW): The ruins of the *abbey,* founded in *c.* 1187 by John de Courcy, display a fine apse with high E. windows, remains of the transept, and parts of the abbey.

Kilclief (about 12 m. NW): The *tower house* was a 15C fortified episcopal residence, and was built under John Sely, Bishop of Dow.

Killough (about 6 m. SE): Ruins of the 10&11C *St.John's Point Church.*

Killyleagh Castle (about 7 m. NE): Built in the 17C on an earlier, Norman site. The famous botanist Sir Hans Sloane (1660–1753), whose collections formed the nucleus of the British Museum, was born in Killyleagh.

Saul (2 m. NE): It is said that St.Patrick landed here in 432 and that he founded the first monastery in 440 (scant remnants). The modern *Memorial Church of St. Patrick,* with its round tower, stands on the hill. The Catholic *St.Patrick's Church* is on the adjoining hill of Slieve Patrick, with a granite statue of the saint.

Strangford (about 9 m. NE): The unique *Castleward House* (1763–80) is at the entrance to Lough Strangford. It was because of differences of opinion with his wife that Lord Bangor had the S. section built in neoclassical style, and the N. section in Gothick.

In the park there are older *towers* (16C) and *Audley's Castle* (*c.* 1500) is nearby.

Drogheda
Louth/Ireland   p.326□E 11

This harbour town with its 20,000 inhabitants lies on the mouth of the Boyne. It is

a Viking foundation (911), and was a flourishing trading centre as early as the 10C. It was often a seat of the Anglo-Irish parliament in the Middle Ages. Oliver Cromwell devastated the heavily fortified town in 1649, and banished the survivors to the Caribbean island of Barbados. Drogheda ('ford bridge') is still a bastion of Irish nationalism. A number of medieval sights still survive in spite of the damage.

Magdalene Tower: The 15C Magdalene Steeple to the N. is a remnant of the Dominican monastery of *St.Mary Magdalene* founded in 1224. Nearby is the surviving *tower* of a 15C Augustinian monastery, founded in 1206.

St.Lawrence's Gate: The crenellated E. tower with its two flanking *round towers* and its projecting *gate* (13C) is the only one of the 10 city gates to survive. It takes its name from the *monastery of St.Lawrence,* which used to adjoin it but of which nothing remains.

Also worth seeing: The old *Tholsel* (town hall) dates from the 17C and is today a bank. The Catholic *St.Peter's Church* (West Street) was built in 1628–81, and in its N. transept it preserves the head of Archbishop Oliver Plunket (executed at Tyburn in 1681). The Protestant *St.Peter's Church* (William Street) with parts of a medieval predecessor was built in 1748–92. The Anglo-Norman motte of *Mill Mount* with its traces of prehistoric gallery tombs is on the S. bank of the Boyne. The remains of the S. *town wall* can be seen at the Protestant *St.Mary's Church.*

Environs: Brugh na Boinne (3 m. W.) The most significant *prehistoric burial ground,* in the Boyne valley, is worth a visit. The mounds are *megalithic tombs* from *c.*

Downpatrick, St.Patrick's Cathedral

Mellifont Abbey (Drogheda)

2500 – 1800 BC (Bronze Age), some of which resemble the prehistoric beehive tombs of Mycenae (Greece) and of the Iberian Peninsula. Those most worth seeing are the tumuli of Dowth, Newgrange and Knowth.

Megalithic tomb of Dowth: The Dowth tumulus (a mound tomb) is about 230 ft. in diameter, and has a corridor (Dromos) 23 ft. long and a central chamber with a round, conical vault and tomb niches.

Newgrange: This is one of the best-preserved passage graves in Europe. The burial mound is some 280 ft. in diameter and some 43 ft. in height. The passage grave, some 59 ft. long, leads to a cruciform main chamber, which has both a corbelled vault some 19 ft. high and some ornamented niches (spiral and semicircular patterns). The hill was surrounded by a circle of menhirs formerly consisting of 38 standing stones (12 stones, decorated with motifs, survive).

Knowth: Since 1968 intensive excavations have been in progress in this massive tumulus, which is some 700 ft. in diameter, with main and subsidiary chambers.

Duleek (about 5 m. SW): Old monastery foundation of St.Patrick (5C), and the remains of a 13C *Augustinian priory* with a 15C tower. Nearby are old *tombstones* and a *high cross* with reliefs (10C). The *Dowdall Cross* is richly decorated with Saints and was erected *c.* 1601 for Dowdall, the judge.

Mellifont Abbey (about 7 m. NW): The first and most important *Cistercian abbey* in Ireland was founded in 1142 by St. Malachy (Malachias) and by French monks from the mother house of Clairvaux (France). 'Melli-font' means 'source of honey'. Originating from here, 38 daughter houses were built all over Ireland, and they supplanted the existing form of Irish monasticism. The ruins of the cruciform monastery church dating from 1157, with its annexes of 1225, survive. The S. cloister dates from *c.* 1200; beside it is the oc-

tangular two-storeyed lavabo, the 14C chapterhouse, and the well defended gatehouse.

Monasterboice (about 7 m. NW): The name of the ruined monastery ('Monastery of Boice') points to its early Christian founder, Buithe (6C), a follower of St. Patrick. A 10C round tower (without a roof) and two insignificant 13C churches still survive from the monastery, which was devastated on several occasions. However, the famous *crosses,* among the finest in Ireland, are worth seeing. The *Muiredagh cross* (the S. cross) from the 10C is named after Abbot Muiredagh (d. 923). This sandstone cross, about 15 ft. tall, is decorated with beautiful Biblical scenes on both sides (Old and New Testament). The *W. cross,* decorated in relief, is also 10C. The *N. cross,* (damaged, modern pedestal) is simpler in style.

Naul (about 9 m. S.): This is the site of the fine prehistoric *passage grave of Fourknocks,* with a central chamber and tomb niches dating from *c.* 1800 BC.

Termonfeckin (about 6 m. NE): Ruins of a three-storeyed *Tower House* with fine win-

Drumlanrig Castle

dows. There is a *cross,* with scenes of the Crucifixion, in the graveyard of *St.Feckin's Church,* where there are traces of an early Christian monastery dating from 664.

Drumlanrig Castle
Dumfries and Galloway/
Scotland   p.324 ☐ G 9

This castle stands a few miles from Thornhill and was built for the first Duke of Queensberry in 1679–89. However, frightened at the high cost, the duke only spent a single night in his new castle. In 1810, the castle was inherited by the Scotts of Buccleuch and is still in their possession today. Sir William Bruce was the architect of this splendid building. The castle, unaltered for 300 years, is a fine example of the transition from fortified building to palace. The arrangement round an inner courtyard and the massive corner towers are old features taken from castles. On the other hand, that splendour which is now also visible in the outer façade is new. William Bruce worked with all the resources of the Renaissance, using arcades on the ground floor, and also employing Corinthian pilasters and rows of pedimented windows. The corner towers make a ponderous impression. Each of them is decorated with three ornate round turrets, while the round staircase towers have baroque lead domes. The castle's pretensions are emphasized by the projecting central section, with the main entrance and a large ducal coronet. The castle was intended as a symbol of the duke's power and position as one of the most important lords in the land. The interior is correspondingly costly. From the wood-carved ornaments by Grinling Gibbons in the drawing-room, the iron columns of the staircase, to the exquisite picture collection — nothing is missing from this aristocratic display. Van Dyck, Hans Holbein and Rembrandt are all represented, as are Ramsay and Gainsborough.

Environs: Durisdeer (4 m. NE): The little church (1699) here has the monument to the second Duke of Queensberry by Van Nost (1711).

Durisdeer (Drumlanrig), tomb

Manasterboice (Drogheda), High Cross

Mennock (9 m. NW): The Museum of the Scottish Lead Mining Industry is in an old miner's hut in this small village. It documents the history and technology of lead mining.

Thornhill (2 m. S.): The *museum* has mementoes of the Covenanters and of Robert Burns.

Dublin/Baile Atha Cliath
Dublin/Ireland   p.326□E 12

Dublin ('Black River') has some 660,000 inhabitants, is the capital of the Republic of Ireland (Eire), and is the economic and cultural centre of the country. The Gaelic cognomen 'Baile Atha Cliath' means 'river ford city' and refers to the river Liffey, which flows through the city and on into Dublin Bay.

History: Traces of prehistoric tombs (in Phoenix Park) are evidence of pre- and early Celtic habitation (from the 2nd millennium BC onwards). The city was really founded in the 9C by the Vikings (Norwegians), who built a fortified base. King Brian Boru defeated the Vikings at the battle of Clontarf (now a suburb of Dublin) *c.* 1010; however, the city remained Norse. The Anglo-Norman Strongbow took the city in 1170, but King Henry II claimed it as a possession of the English crown. From then on, Dublin was the most important English military base in Ireland until its independence in 1921. Up until the 17C it was a small fortified city of some 9,000 inhabitants and it was not until the 18C that Dublin recovered from the devastation wrought by Oliver Cromwell (*c.* 1650). Under the 4 Georges (18/19C) it experienced a tremendous upsurge and it was regarded as the second largest city in Britain—the population was then about 200,000. Its splendid Georgian buildings earned it the title of the 'Athens of the West'. After the potato famine of 1845–9 (wave of emigration to America), Irish nationalism grew and Dublin became its centre (Sinn Fein movement of 1905). The Irish Free State, with its capital Dublin, was recognized in 1921, and on 18

Dublin, Four Courts

April 1949 the sovereign republic of Eire was proclaimed in Dublin (Eire left the Commonwealth), and the aim of the republic was a peaceful reunification with Northern Ireland. A number of world-famous writers were born in Dublin, including Jonathan Swift (1667), Oscar Wilde (1854), George Bernard Shaw (1856), William Butler Yeats (1865), Brendan Behan (1923) and James Joyce (1882). The latter's epoch-making novel 'Ulysses' is also set in Dublin.

Christ Church Cathedral (Winetavern Street): This, the oldest (Protestant) church, was built in 1038 by the Viking King Sigtryg ('loyal to victory') and by Dunan, the first Bishop of Dublin. After its destruction, the Norman Earl Strongbow had a new, larger church built in *c.* 1172. It was expanded in the 14C and was extensively rebuilt in *c.* 1871. The large *crypt* underneath the full length of the nave survives from the Norman church, and has numerous old fragments. The N. and S. transepts were added in Romanesque style under Strongbow. In the *nave* and *choir*,

which were rebuilt in the 19C, are some old *effigies,* the reputed *tomb* of Strongbow (13C), and *tomb slabs* from bishops' and nobles' tombs (13–17C).

St.Audoen (High Street): This, the oldest surviving medieval parish church in Dublin, is in the old city centre and dates mainly from the 12C. Interesting features include the fine *portal* (1190), the *nave,* and the *tower* with the oldest *bells* in Ireland (dating from 1423); there are also a Norman *font* (*c.* 1192) and various *side chapels* (some from the 15C). Near the graveyard are remains of the original *city fortifications* (St.Audoen's Arch).

St.Mary (Mary Street): Inside the Protestant church of 1695, which stands on the site of St.Mary's Abbey, there are fine *wood carvings* and an 18C *organ.*

St.Michan (Church Street): This church dedicated to St.Michan, the Dublin Saint, was built in 1685 on the site of the earlier, Danish building erected as long ago as 1095. The present church has a rectangu-

Leinster House

Christ Church Cathedral

Four Courts, central dome

lar ground plan and a *W. tower*. In the church are two fine 18C *organs* (said to have been used for the first performance of Handel's 'Messiah' in 1742), an interesting 18C litany desk' and a 12C *tomb* of the church's founder. The 17C *crypt*, which contains mummies, is also worth seeing.

St.Patrick's Cathedral (Patrick's Street): This cathedral church (since 1213), which is today Protestant, was built in *c.* 1191 in the form of a wide cross. It was extensively altered in Early English style in the 13C. The *Lady Chapel* at the E. end was added in 1270, and the large angular *tower* in *c.* 1381. The *bell tower* (250 ft. tall) dates from 1794. After being devastated and desecrated by Cromwell's troops on several occasions in *c.* 1650 (it was used as a horse stable), the cathedral was thoroughly restored in 1864–9 by Th.Drew at the ex-

pense of Sir Benjamin Guinness, the Dublin brewer. The *tombs* of important families and figures are especially interesting. They include not only the imposing *monument* to Richard Boyle (1566–1643) who rose to be Earl of Cork, but also the *tablet* to Jonathan Swift (1667–1745), the famous writer and Dean of St.Patrick. The writer of 'Gulliver's Travels' composed his own epitaph, characterising his life: 'He lies where furious rage can rend his heart no more; go, wanderer and, if you can, follow the one who unyieldingly fought for freedom!' The banners and arms of the Order of the Knights of St.Patrick, which was founded in 1783, may be seen in the *choir*. In the door to the *chapterhouse* is the 'reconciliation hole' (cut 1491), where the Earls of Ormond and Kildare shook hands without having to look at one another after a dispute. Not far from the church, in St.

Marsh's Library (St. Patrick's Park)

Patrick's Park, is *Marsh's Library*, built by Archbishop Marsh *c.* 1707. This was the first public library in Ireland, and has a large collection of religious and ancient works.

St. Werburgh (Werburgh Street): The present church was built *c.* 1715 on the site of an early Norman church (St. Martin), and for a long time it was the *castle church* of Dublin Castle. Inside, in the entrance hall, are the *monument* (vault) to the Purcells, a noble family, and also a fine Gothic *wooden pulpit*. There are also *figures of Saints* in the niches, and a vaulted *crypt* with the tomb of Lord Edward Fitzgerald, 1798, the freedom fighter of the 'United Irishmen'.

Academy House (Dawson Street): This building erected in 1770 by J. Ensor and extended in 1852 is the seat of the Royal Irish Academy. The *library* contains valuable original manuscripts, including the 17C historical work the *Annals of the Four Masters,* the very early *Cathach Psalter* (C/7C), the 11C *Book of the Dun Cow*, and the *Stowe Missal* from the 9C.

Dublin Castle (Castle Street/Palace Street): The *motte* was built by the Normans and extended in 1208-20 under King John; only the SE *Record Tower* survives. The SW 14C *Bermingham Tower* was rebuilt in *c.* 1777, and part of it was used as a prison. The other buildings of the castle are grouped around two *courtyards* and date from the 18&19C, when the castle was the seat of the Lord Lieutenant, the governor. In the *Upper Castle Yard* are the *Office of Arms* with its bell tower and the *Heraldic and Genealogical Museum* (Bedford

Tower). The *State Apartments,* with their *Throne Room* and *St. Patrick's Hall,* are worth seeing; fine 17C wooden panelling and allegorical ceiling paintings. The Irish President is inaugurated in St. Patrick's Hall every seven years (the first inauguration was that of Douglas Hyde in 1938). The neo-Gothic *chapel* of 1807 in the *Lower Yard,* with its stone ornament and wood carving, is also worth visiting. Today it serves as the Catholic *chapel of the Holy Trinity.*

City Hall (beside the castle): A domed building by Th.Cooley (*c.* 1770), it has some interesting *mementoes* of the city's history (including the 'Club and Sword', the emblems of the city). The building was formerly used as a stock exchange.

Four Courts (Inn's Quay): The neoclassical High Court of Justice of Ireland, with an *arcaded front* 450 ft. long, was built by J.Gandon in 1786–1802. The W. wing was built by Th.Cooley in 1776–84. The 'four courts' surround the large *central dome* with its high Corinthian *portico* (statues).

The façade bears allegories by the sculptor E.Smyth: Iustitia, Prudentia, Potentia and Gratia. The building was much damaged by the uprising of 1922, but was rebuilt in its original form.

Leinster House (Kildare Street 20): Built by R.Castle in 1745 for the Earl of Kildare (Duke of Leinster), it is today the seat of the *Irish Parliament* (in Gaelic: Dail Eireann). It is said to have been the model for the American White House, built by J.Hoan, an Irishman. Nearby are some fine 18C Georgian and 'Dutch' *mansions* (Molesworth Street), and *Merrion Square* (Georgian). The adjoining buildings of the *National Museum,* neo-Renaissance, *c.* 1890; of the *National Library* opened in 1877; and of the *National Gallery* (1864), are described under Museums.

Old Parliament House (Westmoreland Street): The former *parliament building* opposite Trinity College was built in 1792–4; the E. wing dates from 1785, the W. wing from 1794. It has been the seat of the *Bank of Ireland* since 1804. The imposing

National Museum

classical (Georgian) building with its powerful *colonnades* and *porticoes* was robbed of its function after the dissolution of the Irish Parliament by the 'Act of Union' of 1800. Not only the old *parliament chamber*, but also the *House of Lords* with its splendid Waterford chandelier (1788), Huguenot wall hangings (18C), and the silver mace of the Speaker of the House of Commons (1733), are worth a visit. In the adjoining *College Green* are statues of nationalist orators and champions of 'Young Ireland' (1848).

Trinity College (College Street): The *University of Dublin* was founded as early as 1592 by Queen Elizabeth I as a bulwark of Anglo-Irish Protestantism and as an elitist seat of higher education, placed on a level with Oxford. However, most of the surviving buildings date from the 18&19C (Georgian). Catholic students were only admitted from 1873 onwards, women from 1904. The magnificent *façade* dates from 1752 (Keene/Sanderson), the *Examination Hall* on Parliament Square from 1781, the *chapel* with its fine stucco ceilings by Stapleton from 1790, and the restored *Dining Hall* (with portraits) from 1740. It is said that a *monastery* (Priory of All Hallows), founded *c.* 1163, stood on the site of the 19C *bell tower*.

The *Old Library* (Trinity College Library) of 1712–32 stands in Library Square (second quadrangle), and is of considerable interest. In addition to the rich treasure of more modern writings, it houses the oldest and most valuable of Ireland's *manuscripts*:

1. The *Book of Durrow* (*c.* 670) is the oldest evangelistary. It originates from Durrow monastery near Tullamore, and has richly decorated Irish majuscules and intertwined decorative motifs.

2. The famous *Book of Kells* (8/9C), a splendidly illuminated manuscript (animal, bird and serpent motifs), probably originates from the Scottish monastery on the island of Iona, founded by St.Columba in *c.* 563.

3. The *Book of Armagh* (*c.* 807) is a rare copy of the New Testament and of the

Trinity College

Custom House

'Confessions' of St. Patrick. This small book is written in minuscules.

4. The *Book of Leinster* (12C) contains the ancient Irish epic 'Tain Bo Cuailgne' (Theft of the Bulls), probably composed for the King of Leinster. Mention should also be made of the 8C *Book of Dimma*, which is a pocket evangelistary, the 7/8C *Book of Mulling*, and an old *Irish harp*. The adjoining *New Library* with its fine sculpture by Henry Moore was built in modern style in 1967. Beside the university is the Georgian *Provost House* dating from 1759, the provost's residence.

Museums: Municipal Gallery of Modern Art (Parnell Square): The modern *art gallery* founded by Sir Hugh Lane is housed in this mansion (built 1762). The collection includes some well known works, particularly by Impressionists. In the *Lane Room* (Room 4) there are works by Renoir (1841-1919), Manet (1832-83), Monet (1840-1926), Corot (1796-1875), Degas (1834-1917), Courbet (1819-77), and others. The *Stained Glass Room* has some important pieces of the Irish art of glass-blowing (Hone, Clark). In the *Yeats Rooms* are paintings by J.B.Yeats (1871-1957), the brother of the famous poet.

National Museum (Kildare Street): The *Irish antiquities* department, displaying exhibits dating from the Stone Age to the early Middle Ages, is one of the most significant in Europe. The Bronze Age (*c.* 2000-600 BC) gold brooches, clasps and other jewellery are worth seeing. Valuable *church utensils* survive from the early Middle Ages, including the 8/9C *Ardagh Chalice* with its rich filigree and glass. Also note:

Mansion House

the 7C bronze *Tara Brooch,* with amber and small glass stones; the profusely decorated *'Moylough reliquary'* from Sligo; small Scandinavian (Viking) utensils; *Celtic crosses* (Lismore Cross, Inisfallen Cross, Cross of Cong and others) from the 11/12C; *shrines* (e.g. that of St.Patrick and the 'Cathach shrine'). At the entrance there are copies (by J.Fooley) of the major Celtic crosses of the 7–12C. There is also a collection of 18C gold in the *Art and Industrial Division.* The adjoining *National Library* contains some 1 million volumes, including works on botany, zoology and art; there is also the 'Joly Collection' of old prints of Ireland.

National Gallery (Merrion Square): Opened in 1864, it was founded by William Dargan, the Irish railway magnate, with donations by Sir Hugh Lane and G.B.Shaw. It has some 2,000 masterpieces and today presents an imposing overall view of the development of European painting from the 14C to the 20C. The most significant section is the collection of 15–18C *Italian painters* (in rooms 35, 21, 9, 36), including Lippi, Mantegna, Uccello (room 35); Ghiberti, Fra Angelico, Ghirlandaio (room 21); Tintoretto, Bellini, Titian, Veronese, Palmezzano (room 9); Guardi, Canaletto, Tiepolo (room 36). *Spanish School* (room 39): El Greco, Murillo, Zurbaran, Ribera, Goya. *Dutch and Flemish Schools* (rooms 16–20 and 47): Ruisdael, van Goyen, Claesz, Rembrandt, de Witte, Hals, Ruysdael, Steen, van der Weyden, Ysenbrandt, Brueghel the Younger, Jordaens, van Dyck, Rubens and others. *German School* (room 15): Cranach the Elder, Faber, Huber and others. There are also major *English* (Hogarth, Reynolds,

Gainsborough), *Irish* (father and brother of W.B.Yeats), and *French paintings* (Chardin, Lorrain, Poussin, Clouet, Delacroix, Sisley, Monet, Corot and others). In addition, there are a number of *icons* (Novgorod) and *enamels*.

Also worth seeing: The *General Post Office* (O'Connell Street), today the main post office, was built in 1814–18 (restored in 1929), and played an important part in the struggle for Irish independence. *Parnell Square:* Fine 18C Georgian *houses*; the 'Liberation of Ireland' (bronze, 1971, birds flying upwards) in the *Garden of Remembrance* (1966); next to it is the *Rotunda Hospital* (1764), and another *rotunda* (rebuilt) dating from 1786, with a garlanded frieze. *Belvedere House* (Great Denmark Street) belonged to the Earls of Belvedere and has been a *Jesuit school* since 1840 (fine rooms, e.g. the Apollo Room, the Diana Room, the Venus Room). The beautiful domed *King's Inn* (1795–1817) is near the elegant Georgian *Henrietta Street*. The *Mansion House* was built in *c.* 1705 in Queen Anne style with Victorian additions. It has been the residence of the Lord Mayor of Dublin since 1715. There are numerous pretty 18C Georgian *houses* around the adjacent *St. Stephen's Green*, and also some in Grafton Street. The *Custom House* (1781–91, on Beresford Place, right bank of the river) is one of the finest buildings by James Gandon, the Dublin architect. Note E.Smyth's *statues* on the *S. façade,* the arms of Ireland, the allegorical masks of the Atlantic and the 13 largest Irish rivers (both sides of the dome), and the allegory of Trade on the dome. The *Abbey Theatre*, re-opened in 1966 after the fire of 1951, is located nearby, in Lower Abbey Street which is near the river. Major plays by Yeats, Synge, O'Casey and others had their premières in this theatre, which was founded by W.B.Yeats and his associate Lady Gregory and played an important role in Irish literature of the period. *Phoe-*

nix Park, the largest town park in Europe, dates from the 17C, and is in the NW suburbs of Dublin. It contains the *Military Infirmary* of 1787 and the 223 ft. obelisk of the *Wellington Testimonial* (1817). *Marino Casino,* in the suburb of Marino, is a small 18C pavilion, built by Sir William Chambers for the Earl of Charlemont.

Environs: Ballsbridge (2 m. SE): The interesting *Chester Beatty Library* with its notable Oriental exhibits (cuneiform tablets, Egyptian-Greek papyri, biblical manuscripts, miniatures etc.) is here. It is the collection of Chester Beatty, the mining millionaire, who died in 1968.

Dalkey (9 m. SE): The fine ruins of the 16C *Archbold's Castle* (three-storeyed granite tower). The remains of an early Christian *church* (with a Martello tower) is on the rocky, offshore *Dalkey Island*. To the S. of Dublin there are several prehistoric *tombs* and *dolmens* or *passage tombs* (at Kilmashogue, Kiltiernan, Tibradden).

Dun Laoghaire (7 m. SE): Since 1834 it has been one of Dublin's harbours, with an important ferry connection to Great Britain. It takes its name from the Irish king Loagheire ('Castle Loagheire'), who built a castle here in the 5C (no remains survive). On the coast there are a number of *Martello Towers* (watchtowers), including that of the writer James Joyce (today it is a *museum* devoted to him). Nearby, *Monkstown Castle* has a two-storeyed central tower and is 13–15C.

Dunsoghly Castle (about 2 m. NW): Built by Plunkett in the 15C, with a fine rectangular main tower (oak ceiling) and a 16C chapel.

Finglas (2 m. W): A 12C *cross* and a few remains of the *monastery of St. Finian*.

Howth (about 10 m. E.): This small harbour on Dublin Bay has a 13C church, *St.Mary's*, rebuilt in the 14&15C, with a fine *tomb* (1470) in the S. aisle. *Howth Castle* was built in *c.* 1564 around an older keep (rebuilt in 1738).

Dumfries, Old Bridge

Dumfries

Dumfries and Galloway/
Scotland   p.324□G 9

This town near the mouth of the Nith, a
Royal Burgh in the 12C, was frequently
fought over. Edward I took it for England
in 1300, and six years later Robert the
Bruce gave the signal for the rebellion
against the English when he slew Sir John
Comyn, the king's emissary, before the
high altar of the Franciscan church. The
English were victorious again in 1448,
1536 and 1570, while in 1745 Charles Edward Stuart was rebuffed. From 1791–6,
Robert Burns lived in Dumfries. During
the Second World War it served as the Norwegian military headquarters.

Burns's House: The house where the

poet spent the last three years of his life has
been altered to form a memorial.
Manuscripts and personal mementoes are
on display in addition to the decorations,
most of which are original.

Midsteeple: Built in 1707, it was used as
a prison and court until 1867. There is a
relief of Dumfries in Burns's day.

Old Bridge: This six-arched footbridge
was built in 1431 as the replacement for
a wooden bridge built by Devorguilla Balliol in the 13C. Although this stone bridge
was itself damaged by a flood in 1620, it
was rebuilt with almost no alterations and
with the use of the original stones. It is the
second oldest stone bridge in Scotland after the Brig o'Balgownie in Aberdeen.

Also worth seeing: *St.Michael's* was built

in 1744–54 and in the churchyard is the mausoleum of the Burns family. The *Burgh Museum* is housed in an 18C windmill and is devoted to the history of the region. *Lincluden Abbey* was built as a Benedictine house in the 12C. The small abbey church was rebuilt in the 15C, and the choir and parts of the S. aisle are its chief surviving features. The richly decorated tomb (1430) of Margaret, Countess of Douglas, the daughter of Robert III, is also worth seeing.

Environs: Caerlaverock Castle: (6 m. S., on the E. shore of the Nith estuary) The most unorthodox castle in Scotland. Triangular in form with sides of equal length, it dates back to 1290 and has had an extremely eventful history as a result of its exposed site on the N.shore of the Solway Firth. Edward I took it for England in 1300, but 12 years later Eustace Maxwell regained it for the Scots. It was completely destroyed in 1355. The Covenanters captured it in 1640 after 13 weeks' siege. The base of the gatehouse and of the W.tower, and also the bottom of the S.tower, are among the oldest parts of the castle. The rest of the present building dates from 1425 onwards, with old masonry having been re-used.

The interior was quite comfortable despite the forbidding exterior. Bit by bit, living quarters were erected on the inside of the W. and E. faces and along the E. side is the four-storeyed *mansion* commissioned by the Earl of Nithdale in 1634. Its façade is an outstanding example of the development of the Renaissance in Scotland. The tympana are decorated with allegorical and heraldic motifs, while the ground floor rooms have tunnel vaults.

Glenkiln: 6 m. to the NW are 'the Moores in the moor'. Sir William Keswick collected sculptures by Henry Moore, Epstein and Rodin and erected them in the open landscape: . The showpiece of the collection is Moore's *King and Queen* dating from 1952.

Ruthwell Cross: 5 m. to the E. of Caerlaverock Castle is an 18 ft. high cross, which betrays Irish influence. It dates from the 8C and its runic inscription is the oldest known example of Old English.

Caerlaverock Castle (Dumfries)

Sweetheart Abbey: The ruins of the abbey founded by Devorguilla Balliol in 1273 are to be found 7 m. to the S. The abbey owes its name to the fidelity of its foundress, who preserved her husband's embalmed heart for 16 years in an ivory chest in order that it could be buried in the monastery together with her own body. But the history of the Cistercian abbey is less peaceful. It was constantly involved in the confused Anglo-Scottish disputes. In addition, the whole building burned down in 1381, and finally, in 1547, the abbey was dissolved by the Scottish king and the abbot was expelled to France. In 1609, the reformers caused the abbey's paintings, books and documents to be publicly burned in Dumfries market place. Practically nothing has survived of the monastery buildings except for the *W.gate*. On the other hand, the remains of the red sandstone *church* still make a vivid impression, for the choir, transept and S.aisle have largely survived. The 89 ft. tower over the crossing, and the sturdy W.front, are two further silent witnesses to the building's former prosperity.

Dunblane
Central/Scotland   p.324☐G 8

This was a spa in the 19C, and has some picturesque 17C houses. The 16C single-arched bridge across the Allen is also worth seeing.

Cathedral: This cathedral, built from 1233 onwards, is one of the few large churches in Scotland to have survived relatively well, and this is due to comprehensive restoration of 1892–1914. The oldest part of the building is the square *tower*, which was originally free standing and whose lower Norman section must date from the 11C. It was built by Bishop Clement on the site of an earlier Celtic church. The ground plan is unusual: a choir with no side aisles and no transept, whereas the nave has side aisles and the old tower is incorporated in the S.aisle. After the Reformation, only the choir continued to be used as a parish church, while the nave was allowed to fall into disrepair. Its roof collapsed in the late 16C. However, the W.fa-

Dunblane, Cathedral

çade, with its recessed portal and three narrow Gothic lancet windows, survives. Above it is the famous *Ruskin Window*, which can only be seen from the outside. It is a particularly happy chance that the carved early-15C *choir stalls* have survived. This is one of the very few examples in Scotland to have survived to reveal how choir stalls were built at that time. In the N.aisle is a stone with a Celtic cross, probably dating from the 9C. Three tomb slabs with blue decoration commemorate Margaret Drummond, the consort of James IV, and her two sisters. All three were poisoned in Drummond Castle in 1502.

Environs: Ardoch Roman Camp (6 m. N.): The 2C Roman camp is one of the largst Roman buildings in Britain and accommodated up to 40,000 men in its heyday. The ramparts and stone foundations provide a good impression of the camp's arrangement.

Doune Castle (4 m. W.): One of the largest, best preserved and best restored examples of a 14C fortress. It was in 1419–24, under the Duke of Albany, that the castle reached its maximum size. The living quarters arranged around the inner courtyard date from that time. Although the large tower (105 ft.) reached its full height, the residential quarters never rose to their planned 39 ft. After the execution of Murdoch, Duke of Albany, the castle was confiscated under the Stuarts in 1425 and served for a time as a royal residence. Charles Edward Stuart used it as a camp for prisoners in 1746, and after this it was uninhabited until 1833 and fell into disrepair. In 1883, under the 14th Earl of Moray, it was rebuilt in its present form. *Doune Park Gardens* were laid out by the 10th Earl of Moray in the 1st half of the 19C. The park had a pinetum added in 1860. Another item of interest is *Doune Motor Museum*, with its collection of vintage motor-cars belonging to the present Earl of Moray.

Drummond Castle (10 m. N.): Although it dates from the 15C and has a battlemented tower in good condition, it is mainly of interest for the gardens created by the 2nd Earl of Perth. Essentially baroque, these were laid out on terraces in the 17C using Italian and French models. The house and grounds are particularly famous for their rare trees and plants. The sundial giving the time in various European capitals dates from 1630.

A few miles to the E. of the castle is the *Strathallan Air Museum*, with a collection of vintage aircraft, both civilian and military. Many of them are still airworthy and are flown on display from time to time.

Dundalk

This lively harbour town has some 25,000 inhabitants and is situated on the bay of the same name. It is named after the ramparted fortress of *Dun Dealgan* (to the W.) inhabited by the town's mythical founder, the Celtic hero CuChulainn. The legendary duel between him and Ferdia, his childhood friend, is the subject of the famous epic 'Tain Bo Cuailgne' (Theft of the Bulls). His reputed tombstone is some 3 m. S. of the town.

However, the *walls* of Dun Dealgan which are visible today are the work of Betram de Verdons, the Norman who founded the town anew (12C). Much fought over in the Middle Ages, the town still boasts the 13C Protestant *Church of St. Nicholas,* rebuilt 19C, and a (bell) *tower* (15C) from a 12C provost's residence.

Environs: Aghnaskeagh Cairns (about 6 m. N.): Prehistoric *burial site.*
Ardee (about 14 m. SW): This small town of 3,000 inhabitants has two ruined castles. *Ardee Castle* was built in *c.* 1207 by Roger de Peppard the Norman and has

Dunblane, Cathedral, nave

Celtic High Cross

Choir stalls

15C additions. Today it is the Court House. *Hatch's Castle* in Market Street is a fortified 13C residence. Parts of a medieval church (13/14C) survive in *St.Mary's Church*. Nearby, to the E., are the ruins of *Roodstown Castle*, a four-storeyed tower house in good condition, with fine 15/16C windows.

Carlingford (about 14 m. E.): This is only a small harbour today, but it played an important part in the Middle Ages, as is shown by *King John's Castle* with its strong 13C fortifications; other sights are the 15C tower house called *The Mint* with ancient windows, *Taaffe's Castle* (a rebuilt 16C keep), the old town hall called *The Tholsel* (town gate with tower room) from the 16C, and the remains of a *Dominican house* (The Abbey) founded in *c.* 1305 and rebuilt in the 16C, with church nave, choir and tower over the crossing.

Carrickmacross (*c.* 13 m. W.): N. of here are the remains of *Donaghmoyne Castle* (*c.* 1193), with ramparts and sections of wall.

Castlebellingham (about 7 m. S.): The round tower of *Dromiskin* survives from an old monastery founded by Lughaidh, a follower of St.Patrick (6C). Nearby are a 13 –15C *ruined church* and parts of a *cross*. To the W. are the remains of the 15–17C *Mansfieldstown Church*, and to the S. are the remains of the Norman *Greenmount Motte*.

Inishkeen (about 5 m. W.): A 12C *round tower* still survives from a monastery founded by St.Dega (7C).

Louth (some 6 m. SW): St. Mochta founded a monastery in the 6C near this town which bears the county's name. The small 12C church called *St.Mochta's House* is a simple rectangular stone building (restored). Nearby are the ruins of the 14/15C *Louth Abbey*.

Proleek Dolmen (about 3 m. NE): This prehistoric *monument* consists of an enormous coping slab (about 40 tons) supported by three upright stones.

Roche Castle (Castleroche, about 6 m. NW): These ruins dating from *c.* 1236 were an old *border fortress* against th neighbouring province of Armagh (fine in ner courtyard).

Dundee
Tayside/Scotland   p.324☐H

This, the fourth largest town in Scotland was once among the oldest settlements i the country, but nothing has survived o the medieval buildings, because the Eng lish repeatedly razed the town to the ground, most recently by the work o General Monck in 1651. The entire inne town was rebuilt after World War 2.

St.Mary's Tower: This old church tower 154 ft. tall, is the only 15C building. How ever, it is one of the finest church tower in Scotland. In 1651, when Genera Monck besieged the town, the survivin defenders fled to the tower in the hope that they would be safe within the precincts o the church. However, General Monck caused the books from the city library to be piled around the tower and set on fire.

City Museum and Art Gallery: The city museum contains exhibits devoted to archaeology and local history, including a sextant dating from 1555. The adjoining art gallery has Dutch, French and English paintings besides Scottish ones.

Tay Rail Bridge: This 2m. long bridge across the Firth of Tay was an importan landmark in British bridge building. For mally opened on 31 May 1878, it was a that time the longest bridge in the world The young Thomas Bouch designed a graceful, but unstable, iron girder structure supported by 85 brick pillars. Construc tion took six years and a mere year and a half after it was completed, on 28 Decem ber 1879, the bridge collapsed in a storm whilst a train carrying 75 passengers wa

Dundee, St. Mary's Tower

Dunfermline, Abbey ruins

crossing. The engineer had not taken wind forces into account. The present bridge was built between 1883 and 1888 and has withstood all that nature can throw at it.

Environs: Claypotts Castle (3 m. NE): A fine example of a 16C Scottish tower house. This tower has a Z-shaped ground plan and massive round towers at its outer corners. There are firing slits instead of windows on the ground floor; this was probably necessary because in the late 17C the tower was the residence of James Graham of Claverhouse, known as Bonnie Dundee, who was later a Jacobite commander at the Battle of Killiecrankie, where he fell.

Glamis Castle (12 m. N.): This is another prime example of a tower house with turrets built on corbels and a separate staircase tower in the corner between the two wings. The castle originates from the 11C. King Malcolm is said to have died here in 1034. The present castle dates from 1675 –87, and the title of the Lyon family dates from 1372. The Lords of Glamis had their share of vicissitudes. On 3 December 1540, a Lady Glamis was burned as a witch in Edinburgh at the king's direct instigation. In 1677, the Lords of Glamis were given the title of Earl of Strathmore and Kinghorne. The 14th Earl of this line was the grandfather of Queen Elizabeth II. Both the Queen Elizabeth the Queen Mother and Princess Margaret were born at Glamis. The castle is chiefly worth seeing for its luxurious interior decoration and for the wood panelling and painted ceiling in the castle chapel.

Dunfermline
Fife/Scotland   p.324☐G 8

This linen-weavers' town N. of the Firth of Forth was Scotland's capital for 600 years. A number of Scottish kings lie buried here. James I of Scotland was born here in 1394, and Charles I in 1600. Andrew Carnegie (1835–1919), the Pittsburgh steel multimillionaire, also came from Dunfermline; he founded Carnegie Hall in New York and also some 3,000 libraries the world over.

Glamis Castle (Dundee)

Dunfermline, frescoed vaulting

Abbey: The monastery was founded by Queen Margaret in 1074 and flourished under Benedictines from Canterbury. Through openings in the floor of the abbey church, it is still possible today to see some parts of a small Romanesque church, which has a semicircular apse and was built by order of King Malcolm III for his wife and for the monastery at about this time. The remains of a still older Celtic chapel can also be seen through these openings. In its present form, the *church* consists of two parts. To the W. is the aisle of the medieval abbey church, which was built under King David I in the first half of the 12C and was consecrated in 1150; whereas the E. section dates from 1821, although it stands on the foundations of the medieval church. The original E. section, together with the abbey, was almost completely destroyed by the soldiers of King Edward I of England in 1303. The neo-Gothic new building was built by William Burn in 1817–21. Despite all the devastation, the surviving old section is one of the most beautiful examples of a Norman interior in the whole of Scotland. Its massive Romanesque columns are about 4 ft. 6 in. in diameter, some 29 ft. tall, and richly decorated. The galleries on both sides of the nave were originally connected by a corridor on the W. gable. The rich stone ornaments in the aisles date from the 13C. The fountain on the 2nd pillar of the S.aisle also dates from this period. 16C paintings have been uncovered on the vault of the N. transept; they include depictions of the Apostles Peter, John and Andrew. The Reformation meant that little survived either of the 26 original altars or of the stained-glass windows, of which the Durie Window still contains some original sections. The W. façade above the portal dates, in its present form, from the 15C. The battlemented main tower, 100 ft. tall, replaces the old tower which fell down in 1753. The importance of the town and church is clear from the numerous *royal*

tombs: Malcolm III (1093), Duncan II (1094), Alexander I (1124), David I (1153), Malcolm IV (1165), Alexander III (1286), Robert the Bruce (1329) and Robert III (1406) were buried here. St. Margaret (1093) and her son Edward (1093) also rest here. The monastery was rebuilt after the devastation of 1303, and the guesthouse even became a palace for King James VI and his wife Anne. However, all these buildings are now ruined.

Environs: Aberdour Castle (6 m. SE): The ruins of this castle, which dates from the 14C and reached its maximum extent in the 16&17C, stand on the coast. Some of the better-preserved sections are roofed over to protect the wall paintings.

Inchcolm Island: The best-preserved monastic ruins in Scotland lie off the beaten track on this small island. The abbey was founded by King Alexander I (1078–1124) and was taken over by Augustinian monks from Scone. The tower and parts of the S. aisle are all that survives of the *abbey church,* but the 13C *monastery buildings* are in astonishingly good condition, because they were used as domestic buildings by the family of the Earl of Moray, the half-brother of Mary Queen of Scots. The early medieval *St.Colm's Cell,* the only surviving hermit's cell in Scotland, is to be found not far from the monastery.

Dungannon
Tyrone/Northern Ireland   p.326☐D 10

This small town (about 7,500 inhabitants) was for a long time the residence of the O'Neills, Earls of Tyrone. The *castle,* destroyed in 1602, was rebuilt in *c.* 1790. The Protestant *church* is roughly contemporary.

Environs: Arboe (about 12 m. NE): On the W. shore of Lough Neagh is the famous *High Cross of Arboe* (9C). This cross, over

16 ft. tall and now restored, is decorated with numerous biblical motifs.

Ardress House (about 8 m. SE): This *farmhouse* to the E. of Moy, with its fine Georgian interior (drawing room) and its picture collection, dates from 1660.

Beaghmore (about 16 m. NW): Prehistoric *stone circles* (*c.* 1800 BC) with grave mounds.

Castlecaulfield (about 3 m. W.): Remains of a *house* dating from 1619; a *village church* with a portal dating from 1685.

Cookstown (about 11 m. N.): S. of the town are the remains of the early Celtic ring-shaped *Tullaghoge Fort*, with a rampart and ditch. In the early Middle Ages this was the centre of the 'Ulster clan' of the O'Neills.

Donaghmore (2 m. NW): A 11C *high cross* points towards an *abbey* said to have been founded by St. Patrick (hardly any traces survive).

Dungiven
Londonderry/Northern Ireland   p.326☐ D 9

In this beautifully situated small town are the remains of a *castle* of the O'Cahans (15C), and also the *fortifications* of the London settlers, dating from 1618. To the S. is the ruined church of the Augustinian house of *Dungiven Priory,* (*c.* 1100). The single-aisled church had a choir added to it in the 14C. The tomb of an O'Cahan knight, dating from 1385 (in the S.choir), is worth seeing; the dead man is wearing Irish dress, and beside him are 6 Irish warriors.

Environs: Banagher (about 6 m. SW): Ruins of the 12C *Old Church* with a fine Romanesque portal (10C) and Romanesque and Gothic windows. The 12C *saint's tomb* in the graveyard has a similar design to that in Bovevagh.

Bovevagh (about 2 m. N.): The remains of the medieval *Bovevagh Church* (13/14C)

with an interesting 12C saint's tomb in the form of an ancient Celtic oratory.

Maghera (about 14 m. SE): Remains of an 11/12C *parish church* with a fine W.portal (Crucifixion).

Dunnottar Castle
Grampian/Scotland   p.324☐ I 7

Situated on a 165 ft. high crag jutting out into the sea to the S. of Stonehaven, this ruined castle was once the seat of the Marischals of Scotland. The site of a ruined Celtic monastery, the rock was fortified under King William the Lion (1165 – 1214), and Bishop Wishart consecrated a church here in the late 13C. In 1297, William Wallace, the Scottish champion, took the rock, which had been occupied by the English, and burned down the church together with the Englishmen who had fled thither. Finally, Sir William Keith, the great Marischal, disputed the rock with the Bishop of St.Andrews and the dispute had to be settled by Pope Benedict XIII. The fortress reached its maximum size in the first half of the 17C, in keeping with the political power enjoyed by the Marischals of Scotland. Almost the entire rock was built over at that time. Finally, in 1652, Dunnottar was the last Scottish stronghold. The fortress's fate was then sealed in 1716, when it was seized by the Crown after the Jacobite rising had been put down. Two years later, the fortifications were dismantled and the castle destroyed. Today, only the *Drawing Room* on the first floor of the N.wing, and a number of *vaults,* are worth seeing.

Dunstable
Bedfordshire/England   p.332☐ K 14

This industrial town in the S. tip of Bed-

Durham, Cathedral

fordshire stands on the site of an *Augustinian priory* founded by Henry I. Part of its monastery church still survives. The town's industry developed from straw processing, for which it was a centre in the early 18C.

Church of St.Peter: Its *aisle* and the large *portal* are Norman. They were part of the Augustinian priory church built *c.* 1150. The entire E. end of the church was unfortunately damaged in the 16C, but the *W. front* survived and is an outstanding example of the transition from Romanesque to Early English. The richly decorated *NW portal* is 13C, while the *choir screen* is 15C. In 1533, in defiance of the Papal interdiction, Archbishop Cranmer here pronounced the annulment of the marriage between Henry VIII and Catherine of Aragon, thereby creating the necessary precondition for the Act of Supremacy of 1534, by which Henry VIII declared himself head of the Anglican church and finally completed the break with Rome.

Environs: Edlesborough (5 m. SW): The oldest sections of the large *Church of St.Mary,* occupying an isolated hill top site, date from the 13C. It was rebuilt and extended in the 14&15C, and restored in the Victorian period. There are some outstanding Gothic wooden furnishings, such as the canopied pulpit, the choir screen, and the beautifully decorated misericords of the choir stalls. The paintings in the nave are Victorian, as are the stained-glass windows, the work of Warde and Hughes.

Leighton Buzzard (9 m. NW): The large, cross-shaped *Church of All Saints* has a central tower and dates from the 13C. The oldest feature is the 13C font. The beautifully worked misericords of the choir stalls, and the outstanding wooden roof, are both 15C. The wrought-iron work of the W. portal is by Thomas of Leighton, who also made the screen for the monument to Edward I's wife in Westminster Abbey.

The medieval graffiti on the columns and walls are particularly impressive. The glazing of the church dates from the 19C and is by C.E.Kempe.

Wing (12 m. W.): The *Church of All Saints* is one of the most interesting churches from the Anglo-Saxon period, since there are only three other churches with a Saxon apse and a crypt underneath it. The apse is eight-sided, and the vaulted crypt has a hexagonal central area with a narrow ambulatory around it. The four arches of the nave are also Saxon, while the rest was built in the 13C. The W. tower was added in the 14C, and the S. aisle was rebuilt at the same time. One year later the present windows were installed and the clerestory added. The choir screen is 16C, while the pulpit dates from the early 17C. The church contains numerous monuments, including two outstanding examples from 1552 and 1590 for the Dormer family. *Ascott House* is a half-timbered house built as a hunting lodge in 1870. Today it contains a picture collection, fine furniture and old Chinese porcelain. The collection was assembled by Anthony de Rothschild.

Woburn Abbey (12 m. NW): This old *Cistercian abbey* was dissolved by Henry VIII in 1539, and ownership was transferred to John Russell, who later became the first Earl of Bedford. It was under William III that the Earl became the Duke of Bedford and established his residence at Woburn. Isaac de Caux was the first to enlarge the house and John Sanderson and Henry Flitcroft rebuilt it in the 18C. Towards the end of that century Henry Holland added the finishing touch in the form of the E. façade. Today the house contains an important picture collection with works by Canaletto, Gainsborough, Rembrandt, Reynolds, van Dyck and Velazquez. The collection is supplemented by fine 18C furniture, both French and English, and by valuable silver from the same period. Its extensive *grounds* are today a safari park.

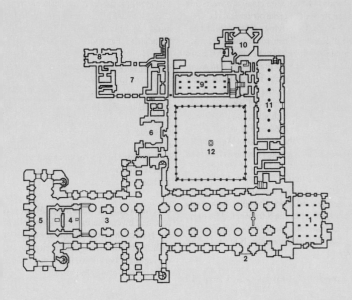

Durham Cathedral 1 Galilee Chapel (vestibule) **2** N. portal (with 12C knocker) **3** bishop's throne **4** high altar **5** Chapel of the Nine Altars **6** chapterhouse **7** deanery **8** crypt **9** old library (formerly refectory) **10** monastery kitchen **11** library (formerly dormitory) **12** cloister

Durham

Durham/England   p.328□I 10

This city was founded in the 10C by Saxon monks who had fled from Lindisfarne, and was fortified in the 11C by William the Conqueror. It enjoyed a heyday after the bishop's seat was moved here from Chester-le-Street in 995. In the early 19C its economy benefited from the mining of hard coal in the surrounding area. The city's university, founded in 1657 and refounded as a working establishment in 1832, is the third oldest in England after Oxford and Cambridge. Today, its architectural monuments make Durham one of the most interesting cities in England.

Cathedral (above the loop of the Wear): One of the most important Norman cathedrals in England, and one of the purest in style. Built on the site of an earlier building which was part of the original Benedictine monastery. Construction began in 1093 by order of Bishop Carilef of Durham, and was largely complete by 1133, under Bishop Flambard. The *Galilee Porch* was added in the late 12C, the *Chapel of the Nine Altars* dates from the 13C, and the *bell tower,* about 230 ft. tall, was rebuilt in the second half of the 15C. On the 12C portal is a 12C *door-knocker* in the form of a grotesque face with an iron ring in its mouth, where escaped criminals could find sanctuary from the clutches of the law.

Interior: The nave has massive *piers*, richly decorated with zigzag ornament; the vault is the oldest surviving early Gothic example in Europe. The earliest known Romanesque *ribbed vault* is to be found in the two aisles of the choir. Fine 12/13C *wall paintings* cover the church. The choir has splendid 17C *choir stalls*, the 13C *bishop's throne* incorporates the tomb of Bishop Hatfield and, above the high altar, the *altar screen* was built in *c.* 1380 and is attributed to Henry Yevele, the architect of Westminster Abbey and Canterbury Cathedral. Behind the high altar is the tomb of St.Cuthbert, the first Bishop of Lindisfarne, who died in 687. The tomb was unfortunately mutilated in 1540. Prior Castell's Clock, made in *c.* 1500, is in the S.transept. The tomb of the Venerable Bede (673–735), the first known English chronicler, is in the Galilee Porch.

Cathedral Library (reached from the cloister on the S.side of the cathedral): Housed in the former Benedictine abbey (dormitory and refectory), it contains the cathedral's unique treasury. Note: Saxon *stone crosses* from Northumbria. The 11C two-volume *Carilef Bible*, which belonged to the founder of the cathedral and has splendidly illuminated miniatures. The 10C *stole* of the Bishop of Winchester. The restored *wooden sarcophagus* of St. Cuthbert, in which he was brought to Durham in 999, and the Saint's *pectoral cross* and *stole.*

Durham Castle (opposite the cathedral): Founded by William the Conqueror as a system of fortified earthworks, it was later much expanded and became the seat of the 'Prince Bishops' of Durham, whose sway extended as far as the Scottish border. Of particular interest inside: the 13C *Great Hall,* today the refectory of the university. The Norman *castle chapel* (1072). The unique Norman *gatehouse,* has no counterpart in Great Britain. A *Renaissance stair-*case (1662) leads to a 15C gallery. Since 1832 the castle has served as the main building of the university, which was re-founded at that time.

Gulbenkian Museum (Elvet Hill Road, part of the university): The only museum in England to specialize in *Oriental art and archaeology.* The collections include: porcelain, ivory and jade, paintings and textiles from China; sculptures from various materials, weapons, and wall hangings from Japan; Muslim ceramics and archaeological finds from Egypt, dating back to the 15C BC.

Durham Light Infantry Museum (reached by car via Framwellgate Peth in the NW of the city): A military museum dedicated to the history of the city's infantry regiment (weapons, uniforms, orders, descriptions of battles, etc.).

Also worth seeing: *St. Oswald's Church* (Church Street), late medieval. The *Market Place, St. Nicholas's Church* and the *Town Hall.* The town also has some fine *bridges* spanning the Wear: *Elvet Bridge* (12C). *Prebend's Bridge* with an excellent view of the cathedral (a favourite place for taking photographs). *Framwellgate Bridge.* In the W. of the city is *Neville's Cross,* commemorating the battle of 1346 in which the invading Scots were crushed and their king, David II, taken prisoner.

Environs: Brancepeth (5 m. SW): Beside the *castle* is the notable *Church of St. Brandon* (13–15C) with monuments to the Neville family (14–16C) and fine carved wood.
Chester-le-Street (about 6 m. N.): Built on the site of a Roman fortress. From 883 it was the resting place of St.Cuthbert of Lindisfarne, and until 995 it was the seat of a bishop, who then moved to Durham. The 13/14C *Church of SS.Mary and Cuth-*

Durham, Cathedral, portal

bert is worth seeing (fine tower, attached hermit's cell; inside are 14 tombs of the Lumley family, mostly from the late 16C). To the E. of the town is *Lumley Castle,* dating from the end of the 14C.

Finchale Priory (about 4 m. N.): A *Dominican house* founded in 1196 as a dependency of Durham. Today all that remains are 13&14C ruins. There are visible remnants of the prior's house, the kitchen, the refectory and the chapel.

Houghton-le-Spring (about 6 m. NE): The 13&14C *church* contains the tomb of Bernard Gilpin, the so-called 'Apostle of the North', who died in 1583.

Lanchester (about 8 m. NW): The 12&13C church is worth visiting; the blind arcades on the N. side employ Roman columns. There is a late Roman altar in the porch. Only a few remnants, near the road leading to Weardale, survive from the Roman fortress of *Longovicium,* from which the ancient spoils derive.

Sherburn Hospital (about 2 m. E.): The 13C *gatehouse* survives from a hospital founded by the bishops of Durham in 1181.

Eastbourne
East Sussex/England   p.332☐L 16

A Crown possession under the Saxons, it was later acquired by three Sussex families. Its development into a seaside resort began in the late 18C, and within a 100 years it was established as such.
The town presents a fine vista when seen from the sea: it is flanked by *Beachy Head,* below which there is a *lighthouse.* The *Seven Sisters,* a series of splendid chalk cliffs, are a particular attraction.

Parish Church of St. Mary: A Saxon church rebuilt by the Normans.

Church of All Souls: A 19C neo-Byzantine church.

Lamb Inn: This 13C pub, formerly used as a smugglers' lair, was once connected to St. Mary's Church by a secret passage.

Pilgrims Inn: 14C, partly timber.
During the Napoleonic wars, numerous forts were built to defend the S. coast. Two of them survive today, although they are no longer used as forts.
The **Redoubt** has a *treasure island village* for children, an *aquarium,* a *grotto* ('The

Blue Temple'), and the Sussex *Combined Services Museum.*
The **Wish Tower** was one of 74 Martello Towers built along the coast, and today houses the *museum* of the Royal National Lifeboat Institution.

Towner Art Gallery: This pretty building is late 18C. Most of the works on display are by British painters of the 18&19C, but there are, for example, also some pieces by Picasso and Henry Moore.

Also worth seeing: Eastbourne has numerous attractive and well laid-out parks, including *Gilgridge Park* and *Motcombe Park.*

Environs: Eastdean (2 m. W.): A *church* with a Norman *tower.*
Michelham Priory (6 m. N.): A 13C *Augustinian priory* with a 14C moat. Today this building, which was converted into a farmhouse in the 16C, contains a collection of old glass, wrought-iron, furniture and forge tools.
Pevensey (3 m. E.): William the Conqueror landed here in 1066. *Pevensey Castle,* formerly a Roman fort, was extended by the Normans and was used to protect a harbour which no longer exists today. Besieged by Simon de Montfort in the 12C,

the castle later fell into disrepair. *St. Nicholas's Church* dates from the 13C. The *Court House,* once a prison and town hall, is today a museum of local history.

Ecclefechan
Dumfries and Galloway/
Scotland
                                    p.324☐H 9

This village, just across the Scottish border, was the home of Thomas Carlyle (1795–1881), the historian, literary critic and writer who became rector of Edinburgh University in 1865. This Scottish moralist wrote a biography of Frederick the Great and translated Goethe's 'Wilhelm Meister'. Goethe himself called him 'a moral force of great significance', and Kaiser Wilhelm II sent a wreath for Carlyle's tomb on what would have been the hundredth birthday of this mediator between Anglo-Saxon and German culture. The tomb is not in Westminster Abbey as originally planned, but is to be found here, in the churchyard of his native village.

Eastbourne, parish church of St. Mary's

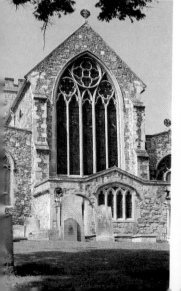

Environs: Gretna Green (4 m. SE): This village owes its fame entirely to 18C Scottish legislation, by which a marriage was valid if a couple at least 16 years old had declared to witnesses their desire to marry. Parental consent was not required for the marriage, neither was a registrar necessary. Gretna Green, as the southernmost border village, received a flood of eloping couples and any large room was used for the ceremony, from the town hall through various inns to the village smithy. Parliament set up the first obstacle to this in 1856 by stipulating a three-week waiting period. From 1939 onwards, a priest or a registrar was also required for the marriage ceremony to be valid for both parties. When, in 1969, the required age was reduced from 21 to 18, the village finally lost its attraction. Today there is only a historical charm in visiting the marriage smithies, which have some documents which are hundreds of years old.

Lockerbie (4 m. NW): SE of the town, on Birrenswark Hill, are the remains of a *Roman castle* with extensive fortifications.

Ecclefechan, Thomas Carlyle's tomb

Edinburgh, view over city

Edinburgh
Lothian/Scotland   p.324☐H 8

This city of kings, the queen of Scotland's cities, dates back to pre-Roman times when Pictish hunters settled here. The Romans had a fortified camp on the castle rock, and this became a kind of fortress in the 5C. King Edwin of Northumberland extended this fortress and gave it its name: 'Edwin's Burgh'. But it was not until the rule of Malcolm III Canmore (1057–93) that the first proper fortress was built here. Duncan I was murdered by Macbeth, and Duncan's son was the last purely Gaelic king and the founder of the dynasty of the Scottish kings. His wife Margaret, later canonized, built a chapel at the highest point of the castle rock in *c.* 1090, and this is the city's oldest building today. The present High Street was laid out as a market street at about the same time. In 1128, King David I brought Augustinian monks to his residence and founded Holyrood Abbey. However, over 300 years were to pass before Edinburgh finally replaced Perth as the capital of Scotland in 1437. Work on Holyrood Castle began in *c.* 1500, and the first printing shop in Scotland was established in 1507 by the royal prerogative of James IV. Flodden Wall was built after the defeat inflicted on James IV at Flodden Field in 1513. The new city wall surrounded the city for the next 250 years. Some remains of it may still be seen near Grassmarket. Henry VIII caused the castle and city to be destroyed in 1544 and 1547 because he was unable to obtain Mary Stuart as his daughter-in-law. Mary Stuart, who had fled to France, returned from exile in 1561 to begin her seven tragic years

Edinburgh, Castle Hill

in Scotland. 22 years later, the city council founded the university.

In 1603, Mary Stuart's son James VI became James I, King of England, and moved to London along with the entire royal household. Over 100 years later, in early 1707, the Scottish parliament was dissolved, and the end finally came for Edinburgh as the capital of an independent Scotland. But trade, science and art simultaneously experienced such an upswing that the city was able to retain its reputation as Scotland's metropolis even without having a royal court. 53 years later, Nor' Loch, the lake below the castle rock, was drained, and in 1767 work began on building the New Town to the plans of James Craig. It was in 1822 that King George IV paid his memorable visit to the city when he initiated the reconciliation of England and Scotland. The industrial age finally broke for Edinburgh in 1836 when the railway was introduced.

Edinburgh Castle: The castle rock 440 ft. high is a volcanic rock with steep cliff walls. Its strategic location must have had a magical attraction for the builders of the castle. The possession of this rock must have been regarded as a kind of status symbol, and this would explain why the Scottish kings were so attached to it, and why the English repeatedly attempted to gain control of the castle and rock. They first achieved this in 1174, when William I had to open the gates to Henry II. The castle was once again in English hands from 1296 until the Earl of Moray succeeded in recapturing it in 1313. On the other hand, Kirkcaldy of Grange withstood a five-year siege by the English from 1568 onwards while Mary Queen of Scots was being held cap-

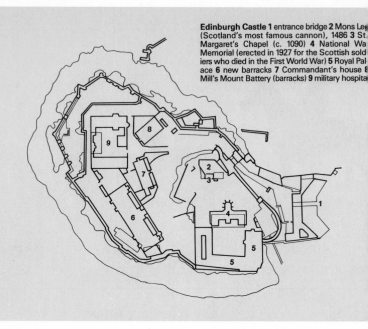

Edinburgh Castle 1 entrance bridge **2** Mons Meg (Scotland's most famous cannon), 1486 **3** St. Margaret's Chapel (c. 1090) **4** National War Memorial (erected in 1927 for the Scottish soldiers who died in the First World War) **5** Royal Palace **6** new barracks **7** Commandant's house **8** Mill's Mount Battery (barracks) **9** military hospital

tive by the English. Cannons brought from England finally compelled him to surrender the castle. Cromwell took the castle in 1650, but it did not open its gates to Charles Edward Stuart in 1745. He had to content himself with Holyrood Palace. A drawbridge, portcullis and watchtowers still adorn the access to the castle rock, but although some of the walls are up to 16 ft. thick, the fact cannot be disguised that nearly all of this is a 19C reconstruction. For example, *Argyll's Tower* is on the site where the Constable's Tower stood before the surrender of 1573. The first Marquis of Argyll and his son were incarcerated in this tower in 1660 before being put to death. *Argyll Battery* provides the best view not only of Princes Street and New Town, but also across the Forth as far as the coast of the Fife peninsula. Since 1861, the Time Gun on *Mill's Mount Battery* has

been fired at 1 p.m. every day except Sundays. The highest point of the rock is reached after Foggy Gate and is the site where the fortress of King Malcolm III Canmore must originally have stood. *Mons Meg*, the most famous cannon in Scotland, cast in Mons in Belgium in 1486, stands here today. All that survives from the time of King Malcolm is *St.Margaret's Chapel* (dedicated to his queen), built *c*. 1090. This chapel, some 29 ft. long and 13 ft. wide, has a tunnel vault and a semicircular apse. At the chancel end of the aisle are two Romanesque arches, one above the other. The zigzag *frieze* in this double chancel arch is especially characteristic and places the structure among the early Celtic chapels. The glass windows, the work of Douglas Strachan, date from 1921. Further to the S. we find the *National War Memorial*, built by Robert Lorimer in 1927

Edinburgh Castle

for the Scottish soldiers who fell in the First World War. Behind this is the real *royal palace*. Only the E. section still dates from the 15C, while the rest was built under Queen Anne in the early 18C. In the S. corner of the old section is the tiny wood-panelled room where Mary Queen of Scots gave birth to James VI in 1566. The 'Honours of Scotland', the insignia of the throne, are on display in the *Crown Room*. They were rediscovered in 1818 at the instigation of Sir Walter Scott, after being concealed in 1707 following the dissolution of the Scottish parliament. The main objects of interest in the castle's royal chambers are the *sceptre* which James IV received from Pope Alexander VI in 1494, the *sword* granted him by Pope Julius II in 1507, and James V's golden *crown* set with well over 100 pearls and precious stones. The *Old Parliament Hall* on the S. side of

the inner courtyard was the assembly hall of the Scottish parliament. This hall decorated with old weapons is today used for State receptions.

St.Giles Cathedral: Except for the crown of its tower, this building, also known as the High Kirk of Edinburgh, is of no interest from the outside. In fact it is not unlike the house of a wealthy citizen and it fits in with the rest of the High Street without giving any hint of the history that lies behind it. 215 ft. long and nearly 115 ft. wide, it dates back to a 9C church. This was followed *c.* 1120 by a Norman church, destroyed in 1385 by Richard II of England. The octagonal columns which support the tower are survivals from this Norman church. All the rest of it was built between 1387 and 1495, when the tower was completed. The church attained the rank of a collegiate church under James III in 1466. At that time it had 44 altars which, along with the other furnishings, were destroyed by the Reformers 100 years later. John Knox began his activities here. The first Reformed church service was held in the church in 1561. St.Giles was an episcopal cathedral for the last time in 1660–88, before then being divided into four separate sections for four different confessions. The interior is as peculiar as the exterior. There is a clearly discernible nave with two aisles on each side, and there are two slight transepts separating the nave from the choir. The latter two sections are of equal length. However, little else of its design is clear-cut. Various features have survived from the different periods of reconstruction, annexes have been added, and aisles have been closed off to form chapels and in some cases opened again. The result of all this is a dismembered church, whose strict Gothic style is of a bleakness which might, at most, meet with the approval of John Knox. Only the crown of the tower, the landmark of the old part of the city, betrays the artistry of the old architects. It is formed from eight arched buttresses supporting a slender pinnacle. Although the crown of the tower is of stone, it gives an impression of lightness not otherwise typical of the crowns of Scottish towers. Inside are a number of interesting monuments, including that to the Duke of Montrose, whose execution was ordered by the Marquis of Argyll. It will have been of little comfort to the Duke that Argyll later suffered the same fate; both now lie buried in the same church. The stained-glass windows date from the 19&20C, and the pillars are decorated by the colours of the most famous Scottish regiments. The *Chapel of the Thistle* (1909) was designed by Sir Robert Lorimer and is in late Gothic style. This chapel, decorated with a net vault, coloured bosses and carved oak stalls, was built for the oldest and most distinguished Scottish order of

Edinburgh Castle, entrance bridge

knights, the Order of the Thistle, founded by James III in 1470. It has only sixteen members at any one time. At present these include the Queen and Prince Charles.

Canongate Church: This church was built by James Smith in 1688 as a parish church, because James II had forbidden the parishioners to enter Holyrood Abbey. Tradition has it that the remains of Rizzio, Mary Queen of Scots' lover murdered at the instigation of her husband, lie buried in the SE corner of the church. Restored in 1951, the church is interesting for its heraldic ornaments. Adam Smith, the economist and philosopher (1723 – 90, author of the 'Wealth of Nations'), and the Edinburgh poet Robert Fergusson (1750 –74), are buried in the graveyard adjoining the church.

Greyfriars Church: This Franciscan

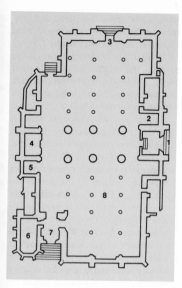

Edinburgh, St. Giles' Cathedral 1 N. portal **2** St. Eloi's Chapel, with the tomb of the Marquis of Argyll **3** W. portal **4** organ **5** tomb of the Marquis of Montrose **6** Thistle Chapel (1909) **7** SE portal **8** choir

Holyrood Palace

church in Candlemaker Road dates from 1620. It formerly belonged to a Franciscan monastery built in the 15C. In 1679, the churchyard associated with the church was used as a prison for 1200 Covenanters after the battle of Bothwell Bridge.

Holyrood Abbey: Only ruins survive of this, the most important and beautiful church in Edinburgh. The church of the Augustinian Abbey of the Holy Cross was founded in 1128 by David I, the son of St. Margaret, as a token of gratitude for having had his life miraculously saved when about to be gored by a stag. The ruins at the NE corner of Holyrood Palace today still bear witness to the abbey's former splendour. The twin-towered *W. façade* has a richly-decorated, carved portal with an open gallery above it. The two corner towers have a double row of pointed blind

arcades, an early-13C Gothic masterpiece. The processional portal between the church and the former cloister is Norman. David II, James II, James V and Darnley were all buried in the church. James II, III, IV and V were married here, and the coronation of Charles I was celebrated here in 1633. The roof fell down in 1768, and after that the church fell into disrepair.

Magdalen Chapel: This chapel in Chambers Street, together with a home for the aged with seven occupants, was founded by Jenet Rynd in 1547. These seven were entirely provided for, but in return they had to pray for hours, day in and day out, for the foundress and her husband. The last inhabitant died in 1665, and after this the chapel was for a long time used as a morgue. Its finest feature is the large *stained-glass window*. This is the only window in the whole of Scotland which dates from before the Reformation and has remained in its original position.

Old St.Paul's Church: This church in Carrubber's Close became the parish church for the St.Paul's parish of Bishop Rose in 1689. When the Episcopal church was disestablished, the Bishop left St.Giles cathedral along with his followers. The parishioners, who were loyal to the Stuarts, did not recognize William of Orange's succession to the throne, and therefore founded the Episcopal Church of Scotland. The present church was erected in 1883 on the site of a wool store which had been used as a church until that time.

St.Mary's Episcopal Cathedral: This cathedral was founded as a counterpart to St.Giles and was begun in 1874 to plans by Sir George Gilbert Scott. Completed in 1917, it is the largest Gothic church built in Scotland since the Middle Ages and has a 275 ft tower.

Holyrood Palace: This palace was built by James V, the father of Mary Queen of Scots, in order to provide a building to succeed the guest house belonging to the monastery. He had the NW tower house built in 1528-32. At that time, it had round towers at its four corners, and also battlements. These were adjoined by a modest W. wing. It is in this tower house that the historic apartments of Mary Queen of Scots and Lord Darnley are situated, and also the secret stairway by which Rizzio's murderers entered. After James VI moved to England in 1603, the palace was never a royal residence again for any length of time. In 1650, Cromwell occupied the building, and Charles II rebuilt it in 1671-9, expanding it to its present size. The plans for this were the work of Sir William Bruce, and the work was supervised by Robert Mylne. In the course of this

work, a SW tower was added and connected to the NW tower by a two-storeyed central section with a balustrade. The portal of this section is framed by twin Doric columns and a small dome with a royal crown. The façades of the inner courtyard are classically articulated, being divided in three and decorated with Doric, Ionic and Corinthian pilasters. Although Charles II never lived in this palace, it was decorated in the very best possible style of the time. The Dutch artist Jakob de Wet painted the ceilings, while the lavishly decorated door frames and fireplaces are the work of Jan Vansantvoort. The tapestries came from Brussels and Paris, while most of the furniture is Scottish. The picture gallery is also the work of Jakob de Wet, who painted the 'portraits' of 111 Scottish monarchs within the course of three years. Their similarity is due less to historical veracity than to the fact that the painter had no copies to paint from. Prince Charles Edward Stuart held court in the palace in autumn 1745 because the gates of Edinburgh Castle remained closed to him. Now the palace is the Queen's official residence when she visits Edinburgh. Some of the present decorations date from the time of Charles II, whereas the State rooms were completely refurbished under George V. They are now decorated with French and Flemish tapestries and 18C furniture. Lord Darnley's rooms in the old N. tower (an audience room, a bedroom and a dressing room) were decorated when the palace was rebuilt under Charles II. The rooms of Mary Queen of Scots (bedroom, dressing room and audience room) were similarly treated; only the oak ceilings still date from Mary's reign.

Royal Mile: The Royal Mile connects the two chief attractions of old Edinburgh. To the W. is the castle, the symbol of temporal

Edinburgh Castle, Royal Palace

John Knox's House

power exercised by the Sovereign, and to the E. is the abbey, the symbol of divine power exercised by the Church. People of influence established their residences along the connecting line between the two. Since it was so important to live here, the number of storeys in these houses, which were known as 'Lands', rose from 10 to 15 in the 17C, making them the first high-rise buildings in Europe. The course of the Royal Mile has not changed in 800 years, even though it is now made up of sections bearing four different names: Castle Hill, Lawnmarket, High Street and Canongate. From W. to E., the most important buildings in the Royal Mile are: *Riddle's Court*, on the S.side of Lawnmarket, formerly belonged to John MacMarren, a city treasurer who was shot dead by a schoolboy in 1595 because he planned to shorten the holidays of the Royal High School by one day. The

philosopher David Hume later lived here (1711–76). Coming immediately after this is *Brodie's Close*, the house of William Brodie, the clergyman who made notable efforts on the city's behalf as a city councillor by day, and 'earned' extra wages as a burglar by night. He was discovered attempting to plunder the city tax office, and in 1788 had the benefit of the improved gallows, the use of which he had himself previously advocated on the city council. Not even his iron collar, which he hoped would preserve him, could save him from death. But he became immortal as the hero of a novel when Robert Louis Stevenson modelled Dr.Jekyll and Mr.Hyde on him. *Gladstone's Land* on the N.side of Lawnmarket is the best example of a 17C Edinburgh town house. This house, with its arcaded ground floor, its outdoor staircase, its crowstep gables and its painted ceilings,

Sarcophagus

has contemporary furniture and is now in the care of the National Trust. A fact of particular interest is that it has two exterior walls. One of the Gladstones extended the house in 1617, and in so doing simply incorporated the old outside wall and its windows into the new house. Another early-17C building is *Lady Stair's House* (1622). Today it contains collections of manuscripts by Robert Burns, Sir Walter Scott and Robert Louis Stevenson. Near the W. portal of St. Giles Cathedral, *The Heart of Midlothian*, a heart-shaped pattern in the street, marks the entrance to the old *town hall* built in 1466, which, under the name of the 'Old Tolbooth', was the setting for the opening of Scott's 'Heart of Midlothian'. Behind the cathedral is *Parliament House*, where the Scottish parliament met from 1639 until its dissolution in 1707. The parliament hall has a beautiful

dragon-beam ceiling and fine paintings. The large S. window shows the ceremonial appointment of the Court of Session by James V in 1532. *John Knox's House*, one of the most picturesque buildings in Old Edinburgh, is on the N. side of the High Street. This building (1490) was John Knox's residence in 1561–72, and was for a time used as a clergyman's house by the Tolbooth parishioners. It was from here that the Reformer began the movement which turned Scotland into what T.S. Eliot described as a 'country ruined by religion'. In contrast to the churches cleared out by John Knox, the Renaissance decoration of his house is still largely intact. The wooden galleries and an oak ceiling painted in *c.* 1600 are especially fine. *Moray House*, on the S. side of Canongate, was built in 1628. Charles I lived here, and Cromwell made it his headquarters. The Treaty of Union of England and Scotland was signed in the garden house of this building in 1707. On the N. side of Canongate is *Canongate Tolbooth,* the old town hall of the parish of Canongate. This parish was founded by David I in 1143 and remained independent until 1856. It has a clock and bell tower built in 1591. Inside, the great hall was used as a council chamber and court; in the basement there were prison cells. Today the city uses it for exhibitions. *White Horse Close* forms a worthy end to Canongate before the latter leads into the square outside Holyrood Palace. The former 17C stagecoach inn was the point of departure for the journey to London. Outstandingly restored in 1965, it consists of a group of typical 17C buildings arranged around a long courtyard.

New Town: Edinburgh's neoclassical New Town is the result of a competition to plan a suburb organized by the city council in 1766. The prize was won a year later by 26-year-old James Craig, who employed a very simple basic concept: a straight street (George Street) running along the ridge of a hill opposite the castle rock was to be flanked to the N. and S. by parallel streets, while to the E. and W. there was to be a square, each square having a church. One of the churches was to be dedicated to St. Andrew, the other to St. George: a symbol of the union of Scotland and England. Within this rectangle, the streets running lengthwise repeat this imagery and are called Thistle Street and Rose Street. The houses were all planned so as to open away from the hillside, and the view southwards from Princes Street to the castle and old city was to remain free, as was the view from Queen Street northwards to the Firth of Forth. This is the reason why Princes Street today still only has houses on its N. side. The Georgian New Town, with an

St. Giles' Cathedral ▷

area of over 740 acres, is today the largest classified historical monument in Great Britain, and rightly so, because it was probably only by placing it under a preservation order that this unique combination of Georgian suburb and medieval old city could be conserved. The most important buildings in the New Town are: the *Register House* at the E. end of Princes Street, which was built in 1774–89 to plans by Robert Adam and finally completed by Robert Reid in 1827. The house contains the main Scottish archive, with documents dating back to the 13C. The *Scott Monument* on the S. side of Princes Street was built in 1844 to a design by George Meikle Kemp. This neo-Gothic monument is 195 ft. tall, and its central feature is a statue (by Sir John Steell, 1846) of Sir Walter Scott and his dog. The numerous niches contain over 60 figures from Scott's novels and ballads. The monument may be climbed. *Charlotte Square* at the W. end of George Street is undoubtedly the most beautiful square in the whole New Town. This square, which has fortunately survived in its entirety, dates back to a design

by Robert Adam in 1791. It was named after George III's queen. Everything is still as the architect planned it, from the classical façades through the pavements (which are arranged to make it easier to enter a coach) to the street lamps. Not for nothing is the N. side of the square regarded as being among the finest street fronts in Europe. Neither is it mere chance that the National Trust of Scotland has its headquarters here (No.5). The Trust has fortunately also acquired No.7, and this offers the visitor an excellent impression of a late-18C interior.

Museums:

National Portrait Gallery of Scotland (Dublin Street): Founded in 1882, the purpose being, as the official description has it, to display Scottish history by showing the portraits of its main figures. The gallery contains a brilliant collection of portraits of prominent Scots from the mid 16C up to the present day. The painters include artists such as Reynolds, Gainsborough, Epstein and Kokoschka.

Museum of Childhood

National Museum of Antiquities: Housed in the same building as the National Portrait Gallery, it offers an outstanding cross-section of the cultural history of Scotland from the Neolithic period up to the beginning of modern times. The museum was founded as long ago as 1781.

Royal Scottish Museum (Chambers Street): This museum displays sculptures from all over the world, and also an archaeological, ethnological, geological, technological and scientific collection. Its scope ranges from early forms of art to the technology of space travel. This is Great Britain's largest combined science and art museum, although it does not include paintings.

National Gallery of Scotland (Mound Street): Housed in a building built by William Henry Playfair in 1845–58 in classical Greek style, it is one of Europe's major art galleries. Apart from an extensive collection of Scottish paintings, the museum also has excellent works from England and the Continent, ranging from Rubens to Van Gogh.

National Library of Scotland (Cowgate): Founded in 1682 by the university's faculty of law. Since 1710 it has been a copyright library, receiving a copy of every book published in Great Britain. Its most valuable treasure is a Gutenberg Bible dating from 1456.

Other museums worth seeing:
The *Wax Museum* in the High Street (No.142) was established in 1976. It has over 100 waxworks of important historical figures. The *Museum of Childhood* is also in the High Street, opposite John Knox's House. This museum has a unique collection of historical toys, books, pictures and items of furniture from several centuries. Particular emphasis is placed on children's education and children's art. *Huntly House,* opposite Canongate Tolbooth, dates from the 16C and contains important exhibits connected with local history. The *Gallery of Modern Art* stands in the grounds of the Botanical Garden and displays 20C paintings, sculptures and drawings, the emphasis being on modern Scottish art.

Edinburgh Castle, screen

St. Giles' Cathedral, royal coat-of-arms

Environs: Craigmillar Castle (4 m. SE): This castle was one of Mary Queen of Scots's favourite places of residence. The inner section of the building is an L-shaped tower house built in 1374, with a great hall on the first floor with four staircases leading up to it. In 1427 a curtain wall was added with round corner towers, the earliest such arrangement in Scotland. The English led by Hertford destroyed the castle in 1544, but the Stuarts immediately rebuilt it. The living quarters, which are not part of the core of the castle, date from the 17C.

Cramond (6 m. N.): This little coastal town was founded by the Romans and was known as Caer Almond at that time. The camp on the mouth of the River Almond was built in *c.* 142 AD at the behest of Emperor Antoninus Pius, the builder of the Antonine Wall. Septimius Severus probably used it in 208 as the starting-point for his punitive expedition against NE Scotland. The walls, about 5 ft. high, of a *Roman house* have survived. The coins, pottery and other finds which have been excavated are now on display in the *Huntly House Museum*. The village also contains numerous well-preserved 18C houses.

Dalmeny (9 m. NW): This is the site of the best-preserved Norman *parish church* in Scotland and is still used as such today. With the exception of the tower, whose predecessor fell down in the 15C, and also of the transept, it is 12C. Note the richly decorated S. portal with its 5-arched arcade, the semicircular apse and the two round chancel arches with their chevrons, a motif which is repeated in the round window arches.

Lauriston Castle (4 m. NW): This castle does not merely provide a good view of the Firth of Forth. The oldest section, a tower house with corner turrets and crowstep gables, was built around 1590 for Archibald Napier, whose son John introduced logarithms. The castle was later

Edinburgh, St. Margaret's Chapel

lived in by John Law (1671–1728), who founded the Bank of France, was the French minister of finance, and went bankrupt.

After 1823, the castle was enlarged by Thomas Allan, and some of the furniture installed at that time may still be seen today. Other items on display are Flemish wall hangings, pottery, and 17&18C paintings.

Eilean Donan Castle
Highlands/Scotland   p.324□F 6

Eilean Donan stands on a small rocky island at the strategically important intersection of three sea-lochs (Loch Duich, Loch Long and Loch Alsh). From the land, the castle can only be reached by a small stone bridge. This sea-girt 13C castle has had a most eventful history. After the defeat of the Norwegian King Haakon (1263), the castle fell to the Earls of Desmond and then the Earl of Moray, who was in the habit of decorating the battlements of his castle with his opponents' severed heads. For two centuries it was the family seat firstly of the MacKenzies, and then of the Huntly family. In the spring of 1719, three English warships razed the castle to the ground with their gunfire. It was not until 1912–32 that it was rebuilt in its original form, and today its romantic exterior makes it probably one of the most-photographed castles in the whole of Scotland.

Elgin
Grampian/Scotland   p.324□H 6

Nothing about this small city hints at its eventful history. The former centre of the 'Garden of Moray', it had a splendid cathedral when Alexander Stewart, the brother of King Robert III, began pursuing his evil practices in the NE of Scotland. Punished for this by being excommunicated by the bishop, the 'Wolf of Badenoch' took his revenge by setting fire not only to the church but to the whole city. The city was alight again in 1452, and the followers of John Knox later wreaked almost as much havoc as Cromwell's troops were to do. The ruins of the cathedral are an eloquent testimony to this devastation.

Cathedral: Founded in 1224, the double side-aisles are not original features, and the church had only a simple timber ceiling. After a fire in 1270, it was rebuilt all the more splendidly. In accordance with the French model, there were double side-aisles, and the chancel and sanctuary were lengthened and provided with side-aisles and stone vaults. The octagonal chapter-house was connected to the N. aisle of the choir, and the raised chancel ends in a double row of early Gothic lancet windows. The chancel was separated from the nave by a rood screen. The tower over the crossing was taller than the spires of the twin-towered façade. It was to this massive central tower that the cathedral owed its title of the 'Lantern of the North'. After the cathedral's completion, its bishop was probably right in asserting: 'My church was the ornament of the realm, the glory of the kingdom, the delight of foreigners.' After the fire, the cathedral was once again completely rebuilt and decorated with rich interior furnishings, most of which came from France and Flanders. All this splendour was destroyed by the iconoclasts of the Reformation. The final collapse of the cathedral began in 1567 when the Duke of Moray had the lead removed from the roof in order to pay his mercenaries. However, the death throes of the proud building lasted until Easter Sunday 1711, when the central tower fell down, bringing the walls and arcades of the nave down with it. Only

Eilean Donan Castle ▷

the chapterhouse has remained comparatively undamaged throughout the centuries.

Bishop's House: The town residence of the Bishop of Moray, built in 1406, formerly stood to the SW of the cathedral. The coats of arms of Bishop Patrick Hepburn (1535–73) and of Robert Reid (1541–58), the Bishop of Orkney and Abbot of Kinloss, both still survive.

Spynie Palace: The ruins of this feudal bishop's castle to the N. of Elgin bear witness to the former power of the bishops, who were often also the advisers of the Scottish king. The stone tower, built in *c.* 1470, is an impressive feature.

Environs: Craigellachie (7 m. SE): To the N. of this little village is one of the finest early-19C bridges. Built by Thomas Telford, it dates from 1812. He ordered the middle section, which is about 160 ft. long, to be cast in Wales, which caused a technical sensation at the time.
Dufftown (10 m. SE): Here the visitor can

see 'what it is that makes a Scotch man happy'—no exaggeration, given that the whisky capital of the Highlands 'stands on seven stills'. The finest example for the visitor is the Grant's Balvenie distillery, where not only the modern whisky distillery, but also the original 19C plant, is on view.

Ely
Cambridgeshire/England   p.328☐L 1

This small city on the W. bank of the Ouse derives its name from 'eel island'. It stands on an island some 9 m. long surrounded by what was inaccessible marshland which could only be crossed with guides who knew the area, and then only at certain times. Hereward the Wake retreated to this narrow ridge of land when fleeing from William the Conqueror and the Normans.

Ely Cathedral 1 W. portal (Galilee porch) **2** SW transept **3** former cloister **4** Monks' Door **5** sacristy **6** S.tranept **7** octagon (over the crossing) **8** N. transept **9** St. Edmund's Chapel **10** Lady Chapel **11** St. Etheldreda's shrine

Elgin, Cathedral, ruins

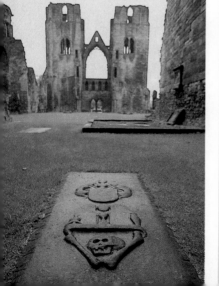

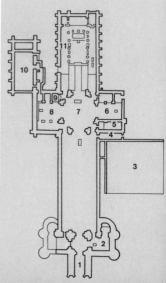

and there he held out until in 1071 a path specially built across the marsh on bundles of brushwood enabled him to escape.

Cathedral: Its history dates back to the year 673 when St.Etheldreda, the queen of Northumbria, founded a monastery here and became its abbess. Abbot Simeon began building the present church in 1083. The E. end and the two transepts were completed by 1106, and three years later the church became a cathedral. The Norman nave was finally completed *c.* 1190. Bishop Eustace had the W. portal, the *Galilee Porch,* built in the early 13C, and from 1229 onwards Bishop Hugh of Northwold lengthened the choir by adding six Early English bays, whose purpose was to provide a more appropriate setting for the shrine of St.Etheldreda. The Norman tower over the crossing collapsed in 1322 and destroyed some sections of the W. choir. Alan de Walsingham replaced it by a magnificent Gothic *octagon,* and built the three W. bays of the present choir in Gothic style. Seen from the outside, the finest section of the cathedral is certainly the *W. façade* with the lavish *Galilee Porch,* the *W. tower* and the small *SW transept.* The exterior of the octagonal tower over the crossing is also one of the high points of medieval architecture.

The interior creates an overwhelming impression of size. Because of its height, the nave, with its 12 late Norman *bays* built between 1106 and 1189, does not feel ponderous, but rather gives a foretaste of the Gothic style which is to come. This impression is only slightly disturbed by the painted ceiling which was added in the 19C instead of the original, undecorated wooden one. The aisle windows have also not survived untouched. On the N. side the windows are Gothic, whereas the original Norman form has been restored on the S. side. On the other hand, the various *portals* have not been altered: these are the *Prior's Doorway* (1140), the *Monks' Door* and the *S. portal.* The oldest section of the cathedral is the *transept,* built from 1083 to 1107. The original painted roof survives in the S. transept, while St. Edmund's Chapel in the N. transept has a 12C fresco depicting the martyrdom of St.Edmund.

Ely, Cathedral

By far the most beautiful part of the cathedral is the famous *octagon* above the crossing. The crossing is formed of four wide and four narrow arches. The *lantern* built of oak (the oak for the corner posts, which are a good 65 ft. long, was collected from all parts of the kingdom) is among the finest examples of English Gothic. The stellar vault of the lantern appears to be suspended weightlessly. E. of the crossing, the *choir* is separated off by a 19C screen. The choir has numerous monuments dating back to the 12C. The *Lady Chapel* was begun in 1320 and completed in 1353. It is not attached to the E. of the church proper, as would otherwise usually be the case, but to the NE corner of the N. aisle.

King's School: The history of this school, which was refounded in 1543, goes back to the time when King Edward the Confessor (1042–66) attended the monastery school in Ely.

Today the school uses the remains of the monastery buildings and the *Prior's House* with its Gothic *Prior Grauden's Chapel*, which was built in 1321–41 and has a fine 13C crypt. Another part of the school is in *Ely Porta*, the large S. gatehouse, whose construction was begun in 1397. The large 14C *tithe barn* is today the school dining-room. The headmaster lives in a 12C house with a fine Norman portal.

Ennis
Clare/Ireland   p.326 □ B 12

This, the county town of Clare, has some 6,000 inhabitants and stands N. of the N. arm of the Shannon (the Gaelic word 'ennis' means 'shore'). The town has preserved its ancient appearance, with narrow alleyways and buildings from the 18&19C.

Ennis Abbey (Church Street): The ruined

Franciscan monastery was founded by the king of Thomond in 1240 (with later additions). The surviving features of the *church* are the tall *tower* above the *transept* (both 15C), and the fine *E. window*, which has five sections and a pointed arch (13C). There are also the *cloister* and some good 15C *carvings*, especially the *king's tomb* (the MacMahon tomb) which has a relief of the Passion dating from *c.* 1470. Some 600 pupils and 300 monks lived in the monastery in its heyday in the 14&15C.

Also worth seeing: The classical *Court House* dates from 1852. Daniel O'Connell, the well-known campaigner for Irish independence, was active in Ennis from 1828–31 as an M.P. for Clare. In the town centre there is a *column* dedicated to him, with a statue.

Environs: Clare Abbey (also known as Killone Abbey, about 1 m. S.): Ruins of the *Augustinian abbey*, with a well-preserved tower which is a landmark. The abbey was founded by Donal O'Brien, the King of Munster, in *c.* 1195.

Cliffs of Moher (about 25 m. NW): The cliffs rise over 800 ft. above the Atlantic. At the top of the cliffs is the *O'Brien tower* (1835), with a wonderful view of the sea.

Corrofin (about 9 m. NW): S. of here are the notable remnants of the *Abbey of St. Tula* (also known as 'Dysert O'Dea') founded in the 7/8C. The 12C Romanesque church has a fine carved S. portal, tracery windows dating from the 13&14C, and a ruined round tower. There is a good 12C limestone high cross, with a Crucifixion and linear and interlaced ornamentation.

Danganbrack (about 9 m. SE): Nearby is *Knappogue Castle*, a 16&17C tower house belonging to the MacNamara family, with a fine keep. Medieval banquets are held here in summer.

Dromoland Castle (about 6 m. SE): Now a hotel, it was built in neo-Gothic style in 1826, and stands on the site of an ancient Celtic royal castle of the O'Brien family.

Kilfenora (17 m. NW): The remains of what was an important *monastery* (seat of a bishop since 1152), with the 12C ruins of *St. Fachtna Cathedral*. The nave has been incorporated into a Protestant church, and the roofless choir is decorated with carved capitals, reliefs of bishops, and a monument (13–15C). Also of note are the three *high crosses* (12C) in the churchyard, with ornaments and figures (limestone).

Leamaneh Castle (about 14 m. NW): This ruined castle has a keep with arrow slits (15C), and a tower house with fine windows (17C). The inscription on the door (1643) refers to Conor O'Brien, the lord of the castle, his legendary wife Maire Ruadh ('Red Mary'), and Cromwell's attack in 1651.

Quin Abbey (about 6 m. SE): The *Franciscan abbey* was built *c.* 1400 on the site of a 13C *Norman castle*. With its fine arcaded cloister and its surviving walls and towers, it is among the finest Franciscan houses in Ireland. The tombs of the Mac-

Namaras are in the *church*. On the opposite bank of the river is the ruined 13C *St. Finghin's Church*.

Tulla (about 6 m. E.): Nearby, at *Magh Adhair,* are the remnants of an ancient Celtic *coronation site* for the kings of Thomond, with ramparts and ditch.

Enniscorthy
Wexford/Ireland   p.330☐D 13

This charming old trading town has some 6,000 inhabitants and an imposing 13C Norman *castle*. However, all that survives of the original fortress is the square *keep,* flanked by towers. Today this houses a museum of local history and folklore. The other buildings date from the 16&19C. The neo-Gothic *St. Aidan's Cathedral* was built about 1843.

Environs: Ferns (about 7 m. NE): This small village was the capital of Leinster before the arrival of the Normans. St. Edan founded a monastery here in the 6C. After being destroyed, it was rebuilt as an Au-

Quin Abbey (Ennis)

Dromoland Castle (Ennis)

gustinian priory in *c*. 1160. Some remains of the monastery church with its rectangular bell tower (later completed as a round tower with fine pointed arches) can still be seen. The Protestant *cathedral* (1817) was built on the site of a 13C Norman church which was burned down in 1577. The Norman *Ferns Castle*, standing on the site of the old residence of the kings of Leinster, also dates from the 13C. Some sections of the castle—its fine central keep and chapel, and also the SE tower and several corner towers—are still in good condition.

Enniskillen
Fermanagh/Northern Ireland   p.326□D 10

This charming holiday resort, the county town of Fermanagh, has a population of about 8,000 and lies on the river Erne, the river connecting Upper Lough Erne wit Lower Lough Erne. It is today sti regarded as the centre of the Anglo Protestant 'planters', who settled here i the 17C. A 15C *keep* and the *water gate* da ing from 1580, with a *museum*, still surviv from the *castle* of the Maguires. The Pro estant *cathedral* dates from the 17&18C an houses the *colours* of the famous royal reg ments of Enniskillen. To the W. are *Po tora Royal School*—founded in 1608, it i rich in tradition and has buildings datin from 1777—and *Portora Castle* (1615). T the S., on the shore of Lough Coole, is th neoclassical *Castle Coole*, built by J.Wya in *c*. 1785, with fine stucco and charmin grounds.

Environs: Caldragh (about 22 m. NW on Boa Island): Strange, probably paga *stone sculptures* (statue of Janus) from th 5&6C (by the village graveyard).
Crom Castle (about 22 m. SE): This ca tle on the E. shore of Upper Lough Ern dates from about 1611, at the time of th 'planters'; a new house was built here i the 18C after a fire.
Florence Court (about 9 m. SW): Thi castle was built for the Earls of Coole (fro Enniskillen) in about 1760.
Killadeas (about 7 m. N.): In the grav yard are interesting 7&8C *stone sculpture* including the 'Bishop's Stone'.
Tully Castle (about 16 m. NW): Thes ruins on the W. shore of Lower Loug Erne date from about 1610, during th time of the plantations. Nearby, on *Inis macsaint Island* in the lough, are a 11&12C ruined church with a simple hig cross (without a wheel).
White Island (about 12 m. NW): On thi island is a 12C *ruined church*, with Romanesque S. portal and fine stone carv ings (clergymen, warriors, sacrificia animals) dating from the 8&9C, some wit pagan motifs. On the mainland, on the shore, are the ruins of *Old Castle Archda* (1615), and additions (1773).

Enniscorthy, view of town

Evesham
Hereford and Worcester/
England   p.332□H 14

This little town in the Avon valley grew up round a large and rich *Benedictine abbey,* founded in the 8C. All that survives of the abbey today are some 11C foundations, some Norman remains, and the bell tower of 1533. The free-standing *tower* is an outstanding example of late Gothic. It was in 1265, to the N. of the town, that the battle took place in which Prince Edward, later to become King Edward I, defeated Simon de Montfort. An obelisk erected in 1845 commemorates the battle. In the former garden of the abbey, on the site where the high altar formerly stood, is a memorial stone to Simon de Montfort, who is buried here.

Almonory Museum: This museum in a 14C half-timbered house displays exhibits from Roman and Saxon times, and also from the Middle Ages.

Environs: Bredon (12 m. SW): The *Church of St. Giles* dates mainly from the 12C, and like most Norman churches it has a central tower. Inside, some medieval tombs and remains of 15C glass are the chief items of interest. There is a sizeable 17C monument, richly decorated with columns, cherubim and heraldic ornamentation.
Pershore (11 m. W.): The remains of the *abbey church* today serve as a parish church, and are dedicated to the Holy Cross. It dates back to a Benedictine abbey which existed as long ago as the early 10C and was probably originally built for St.Eadburga. Edward the Confessor seized a large part

of the abbey's revenues in order to finance the building of Westminster Abbey. The choir, the crossing with the massive central tower, and the S. transept, still survive from this once proud abbey church. The Lady Chapel and the nave were destroyed after the dissolution of the monasteries, and the N. transept fell down in the 17C. The choir dates from 1223 in its present form, the vaulting from the early 14C. The early Gothic tower, built c. 1330, rests on massive Norman arches, and has four lancet windows on each side of its top storey. The pinnacles at each corner are of later date. Impressive features in the interior are the vaults in the side aisles, the fine triforium, and the clerestory built in 1239.
Wickhamford (2 m. SE): The Parliamentary troops, led by Colonel Henry Washington, defeated the Royalists here in 1646. The Colonel belonged to the same family as George Washington, the first President of the United States. The coat of arms of the Washington family, with its three stars and two stripes, served as a model for the American national flag. This *coat of arms* can still be seen above the tomb of Penelope Washington, the Colonel's daughter, in the church of Wickhamford.

Exeter
Devon/England   p.332☐G 16

This, the county town of Devon, was the Roman *Isca Dumnoniorum* founded in c. AD 50, and under the name of *Escancestre* it was the capital of the kingdom of Wessex. There was a monastery with a Saxon abbey here in c. 680, and in c. 876 the Danes stormed the town for the first time. They succeeded in doing this again in 1003, and in 1068 the town, which had in the meantime been fortified, had to submit to William the Conqueror after a fairly long siege. Exeter became a diocesan city

in 1050, and in 1205 it was given its first mayor. In 1497 Perkin Warbeck besieged the city. During the Civil War it changed hands several times. William III was crowned within its walls in 1688. Most of the medieval part of the city was reduced to ashes in May 1942.

Cathedral: Athelstan founded it in 932 as a monastery church dedicated to St Peter. In 1112-1206 a large Norman church was built, whose two sturdy *towers* were incorporated into the transept of the present cathedral. Work on altering and enlarging the Norman church began at the S. end c. 1270 under the supervision of Bishop Bronescombe. The *W.façade*, with its lower tier of carved figures, was completed a little less than 100 years later, c. 1360. The upper series of figures was not added until the late 15C, when the upper section of the towers were also rebuilt and heightened. The *rows of figures* on the W. façade reflect the medieval scheme of things: the Evangelists, the Apostles, the Patriarchs and Prophets are assembled around King Athelstan, Athelbert, Alfred and William. Inside the cathedral, the visitor is captivated by the simplicity of the Decorated design. The massive clustered columns, standing close together, combined with the narrowly fanned vault and the stone choir screen dating from 1320, result in a subtly graduated spatial effect. Opposite the entrance on the N. side is the impressive *Minstrels' Gallery* built by Bishop Grandison, where angels are seen playing various musical instruments. In the SW corner is the flag from the sledge of Captain Scott, the great Antarctic explorer (1868-1912). In the *N. transept*, which is the ground floor of the Norman *St.Paul's Tower*, there is a 15C fresco of the Resurrection. The life-size statue of the painter James Northcote (1746-1831) is by Chantrey. The early Gothic *chapterhouse*, with its ceiling completed in 1478, adjoins the S. transept which contains the tomb of Hugh Courtenay

ay, Earl of Devon, who died in 1377. The
finest furnishings in the cathedral are in
the *choir*. The choir stalls themselves are
Victorian, but the misericords dating from
about 1250 have fortunately survived.
They are the oldest in England and depict
such secular motifs as a king sitting in boil-
ing water. The bishop's throne is a most
unusual masterpiece: it is some 60 ft. high,
was completed *c*. 1320 and is decorated
with an abundance of carved animal and
human heads. Numerous monuments to
the important bishops of Exeter are another interesting feature of the choir. There
are more such monuments in the *Lady
Chapel*, including that to Bishop Bronescombe, who began the rebuilding of the cathedral.

The *cathedral library* is housed in a wing
of the rebuilt bishop's palace. It contains
some Saxon manuscripts, but its greatest

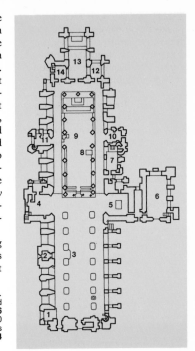

Exeter Cathedral 1 St. Edmund's Chapel 2 N.
portal 3 Minstrels' Gallery 4 St. Paul's Tower and
N. transept 5 St. John's Tower and S. transept 6
chapterhouse 7 sacristy 8 bishop's throne, 1320
9 choir 10 St. James's Chapel 11 St. Andrew's
Chapel 12 St. Gabriel's Chapel 13 Lady Chapel 14
St. John the Evangelist's Chapel

Exeter, Cathedral, fan vaulting

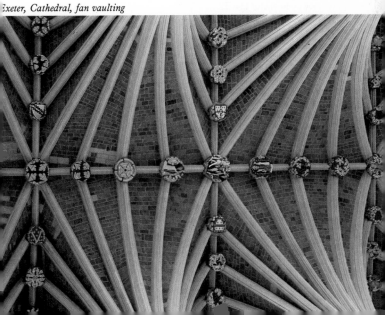

treasure is the *Codex Exoniensis*. This manuscript written between 950 and 1000 is the most extensive single source of Old English poetry from the Anglo-Saxon period. This manuscript was presented to the library by Bishop Leofric.

St.Nicholas Priory: The following still survive: the crypt completed in 1087, a 13C kitchen, a guest room with ceiling frescos, and the 15C tower. The garden is decorated by a 7C Celtic cross.

Guildhall: Mentioned in a document dating from 1160, and therefore regarded as the oldest municipal building in England. Its oldest sections were built in *c.* 1330, and the great hall was completed in 1464. The building is chiefly impressive for its splendidly worked corbels and the wainscots dating from 1594.

Museums: The *Royal Albert Memorial Museum and Art Gallery* is devoted to art, natural history and local handicrafts. There are silver and pottery, and local costumes dating from about 1750 onwards. The most important works in the picture gallery are by Reynolds and Turner. The *Rougemont House Museum* illustrates the county's history and prehistory. The *Maritime Museum*, which is housed in some old warehouses on the river bank, deals with the history of shipping.

Environs: Crediton (9 m. NW): This is the birthplace of St.Boniface (673–754), the apostle of the Germans, who is buried in Fulda. From 909 to 1050 it was the diocesan seat of the counties of Devon and Cornwall. The *Church of the Holy Cross* dates from the 8C and has a Norman font. The crossing, the central tower, and parts of the choir, date from the 12C.
Cullompton (12 m. NE): The *Church of St.Andrew* is a well-built Gothic church with a magnificent W. tower dating from 1545. The gargoyles and turrets are outstanding. Impressive features inside are the clerestory and the beautifully vaulted second aisle, donated by John Lane in 1525.
Tiverton (16 m. N.): Only two towers still remain of the *castle* built by the first Earl of Devon in *c.* 1105. The massive gatehouse on the E. side dates from the 14C. The *Church of St.George* is 15C, but was extensively restored in the 19C. The rich decoration of the Greenway Chapel, which dates from 1517, bears witness to the profitability of the wool trade. The richly decorated Gothic S. portal of 1517 was donated by John Greenway. *Blundell's School* (1604) was also founded by a rich clothier. Some 2 m. NE is *Knightshayes Court*, built about 1870 by the architect William Burges; it has a fine collection of pictures.

Exeter, Cathedral, W. window

Falkland Palace
Fife/Scotland   p.324□H 8

The oldest parts of the Stuarts' hunting lodge date from the time of King James III (1460–88), although there was probably an earlier building on the site, for an escutcheon at the gatehouse—with the red lion of the Earl of Fife of the house of Macduff —shows that there was a castle here from 1120. The red lion of Scotland was first associated with the place in 1437, when James II took over the castle. After variou alterations the three-winged building ac quired its present form (1530–40). Mar Stuart often stayed here. Charles II (163 –85) was the last monarch to live in the pa ace. He handed it over to the administra tion of the Marquis of Bute, whose famil

Falkland Palace, Stuart hunting lodge

transferred it to the National Trust in 1952. The *S. wing*, built by James IV and converted by his son, was restored by the Marquis of Bute in 1887 and made habitable again. Its façades are an indication of its architectural history: the street front is still Gothic, while the façades looking on to the courtyard (1537–42) are articulated in the French manner—elegant early Renaissance columns and medallions with heads. The *Chapel Royal* is also in the S. wing. Built 1501 – 12, it is furnished with Flemish tapestries and has a ceiling repainted in 1633. Also very fine are the royal stalls with their delicate columns and arches, and the oak panelling behind the altar. Mary Stuart's father died in the *King's Bed Chamber*, in the central part of the E. wing. Recently, this room has been reconstructed to contemporary plans and it has a gilded four-poster from the time of James VI. The *gatehouse* with its two round towers looks more war-like than it is—interestingly, it was built some two years after the tennis court in the park. The latter, built in 1539, is the second-oldest surviving royal tennis court, after that of Hampton Court. The

gardens, although referred to as early as the 15C, did not acquire their present form until after 1628.

Farnham

Surrey/England   p.332☐K 15

This flourishing town originated as part of the estate of the Bishop of Winchester. A few interesting Georgian houses are preserved in West Street; the most beautiful are *Willmer House* (1718) and *Sandford House* (1757).

Farnham Castle: The Romanesque *keep* was begun in 1138 by Henry of Blois, nephew of William the Conqueror and brother of King Stephen, after he had become Bishop of Winchester. However, in 1155 Henry II knocked down everything Henry of Blois had built and today only the foundations of this massive tower remain. The castle proper was started around 1170. The *Great Hall*, completed around 1175 and restored in 1677, has survived,

Falkland Place, royal coat-of-arms

Gatehouse

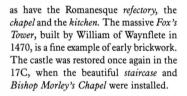

Farnham, half-timbered house

Faversham, Guildhall

as have the Romanesque *refectory*, the *chapel* and the *kitchen*. The massive *Fox's Tower*, built by William of Waynflete in 1470, is a fine example of early brickwork. The castle was restored once again in the 17C, when the beautiful *staircase* and *Bishop Morley's Chapel* were installed.

Farnham Museum: Housed in Willmer House, which is Georgian; it contains a collection of archaeological finds, 17&18C furniture, and local history exhibits.

Environs: Aldershot (*c.* 3 m. NE): This little town did not achieve importance until 1855, when it acquired a large garrison. Its three museums are devoted to aspects of military history. The *Airborne Forces Museum* contains paratroop equipment from the last 60 years. The *Royal Army Dental Corps Museum* traces the development of

dental care in the army since 1620. The *Royal Army Medical Corps Historical Museum* documents the development of medical care in the army.

Church Crookham (*c.* 4 m. N.): Lord Harding opened the *Gurkha Museum* here in 1974. It contains mementoes of Gurkha regiments from 1815 onwards.

Haslemere (*c.* 12.5 m. S.): Of interest here, apart from a few Georgian *houses*, is the *Educational Museum*. Set up in 1888, it is devoted principally to geology, zoology and history. Of particular interest is its collection of British birds. Arnold Dolmetsch's collection of old English musical instruments is housed in *Jesses House*; the Dolmetsch Festival is an annual event during which early music is played on original instruments.

Waverley (*c.* 2.5 m. S.): England's first *Cistercian Abbey* was built here in 1128 in

Faversham, St. Mary of Charity

14C wall painting

a style of the utmost simplicity. Now only part of the transept remains.

Faversham
Kent/England   p.332□L 15

This picturesque little town has its roots in both Roman and Saxon settlements.

Church of St. Mary of Charity: Built on a cross-shaped ground plan with Norman arcades and windows and an 18C bell tower. Inside, 14C *wall paintings* have survived on one of the pillars; the fine *carvings* date from the 15C.

Ospringe Church: This little church with a modern tower was built in the 13C.

Also worth seeing: The town's most

beautiful *old houses,* dating from the time of the Tudors and Stuarts, can be seen in Abbey Street and in the market square, where the *Guildhall* (Tudor, restored 1814) also stands. Also worth mentioning is *Arden's House,* the home of mayor Thomas Arden, whose murder by his wife and her lover inspired the play *Arden of Faversham* (1592; claimed by some to be an early work of Shakespeare's). At *Judd's Folly Hill* there was once a Roman settlement. The *Maison Dieu* (Ospringe) now contains a Local History museum.

Environs: Lynsted (*c.* 2 m. W.): The *church of St. Peter and St. Paul* is Perpendicular and has fine tombs; beautiful Tudor houses.
Otterden Place (*c.* 5 m. S.): House from the time of Henry VIII. Closed to the public.

Fishguard/Abergwaun
Dyfed/Wales   p.330☐F 14

A little port in Fishguard Bay with about 5,000 inhabitants. It is now an important embarkation port for the ferry to Ireland. The community, divided into an upper and lower town, stems from a Norwegian foundation (11C).

Environs: Dinas Head (c. 5.5 miles NE): One of the best-preserved prehistoric camps can be seen on the spit of land called Dinas Head. Known as *Carn Ingli,* it consists of a series of stone walls between the rocky crags. Near Dinas (towards Newport) is *Cerrig-y-Gof,* with an interesting group of five burial chambers .
Llanychaer (c. 3.5 miles SE): Further remains of megalithic stone tombs are to be found at *Parc-y-Maerw.* A nearby vantage point has a splendid view of Fishguard Bay, Newport and the Dinas Head peninsula. Inland (to the SE) is the splendid scenery of the *Preseli Mountains* (Welsh: Mynydd Preseli) with a magnificent view

from *Presely Top* (Welsh: Y Foel Cwm Cerwyn), the highest point (1,962 ft).
Mynachlogddu (near Maenclochog, c. 12.5 m. SE): In the S. of the region lies the prehistoric stone circle of *Gors Fawr.* The religious circle consists of 16 stones with two outliers. Nearby there is also a church ruin on the site of the old pilgrimage place of *St. Teilo Well* (Welsh: Llandeilo), where there was formerly a healing spring.
Nevern (c. 2 m. NE of Newport): The interesting *village church* is dedicated to St. Brynach, a contemporary of St. David (6C). The church tower is of Norman origin (12C) and most of the masonry and the windows are Perpendicular (15C) (restored c. 1864 & 1952). At the entrance to the churchyard there is a mounting block, formerly used for mounting horses. Near the 19C porch is the early Celtic *Vitalianus Stone,* a fifth century tombstone with Latin and Ogham inscriptions. The *Great Cross* dates from c. 1000, is 13 ft. high and decorated with a pattern of interlaced ribbons on all four sides (to symbolize eternity). A window sill in the apse has a carved stone (5C) inscribed in Latin (fragmentary). The

Nevern (Fishguard), village church

E. front of the N. transept has a 6C votive cross, which probably came from the original Celtic pilgrimage church (on the pilgrim route to St.David's). In the S. transept is the *Maglocunus Stone* (5C) inscribed in Latin and Ogham and nearby there is a stone with a bas-relief of a cross and ribbon patterns. About 200 yds W. of the church and cut into the rock next to the path is a *Pilgrim Cross* with a niche, which probably dates from 5–6C.

Newport (Welsh: Trefdraeth; *c.* 9 m. NE): This little town at the mouth of the river Nevern in Newport Bay was founded *c.* 1100. Parts of its moated 13C *castle* have survived, including the gateway with flanking tower, part of the curtain wall and a round tower, which adjoin a building of 1859.

Pen Caer: This rocky peninsula to the W. was inhabited even in prehistoric times. Numerous dolmens (prehistoric stone burial chambers), stone circles and earthworks around *Llanwnda* (*c.* 2 m. NW) and *Goodwick* (*c.* 1 m. NW) testify to this fact. In Goodwick there is also an ancient little *church* and churchyard (13–14C). A memorial stone at *Carreg Wastad Point* (NW of LLanwnda) recalls the last landing by French invading forces in 1797; these surrendered to the Welsh peasant army after 3 days. On the promontory of *Strumble Head* (*c.* 5 m. NW) lies *Gaer* (or *Garn Fawr*), one of the most remarkable prehistoric stone fortresses in Wales, with ramparts, moats and remains of stone huts. Remains of megalithic burial chambers are also to be found at *Abercastle* (*c.* 6 m. SW) on the W. coast (near Mathry). At a spot called *Carreg Samson* 3 upright stones support a massive *covering stone* (*c.* 17 x 10 ft.). According to local tradition, anyone who spends the night in such a Cromlech (barrow) will either go mad or become a poet.

Pentre Ifan (*c.* 6 m. E.): Here is one of the largest and most beautiful *dolmens* in Wales. The covering stone (*c.* 16 ft. long) is borne by supporting stones 7.5 ft high. The burial site covered an area (still easily recognizable) of *c.* 38 x 57 ft. Apart from the dolmens there are also a portal of 3 stones and stones of the semicircular forecourt. The 33 stones of Stonehenge in Wiltshire are also thought to come from the

Nevern (Fishguard), large High Cross

Fishguard

E. of the Preseli Mountains. On the ridge of the *Preseli Hills* is an ancient path called Ffordd Ffleming.

Flint
Clwyd/Wales   p.328□G 12

This coal- and lead-mining town (with chemical works) on the mouth of the River Dee played an important role in medieval times.

Castle: King Edward I of England (1272 – 1307), after his invasion of Wales (*c.* 1277), built this the first of his castles against the rebellious Welsh. He then built the castles of Rhuddlan (see Denbigh), Conwy, Beaumaris (see Anglesey), Caernarvon, Criccieth (see Lleyn Peninsula), Harlech, Bere and Aberystwyth. The ground plan of Flint Castle is roughly square with thick double walls and a tower at each corner; a tower to the S. outside the walls served as the keep and has its own protective walls and drawbridge. The castle is the setting for a scene in Act III of Shakespeare's play 'Richard II'.

Environs: Hawarden (*c.* 6 m. SE, towards Chester): Ruins of a *castle* dating from 1300 (reign of Edward I) with public park; also *Gladstone Castle* of 1752 and the *parish church* with a Gladstone monument. *St. Deiniol's Library* contains over 60, 000 volumes (including old documents). Near Hawarden are the ruins of *Ewloe Castle* from 1257 (Welsh-Norman). **Holywell** (*c.* 4 m. NW): This little town, a place of pilgrimage since ancient times (6–7C), is known as the 'Welsh Lourdes'. St. Winefride (Gwenfrewi), who was beheaded in the 7C, is honoured here. St. Winefride's Chapel, above the old healing spring, is a fine 15C late Perpendicular building (pilgrimage in June and Nov.). Nearby, towards the coast (at Holywell

Junction), are the remains of *Basingwerk Abbey*, an old Cistercian abbey of 1150 in Early English style. Parts of the S. transept and wing, cloisters with parts of the dormitory, refectory and the gatehouse have survived.

Mold (*c.* 6 m. S.): The parish church of *St. Mary* is Perpendicular from the 15C and has a beautiful roof, good stained glass and animal carvings from that time.

Northop (*c.* 3 m. S.): The church was built by the mother of Henry VII in the 15C (church tower in Somerset style, beautiful tombstones).

Whitford (*c.* 8 m. NW of Flint): Near the village stands *Maen Chwyfan* (or Achwyfan), the tallest free-standing Celtic cross in Britain. This decorated stone cross is 11 ft. high and dates from the 10–11C.

Folkestone
Kent/England   p.332□L 15/16

This former fishing and smuggling village achieved importance in the 19C as a bathing resort and Channel port.

St. Mary and St. Eanswythe: Founded by Eanswythe, granddaughter of Ethelbert, the first Christian king of Kent. The present church dates from the 13C and contains the relics of the founder in her *chapel*. A stained-glass window and a statue commemorate Folkestone's greatest son, the physician William Harvey (1578– 1657), who discovered the circulation of the blood.

Christ Church: Built in 1850, it was destroyed in an air raid of 1942. The tower was later rebuilt as a memorial.

Also worth seeing: Along *the Leas* stand Victorian hotels and guest houses. At the

Lympne Castle (Folkestone)

Folkestone, Christ Church, tower

Hythe, St. Leonards' Church

W. end is the *East Kent and Folkestone Art Centre,* a private gallery mounting consistently good exhibitions. The *Civic Centre* is a fine modern building of original design. *Caesar's Camp,* a hill to the N., provides a magnificent panoramic view. Also worth seeing is the picturesque *Old Town* around the harbour.

Environs: Hythe (*c.* 4 m. SW): This town, one of the 5 Cinque Ports, was later drawn into the line of defence against Napoleon. *St. Leonard's Church,* which dominates the town, is characterized by the splendid chancel which is considerably higher than the nave; beneath the church the crypt has human bones, whose origins are unknown.

Lympne Castle (6 m. W.): Remains of a medieval castle. *Stutfall Castle* consists of the remains of a Roman fort.

Saltwood: Just over half a mile from Hythe lie the ruins of this Norman *castle,* whence, in 1170, the four knights rode out to murder Thomas Becket.

Forth Bridges
Lothian/Fife/Scotland   p.324☐G 8

Queensferry, on the S. side of the Firth of Forth, marks the ancient ferry link used by Queen Margaret in the 11C (hence the little town's name). Hawes Pier, the old ferry pier from the last century, lies directly below the giant railway bridge. Close by is the picturesque Hawest Inn from the 17C. Old photographs inside show the building of the bridge, which is *c.* 1.5 m long. Also worth seeing is the Carmelite chapel. Founded in 1330, the present

Fort William, Inverlochy Castle

building with central tower and barrel vaulting dates from the 15C. It is the only Carmelite church in the whole of Britain to have survived the ravages of time and still to be used as a church.

Forth Railway Bridge: This massive steel construction was built with the Tay Bridge disaster of 28 December 1879 in mind. Built 1883–90 to plans by the engineers Sir John Fowler and Sir Benjamin Baker, the bridge is *c.* 2,800 yards long. The 3 main pylons are *c.* 363 ft. high and the headroom above the water is *c.* 152 ft; the two main spans are *c.* 1,757 ft. Safety was the highest priority and to this end steel tubes with a diameter of nearly 12 ft. were used for the lower compression chords alone. As inferior materials had contributed to the Tay Bridge collapse, special attention was paid to the quality of steel

used here. To this day, over 90 years after its completion, not one piece of steel has had to be replaced.

Road Bridge: The Forth Road Bridge was opened in 1964. It is nearly 2,000 yds long in all, the central span being 3,300 ft. The carriageway hangs like a filigree ribbon between the 2 slender pylons, thereby contrasting markedly with the heaviness of the old railway bridge and highlighting 70 years of technological advance.

Fort William
Scottish Highlands   p.324 □ F 7

This little town at the foot of Ben Nevis, (which at 4,406 ft. is the highest mountain in the British Isles), dates back to the time

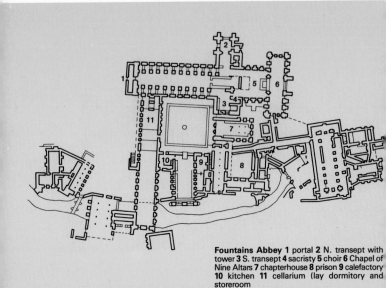

Fountains Abbey 1 portal **2** N. transept with tower **3** S. transept **4** sacristy **5** choir **6** Chapel of Nine Altars **7** chapterhouse **8** prison **9** calefactory **10** kitchen **11** cellarium (lay dormitory and storeroom

of Cromwell. In 1655 General Monck had the first stockade built. This then acquired stone walls under William of Orange in 1689. In 1715 the fortress was extended to such an extent under General Wade that the Jacobites were unable to capture it either then or 30 years later. It was not until 1864 that the fort was finally defeated —by the railway—and it was then converted to a locomotive depot. Remains of the fort are still to be found near the station.

West Highland Museum: This museum has not only a superb local history collection but also numerous Jacobite exhibits and a good tartan collection.

Inverlochy Castle: This dates back to the 13C, as does Comyn's Tower, a round tower with walls 10 ft. thick; most of the castle is 15C, however. The Earls of Mar

and Caithness lost a battle near the castle in 1431.

Neptune's Staircase: About 4.5 m. NW at the end of the **Caledonian Canal** is the first of the series of 8 locks to counter the height difference of some 67 ft. between Loch Linnhe and Loch Lochy. The canal follows the fault-block depression of Great Glen between Loch Linnhe and the Moray Firth. The series of lochs (Loch Lochy, Loch Oich and Loch Ness), like a string of pearls, made it possible for only 20 m. of the 60 m. stretch to have to be developed as a canal. The entire height difference of 108 ft. is negotiated by 29 locks. The canal, which is 17 ft. deep and 50 ft. wide, was begun by Thomas Telford in 1804 and completed in 1822. From 1834–47 it was extended again, because it could no longer cope with the traffic. Today the canal is

Fountains Abbey, ruined abbey and church

nly of importance to pleasure craft. The
echnical installations, however, are still as
nteresting as ever.

** ountains Abbey**
orth Yorkshire/England   p.328□ I 11

---

ountains Abbey (near Studley Royal):
ounded with the permission of the Arch-
ishop of York in 1132 by monks from
t.Mary's Abbey in York who wanted to
scape the latter abbey's decadence. They
dopted the Cistercian rule and were sup-
orted by Bernard of Clairvaux. In the fol-
owing period the monastery flourished
nd extended its sphere of influence over
ne surrounding areas, until, at the time
f its dissolution in 1539, in the course of
enry VIII's separation of the Church of

England from Rome, it was one of the
largest and richest monasteries in England.
Henry's plan to make the abbey the episcopal church of a new diocese in Lancashire foundered, however. In 1611 parts
of the abbey (including the hospital) were
torn down and the stone used for the building of Fountains Hall.
Today the church has survived (only the
roof is missing) along with the ruins of the
adjacent buildings; of the hospital, however, there remain only traces.
Church: Total length of 360 ft, it has a nave
with two aisles, transept and a long chancel. Pillars and arcade arches of the *nave*
are late Romanesque (transitional style).
Above the N. transept stands a 15C tower
in Perpendicular style (168 ft. high). Behind the *chancel,* with a nave and two aisles
(Early English), is the *Chapel of Nine Altars,* built 1203–47, which is also Early

Fountains Abbey, ruins

English (of interest here is the huge E. window).
Other monastery buildings: S. of the nave is the cloister, whose sides are *c.* 134 ft. long; the E. walk has 4 beautiful Norman-Romanesque *arches*, which open to the *chapterhouse* (remains of marble pillars). The E. side of the building has tombs of abbots. S. of the chapterhouse are remains of the *Base Court* and the *dormitory*, behind which (partly over the River Skell) the *hospital* used to be. S. of the cloister is the monks' *calefactory*, behind which is the former *refectory*, built predominantly in Early English style. W. of the cloister is the 335 ft. long *cellarium*, half of which was used as the dormitory for the lay brothers and the other half as a storehouse. To the W., partly built over the River Skell, are the lay brothers' *sick bay* and the *guest-house;* also of interest is the old *bridge*.

Studley Royal: An extensive park laid ou[t] in 1727 and adjacent to the abbey, it ha[s] many surprising vistas and beautiful views. Of particular interest among the building[s] and monuments are the *Octagon Tower, th[e] Temple of Piety,* a *statue of Neptune* in th[e] *Moon Pond,* and the *Temple of Fame,* i[n] front of which is a *statue group* of Hercule[s] wrestling with the giant Antaeus.

Fountains Hall (W. of the park): [A] Jacobean-Renaissance mansion, built i[n] 1611 with spoils from the abbey hospita[l]. Beautiful furniture inside, interestin[g] sculpture in the chapel (Judgement o[f] Solomon) and an old stained-glass windo[w] with coat-of-arms. In the adjoining *mu[-] seum,* there are valuable pieces from the ab[-] bey and a model of the whole abbey as i[t] was in 1539.

Framlingham
Suffolk/England   p.328 □ M 1[ ]

This old country town has a triangula[r] market place and some old houses, such a[s] the 16C *Crown Inn* and the 17C *Ancien[t] House.*

Castle: This was built *c.* 1190 by Roge[r] Bigod, 2nd Earl of Norfolk, and was th[e] most modern fortress in S. England at th[e] time. The layout included a massive *cu[r-] tain wall* with projecting square *towers.* I[n] 1215 King John captured the castle but di[d] not destroy it. In the reign of Edward [I] (1272–1307) the fortress was at its larges[t] with no fewer than 13 towers. Mary Tudo[r] resided here in 1553 until her successio[n] was finally secure. Within the old walls o[f] the ruined castle stands *Poor House,* whic[h] was formerly the Great Hall and had bee[n] converted by Pembroke Hall, Cambridg[e] in 1636, in order to fulfil the condition o[f] a legacy, which had given them possessio[n] of the castle.

Framlingham, Castle

St.Michael: This originated in its present form in the mid 15C and is predominantly Gothic. Of the preceding Early Gothic church there are just a few remains. The nave has a well-designed *dragon-beam roof.* The church contains numerous *tombs,* including that of Henry Howard, Earl of Surrey, who was hanged by Henry VIII in 1547, also that of Thomas Howard, 3rd Duke of Norfolk, and of Henry Fitzroy (bastard son of Henry VIII) and his wife Lady Mary Howard.

Environs: Dennington (*c.* 3 m. N.): The Gothic *Church of St.Mary* has a sanctuary dating from the preceding church and a W. tower. The sides of the 15C stalls are decorated with good carvings. The choir screen is 16C, as is the stained glass. The tombs in the church date back to the 15C.
Saxtead Green (*c.* 2.5 m. W.): *The Wind-*

mill is a superb example of an East Anglian post-mill, the whole mill casing of which rotates around a central axle to face the sails into the wind. The mill is completely intact and stands on historic ground—there was a mill here as early as 1309. The present mill, built in 1796, was in operation up to 1947.

Frome
Somerset/England   p.332□H 15

This little town dates back to Anglo-Saxon times and has preserved its old character with steep, narrow alleys and old stone houses. In 1685 there were many hangings here following the Duke of Monmouth's uprising. The *parish church* dates back to the 13C, but was extensively restored in 1866.

Environs: Longleat House (5 m. SE): This great country house was built from 1568 in early Renaissance style by Robert Smythson for Sir John Thynne. In 1807–11, under Sir Geoffry Wyatville, the *Stable Court* was built on, the main staircase converted and various other things altered inside. The great park was laid out by Capability Brown. The complex, one of the finest Elizabethan country houses, has a *library* with a superb collection, including a First Folio edition of Shakespeare's plays, a Fust and Schoeffer Bible of 1462, autograph letters written by Queen Elizabeth I and a charter granted to Glastonbury Abbey in 681. The house contains superb furniture, including Talleyrand's desk, on which the Treaty of Vienna was signed in 1815. Of the paintings, the most valuable is probably Titian's 'Holy Family'.

Furness Abbey
Cumbria/England   p.328□G 11

Furness Abbey: Founded in 1127 by

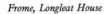

Frome, Longleat House

monks from Savigny in Normandy at the behest of Stephen, later King of England (1135–54). Around 1147 the Cistercian rule was adopted and the abbey's sphere of influence extended over the whole area N of the abbey as far as Windermere. The second largest abbey in England after Fountains Abbey, it was one of the first important English monasteries to be dissolved in the course of the Reformation. It fell into decay following the Dissolution and was destroyed by a fire. The ruins remaining today give a good impression of its architectural development from the 1–15C.

Church (main entrance through N. transept): The entire outer length is about 320 ft. It has a cross ground plan with nave, transepts and chancel; there was originally a tower over the crossing. The nave was built in Romanesque transitional style (1145–90). The remains consist of the S. wall of the S. aisle. On the ground there are the remains of nave *pillars* (9 on the N. side, 5 on the S. side; alternately round and bundled). Walls between the aisles and transept show the original height of the roof. At the E. end of the N. aisle there are a few unusual carved *plaques* and at the E. end of the nave there are ground traces of the former *chancel wall*. In front of the nave to the W. is a keep-like *tower* in late Gothic Perpendicular style, which has a beautiful late Gothic W. window (the tower may be climbed by a stair). Of the original four pointed arches which bore the crossing tower, only that on the chancel side has survived. The E. wall of the *transept* is adorned with beautiful pointed arches supported by bundle columns; of the *c.* 33 ft high *window* of the N. transept there remains just the frame; beneath this there is a beautiful four-layered *portal*. The best preserved part of the church is the *chancel*: In the S. wall there are four superb sedilia (priest seats let into the wall), roofed by high Gothic baldachinos in Decorated Style; next to these, also roofed by a bal dachino of the same style is the piscina (basin for washing the Communion vessels). At the E. end of the chancel is a late Gothic Perpendicular window, which is *c.* 57 ft. high. The outer side of this window has two figures—probably the church founder Stephen and his wife Maud (according to strict Cistercian rule, however, the setting up of statues, in a monastery church was forbidden). Also of interest in the chancel are the other windows. From the chancel you can get to the sacristy, which also contains an old piscina.

Other monastery buildings: From the S. aisle there is access to the former *cloister,* of which little remains. On its E. side another highlight of the abbey ruins consists of the Romanesque-transitional *arches,* borne by columns with lovely leaf capitals. Through the middle arch (the side arches formerly had bookcases) you can get to the *Chapterhouse* (built *c.* 1220–40 in Early English style) of a kind almost unique in England. The walls have running arcades, whose capitals are richly

worked. Of the columns, which used to support the now-collapsed roof, one is still intact (there are remains of others). S. of the above-mentioned arches is the entrance to the former *monks' dormitory* (200 ft. long with beautiful pointed arch windows in the walls). S. of the cloister is the old *refectory,* behind and adjacent to which is the *hospital* (in whose *chapel* are 2 pictures of knights in armour from the 12C, the only depictions of their kind in England). E. of the chapel are the remains of the octagonal *kitchen,* and a few steps further on are the ruins of the *Abbot's dwelling.* To the N. of the monastery complex is the *chapel* at the old abbey gate (Romanesque portal, a few beautiful pointed arch windows and 3 sedilia inside).

Environs: Dalton-in-Furness (*c.* 1.3 m. N.): Interesting 14C *tower.*
Millom (*c.* 5 m. NW): *Holy Trinity* church was founded in Norman times and later extended. Inside are tombs of the Huddleston family, the oldest with beautiful alabaster carving of 1494.

Furness Abbey, view of ruins

Gainsborough
Lincolnshire/England   p.328☐K 12

Old Hall: This large town house, originally built in the Middle Ages and traditionally the place where Sweyne (father of the Danish king Canute) was murdered, was destroyed in the War of the Roses between the houses of York and Lancaster in the mid 15C. It was rebuilt in its present form (part brick, part half-timbered) *c.* 1500 and towards the end of the sixteenth century became the meeting place of the Dissenters (Puritans, predecessors of the Pilgrim Fathers). Inside the house is a *museum* with interesting period furniture, a collection of paintings, a puppet exhibition, and period costumes. Also of interest are the original decorations in many of the rooms and the kitchen, which has been maintained in its original condition.

Also of interest: *All Saints Church* with a late Gothic Perpendicular tower. The *John Robinson Memorial Church* of the Congregationalists (completed in 1897).

Environs: Blyborough (*c.* 7.5 m. NE): The church of *St.Alkmund* is Early English; the chancel arch dates from the time of construction.

Coates-by-Stow (*c.* 6.5 m. SE): The church of *St.Edith* was originally Romanesque and without aisles; the S. portal and the font date from the time of construction. Perpendicular chancel, the gallery of which has survived. Also of interest inside are the remains of the medieval glass paintings, a late Gothic pulpit from the 15C and a tombstone from the time of Cromwell.
Harpswell (*c.* 6 m. E.): The tower of the church of *St. Chad* dates back to Anglo-Saxon times, while the aisle was added in the 14C. Of principal interest inside is the Romanesque font and, on the N. side of the chancel, the tomb plaque of the Whichcot family with a depiction of a knight and his lady.
Kirton in Lindsey (*c.* 8.5 m. NE): The church of *St.Andrew,* originally Romanesque and later altered, was restored in the 19C; W. tower and S. portal are Early English. Of interest inside is the Romanesque portal in the chancel.
Stow (*c.* 6 m. SE): The church of *St.Mary* is Anglo-Saxon, although the nave was later converted to Romanesque; crossing tower. Of interest inside is the Romanesque chancel and beautiful Romanesque arches in the nave, as well as the early Gothic font and the remains of medieval wall paintings in the N. transept, which depict St. Thomas à Becket.

Galway

Galway/Ireland   p.326☐B 12

This lively trading port in Galway Bay (pop. *c.* 30,000) is capital of W. Ireland and the Gaeltacht. It has had a university since 1849, which promotes the revival of the Irish language and culture.

History: The town developed around the castle, which was founded in 1232 by the Anglo-Norman Richard de Burgh. During the Middle Ages it was an English bastion in the Gaeltacht and until the mid 17C the town was in the hands of 14 English families, known as 'the Tribes of Galway'. Following Oliver Cromwell's brutal occupation of the town in *c.* 1650 (devastation, expulsion, enslavement) the town lost its importance.

St.Nicholas (Shop Street/Market Street): The principal parish church of the Church of Ireland, it was built in 1320 and later considerably altered (15&16C). Of interest are the *W. gate* (15C), the *S. portal* (16C),

the *tower* (1500), the *Chapel of the Sacrament* (1538), a beautiful 16C *altar*, a 15C *lectern* and various tombs (15–17C). The *Lynch Stone* (N. of the church) commemorates Mayor James Lynch (1493), the reputed 'initiator' of 'Lynch Law'. It is said that, finding no hangman, he hanged ('lynched') his own son.

Lynch's Castle: This restored mansion in Shop Street, which now houses a bank, dates from the 16C and was the seat of the Lynch family. It has beautiful *windows* and portals and an exhibition of the town's and its own history. The exterior has Gothic gargoyles and escutcheons (Henry VII).

Also worth seeing: The *Franciscan monastery* in Francis Street (with a new church of 1849), which was built next to the old town walls in the 13C. The church contains 17C sculptures on the tomb of Sir Peter French; further 17C tombs in the churchyard. The town square, *Eyre Square*, is dedicated to the American president J.F.Kennedy, of Irish descent, who was triumphantly received here in 1963. Of in-

Gainsborough, All Saints' Church

Galway, Lynch's Castle, coat-of-arms

terest is the curious *monument* to the Gaelic writer Patrick O'Connor (1882-1923). The *Spanish Arch,* an archway near the harbour, is indicative of the once-flourishing trade with Spain.

Environs: Annaghdown (*c.* 8 m. N.): The remains of the monastery founded by St. Brendan in the 6C lie to the E. shore of Lough Corrib and consist of a 15C *cathedral* (older parts of the building—windows and an archway—date from 1200). A *priory* of 1195 has a fortified Romanesque church and cloister.
Claregalway (*c.* 6 m. NE): Ruins of a *Franciscan monastery* of 1290 with chancel windows, tower and N. transept (15C).

Glasgow
Strathclyde/Scotland   p.324□G 8

This city on the Clyde estuary was founded by St. Mungo who built a small church on the site of the present cathedral in 543. As the place was called Glas Cau (Celtic for 'Green Place') the settlement took the same name. In the 12C a Romanesque church was built here and this then had to make way for the present cathedral (built 13–15C). In 1451 Glasgow acquired Scotland's second university through Bishop William Turnball. In 1568 Mary Stuart was defeated near Queen's Park. In 1611 the city finally achieved the status of a Royal Burgh. The Reformation appears to have divided the city: the new faith was adopted while the Catholic bishop remained in office. In 1615, however, John Ogilvie, a Catholic priest canonized in 1976, was hanged for his faith. Cromwell ruled the city comparatively leniently in 1650–1 and, in 1745 the Young Pretender, Charles Edward Stuart, was not greeted with open arms. The Glaswegians were obliged to give him financial support, but reclaimed the money from London for their good conduct. The city centre, once the area around the cathedral, had meanwhile shifted to Glasgow Cross. (George Square, today's city centre, was at that time open space.)

The city then grew very rapidly in the 18C, becoming a centre for trade with North America and a metropolis of the tobacco trade. The real masters were now the Tobacco Lords whose clippers sailed backwards and forwards between the Clyde and Virginia. Already in 1755 there were about 400 trading ships stationed on the Clyde. In order to provide themselves with the right standing, the Tobacco Lords had part of Trongate paved. These 'plainstanes' were not only the city's first pavement, but they were also only allowed to be used by those who had paid for them! James Watt invented the steam engine here in 1769 and thereby provided the 'spark' which was to ignite the Industrial Revolution. He was Glasgow's chief engineer at the time when the 20 mile stretch of the Clyde up to the firth was deepened to enable seafaring ships to sail as far as Glasgow. This enabled the world's largest dockyard to be built in Glasgow. In 1812 the paddle-steamer 'Comet', the world's first seaworthy steamer, was launched. In the mid 19C 80% of steamers built in Great Britain still came from the Clyde dockyards. Such vessels as Tsar Alexander's yacht the 'Livadia' and the 'Queen Elizabeth II', one of the last great luxury trans-Atlantic liners, were built on the Clyde, which was a prestigious name in shipping.

Glasgow, always a trading town, later became an industrial town, whose growth had more to do with the state of the market than with politics. Although the city was never actually destroyed, there is scarcely any old architecture, as the old was always in the way of the new and was therefore uncompromisingly torn down. Even comparatively recentlywhole districts have

Glasgow, Cathedral of St. Mungo

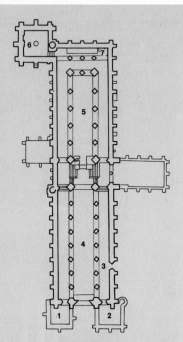

Glasgow, Cathedral of St.Mungo 1,2 former tower of W. façade **3** SW portal **4** nave **5** choir **6** sacristy **7** tomb of Archbishop Law

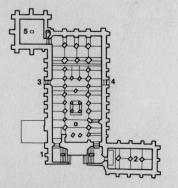

Lower Church 1 NW portal **2** Blacader's Crypt **3** NE portal **4** SE portal **5** chapterhouse

been torn down for 'redevelopment', with little consideration as to what may have been lost.

Cathedral of St. Mungo: Considering Glasgow's readiness for demolition and destruction, it is remarkable that this cathedral should be the only one in Scotland, apart from Kirkwall's, not to fall victim to the iconoclasts or the soldiers of the English Crown. Only the two towers of the W. façade failed to survive the times, but not because of the Reformists or the soldiers, but because of the artistic sensibility of the last century. As the two towers were different in height, structure and style, and therefore deemed to be unsuited to the rest of the building according to the taste of the time, they were removed in 1846. Plans to replace them with neo-Gothic towers were never carried out. The whole of the remaining building thus dates from the time of construction (1197–1480). The cathedral stands on the site of Glasgow's first cathedral, founded by King David I and Bishop Achaius in 1136 and burned to the ground in 1196. The new building was begun under Bishop Jocelin; under Bishop Bondington the crypt, chancel and tower were completed by 1258. By 1425 Bishop Lauder had added the chapterhouse below the sacristy; Bishop Cameron completed the sacristy in 1445. The nave mainly dates from the 13&14C and was finally completed in 1480. The beamed roof in the nave and chancel replaced a barrel vault, for which the side walls were too weakly constructed. Towards the end of the 15C Bishop Blacader planned a large S. transept, only the crypt of which (Blacader's crypt) came to fruition. The last Roman Catholic archbishop, James Beaton, foresaw future developments correctly and, in 1560, he managed to take the cathedral's treasure and archives to France before they could fall into the hands of the iconoclasts. To this day neither treasure nor archives have returned. The cathedral's rich fur-

Cathedral of St. Mungo

nishings fell victim to the Reformation, whose zealots 'cleansed' the cathedral of the 'testimonies of idolatry'. The destruction of the building itself was prevented by the intervention of the trade barons. As a concession to the Reformation the cathedral was divided into three parts, since which time the chancel, nave and main crypt have each formed a separate parish church.

In spite of the long period of construction lasting 283 years, the building, which is *c.* 336 ft. long, is astonishingly homogeneous. Early English Gothic, with narrow windows and doorways, predominates, along with such typically Scottish features as the tower with ambulatory. The nave and choir are not only of equal width, but also practically of equal length. They are separated by a screen beneath the crossing. The chancel is *c.* 3 ft. higher than the *nave,* which is impressive for its splendid proportions, double-arched triforium and fine clerestory. The walls have numerous monuments and regimental emblems. The stained-glass windows, dating from Victorian times, were replaced by modern glass in 1950–8. The rectangular *High Church* (the old choir) with its ambulatory and series of chapels is in effect a second storey. The superb rood screen, through which you enter this church, has fine corbels with depictions of the Seven Deadly Sins. Here too the triforium is particularly splendid, the capitals of the pairs of columns having exquisite decoration. The pulpit, dating from *c.* 1600, was originally destined for the Lower Church. The High Church concludes with a straight E. wall with four extremely tall, slender lancet windows. The SE chapel has the tomb of Archbishop Law of 1632. The sacristy adjoins on the N. side and seems to contain all the beautiful features of Gothic style. The central column is adorned with the arms of the builder, Bishop Cameron. To the S. of the rood screen a stair leads down to *Blacader's Crypt*, which represents the final attempt to provide the church with a transept. Of interest here are the finely carved ceiling bosses.

Beneath the former choir and with the same ground plan lies the *Lower Church*, which would seem to be a crypt because of its position, but which is actually above ground. This, without doubt the most beautiful part of the whole cathedral, is the masterpiece of Scottish early Gothic. Bundles of pillars with scroll decorations on the capitals, lancet windows, fan vaulting and the many coloured ceiling bosses make for a use of space that is without equal. Also beautifully designed is the *chapterhouse*, which adjoins at the N. corner of the Lower Church. This room lies immediately below the sacristy and is borne by a central pillar, which is richly adorned with heraldic decorations.

Necropolis: The 'City of the Dead', Glasgow's largest cemetery, on Fir Park Hill, is right next to the cathedral. It was laid out in the 18C and provided the rich merchants and industrialists of the 19C with a place like no other for the final self-representation; Greek, Egyptian, Indian, Chinese and European from the most diverse epochs—there is no style which is not represented here.

Since 1825 the last resting-place of the Glaswegians has been watched over from a Doric column by the Reformer John Knox.

St. Andrew's: Built 1739–56, this church is one of Scotland's earliest classical buildings. The fine mahogany stalls were donated by the Merchants' Guild.

St. Vincent Street Church: Built by Alexander Thomson in 1859. The architect, known in Glasgow as 'the Greek', built everything from villas to warehouses in a style which he believed was that of the ancient Greeks. The church is a kind of

Cathedral of St. Mungo, Blacader's crypt, ceiling

Greek temple, whose exterior is characterized by Egyptian-style pylons, over which rises a campanile-like tower. The colonnades, pinnacles and idiosynchratic dome are quite unique. The interior is also characterized by the exotic. The portico has a running gallery resting on wrought-iron columns, the capitals of which are decorated with acanthus and palm leaf motifs. Blue, red and brown seem to be the colours which Thomson considered typically Greek—the modern visitor may, however, detect a mixture of Egyptian, Greek and other classical components.

City Chambers: The foundation stone of Glasgow's new Town Hall on George Square was laid in 1883. Five years later William Young's magnificent building was opened by Queen Victoria. Mercantile and civic self-confidence joined in the desire to express their own conception of themselves through the abundance and expense of the materials employed. Thus the twin columns in the entrance hall are of hand-polished red granite adorned with dark green marble capitals, and the barrel vaults

are decorated with Venetian mosaics. In the staircases Brescia marble competes with Carrara marble, alabaster replaces the granite, and rosewood and mahogany are just good enough to be used instead of oak. The banqueting hall with its coffered barrel vault and wall pictures by local artists is a paradigm of Victorian pomp.

Kibble Palace: This conservatory in the Botanical Gardens was built by Joseph Paxton in 1873. The Scottish mini glass palace consists exclusively of wrought-iron Victorian columns and arches and glass. The round-domed building was first used as a concert and assembly hall and now houses a unique collection of tropical tree ferns.

Provand's Lordship: Glasgow's oldest surviving house was built *c.* 1471 and is the last remnant of Cathedral Square, formerly the heart of the city. This typical 15C town house, with its mighty walls, dissimilar windows and beautifully-stepped corbie gables, was built for William Baillie, a titular canon.

Cathedral of St. Mungo, sacristy, coat-of-arms

Tolbooth Steeple

St. Mungo, crypt, tapestry

The house has 17C furniture and is now a museum of Scottish history.

Tolbooth Steeple: The tower of the former town hall—at the crossing of Trongate and High Street—dates from 1626. It is 114 ft. high, has 7 storeys, and an open balustrade with a cross at the top. The old town hall to which it belonged was torn down long ago. The medieval market cross diagonally opposite is a modern copy of the original.

Merchants' House: This building of 1874 is the seat of the oldest chamber of commerce and industry in Britain. Its Victorian banqueting hall is of interest for its coloured glass windows.

Museums:
Old Glasgow Museum: This is housed in the People's Palace, opened in 1898 in Glasgow Green, the largest park on the bank of the Clyde. It provides an excellent impression of the 800-year development of the city of Glasgow.

City Art Gallery and Museum: This is not only the city's most important museum, but it is also one of the most superb municipal art collections in Britain. Opened in 1901, the museum was endowed with one of the largest private art collections of all time by Sir William Burrell in 1944. The collector, who sold his merchant fleet in 1917, devoted the rest of his life up to his death in 1958 to collecting works of art. Flemish, Dutch and French masters are represented along with the most valuable sculptures and Egyptian reliefs, Persian carpets and Flemish tapestries, stained glass and ceramics; there are

Art Gallery and Museum

also Greek, Persian and even Mesopotamian antiquities. The museum additionally has a weapons collection and an outline of the history of Clyde shipping.

Hunterian Museum: This museum contains archaeological, zoological and anatomical collections. There are also collections of old manuscripts and early printed books, as well as a famous coin cabinet. The paintings include works by Rembrandt, Rubens, Chardin and Whistler, as well as Scottish painting from the late 19/early 20C.

Pollok House: A Georgian mansion designed by William Adam for William Sterling Maxwell of Pollok *c.* 1740. The latter gathered Britain's most valuable collection of Spanish painting together in this house. The museum's collection is rounded off by valuable Spanish glass, porcelain and oriental furniture.

Museum of Transport: This is to be found in the district of Pollockshields and has a collection of Scottish steam locomotives, omnibuses, trams, cars, fire engines and bicycles.

Regimental Headquarters of the Royal Highland Fusiliers: Displayed here is the history of this famous Scottish regiment and of the Highland Light Infantry.

Glastonbury
Somerset/England   p.332☐H 15

There was already a trading centre here in

the 2C BC, but no remains have survived. As the Romans only destroyed things here and built nothing, there are no longer any traces either of them or of their predecessors.

The story is not altogether different as regards the remains of England's oldest Christian community, which once occupied the site where ruins of a large medieval *abbey* now stand.

Abbey: This Benedictine abbey, plundered by Henry VIII, was once England's largest monastery complex and is now its most famous ruin. According to legend it was here that Joseph of Arimathea brought and buried the chalice used at the Last Supper and in which the blood of the crucified Christ had been collected. It was around this Holy Grail that King Arthur gathered together his famous Round Table, the grail being the holiest centre of the kingdom. If one is to believe the tradition, England's first church, *Vetusta Ecclesia,* stood here in the 1C. St.Patrick is reputed to have found his last resting place here in 463. King Ina is reputed to have built a larger church in 708, which (here the records begin) became a *Benedictine Abbey* in 940, the first abbot being St.Dunstan. The importance which the abbey attained almost immediately is shown by the tombs of the Saxon kings Edmund the Magnificent (946), Edgar (975) and Edmund Ironside (1016). Until 1154 the Abbot of Glastonbury was also Archabbot of England. In 1184 the entire complex was destroyed by fire. In order to finance its rebuilding the monks seized upon a ruse, claiming to have discovered the tombs of Joseph of Arimathea and King Arthur. The resulting pilgrim attraction provided them with the necessary funds. These were plentiful enough to allow England's largest monastery of the time (the abbey church alone was over 360 ft. long) to be completed by 1303. It was finally dissolved by Henry VIII in 1539, who plundered it and

had its last abbot hanged. The decaying buildings served as a convenient quarry for the surrounding area. Still surviving today are parts of the two *E. crossing pillars,* part of the S. and E. *outer chancel wall,* remains of a *chapel* from the N. transept and part of the *Chapel of the Virgin* and a *Galilee* adjoining the W. wall. The Chapel of the Virgin Mary is also the oldest part of the later building. It was built in 1186, and its round arches are Norman while the neighbouring arcades herald Gothic with their pointed arches. Two portals still preserve their archivolt figures with the Annunciation, Nativity and Massacre of the Innocents. The quality of the work is an indication of the care and skill of the monastery's builder.

The only almost undamaged building of the abbey is the *Abbot's Kitchen* from the late 14C. This square building with its octagonal pyramid roof is one of the best preserved medieval kitchens in Europe.

Lake Village Museum: In prehistoric times Glastonbury was a lake village, as the Bristol Channel still extended this far. The Iron Age remains of this lake settlement are on display in a 15C house.

Glendalough

Wicklow/Ireland   p.326 □ E 1

The 'Delphi' of Ireland is picturesquely situated in a narrow, wooded valley in the Wicklow Mountains. The name Glendalough means 'Glen of the Lakes', referring to the two little mountain lakes, Upper and Lower Lake. St. Kevin, the legendary Celtic saint, built his first secluded settlement here around 600 which was soon followed by a monks' settlement. The high-born hermit was, like St.Francis of Assisi, known as a mystic and

Cathedral of St.Mungo, W. window

animal lover. For some 600 years the extensive monastic area played an important role in the religious life of Ireland. Restorations were carried out in the 19C and around 1912.

Lower Lake Area: The most impressive building is **St.Kevin's Church** (11/12C): The little single-celled church interior (oratory) has a beautiful *console roof* of loosely overlapping stones in the shape of a 'capsized boat'. A *barrel vault* supports the stone roof. Inside is a *Celtic Cross* (12C) with a depiction of an abbot (perhaps the canonized Abbot O'Toole) and geometric patterns. Because of the small *round tower* (bell tower) added onto the W. side in the 12C, the church acquired the nickname 'Kevin's Kitchen' as the tower looks like a chimney. Next to this is the so-called **cathedral** (11C) with chancel, sacristy (12C) and a 12C Romanesque N. gate. The church (restored in the 19C) contains early Christian *tombstones;* also of interest is *St. Kevin's Cross* (12C), an 11 ft high granite monolith. A particular emblem of Glendalough is the 11C **Round Tower.** The entrance to the over 100 ft tower is about 10 ft above the ground; it has 4 windows facing the various wind directions and a beautiful (restored) *conical roof.* The tower is surrounded by an old *cemetery* with numerous interesting (early Christian/medieval) *tombstones.* Nearby is the **Priest's House,** possibly a 12C funerary chapel, with a beautiful Romanesque *portal relief.* **St Mary's Church** (next to the Round Tower) is a little Romanesque church of the 10/11C with chancel and N. portal. Outside the *ring wall* (cashel) surrounding the cemetery stands the Romanesque church of **St.Saviour's** with very beautiful work by stonemasons (chancel arch, E. window). The little church is supposed to have been built by Abbot St.Laurence O'Toole in the 12C (restored 1875). Near the hotel (eastwards) is **Trinity Church** (11/12C) with a former W. tower and S. portal.

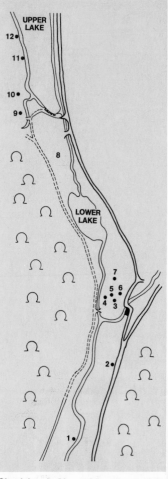

Glendalough, Monastic settlement **1** St. Saviour's Church **2** Trinity Church (11&12C) **3** Cathedral (11C) with 12C choir and sacristy **4** St. Kelvin's Church (11/12C) **5** Priest's House **6** Round Tower (11C) **7** St. Mary's Church (10&11C) **8** car park **9** Reefert Church (11C) **10** St. Kevin's Cell (9&10C) **11** St.Kevin's Bed **12** Temple-na-Skellig (11C)

Upper Lake Area: St. Kevin's original settlement probably lay on the less easily accessible S. bank of the Upper Lake,

Glendalough, Round Tower

Reefert Church

where the remains of the Romanesque **Reefert Church** (11C) are to be found. The name reefert ('king's tomb') refers to the burial place of the old-Gaelic nobles. Neighbouring **St.Kevin's Cell** is a dilapidated early Christian 'beehive hut' of the 9/10C. On a cliff over the shore of the lake is a cleft called **St.Kevin's Bed,** where the saint is said to have meditated (also St. Laurence O'Toole in the 12C). Also only accessible by boat is the little cliff church **Temple-na-Skellig,** a small, 11C rectangular (restored) building with a little window (E.), where St.Kevin's first hermitage may have stood. Very recently a new 'Brotherhood of St.Kevin' was set up here, the goal of which is the final reconciliation between the English and the Irish ('Order of Peace').

Glenfinnan Monument
Scottish Highlands   p.324☐F 7

This monument, commemorating the Jacobite uprising of 1745, was erected by Macdonald of Glenaladale in 1815. It stands on the spot where, on 19 Aug. 1745, the Marquis of Tullibardine raised the standard of Charles Edward Stuart, calling the Highland clans to arms. The rather unattractive, but widely visible, Scottish national monument consists of a column bearing a statue of a Highlander by Greenshields. The event is commemorated on plaques in Latin, Gaelic and English.

Gloucester
Gloucestershire/England   p.332☐H 14

This, the principal town of the county of Gloucestershire, lies on the E. side of the Severn and is connected to the sea by its own canal. The old trading city goes back to Roman *Glevum* and Anglo-Saxon *Caer*

Glou. It achieved importance through being the lowest crossing-point of the Severn. The city acquired its first constitution under Henry II in 1155, and King John 'Lackland' (1199–1216) is supposed to have preferred it to London, while Henry III was even crowned here in 1216. During the Civil War the city sided with the Parliamentary Party and the Royalists were unable to capture it in 1643.

Cathedral: A not inconsiderable role in the city's importance was played by the *Benedictine Abbey of St.Peter,* which existed up until 1540. From 681 to 790 it was a monastery for men and women, from 823 a college for secular priests and from 1022 it was again a Benedictine monastery. The building of the large monastery church was begun and the monastery complex was continually extended until it was finally dissolved by Henry VIII, who handed it over to secular priests and raised it to the rank of cathedral. The actual initiator of the building of the church was Abbot Serlo, who pushed the building through so that it could be consecrated in 1100. In 1327 King Edward II, who had been murdered in Berkeley Castle, was interred in the monastery church, his body having found no rest either in Bristol or Malmesbury. His *tomb,* created shortly after 1330, with a stylized alabaster head, soon become the goal of a pilgrimage, which was fervently promoted by Edward III. The profits from this pilgrimage enabled the monks to complete the existent Gothic parts and continually to extend the abbey. The choir was vaulted from 1337–51, the cloister was built from 1351–1412, the W. façade was built from 1420–37 and by 1450 the 13C tower was replaced by the 225 ft. central tower. The Lady Chapel was finally completed by 1498.
The *nave* itself clearly shows the transition from Romanesque to Gothic. The N. aisle

Cathedral, tomb of Edward II

TOMB OF
EDWARD · II

is still completely Romanesque, having been stabilized by the adjoining cloister and not needing renovation like the S. aisle (up to 1318), which then acquired its Gothic windows. Particularly impressive are the massive cylindrical *columns,* which principally support the weight of the roof. The great *organ casing* was made in 1663 and is the oldest of all England's cathedrals. It is also repeatedly apparent in the *choir* that Romanesque features were reworked by architects with Gothic sensibilities. This concern was not detrimental to the building, however, but on the contary led to the development, in connection with the fine vaulting, of one of the earliest and most beautiful early Gothic interiors in England. The 74 x 40 ft. *E. window* was constructed at the behest of Lord Bradestone in 1352 to commemorate the Battle of Crécy. The beauty of this window (still preserving its original glass) is barely tarnished by the fact that the Norman apse had to be removed for it. The *choir stalls* also date from the 14C, and its misericords are developed as powerful grotesques.

The choir contains numerous remarkable *tombs,* the most important of which, apart from Edward II's, is that of King Osric the founder of the abbey. At the entrance to the presbytery stands the tomb of Robert Carthouse, the eldest son of William the Conqueror, who died in 1134. This is adorned with a painted oak figure of around 1290.

The *Lady Chapel,* which was not started until a century after the completion of the great E. window, had to conform to the dimensions of the latter. As a result a lower but harmonious chapel was constructed with fine vaulting, splendid tracery windows and a beautiful paved floor. The Lady Chapel was also given a magnificent *E. window,* which has preserved much of its original glass and shows the Tree of Jesse. In the *central tower* there hang no fewer than 10 bells, 4 of which date from

Gloucester Cathedral 1 W. façade **2** S. portal **3** cloister **4** Lavatory **5** altar **6** choir **7** N. transept **8** S. transept **9** St. Paul's Chapel **10** St. Andrew Chapel **11** presbytery **12** tomb of King Edward **13** high altar **14** War Memorial Chapel **15** E. window **16** St. Stephen's Chapel **17** Lady Chapel chapterhouse

Cathedral

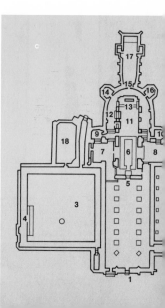

re-Reformation times, including 'Great
~~eter~~' of 1420.

~~T~~he *cloister,* completed in 1412, is equally
~~i~~mpressive for its beauty as for its good state
~~o~~f repair. Its fan vaulting is the first of its
~~k~~ind in England and was the invention of
~~G~~loucester's stone masons. The N. part,
~~t~~he monks' lavatorium, is particularly im-
~~p~~ressive. The S. side was the scriptorium,
~~a~~ sort of monks' study. The *monastery li-*
~~b~~rary preserves a Coverdale Bible of 1535
~~a~~s its most valuable treasure, and some re-
~~m~~ains of a 10C Anglo-Saxon manuscript.

~~C~~hurch of St. Mary-de-Lode: This
~~s~~tands on Roman foundations and has a
~~l~~ow Norman sanctuary. Just N. of the
~~c~~hurch 4 11C arches mark the spot where
~~S~~t. Oswald's Priory once stood, which was
~~f~~ounded in 909 and destroyed in 1643.

~~C~~ity Museum: This is dedicated to the
~~a~~rchaeology and natural history of the area
~~a~~nd contains such valuable pieces as the
~~b~~ronze mirror of Birdlip from around AD
~~2~~5 and a group of Roman statues, made in
~~B~~ritain between AD 100 and 250. Also on
display is a collection of ceramics, furniture, silver and glassware.

Bishop Hooper's Lodging: The bishop
spent his last night here, before dying as
a martyr. A *Folklore Museum* is now installed in the house, demonstrating, among
other things, various methods of fish-
catching in the Severn. The history of the
Gloucester Regiment, from its foundation
in 1694 to the present day, is also por-
trayed.

Environs: Ashleworth (4.35 m. N.): The
little *Church of SS Andrew and Bartholomew* dates back to the 13C. Its tower
is early 14C, the octagonal font 15C. The
Holy Water font at the entrance also dates
from pre-Reformation times. Next to the
church stands the old *tithe barn* of the 15C.
Elmore Court (*c.* 4 m. SW): This *country mansion* dates from Elizabethan times,
but has Georgian additions. The staircase
and a few fire-places are still wholly
Elizabethan, and some of the furnishings
also still date from this time. The house
contains a collection of old manuscripts.

~~C~~athedral, effigy of Edward II, detail

City Museum, Rufus Sita's gravestone

Cathedral choir stalls

Great Witcombe Villa (*c.* 4 m. SE): This Roman *mansion,* commanding fine views, is astonishingly well preserved. Excavations have revealed that walls up to 6.5 ft. tall had survived the centuries. Mosaic pavements and part of a bath were also found.

Kempley (15 m. NW): The little Norman *church* was built around 1100 and contains beautiful frescos from around 1150.

Westbury-on-Severn (11 m. SW): *Westbury Court* has a beautiful old garden, laid out as early as around 1700.

Gort

Galway/Ireland p.326□B 12

This little town can be used as the base from which to visit interesting places in the vicinity.

Environs: Ballylee castle (*c.* 0.5 m. N.) This 16C *tower house* was made famous by the Irish poet W.B. Yeats (Nobel Prize 1923), who settled here 1920–9. It now houses a small *Yeats Museum* . Not far away is *Coole Park* (with the romantic Coole Lake) which belonged to his literary friend Lady Gregory. Nearby are the ruins of *Kiltartan Castle* (13C) with defensive walls (to the S.) and the ruins of *Tullira Castle*), 17C tower house with rebuilding dating from 1882 (to the N.

Kilmacduagh Monastery (*c.* 4 m. SW) This monastery was founded as early as the 7C by the King of Connacht for the Celtic Saint, Colman MacDuagh (the Gaelic name means 'Church (kil) of MacDuagh') The remains of the *cathedral* (11–12C) with beautiful portals from the 12&15C have survived; the N. *transept* has 17C sculptures. To the NE is the church of *St. John*

Cathedral, tomb of William the Conqueror

(probably 12C), *O'Heyne's Church* from the 13–15C and, to the E., the church of *St.Mary* of 1200 with a 15C S. portal. Also of interest is the well-preserved *Round Tower ('Leaning Tower')*, 114 ft. high from the 12C. Nearby the 13C *Glebe House* was probably the former abbot's residence.

Lough Cutra Castle (*c.* 3 m. S.): This *castle*, delightfully situated on Lough Cutra, was built in neo-Gothic style by John Nash in *c.* 1820. Inside there is beautiful 17–19C furniture.

Grantham
Lincolnshire/England   p.328 □ K 13

St.Wulfram: Mostly built in the 14C in Decorated style (the N. aisle is earlier). The tower, *c.* 312 ft high, and also Decorated, has become a town landmark. Beneath the *Lady Chapel* the double crypt of 1340 has a beautiful vault; the *S. porch* has late Gothic decorations. Of interest inside is the late Gothic *Chantry Chapel* in the N. aisle and the *font*, also late Gothic, with richly-carved biblical scenes.

Angel and Royal Hotel: This inn, built as early as the 14C, originally belonged to the Knights Templar but was later taken over by the Order of St.John of Jerusalem (Knights Hospitallers). The beautiful two-storeyed *façade* has an arcade in the middle and is flanked by two arched windows (window frames are later).

Grantham House: Originally a Gothic mansion from the late 14C, it was extended *c.* 1570 in Elizabethan style and extensively converted in Georgian style in the 18C.

Grantham, Church of St. Wulfram, font   *Crypt*

Margaret, daughter of Henry VII, and later wife of King James IV of Scotland, stayed here in 1503.

Museum: This contains interesting objects pertaining to the history and archaeology of the town since 2000 BC. Of particular interest are the exhibits commemorating the great physicist Sir Isaac Newton (1642–1727), who was born at Woolsthorpe Manor, S. of the town.

Also worth seeing: The *Guildhall*, with a *statue* of Newton outside. The 16C *Grammar School*, which Newton attended. The *Beehive Inn*, one of the town's oldest inns (with a real beehive as its sign).

Environs: Ancaster (*c.* 6 m. NE): Roman *Causennae*, a station on the London-Lincoln road (excavated remains of the old *town fortifications*).

Belton (*c.* 2.5 m. N.): The church of *Sts.Peter and Paul*, originally Romanesque, has been repeatedly altered—for the last time in 1816 when a new chapel designed by J. Wyattville was added. Also worth seeing is *Belton House*, a mansion built 1685–8 to the designs of Christopher Wren. Inside: beautiful period furniture and a valuable collection of paintings; also of interest is the 'Chinese Bedroom'. A Horse Museum is now housed in the old stable buildings.

Belvoir Castle (*c.* 6 m. W.): *Castle* of the Dukes of Rutland; originally a fortress, repeatedly converted since the 17C. Inside is a very interesting art collection with pictures by Rembrandt, Rubens, Holbein and English masters of the 18C.

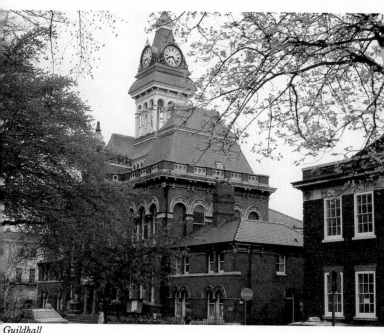

Guildhall

Boothby Pagnell (*c.* 4 m. SE): A fortified *mansion,* built as early as 1178, has an interesting hall on the vaulted ground floor.

Bottesford (*c.* 7.5 m. NW): The church of *St.Mary* was built in the 13C and later altered. Inside there are a few interesting medieval tombs.

Caythorpe (*c.* 7.5 m. N.): The church of *St.Vincent,* is a Gothic building of the 13C with a crossing tower; of interest within are the pointed arches of the nave and remains of medieval wall paintings.

Folkingham (*c.* 10 m. E.): The church of *St.Andrew,* originally Romanesque, later converted; Early English chancel and beautiful Perpendicular tower. Of interest are the late Gothic windows.

Honington Camp (*c.* 5 m. N.): Remains of an Iron Age hill fort (one of the few in Lincolnshire) whose defensive moats and ramparts have survived.

Hough-on-the-Hill (*c.* 6.5 m. N.): The W. tower of *All Saints Church* is Anglo-Saxon; also of interest is the little staircase tower. Inside there are early Gothic columns in the aisles and pointed arches on the N. side of the chancel.

Irnham (*c.* 8.5 m. SE): The church of *St.Andrew,* originally Romanesque, has later Gothic alterations. Inside is the interesting tomb slab of Sir Andrew Luttrell, d. 1390.

Osbournby (*c.* 10 m. E.): The church of *Sts.Peter and Paul* is mainly in the Decorated style of the 13C. Inside there is a beautiful Romanesque font and interesting late medieval woodcarving.

Sempringham (*c.* 10 m. E.): The church of *St.Andrew* was originally Romanesque (nave arcades and portals); the chancel was not added until the 19C.

Woolsthorpe Manor (*c.* 6 m. S.): House

Angel and Royal Hotel

in which the physicist Sir Isaac Newton was born.

Great Malvern
Hereford and Worcester/England   p.328☐H 14

Great Malvern is the most important of the 7 villages called Malvern which occupy the lower part of the Malvern Hills, gently rolling countryside which reaches a height of *c.* 1,500 ft. From its highest point, the 1518 ft Worcestershire Beacon, three cathedrals can be seen — Worcester, Hereford and Gloucester.

Priory Church: This church dates back to a Norman building of the 11C, remnants of which are still discernible inside. The Romanesque arcades date from the 12C;

the rest is 15C Gothic. The tower is a copy of Gloucester Cathedral's. The church is known for its superb *stained-glass windows* from the 15&16C. The chancel windows (20 ft. high) and the windows in St.Anne's Chapel are particularly fine. The window in the N. transept shows Prince Arthur, son of Henry VII.

St.Giles: This 12C church in the village of Little Malvern was part of a Benedictine monastery. Renovated in the 14C, only the central tower and the E. part have survived. The *stained-glass window* in the E. wall dates from the 15C and depicts Edward IV with his family.

Environs: Eastnor (9 m. S.): The *Church of St.John the Baptist* dates from the 12C and has a 14C tower; it was extensively renovated in neo-Gothic style by Sir Ge-

Great Malvern, Priory Church, window detail

orge Gilbert Scott in 1852. The glass window in the E. wall is by C.E. Kempe. *Eastnor Castle* was begun in 1810 by Sir Robert Smirke, who built the British Museum. He constructed a neo-Gothic (Gothick) complex with massive, battlemented round towers at the corners, which appear authentically Norman. The hall, which is 60 ft. high and 67 ft. long, was arranged by Sir George Gilbert Scott; the library is the work of George Fox. The castle now houses a collection of weapons, as well as valuable tapestries and paintings. **Herefordshire Beacon** (2.5 m. S.): The Iron Age *hill fort* is impressive for the extent of its moat and ramparts. The Romans had a look-out station here and in Norman times there was a castle on the same site. **Ledbury** (10 m. SW): *St.Michael and All Angels* dates back to the 11C, but the present church building dates mainly from the late 13/early 14C. The lower part of the free-standing tower also dates from the 13C, while the upper part was renovated in 1734.

The windows, of 1895–1904, are by C.E. Kempe. The church's most valuable possession is the sculpture of a priest in an attitude of prayer (second half of the 13C).

Great Yarmouth
Norfolk/England   p.329☐M 13

Used by the Romans and once an important herring port, the town is Norfolk's most popular holiday resort today. It stands on a long peninsula with the sea on one side and the confluent mouths of the rivers Bure, Yare and Waveney on the other. The grid network of narrow streets and little al-

Great Malvern, Priory Church, window detail

leys contains some old houses which go back to the 14C. The most beautiful part of the town, known as *The Rows,* lies between Hall Quay and the Market Place.

St. Nicholas: This large parish church (262 ft. long) was totally gutted by fire in 1942 and now its 12C origins are only apparent from the exterior. The lower part of the *tower* dates from that time, while the *W. façade* was built in early Gothic style. The church was restored by Stephen Dykes Bower from 1957–61, who reduced the number of arcades in the nave and installed new ones in the chancel. The Norman *font* and the Georgian *pulpit* were taken from other churches. The *stained glass* was created by Brian Thomas; the *choir screen* is by Stephen Dykes Bower.

Town Wall: In the 13&14C the town was encircled by a strong wall with no fewer than 16 towers and 10 gates. Parts of this fortification system (intact into the 17C) can still be seen in Blackfriars Road.

Elizabethan Museum: This is housed in an Elizabethan house with a Georgian façade. Its rooms have beautiful panelling, 16C furniture and domestic items from the 17–19C. There is also an interesting collection of glass.

Tolhouse (Middlegate St.): Great Yarmouth's *Town Museum* of local history is housed in the former prison (14C, restored in 1961 following bomb damage in World War 2).

Environs: Burgh Castle (3 m. W.): The Roman *fortification system* was developed *c.* AD 300 to control the extensive natural

Greenhead, Hadrian's Wall

harbour at the confluence of the Yare and the Waveney. On the inland side there are the remains of 3 defensive walls, whose mortar has survived the centuries. To the S. the Normans built a *castle*, remnants of which can be seen.

Caister-on-Sea (*c.* 4 m. N.): The site of a fortified Roman *settlement*, which was founded in the 2C and held until the withdrawal of the garrison. Excavations, however, have revealed only part of the S. gate, part of the defensive wall and remains of a larger building. The Saxons at first destroyed the settlement and then occupied it themselves. After being destroyed once more, this time by the Danes, the Normans rebuilt it. The *castle*, an impressive ruin, was built 1432 - 5 for Sir John Fastolf (Shakespeare's 'Falstaff'). It now houses a *Motor Museum*.

Fritton (*c.* 7.5 m. SW): *St. Edmund* , a thatched church, was already founded in Saxon times. The sanctuary pavement was laid around 750. The round tower dates from the 11C, the font from the 15C. 12C frescos were discovered in the apse.

Greenhead / Hadrian's Wall
Northumberland / England   p.328☐H 10

Hadrian's Wall: This is not only the most important Roman structure in Britain, it is also the best preserved example of a Roman frontier fortification in the world. Built on the orders of the Emperor Hadrian (AD 117–38) in 122–30, it formed the N. defences of the Roman Empire against the Picts. Its length, between Wallsend-on-Tyne in the E. and Bowness-on-Solway in the W., is about 73 m. Built

Hadrian's Wall, E. stone section

first excavation and research was carried out by William Camden in 1586; finds from this and subsequent excavations are to be found principally in the museums of Carlisle, Newcastle, Housesteads, Chesters Fort and the local excavation zones.

Environs: Birdoswald (*c.* 2 m. W.): Remains of the Roman frontier fortress of *Camboglanna* (once the largest fortress on the wall), parts of the fortress walls, gates and towers and a part of Hadrian's Wall itself are visible today.

Gilsland (*c.* 1.5 m. NW): Well preserved section of the wall along with two *Roman altars with inscriptions*.

Haltwhistle (*c.* 3 m. SE): The church of the *Holy Cross* was built in the 13C on top of an earlier building of 1178; of interest within are beautiful old memorial plaques, a hexagonal 17C font and a three-seated sedilia in the choir; the E. window is by William Morris.

Lanercost Priory (*c.* 6.5 m. W.): Built by Robert Vaux in the mid 12C for Augustinian canons using stone from Hadrian's Wall; the Jupiter Altar inside dates from this time. In 1740 the nave and S. aisle were converted into a parish church. Inside there are the beautiful 12C arcades and remarkable windows by Sir Edward Burne-Jones. Near the church a *bridge* over the River Irthing dates from Tudor times (15C).

Over Denton (*c.* 2.5 m. W.): With a small, predominantly Norman-Romanesque *church*, which was probably built as early as Anglo-Saxon times (architectural remains from this time have survived) using materials from Hadrian's Wall. **Vindolanda Roman Excavations** (*c.* 6 m. E.): Remains of a Roman *frontier fort* and civil buildings. In the excavation area exact reconstructions have been made of parts of Hadrian's Wall. The adjacent *Chesterholm Museum* contains interesting

of stone in the E. and originally *c.* 20 ft. high, it is made of turf in the W., where it is *c.* 13 ft. high. On the N. side there is a moat (on average 30 ft. wide and 10 ft. deep) and on the S. side the *vallum*, a broad, straight trench, about 20 ft. wide and 10 ft. deep, which was fortified on both sides by an earth wall. Between the vallum and the wall there was a military road 20 ft. wide. There was a series of 17 forts at intervals of about 5 m. and between these there were fortified mile-castles every Roman mile, which were interconnected with watch towers. The wall was guarded principally by Roman auxiliaries from all provinces of the empire (regular troops were only used in emergencies).

Damaged by invading Picts in the 2&3C, it was rebuilt; it was damaged for the last time in 383. Part of the wall was used for building the Newcastle-Carlisle road. The

Hadrian's Wall, watch station

Lanercost Priory (Greenhead)

excavation finds (including leather footwear, items of clothing, jewellery and objects of everyday life; everything has been excellently preserved owing to the favourable conditions provided by the soil).

Greenock
Strathclyde/Scotland   p.324☐F 8

This industrial and trading town on the S. bank of the Clyde was the birthplace of James Watt (1736–1819), inventor of the steam engine. The oldest dock on the Clyde was built here in 1711 and in 1859 the last great wooden ship was launched from here. In 1940–5 this was the main naval base of the Free French. A large granite cross on Lyle Hill overlooking the town is a memorial to those French sailors who

gave their lives in the battles in the Atlantic.

Old West Kirk: This church, built in 1591, was the first church to be built after the Reformation and also the first Presbyterian church to be officially recognized by Parliament. The church originally stood elsewhere until, in 1920, standing in the way of industry, it had to be removed to its present location. Rebuilt using the old materials, it contains stained-glass windows by Burne-Jones, Morris and Rossetti.

James Watt Memorial Building: Built by William Blore in 1835, it contains mementoes of James Watt, an art gallery and the MacLean Museum with model ships and natural history exhibits.

Environs: Port Glasgow (3 m. E.): This

Doughty Museum (or *Welholme Galleries* (in the Town Hall): Well worth seeing is the collection of over 60 *model ships* from the 18–19C (some were made by French prisoners of the Napoleonic Wars); also old fishing cutters. The *Doughty Collection* has valuable old Chinese porcelain; a small collection of paintings has pictures of local interest.

Also worth seeing: *Fish market:* Today Grimsby is the most important fishing port in England.

Environs: Caistor (*c.* 11 m. SW): This village was built on top of the remains of an old Roman fort. Of interest is the parish church of *Sts. Peter and Paul.* The W. tower is pre-Romanesque; inside, the beautiful Decorated arches are 13C. Also of interest are the medieval stone figures from the 13–14C and glass paintings from the 19C, some of which are by C.E. Kempe. **Cleethorpes** (adjoining Grimsby to the SE), with the church of Old Clee, (*Church of the Holy Trinity and St. Mary.)* The W. tower comes from the original Anglo-Saxon building; nave colonnades are Romanesque. Of interest inside is the Romanesque *font* and an *inscription* of 1192 on a column, which commemorates the reconsecration of the church by the Bishop of Lincoln.
Rothwell (*c.* 10 m. SW): The church of *St. Mary Magdalene* has a pre-Romanesque W. tower; inside are beautiful Romanesque columns and richly decorated arches.

own was Glasgow's port until the 18C. In 1762 the world's first dry dock was built ere by James Watt. Somewhat lost between two docks lies *Newark Castle,* the own's oldest structure. This was built rom 1597 on the remains of an older complex from the 15C. With its corbies and gabled windows, consoles and turrets, the well preserved castle of the Maxwells is a good example of Scottish Baronial style of the late 16/early 17C.

Grimsby
Humberside/England   p.328☐K 12

St. James: The town's parish church, built in Decorated Style in the 13C but later greatly altered (tower rebuilt in 1365 in Perpendicular style, chancel renovated at the end of the 19C).

Guildford
Surrey/England   p.332☐K 15

The county town of Surrey was first recorded as a borough in 1131, although it had already existed as a settlement at the ford over the Wey at the time of King Alfred (before 900). The High Street is still flanked by picturesque old *houses.*

Royal King Edward VI Grammar School: Founded in 1557 and still used as a school. The *school library* was founded by Bishop Parkhurst in 1573 and contains 89 chained old folio volumes.

Cathedral: Designed for the diocese of Guildford by Sir Edward Maufe in 1927, although building did not begin until 1936. Consecrated in 1961, it was completed in 1964. The interior is very simple, in a neo-Gothic style. Sculptures are by Eric Gill, Vernon Hill and Alan Collins; the *stained-glass windows* by Moira Forsyth and Rosemary Rutherford.

Holy Trinity Church: Extensively rebuilt in the mid 18C after the tower had collapsed and destroyed the church. Inside are the tomb of Archbishop Abbot, who died in 1633, and the memorial to Speaker Onslow, who died in 1768.

Archbishop Abbot's Hospital: This Jacobean brick house at the end of the High Street was donated to the poor people of his hometown by George Abbot,

Archbishop of Canterbury, in 1619. The layout consists of a *gatehouse* with four towers and a *courtyard* around which the living quarters are grouped. The hospital, originally designed for a warden, 12 brothers and 10 sisters, now serves as a home for the elderly, in which the men, proud as ever, still wear the flat Tudor hat and coats with the silver arms of the Archbishop. The hospital's *chapel*, built in 1621, has interesting stained-glass windows and portraits of Calvin, Wyclif and Foxe.

Museum: Collected in a 17C brick house are mementoes of Lewis Carroll, the author of 'Alice in Wonderland'. In reality the Revd. Charles Dodgson, he died during a visit to Guildford and is buried in the town cemetery.

Women's Royal Army Corps Museum: Exhibits include uniforms, mementoes, decorations and medals from World Wars 1&2.

Environs: Clandon Park (*c*. 2 m. E.):

Guildford, High Street

Built in classical style for the 2nd Lord Onslow by the Venetian architect Giacomo Leoni from 1731-5, the unimpressive exterior does not prepare you for the splendid interior. The two-storeyed entrance hall has two stunning tiers of Corinthian columns and a richly decorated stucco ceiling with detached figures of angels and slaves. Complementing this Rysbrack created the antique-style fireplace with reliefs of Bacchus and Diana. The wallpaper and stucco decorations are preserved in their original form throughout almost the entire house. The furnishings, however, of valuable furniture, tapestries, mirrors and porcelain (Gubbay Collection) come extensively from Little Trent Park in Hertfordshire. Of particular value is the collection of Chinese porcelain birds from the 17&18C.

Compton (3 m. SW): The church of *St. Nicholas* dates back to Norman times. With its shingled W. tower, which may be Anglo-Saxon, and Norman nave roof, it is typical of the older churches in the county. It is of particular importance owing to its extremely rare two-storeyed Romanesque *sanctuary*. The sanctuary itself is vaulted and above this there is a chapel, which is open at the chancel end. The round-arched wooden concluding balustrade was made around 1180.

The *Watts Mortuary Chapel* is a small Byzantine cruciform domed basilica with a Norman stucco portal and Art Nouveau angels. The building was begun in 1896, when one of England's most popular painters, George Frederic Watts, still had 8 years to live. The chapel was built by the painter's wife, who with her ceramics pupils made terracottas for the chapel. The interior is furnished in Art Nouveau style with choruses of angels and the Tree of Life. The *Watts Gallery* has *c.* 150 of the artist's pictures.

Godalming (*c.* 4 m. S.): The home town of the writer Aldous Huxley (1894-1963). The large, cruciform church of *Sts. Peter and Paul* goes back to Norman times, although most of the present fabric dates from the 13C. The *Borough Museum,* housed in *Hundred House,* was built in 1814 and stands on the site where for 1,000 years the fortunes of the county were decided. The museum's exhibits are dedicated to the history of the town and county and to archaeology.

Loseley House (*c.* 1.5 m. S.): This Tudor mansion was built for Sir William More 1561-9 with stone from Waverley Abbey. The N. wing with the Great Hall (beautiful panelling, grotesques and 'trompe l'oeil' perspectives) has survived.

H

Haddington
Lothian/Scotland   p.324 □ H 8

Probably the most interesting small town in Scotland, Haddington was elevated to the status of Royal Burgh by David I in the 12C. Alexander II was born here in 1198 and John Knox the Reformer in 1505. To-day the numerous town houses from the 17&18C make the town a delight; an offi-

cial list names no fewer than 129 architec-turally or historically important buildings

St.Mary's: This cruciform church has a 14C central tower. The nave is used as a parish church; the chancel and parts of the tower have been restored. There are some interesting baroque tombstone slabs in the graveyard beside the church.

Abbey Church: This church, also cruci-

Haddington, St.Mary's Church, façade

form with a central tower, dates from the 16C. Its W. front is impressive for the double gate arch. Jane Welsh Carlyle, wife of the writer Thomas Carlyle, is buried in the chancel.

Haddington House: Dating from the early 17C this is the oldest surviving residential house in the town. Today it houses the municipal museum.

Town House: (or Town Hall): Built by William Adam in 1748, it is a good example of the bourgeois classicism which Adam advocated. The tower, 170 ft. tall and built in 1831, is by Gillespie Graham.

Also worth seeing: The *High Street* is of interest for its ensemble of buildings. In 1962, as part of the restoration work, the first attempt was made to coordinate the painting of a whole row of houses. The *Poldrate Mill* is a three-storeyed corn mill with an undershot mill wheel. It dates from the 18C and is still in operation today. *Mitchell's Close* is a good example of successfully-restored 18C houses. The stepped gables and pantile roofs have been restored in conformity with the original.

Environs: Dunbar Castle (9 m. E.): The ruins of this castle from the 13C no longer bear any sign of the part it played in the wars of independence. Under the command of Black Agnes, the Countess of March and Dunbar, the castle survived a six-week siege by the English in 1339; in 1544 the Earl of Hertford succeeded in conquering the town but not the castle. It was not until 1570 that the Earl of Moray managed to destroy the fortress. In 1650 the decisive battle between Cromwell and the Covenanters took place here. Of the latter, over 3,000 were slain and some 10,000 were taken prisoner.

Hailes Castle (3 m. E.): Ruins of a 13C castle. Mary Stuart was here with Bothwell

in 1567. The building was destroyed by Cromwell in 1650. Features of interest include the two towers with dungeons into which the visitor can descend to get some idea of medieval imprisonment.

Tantallon Castle (6 m. NE): This, the castle of the Douglas Clan, was built in *c.* 1375 on the cliffs of a small peninsula. The lords of the castle pursued a mischievous policy of vacillation between the Scots and the English and, as a result, the fortress was besieged by the Scottish king on several occasions, e.g. by James IV in 1491 and James V in 1528. The castle was extended and reinforced from 1529 onwards, but this proved to be of no avail in 1651, when General Monck bombarded it for 12 days before ordering its storming. Despite all the devastations, the ruins are still very imposing today. The blind wall, 49 ft. tall and some 13 ft. thick, defends the landward side and is overlooked by sturdy towers in the middle and on both flanks. The E. tower had five storeys; the W. tower had six. The three sides facing the sea were well defended by cliffs 100 ft. high. In front of the blind wall, looking inland, there was

Tantallon Castle (Haddington)

Haddington, St. Mary's Church

a three-tier system of defences consisting of ditches, drawbridges and bulwarks.

Halifax

West Yorkshire/England   p.328☐I 12

Halifax was a settlement in Anglo-Saxon times (if not before) and wool-processing is documented as having been carried out here since 1275. Halifax became famous from the 14C onwards as a result of the town's gibbet, a predecessor of the guillotine, which was used to behead wool thieves. Hence the following phrase, 'From Hell, Hull and Halifax, Good Lord deliver us'. Today Halifax is an industrial town.

St.John the Baptist: The town's parish church, whose building materials date largely from the 15C, with a fine Perpendicular tower. The W. portal is of particular interest and has the wooden figure of a beggar known as *Old Tristram* (17C, to judge from the style of its clothing).

Piece Hall: The town's former cloth market, completed in 1779. Three-storeyed and built around an enormous square courtyard, it has over 300 rooms. Today it is occupied by numerous wholesalers.

Wainhouse's Tower: A tower some 295 ft. tall, which was planned as a factory chimney but never used as such. From the platform at the top, the visitor has a commanding view over the town and its environs. It is arguable that the tower shows that even in the 19C there was an awareness of the need for environmental protec-

Haddington, St. Mary's Church, tombstone (l), portal (r)

...ion and that the builder, who owned a ...yeing factory, wanted to protect the peo-...le living nearby from the factory's un-...ealthy exhaust gases. However, legend has ...: that rivalry between two competing ...manufacturers was the real reason for ...uilding the tower.

Shibden Hall: A mansion with fine half-...imbering from the 15–17C. Today it is an ...nteresting *Folk Museum*. Old craftsmen's ...vorkshops, including a smithy, a harness-...naker's, a wheelwright's, a nail-forge, as ...vell as an apothecary's shop and a brew-...ry, have been reconstructed in accordance ...vith the originals in the barn and the out-...buildings. There is also a collection of old ...oaches and carts on display.

Also worth seeing: The *Town Hall,* built ...n the 19C in Italianate neo-Renaissance style (the clock tower is about 200 ft. tall). *Old Cock Hall* is 16C and has old oak fur-niture and stained-glass windows. *Bank-field Museum* exhibits old textile-processing machines and the original blade of the gib-bet mentioned above.

Environs: Brighouse (about 3 m. E.): A notable *Art Gallery,* one room of which is given over to H.P. Jackson, a local wood-carver.

Hepton Stall (6 m. SE): A village with in-teresting buildings and an octagonal *chapel* dating from 1764 in Northgate. The old *school,* from the 17C, today contains the *lo-cal museum.* Since 1854 all that has re-mained of the old 15C *church* is its outer walls.

Huddersfield (about 6 m. SE): Next to the *railway station,* which is built in classi-cal Greek style with eight columns on the main front, is the *Tolson Memorial Museum* (in Ravensknowle Park), which is worth visiting for its Roman archaeological finds and exhibition on the development of textile processing. The *Art Gallery* (Princess Alexandra Walk) has a good collection of modern sculptures, including works by Epstein and Moore.

Kirkburton (about 12 m. SE): A fine *church*, most of which dates from the 12C.

Mirfield (about 6 m. E.): Old tradition has it that the tomb of the medieval hero Robin Hood is in *Kirklees Hall nearby.*

Todmorden (about 9 m. W.): *Todmorden Hall,* over 300 years old, is today a post office. Allegorical figures of Yorkshire and Lancashire can be seen in the gable of the *Town Hall*—the border between the two counties formerly ran right through this building.

Halstead
Essex / England   p.332☐L 14

This little town on the upper reaches of the

Colne has a homely character; there ar[e] some fine old houses.

St. Andrew's: This church, dating bac[k] to the 14&15C, was largely rebuilt in th[e] 19C. The *altar panels* by Sir Arthur Blom[field date from 1893. The church contain[s] various *tomb monuments,* in particula[r] those of the Bourchier family.

Blue Bridge House: This house datin[g] from the Queen Anne period was built i[n] 1713 by order of John Morley on the bas[is] of an already existing house. Today it con[tains a collection of *bird paintings* from th[e] 18&19C.

Environs: Castle Hedingham (6 m[.] NW): This small town was built aroun[d] the once-massive Norman *castle*, which th[e] Earls of Oxford had built in *c.* 1130. Th[e] sturdy keep, four storeys tall, has survive[d] almost undamaged from the original cas[tle. The walls of the keep, some 13 ft. thick[,] are decorated on the inside with zig-zagge[d] arches. There is a 15C bridge across th[e] castle moat. The church of *St. Nicholas* i[s]

Halifax, Town Hall

Door

Norman, although the clerestory was added later; the tower was not built until 616. The N. and the two S. portals are also Norman. The nave has a double dragon-beam ceiling. The choir screen and choir stalls with their splendidly carved misericords are 14C.

Great Bardfield (12 m. W.): The church of *St.Mary the Virgin* dates from the 14C, while the W. tower and chancel are Norman. Interesting features include the remains of 14C stained-glass windows and the stone-built choir screen of the same date.

Little Maplestead (4 m. NE): The church of *St.John the Baptist* is the smallest and latest-built of the four round medieval churches in England. Its round central section is only some 30 ft. in diameter. The church was built by the Knights Hospitaller in *c.* 1340. The E. side of the chancel has an apse and dates from the same period.

Wethersfield (8 m. W.): The church of *St.Mary Magdalen* dates back to the 13C and was rebuilt and enlarged in the 14&15C. The nave and the well-

proportioned clerestory date mainly from the 15C. The church contains the remains of Gothic stained-glass windows and some well-designed 15C tomb monuments.

Harlech
Gwynedd/Wales   p.328☐G 13

Harlech, with some 1,200 inhabitants, is historically the town of Welsh nationalism. It has a compact medieval townscape with an imposing ruined castle.

Castle: Built in this strategic location in *c.* 1283 by Edward I, who conquered Wales. This square building has corner towers and is protected by a wide ditch on the land side. The water of the estuary came up to the castle walls on the seaward side of the building. (The sea has retreated since the castle was first built.) The visitor standing on the well-preserved walls has a good panoramic view of the *gatehouse* (in the S.), the *inner courtyard,* and the foundation walls of the castle hall and bakery.

Halstead, Church of St.Andrew, altar

The Welsh rebel Owen Glendower took refuge here about 1404 and proclaimed himself Prince of Wales.

Environs: Llanaber (about 11 m. S.): In this coastal village we find the region's most interesting church, which stands right by the sea front. The church of *St. Mary* was built in the early 13C in Early English style with gateway, columns and fine ornaments. The E. window consists of a single lancet arch. Prehistoric and ancient Celtic finds have been made in the vicinity, particularly at the site called *Carneddan Hengwm*. **Llanenddwyn** (about 6 m. S.): This village has a Perpendicular *church* dating from 1593, a chapel from 1615 and a circular graveyard. Nearby is *Cors-y-Gedol*, a mansion from 1576. Outside the town, at *Dyffryn Cairn*, there is a neolithic burial mound with two partially surviving burial chambers.
Maentwrog (about 9 m. NE): The village takes its name from the early Celtic St. Twrog (6 – 7C), whose ancient stone ('maen') is in the graveyard.
Portmeirion (about 5 m. N.): Sir Clough Williams-Ellis' Italianate village folly, with harbour, bell tower, brightly coloured cottages, restaurants, etc.
Tomen-y-Mur (about 9 m. NE): These Roman remains are to be found near the dammed reservoir of Trawsfynydd, where there is a nuclear power plant. Some scant remains of the Roman camp (from 78–135) still survive along with Celtic and Norman ramparts.

Harris and Lewis (I)
Scotland   p.322 □ E 4/5

Harris and Lewis, one and the same island, are separated from one another by a roadless mountain barrier 7 m. wide. From the cultural point of view they therefore developed as if they were two different islands,

e.g. the Gaelic spoken in the two parts of the island actually differs in sound. Harris has given its name to Harris Tweed, a woven woollen cloth known the world over.

Rodel: The only medieval church in the Outer Hebrides stands in a fishing village on the S.tip of Harris. The cruciform church of *St.Clement*, built in *c.* 1500, was a fitting burial site for Alastair Crotach MacLeod, the clan leader (1528). The curious fertility carvings half-way up the church tower, a particularly interesting archaic element of possible Irish origin, are the only examples of their kind in Scotland.

Carloway: This *refuge keep*, 2 m. S. of the village and one of the best-preserved in the whole of Scotland, was built in the 2C BC. The inner courtyard is 25 ft. across and the outer walls survive up to a height of 30 ft.

Callanish: The *standing stones* are the Scottish counterpart of Stonehenge. They have stood in the marshy soil here for over 3,500 years. A circle of stones, some 39 ft in diameter, forms the inner chamber around a central monolith some 16 ft. tall. An avenue 272 ft. long and 26 ft. wide leads towards the central chamber. The stone circle itself is formed by 13 menhirs.

Also worth seeing: 2 m. S. of *Barvas* is a genuine Hebridean house (Black House), which has been restored as a museum. Exhibits illustrating the folklore and history of the area have been assembled in an interesting small museum in *Shawbost*.

Harrogate
North Yorkshire/England   p.328 □ I 11

The town experienced its heyday in the

Harlech, Castle

19C when it was one of the most important spas in England, with 88 springs whose waters were rich in sulphur and iron. Today it is a much-frequented holiday resort and conference town. Its extensive parks have earned it the name of Britain's floral resort. The *Royal Baths*, the former building for cures and treatments, is worth seeing—today it is used as a conference and exhibition centre. The *Museum of Local Antiquities*, with its collections of local interest, is housed in the former *Royal Pump Room*, the tap room built in 1842 above the most important of the sulphur springs.

Environs: Cowthorpe: (some 7 m. E.): A notable *church*, built from the spoils of a former building. Unusual supporting arches on the tower.

Fewston (about 9 m. W.): The church dates originally from the 13C, although the present building is Jacobean. Nearby is *Swinsty Hall*, a fine 16C building.

Hilltop Hall (*c.* 3 m. S.): Formerly a hostel for monks on the way from Kirkstall Abbey to Fountains Abbey. Built in mixed style in the 15C.

Knaresborough (some 4 m. NE): There are various sights in this town in the deeply carved-out valley of the Nidd. The church of *St.John the Baptist* was first mentioned in 1114. The nave and aisles are 15C Perpendicular, while the tower and chapels are Early English from the 12C. The sacristy has two life-sized pictures of Moses and Aaron painted on wood and dating from the 15C. The 15C *Chapel of our Lady of the Crag*, a chapel hewn from the rocks above the River Nidd, is unique of its kind in England. The 14C *castle* was devastated in the Civil War (17C). The three-storeyed castle keep (square-shaped, with sides about 56 ft. long; dungeon beneath) and the remains of the main gate, still survive from this building which was originally fortified with 11 towers. *Manon House*, a 13C mansion. Inside is a bed in which Oliver Cromwell slept. *St. Robert's Cave*, the cave of St. Robert the hermit (1160–1218).

Nun Monkton (about 6 m. E.): A fine *church* in late Norman/Early English style, with a fine Romanesque portal.

Pannal (about 2 m. S.): The 13C church of *St. Robert of Knaresborough* is worth seeing. The oldest sections are the chancel and tower. Inside there are some fine tombs of the Bentley family. The first window in the S. side has a notable old stained-glass window probably depicting the priory of St. Robert of Knaresborough, of which the church formed a part from 1348 onwards.

Ripley (*c.* 4 m. N.): Inside the fine 15C church of *All Saints* are some excellent tomb monuments of the Ingilby family. The medieval shroud of a knight (black taffeta with a coat-of-arms) is in the NE corner of the church. *Ripley Castle*, which has been the Ingilby family seat since 1350, is built in the Tudor style. The portal and tower date from the 15–6C. The interior decoration is worth seeing.

Rudding Park (*c.* 3 m. SE): A fine *park* laid out by Repton with a Regency *mansion*.

Spofforth Castle (*c.* 5 m. SE): A fortified 14C *mansion*, belonging to the Percy family (it was the birthplace of Harry Hotspur) and built on the site of an Anglo-Saxon building. Finally devastated in 1604 after many destructions and reconstructions. There are fine pointed-arched (Gothic) windows in the Great Hall. Another feature worth seeing in the town of Spofforth is the *church*, built in the late-Norman Transitional style. Inside are the remains of an ancient market cross.

Wetherby (*c.* 9 m. SE): Inhabited in Roman times. Sights include a picturesque *bridge* and the remains of a *castle* from the time of Henry I (1100–35).

Hartlebury Castle
Hereford and Worcester/England   p.328☐H 14

The Bishop of Worcester has had a *residence* here for more than 1,000 years. The present house was built in 1675 beside a medieval *castle* protected by a rampart and moat. The residence contains a large portrait gallery and an 18C rococo hall. The *library* by Richard Hurd (1720–1808), and also the *county museum*, are housed in the castle.

Environs: Bromsgrove (12 m. E.): The church of *St. John the Baptist* has a 14C tower and numerous tomb monuments from the 15&16C. Most of these are made of alabaster and dedicated to members of the Talbot and Stafford families.

Chaddesley Corbett (6 m. NE): The church of *St. Cassian* has a Norman nave, while the remainder of the church was built in the 14C. The early Norman font, decorated with serpents, dragons and other beasts, is especially worth seeing. Some tomb monuments dating back to the early 14C are also of interest.

Great Witley (*c.* 11 m. SW): The church of *St. Michael and All Saints* was formerly part of Witley Court, the seat of Lord Foley. The previous medieval building was torn down in the early 18C and a baroque structure was then erected on the old foundations in 1735. The unorthodox ground plan shows two small transepts at the E. end level with the altar; the tower rises above the entrance at the W. end. Only a small part of the outstandingly good interior decoration is local. The

Battle (Hastings), Abbey

Bateman's (Hastings), Rudyard Kipling's house

magnificent stained-glass windows, which were designed by Francesco Sleter the Venetian and built by Joshua Price in 1719, were purchased by Lord Foley from the heirs of the Duke of Chandos, Marlborough's paymaster. The magnificent painted panels on the ceiling are the work of Antonio Bellucci and came from the same source (it is likely that the organ front did too). All the rich stucco decorations are in gold, as is the background of the altar panels. The S. transept contains the monument to the first Lord Foley, built by Michael Rysbrack in the first half of the 18C.

Hastings
East Sussex/England   p.332 □ L 16

Today Hastings is a popular holiday resort along with *St. Leonards,* although the latter is mainly residential. Hastings was once an idyllic fishing village, whose memory comes alive when the visitor wanders through the narrow streets of the old town with its pretty 16C half-timbered houses. During its heyday in the Middle Ages, Hastings was one of the five Cinque Ports and a base of the Royal Fleet. It was consequently the frequent target of French attacks, especially during the Hundred Years' War (1337–1453). The town's importance diminished as the harbour silted up.

St. Clement's and All Saints: This fine medieval church was built in the Perpendicular Style in the 14C.

Castle: The remains of the castle built by William the Conqueror after the Battle of

Bodiam Castle (Hastings)

Hastings in 1066 occupy *Castle Hill*, high above the old town.

St. Clement's Caves: These sandstone caves go back some 65 ft. into *West Hill*, a spur of *Castle Hill*.

Fisherman's Museum: This house built near the harbour in the 19C was really intended to be a chapel. Today the *Enterprise* may be admired here. It is the last fishing boat built in Hastings. Fishermen's children are still baptized on its deck.

Museum and Art Gallery: This museum in Cambridge Road shows Lord Brassey's *Pacific Collection*.

White Rock Pavilion: An *embroidered tapestry*, worked by the Royal School of Needlework 900 years after the Battle of Hastings, depicts events of English history after 1066.

Also worth seeing: *Bottle Alley*, the shore promenade, whose walls are covered with innumerable colourful glass fragments. The *Conqueror's Stone* commemorates William the Conqueror, who is said to have once breakfasted on it. Also of interest is the *fishing quarter*, where the boats have to be pulled up onto the beach for lack of a harbour. The nets are dried in tower-like buildings or net-lofts, which were erected in this fashion in the 16C because the fishermen had to pay a high rent and so built upwards for economy. Numerous Georgian and Regency houses are ranged side by side along the shore promenade towards *St.Leonard's*. The *flower clock*, made up of over 30, 000 plants, in the *White Rock Gardens* is a magnificent sight. Here also there is a *miniature Tudor village*.

Environs: Bateman's (*c.* 10.5 m. NW): Here is the house (built in 1634) where the writer Rudyard Kipling lived 1902–36.

Battle (6 m. NW): This picturesque town, some of whose houses date from the 13–14C, was the site of the *Battle of Hastings* in 1066, in which the Saxon King Harold II was defeated by his Norman opponent William, and England then came under Norman rule. William vowed to build a church here if he won. However, nothing has survived of this. *Harold's Stone*, erected in 1903, marks the site of the former high altar and the place where he died. The massive *entrance gate*, belonging to the Benedictine monastery which William later built around the house, is a major point of interest in the town today. Also worth seeing are *St.Mary's Church*, which is a 12C Norman building, and the *Battle Historical Society's Museum*, which offers an extremely rich collection documenting the history of Sussex from earliest times to today.

Bodiam Castle (9 m. N.): This square 14C *castle*, with battlemented towers and surrounded by a moat is picturesquely lo-cated. It was never besieged, and today is an impressive example of a castle built with more attention to domestic comfort than previously.

Brede Place (5 m. NE): A castle-like building from the 14C with a fine weapon collection; there is also some work by the sculptress Claire Sheriden. Interesting chapel.

Burwash (11 m. NW): *Rampyndene* is a typically rural half-timbered building with a large roof and chimney (17C).

Fairlight (1 m. E.): You can take a delight-ful walk over the *Firehills* into this little village.

Haverfordwest/Hwlfford
Dyfed/Wales   p.330□F 14

This small town (with some 9,000 inhabi-tants) is located at the point where the Western Cleddau flows into the ria which has Milford Haven at its mouth. It was founded by the Vikings. The Normans built a *castle* here in the 12C to defend the

Haverfordwest, St.Mary's Church, capital

andsker (the division between the English- and Welsh-speaking areas), which was extended in the 13C. The castle was razed by Oliver Cromwell in 1648. Its ruins house a *museum* of the town's history in a 19C building.

St.Mary's: The *nave* is the oldest part of the church and dates from 1170 (the intermediate arcades from 1240). The *capitals* have superb carvings of grotesques, figures and heads, etc., e.g. a monkey playing the harp, a lamb biting a serpent in the head (victory of Good over Evil), and a monk with a beer mug on his head. Notable features include the *oak ceiling*, a Perpendicular clerestory in the nave, carvings on the 15C *Mayor's Bench,* and the fine Early English *S. portal*. There is also a *sarcophagus slab* with the figure of a pilgrim (*c*. 1450; by the SW window). Only sparse remains survive of an old *monastery* near the hospital.

Environs: Dale (about 12 m. SW): This romantic fishing village is on the S. tip of the peninsula. It contains an old restored *castle*, whose original S. wing still survives. From the cliffs some 2 m. S. of Dale, the visitor may enjoy a splendid view of the open sea and Milford Haven Bay with lighthouses.

Llawhaden (8 m. NE): The ruins of the old *bishop's castle* of Llawhaden are to be found here in the idyllic valley of the Eastern Cleddau. The bishops of St.David's had this castle built in the 13C to protect their estates. A fine gateway and a gatehouse with slender towers, the S. wall with two towers, and the castle chapel and tower, have survived. Behind the old Cleddau bridge we find the 13C *parish church* (rebuilt in the 14C) with an old and new tower and a fine pulpit. Nearby, to the S., is *Blackpool Mill* the only tide-driven mill in Great Britain (built in 1813).

Marloes (9 m. SW): Here we find remnants of a prehistoric *castle on a cliff* with a three-tier line of ramparts and ditches. The names of the offshore islands of *Skomer, Skokholm* (derived from Stockholm) and *Grassholm* point to the fact that it was inhabited by the Norsemen in the 11C. These islands are a Nature Reserve

Haverfordwest, St.Mary's Church

Oak ceiling

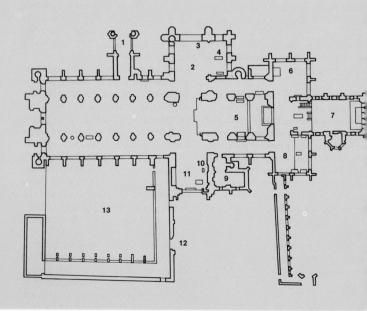

Hereford Cathedral 1 Bishop Booth's portal **2** N. transept **3** tomb of Bishop Thomas Charlton **4** tomb of Bishop Thomas Cantelupe **5** choir **6** NE transept **7** Lady Chapel **8** SE transept **9** sacristy **10** altar **11** S. transept **12** ruined chapterhouse **13** cloister

and there is a bird observatory on Skokholm.

Milford Haven (*c.* 6 m. S.): This small town of some 15,000 inhabitants was founded in the 18C by returning American immigrants (Quakers). It is located on the natural harbour of the same name. Geologically speaking Milford Haven is a drowned river valley, up to 2 m. wide and 20 m. long, with numerous branches. It has up to five large bays, 16 smaller creeks and over 15 good shipping lanes.

Narberth (about 9 m. E.): Remains of a poorly-preserved *castle* with corner towers can be seen in the S. of this little town. Legend has it that the Celtic prince Pwyll

resided here and once exchanged his rul for that of Arawn, the king of the dea (Book of Mabinogion, chapter I).

Picton Castle (about 4 m. E.): The well preserved castle, with its park, dates fro the 13C. The interior decorations are Ge orgian from 1740. An interesting pictur gallery with works by Graham Sutherland

Roch Castle (about 6 m. NW): This 13 castle stands on the road to St.David's an is today the residence of Lord Kehswoo

---

Hereford

Hereford and Worcester/England p.332☐H 1

This old town on the left bank of the Wy was the seat of the bishop of Lichfield i 672. In the Middle Ages this little tow had a 'firm castle with many towers' im

Hereford Cathedral

mediately above the river, but nothing has survived of this.

Cathedral: Dedicated to St. Mary and St.Ethelbert, legend has it that the church owes its existence to an apparition. The spirit of St.Ethelbert, who was murdered by Offa of Mercia in 794, is said to have appeared and called for a church to be built to atone for his murder. Thus the church was built in 825 above the tomb of the saint and became the first church in the region to be built of stone. When the Welsh came in 1056 the church and town were burned down; the Norman bishop Robert de Losinga had the church rebuilt in 1079. His successor, Bishop Reynelm (1107–15), created the first church to have a nave from this round church. The initial work on the Lady Chapel was carried out under William de Vere (1186–99); the E. end was finished in *c.* 1220. The large N. transept was completed by *c.* 1260. The church is some 360 ft. long and the central tower rises some 180 ft. above the Norman crossing; the tower was built by Bishop Adam of Orleton (1312–27), as was the chapterhouse, only ruins of which survive. The W. tower fell down in 1786 and pulled the W. part of the Norman nave down with it. The opportunity was then taken to rebuild the nave and the W. front in the neo-Gothic style.

Although so much building has been done over many centuries, the cathedral has a surprisingly clear *ground plan*. The nave and choir each have two aisles; two smaller transepts are inserted between the choir and the Lady Chapel and there is a larger transept at the level of the crossing which has sturdy arches supporting the tower. On the S. side is St.Ethelbert's Chapel, which

Hereford, Cathedral, nave

is a transept reduced in size by the sacristy. The *nave* is still impressively Norman despite the alterations arising during the reconstruction work after the W. end fell down. The massive pillars and the connecting arches with their rich decorations still give a vivid impression of the nave's former appearance. The *transepts* show a strong early-Gothic influence, and the oak chancel was built about 1610. The large *N. transept* is also early Gothic, with some 15C stained-glass windows. Bishop Thomas Cantelupe was interred here in 1282, and his tomb at one time attracted large flocks of pilgrims. The bishop's shrine shows some notable figures of Knights Templar of whom he was Grandmaster. Bishop Thomas Charlton, who died in 1344, lies here in a tomb with a baldacchino. The *S. transept* still has a very Norman character; on the E. wall there a

triptych which was built in 1530. The *choir* is a captivating feature, with its splendidly designed triforium and the Early English clerestory. The latter dates from the early 13C, as does the vault. The bishop's throne and the choir stalls both date from the 14C. The early English *Lady Chapel*, completed in *c*. 1220, impresses by the five lancet windows in the E. wall. Some of the windows have 14C stained glass. In addition to numerous bishops' tombs, the cathedral has two very precious items. One of them is Richard of Haldingham's *Mappa Mundi*, a medieval map of the world, which is not only one of the largest, but also one of the best-worked maps in Europe, and was probably painted on parchment in Lincoln in about 1275. The centre of the map is Jerusalem, and it depicts the medieval concept of the world outstandingly well. The other precious item is the *chained library*, the largest of its kind in the world. Some 1500 books, some of them manuscripts and others early printed works, are locked to the shelf with chains in such a way that although they could be taken out and read, it was not possible to take them away. The shelf for the chained library was built in 1611; more than 70 of the books here were printed earlier than 1500.

City Museum and Art Gallery: This museum shows some exhibits from the Bronze Age, Iron Age, and the Roman Castra Magna (5 m. NW). Apart from scientific and geological finds from the environs, the exhibits include ceramics and glass, and also watercolours by local artists.

Environs: Kilpeck (5 m. SW): The small Norman *church* of 1145 is quite unique. Impressive for its exceedingly rich decoration, this very decoration is in itself a problem, for it seems to have no direct connection with similar forms in Normandy; rather, it seems to be bear some relationship to the cathedral of Santiago de Com postela in N. Spain. Probably the most impressive feature is the *S. gate*, whose columns (double column on the right) and staggered arches show an excess of individual interwoven motifs (plants, flowers, fruits, serpents and dragons). The *chancel arch* is of similarly outstanding design.

Hermitage Castle
Borders/Scotland   p.324□H 9

This castle in the formerly wild earldom of Liddisdale dates back to the early 13C and initially belonged to the Soulis clan. In 1320 Robert the Bruce seized the castle, which then came into the possession of William Douglas, Knight of Liddisdale. The lords of this powerful Border clan were little disturbed by the fact that they first had the Scottish and then the English king as their feudal lord. The Soulis clan were successful with this policy of vacillation until 1491. The oldest parts of the building, an L-shaped tower house and a domestic building around a narrow courtyard, date from the initial period of Douglas rule.

The castle was much extended in *c.* 1400, with additions at both E. and W. ends. The corners of these wings were secured by four sturdy *defensive towers*. A new well was dug in the SE tower; kitchen and bakery were housed in the SW tower. The towers, connected by blind walls, have a Gothic arch with a gate on each of the N. and S. sides. James IV of Scotland brought the policy of vacillation to an end in 1491 when the Douglas clan had to cede the castle to Patrik Hepburn, Earl of Bothwell, who was loyal to the king. The castle was officially confiscated in 1540 because of the clan's relations with England. The building fell into ruins from the 17C onwards, before being restored by the Duke of Buccleuch in 1820.

Hereford, Cathedral, triptych

Environs: Hawick (9 m. N.): A notable collection on the history of the Border region is on show in the *municipal museum*.

Hertford
Hertfordshire/England   p.332□K 14

This old town on the Lee still has a large number of 16&17C houses in the town centre. Fore Street has houses decorated with stucco.

Hertford Castle: Building began in *c.* 1100. The castle belonged to the crown until the reign of Elizabeth I. (Edward III kept the dead body of his mother, Queen Isabella, lying on a bier in the castle for three months.) David Bruce, King of Scotland, King John of France (after the Battle of Poitiers) and Henry Bolingbroke, Duke of Lancaster, were all incarcerated here. In the reign of James the castle was sold to William Cecil, the Earl of Salisbury, and his family is still in possession of the building. Only an octagonal tower and remnants of the blind wall survive from the 12C building. The gatehouse dating from 1465 was rebuilt in the 18C.

Museum: This is housed in a 17C halftimbered building. Exhibits include archaeological finds, geological specimens as well as examples of handicrafts; there is also an exhibit on the history of the Hertfordshire regiment.

Environs: Broxbourne (6 m. SE): The church of *St.Augustine* dates from the 15C and has an octagonal Norman font. One peculiar feature is that nave and chancel are not separated by a triumphal arch. The church contains numerous tomb monuments and memorial tablets.

Waltham Abbey (12 m. SE): The *Abbey Church of the Holy Cross* is all that remains of a Norman monastery founded by Harold in 1060. Harold was buried in the monastery after the Battle of Hastings in 1066. All that has survived of the Norman church is the nave and aisles. The S. Chapel was not built until the 14C; the W. tower is 16C. Sir E.J. Poynter painted the ceiling of the nave. The tripartite E. window, rebuilt in 1861 to a design by Sir Edward Burne-Jones, has a superb Tree of Jesse.

Ware (3 m. NE): The centre of this town has preserved much of its old character. There are still numerous half-timbered houses from the 16&17C. 15C houses, in which the Bluecoat school was housed (1674–1761), still stand in *Bluecoat Yard*. Small houses built in 1698 for nursemaids and children stand opposite. John Scott, the Quaker poet, lived in the elegant *Amwell House* built of red brick. The Council Office is housed in the remains of an old *Franciscan priory*, founded by Thomas Wake in 1338.

Hexham
Northumberland/England   p.324 □ I 1

Hexham, a bishopric from 678 onwards under the Anglo-Saxon *Hagulstald,* was completely destroyed by the Danes in 1810. In 1464, during the Wars of the Roses, Edward IV and his Yorkshire troops defeated the units from Lancashire under Henry VI.

Hexham Abbey (also known as *Priory Church* or *St. Andrew*): An Anglo-Saxon monastery, originally founded on this site by St.Wilfrid in 678, was destroyed as early as the mid 9C. It was rebuilt from 1113 onwards by the Archbishop of York for Augustinian canons, and work on the present church began *c.* 1180 in splendid Early English style (it is known to the experts as a 'textbook of Early English architecture'). The nave, destroyed by Scottish troops in 1296, was rebuilt in 1908. The E. façade dates from the 19C.

Particularly noteworthy features inside include: the old *staircase* in the S. transept with its direct access to the monks' dormitory so that the monks could perform their night offices without making a detour; an ancient *tombstone;* and an 8C Anglo-Saxon *cross.* The magnificent *choir* contains the old stone *bishop's seat* known as 'Wilfrid's Throne' from the first church of the earlier monastery. From the same period come the *'frith stool'* ('peace stool') which offered safety to law-breakers on the run, and the 15C *choir wall.* In the original *crypt* of the old Anglo-Saxon church ('Wilfrid's Crypt'), Roman building materials were used.

Also worth seeing: *Moot Hall* (14C) was formerly the official seat of the bailiffs of

Hexham, view

the Archbishops of York. The 14C *Manor Office* served as the bailiffs' prison and is unique in England. *Shambles,* a market hall supported on columns, dates from 1766.

Environs: Blanchland (*c.* 9 m. S.): An 18C village built on the site of a Premonstratensian monastery founded in 1165. Today the *chancel* and *N. transept* of the former monastery church form the parish church of *St.Mary the Virgin.* Immediately adjacent are the old *porch* and the monastery's *storage building,* which is now a guest house.
Carrawburgh (*c.* 10 m. NW): Remnants of the Roman castle of *Brocolitia* (a temple of Mithras from the 3C AD was uncovered in 1950).
Chollerford (*c.* 6 m. N.): Excavations of the Roman camp of *Cilurium* (Chesters

Fort) on Hadrian's Wall. Items surviving include an almost complete *watchtower.* The best-preserved *thermal baths* in England are on the bank of the N. Tyne. There are remains of a *bridge* across the N. Tyne, which carried the wall and military road across the river. The *museum* has a good collection of excavation finds.
Chollerton (*c.* 7 m. N.): Fine *church,* with a nave borne by Roman columns; the font was formerly a Roman altar).
Corbridge (*c.* 2 m. E.): Capital of the Kingdom of Northumbria in the 8C. 13C *parish church* (Anglo-Saxon tower; Roman spolia inside) and a fortified 14C *parsonage.* About 1 mile W. of the town are the remains of the Roman military camp of *Corstopitum,* a border fortress from the 1C AD, which was extended in the 3C AD into a base-line town for the garrisons of Hadrian's Wall. Notable excavation finds

in the *museum* include many inscriptions and the famous 'Corbridge Lion'.

Housesteads (*c.* 12 m. NW): The finest of the Roman forts on Hadrian's Wall, *Vercovicium* spread over about 5 acres, garrisoned some 1,000 men; granaries and soldiers' billets survive. Interesting excavation finds in the *museum*.

Langley Castle (*c.* 7 m. W.): A fortified 14C *mansion*.

Simonburn (*c.* 7 m. NW): The 13C church of *St.Mungo*, whose choir was restored by the famous architect Anthony Salvin in 1863. Remains of an Anglo-Saxon cross.

Warden (*c.* 2 m. NW): An interesting *church* with an Anglo-Saxon tower; an ancient Roman arch has been integrated into the building).

Hitchin
Hertfordshire/England   p.332□K 14

This old trading town has several houses from the 16&17C. George Chapman, the great Homer translator, was born here.

St.Mary's: The large parish church dates mainly from the 14&15C; the lower part of the *W. tower* goes back to the 12C. The *choir screen* and the stone *font* are 15C. The *tomb monuments* are late 15C, and there is an especially beautiful tombstone slab from 1478; a tomb monument of 1697 may be by William Stanton of Holborn.

Environs: Ashwell (12 m. NE): This little town is impressive for its numerous old *half-timbered houses*, some of which date back to the 16C. The church of *St. Mary's* dates from the 14C. One of the walls of the tower has a rare sgraffito of old St. Paul's Cathedral. There are two tapestries by Percy Sheldrich. The *Ashwell Village Museum* began with the collection formed by two schoolboys in the 16C. The museum documents village life in England and its development from Prehistoric times until today.

Knebworth (8 m. S.): The church of *St. Mary* was originally Norman but was later extended. There are some *tomb monuments* worth seeing, including two by Edward Stanton from *c.* 1700, and one with the figure of Lytton Lytton, by Thomas Green of Camberwell in *c.* 1710. *Knebworth House* was begun by Sir Robert Lytton in 1492. Although partially destroyed in 1812, many of the old building materials have survived. The large Tudor hall (with Jacobean ceiling) has survived undamaged and is particularly beautiful. In 1843 the first Lord Lytton rebuilt the outside of the house in Gothic style. Today the building contains valuable furniture from the 17&18C, a portrait collection, and mementoes and manuscripts of Sir Edward

Housesteads (Hexham), remains of the Roman border fortress of Vercovicium

Bulwer-Lytton the novelist and author of 'The Last Days of Pompeii'.

Howden
Humberside/England   p.328☐K 11

St.Peter: A former collegiate church, built mainly in the 14C, it has a cruciform ground plan with a massive tower over the crossing; the chancel has been in ruins since the end of the 17C. Inside there are interesting *tomb monuments*, some of which are medieval. S. of the church are the remains of an octagonal *chapterhouse*.

Environs: Carlton Towers (some 8 m. SW): The *castle* of the Dukes of Norfolk, originally built in 1614, was rebuilt in 19C Victorian neo-Gothic.

Eastrington (*c.* 4 m. NE): The church of *St. Michael* was originally pre-Romanesque but later extensively altered in Romanesque style. Inside is the splendid tomb monument of a judge who died in 1546 and is shown in his robe and armour.

Goole (*c.* 2 m. S.): Since the 19C this has been a port on the lower reaches of the River Ouse. The church of *St. John* was built by the 'Aire and Calder Navigation Company' in 1843 (inside are many memorial tablets to ships and their crews lost at sea). The *Lowther Hotel* in Aire Street is also worth seeing (18C Georgian Renaissance style).

Rawcliffe (*c.* 5 m. SW): The former home and burial place of Jimmy Hurst, a famous eccentric, who attempted to fly using wings he himself built (reign of George III, 1760–1820).

Huntingdon
Cambridgeshire/England   p.328☐K 14

Oliver Cromwell's birthplace, it dates back to the Romans, together with its suburb of Godmanchester. The *E. and W. gates* of the Roman garrison have been excavated, as have the *baths*.

St. Mary the Virgin (Godmanchester): This church built of cobblestones was erected in the 13C; its stone *tower* is 17C. The church was extended and rebuilt in the 14C; the *clerestory* is 15C. The *choir stalls* with their beautifully-carved misericords date from the same time.

All Saints: This late Gothic church, much restored, contains the *register* where Cromwell's birth and baptism are entered (rescued from the devastated church of St. John).

Hinchingbrooke House: This dates back to an early-13C Benedictine convent. After the Dissolution of the Monasteries it came into the possession of the Cromwell family. Sir Richard Cromwell, Oliver's grandfather, converted the building and made a Tudor house out of it. Queen Elizabeth I was received here in 1564, and the possession was sold to Sir Sidney Montagu in 1627. The building, used as a school today, may be visited.

Cromwell Museum: This is accommodated in the house where Cromwell once went to school. The house dates from the *Hospital of St. John* founded by David I of Scotland in the early 12C. This hospital was converted into the town's school in 1565. Today it houses numerous mementoes of Cromwell.

Environs: Buckden (5 m. SW): The church of *St. Mary*, near the former bishop's palace, is Gothic in period and has a tower with a fine spire and a two-storeyed entrance hall on the S. side. The 17C pulpit, and some remains of the medieval stained-glass windows, are worth seeing. **Buckden Palace** was used as a residence by the Bishops of Lincoln from the early Middle Ages until 1838. The oldest surviving parts of the building are the large tower and the inner gatehouse. Both come from the building commissioned by Bishop Rotherham in the 15C. Bishop Russell completed the building.
Catherine of Aragon lived here 1534–5 before being taken to Kimbolton Castle.
Kimbolton Castle (10 m. W.): From the early Middle Ages, this castle was used by Henry VIII from 1535 as a prison for his divorced wife, Catherine of Aragon, until she died. Parts of the building fell down in 1707, whereupon the first Duke of Manchester commissioned John Vanbrugh to reconstruct the complex. By 1714, Vanbrugh had built the present rectangular building with its courtyard. Robert Adam added the outer gatehouse in 1766.
  Papworth St. Agnes (7 m. SE): The *Manor House* is largely Elizabethan and was owned by William Mallory. The building was rebuilt in 1660.
St. Ives (7 m. E.): The ruins date back to the foundation of the daughter monastery called Ramsey (969). In *c.* 1050 this became a small *priory* dedicated to St. Ivo, a Persian bishop. However, nothing has survived of the priory apart from remains of walls. The six-arched *bridge*, built across the River Ouse in 1415, has stood the test of time well.

Inveraray Castle
Strathclyde/Scotland   p.324□F 8

Inveraray is the old county town of Argyll. The castle is the seat of the Dukes of Argyll, the chiefs of the Campbell clan. At the time of the Jacobite risings the Campbells took the side of England in order to gain sanction for their struggle with their arch-enemies, the MacDonalds. Their en-

mity towards the Stuarts had begun when the Marquis of Montrose burned Inveraray in 1645, and the Stuarts had two members of the Argylls executed in Edinburgh in 1681 and 1685.

Inveraray is one of the few examples in Scotland of a castle unscathed by war, but demolished on the orders of the lord of the castle himself. In the mid 18C, Archibald, Duke of Argyll, was no longer pleased with his old ancestral seat on Loch Fyne. He had

Inveraray Castle

Inverness, Inverness Castle

it torn down along with the village around it, and gave Robert Mylne the commission to rebuild the village a little way from the castle. Inveraray thus became the first completely planned castle in Scotland. The classical *church*, completed in 1795, was divided in two by a wall: one half for the church service in English, and the other for that in Gaelic.

The classical *castle* with its medieval elements was designed by Roger Morris in 1744, and Robert Mylne both supervized the building and designed the interior. The tapestry and dining-room, both dating from 1780, are his work. Since money was no object, French decorators were hired to paint the ornaments on the walls and ceilings. Guinand was responsible for the grisaille figures, and Girardy for the garlands of flowers and arabesques. The Beauvais tapestries were woven in 1785.

There are some fine paintings by Gainsborough, Ramsay and Raeburn. All this, and numerous exhibits relating to the history of the family, together with documents dating as far back as 820, can today be admired again following the restoration of the castle after a fire in 1975.

Inverewe Gardens
Highlands/Scotland   p.324☐F 5

In 1862 Osgood MacKenzie began to lay out a tropical *garden* on what was then a bare W.-facing slope. Behind a windbreak of stone-pines and Scotch firs, MacKenzie planted subtropical plants, palms and shrubs from almost the entire Empire on topsoil especially carted in. His achievements with hortensia and magnolia were

The city

quite outstanding, thus showing, with genuine Scottish tenacity, what can be done if only it is properly begun.

The garden is today looked after by the National Trust and is one of the sights of Scotland.

Inverness
Highlands/Scotland   p.324☐G 6

Lying at the end of the Great Glen, in the 6C it was the site of the capital of the Pictish kingdom. St.Columba visited the Pictish king Brude here in 565. Macbeth's castle probably stood here in the 12C. The first *castle* was built by King David I in *c.* 1141 and William the Lion surrounded it with a rampart and moat in 1180. Cromwell had *Sconce Fort* built in 1652-7 in or-

der to control the Highlands more firmly. Prince James Francis Edward was proclaimed King James VIII in Inverness castle in 1715, but this did no good either to him or the Jacobites. The town became Jacobite again for a year in 1745&6 until the Duke of Cumberland, in the tried and tested Scottish tradition, finally had the castle burned down after the battle of Culloden on 17 April 1746.

Tour of the town: *Abertaff House,* the oldest house in the town, dates from 1592 and has one of the few surviving outside spiral staircases. Today it is used by the Highland Association for the preservation of the Gaelic language and culture. The *Town Hall* built in 1878-82 is wholly Victorian. It is mainly of interest for its old *market cross* with the stone of the tubs (Clach-na-Cudainn), on which women

Inverness, Victorian Town Hall

could place heavy loads or water-buckets. Apart from the modern 19C *castle,* there is also the *museum,* where archaeological finds, Jacobite mementoes, objets d'art and weapons from the Highlands are on display. *St. Andrew's Cathedral* was built in 1866–71. Its font is a copy of the famous 'angel font' in Copenhagen.

Outside the town, to the E., is the site of the *Battle of Culloden,* where the last hopes for an independent Scotland under Jacobite rule perished in the blood of the Highlanders. A National Trust information centre provides an audio-visual depiction of the battle; the *stone pyramids* which the individual clans built to their dead along the road indicate the mass graves. A simple stone to the dead of the Duke of Cumberland with the inscription: 'The English were buried here' is the only symbol of unity.

Environs: Beauly (6 m. W.): The Frasers of Lovat, a Norman family, lived here. In the 12C they introduced Anglo-Norman (an Old French dialect) as the official language for their area of jurisdiction and thus created a linguistic island within a Gaelic-speaking area. Sir John Bissit of Lovat founded a Valliscaulian *priory* in 1230. The associated *church* was built in the 14–16C, while the present façade dates from about 1530.

Cawdor Castle (about 7 m. NE): According to Shakespeare, Macbeth was a Thane of Cawdor. If one were to believe the tradition, the murder of Duncan was in Cawdor Castle (1040). But this cannot be true, since the castle was only built in 1454. The *drawbridge* and the massive *central tower* are both of interest. Today the castle is lived in by Earl Campbell of Cawdor, but can be visited.

Leith Hall (Inverurie)

Maiden Stone (Inverurie)

Fort George (about 9 m. NE): The fort was built after the battle of Culloden and is one of the best-preserved examples in Europe of an 18C fort with gun emplacements. It was named after King George II and it is still in an excellent state. Inside there is the *regimental museum* of the Queen's Own Highlanders.

Inverurie
Grampian/Scotland   p.324☐H 6

There are several medieval sights scattered around this small town at the confluence of the Urie and the Don. In the middle of the town is the *Brandsbutt Stone,* a massive, irregular block with Ogham writing and Pictish symbols. The *local history museum* is also worth a visit.

Environs: Leith Hall (about 8 m. NW): The oldest sections were built around 1650, while the E. and the S. wings were built or raised in 1756. The choir with the Renaissance façade was built in 1868. Leith Hall was the seat of the Leith family for 300 years and is today maintained by the National Trust of Scotland.
Loanmead Stone Circle (5 m. NW): This circle of stones dates from between 1800 and 1600 BC and has a circular burial site at its centre.
Maiden Stone (4 m. W.): The most famous early Christian monument in Aberdeenshire is on Drundurno Farm. The stone is decorated with Celtic symbols and ornaments on one side, and bears Pictish symbols on the other.
Pitcaple Castle (3 m. NW): The oldest parts of this *small castle* with its Z-shaped ground plan date back to the second half

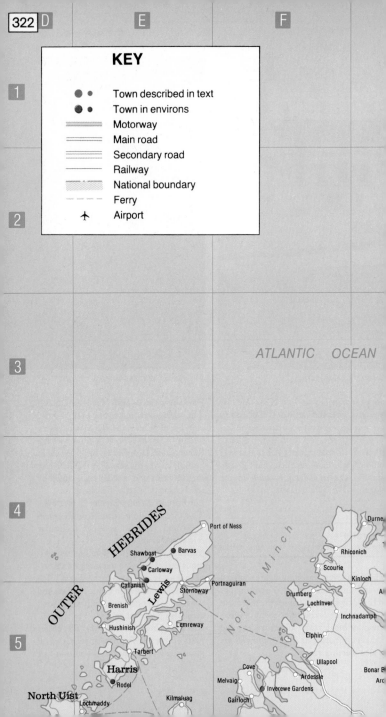

Unst

Dalsetter

Yell   Funzie

Burravoe

S H E T L A N D

Mainland   Laxo   Brough

I S L A N D S   Walls

Girlsta

Scalloway   Lerwick

Broch of Clickhimin

Broch of Mousa

Rerwick

Jarlshof

Westray

Egilsay   Sanday

Birsay   Broch of Gurness

Mainland

Skara Brae   Maeshowe

Stromness   Kirkwall

Orphir

O R K N E Y

I S L A N D S

Hoy   **South**

Ronaldsay

Pentland   Firth

Scrabster

John o'Groats

Thurso   Castletown

Dalhalvaig   *NORTH SEA*

Achavanich   Wick

Kinbrace

Dunbeath   Lybster

Berriedale

hbeg   Helmsdale

Dunrobin
Castle

onoch Firth

Wilkhaven

Moray Firth

to Aberdeen

N

30km

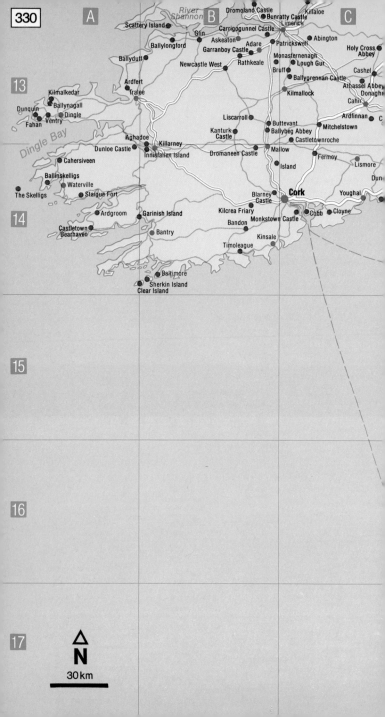

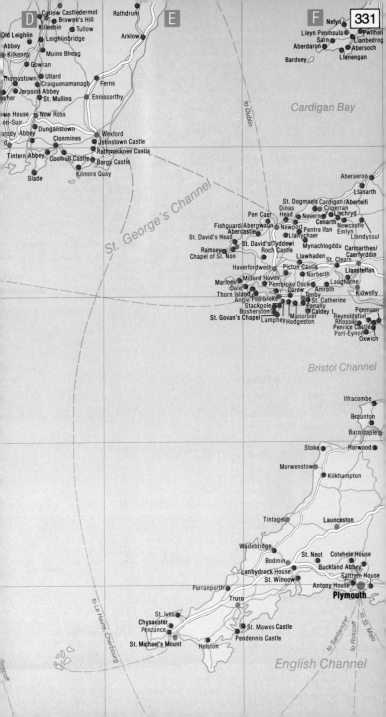

D

Carlow Castledermot
Browne's Hill
Killeshin
Tullow
Rathdrum

Old Leighlin
Abbey
Leighlinbridge
Kilkenny
Muine Bheag
Arklow

Gowran
Thomastown
Ullard
Craiguenamanagh
Ferns

Jerpoint Abbey
St. Mullins
Enniscorthy

ther
New Ross
own House
on-Suir
Dunganstown
Wexford
irdy Abbey
Clonmines
Johnstown Castle

Tintern Abbey
Coolhull Castle
Rathmacknee Castle
Bargy Castle

Slade
Kilmore Quay

E

to Dublin

F

Nefyn
Lleyn Peninsula
Pwllheli
Sarn
Llanbedrog
Aberdaron
Abersoch
Llanengan
Bardsey

Cardigan Bay

Aberaeron
Llanarth

St. Dogmaels
Cardigan/Aberteifi
Dinas
Head
Cilgerran
Lechryd
Pen Caer
Neverne
Cenarth
Newcastle
Emlyn
Fishguard/Abergwaun
Pentre Ifan
Llandyssul
Abercastle
Newport
Llanychaer
St. David's Head
Mynachlogddu
Carmarthen/
Caerfyrddin
St. David's/Tyddewi
Roch Castle
Llawhaden
St. Clears
Ramsey
Haverfordwest
Picton Castle
Llansteffan
Chapel of St. Non
Narberth
Laugharne
Marloes
Milford Haven
Kidwelly
Dale
Pembroke Dock
Carew
Amroth
Thorn Island
Tenby
Angle Pembroke
St. Catherine
Penmaen
Bosherston
Penally
Reynoldston
Stackpole
Caldey I.
Rhossili
St. Govan's Chapel
Lamphey
Manorbier
Penrice Castle
Hodgeston
Port-Eynon
Oxwich

Bristol Channel

Ilfracombe
Braunton
Barnstaple

Stoke
Horwood
Morwenstow
Kilkhampton

Tintagel
Launceston

Wadebridge
Bodmin
St. Neot
Cotehele House
Lanhydrock House
Buckland Abbey
St. Winnow
Saltram House
Perranporth
Antony House
Truro
Plymouth

St. Ives
Chysauster
Penzance
St. Mawes Castle
St. Michael's Mount
Pendennis Castle
Helston

to Le Havre, Cherbourg
to Santander
to Roscoff
to St. Malo

English Channel

St. George's Channel

of the 15C. Three monarchs (James IV, Mary Queen of Scots and Charles II) visited it. It is still in family hands, but open to the public.

Iona (I)
Strathclyde/Scotland   p.324☐E 7

This tiny island off the SW tip of Mull was the cradle of Scottish Christianity, and for centuries it was the intellectual centre of the country and the last resting place of Scottish kings. St.Columba landed here in 563 to proclaim Christianity to the Scots. He was an Irish prince wearing a penitential robe and accompanied by twelve men. When he died in 597, he left behind a church of wood and clay, whose foundations have not yet been clearly located, for times were always harsh on Iona. In 794 and 801 Vikings devastated the monastery and in 806 they slew sixty-eight monks at once in Martyrs' Bay. The sarcophagus of St. Columba was then taken to its Irish home in the monastery of Kells. The Vikings laid the island waste again in 825 and 986. In 1093, the Norwegian king Magnus Barefoot finally gained control over it and it did not come under Scottish rule again until 1266. There was no monastic life to the island from 1561, when the Scottish parliament dissolved the monasteries, until 1938, when the Iona Community recommenced its work. The island only returned to its true purpose when Christians of various denominations combined themeselves into an order in the spirit of St.Columba. The island is now a nucleus of social commitment again, as it was 1400 years ago and the restoration of the abbey is an outward sign of this.

Benedictine Nunnery: This was founded by Reginald MacDonald of Islay and lasted from 1203 to 1561. Some parts of the *refectory* and *cloister* have survived,

as have some remains both of the *choir* of the nunnery church and of the *sacristy.* The 15C *MacLean's Cross* is decorated with Irish ornaments. It was built by or for a MacLean of Duart.

Reilig Odhrain: The *kings' graveyard* is the oldest Christian graveyard in Scotland. No less than 48 Scottish, four Irish and eight Norwegian kings have their last resting place here. Kenneth MacAlpine, who united Scotland, rests here, as do King Duncan and his murderer Macbeth. Shakespeare's 'Icolmkill', the charnel house of the ancestors, means the 'island of Columba's cell', and this in turn is the Gaelic name of the island of Iona. Unfortunately, nothing has survived of the tombs. The kings were interred in Dunfermline Abbey from the 11C onwards. The old tomb slabs cover the graves of 13&14C chieftains.

St.Oran's Chapel: The *graveyard chapel* was probably built as early as the 8C. In its present form it most probably dates from the time of Queen Margaret in c. 1080. If tradition is to be believed, the chapel is on the exact site where St Columba built his first church—however it has not been possible to prove this.

Benedictine Abbey: Even the entrance is unique. The 'Street of the Dead' once led from Martyrs' Bay to the abbey. Some 330 ft. of this old burial way have been uncovered in front of the cathedral. By the road is the enormous 12C *St. Martin's Cross.* Priests once preached at the cross, which is about 14 ft. tall and is decorated with scenes from the Bible and Irish ornamentation. Apart from Kildalton in Islay, this cross is the only Celtic cross in Scotland and is a combination of the Christian cross with the circle as a symbol of the Druid sun god. The nearby *St.John's Cross* is a modern restoration.

Work on the cathedral was begun in the

Iona, Benedictine Abbey

2C. It shows Romanesque and early Gothic elements. The stumpy tower over the crossing, supported by four Romanesque arches, rises to 70 ft., exactly the same as the width of the nave. The church fell in ruins from 1561 onwards, and so did the attached monastery. It was only after the 8th Duke of Argyll presented the monastery to the Church of Scotland in 1899 that the reconstruction of the cathedral was undertaken, continuing until 1910. Work on restoring the cathedral has been in progress since 1938.

Ipswich
Suffolk/England   p.332☐L 14

This, the county town of Suffolk, lies on the mouth of the Orwell and was inhabited in prehistoric times. The Saxons called it *Gipeswic;* the Danes plundered it in 991 and 1000. King John gave the town its first political constitution in 1199. The town enjoyed a heyday in the 16C when it was one of the most important wool ports. Cardinal Wolsey was born here in 1475, and the painter Thomas Gainsborough also lived here (1727–88).

Church of St.Mary-le-Tower: This is the town's parish church and was rebuilt in the second half of the 19C. Its *tower,* about 190 ft. tall, is impressive.

Church of St. Margaret: This Gothic church attained its present form in the 15C. Its double *dragon-beam* ceiling and the *clerestory* (also 15C) are impressive.

Christchurch Mansion: This Tudor

country house was built in 1548–50 on the site of a 12C Augustinian priory and rebuilt in 1675 after a fire. Today the building serves as a *museum* which, in 36 rooms, displays an extensive collection of furniture, antiques and paintings, mainly by artists from the county of Suffolk. The picture collection includes works by Churchyard, Constable, Gainsborough, Munnings and Steer.

Ipswich Museum: This contains a fine collection devoted to the county's history and natural history. Its exhibits range in time from prehistory to the Roman occupation of East Anglia, and the Middle Ages. The museum's contents are rounded off by a collection of tropical and indigenous birds.

Environs: Aldeburgh (about 19 m. NE): This seaside resort which is today mainly known for its music festival was once an important harbour. A number of well-preserved houses date from its time as a port, including the *Moot Hall,* a 16C half-timbered building. The Perpendicular *Church of St.Peter and St.Paul* is 16C. Its W. tower and the font inside date from the 14C.

Butley Priory (16 m. NE): The *Gate House* is 14C and was once part of an Augustinian priory, which was founded by Ranulf de Glanville in 1172. It is worth seeing for its numerous coats-of-arms carved from stone, including those of England and France and the three crowns of East Anglia. Many of the principal families of East Anglia also have their coats of arms here.

Freston Tower (5 m. S.): This six-storeyed *tower house*, built of brick and having a continuous spiral staircase, dates from *c.* 1550.

Grundisburgh (8 m. NE): In the nave, S. aisle and a chapel of the early Gothic *Church of St.Mary,* there is an outstanding hammerbeam ceiling which is decorated with a large number of angels. There

is a 13C fresco of St.Christopher which is worth seeing.

Hadleigh (11 m. W.): This little town was once a centre of the wool trade, and still has some fine old *houses* from the 15&16C as well as some Georgian ones. The *Church of St.Mary* dates from the 14C, while the W. tower with its spire was built in the 15C. The font is 14C, whereas the choir screen and the carved pew-ends date from the 15C. The organ case is early 18C. The *Deanery Tower* dates from 1495 when it was a gatehouse for the palace of Archbishop Pykenham. Inside is an octagonal prayer room with brick vaulting.

Kersey (12 m. W.): This beautiful old weaving village is impressive for its numerous fine *half-timbered houses*. The *Church of St.Mary* has a 15C W. tower, but the church itself was largely rebuilt in the 19C. The oldest of the interior furnishings is the font, which is Gothic and decorated with carvings of angels. There is a fresco of St.George and the dragon.

Orford (22 m. E.): The *castle* was built by Henry II between 1165 and 1173. The 18-sided polygonal keep still stands; three corner towers are incorporated in it. However the outer fortifications—curtain wall and towers—have been destroyed.

Woodbridge (8 m. NE): Numerous old *houses* dating from the 15&16C. The large *Church of St.Mary* is Perpendicular, and its somewhat ponderous W. tower was added in the 15C. The font with the symbols of the seven sacraments dates from the same period. A monument to a local family dates from the 17C and is decorated with some good figures.

Jersey (I)
Jersey/England   p.332☐H 1

Jersey, the largest and southernmost of the

Ipswich, Church of St.Margaret

Channel Islands, was Norman during the Middle Ages and remained a part of England in 1450, along with the other Channel Islands, when Normandy itself fell to France. The islands are subject to the Crown but owing to their historical background they have a political constitution of their own. French is an official language.

St.Helier: The capital of Jersey is also the home of the *Jersey Museum,* which is devoted to archaeology, history, art history, and handicrafts. The development of the islands is shown from the earliest times up to the present day. An art gallery is attached, containing the works of local artists.

Hougue Bie: The Stone Age *chamber tomb* dates from *c.* 2000 BC. It consists of an arrangement of large stones from the nearby coastline, and is designed in such a way that the central chamber can be reached via side chambers. The entire complex was covered over with gravel and earth and formed a high burial mound. When the tomb chamber was opened by

archaeologists in 1924, it turned out that it had unfortunately already been plundered. The *Church of Notre Dame de la Clarté* stands on the hill. It is 12C and was probably built to mark the triumph of Christianity over heathendom. The *Jerusalem Chapel* was added in 1520 by Dean Mabon when he returned from a pilgrimage to Jerusalem. In the crypt of the chapel there is a copy of Christ's sepulchre from the Church of the Holy Sepulchre in Jerusalem. The *German Occupation Museum* has a collection of exhibits from the time of the Nazi occupation during the Second World War. The *Agricultural Museum* shows how agriculture has developed on the island.

Jervaulx Abbey
North Yorkshire/England   p.328☐I 1?

Cistercian abbey: It was founded in 1156, and in its heyday it commanded the entire upper valley of the Ure. The monks of the abbey were well-known as good

Jervaulx Abbey, ruins

horse breeders. The abbey fell into disrepair very rapidly after the Dissolution, and Adam Sedburgh, its last abbot, was hanged at Tyburn in 1537 for taking part in the 'Pilgrimage of Grace'. The site of the abbey church was not even known until 1805, the year when excavations began; the open remains of the monastery buildings were for centuries used as a quarry.

All that still remains of the *church*, which was originally 280 ft. long, are some low sections of the exterior walls, two altars, the bases of some pillars, and the raised site of the high altar. In the *chapterhouse*, built in the 12C Early English style, the portal is of particular interest. There are two beautiful round-arched windows to the sides of it. There are 15 different *stonemasons' marks* scattered all over the abbey.

Environs: Bedale (some 6 m. E.): Of interest is the 13&14C church of *St.Gregory* with its massive tower. The latter was formerly used for defence. *Bedale Hall* (18C Georgian) today houses a museum of local handicrafts.

Masham (about 5 m. SE): This town has a fine *church* (12–14C; the substructure of the tower is Norman and there is an octagonal roof). Inside, above the chancel arch, is a painting which is thought to be part of a Nativity by Reynolds which was destroyed by fire in 1816.

Middleham (about 4 m. NW): Apart from the church of *St.Mary and St.Alkelda* (originally built in *c.* 1280 and later enlarged; fine windows in the aisles, 15C), another building worth a visit is *Middleham Castle*. Founded by the Normans, it was the place where King Edward IV was held prisoner in 1469 by the Neville family, to whom the castle belonged from the 13C onwards. It was devastated by the Parliamentarians in 1646 during the Civil War. The surviving features include the keep, the chapel and the great hall.

Well (about 6 m. SE): Known for its *Roman baths* (the largest in England after those at Bath). In the *church* are some fine monuments to the Latimer family (one of them is said to have slain the 'largest dragon in the world' in the neighbourhood).

West Tanfield (about 7 m. SE): The remains of a *castle* (a 15C tower and gateway with a fine Perpendicular window survive). The *church* (originally Norman, now Perpendicular) is worth a visit. Inside are the notable tombs of the Marmion family. These were restored in the 19C, in some cases not very well.

Jervaulx Abbey, base of pillar

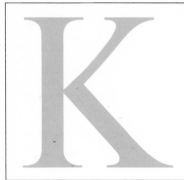

Kells/Ceanannus Mór
Meath/Ireland   p.326□D 11

This small town grew up around an early
Christian monastery founded by St.
Columba (St.Colum-cille) in the 6C. It has
a series of interesting early medieval
features.

St. Columba's House: This interesting
9C *stone oratory,* with a rectangular ground
plan, vaulting and stone roof, is a striking
example of old Irish religious architecture.
It has an attic and has been partly rebuilt
(entrance).

Round Tower: This was part of the old
monastery, now in the churchyard, and
must date from the 11C. Over 90 ft. high,
it was a place of refuge. Now its cap is missing and it has 5 windows. The famous
Book of Kells (8/9C), was written in Kells
monastery and is now in Trinity College,
Dublin.

High Crosses: The *South Cross,* near the
round tower, dates from the 9/10C and is
dedicated to St.Patrick and St.Columba.
The 11 ft. high cross is decorated with lavish biblical scenes (Fall of Man, Abel,
Fiery Furnace, Daniel, Abraham, David,

Feeding of the 5, 000, Apocalypse and
others). There are three other *high crosses*
in the graveyard (10–12C), including the
East Cross depicting the Crucifixion. The
Market Cross (10C) in the middle of the
town is richly decorated (frieze with horse
and foot soldiers; biblical scenes).

Environs: Castlekeeran (*c.* 3 m. NW):
Sparse remains of a *monastery* founded by
St.Kieran in the 6C, with ornamented high
crosses (near the church ruins). Nearby is
an *Ogham stone* with inscription (*c.* 7C).
The nearby *St.Kieran's Well* is still a place
of pilgrimage (in August).
Oldcastle (*c.* 13.5 m. NW): SE of the village is a *prehistoric burial place* with about
30 gallery graves with main and side chambers from the 3–1C BC. The hill of *Slieve-
na-Calliagh* (Loughcrew Hills) is one of
Ireland's most impressive burial grounds
(with ramparts, standing stones and
earthworks).

Kelso
Borders/Scotland   p.324□H

A beautiful small Border town at the con

Kelso, Floors Castle

fluence of the Teviot and the Tweed, described by Sir Walter Scott as Scotland's most romantic village. The English occupied the town in 1522, 1544 and 1545 and could only be dislodged by the Scots with difficulty.

Kelso Abbey: The oldest and richest abbey in the Borders was founded by King David I (1084–1153), who, in 1116, summoned monks from France and then settled them in Selkirk. 12 years later they came to Kelso when David established a new abbey here. For centuries the abbey grew and prospered undisturbed; indeed its influence grew so strong that its abbots even challenged the supremacy of St. Andrews. In 1460 James III was crowned king in the abbey church, but after the death of James IV at the Battle of Flodden Field the abbey's fate was sealed. Scottish chieftains fought over its ownership and in 1523 it was set ablaze by the English. In 1545 it was used as a refuge and the last 102 defenders were hauled out of the main tower and executed. The proportions of the abbey church are in accordance with the importance of the monastery, with transepts at both ends of the nave arranged in the style of Romanesque churches on the Rhine (Worms). The ground plan, in the form of a double cross with a tower at the W. and E. ends, can no longer be discerned from the ruins, but is recorded in an old document in the Vatican. Parts of the *W. façade, W. transept* and *W. tower* are preserved, as are remains of the *nave.* Particularly impressive is the 800 year old W. façade with its two-tiered Norman windows, the stump of the main tower and 2 smaller side towers. The great tower was borne by four 50 ft. high pointed arches, two of which remain. Although not entirely pure in style, the façade nevertheless betrays Lombard influence. Unfortunately nothing remains of the abbey buildings.

Floors Castle: Sir John Vanbrugh and William Adam were the architects of this castle, begun for the 1st Duke of Roxburgh in 1718. In 1838 – 49 it was altered in romantic Tudor style by William Henry Playfair along the lines of Heriot's Hospital, built in Edinburgh in 1616. It was then that it acquired its 365 windows, one for each day of the year. The interior furnishings are mostly those brought by the wife of the 8th Duke of Roxburgh on the occasion of her marriage. According to tradition, a 500 year old yew tree in the castle park marks the spot where King James II was killed by an exploding cannon in 1460.

Also worth seeing: *The Cross Keys Hotel* is a good example of an 18C mail-coach inn. *Ednam House,* built in 1761, has an Italian rococo ceiling. *Rennie Bridge* was built as a five-arched bridge over the Tweed in 1800-3 by John Rennie; the 1811 Waterloo Bridge in London, pulled down in 1934, was copied from it.

Environs: Mellerstain House (*c.* 7 m. NW): This is a good example of an 18C Scottish mansion. The building was begun by William Adam around 1725 and completed by Robert Adam in 1770–8. Original stucco and painting inside, and most of the furnishings date from the time of construction. Its park is also worth seeing.

Kendal
Cumbria/England   p.328□H 1°

Holy Trinity: Originally 13C, the present church is mostly Early English; the oldest part of the building is on the SE side. Inside there are two pairs of aisles, both the same length as the nave. Of interest are the remains of *frescos* and 4 *chapels* with beautiful oak; the oak ceiling of the church has been completely renovated apart from a few individual details. At the E. end of the N. aisle are the colours of the Westmorland

Kelso, countryside

Regiment from 1755 to 1881; also of interest are the sword and helmet of 'Robin the Devil', a member of the Philipson family, who distinguished himself by his boldness during the Civil War.

Castle: Built in the 12C, it is now in ruins (remains of the walls and moat; a round tower and remnants of two other towers and the keep are recognizable). The castle was probably the birthplace of Katherine Parr, the sixth wife of Henry VIII (1509 –47).

Abbot Hall: Georgian mansion built in 1759 by the architect John Carr of York. The ground floor has the *original furnishings* from the time of construction (beautiful period furniture); on the upper floor is a collection of works by modern painters and sculptors. In the former stables is the *Museum of Lakeland Life and Industry* with collections concerning the crafts and industries of the Lakes.

Also worth seeing: *Castle Dairy*, which served the purpose its name suggests, was built in Tudor-Renaissance style in 1564. The *Town Hall* contains pictures by the great English painter George Romney (1734 – 1802) and the prayer-book of Katherine Parr. *Kendal Museum* with exhibits related to local natural history and archaeology.

Environs: Cartmel Fell (*c.* 7 m. SW): With the church of St. Anthony (early 16C); of interest inside is the three-tier pulpit and beautiful old stained glass.
Crosby Garrett (*c.* 15 m. NE, near Ravenstonedale): Remains of 3 *Iron Age settlements* (occupied up to the Roman inva-

Levens Hall (Kendal), park

sion); foundation walls of rectangular huts and the rampart surrounding the whole complex survive.

Levens Hall (*c.* 5 m. S.): Splendid 16C *mansion* (Elizabethan), the core of which is a 13C fortified tower house. Interesting period furniture and 17C panelling inside. The unusual *park* (laid out in 1689 by the French landscape gardener Beaumont) includes a collection of old steam-engines and locomotives (guided tours during opening hours).

Sizerburgh Castle (*c.* 3 m. S.): Ancestral home of the Strickland family since 1239; the present building has a 14C defence tower and additions from later periods (notably 15, 16 and 18C). The interior includes beautiful ceilings and wall panelling.

Witherslack (*c.* 9 m. SW): The *Church of St. Paul* was built in late Gothic style in 1669 (altered in the 18&19C); beautiful wood and stained glass from the time of construction.

Keswick
Cumbria/England   p.328□H 10

Church of St. Kentigern (in Crosthwaite): Local parish church, built in the early 16C in Perpendicular style on the site of a pre-Norman building (its patron saint was a 6C Bishop of Glasgow, to whose diocese Keswick once belonged). Restored by Sir Gilbert Scott in 1845. Inside is an interesting old *font* (1390, with the arms of Edward III; 8 side panels bear lettering, some of which is still undeciphered); also of interest are the *windows* (on the left, above, is St. Anthony with a cross in the shape of a Greek T); also a *monument* to the English poet Robert Southey and in the choir is the *tomb* of Sir John Radcliffe and his wife.

Also worth seeing: *Moot Hall* (market place, 1813). *Greta Hall,* where Robert Southey lived from 1803–43. *Fitz Park Museum,* with an interesting model of the Lake District and many mementoes of Wordsworth, Southey and Ruskin (including original letters).

Environs: Carrock Fell (*c.* 10 m. NE): Remains of an Iron Age *hill fort.* The ramparts survive and take in, on the E. side, a few stone cairns which were built over Bronze Age graves.

Castle Rigg Stone Circle (*c.* 2 m. E.): *Stone circle,* some 4–5000 years old, with a diameter of about 100 ft; 38 stones are still standing. Experts believe it was probably used for religious purposes.

St. Herbert's Island (on Derwent Water S. of Keswick): Remains of a 7C *hermitage* in which Herbert, a contemporary of St. Cuthbert, lived.

Keswick, Church of St. Kentigern

Sarcophagus of Sir John Radcliffe and his wife

Kidwelly/Cydweli
Dyfed/Wales   p.332☐F 14

This ancient town with a decayed harbour, at the mouth of the river Gwendraeth in Carmarthen Bay, is one of the oldest Norman towns in Wales (founded 1094).

Castle: The wood and earth castle was built around 1100 and was altered several times in the 13&14C. Set on a hill, it has a splendid *gatehouse* leading to the outer *ward*. The *inner ward* (built around 1280) is almost square and has a strong *round tower* at each corner. The gate opened in the S. wall and in the N. wall there was a small postern. On the upper floor of a tower is a pretty *chapel*. The ruins of the *Great Hall* are still visible, while the *kitchen* with fireplace is still well preserved. In the

water, between the castle and the medieval *bridge* (14C), are the foundations of a medieval *mill*.

Also worth seeing: The 13&14C *parish church* (greatly altered in the 19C) dates back to a Benedictine priory. It is cross-shaped (English type) with a tower and has a beautiful font with a stone seat. Contained here is the tomb of a 13C lady of the castle. Nearby (Causeway St.is the *Prior's House* (13C) a much-altered remnant from the old priory.

Kildare
Kildare/Ireland   p.326☐D 12

This little country town (some 34 m. SW of Dublin) grew up around a convent founded by the Irish St. Brigid.

St.Brigid's Cathedral: Brigid, the 'Virgin of the Gaels', built her convent around 480 on a pagan religious site. Following its destruction by Vikings (9C) a Gothic *church* was built around 1200. In 1686 the *choir* was rebuilt and in about 1875 the entire church was restored. The cruciform church has beautiful *pointed arches* and old *tombs* (13–16C). Its *round tower* (108 ft. high) has a Romanesque gate; the battlements are 18C. In the graveyard are a (damaged) *cross* and the remains of an old *Fire House* for the 'Eternal Light' of the originally mixed Celtic community.

Also worth seeing: On the edge of the town (towards Nurney) are the ruins of the Franciscan *Grey Abbey* (1260). Hardly any traces remain of *Kildare Castle* (11&12C). In the suburb of Tully is the famous *National Stud* with its interesting *Japanese Gardens.*

Environs: Naas (*c.* 12.5 m. NE): This racing town was once the capital of the Kings of Leinster. A *keep* and other parts of a 12C *Norman castle* still stand.

Old Kilcullen (*c.* 7.5 m. E.): Traces of an old monastery survive here: remains of a *Round Tower* and parts of 3 tall *granite crosses* decorated with figures (9C). Near the town is the *burial mound of Dun Ailinne,* seat of the first Kings of Leinster.

Kilkenny
Kilkenny/Ireland   p.330☐D 13

This small industrial town (pop. *c.* 17,000) in the Nore valley is the centre of County Kilkenny. It has preserved its medieval character very well and is one of Ireland's most charming towns. Its venerable buildings (in fact built of limestone) have earned it the nickname of the 'Marble City'.

History: The Celtic St.Canice (Gaelic Chainnigh) founded a monastery in the 6C, as the town's Gaelic name Cill Chainnigh ('Church of Canice') suggests. The Anglo-Norman invaders under Strongbow built a *fortress* on the river in 1172, which was added to under William the Marshal in 1204. Under James Butler, Earl of Or-

Kilkenny, Kilkenny Castle

monde (around 1391) Kilkenny held sway over wide stretches of S. Ireland and became the regional capital. The town was often the seat of the Anglo-Irish parliament. In 1366 the famous 'Statutes of Kilkenny' were passed here, forbidding the Anglo-Norman population, under penalty of death, to marry anyone of the Irish race or to speak Gaelic. Those Irish driven from the Old Town settled in the suburb of Irishtown. From 1642–8 the Irish Confederation Parliament met here, representing a kind of early Irish national parliament. Their goal was the religious freedom of the Irish Catholics and the end of England's policy of colonization. This historic new beginning was crushed by Cromwell's troops in 1650.

St. Canice's Cathedral: This church, situated in Irishtown, is one of Ireland's most beautiful and best-preserved cathedrals. It was built in 1251–86 in Decorated Style on the site of the first monastery founded by St. Canice. The *central tower* was rebuilt after its collapse in 1332. Of interest are the battlemented *walls* and quatrefoil *cloister windows,* as well as the old 100 ft. high *Round Tower* to the S. (new roof). The interior contains beautiful monuments and tombs. The old *Bishop's Tomb* lies behind the high altar, the S. transept contains the tombs of the Earls of Ormonde (16&17C). Also of interest is the black *marble font* of the 12C, *St. Kieran's Chair* and the ribbed *cloister vaulting* of 1465. Next to the cathedral is *St. Canice's Library* with an important collection of psalters, including the 'Red Book of Ossory' and other rare editions from the 16&17C.

Black Abbey (Abbey St.: This Dominican Abbey, incorporating *Black Friars Church*, was founded by William the Marshall in 1225. Rebuilt in the 19C, the church retains some older sections: the 13C nave, the S. transept (14C) and the tower over the crossing, added in 1517. Inside is a 15C *alabaster statue* and a medieval *wooden statue* of St. Dominic; in the old graveyard are 15–17C *tombs*.

Franciscan Friary: Of this 13C monas-

Kilkenny Castle

tery there remains only the original *choir*. This was enlarged in the 14C, with the addition of interesting *windows*. The tall tower over the crossing (1350) is one of the earliest Franciscan towers in Ireland.

Kilkenny Castle: The castle stands in the High Town, on the site of Strongbow's original fortress of 1172. Despite repeated alterations and restorations (particularly by W. Robertson, 1826) it has retained its impressive medieval character. Three of the massive cylindrical *towers* are 13C, the beautiful *gateway* and gate are late-17C. From 1397–1967 the castle belonged to the Butler family. The famous *Butler Archives* (castle library) are now in the National Library in Dublin. Nearby are the 18C outbuildings and stables, where interesting jewellery and weaving are produced in the *Kilkenny Design Workshop*.

Rothe House (James Street): The splendid Tudor *town house* (1594) of a merchant, Rothe, is probably the finest building in the town. It consists of 3 parallel sections with 2 *inner courts* and beautiful 16C *half-timbering*. The *museum* of the Archaeological Society, with collections relating to local history, has been housed here since 1966.

Also worth seeing: *Kilkenny College* was founded in 1666. The building, with a 100 ft. Round Tower on the S. side of the church, dates from 1782. *Shee's Hospital* with a small chapel was built in 1581 as a place of refuge for the outlawed Catholics. The Catholic priest's seminary, *St.Kieran's College*, houses a small *museum* with medieval finds from the diocese of Ossory. The *Town Hall* (Tholsel) was originally built as an exchange in 1761. On the upper floor is a well preserved *assembly room* and a *collection of historical documents* concerning the town's history (including the 13C 'Liber Primus'). *Kyteler's Inn* (1324) is one of the oldest houses in

Kilkenny and is now, following restoration, again in use as an inn. One of its owners, Alice Kyteler, is supposed to have only narrowly escaped being burned as a witch in the 14C.

Environs: Callan (*c.* 9 m. SW): Remains of *St.Mary's Church*, built around 1460 (W. tower preserved) and of an Augustinian monastery founded around 1462. Nearby Slievenamon Hill (2,368 ft.) appears in the Old Celtic saga of King Finn MacCool and the hero Dermot (compare Siegfried's Saga).

Gowran (*c.* 7.5 m. E.): The town has an interesting (now Protestant) *church* of 1275 with numerous medieval sections and tombs.

Jerpoint Abbey (*c.* 12 m. SE): One of the most beautiful ruined monasteries in Ireland. The Cistercian abbey was founded in 1180 by the Lord of Ossory. The Romanesque choir and transept have beautiful capitals; the nave is later. The impressive angular tower rising above the crossing and crowned by battlements, and the *cloisters* with fragments of arches date from the 15C (richly decorated double columns). Inside are interesting *tombs*, including a bishop's tomb (1275) in the N. of the choir (figures of knights). To the E. of the cloister lay the sacristy, chapterhouse, dormitory, refectory and kitchen.

Kells (*c.* 7 m. S.): In the village are the remains of a strongly fortified *Augustinian priory* of 1192. In the second inner court the Lady Chapel of the church still stands. Close by (to the S.) is an interesting medieval *Round Tower* (roof missing), next to the remains of a church and a 9C cross adorned with geometrical motifs.

Knocktopher (*c.* 15 m. S.): Of interest here are a medieval tower, a Romanesque *portal* and 15–17C *tombs* from the old village church (Gothic).

Thomastown (*c.* 10 m. SE): This was

Jerpoint Abbey (Kilkenny)

Killarney, Cathedral

founded in the 13C by the Norman lord Thomas (FitzAnthony). There are still *towers from the fortifications* by the bridge over the Nore and remains of a 13C Protestant *church* with modern additions. The *stone altar* in the nearby Catholic church comes from Jerpoint Abbey.

Killarney

Kerry/Ireland   p.330 □ B 14

This popular holiday resort lies in enchanting countryside by Lough Leane, at the foot of Ireland's highest mountains, Macgillycuddy's Reeks (Carrauntoohill, 3,414 ft.).

Muckross Abbey (*c.* 2.5 m. S. of the town centre): This Franciscan abbey was founded by the MacCarthys in about 1340 (14C additions). Of interest are the massive square *tower*, the *E. window* of the ruined church and the small *cloister* with round and pointed arches. In the *choir* are the tombs of the MacCarthys and other noble families. Nearby lies *Muckross House*, built in Elizabethan style in 1843. Inside is a beautiful collection of crafts, furniture, paintings and a folklore museum.

Ross Castle (*c.* 2 m. SW of the town centre): The 14&15C ruined castle stands on the Ross Island peninsula on Lough Leane. The *keep* provides a beautiful view over the lake. Also preserved are the outer walls with *corner towers*.

Cathedral: The Catholic cathedral (New Street) was built in 1846–55 in imposing Gothic Revival style by Pugin. It is the

Killarney, Jaunting Car

finest Catholic church of its kind in Ireland.

Environs: Aghadoe (*c.* 4 m. NW): This lakeside village contains remains of a 12&13C *monastery church*: a Round Tower, portal and window from the 13C and an Ogham stone (5/6C) in the W. wall of the choir. Nearby are the ruins of *Parkavonear Castle* (13C), probably a former bishop's residence.
Dunloe Castle (*c.* 6 m. NW, at the NW end of Lough Leane): This *fortress* dates from around 1215 and was completely renovated as a hotel. In the castle park are medieval ruins and a group of *Ogham stones* (5/6C).
Innisfallen Island (*c.* 2.5 m. SW): On this island on Lough Leane, which has splendid trees, are the remains of *Innisfallen Abbey*, founded by St.Finian in the 7/8C. 13C

sections still stand, including the W. part of the church with a beautiful W. portal. Near the shore is a small 12C *oratory* (early medieval prayer house) with a Romanesque portal (decorated with animal heads).

Kilmallock
Limerick / Ireland   p.330 □ C 13

This once well-fortified little town was founded by the FitzGerald family and was the seat of the White Knights, the Earls of Desmond, up until the 16C.

Dominican Church: Monastery and church were founded by the FitzGeralds and considerably extended in the 14&15C. Worth seeing are the ruined 13&14C church with a beautiful 5-arched E. window, S. transept, ruined tower, the remains of cloister and living quarters and the tomb (1608) of the last White Knight, 1608.

Also worth seeing: The former parish church of *St.Peter and St.Paul* (collegiate) dates from the 13–15C. There are the remains of a Round Tower and the S. portal (15C). Of the old town fortification there survive *Blossom Gate,* parts of the *town ramparts* with 2 *fortified houses* and the *keep* of the 15C *King's Castle,* which was destroyed by Cromwell.

Environs: Ballygrennan Castle (3 m. N.): Well preserved and extensive castle with a 16C central tower (17C additions). **Bruff** (*c.* 4 m. N.): Important *prehistoric finds* were made to the N. of the village by the shore of little Lough Gur. These included megalithic tombs, stone circles, remains of hill forts and foundations of houses.

King's Lynn
Norfolk/England   p.328☐L 13

The old port on the Great Ouse was originally called Bishop's Lynn and was a walled town. Of these *town walls,* however, there remains but little—the *S. gate* (1520) still stands.

Chapel of St.Nicholas: Founded in 1146 about half a mile N. of the Church of St. Margaret by Bishop Turbus, who wanted thereby to create a new town centre. The oldest houses around it date from the 14C. The large chapel dates in its present form from the mid 15C, only the *SW tower* being older. This, however, has a later spire (1869). Note the *S. portal* and the *roof.*

Church of St. Margaret: This was founded around 1100 by Bishop Losinga. It acquired its two W. towers in the 12C

and was partly rebuilt in the 13C. In 174 it was altered once more by Matthew Bret tingham. The *choir screen,* parts of the *choir stalls* and good *misericords* date from the 14C. The *pulpit* is early Georgian, whil the *organ* dates from 1754. The most un usual features of the interior are 2 *brasses* amongst the finest examples in England which were made in Holland or Germany The older one was made for Adam de Wal soken, who died in 1349, and consists c a circle of scenes from everyday life. The second was made for Robert Braunche who died in 1364, and is called the Peacoc Brass after the scene depicting a feast give by Braunche for Edward III.

Guildhall of the Holy Trinity: Built i 1421, it is chequered with different type of stone. First added to in Elizabetha times, in 1895 the *Town Hall* was built on The treasury contains some fine items *King John's Cup* (14C) is the oldest surviv ing secular chalice. This fine piece is deco rated with enamels of hunting scenes Hardly less fine are *King John's Sword,* beautiful *chain of office* of 1512 and th *Nuremberg Cup* of *c.* 1600.

Lynn Museum: This displays collection devoted to local geology, archaeology an history.

Museum of Social History: A museum of crafts and applied art.

Environs: Castle Rising (*c.* 4.5 m. NE) Perhaps the most interesting village in th county, this was once an important port be fore the sea receded. Its importance to th Normans is indicated by the *castle.* This stands within a 66 ft. high ring of earth ramparts, one of the most impressive of its kind in England. Its origins are still not en tirely clear, but it is certain that during th time of the Roman occupation there had been a stronghold here with a ring of ram parts. Around 1150 William de Albini

Earl of Sussex, who was married to the widow of Henry I, built a castle within the existing ramparts. Around 1330 the castle became the residence of Queen Isabella, mother of Edward III. In 1544 it was inherited by Thomas Howard, Duke of Norfolk, whose family still own the castle to this day. *Trinity Hospital* was founded in the 17C by Henry Howard, Earl of Northampton, during the reign of James I, and was completed before 1617. The Jacobean almshouse consists of 9 houses arranged around a court, a common room and a chapel. It was built as a home for old ladies, who on Sundays still wear dress dating from the time of the Hospital's foundation.

North Runcton (3 m. S.): The *Church of All Saints* is one of the county's most beautiful early-18C churches. It was designed by Henry Bell and completed in 1713. The interior is dominated by *Ionic* columns and the whole interior furnishing is also by Henry Bell.

Sandringham (c. 7 m. NE): *Sandringham House,* a country house belonging to the Queen, was built in 1867–70 for Edward VII. It stands in a beautiful park with various gardens *(Rose Garden, Water Garden)* and is open to the public in the summer when the Queen is not in residence. There is also a small *church* in the park, which contains, among other things, a monument to Edward VII (with a beautiful silver altar).

Wiggenhall (c. 7 m. SW): The *Church of St. Mary Magdalen* dates back to the 13C. The *tower* is from this time, while the rest of the church was altered in Gothic style in the 14C. Fragments of the 15C *stained glass* are preserved; the *pulpit* is early-17C. The *stalls,* the *panelling* and the painted *grille* are Jacobean.

Kingston-upon-Hull
Humberside/England   p.328☐K 11

This town, generally known as 'Hull', was called 'Wyke-upon-Hull' until 1293; it has had a town charter since 1299 and was heavily fortified in the 14C. Shipbuilding and the fishing industry have brought the

Castle Rising (King's Lynn)

King's Lynn, Church of St. Margaret

town wealth over recent centuries; today Hull is one of England's most important sea and ferry ports.

Holy Trinity (Market Place): Built mainly in the 14&15C in Perpendicular style, completed in 1492. This is one of England's largest parish churches and has a cruciform ground plan and massive tower over the crossing. A feature of the church is its superb, richly decorated large Gothic *windows* on all its façade.

Maister's House (High Street): This Palladian house was built for the Maister family (merchants) in 1744. Of particular interest within are the Palladian *entrance hall* and the *staircase*, also the contemporary *wrought iron* by Robert Bakewell.

Trinity House (Trinity House Lane): Originally built as early as 1369 for the guild controlling pilotage of the Humber. The present building of 1753 houses the *Navigation School,* founded in 1787 (the oldest mariner's school in the world; the cadets still wear the historic English sailor's uniform of the 18C).

Wilberforce House (High Street): Merchant's house, built in the 17C in Elizabethan style; William Wilberforce (1759–1833), whose Abolition of Slavery Act of 1807 officially rid the British Empire of slavery, was born here. The house, still furnished in part with original period furniture, today contains a *museum* concerning the history of slavery and with an interesting collection of puppets and toys.

Forens Art Gallery (Queen Victoria Square): The town's art gallery, opened in 1928. It contains an extensive collection of European masters (including Canaletto, Guardi, Hals, Maffei) and a collection of modern English painters and sculptors (Henry Moore). Also of interest are the works by the 19C 'Marine Painters'.

Town Docks Museum (also *Maritime Museum;* Hessle Road): Museum of deepsea fishing (particularly whaling) and shipbuilding, housed in the former Dock Offices of Hull since 1975.

Transport and Archaeological Museum (High Street): The transport and communications section displays an impressive collection of old vehicles (automobiles, tracked vehicles, bicycles). The *Mortimer Archaeological Collection* exhibits, next to material concerning the history of Hull's whaling, superbly preserved Roman floor mosaics from the 4C (from Rudston, W. of Bridlington, and from Brantingham).

Also worth seeing: The 14&15C late Gothic *Church of St.Mary* (corner of Lowgate/Chapel Lane). *Charter House Hospital* of 1384, rebuilt in 1780 after being destroyed in the Civil War. *Guild Hall* (A. Gelder Street), the Town Hall with a splendid façade (contains a valuable collection of old documents concerning the history of the town). The *Wilberforce Monument* (in front of the Technical College) in commemoration of William Wilberforce (100 ft. high column). *'King Billy'* (S. of the Market Place), the local nickname for the gilded equestrian statue of William of Orange (late-17C). *Robinson Crusoe Plaque* (in the Queen's Gardens) commemorates the character from Daniel Defoe's novel (he set out from Hull). *Humber Bridge* (W. of the town centre), a suspension bridge over the Humber, opened in 1981 (without a central support; with a span of over 4,600 ft. it is the longest bridge of its kind in the world).

Environs: Burton Constable Hall (c. 7 m. NE): Elizabethan *mansion* built in 1570; extended and altered in the course of the 18C by Robert Adam amongst others. A puppet museum and a collection

Kingston-upon-Hull, Holy Trinity

Timoleague (Kinsale), Franciscan Priory

of old vehicles are two of the attractions to found in the grounds.

Cottingham (*c.* 1.5 m. NW): With the Gothic *Church of St. Mary the Virgin* (13 –15C).

Hedon (*c.* 5 m. E.): With *St. Augustine's Church*, known as the *'King of Holderness'* (nave 14C, choir mainly 13C). Inside are interesting Gothic windows and a richly decorated 14C font.

Patrington (*c.* 13 m. SE): With *St. Patrick's Church*, the *'Queen of Holderness'* (14C; particularly beautiful tower over the crossing; inside note the Easter Sepulchre on the N. side of the choir).

Skidby (*c.* 5 m. NW): With an *Agricultural Museum* housed in an old *windmill.*

Swine (*c.* 2 m. N.): The *Church of St. Mary* was the choir of a Cistercian convent church founded in the 12C; inside is a beautiful late Gothic E. window (1531).

Welwick (*c.* 15 m. SE): *Church of St. Mary* (originally Romanesque, rebuilt as 14C Gothic; in the N. aisle is an interesting medieval monument).

Kinsale

Cork/Ireland   p.330☐B 1

This picturesque little harbour on the estuary of the river Bandon played an important role in the 17&18C as an English naval base. In 1601 the Irish and Spanish forces were defeated here by the English (Lord Mountjoy).

St. Multose: This cruciform Protestant parish church dates from the 13C and has a massive *NW tower,* which was restored in the 18&19C. Also of interest are the medieval *font* and *tombs* from the 16&17C

Also worth seeing: *Desmond Castle* or *French Prison* is 16C. This town house, used at times as a prison, has beautiful windows, gates and coats-of-arms. The *Almshouse* with a red brick portal was built in 1682 and the 'Dutch' style former *Court House* in 1706; a small museum of local history and culture is now housed here. The crooked streets contain numerous 18C Georgian buildings.

Environs: Bandon (*c.* 12 m. NW): This town on the river of the same name was founded in 1608 by the adventurer and later Earl of Cork, Richard Boyle (see Youghal). *Kilbrogan Church* (1610) is one of the earliest Protestant churches in Ireland. Parts of the 17C *town walls* are also preserved.

Timoleague (*c.* 12 m. W.): The name means 'St.Molaga's House' and dates back to the saint's monastic foundation. Of the 13&14C *Franciscan Priory* there remains a roofless ruined church with S. arches and a slender tower.

Timoleague (Kinsale)

Kinvarra

Galway/Ireland   p.326☐B 12

A little port at the SE corner of Galway Bay with *Dungory (Dunguaire) Castle* on a rocky island in front of it. In the summer medieval banquets are held in the well- fortified tower. In the village are the ruins of a medieval *parish church* (*c.* 14C).

Environs: Ballyvaghan (*c.* 15 m. W.): Near this coastal village, in the barren karstic landscape of the Burren, there are numerous *megalithic tombs* testifying to prehistoric settlement. Here too is *Newtown Castle,* a 16C tower house.

Corcomroe Abbey (*c.* 4.5 m. W.): Of the 12C former Cistercian abbey there remain the ruined *church* with a five-arched E. window, 15C *tower* and *gateway.* Also

worth seeing is the *tomb* of King Conor O'Brien with beautiful carving (about 1267).

Kilcolgan (*c.* 5.5 m. NE): The ruins of *Tyrone House* (1779) and *Drumacoo Church* with beautiful 13C parts are worth seeing. To the SE are the ruins of the pre-Norman monastery church of *Kiltiernan,* surrounded by a wall (*c.* 11C).

Kirkby Lonsdale

Cumbria/England   p.328☐H 11

Church of St. Mary the Virgin: Built under King Stephen (1135–54), later altered. Inside note, on the N. side of the nave, 3 richly decorated and original *columns,* which alternate with clustered pillars; also worth seeing are the octagonal

17C *pulpit* and various 18C *panels*. The *graveyard* offers a wonderful view.

Also worth seeing: *Devil's Bridge* over the river Lune, with elements from the 13C. 17C *Manor House; Fountain House* (18C).

Environs: Casterton (*c.* 1 m. N.): To the N. of the village is a prehistoric *stone circle* (20 stones still standing).
Middleton Hall (*c.* 5 m. N.): Late-14C *mansion* (enlarged, with the addition of a wall and inner court, 15C). On open land close to the house is a Roman *milestone* (discovered 1836; 'No. 53 [LIII]' on the road to Carlisle). Also nearby is an old *cross*, called 'The Standing Stone of Whilprigg'.

Kirkcaldy
Fife/Scotland   p.324□H 8

The birthplace of Robert Adam, the architect, and Adam Smith, the economist, it has been a Royal Burgh since 1450. By

the harbour and in the adjacent alleys is a series of picturesque 17C houses, which now belong to the National Trust. The tower of the *parish church* dates from the 13C. The town's 3 museums are of interest: The *Town Museum* with an adjoining art gallery, the *John McDougall Stuart Museum* and the outstanding *Industrial Museum*.

Ravenscraig Castle: A little to the NE of Kirkcaldy are the impressive ruins of Ravenscraig Castle. Built by James II in 1460–3, it is protected by a deep moat carved out of the rock. The walls, built of rows of carefully hewn stones, are impressive and speak for the care of the builders. The castle is probably the first in Britain to have been specifically designed for defence by firearms. It was the ancestral home of the Sinclair family and the Earls of Orkney.

Environs: Burntisland (6 m. SW): The *church,* dedicated to St.Columba, is well worth seeing. It was built in 1592 as a copy of the old North Church in Amsterdam;

Kinvarra, Dungory Castle

the octagonal tower dates from 1749. The galleries with their emblems of the guilds are 17C. In 1601 the General Assembly of the Church of Scotland met in St.Columba and agreed to accept the Authorized Version of the Bible. This version was printed in 1611.

Knutsford
Cheshire/England   p.328 □ H 12

This little town on the NE edge of Cheshire's salt-mining area still has a series of old houses, including a few very fine Georgian and Victorian ones.

Church of St. John the Baptist: This classical brick church (1740–4) stands on the site of an earlier church of 1581. The *W. tower* has urns at each corner of the parapet.

Environs: Great Budworth (c. 7 m. W.): The *Church of St.Mary and All Saints* with its massive W. tower dates from the 14&15C. The choir stalls and the font are 15C. Sir Peter Leycester (1678) and Sir John Warburton (1575) are buried here.
Lower Peover (3 m. S.): The *Church of St. Oswald* is built of wood (except for its sandstone tower), but still dates from the 13C. The interior is impressive for its well-arranged wooden columns, wooden arches and timbered roof. Its dark oak contrasts superbly with the whitewashed walls. Font and pulpit are Gothic.
Mobberley (c. 2.5 m. E.): The *Church of St.Wilfrid* dates back to the 13C, but was probably not completed until the 15C. Impressive 15C ceiling over the nave, well-preserved choir screen from the same time and a few fragments of stained-glass windows. A fresco depicts St.Christopher. The most recent addition is the tower of 1683.
Tatton Park (c. 2.5 m. N.): The former ancestral home of Lord Egerton. It originally consisted of a smaller house from the time of Charles II. This was enlarged by Samuel Wyatt in the late 18C. The *garden* was laid out by Joseph Paxton, whose plan for an artificial lake was not carried out. There is, however, an orangery and a

Kirkcaldy, Ravenscraig Castle

Japanese garden with an original Shinto temple, which was imported from Japan in 1910 and set up by Japanese craftsmen. The series of terraced gardens is arranged in front of the S. façade of the house, which is dominated by 4 massive classical columns. The interior of the house today contains an interesting collection of Victorian furniture and paintings by Canaletto, van Dyck and others.

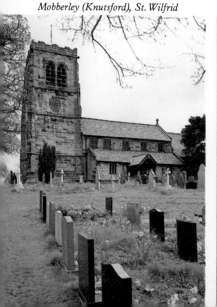

Mobberley (Knutsford), St. Wilfrid

Ceiling

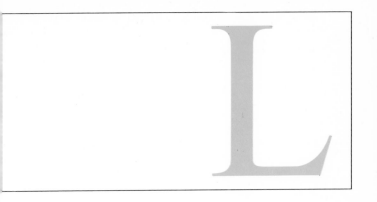

Lampeter/Llanbedr
Dyfed/Wales   p.328□G 14

This small town in the valley of the river Teifi (in Welsh: 'Llan-bedr' = 'St.Peter') has been the site of *St.David's College* since 1822. This is now part of the University of Wales but was founded by the Bishop of St.David's as a theological college. The interesting Gothic Revival college buildings, which are by Cockerell (1827), remind one of Oxford. The town is also well known for its annual horse market, held in May. Lampeter is a good base for a tour of the hills of central Wales (about 500 sq.miles in area).

Environs: Llanddewi Brefi (about 7 m. NE): This town has a 12&13C *church*, rebuilt in the 19C. An important synod was held here in Celtic times (6C) to oppose the Pelagian heresy. St.David (St. Dewi), the patron saint of Wales, made a speech at the synod. The *tombstones* and *carved crosses* in the churchyard, some of them bearing inscriptions, date from this early Christian period.

Llanfair Clydogau (about 3 m. NE, in the Teifi valley): Disused *silver mines*. There is a fine 14C font in the *village church*.

Pontrhydfendigaid ('Bridge of the saint's ford', about 13 m. NE). A single-arched 17C *bridge over the Teifi* survives.

Pumpsaint (about 6 m. SE): On the main road to Llandeilo, it has the remains of old *gold mines* (some of the galleries survive) which were worked as early as Roman times (the Dolaucothi mine).

Strata Florida Abbey (about 12 m. NE): The impressive and isolated ruins of one of the most famous abbeys and sites of pilgrimage in Wales (in Welsh: 'Ystrad Fflur' = 'Valley of the Flowers)'. This once rich Cistercian abbey was founded in *c.* 1164 and was regarded in the 12&13C as the 'political, religious and educational centre of Wales'. The surviving parts of the abbey church—Early English in style—include the round-arched portal with five archivolts on what was the W. front, the old 14C pavement tiles in the S.transept (formerly in the sanctuary), the transept chapels (three on each side) with their pavements and carvings, and the cloister, with alcoves, S. of the church (15C). Further features are the chapterhouse and the 13C sacristy. Some old tombstones survive from the former *graveyard,* including a monument to the Welsh bard Dafydd ap Gwilym (14C).

Tregaron (about 11 m. NE): A small market town and a starting point for trips to the lonely and beautiful hills (E. towards Abergwesyn).

Tynygraig (about 15 m. NE): In the *church* is a Celtic *tombstone* with a fine raised cross and an inscription.

Lancaster
Lancashire/England   p.328☐H 11

Priory Church of St. Mary: The first church was Saxon and the W. *portal* dates from this period. Perpendicular additions and alterations were made in the 14&15C. The powerful *tower* was built in 1759. Two features of particular interest inside are the richly decorated oak *choir stalls* (*c.* 1340) and the Jacobean *pulpit* by Louis Rubiliac, the French sculptor.

Castle: The first fortification on this site was built by the Romans and was taken over by the Saxons in the Dark Ages. In 1102 the Normans replaced the old wooden tower with a stone keep. Under King John (1199–1216), the building was enlarged to include a rampart, round

towers and a massive gatehouse; thereafter the main additions were within the castle (including a banqueting hall and the residential section). This was a stronghold of Parliamentary troops in the Civil War, and was mainly used as a prison. In the 18C it was also the seat of a court. An outstanding feature is the *keep* which is some 80 ft. high, with walls over 10 ft. thick. From one of its turrets, known as *John of Gaunt's Chair*, the Spanish Armada was sighted in 1588. The castle also incorporates the *Shire Hall* which has over 100 shields bearing coats of arms.

Lancaster City Museum: This is housed in the *Old Town Hall*, which was built in 1781 and rebuilt in 1873. Note the department of archaeology and history (with some Roman inscriptions, prehistoric finds, and a collection of model ships) and the art gallery (ceramics, porcelain, period furniture, paintings, drawings, etc.). The museum also has mementoes of the King's Own Royal Lancaster Regiment.

Also worth seeing: *St. John's Church* (Ge-

Lancaster, Priory Church of St. Mary

orgian, 1734). The *Friends' Meeting Hall* dating from 1690, a meeting place for the Quakers, who were founded by George Fox in the 17C. They referred to themselves as 'Friends'. The old *Custom House* of the former harbour of Lancaster was built in the 18C. On its façade are Ionic columns, each one worked from a monolith. *Skerton Bridge* across the river Lune (1787/8).

Environs: Borwick Hall (about 7 m. N.): Elizabethan, it dates from 1595, although it incorporates sections of an older building. It has not been altered since. There is a fine *park*.

Carnforth (about 7 m. N.): Contains the *Steamtown Railway Museum,* with over 30 original English and foreign steam locomotives. There are trips during the summer and on public holidays.

Heysham (about 4 m. W.): Part of the church of *St. Peter* is Saxon. It was altered both under the Normans and also on several subsequent occasions up until the 17C. There is an oustanding 10C tombstone which is decorated with human and animal figures. In the adjoining *graveyard*

are the richly carved shaft of a 9C cross, and also a stone sarcophagus probably dating from the 11–13C. To the W. of the church are the ruins of *St. Patrick's Chapel,* probably built by Irish missionaries in the 5C. Further to the W. again are six *tombs* hewn from the rock.

Hornby Castle (about 9 m. NE): A medieval *castle* with a 13C tower in good condition.

Leighton Hall (about 8 m. N.): Originally built in 16&17C neoclassical style, a fine neo-Gothic façade was added to it in *c.* 1800. Inside there is some good period furniture.

Largo Bay
Fife/Scotland   p.324☐H 8

Fishing villages are ranged along the S. coast of the county of Fife like pearls on a string.

Largo: *Lower Largo,* with the harbour and a statue of Robinson Crusoe, lies at the cen-

Priory Church of St. Mary, choir stalls

Lancaster, Castle

tre of the largest bay. The statue commemorates the fact that the man on whom Daniel Defoe based his character was born here. There was once a 16C castle, but only a *round tower* with a conical roof has survived. There is a *church* in *Upper Largo* at the foot of Largo Law, a hill which is 980 ft. high and offers an excellent all-round view. The church has a 16C tower and choir. There is a *Celtic cross* near the entrance to the graveyard.

Elie: Garnets may be found on the beach. *Gillespie House* may be distinguished by its colonnaded entrance, built in 1682. The *parish church* is 17C, as are some pretty *Little Houses*.

St.Monance: This is probably the most picturesque of Fife's fishing villages and has some charming *Little Houses* by the sea front and on the cliffs. A particular feature is the Gothic *Church of St.Monan*, which King David II had built *c.* 1362. It has a compact square tower and an octagonal steeple, the roof is groined. The King built the church in gratitude for his recovery

from a wound at the Saint's sarcophagus.

Pittenweem: Here too we find picturesque *Little Houses* around the harbour. The town takes its Gaelic name from the cave near the harbour. It was here, in the 12C, that Irish and Scottish monks erected a shrine to St.Fillan. A *priory*, connected to the cave by a shaft, was built here in 1141 and restored in 1935. The square tower of the *parish church* has a distinctive balustrade (1591).

Largs
Strathclyde/Scotland   p.324☐F 8

This small town on the W. shore of the Firth of Clyde has seen tempestuous times. The decisive battle against the Norwegians was fought here in 1263, when Haakon lost the Hebrides and the Isle of Man. The battle lasted two days, sometimes on ships in the Clyde, sometimes on land, until Alexander III succeeded in bringing 400 years of Norwegian rule to an end. A *round tower*

Largo Bay, Upper Largo, church

S. of the town, near Bowen Craig, commemorates this important battle.

Skelmorlie Aisle: In 1636, this side aisle of the old parish church of *St.Columba* was converted into a *mausoleum* for Sir Robert Montgomerie and his wife. At the same time a painted roof was added. The mausoleum is regarded as one of the best Renaissance buildings in Scotland. The *monuments* to the Boyle family of Kelburne were added later and are of interest.

Also worth seeing: The museum of the historical society contains exhibits on local history.

Environs: Great Cumbrae (0.5 m. W.): The island of Great Cumbrae lies opposite Largs and is separated from the mainland by a half-mile channel. **Millport**, the main town on the island, has a *museum* devoted to the area and a *Marine Biological Station* with a good aquarium.
Saltcoats (7 m. S.): The *Harbour and Maritime Museum* also deals with the area in general and with the sea. 25 fossil tree trunks are uncovered when the tide is out.

Launceston
Cornwall/England   p.331 □ F 16

This, the former capital of Cornwall, was once known as *Dunheved*. On one of the hills overlooking the town are the ruins of a Norman *castle*. Its massive, circular keep is still most impressive today. George Fox, the founder of the Society of Friends (the Quakers), spent a year behind bars in this castle in 1656 because the population utterly rejected his message of salvation.

Church of St.Mary Magdalene: The oldest section is the 14C *SW tower* with its beautifully hewn stones. The church itself was built in 1511–24 under Sir Henry

Trecarrel. It has uniquely captivating Gothic quatrefoil carving on the walls, with abundant *heraldic motifs*. The church's patron saint is depicted as a recumbent figure in a niche of the E. wall, surrounded by angels and musicians. The finest item among the furnishings is the *wooden pulpit*, which is decorated with subtle filigree carving and is one of the very few pulpits to have survived the Reformation.

Leeds
West Yorkshire/England   p.328 □ I 11

There was a ford across the river Aire here in Roman times, but it was not until the 18C that the city became a centre of the cloth trade. The first railway line in the world was opened here in 1758, transporting coal from Middleton to the river Aire in Leeds; the draught horses were replaced by two steam locomotives as early as 1812. With over 500,000 inhabitants, Leeds is today the sixth largest city in England and

Launceston, castle ruins

is the centre for the manufacture of ready-to-wear clothing.

Church of St. Peter (Kirkgate): This is the city's parish church. The present building dates from 1841 (its original predecessor was mentioned in the Domesday Book). Inside, note a fine *alabaster slab* (Christ and the 12 apostles; mosaic inlay) on the high altar; a good E. *window* in the choir and *monuments* to distinguished citizens of Leeds scattered throughout the church.

St. John's Church (New Briggate): Its building was financed in 1634 by John Harrison, a rich merchant and alderman of the city. The church has a painting of the founder presenting a jug of gold coins to King Charles I, who was held prisoner in Leeds at that time. It is Tudor in style with late Gothic influences. Inside are beautiful old *pews* and a good *Renaissance window*.

Town Hall (The Headrow): This was built in the late 19C in monumental neo-Gothic Victorian style. There is a *clock tower* some 200 ft. high above an imposing colonnaded front. The steps leading up to the main entrance are flanked by lions. At the entrance is a *bronze plaque* in memory of Joseph Aspdin, one of the inventors of Portland cement.

Civic Hall: Standing behind the Town Hall, it was opened in 1933. On its two towers are figures of owls (the creatures on the Leeds coat-of-arms), and inside are monuments to famous men from Leeds and Yorkshire.

City Art Gallery (opposite the Town Hall): This includes a picture gallery with notable works by English masters, including Constable and Gainsborough. The sculpture collection has works by Jacob Epstein and Henry Moore. The latter studied at the Leeds School of Art, and the Art Gallery encouraged him in his youth.

Also worth seeing: *St. Anne's Cathedral* (Cookridge Street), the city's Roman Catholic cathedral. *St. Aidan's Church* (Roundhay Road), consecrated in 1894, with fine mosaics (scenes from the life of St. Aidan). *St. George's Church* (near Park Street), built in Gothic style. *Holy Trinity Church* (Boar Lane), built *c.* 1720; it is the only significant Georgian church in Leeds. Inside are some fine wood carvings. *St. Matthew's Church* (Holbeck) with an obelisk in memory of Matthew Murray, who built the first steam locomotive on the Middleton-Leeds line. *Mill Hill Chapel* (near City Square), rebuilt in 1847. Joseph Priestley, who discovered oxygen, was active here in 1767–78. *Corn Exchange* (Kirkgate), a monumental 19C Victorian building. *City Varieties* (Headrow), the oldest and one of the last surviving music halls in England. Charlie Chaplin performed here as a young man.

Leeds Library (Commercial Street), founded in 1768, the oldest library of its kind in England. *Brotherton Library* (in the university, reached via Woodhouse Lane), with a valuable collection of rare books and autographs, including letters written by the Brontë family. In the centre of Leeds there are also some good arcaded streets (Thornton's Arcade, Queen's Arcade, Country Arcade, Grand Arcade, Market Arcade).

Environs: Adel (about 6 m. NW): Adel has one of the finest Norman *churches* in Yorkshire. It dates from the 12C and has a richly carved portal; inside there is a magnificent Norman chancel arch.

Bramham (about 9 m. NE): With a fine 13C *church* and *Bramham Park*, built in Queen Anne style in the early 18C. Inside are paintings, some by Reynolds. The park is laid out along the lines of Versailles.

Harewood (about 8 m. N.): The most interesting feature, apart from the *Church of*

Leeds, Town Hall, façade

Civic Hall

Civic Hall, clock

All Saints (fine alabaster tombs), is *Harewood House*, a mansion built in 1759–67 in neo-Corinthian style. Inside, the decoration of the individual rooms is of interest: the music room has Chippendale furniture and ceiling paintings by Angelika Kauffmann. There are fine works by Gainsborough and Reynolds in the gallery. The Green Drawing Room and the Rose Drawing Room contain a collection by Italian masters. In the park are the remains of a fortified 14C *gatehouse*.

Kirkstall Abbey (about 3 m. W.): A *Cistercian abbey* completed in Norman style in 1181. It is a daughter house of Fountains Abbey, and was dissolved in 1540. Restoration began in 1890. The ideal ground plan of a medieval monastery is clearly apparent here: to the W. of the cloister are the dormitory of the lay brothers, the kitchen, the refectory and other rooms, and to the E. are the monks' dormitory and the chapterhouse, with the hospital and abbot's house behind them. The church is in good condition (only some parts of the roof and tower are missing), and is built in typical Cistercian manner without any pronounced exterior ornament. In the 15C the battlements and windows were altered and added to in Perpendicular Style, and the height of the tower was raised in the 16C. The *Abbey House Museum* is in the former gatehouse. Its exhibits include finds excavated from the abbey, and also a comprehensive museum on the traditions of Leeds and its environs.

Oakwell Hall (about 7 m. SW): 16C Tudor; inside there is an old oak staircase leading up to the gallery.

Otley (some 11 m. NW): Situated in Wharfedale, Otley has had market regulations laid down since 1222. *All Saints Church* was founded in the 7C. The choir is Norman, the rest 15C. There are some notable monuments, including that to the first Lord Fairfax and his wife. Remains of three Saxon crosses. Otley is the birthplace of Thomas Chippendale (1711–79), the cabinet-maker who gave his name to a style of furniture.

Tadcaster (about 14 m. NE): It was inhabited in pre-Roman times, and was called 'Calcaria' under the Romans. The 15C *church* is of note. It has a fine battlemented tower, and inside there is a notable Norman chancel arch. There is also the *Ark Museum*, housed in a late medieval house beside the church. It has a good collection on the history of the art of brewing.

Leicester

Leicestershire/England   p.328□I 13

This is one of the oldest towns in England. In Roman times it was known as *Batae Coritanorum* and was the main town of the Coritani. It was an important Norman for-

Leeds, Holy Trinity Church

ress in the Middle Ages, and a frequent esidence of English kings in the 14C.

Jewry Wall (St. Nicholas Circle): This wall, some 20 ft. high, is the last remnant of Roman Leicester. One theory has it that t is part of a public bath built in the fo-rum of the ancient city, while according to another theory it is part of a temple. There are finds from the excavations in the ad-joining *Museum of Archaeology*. Amongst these, the coloured floor mosaics and street pavements are especially interesting. There are also many exhibits on the archaeology of Leicesterhire until the 15C.

Cathedral of St. Martin (High Street): Originally Romanesque, altered in Gothic style in the 14C, and most recently rebuilt in the 19C to plans by David Brandon, G.F.Bodley and G.E.Street. Inside, there is an interesting *monument* built and signed by Joshua Marshall in 1656.

Church of St. Margaret (St. Margaret's Way): This was formerly part of the pre-bend of the Bishop of Lincoln. The S. ar-cade of the nave and the S. portal date from the original 13C church. The rest of the church is in the Decorated and Perpendic-ular styles of the 14&15C. Restored by Sir Gilbert Scott, and later also by G.E.Street, in the 19C. The stained-glass windows dat-ing from 1840 are by Thomas Willement.

Church of St. Mary de Castro (Castle Street): Built *c.* 1150 as the chapel of the Norman castle. Enlarged in the Early Eng-lish style in the 13C. A fine *spire*. King Henry VI (1422–61) was knighted here.

Church of St. Nicholas (St. Nicholas

Street): This, the oldest church in the city, was built in Saxon times using Roman bricks (this is apparent in the clerestory). Rebuilt by the Normans, the choir is Early English, while the tower is early Romanesque. Much altered in the 19C.

Guildhall (Guild Hall Lane): The Guildhall was used as a town hall from the 17C onwards. In the Middle Ages it was the property of the Guild of Corpus Christi. Work on the half-timbered structure began in 1340, and in the 15&16C it was rebuilt in Tudor style. Inside, the *Great Hall* is worth viewing, as is the *city library* which dates from no later than 1587 and possesses the *Codex Leicestrensis,* a valuable 15C Greek manuscript of the New Testament.

Museums: *Belgrave Hall Museum* (Thurcaston Road), accommodated in an 18C country house built in Queen Anne style. A notable collection of old coaches and agricultural implements. *The Magazine* (The Newarke): A 14C guard house, today the museum of the Royal Leicester Regiment. *Newarke Houses Museum* (The Newarke): This is the city museum, with exhibits concerning the city's history since 1500 (including woven and knitted goods, toys, clocks, and musical instruments). *Leicester Museum and Art Gallery* (New Walk): Offers a survey of 300 years of English painting, including sporting pictures. There are also collections of ceramics, glass and silver, and a good section devoted to the natural history and geology of Leicestershire. The *Leicestershire Museum of Technology* (Corporation Road): A technical museum, including four late 19C side-lever engines; an interesting collection of old horse carriages and motorcycles. *Roger Wygston's House* (St.Nicholas Circle): Built in the 15C, with an 18C façade; today it is a *costume museum.*

Also worth seeing: *All Saints' Church* (High Cross Street). Its façade is 13C and it has a fine Romanesque W. portal. The

chapel of *Trinity Hospital,* founded in 1131 (The Newarke). All that survives of the *castle* by the River Soar is the restored great hall; on this site there is a modern statue of Richard III, who was defeated W. of the town at Bosworth Field in 1485. *Abbey Park* (St.Margaret's Way), with the ground plan and remains of the walls of the abbey of the Grey Brothers, founded in 1143. Cardinal Wolsey died here in 1530. The *Clock Tower* (1866) stands in the town centre and has statues of four of Leicester's benefactors.

Environs: Gaddesby (about 7 m. NE): Inside the late-14C church of *St.Luke* there are some beautiful oak pews, which are contemporary with the building of the church.
Kings Norton (about 6 m. SE): The church of *St.John the Baptist,* neo-Gothic built in 1760–75 by John Wing the younger from Leicester.
Loughborough (about 10 m. N): This is famous for its bell foundries. In the *War Memorial Tower* there is a chime of 47 bells.
Market Bosworth (about 12 m. W.): This is the site of the final battle of the Wars of the Roses, between Richard III and Henry Tudor in 1485 (there are information boards and marked paths on the battlefield).
Prestwold Hall (about 11 m. N.): A 19C mansion with fine marble inside.

Letterkenny
Donegal/Ireland   p.326☐D

This, the largest town in Donegal, has 5,000 inhabitants and lies at the end of Lough Swilly, a long sea lough, at the mouth of the River Swilly. This agricultural centre has the beautiful Catholic *Cathedral of St.Eunan,* built of sandstone and dating from *c.* 1890.

Environs: Buncrana (about 22 m. NE):

Buncrana Castle, built *c.* 1716. There is also the three-storeyed *O'Doherty's Keep* at the bridge over the Crana. This 14C keep was part of a Norman castle.

Conwal Church (about 2 m. SW): A medieval church with interesting tombstone slabs (reliefs of the Cross) from the early Christian period.

Creeslough (about 22 m. NW): *Doe Castle* was built in the 16C and largely restored in the 18&19C.

Grianan of Aileach (about 11 m. NE): This, the ancient Celtic *royal seat* of the O'Neill Princes of Ulster, lies at the neck of the Inishowen peninsula, near the present-day border town of Bridge-End, and dates from the 5–12C. The concentric fort with three rings of ramparts known as *Aileachs Palace* was devastated *c.* 1000 by the High King Brian Boru of Munster. The earth hill fort offers a splendid view and was restored by Dr.Bernard of Derry in 1870, or, more accurately, reconstructed in accordance with his own views.

Fahan (about 19 m. NE): St. Mura founded a *monastery* here in the 7C, and a modern *church* has been built on its site. The interesting early Christian cross slab of Fahan Mura, dating from the 7&8C, survives. This tall cross slab is a funerary stela and bears an image of the Cross with intertwined ornaments and a Greek inscription. It is an example of the transition from the cross slab (stone slab) to the fully formed high cross.

Raphoe (about 9 m. SE): The Protestant *St.Eunan's Cathedral* was rebuilt in *c.* 1700 and has old Romanesque stone fragments (10C) and some other structural components from the 15–17C. The ruins of the adjacent *castle,* with its corner towers, date from 1636. Nearby, towards the S., there is a well-preserved prehistoric *stone circle* with over 60 stones on the peak of a hill.

Rathmullan (about 12 m. NE): On the W. shore of Lough Swilly are the remnants of a 15C *Carmelite friary* founded by Mac-Sweeny.

Lewes
East Sussex / England   [p.332□K 16

This small town is best explored on foot because its streets rise steeply and are very narrow. In 1264 it was the site of the battle of Lewes, in which King Henry III was defeated by his barons led by Simon de Montfort; a defeat which led to the birth of the English parliament. The town was a bastion of the persecuted Protestants during the rule of Queen Mary (1553–8).

St. Anne's Church: Built in the 12C, with an altar and a 17C pulpit. A fine Norman font.

Church of St.John the Baptist: Structural elements from the 12–18C, with extremely beautiful stained-glass windows.

St. Michael's Church: Rebuilt in the 18C, with a 13C round tower and some further splendid stained-glass windows.

Castle: All that survives of this today are the 14C barbicans, parts of the walls, and the remains of the Norman keep.

Also worth seeing: Smart little Georgian houses are scattered all over the town. Note *Anne of Cleves' House,* 16C, the home of Anne of Cleves after she was divorced from Henry VIII. Today it is a *museum,* where contemporary decorations and a collection of splendid wrought iron are on display. The Elizabethan *Barbican House* is today the *Museum of the Sussex Archaeological Society,* where Roman, Saxon and medieval items can be seen along with some paintings and drawings. John Evelyn lived for a time in *Southover Grange,* which has an outstanding 16C fireplace. John Paine lived and worked from 1768–74 in *The Bull* (15C). Today it is a restaurant.

Environs: Firle Place (5 m. SE): The

House of the Gage Family was restored in the 18C in its original Tudor style. Today it is a *museum* where furniture (Louis Quinze), porcelain and pictures by famous artists are on display. General Gage, who fought in the American War of Independence, came from this family.

Glynde (2 m. E.): *St.Mary's Church.* Its exterior, and also its inner decoration, date from the 18C, while the stained-glass windows are 17&18C. *Glynde Place:* A 17C *house* restored in the 18C. Bronzes and paintings (some by Rubens and Lely), and also embroidery, are displayed in the panelled gallery.

Mount Caburn (3 m. SE): An Iron Age *fort* enlarged by Normans.

Lichfield

Staffordshire/England   p.328☐I 13

This, the birthplace of Samuel Johnson, became the seat of a bishop in 672 when St.Chad of Repton came here. The saint's tomb became a pilgrimage site and pilgrims' donations made it possible to begin the cathedral. The town flourished in the Middle Ages and was granted no less than six royal letters patent, the first being granted by Richard II in 1378. In 1553, Mary I granted the town the privilege of being allowed to exercise its own jurisdiction.

Cathedral: This church dedicated to St. Mary and St.Chad is one of the smaller English cathedrals, but one of the most beautiful. It is also the only one to have three massive towers. Built from 1195–1325, it stands on the site of two earlier churches. The first was built by Bishop Hedda in *c.* 700, while the other probably dates from about the turn of the millennium. The oldest sections of the present cathedral are the three *W. bays* of the choir, and the *vestry,* completed by 1208. The remainder of the *choir,* the *transepts* and the *chapterhouse,* all Early English, had been added by 1250. The early Gothic *nave* was completed by 1280, and the *Lady Chapel,* also early Gothic, by 1325. In 1643, the

Lewes Castle

Roundheads led by Lord Brooke besieged the Royalists, who were eventually defeated. Just three years later Cromwell's troops shot the main tower to pieces, and partially destroyed the interior. After the restoration of the monarchy in 1660, work on restoring the cathedral was begun under Bishop John Hackett (1662–9), and the work was provisionally completed in 1950 when the cross was replaced on the central tower.

The *exterior* of red sandstone is mainly remarkable for its superb *W. façade*—no fewer than 113 saints, carved from the stone, fill four galleries between, beside and above the three portals. The enormous *central window* is divided into six lancets which, like the sculptures, are actually modern replicas of the weather-worn stone of the originals.

The *interior* has a clear and distinctive cross-shaped arrangement. The choir and nave each have two aisles and the same number of bays. But the nave is some 30 ft. shorter than the choir. The two transepts each project beyond the crossing by one bay; the vestry has been added at the SE corner, the chapterhouse at the NE. Although the nave is shorter, it is not dominated by the choir, since there is no break between the two. Instead the visitor is offered a view of rare beauty down the length of the cathedral to the stained-glass window of the Lady Chapel. The richly decorated *capitals,* the beautiful *triforium,* and the *tracery* on the windows of the clerestory, provide a rare and beautiful example of the beginnings of the early Gothic style. The transepts, which were built earlier than the nave, originally had a higher roof. The stone vaults were not added until the late 15C, and the result is that the window in the S. gable is now only visible from the outside. The other windows are partly early Gothic and partly Gothic proper. The Early English *choir* is not precisely aligned with the nave, for the axis of the nave is turned to the W. by some 10

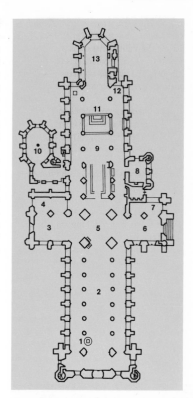

Lichfield Cathedral 1 font **2** nave **3** N. transept **4** St. Stephen's Chapel **5** crossing **6** S. transept **7** St. Michael's Chapel **8** sacristy **9** choir **10** chapterhouse **11** high altar **12** Monument 'Sleeping Children' by Chantrey (1817) **13** Lady Chapel

degrees. Original early Gothic traceried windows have survived on the S. wall of the choir, while the rest was restored in the 18&19C. The E. wall of the S. choir aisle is of particular interest. It contains the 'Sleeping Children' by Chantrey (1817), and the window above this still has the original Flemish stained glass depicting the Trinity. The *Lady Chapel,* with its nine soaring windows and the polygonal apse, is in the finest early Gothic style. The magnificent impression is intensified by the windows, dating from *c.* 1535, from the Cistercian abbey of Herkenrode near Liège; the stained glass was purchased in 1802 for the restoration of the Lady Chapel. The *monuments* to the cathedral's major bishops are scattered throughout the interior.

The *chapterhouse* completed in 1249 is octagonal and has splendid floors, magnificently worked capitals, corbels and bosses. In the upper storey of the chapterhouse is the *library*. Its treasures include an Irish evangelistary of the late 7C and some very early Bibles.

Museums: The *Johnson Museum* is in the house where Samuel Johnson, the great lexicographer (1709–84), was born. He compiled the first significant dictionary of the English language, which appeared in 1755 after eight years of work. Personal mementoes and a collection of important literature about Johnson are on display in the museum. The *Staffordshire Regimental Museum* has uniforms, coats of arms, medals, documents, pictures and battle trophies of the county's regiments. Some of the exhibits also relate to the American War of Independence.

Environs: Elford (4 m. E.): The *Church of St. Peter* has a 16C tower, while the church itself was restored by A.Savlin in 1848 and by G.E.Street in 1870. It is mainly of interest for its plethora of monuments which are decorated with figures, including one of a boy holding a ball and pointing to the spot on his head where he was hit (15C).

Merevale: (12 m. SE): The *Church of St.Mary* was originally built as the 'capella ante portas' of the *Cistercian abbey*, which was founded in the 12C. The church was built in the 13C, but the present structure is mainly 14&15C. The most outstanding decorations are a 14C Jesse window, a 13C tomb decorated with figures, and a medieval organ taken from the mutilated abbey church.

Tamworth (6 m. SE): This town was of great importance during Saxon times. In the 8C, King Offa maintained not only a *royal palace* here, but also a *mint*. The first

Lichfield, Cathedral, portal

Nave

proper rampart was built in *c.* 910, probably by Ethelfreda, a daughter of Alfred the Great. The oldest part of the present buildings, namely the banqueting hall, was built during the time of Henry VIII, while the rest is Jacobean. Local history is documented in the *castle museum.* Some early English coins which were struck in Tamworth during the time of King Offa are the main item of interest. The *Church of St.Editha* dates from the 14C and is dedicated to King Edgar's daughter. It contains some notable monuments and Pre-Raphaelite stained-glass windows.

Limerick
Limerick/Ireland   p.326☐C 13

This city of some 100,000 inhabitants lies where the river Shannon enters its estuary. Shannon Airport, some 14 m. W. of the city, is an important international airport. The five-line verses known as limericks are one reason for the city's fame. Edward Lear

(1812–88), the English painter and poet, was a master of this 'nonsense poetry'.

History: A site on Lough Gur, near the city, was inhabited in the Bronze Age. The city itself dates from a 9C Viking settlement. In the 10C it became the centre of the O'Brien Kings of Munster. Limerick was a bastion of the English from the time of its conquest by the Anglo-Normans in about 1200 up until the 18C. The districts of *English Town* (in the N., with a castle) and *Irish Town* (in the S.) still exist today, separated by the Abbey River.

St. Mary's Cathedral (English Town): This cathedral, which is now Protestant, was built by King O'Brien of Munster *c.* 1180. The *W. portal,* the *nave,* and parts of the *side-aisles and transepts,* still survive from that cruciform building. The choir, the W. tower, the S. transept chapels, and the S. portal, were added in the 14&15C (further restoration in the 17–19C). Inside are some fine *monuments* (15–18C) and interesting carved wooden *choir stalls* with

Limerick, King John's Castle

misericords (15C). There is a fine view from the 15C *bell tower* with its bells dating from 1678.

King John's Castle (English Town): This imposing riverside fortress on the banks of the Shannon was built by the Anglo-Normans in *c.* 1200 for King John. Features surviving from the almost square castle with its four corner towers are the *castle gate* flanked by towers, the *NW and SW corner towers* and parts of the *curtain walls*. Nearby, to the E., are the remains of a *Dominican monastery* founded in *c.* 1230 and rebuilt in the 15C. On the other side of the river, reached by crossing Thomond Bridge, is the so-called *Treaty Stone* commemorating the 'Treaty of Limerick', which granted increased rights for the Irish (1691)—and was not adhered to.

Also worth seeing: The *Custom House* in Irish Town, on the mouth of the Abbey River, was built in the Georgian style in 1769, with a fine façade. The *Town Hall* in Irish Town is a brick structure erected in *c.* 1805. *Kilrush Church* (13C, Barrington's Pier) is a small rectangular building with a W. portal and a rounded E. window. The four-storeyed *Fanning's Castle* (Barrington's Quay) was built in the 16&17C and was the house of a merchant, Fanning. Near St.John's Square is the Catholic *Cathedral of St.John,* a neo-Gothic building dating from 1856–61, with a tower 275 ft. tall. Inside, note a marble Madonna by Benzoni (in the sanctuary) and a splendid crosier with a mitre (in the treasury) dating from the 15C. *Newtown Pery,* a southern Georgian district, was built in the 18C by order of Pery, a rich merchant and politician. The layout of its streets resembles a chessboard. Its sights include the neo-Gothic *Dominican Church* dating from 1860, with a 17C Flemish statue of the Virgin, and also the *People's Park* laid out in the 18C. The *museum* in the People's Park houses local antiquities and primitive finds, as well as documents relating to the city's history. The adjacent *Art Gallery* has a collection of works by contemporary Anglo-Irish painters.

Environs: Abington (some 9 m. SE): The remains of the small 12C Romanesque *Clonkeen Church,* with its beautifully decorated W. portal and round window.

Bunratty Castle (about 11 m. NW): This is the former 15C stronghold of the O'Briens of Thomond, not restored until 1960. It has four corner towers, a spacious banqueting hall, a knights' hall on the top storey, a castle chapel, and bedrooms, and possesses an impressive exhibition of furniture and decorations from the 14–17C. 'Medieval banquets' are held here in summer. Nearby is a reconstructed *folk park* with rebuilt old houses typical of County Clare.

Carrigogunnel Castle (about 7 m. W.): This *castle* is picturesquely sited on the Shannon. There is a splendid view from here. The castle dates from the 15C, and has two multi-storeyed towers, as well as other, 16C fortifications.

Lough Gur (about 12 m. S.): An extensive *prehistoric settlement,* with important cultural finds, lies on the S. and N. shores of this small lake. There are good stone circles, dolmens, megalithic tombs and foundations of houses dating from *c.* 2000 BC (see also Kilmallock).

Monasternenagh (about 12 m. S.): This former Cistercian monastery was built in *c.* 1150, and Mellifont Abbey (see under Drogheda) formed its model. It was protected by the O'Briens, kings of Limerick. Of the *monastery church,* some fine fragments of the interior, including capitals, have survived. The monastery was dissolved in 1541 after first being damaged.

Patrickswell (about 6 m. SW): The ruins of *Mungret Abbey,* an early Christian monastery founded by St.Nessan in *c.* 1550. It has frequently been plundered, but two small churches from the 11&12C survive.

hey each have a simple W. portal, narrow
windows and a W. tower.

---

incoln

incolnshire/England   p.328☐K 12

his was founded in pre-Roman times,
when it was known as *Lindum*. From the
C AD onwards it was a Roman garrison.
he city's present name derives from 'Lin-
um Colonia'. The wool trade made Lin-
oln a flourishing city in the Middle Ages,
nd coins struck in Lincoln have even been
und in Scandinavia. Industrialization led
o an upsurge in economic activity during
he 19C.

Newport Arch (Bailgate): This is the
ormer N. gate of the Roman town, and is
he only surviving example of its kind in
ngland. It was built in the 2C AD. The
., inner side is original, and the remainder
was rebuilt in the Middle Ages. The an-
ient ground level was about 8 ft. below the
resent level.

Cathedral: This is one of the major
Gothic churches of Europe. Work on it began in 1072 under the Normans after the
building of a bishop's palace in the city.
The W. façade survives from the original
cathedral. Following a fire in 1141 and an
earthquake in 1185, work on the present
building began in 1192 under Bishop
Hugh of Lincoln. The main body was
completed in *c.* 1280, the tower over the
crossing in 1311. There have been almost
no further additions or alterations since
that time.

Exterior: The ground plan is in the form
of a cross of Lorraine (nave, two transepts

Lincoln Cathedral **1** W. front with 3 Romanesque portals **2** Morning Chapel **3** late Romanesque font **4** NW transept **5** St.Michael's Chapel
6 St. Andrew's Chapel **7** St. George's Chapel **8**
crossing (with an 280 ft. tower, 1311) **9** SW transept **10** St.Edward's Chapel **11** St.John's Chapel
12 St.Anne's Chapel **13** Galilee porch **14** choir **15**
SE transept **16** Chapel of St.Peter and St.Paul **17**
sacristy **18** S. portal **19** tomb of Queen Eleanor
(1291) **20** Angel Choir (1254–80) **21** tomb of St.
Hugh **22** NE portal **23** Easter sepulchre **24** tomb
of Catherine Swynford and her daughter (1403)
25 NE transept **26** Medicine Chapel (now treasury) **27** chapterhouse (1260) **28** cloister (1300) **29**
library (1674&5)

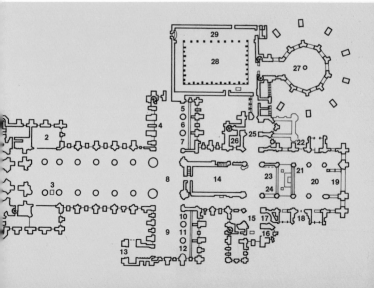

on each side, choir). There is a splendid *W. front* with three Norman portals, and above them a unique *carved frieze* (1145) and two Decorated *towers* 215 ft. high. The *tower over the crossing* rises to 280 ft. and originally had a wooden spire clad in lead. It contains the bell known as 'Great Tom of Lincoln' which weighs about 5.5 tons. The Decorated *W. transept* was built in 1200–35, whereas the *E. transept* is Early English. The *Angel Choir*, so called after the 30 figures of angels in the triforium, was added in 1254–80 (on its N. side, on the easternmost pier, is the figure known as the 'Lincoln Imp'. On the S. side is the richly decorated *Presbytery Portal*, which has a Last Judgement. There are fine gargoyles on the *façade*.

Interior: The rose-windows in the W. transept are especially fine (to the S., the 14C *Bishop's Eye;* to the N., the *Dean's Eye* dating from 1225; both have beautiful 13C stained glass). In the *choir*, which is in unadulterated Early English style, there are splendid oak choir stalls (1380). There is an interesting Easter Sepulchre to the left of the high altar, while the tomb of Catherine Swynford and her daughter, which dates from 1403, is to the right. In the *Angel Choir*, in addition to the figures of angels, there are the tomb of St.Hugh by the choir screen, and the splendid E. window (the oldest of its kind in England), with the tomb of Queen Eleanor (1290) beneath it. The late Romanesque marble *font* to the right of the main portal is also worth viewing.

Since 1960, the treasury has been housed in the *Medicine Chapel* in the N. aisle of the choir. The main items are old Communion utensils, an original copy of the Magna Carta (1215, and the charter of the cathedral's foundation, drawn up by William the Conqueror. The N. arm of the E. transept leads to the *cloister* (a fine old vault dating from 1300; on the N. side is the library built by Sir Christopher Wren in 1674/5). From the cloister, the visitor may enter the ten-sided *chapterhouse* (1250). This is the earliest Gothic building of its kind in England, and has a splendid vault supported by a central column.

Lincoln Castle (Castle Hill): Built by William the Conqueror in 1068, and later considerably altered. Surviving features include the Norman *E. gate* (15C façade; inside there is a fine vault). Three *towers* (Lucy Tower dating from 1200; Cobb Hall 1400; Observatory Tower, built in the 19C for astronomical purposes).

The castle prison dating from 1780 is today the *city archive*.

Jews' Houses: A group of 12C Norman houses belonging to local Jewish merchants and bankers. They include the *house of Aaron the Jew* (Steep Hill; alleged to be the oldest inhabited house in England), the *Jew's House* dating from 1170 (The Strait), and immediately next to it the *Jew's Court*.

Museums: *Greyfriars City and County Museum* (Broadgate): This museum is housed in the 13C former church of the

Lincoln, Cathedral, Gothic tower

Grey Friars. It contains finds from Roman Lincoln, a collection of weapons, and a department of natural history.

Museum of Lincolnshire Life (Burton Road): This is devoted to everyday life in the town and county since the time of Elizabeth I.

Usher Gallery (Linden Road): A collection of paintings (chiefly by Peter de Wint), old clocks, and miniatures. There is also a room devoted to Alfred Lord Tennyson (1809–92), with manuscripts, first editions and personal memorabilia.

Also worth seeing: The 12C churches of *St.Benedict* (Newland), *St.Mary-le-Wigford* (S. of the river Witham), and *St. Peter-at-Gawts* Stonebow (near the River Witham), is the city's former S. gate, built in the 16C above a Roman gate. Above this is the *Guildhall*, a fine half-timbered building with a timber ceiling. The roof houses the 'Mote Bell' (1371) which still summons the councillors to council meetings. The 12C *High Bridge* across the River Witham is the oldest bridge in England to have houses built on it. *Cardinal's Hat* (Gran-

tham/High Street) is a splendid late Gothic house named after Cardinal Wolsey. *Priory Gate* and *Potter Gate*, two old city gates in Pottergate street. *Brayford Pool*, the remains of the Roman river port, from which wool was exported in the Middle Ages.

Environs: Auburn Hall (about 7 m. SW): A 16C brick house. Inside, the staircase and the panelling are worth seeing.

Cherry Willingham (about 4 m. E.): The 18C church of *St. Peter and St. Paul*, with a fine octagonal lantern on the W. side.

Doddington (about 5 m. SW): With an Elizabethan house built in 1593–1600 (a fine façade; inside, contemporary furniture and a good collection of Chinese porcelain).

Foss Dyke (about 4 m. W.): A *canal* built by the Romans in the 1C AD to connect the rivers Trent and Witham (the old towpath has also survived).

Kirkstead (about 14 m. SE): The 13C church of *St. Leonard* formed part of a Cistercian abbey which was founded in the 12C and is now in ruins.

Lincoln, Cathedral

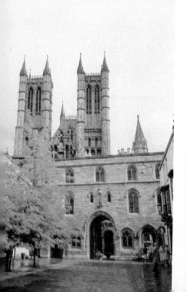

Jew's House

Navenby (about 9 m. S.): Contains the church of *St. Peter* (an especially fine Gothic E. window; inside there is a richly decorated Easter sepulchre on the N. side of the choir).

Snarford (about 9 m. NE): Inside the 12C church of *St. Lawrence* are three 16/17C monuments which are worth looking at.

Linlithgow
Lothian/Scotland   p.324☐G 8

This small town on the S. shore of the Firth of Forth was a Royal Burgh in the 12C. Edward I of England had a fortified *tower* built here in 1302, but the Scots seized this in a surprise attack in 1313. From 1425 onwards, immediately after completing 19 years of imprisonment in England, James I (1394 – 1437) began replacing the old *castle* with a more comfortable one. Margaret Tudor, the 13-year-old bride of James IV, came here in 1504. James IV later died at Flodden Field. Mary Queen of Scots was born here in 1542 and shortly afterwards her father James V died here. This was reason enough for Henry VIII to court the hand of the future Scottish queen for his son Edward, who was just five years old at the time. When Henry's plans did not succeed, he issued the following order in 1544: 'Burn Edinburgh down and raze it to the ground as soon as you have taken and plundered all that you can from it '. Charles I left the castle in 1633, being the last monarch to do so. Cromwell's troops occupied it in 1651 –9. In 1746, the Duke of Cumberland's soldiers, who were billetted here, set their own quarters on fire through carelessness.

Linlithgow Palace: The ruins of the old royal palace are still impressive, being a combination of fortress on the outside and residence on the inside. Because the position of the Scottish kings was always inse-

cure, the palace was built around a square inner courtyard with four corner towers. Little has survived of the former splendour of the interior. Of the tapestries, oak panelling, stucco and frescos, only historical descriptions survive. The panels, with coats of arms showing the insignia of the orders of the Garter, the Thistle, St. Michael, and the Golden Fleece, are but a pale 19C copy, and give only a faint idea of the gilded ornaments which formerly decorated the window gables. Only the *fountain* in the courtyard, with its Renaissance figures and late Gothic ornaments, provides a clue to how people once lived here. The *royal apartments* were all on the first floor, and the *Great Hall*, some 100 ft. long, with a timber ceiling and a fireplace 23 ft. wide, was in the E. wing. The *castle chapel*, with five lancet windows dating from *c.* 1490, is to the S. In the W. wing were the *audience room* and the *private apartments*. A *spiral staircase* in each corner of the courtyard, and another in the N. façade, ensured ease of access.

Church of St.Michael: This is the largest parish church from before the Reformation, and was consecrated in 1242. When the castle was burned in 1424, this church was also partly destroyed and subsequently rebuilt. The oldest surviving section is the *nave* (1497). The *tower* and *apse* were not completed until 1531. Until 1821 the tower had an open stone crown, the present structure being added in 1964.

Environs: Hopetoun House (3 m. NE): The Scottish Versailles. Its square core was built by William Bruce in 1696, and the remainder is the work of William Adam and his sons John and Robert. From 1721–54 they built a palace in monumental baroque style for the Earl of Hopetoun, who was intent on gaining prestige. The two-storeyed façade is articulated by Corinthian pilasters, whilst the attic has balustrades and ornamental stone vases. To

Linlithgow, Linlithgow Palace

the left and right, they added semicircular colonnades with pavilions. Adam's two wings decorated the state rooms with damask, gilded stucco ceilings, and 18C furniture. It is these rooms in particular which make the house worth a visit.

The Binns (2 m. E.): Part of this *mansion*, which is unprepossessing when seen from the outside, was built in 1478. Its stucco ceilings are 17C. The most famous person to live in the house was General Tam Dalyell (1599–1685), who escaped from the Tower of London, served under the Tsar, defeated the Covenanters and, as legend has it, was finally carried off by the Devil. The 17C decorations are worth viewing.

Torphichen Preceptory (6 m. SW): The ruins of a Norman *church* built for the Templars in the 12C. All that remains of this church is the chancel arch. The aisles date from the 13C, and in the 16C a new church was built on the foundations of the first nave. The tower is 15C. A little way behind the preceptory rises *Cairnpapple Hill*, one of the most important neolithic sites in Scotland. Its most interesting feature is that several different layers have survived. The old chamber tombs were expanded in the Bronze Age, but the entire site was plundered in *c.* 1500 BC, and then a new tomb was built, which was later once again enlarged.

Lismore
Waterford/Ireland   p.330☐C 14

This small city, charmingly situated on the river Blackwater, originates from an abbey founded by St.Carthach in the 7C. In the early Middle Ages, before being attacked by Danes and Normans, it was famous for its *monastery school* (St. Colman) and its numerous *churches*.

Cathedral of St. Carthach: The former 12C cathedral was rebuilt as a Protestant church in 1633 after being damaged in about 1600. Parts of the old church still survive: the *chancel arch*, the *S. transept* and some *windows*.

Lismore Castle: This *riverside fortress* was built by King John in 1185, and was repeatedly rebuilt after being damaged on various occasions. Sir Joseph Paxton converted it into a fairytale castle in the 19C, and today it is owned by the Duke of Devonshire. The vault of the *castle church* (12C) and parts of the 15&16C *Bishop's Palace* survive. The famous 'Book of Lismore', a 15C collection of legends concerning Irish saints, was also discovered here, as was the 'crooked staff of Lismore' (11&12C), today in the National Museum in Dublin.

Environs: Dungarvan (7 m. E., with about 5,000 inhabitants): Dungarva boasts the ruins of an Anglo-Norman *ca tle* dating from 1185 (King John). The ke and battlemented walls are still impressiv In the suburb of *Abbeyside*, the only rer nant of a former abbey is a 13C tow which has been incorporated into a Vi torian *parish church*.

Liverpool
Merseyside/England   p.328☐H

Liverpool was founded in the 10C and h been a city since 1207. It first rose to ir portance as a port in the 16&17C and benefited from the Industrial Revoluti during the 18C, growing rich on the sla trade and the blossoming Lancashire c ton industry. Today Liverpool is one of t country's major ports and industrial citi

Metropolitan Cathedral of Christ tl King (Mount Pleasant): The city's F man Catholic cathedral. Construction b gan in 1933 in neo-Byzantine style, t intention being to build the largest chur

Liverpool, Anglican Cathedral

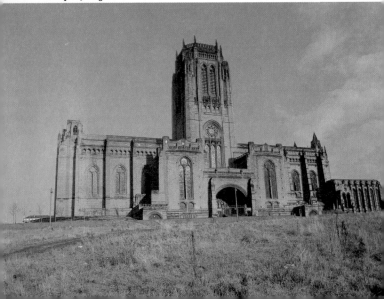

n Europe. The crypt was completed by 939 and, after interruptions caused by the var, work was only resumed in 1962, in ontemporary style. The cathedral was onsecrated in 1967, but it was not entirely omplete at that time. The most impressive feature is the overall concept, which s like a tent with a glass roof, the overall eight being some 330 ft. Of particular ote inside are the stained-glass windows f which ample use is made all over the cahedral (including the roof). The boldness f the cathedral's design makes it one of the nost notable modern buildings in Great 3ritain.

Anglican Cathedral (St.James Road): Also known as *Liverpool Cathedral.* Constructon began in 1904 in neo-Gothic style o plans by Sir Giles Gilbert Scott, who suervised the work until his death in 1960. The cathedral was not consecrated until 971, and is not yet complete. This is the argest Anglican church in Great Britain. t has a peculiar ground plan with a nave, wo transepts and a choir; the tower is some 60 ft. high. Inside, note the *organ* which is in the choir and, with its 9,700 pipes, is thought to be the largest in the world; the *War Memorial Chapel;* and the *stained-glass windows.* The tomb of William Huskisson, who in 1830 became the first person to die in a railway accident, is in the adjoining graveyard of *St.James.*

Church of Our Lady and St.Nicholas (Chapel Street): The oldest parish church in Liverpool. It was built in 1360, but was destroyed in air raids in the Second World War and later rebuilt. There are fine wooden carvings inside.

Town Hall (Dale Street): This was built in neoclassical style in 1754&5. There is a *statue* of the goddess Minerva on the domed tower. The portico is decorated with Corinthian *columns.* The *frieze* which runs around the building is the work of French prisoners at the time of the Napoleonic Wars. Inside there are collections devoted to the city's history (only open to the public in August, but guided tours are available for groups all year round).

Metropolitan Cathedral of Christ the King

St. George's Hall (William Brown Street): Neoclassical in style (1838–54), it has a massive *façade* some 525 ft. in length, and its middle section has sixteen Corinthian columns (about 65 ft. in height). The central *hall* holds some 1,750 people and is today used for concerts, especially organ concerts. The rest of the building houses public institutions (courts and other public authorities).

St. John's Shopping Centre and Market (near Lime Street station): A covered pedestrian precinct and shopping centre whose modern design broke new ground in England. At the centre is *St. John's Beacon,* a tower some 490 ft. in height. Its observation platform gives a panoramic view of the city.

Walker Art Gallery (William Brown Street): This is the most important *collection of paintings* in Great Britain outside London. It covers every period of European painting from the 14C to the present day. The collections are arranged chronologically, beginning with the primitive

Anglican Cathedral, altar

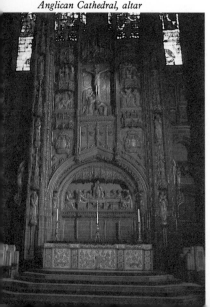

Italians of the 14C, then the Flemish and Italian painters of the 15&16C, and so on. The *Virgin and Child* by Rubens, and the Rembrandt *Self-Portrait* of 1629, are outstanding. A good collection of French Impressionists. The *sculpture collection* includes major works by Rodin and Moore.

City of Liverpool Museum, (near the Walker Gallery): Built in the 19C, and rebuilt after being destroyed in the Second World War. It contains a *department of cultural history* (archaeological collection with Egyptian, Greek and Roman objects; Saxon jewellery; ivories; a porcelain collection; a collection of weapons; old musical instruments, etc.) and a *natural history section* (aquarium, models of houses from all over the world, etc.). On the ground floor there is a *transport museum,* which contains some old locomotives, and a *maritime section*. On the third floor there are a large *planetarium* and a department devoted to the *history of space travel.*

Also worth seeing: *Playhouse Theatre* (Williamson Square), the oldest repertory theatre in England. The present building dates from 1911. The *Central Libraries* (next to Liverpool Museum) have an interesting collection of first editions, manuscripts and incunabula from the 15&16C. *Suddley Art Gallery* (Mossley Hill), with an extensive collection of 18&19C English painters. *Pier Head* on the River Mersey gives a splendid view of the port and city. *Queensway Tunnel* (reached from Dale Street), the first road tunnel under the River Mersey, was opened in 1934 and is among the longest in the world, being 2.5 miles in length.

Environs: Rufford Old Hall (about 18 m. N.): A *half-timbered building* from the 15–17C, with original 17C oak furniture. Today it houses an interesting *local museum* (domestic implements, weapons, porcelain, dolls, etc.).

Speke Hall (about 8 m. SE): A beautiful 15C *half-timbered building* with original interior decoration (the stucco, carved wood and old kitchen are of particular note).

St.Helens (about 16 m. NE): A centre of the glass industry. In Prescot Road there is a comprehensive *glass museum*.

Warrington (about 10 m. E.): Warrington stands on an ancient Roman crossing over the Mersey and has two well-preserved churches *(Holy Trinity* and *St. Elphins).*

Llandeilo
Dyfed/Wales   p.332☐G 14

This small market town in the valley of the Towy (Tywi), and the *castles* in its neighbourhood, looks back on a long Celtish-Welsh history. The heartland of the Rhys family, the princes of S. Wales, was here and in the surrounding area. Rhys ap Gruffydd was recognized as King of South Wales under King Henry II (1154–89). However, hardly any remains survive from this period except for the medieval *parish church* rebuilt in c. 1850.

Environs: Carreg-Cennen Castle (about 5 m. SE): This ruined castle may be reached via the villages of *Ffair-Fach* and *Trap.* The old fortress of the Rhys family dates from the 13C and stands on a limestone crag almost 330 ft. high. There is an extensive view to the E. over the Brecon Beacons National Park. The vaulted underground *escape tunnel,* some 150 ft. long, is of interest. The ruins of the walls and towers, with their square ground plan, are still impressive despite the castle's destruction in the 15C.

Dynevor Castle (about 2 m. W.): In 1856 the Rhys family (Lord Dynevor) built Dynevor Park to the W. of the town. The family has lived in the area since the time of Rhodri Mawr (Roderick the Great) in

the 9C. The ruins of the old castle stand on a rock above the river and consist of an isolated circular keep and a polygonal *enclosure* to the E. Parts of the N. front and of the *ramparts* hewn from the rock also survive.

Llandovery (about 12 m. NE): This pretty little town in the Towy valley lies at the confluence of the Gwydderig and the Bran and still has the ruins of the old 13C *castle* (behind the Castle Car Park). The town also boasts one of the two Welsh-speaking *public schools* (founded in 1848; the buildings are Victorian).

Llanfair-ar-y-Bryn (about 16 m. NE): Contains the 13&14C church of St.Mary. This was partly built from the bricks of a former Roman *fort* on the same site (the earthworks are visible).

Llangadog (about 9 m. NE): Outside this picturesque old town there are some remains from a prehistoric *hill fort* (stone rampart). *Llanwrda* (about 11 m. NE), was the legendary haunt of Merlin the wizard.

Llangathen (about 6 m. W.): Near this town, which has a 13C *church* with a fortified tower, is another *ruined castle* which

Anglican Cathedral, W. window

belonged to the Rhys princes. The *Dryslwyn Castle* (2 m. SW) has been largely destroyed. It was built on the site of a prehistoric settlement. There is a good view across the valley of the Towy.
Talley Abbey: (about 9 m. N.): Ruins of the 12&13C *Premonstratensian abbey*. Parts of the central tower (over the crossing) and of the foundation walls have survived in this idyllic setting. This was the only Premonstratensian abbey in Wales.

Llandrindod Wells
Powys/Wales   p.328□G 14

This town of some 4,000 inhabitants is one of the most popular Welsh spas, with 30 sulphurous and ferrous springs. The *town museum* in Temple Street has some interesting archaeological finds.

Environs: Abbey Cwmhir (about 6 m. N.): The remains of the old Cistercian abbey dating from 1143, with the foundations of an abbey church 243 ft. in length.
Builth Wells (about 6 m. S.): There are a few remains of a *castle* in this small town on the River Wye; as well as a six-arched bridge over the Wye dating from 1779.
Llanbister (6 m. N.), **Llananno** (7 m. N.) and **Llanbadarn** (9 m. N.): Each of these villages has an interesting old *church* with gateways, fonts, choir screens and crucifixes from the 15&16C.
Rhayader ('waterfall'; about 9 m. NW): There is a 12&13C font in the 14C *parish church*.

Llangollen
Clwyd/Wales   p.328□G 13

The town of Llangollen (pronounced Hhlangohhlen) has some 3,000 inhabitants and is charmingly situated in the Vale of Llangollen on the head waters of the river Dee. It has become known the world over

for the annual international eisteddfod which have been held here since 1947.

St.Collen's Church: The parish church whose name is also that of the town ('Llangollen' means 'Saint Collen'), is 14C. The *nave* and *N. aisle* are from the original church, with some later alterations; the *tower* dates from 1749, while the *S. aisle*, the *presbytery* and the *side-chapels* were added in 1863. The richly carved *oak roof* with its angels, birds, flowers and grotesques, is also worth seeing.

Also worth seeing: One curiosity is the richly decorated black-and-white house of *Plas Newydd* standing on Butler Hill. Beautifully situated, in the 18&19C the house was filled by the two 'Ladies of Llangollen' with carved oak, panelling, leather wall hangings, and medieval stained-glass windows.

Environs: Castell Dinas Bran (3 m. NW): The ruins of this fortress stand on the N. bank of the Dee. It was built in c. 1270 by the Welsh prince Gruffyd ap Madoc, but rapidly fell into disrepair (there is a fine view).
Chirk (about 6 m. SE): This village has a fine 15C *parish church* with a tower, an old roof and monuments. To the W. are the remains of *Chirk Castle*. Originally 13C, it has been rebuilt several times since then and it is now square in shape with four corner towers. The rooms inside have fine 17–19C furniture and decorations.
Corwen (about 10 m. W.): This small town has a *parish church* with a Norman font and medieval monuments. Not far away is the prehistoric stone rampart of *Caer Drewyn* (to the N. of the Dee).
Cysyllte (about 4 m. E.): The Dee is spanned here by a massive *aqueduct* with 18 arches, dating from 1800, and by a sandstone *railway viaduct* with 19 arches (19C).
Llandrillo (about 12 m. SW): Bronze Age remains of a *stone circle* are to be found be-

hind this village at *Tyfos Farm* (some of the stones in the circle are still standing).

Valle Crucis Abbey (about 1.5 m. NW): Some interesting remains of the *Cistercian abbey*. The abbey was founded by Prince Madoc in *c.* 1204 and was enlarged in the 14C. It is one of the most important ruined monasteries in N. Wales. The W. side is Early English, with a richly decorated portal, three lancet windows and a rose-window. There is also the chapterhouse which is attached to the E. cloister and has a portal and a ribbed vault. To the N. of this are the 14C sacristy and parts of the dormitory. Near the monastery is the interesting stone column known as *Eliseg's Pillar,* on which there was formerly a cross. This mysterious column, some 7 ft. high, bears a Celtic inscription and is probably 9C.

Lleyn Peninsula
Gwynedd/Wales   p.326☐F 13

The Lleyn Peninsula is in NW Wales, be-

tween Cardigan Bay to the S. and Caernarfon Bay to the N. The Welsh is still strong here and traditional customs are still very much alive.

Pwllheli (about 4,000 inhabitants): This small seaside resort has a railway terminus and is the main town of the Lleyn.

Environs: In *Llanbedrog* (4 m. SW) there is a medieval *church* with a fine choir screen. *Foxhole Cottage,* a picturesque 17C fisherman's house, stands on the coast. *Abersoch* (7 m. SW): *St. Tudwal's Islands,* two small islands offshore from Abersoch named after the Celtic Bishop Tudwal (6C), have some remains of a 12C chapel. *Llangengan* (about 8 m. SW): The *church* of this village on the S. coast is dedicated to St. Engan and has a carved oak choir screen (16C) and fine pews. In the vicinity, near the village of *Llangian* with its pretty cottages, is the Tudor and Georgian manor house of *Plas-yn-Rhiw* (16&18C), built on foundations dating from the 10C.

Aberdaron: This fishing village (some

Clynnog-Fawr (Lleyn peninsula), village church

1,200 inhabitants) at the SW tip of the peninsula contains the beautiful church of *St.Hywyn's,* which stands by the sea and has a Norman portal, 15C arcades inside, and a Perpendicular window. The historical rest house of *Y Gegin Fawr* dates from 1300 and was used by pilgrims on their way to Bardsey Island.

Environs: Bardsey Island (2 m. from Aberdaron): This small island, a pilgrimage site from the 5C onwards, has some scant remains of *St.Mary's Abbey* (13C). The origins of this go back to a building founded by the Celtic St.Cadfan in 516. It is also known as the 'Island of 20,000 Saints' since it was once a popular burial site and 20,000 saints are said to be buried on it. *Sarn* (about 7 m. NE): Near this inland village is the *Cefnamlwch dolmen,* the best-preserved burial site in the peninsula. A peculiar 15C church stands in the village of *Llangwnnadl,* not far away (towards the W. coast).

Nefyn (about 2,000 inhabitants): This small seaside resort on the W. coast has been of importance ever since the Middle Ages (it has had a town charter since 1355). To the S. are a few remains of the prehistoric fortress of *Garn Bodfuan.*

Environs: Llanaelhaearn (about 6 m. NE): On the E. peak of Yr Eifl (The Rivals), at an altitude of 1,750 ft., are the remnants of the important prehistoric settlement of *Tre'r Ceiri* with over 100 hut circles (Cytiau) and a large earthwork (there is a splendid view from the summit).

Clynnog-Fawr (NW coast): A fine late Perpendicular *collegiate church* dating from 1536. It has a porch, a carved wooden roof, a crucifix on the rood screen, and choir stalls. It is dedicated to the Celtic monk St.Beuno (6C), who founded a monastery here.
The small *chapel* SW of the church is said

to stand above St.Beuno's tomb. The nearby St.Beuno's Well was once a healing spring.

Criccieth (about 1,800 inhabitants): This small seaside resort N. of Tremadog Bay has the well-preserved ruins of a *castle* once held by the Welsh prince Llywelyn Mawr (the Great) in *c.* 1200. It was enlarged by Edward I. The massive gatehouse with its two towers, the inner ward and the double moat have survived. Some remains of the outer castle wall, of the Engine Tower from where missiles were launched, and of the Welsh keep still exist.

Environs: Porthmadog (about 4 m. NE): Madog ap Owain Gwynedd, the Welshman who allegedly discovered America, is said to have sailed from here in about 1150 and to have landed in what is now Florida. Tre-Madog (Tremadog) Bay is named after him.

Loch Leven
Tayside/Scotland   p.324□H 8

This large loch in the middle of the Fife Peninsula became infamous as a result of the imprisonment of Mary Queen of Scots for eleven months (starting from 16 June 1567) in the small castle on *Castle Island* at the W. end of the loch. Her husband had been murdered in February of the same year, and only three months later she married her probable murderer and by so doing stirred up her lords against her. While the people marched through the streets of Edinburgh shouting 'Burn the whore!', the queen signed her abdication on 24 July 1567. The scene could hardly have been more dramatic. As her son, who was just one year old, was being anointed King James VI in Stirling Castle, her Protestant stepbrother, the Earl of Moray, had him-

och Leven, Kinross House

lf proclaimed regent. It was under his
rotection that John Knox took possession
the child in order to rescue it from the
dulterous Papist'. But the 24-year-old
ueen did not give up. On 2 May 1568, the
ung Lord George Douglas, the son of the
rd of the castle, helped her to escape. A
ge let her out of the castle, threw the key
vay and rowed her to land, where George
ouglas was waiting for her. He brought
r to Niddry Castle, the fortress of the
amiltons.
st eleven days later she faced her brother
the decisive battle of Langside near
lasgow. This ended in victory for her
other, and Mary was forced to flee head-
ng. On 16 May 1568 a fishing boat took
r across the Solway Firth to England,
vay from her Scottish home for ever. She
as held prisoner in England by Queen
lizabeth for 20 years.

Loch Leven Castle: Its walls date back to
1335. The curtain wall and the three-
storeyed, square keep are also 14C. The
round tower at the SE corner of the curtain wall was added in the 16C.
The castle can be reached by ferry from
Kinross.

Kinross House: William Bruce built this
baroque seat in 1685–93. It stands between
the small town of Kinross and Castle Island and looks directly over Loch Leven
Castle. In 1671, Charles II made William
Bruce, a follower of the Stuarts, court architect. He designed the extensions to
Holyrood Palace. His own country seat
was intended to represent the perfection of
his ideas, as befitted his high position. It
was not for nothing that Daniel Defoe
described the house as 'the most beautiful
and regular piece of architecture in the

whole of Scotland, and perhaps in the whole of England'.

The *park* surrounding Kinross House was laid out by Bruce himself, while the *Fish Gate* at the entrance to the park is the work of Flemish stonemasons.

Burleigh Castle: The earliest part of these ruins 2 m. NE of Kinross was a tower built in 1582 which was once the family seat of the Balfours of Burleigh.

Loch Ness
Highlands/Scotland   p.324☐G 6

This loch is the largest in the Great Glen and has been famous since the 7C, when St.Columba's biographer was the first to report that there was a monster there. Since then this monster has regularly appeared in the media without having ever having been properly observed. It has not yet been possible to prove whether the monster exists or not, not least because the loch, which is only a mile wide, has a maximum depth of 1,070 ft. deep and is over 650 ft. deep for more than two thirds of its 22 mile length. Furthermore, its boggy water is as dark brown as that of most lakes in the Highlands, and divers can hardly see their hands in front of their faces.

Over the centuries, the strategic importance of this loch has been more significant than the plesiosaur which may live in it —hence the remains of two fortresses.

Fort Augustus: Fort Augustus, at the S. end of the loch, and Fort William further S., were built by the English to control the recalcitrant Highland clans. Fort Augustus dates from 1715, being named after the Duke of Cumberland. In 1730 General Wade extended it and had a road built along the S. shore of the loch. In 1744, Charles Edward Stuart (Bonnie Prince Charlie) captured the fort and held it un-

Loch Ness, Urquhart Castle

til the battle of Culloden. The fort w. turned into a Benedictine abbey in 187

Urquhart Castle: This occupies a ke strategic site at the junction of Glen U quhart and Glen Convinth on the N. sho of the loch. The bluff was probably forti fied in about 1200 and it is probably th spot from which Allan Dorward controlle traffic through the Great Glen in *c.* 123 The castle was in English hands in 129 but in 1313 Robert the Bruce recapture it for Scotland. 200 years later, Dona Macdonald of Lochalsh, Lord of the Isle took possession of the castle and probab also assumed control of the surroundi area. Most of the fortress was blown up 1691 to prevent it from falling into th hands of the Jacobites. But the remains the building, once one of the greatest ca tles in Scotland, are still impressive.

The lower storeys of the *gatehouse*, with good tunnel vaulting, still survive, and there is also a NE *tower*. The castle, which covers an area of some 108,000 sq.ft., was accessible from the land only by a drawbridge.

London
p.332☐K/L 15

Contents

HISTORY AND DEVELOPMENT

Numerous finds prove that the area around London was inhabited by the Celts (from *c.* 800 BC onwards). Following Caesar's initial landing in Britain in 55 BC, the Emperor Claudius (10 BC–AD 54) conquered the SE of Britain and founded the military camp of *Londinium* on a strategic ford across the Thames. The camp rapidly developed into a flourishing port and trading post. The area of about 1 square mile which the Romans fortified with a massive rampart corresponds approximately to today's City of London. Around AD 61, the Romans faced an uprising by Boadicea, the warlike Queen of East Anglia, who even succeeded in capturing London. From about 240 onwards, London was the capital of one of the four late Roman provinces of Britain under the Emperor Diocletian

(240–313/16). After the Romans withdrew
from Britain in the early 5C, thus leaving
the way clear for settlement by Angles,
Saxons and Jutes, London became less important and, like the rest of the country, it
suffered severely from continual raids by
Danes and Vikings. The Saxon King
Alfred the Great (848/9 – 899/901) encouraged the arts and culture. The chief
debt owed to him by English literature is
for his translations of and commentaries on
Latin works. He not only saved the country from final Danish domination (he won
the battle of Edington in 878), but also captured London in 886. Canute (995–1035)
and Edward the Confessor (1003–66) both
resided in Westminster, and William the
Conqueror (1027–87) had himself crowned
in Westminster Abbey in 1066 after his victory at Hastings. He confirmed all the
city's privileges and began building the
White Tower as a royal residence. It was
completed and enlarged by his successors.
It was under Henry I (1068 – 1135) that
London finally replaced Winchester as the
capital of England. In 1157, in the stable
courtyard, the Hanseatic League established a base for itself in the city which had
attained wealth and reputation as a result
of trade and commerce. The city was
directly subordinate to the King and, from
1192 onwards, was administered by the
Lord Mayor who was elected by the guilds.
In the 16C, London, with its 500,000 inhabitants, was the largest city in England.
Economic prosperity was increased by the
foundation of the first trading companies
and the first commodity exchange (1567).
During the reign of Elizabeth I (1533–
1603, Queen from 1558 onwards), events
not only led to English dominantion of the
oceans (victory over the Spanish Armada
in 1588), and the beginnings of what was
to be the Empire, but England also em-
barked on the Elizabethan Age, during
which art, culture and literature (William

London, Houses of Parliament ▷

Shakespeare, 1564–1616) flowered, particularly in the capital. In 1665, a devastating plague reduced the population of London by almost 70,000, and in 1666 four-fifths of the city, which had at that time grown far beyond its original limits, were reduced to ashes by the Great Fire. But this only briefly interrupted the city's continuous growth. Over the centuries, London became the centre of the constantly growing Empire, which reached its apogee under Queen Victoria (1819–1901, Queen from 1837 onwards), bringing London power, growth and another cultural and artistic heyday as a result of industrialization and the expansion of international trade. The port was the largest in the country in the early 19C, and the public transport networks were constantly being adapted to increasing requirements. German air raids caused considerable damage in the First World War, and during the Battle of Britain in the Second World War a large part of the City of London was reduced to rubble.

Some 9 million people now live in London and its suburbs, and the city, which is divided into 32 boroughs, covers an area of 620 sq. miles, making it one of the largest of the world's capitals. One reason for its size is the preference of the English for terraced houses and small gardens. As a result less than 5,000 people live in the City of London, while more than half a million flock here for their daily work.

Today London is the capital of Great Britain, Northern Ireland, the centre of the Commonwealth, and also the seat of the Royal Family, an Anglican Bishop and a Catholic Archbishop, the Parliament, the high courts, the major administrative bodies and scientific institutions. Immigrants who have arrived from all parts of the Commonwealth since 1945 have not only created a multifarious mixture of nations, but have also brought their cultures and habits with them, providing the visitor with an enduring impression of the variety of peoples of the former Empire. There are also a plethora of religious and secular buildings of all styles and periods. Among these, those by Christopher Wren (1632–1723), the 'architect of London', are outstanding. Numerous museums and galleries display precious and interesting finds from all parts of the world and from all stages in the development of nature, man and art. Two large opera houses, the National Theatre with three different auditoriums, and 50 other theatres, offer something for every taste. The visitor may discover charming corners and alleyways, such as the reader of the novels of Charles Dickens (1812–70) has learned to love, and he may also wander down distinguished, elegant or simple streets of houses, businesses, and shops. Noisy traffic junctions are to be found next to parks which are oases of tranquillity. Monuments and traces of past greatness are everywhere, as are traditions which are lovingly and faithfully adhered to—and sometimes smiled at by outsiders. The colourful public events and parades offer the onlooker a hint of former greatness and splendour.

RELIGIOUS BUILDINGS

Westminster Abbey: *History.* The present Abbey stands on a site upstream from the City of London which was inhabited even in Roman times. The first church dates back to the 7&8C. Edward the Confessor began rebuilding in 1050–60, and some fragments of his church and monastery are still standing today.

In 1245, Henry III began building the existing church, which later received the mortal remains of the Confessor and served as the coronation and burial place of kings. Thus the monuments to Henry and his family are among the Abbey's greatest treasures.

The plans drawn up in 1245–53 by Henry of Reyns, the first architect, betray French

the Royal Air Force with the Battle of Britain memorial window, numerous flags and the tomb of the 'father' of the R.A.F., Viscount Trenchard (d.1956) **27** tomb of Mary Stuart **28** St.Nicholas Chapel with the marble tomb of Sir John Villiers (d.1606) and the splendid tomb of Elizabeth, Duchess of Northumberland (d.1676) by Robert Adam and Nicholas Read **29** St.Edmund's Chapel with numerous tombs, notably that of William de Valence (d.1496) with a splendid effigy **30** S. ambulatory with the Chantry of Henry V **31** St. Benedicts Chapel with the alabaster tomb of Si-mon Langham (d.1376), the Archbishop of Can-terbury **32** Poets' Corner, with the marble tomb of Geoffrey Chaucer (d.1400), and the tombs of Browning (d.1889) and Tennyson (d.1892); also busts of Dryden (d.1700) and Longfellow (d.1882) **33** S. transept with memorials to Garrick, the historian Macaulay, Barrow and Händel **34** St. Faith's Chapel, with two magnificent 16C tapes-tries from Brussels **35** chapterhouse **36** Chapel of the Pyx, former sacristy with the oldest altar in the church; it was originally the home of the Pyx, a casket in which the trial-plates for the coins and weights of the realm were kept **37** undercroft, mu-seum devoted to the abbey's history **38** door to the cloisters **39** cloisters; on one of the outer arches is a row of figures which forms a Tree of Jesse, and a further archway leads through to the old dormitories, which are now the library **40** Dean's Yard **41** Deanery (no public access) **42** Jericho Parlour (no public access) **43** Jerusalem Chamber (no public access) **44** bookshop

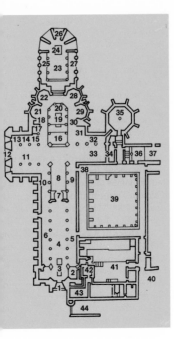

London, Westminster Abbey 1 W. door **2** St. George's Chapel; the former baptistery is now dedicated to those who died in the First World War **3** Tomb of the Unknown Soldier and a plaque to Sir Winston Churchill **4** nave with numerous tablets, including memorials to David Livingstone, Robert Stephenson and Neville Chamberlain **5** S. aisle **6** N. aisle **7** organ gallery **8** choir with memorials to Sir Isaac Newton and Earl Stanhope **9** S. choir aisle **10** N. choir aisle **11** N. transept, sometimes known as the States-man's Aisle, with numerous memorials **12** N. por-tal **13** St.Andrew's Chapel **14** St.Michael's Chapel **15** Chapel of St.John the Evangelist **16** sanctu-ary with high altar; screen with scenes from the life of Christ, and a modern mosaic of the Last Supper by Salvati over the altar **17** Islip Chapel; two storeys, dedicated to the abbot and church architect Islip (d.1532) **18** N. ambulatory **19** St. Edward's Chapel (over the apse of the old church) with the tomb of Edward the Confessor and other monarchs **20** Chantry of Henry V **21** Chapel of St.John the Baptist, with the marble tomb of Thomas Cecil, Earl of Exeter (d.1623) and his wife **22** St.Paul's Chapel, with the tombs of dignitar-ies from the times of Henry V and Charles I **23** Henry VII Chapel, a masterpiece of Gothic ar-chitecture with the King's tomb (**24**), as well as that of his wife and numerous banners of the Or-der of the Bath **25** tomb of Elizabeth I, with her sister Mary ('Bloody Mary') nearby **26** Chapel of

influence: a tall nave with two rows of piers, and a polygonal apse at the E. end with radiating chapels and a cloister along the lines of Reims cathedral. The choir, transepts and the first part of the nave were completed within 10 years. By the end of the century work had proceeded as far as the fourth bay of the nave. At this time the remnants of the Norman church were still standing.

Building work was resumed in the mid 14C and was supervised by H.Yevele from 1360 onwards. He completed the W. sec-tion of the nave (work on pulling down the old nave began in 1375), and he adhered scrupulously to the style in which build-ing had begun a century before. The Henry VII chapel, a model of the Perpen-dicular, was built in 1503 on the site of the Lady Chapel erected by Henry III. Al-though the monastery was secularized dur-ing the Reformation, the buildings hardly suffered any damage. The church was filled with increasingly bombastic monuments. Although some of these are very attractive, their great numbers gradually masked the architectural beauty of the church.

The W. towers, which appear relatively small, were built about 1730 to plans by Hawksmoor. The 19C restoration was not only thorough but also completely marred the external appearance of the church. However, 'the interior was able to preserve more of its original appearance and its old furnishing than any of our other cathedrals... The Abbey is simply the masterpiece of English art, and is a treasure-house richly filled with medieval sculptures and paintings' (Lethaby).

Exterior. The oldest sections are in the E. The chapterhouse (1245–50) with its impressive 14C flying buttresses originally had a flat roof, but now supports a pyramidal one dating from the 19C. The flying buttresses of the Henry VII chapel bear carvings of all kinds of creatures, including the inlaid turrets with their Tudor domes which are richly adorned with crockets. The windows between these turrets are arranged in a zigzag scheme. On the N. side of the nave, the break between the 13C style and the style of Yevele's work is clearly indicated by the difference between the unadorned wall and the tracery of the aisles.

Interior. The nave captivates the visitor both by the unity of the 13&14C elements and by its immense height. The pillar shafts are of dark Purbeck marble throughout; and the capitals, the transept walls and the walls beneath the (new) rose-windows are extensively carved. The Henry VII chapel is one of the masterpieces of late Perpendicular. A fan vault with rich pendent decoration extends over the aisles and the radiating chapels. A superb fan vault, with enormous pendants, covers the nave and reaches a high point in the polygonal vault above the apse. This contrasts with the rich carvings from the second decade of the 16C. These have preserved their

medieval appearance although the vivi[d] colours which once adorned the individua[l] items have faded.

Monuments. Chapel of St.Edward the Con[fessor. Henry III commissioned the build[ing] of Edward's shrine in 1241, before th[e] rebuilding of the Abbey began. The tall[er] lower section containing the tomb is Cos[matesque and dates from 1270. The uppe[r] part, which is richly embellished with pre[cious stones, was stolen during the Refor[mation and later replaced by a wooden one[. Near the shrine are the Coronation Chai[r] and the tombs of the Plantagenet kings[. Walter of Durham made the Coronatio[n] Chair in 1300/1. It contains the Stone o[f] Scone which Edward I seized from th[e] Scots. The chair stands before a 13C ston[e] wall (the rear wall of the altar) decorate[d] by a frieze showing scenes from the life o[f] Edward the Confessor. Close by is the[] tomb of Edward I (d. 1307), a simple, un[adorned tomb without any effigy made o[f] black Purbeck marble. There is a wonde[r]ful gilded bronze effigy of his wife, Eleano[r] of Castile (d. 1290) on her marble tomb[. This effigy, and the one of her father-in[-]law Henry III (d. 1212), are by W.Torel[. More royal tombs occupy the S. wall of th[e] chapel. The tomb of Edward III (b[y] Yevele), bears a hierarchical gilded bronz[e] figure with long hair and beard. The realis[tic figure of Edward III's wife Philippa o[f] Hainault (d. 1369) was carved from marbl[e] by Hannequin de Liege. The double tom[b] of Richard II and his queen Anne of Bo[hemia was made by Yevele and St.Lot i[n] 1394&5, while the figures are by N.Broke[r] and G.Prest. At the E. end is the *Chantr[y] of Henry V,* completed in *c.* 1460. Of th[e] monarch's tomb (1422 – 30), only th[e] wooden base of the effigy survives.

Sanctuary. The Cosmatesque pavemen[t] dates from 1268. Above the sedilia on th[e] S. side (*c.* 1308), there are larger-than-lif[e] pictures of saints and kings. On the N. sid[e]

Big Ben (Houses of Parliament[)

Westminster Abbey, chapterhouse

are the three large medieval tombs of Edward I's brother Edmund Crouchback, Earl of Lancaster (d. 1296), the latter's wife Aveline (d. 1272), and cousin Aymer de Valence (d. 1324). The effigies are canopied, and the tombs are adorned with painted statuettes of mourners. The most recent of the monuments is typical of the Decorated Style in its wealth of figures and decoration.

Ambulatory. The SW altarpiece, with large figures of Christ and Saints and delicate stellar panelling (13C), may possibly be from a medieval high altar. The paint has faded, but was once of high quality. There are numerous memorials and tombs from the 13–18C in the chapels. Particular attention should be drawn to the *effigy of William de Valence* (d. 1296) once covered with Limoges enamel, and to the elegant *effigy of John of Eltham* (d. 1337), which

is made entirely of alabaster and is in the Chapel of St.Edmund at the SW end of the ambulatory. The Chapel of St.John the Baptist contains the impressive 36 ft.-high tomb of Lord Hunsdown and his wife. *Henry VII Chapel.* The nave houses the tomb of the king and his queen Elizabeth of York. This tomb is by Torrigiani (1518). The gilded bronze effigies dating from the Reformation are in charming contrast to the other sculptures in the chapel. The monarchs' likenesses are highly realistic, and the corners of the tombs are adorned with beautiful figures of angels. The richly decorated Gothic stalls with high canopies were built in 1520. In the N. aisle, an impressively realistic effigy of Queen Elizabeth I (d. 1603) rests on her rather modest tomb. The latter is by M.Colt. James I's two infant daughters are buried in the Innocents' Corner. The *tomb of Lady Margaret Beaufort,* the mother of Henry VII, in the S. aisle, was made by Torrigiani in 1513 and is regarded as the first great Renaissance work in England. In 1607–12, C.Cure built the tomb of Mary Queen of Scots, the mother of James I. it bears a captivating effigy of the beautiful and tragic queen. The impressive allegorical *tombs* in the apsidal chapels are by Hubert le Sueur. In the SW one are those of the Duke of Lennox and Richmond (d. 1624), a cousin of James I, and of his wife (d. 1639), and that in the NW one is of George Villiers, Duke of Buckingham, the King's favourite (d. 1628).

Nave and transepts. Of the innumerable memorials on the walls note the following: *Poets' Corner* which is the SE corner of the S. transept. Its main feature is the memorials to great scientists and men of letters, e.g. to John, Duke of Argyll and Greenwich (by Roubillac, 1748/49), to Handel (1761, also by Roubillac), and to the actor David Garrick (1779, by H.Webber). The end wall of the S. transept has 9 ft.-high, late-13C *wall paintings* of St. Christopher and Doubting Thomas. In the

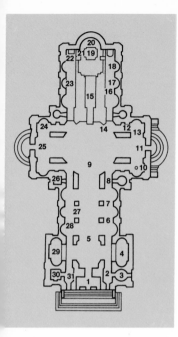

London, St.Paul's Cathedral 1 W. portal **2** SW portal **3** Dean's Staircase, a spiral staircase with splendid wrought-iron gates by Tijou (no public access) **4** Chapel of St.Michael and St.George, since 1906 the chapel of the order of the same name, founded in 1818 and the highest honour for Foreign Office diplomats **5** nave **6** S.aisle **7** 'The Light of the World', Christ with a lantern, a variant by Holman Hunt in his original painting, which is in Oxford and dates from 1900 **8** entrance to library, Whispering Gallery, in which a whisper can be heard at a distance of more than 100 ft, and dome **9** dome with the Thornhill's 8 scenes from the life of St.Paul **10** font by Francis Bird (1727) **11** S. transept **12** entrance to the crypt, said to be the largest in Europe: tombs of Wren, Nelson, Wellington, Holman Hunt and others **13** Chapel of the Order of the British Empire **14** pulpit by G.Gibbons **15** choir **16** S. choir aisle **17** Donne memorial **18** Lady Chapel **19** high altar of Sicilian marble; the splendid baldacchino has a Christ Triumphant and 4 gold angels **20** American Memorial Chapel, dedicated to the 28,000 Americans who were stationed in the British Isles and died on the Continent during the course of the World War 2; their names are displayed on the Roll of Honour opposite the altar. The three windows depict scenes from the life of Christ which glorify the service, sacrifice and redemption of the Christian soldier. **21** wrought-iron gates by Tijou **22** Chapel of Modern Martyrs (1961), dedicated to the martyrs of the Anglican church since

1850 **23** N. choir aisle with carvings by Gibbons **24** N. transept chapel **25** N. transept **26** Lord Mayor sacristy **27** Wellington monument, bronze figures representing Valour and Cowardice, Truth and Falsehood **28** N. aisle, including the memorial for General Charles Gordon, who died during the Mahdi revolt in Sudan in 1885 **29** St.Dunstan's Chapel, which is used for regular daily communion and private prayers **30** All Souls' Chapel with the memorial to Lord Kitchener, one of the greatest of 19C British generals **31** NW portal

N. transept, Sir Francis Vere rests in full armour on a marble slab, supported by four kneeling knights. Dating from 1609, this work is attributed to Colt. Here there also stands the famous *Nightingale Monument* (Roubillac, 1761), in which Joseph Nightingale is trying to ward off the lance threatening his young wife. At the W. end of the N. aisle is the monument to Charles James Fox (Westmacott, 1810–15), with allegories of peace and freedom and a negro in prayer. A contemporary portrait (1385 – 90) on the SW pier by the entrance depicts Richard II, and at the NE end is the monument to Isaac Newton (Kent and Rysbrack, 1731).

Cloister. This dates largely from the 14C and was begun under Henry II. It leads to the Chamber of the Pyx, a remnant of the old abbey (11C) and, through two vaulted ante-chambers, to the *chapterhouse* built in 1245–50. The vault of this octagonal room, which in the 14–16C was used by Parliament as an assembly hall, is supported by a single slender central pillar. Light enters the room through 40 ft. high windows on six sides. The pavement still has its original slabs, some of which show a beautiful rosette pattern. Wall tapestries and seven glass medallions from the 13C may be seen in the Jerusalem Chamber. *Museum in the Norman undercroft.* Wood and wax figures, which were formerly carried in funeral processions, are on display here. Note the life-sized effigy of Edward II, a wax likeness of Charles II as a member of the Order of the Garter, and a beautiful 11C capital from the cloister of the Judgement of Solomon.

St.Paul's Cathedral: *History.* 604 is accepted as the year when the first church was founded on this site. The church which preceded the present cathedral was begun in the late 11C and enlarged and altered in the 14&15C. Old St.Paul's Church was among the greatest churches in Christendom before being destroyed in the Great Fire of 1666: it was 584 ft. long and its tower was 490 ft. high. The church had fallen into disrepair by the early 17C. Then, in 1634, Inigo Jones added a large W. portico with columns 49 ft. tall. In May 1666 Christopher Wren proposed that a new dome be built over the crossing. But the devastation wreaked by the fire of 2–7 September was so disastrous that, after repeated attempts to rebuild the church, the decision was taken to build a completely new one to plans by Wren. His first designs were rejected, and he himself greatly altered the final plans while the work was in progress. The foundation stone was laid in 1675, and in 1771 the entire church, 575 ft. long and 364 ft. high, was complete.

Features. The outstanding feature of the building is its dome, which Wren placed on the Latin cross ground plan with considerable skill. The church itself adheres to the formal tradition of English cathedrals: a nave flanked by aisles with clerestories and vaults supported by flying buttresses; transepts and a choir surrounded by an ambulatory; a tower over the crossing which Wren replaced by the dome spanning the nave and aisles; and two W. towers. In order to adapt the building's proportions to those of the dome, Wren so designed the outer walls that, like the internal walls, they rose above the roof of the side aisles to the height of the nave, screening the flying buttresses, which were out of keeping with a classical design, and giving the cathedral a uniform, massive appearance. The dome, which seems hemispherical from below, rests on a drum with tall windows and a cornice. Beneath this is a a massive colonnade with eight buttresses (every fourth column). At the top of the dome there is a lantern with a golden ball and a cross. However, the exterior is by no means mirrored by the interior. Inside there is an inner stone dome

St.Paul's Cathedral, vaulted ceiling, mosaic

beginning a little below the colonnade of the exterior and its vault barely reaches the base of the outer dome. An enormous cone of stone fills the area between the two domes and supports not only the lead covered timber-work of the outer dome, but also the stone lantern.

Exterior. The exterior has two orders; the portico has a pediment, two tiers of columns arranged in pairs, and is flanked by the W. towers on either side of the nave. These towers are regarded as the most baroque of all Wren's London towers. The semicircular porticoes of the transepts reflect the form of the dome and the E. apse.

Interior. The nave, aisles, transepts and choir have flat, dish-shaped domes above each section of the ceiling, and the main dome rests on eight arches. Thornhill painted frescos on the cupola, contrary to Wren's wishes. The mosaics are 19C. The Whispering Gallery runs 100 ft. above the ground at the base of the inner dome (the outer stone gallery above the colonnaded storey, and the Golden Gallery above the dome, are also accessible). The *choir* has exceptionally fine wooden carvings (fruits, leaves, flowers and angels' heads) by Grinling Gibbons. The original plan was that the choir should be divided by the organ and a separating wall, but this plan was altered. The organ case is now divided and, together with the choir stalls, it stands to either side of the choir. Some of the carvings were used for a splendid arch in the S. transept. The gilded wrought-iron gates, whose position was also altered, are by J.Tijou. The *high altar* and *baldacchino* are modern, the Victorian originals having been destroyed in the bombing. In a S. side-chapel of the choir is the notable *monument to John Donne,* by N.Stone, 1631: it shows the poet standing erect, wrapped in a shroud. There are numerous other monuments, mostly to heroes of the Napoleonic Wars. By each pier in the crossing there are commemorative groups. The bombastic *Wellington monument*

(1857–1912) by A.Stevens is in the nave. The *monument to Lord Nelson* (1808–18) has a realistic figure of the admiral by John Flaxman. At the base of the W. towers there are *chapels* with notable screens by Jonathan Maine (1698). Above the S. one is the *library,* reached via a staircase; fine panelling and cupboards. Wren's various models for the church, and some historical material relating to the old church, are displayed in the *Trophy Room* above the N. one. In the *crypt* is *Nelson's marble sarcophagus,* black in colour, which Benedetto da Ravezzano made in 1524–9 for Wolsey's tomb in Windsor. There is also Wellington's gun carriage, cast by G.Semper in 1852 from melted-down cannonballs.

Southwark Cathedral (Borough High Street, SE1): This church, formerly belonging to the Augustinian monastery of St.Mary Overie, was built in the 13&14C. The Early English style has survived especially in the crossing, where massive piers support the tower, in the choir and in the retro-choir with its four aisles. The nave was rebuilt in the 19C, while the

St.Paul's Cathedral, W. tower

tower over the crossing tower is 14&15C. Later work on it may have been by H.Yevele. The chequered pattern of the parapet is original and has been partly restored. There are numerous *tombs*, including that of John Gower (d. 1408), whose head rests on three of his books and that of Alderman Humble and his wife (1616), both of whom are kneeling under a panelled canopy. There is also the monument to Joyce Austin, Lady Clarke (1633), with an allegory of agriculture and two peasant girls who have fallen asleep after harvest.

Westminster Cathedral (Ashley Place, SW1): This domed Roman Catholic cathedral was built by J.F.Bentley in the Byzantine style in 1895-1903. He used red brick with white stone bands. The marble facing of the interior has remained unfinished and gives the building a sombre, mysterious atmosphere. Eric Gill carved the Stations of the Cross in 1913-18; the rich furnishings and decorations are largely from the 1930s.

All Hallows (London Wall, EC2): Built by George Dance the Younger in 1765-7, the church has a simple interior with a tunnel vault borne by Ionic columns, which frame side aisles vaulted by a coffered ceiling.

All Saints (Margaret Street, W1): This is certainly the most beautiful Gothic Revival church in London, and was built in 1849 –59 under the supervision of W.Butterfield. The outer walls are of polychrome brick; the church is crowned by a brick tower and another tower with a slate spire. Coloured bricks are an unusual feature of the interior and the effect is intensified still further by frescos, mosaics, coloured glass, alabaster and marble. The rear wall of the altar was carved by W.Dyce.

Chapel of St. John: (see Tower).

Christ Church (Newgate Street, EC1): The slender, square tower is one of Wren's best works. The church itself, which was built on the site of the old Greyfriars Monastery, has been destroyed. There is a garden on its site.

Christ Church (Spitalfields, Commercial Street, E1): This massive church (1714-19) is by Hawksmoor. The baroque W. façade is reached by a flight of steps. The portico, which is covered by an open tunnel vault, is the lowest in a series of triumphal arches superimposed on one another and ending in a massive stone tower which was altered in the 19C. Enormous Corinthian columns, with tall bases and rich capitals, separate the nave from the aisles and from the choir. At the W. end there is a gallery with a carved wooden organ frontal (1730).

Holy Trinity (Sloane Street): Built by J.D.Sedding in 1888-90, it is a conspicuous example of the Arts and Craft Movement, with coloured marble, rich decorations by Sedding and his contemporaries, and stained-glass windows by Burne Jones.

Methodist Chapel (Fournier Street, E1): This house of God was built as a chapel in 1743, later became a synagogue as the population changed, and is today a mosque. Galleries rest on Tuscan columns in the simple interior.

Old Church (Old Church Street): Extensively restored after the destruction of 1941. The original More Chapel, with the monument to Thomas More (d. 1532) and other notable monuments, still survives.

Queen's Chapel (Marlborough Place, near Pall Mall, SW1): This church, which was built in 1623-7 as a private chapel for Queen Henrietta Maria, Charles I's Catholic wife, is one of Inigo Jones's masterpieces. The interior is spanned by a coffered vault in white and gold, and the Venetian window in the E. takes up the whole width of the building. Fine decoration from the second half of the 17C.

St. Andrew's (Holborn, EC1): Although the church survived the Great Fire, it was rebuilt by Wren in 1686/7 (although the tower was not completed until 1704). Gutted by fire in 1941, it was restored and fitted with decorations from the Foundling Hospital: font, pulpit, organ (presented by Handel) and the monument to Thomas Coram, the hospital's founder (d. 1751). The two poor-house children above the door (1696) are from a nearby school.

St. Anne and St. Agnes (Gresham Street, EC2): This Wren church (1677–80) is regarded as one of his most successful arrangements of space. The ground plan is a square within a cross whose tunnel-vaulted arms meet in a vault over the crossing borne by Corinthian columns. The wooden rear wall of the altar is original.

St. Anne Limehouse (Three Colt Street,

EC2): Hawksmoor, 1714–24; the tower is a classical adaptation of the Perpendicular style (as it is to be found in Boston, Lincolnshire). In 1853, P.C. Hardwick restored the interior and the W. apse.

St. Bartholomew-the-Great (West Smithfield, EC1): The church consists of the choir and transepts of the old priory church of 1123. The groin-vaulted ambulatory and the round pillars with galleries above them are London's finest example of Norman architecture. The clerestory windows are late-14C; the oriel on the S. side of the choir dates from *c.* 1520. To the N. of the altar, in a canopied tomb bearing an effigy (*c.* 1500), there rests Rahere (d. 1143), the founder of the priory and of the adjoining St. Bartholomew's Hospital.

St. Benet's, Paul's Wharf (Upper Thames Street EC4): This Wren church (1677–85) retains one of the best-preserved of his interiors, and also numerous original *carvings*: a gallery borne by Corinthian columns, a splendidly embellished W. door, pews and choir stalls, reading desk

Southwark Cathedral, nave

All Hallows

and pulpit, an exquisitely worked communion rail, the altar table, and the rear wall of the altar. The simple exterior is of brick, with stone ornament. The tower has a graceful lead dome and a slender spire.

St.Bride's (off Fleet Street, EC4): Built (1670–84), burnt down in 1940, and subsequently rebuilt. It possesses Wren's most famous tower and his tallest (226 ft.), and also his best-known spire (1701–3) with four well-proportioned octagonal and arcaded storeys, each storey being set back and the top one being crowned by an obelisk.

St.Clement Danes (The Strand, WC2): Wren rebuilt the church in 1680–2, and Gibbs completed the tower in 1719. The interior, with its stuccoed vault and the pulpit by Gibbons, was restored after the destruction of 1941.

St.Cyprian's (Clarence Gate, Glenworth Street, NW1): The magnificent interior (1903) is the best-preserved example of Sir Ninian Comper's imaginative recreation

St. Bartholomew-the-Great

of English pre-Reformation liturgical decoration. The open-work choir screen, the stained glass, the font cover, and the hangings, were all personally designed by him.

St. Dunstan-in-the-West (Fleet Street, EC2): This octagonal church was built by J.Shaw in 1829–33. The interior has a stellar vault, restored after being destroyed in 1944. The exterior is crowned by an open-work lantern (Th.Harris, 1671), and two giants strike the quarter-hour on the clock. Statues from the old Ludgate now stand on and within the porch: Queen Elizabeth I (1586) and the legendary king Lud and his sons.

St. George's (Bloomsbury Way, WC1): Hawksmoor, 1716–27; it has a massive Corinthian portico and a tower which is a free copy of the mausoleum of Halikarnassos and is crowned by a statue of George I (who ascended the throne in 1714) as St.George. The theatrical interior with its rich stucco has a square ground plan and is illuminated by a clerestory.

St. George's (Hanover Square, St. George's Street, W1): Built by J.James (1712–24) at almost the same time as the preceding church. It too has a Corinthian portico (the oldest of its kind) with a pediment on which a statue of George I was supposed to stand. The bright interior is divided into a nave and aisles with side galleries. On the E. wall is a *Venetian window* of splendid Flemish glass (1540–50).

St.Helen (Bishopsgate, Great St.Helens, EC3): The church of the St. Helen's Benedictine convent, it was built in the late 13C and has two adjacent naves. One of these was reserved for the nuns, and the other was part of the old parish church. On the N. wall is the nuns' night staircase (1475), and on the N. wall of the nuns' choir is a Easter Sepulchre. The church has a good Jacobean pulpit and numerous im-ressive *brasses* and *monuments,* including those to Sir John Crosby (d. 1476), the church's benefactor and the builder of Crosby Hall, Chelsea; Sir Thomas Gresham (d. 1579), the founder of the Royal Exchange; Sir John Spencer (d. 1605), who was mayor in 1594, and his wife. The monument to Martin Bonds (d. 1643) shows the dead man in a tent. The tomb of Sir Julius Caesar, who was a judge (d. 1636), is the work of N.Stone.

St. James's Garlickhythe (Garlickhill, C4): Rebuilt by Wren in 1674–87, it has a graceful nave, to which a square, balustraded tower was added in 1713. The interior has some good carvings, in particular the pulpit, the W. gallery and the organ by Father Smith. Some beautiful iron swordholders may also be admired.

St. James's (Piccadilly, W1): Wren built the church in 1681–4, when the area surrounding St.James's was beginning to be developed. He saw it as the ideal, sparsely furnished Protestant church, with space for a congregation of some 2000 believers.

The exterior consists of bricks with a stone filling, and the spacious interior (destroyed in 1941, and later restored) has some particularly good *carvings* by Grinling Gibbons: a font with Adam and Eve and the Three Wise Men, and the rear wall of the altar. The organ was brought here from Whitehall.

St. James-the-Less (Thorndike Street, Vauxhall Bridge Road, SW1): This red and black brick church (1860/1) is one of G.E.Street's most original works. The powerful tower rises above the portico and is separate from the church proper. The interior is decorated by red granite columns with foliate capitals, and by walls of brightly-coloured brick. The pulpit is richly worked, and there are some fine stained-glass windows. The fresco above the chancel arch (Day of Judgement) is by G.F.Watts.

St.John's (Smith Square, SW1): Built by Th.Archer in 1714–28, it is one of the most beautiful baroque buildings in London. There are four corner towers and the

St. Bartholomew-the-Great, altar

St. Helen

pedimented porticoes face N. and S. The interior, where four large Corinthian columns support a sturdy cornice, was gutted by fire in 1941 and was later restored as a concert hall.

St.John's Clerkenwell (St.John's Square, EC1): This church, together with St.John's Gate, is the only remnant of the great Order of the Knights of St. John, which Henry VIII dissolved in 1540. The 12C crypt has a ribbed vault and houses the monument to Juan Ruyz de Vergara (d. 1575), whose effigy, together with that of a page, can be seen in full armour on the coffin lid.

St.John's Parish Church (Hampstead): This church, built in 1744–7 and enlarged in the 19C, is picturesquely set at the end of Church Row behind some splendid

wrought-iron railings taken from the house of the Duke of Chandos in Canon, Edgware. Inside there are a gallery, large columns, and a fine 18C pulpit.

St. Katherine Cree (Leadenhall Street, EC3): The choir was built in 1628–31 after Inigo Jones had finished the Renaissance Queen's Chapel and still has a Gothic panelled ceiling with a Gothic ribbed vault on which the coats-of-arms of the London guilds make a fine show. The E. window ('Katherine's Wheel'), a rose in a square frame, originates from Old St. Paul's Church.

St. Luke's Church (The Vinage): This plain brick church was begun in 1630 and enlarged in the late 17C. The E. end is 19C. It has a pedimented portico, 17C glass with coats-of-arms, and monuments, including that to Edward Wilkinson (d. 1568), Elizabeth I's head cook.

St. Magnus the Martyr (Lower Thames Street, EC3): This Wren church (1671–85) has one of the finest interiors in the City of London, with exquisite *wood carving* on the W. gallery and the organ front (Jordan, 1712), the door surround, the choir and the rear wall of the altar. There is also some magnificent *wrought-iron*, such as the communion rail (1683) and the sword stand (1708). The 185 ft. steeple (completed 1705) is borne by a square bell tower.

St. Margaret's (Lothbury, EC2): Built by Christopher Wren in 1686–95, it has a fine spire and particularly good decorations mostly assembled from the furnishings of old Wren churches which were torn down in the 19C. Features worth mentioning are the *choir screen* (1689) from All Hallows Dowgate which was designed by Wren himself, the *pulpit*, and the *font*, which attributed to Gibbons and comes from St. Olave's Jewry.

St. Margaret Pattens (Eastcheap, EC3): This is another of Wren's churches. It has a 200 ft. tower and splendid *carvings*, especially the rear wall of the altar and the communion rail, and the W. screen adorned by royal coats of arms.

St. Margaret's (Westminster, Parliament Square, SW1): Most of this church, which was originally built as a parish church in the shadow of the Abbey, was built in the first quarter of the 16C and radically altered in the 19C. J.James rebuilt the tower in Gothic style in 1735–7. The E. window, which was installed in the church in 1758, was made in the Netherlands to commemorate the impending marriage between Catherine of Aragon and Prince Arthur, Henry VII's eldest son. However, Arthur died, and the Spanish princess became the first wife of his brother, Henry VIII. The church also houses numerous monuments from the time of Elizabeth I and James I.

St. Martin-in-the-Fields (Trafalgar Square, WC2): The narrow tower and spire of Gibbs's church (1722–36) rises steeply from the roof behind a Corinthian portico. Initially the design was strongly criticized, but it later served as a model for innumerable churches throughout the English-speaking world.
The side-chapels and galleries of the interior are divided by large columns which support the stuccoed, vaulted ceiling. The stucco is by the Italian artists Artari and Bagutti, who worked under Gibbs.

St. Mary Abchurch (Abchurch Lane, EC4): The inconspicuous exterior of this Wren church (1681–6) conceals a magnificent interior whose dome rests on three massive arches. The dome may have been painted by Thornhill (1708), while the wall behind the altar is one of Grinling Gibbons's masterpieces (1686). The pulpit with its enormous sounding-board and the

St. Martin-in-the-Fields

richly decorated font cover are both by W.Gray and both date from the same period.

St. Mary Aldermary (Queen Victoria Street, EC4): This church, with its plaster fan vault, was rebuilt by Wren in 1681&2 in the Gothic style. Wren's design was probably not based on the previous church. The tower (1702–4) has four massive piers above which there are turrets decorated with moulded cornices. Some good 17C carved wood inside.

St. Mary-at-Hill (Great Tower Street, EC3): Rebuilt by Wren in 1670–6, it has been frequently altered since then. However, four original columns standing at the corners of a square still support the vault. Other original features include the magnificent *stucco* (1787/8) and the good

17&18C *carved wood*. When W.G.Rogers restored the church in 1848&9, he managed to recreate to perfection the 17C style. The six gilded and enamelled sword holders are probably the finest in the City.

St. Mary-le-Bow (Cheapside, EC2): Rebuilt by Wren in 1670-7, it has the finest of Wren's own spires. Although it burned down in 1941, it was restored to its original form. The old Norman crypt has survived.

St. Mary-le-Strand (WC2): Built by Gibbs in 1714-17, it shows Italian influence, which is mainly apparent in the semicircular colonnaded W. portico. However, the four-storeyed tower follows the Wren tradition and is not part of the original church.

St.Mary Woolnoth (King William Street EC4): Hawksmoor's only church (1716-27) in the City, it demonstrates his boldness and originality. The façade is heavily rusticated not only around the windows but also on the wide double tower. The

St.Mary Abchurch, reredos

magnificence of the interior lies chiefly in the central section, which has four groups of triple Corinthian columns and an elaborately moulded stucco ceiling. Most of the old carved wood survives. Note the wall behind the altar and the organ case which encloses a Smith organ.

St. Pancras Parish Church (Upper Woburn Place, WC1): this church (1819-22, H.W. and W.Inwood) is a supreme example of Greek Revival in England. The octagonal tower is reminiscent of the Tower of the Winds in Athens, while the Ionic temple front and the vestries on both sides, with their caryatids, are modelled on the Erechtheion on the Acropolis. The windows and doors are pedimented. Inside, columns with lotus-flower capitals support the gallery. The decorations are mostly good and they too show unmistakable classical Greek features.

St.Paul's (Covent Garden, WC2): Rebuilt in 1795, after being destroyed by a fire, to the original Inigo Jones design of 1631-8, it takes the form of a temple, with a projecting roof.

St. Peter ad Vincula: (see Tower).

St. Peter upon Cornhill (EC3): This Wren church (1677-87) has a fine tower topped by a cupola and obelisk. Magnificent *wood* inside, including a choir screen by Wren himself extending across the nave and both aisles.

St.Peter's (Vere Street, WC1): Built by Gibbs in 1721-4, this church has a plain, dark brick exterior with stone dressings and a tasteful interior with Corinthian columns on tall bases. Other features: a stuccoed ceiling by Artari and Bagutti; stained-glass windows dating from 1871-89; and an altarpiece by Burne-Jones.

St.Sepulchre (Holborn Viaduct, EC1):

The core of this spacious church was probably rebuilt by Christopher Wren in 1670-7. This, as well as the 15C tower, was radically restored in the 19C. Some excellent furnishings survive, such as the wooden gallery and the organ case.

St. Stephen (Walbrook, EC4): The interior of 1672-9 is the most splendid of all Wren's City churches. The coffered dome covers a square area with an additional section to the W. This dome rests on arches which are supported by clustered Corinthian columns with an entablature. St.Stephen's too has some splendid *woodwork*, including the pulpit, the cover of the font, the organ gallery and the organ case.

St. Stephen's Chapel (see Houses of Parliament).

St. Vedast's (Foster Lane, EC2): Christopher Wren built this church in 1670-3. The elegant tower, with its alternating concave and convex storeys, was added in 1694-7 and betrays the influence of Borromini. The interior had to be restored after a fire. A stuccoed ceiling was added at this time, in accordance with Wren's wishes. The furnishing is good throughout and comes from other Wren churches which have been destroyed.

Spanish and Portuguese Synagogue (Bevis Marks, EC3): The interior of the building erected in 1700/1 resembles the other churches and chapels of the period. It is richly decorated with contemporary woodwork and seven magnificent brass candlesticks.

Temple Church (EC4): A round Norman door leads into the circular, early Gothic nave of the church of the Order of St.John of Jerusalem, which was consecrated in 1185. The nave is surrounded by pointed arches borne by slender pillars of Purbeck

marble. The well-proportioned, oblong chancel was built in 1220-40 and made the church one of the most beautiful buildings of the period. Badly damaged in 1941, the church has been faithfully restored. The monument to Robert de Ros (d. 1227) is the best preserved of the numerous monuments to the knights of the Order. The reredos (1692) was by Wren.

Wesley's Chapel (City Road, EC1): John Wesley founded this simple chapel near his house in 1777. Some good original items of furnishing still survive.

SECULAR BUILDINGS

Apothecaries' Hall (Blackfriars' Lane, EC4): For a long time the apothecaries' guild, founded in 1617, held a monopoly over the sale of medicines in the City of London. Above the entrance to the guild hall, which dates from 1670 and was altered a century later, is the coat-of-arms. The hall is not normally open but it contains some fine panelling and paintings.

St. Mary-le-Strand

Bank of England (Threadneedle Street, EC2): The seat of the country's central bank, founded in 1694, and also the site where its gold reserves are held was begun by J.Soane in 1788 and enlarged by Sir H.Baker in 1924–39. Soane's façade, which has a balcony borne by Corinthian columns, and stone sculptures, remained untouched in the process. Only the entrance hall is open to the public.

Banqueting House (Whitehall, SW1): This historic Palladian building by Inigo Jones is the sole remnant of the Palace of Whitehall, which burnt down in 1698. The *ceiling paintings* in the severe Banqueting Hall with its Corinthian columns, pilasters and balustrades are a masterpiece by Rubens, on whom Charles I bestowed a knighthood for his work. Nine paintings surrounded by gold frames glorify the greatness and wisdom of the Stuarts and depict, inter alia, the apotheosis of Charles I (there is also a bust commemorating the unfortunate king, who went to the executioner's block from this room) and the union of England with Scotland.

Buckingham Palace: The Palace stands at the end of The Mall. Its classical façade (A.Webb, 1913) bears Corinthian pilasters and a balustrade. At the sides and in the centre there are projecting, pedimented sections. Built by the Duke of Buckingham in 1703, it has been in royal hands since 1761. Nash extended it in 1826–30, and it has been the London residence of the Royal Family since 1837, and consequently is not open to the public.

Carlyle's House (Cheyne Row, SW3): Dating from 1708 and still in its original condition, the house was occupied by Thomas Carlyle in 1834–65. It is a typical town house of Carlyle's day and contains personal mementoes of the writer.

Charlton House (Charlton Road): The only Jacobean house still standing in the London area was built in *c.* 1607–12. It ha an E-shaped ground plan and is of re brick with tiles; it has two side towers. The central portico, which rises three storeys is somewhat unusual. Inside, the hall oc cupies two storeys and there is a beautifull carved banister, 17C fireplaces, and con temporary stucco ceilings in the galler and drawing room.

The Charterhouse (Charterhous Square, EC1): The ground plan of the Car thusian monastery, which was founded i 1371 and dissolved in 1573, was excavate during repair work carried out after th Second World War. The oldest existin house is Wash-house Court. This restore 16C building is today an old people's hom and only open by arrangement.

Chelsea Royal Hospital (Royal Hospi tal Road, SW3): Founded by Charles II a a home for war veterans, the Hospital wa built by Christopher Wren from 1682–9 around a court open on the S. side, toward the Thames. J.Soane enlarged it in the 19C in his own personal neoclassical style. Th plain exterior is of patterned brick. In th centre is a portico with enormous Tusca columns. Behind the portico, an octagona vestibule crowned by a lantern leads int the chapel and the hall. The chapel ha panelled walls and the original decoration (reredos, altar screens, organ front). Th refectory (S.Ricci, 1710–15) is in the apse Opposite, on the W. side of the central sec tion, is the simple hall whose end wall i decorated by an allegorical portrait o Charles II by Verrio. The Royal Avenu was opened in 1692–4 and was intende to lead to Kensington Palace, but was onl actually completed to the S. of Kensing ton Road.

The uniforms still worn by the occupant of the home date from the early 18C (blu

Queen Victoria Monumen

winter coat, and red frock-coat in summer).

Chiswick House (Burlington Lane, W4): The villa was built in 1725-9 to plans by the Earl of Burlington in the Palladian style which he introduced to London. Above the low ground floor there is a tall upper storey with a colonnaded portico reached by a double staircase at either side. The interior is by W.Kent. Features include the octagonal, domed central hall and the gallery, which has a frescoed ceiling and is in white and gold.

Clarence House (The Mall, SW1): Built by Nash in 1825 it is decorated with stucco, and is today the Queen Mother's residence. It adjoins St.James's Palace to the W. (see p. 418).

Crosby Hall (Cheyne Walk, SW3): This was built in 1466-75 in Bishopsgate (City of London) as part of the residence of Sir John Crosby, the wool merchant. The hall survived a fire in the 17C and was moved to Chelsea in 1908. Note the large oriel window and the splendid wooden roof.

Custom House (Lower Thames Street, EC3): A 19C building with a neoclassical façade, it is the seat of the London customs office and can be visited by arrangement.

George Inn (Borough High Street, SE1): This picturesque inn was built as long ago as 1677 and was once an important coaching inn.

Gray's Inn (High Holborn, WC1): One of London's four Inns of Court. Sir Francis Bacon (1561-1626) lived and worked here for 50 years, and Shakespeare's 'Comedy of Errors' was given its first performance here in 1594. The splendid 16C hall is only open by arrangement.

Guildhall (EC2): This, the town hall of the City of London, was built in 1411, but was so severely damaged by the Great Fire of 1666 and by bombing in the Second World War that only the crypt (15C, with restored groin vaults) and the walls of the Great Hall have survived. The City's coat of arms is in the porch of the present, playfully designed Gothic brick building. The members of the City Corporation, dressed in traditional robes, hold discussions in the Great Hall, which is also used for banquets. By tradition, the Sheriff is elected on St.John's Day, while votes for the Lord Mayor are cast in June of each year. The wooden ceiling was restored by Sir Giles Scott in 1952. Note the coats of arms and banners of the guilds and the oak balustrades of the galleries. There are also statues of the giants Gog and Magog, and of Churchill, Nelson, Pitt and Wellington; the Royal Fusiliers' Memorial, the oak drawer with the City sword and sceptre, and the S. window (15C).
Guildhall Library. The library has folios of Shakespeare's plays, a document signed by him concerning a house purchase, a map of London dating from 1593, and over 150,000 books on the history of London. See also The Clockmaker's Company Museum (p.427), and the Guildhall Art Gallery (p.429).

Guy's Hospital (St.Thomas Street, SE1): Thomas Guy was a bookseller who later became a speculator. A monument to him was made by Scheemaker in 1733. Guy founded the hospital in 1721 and the three-winged building has scarcely changed since the late 18C. John Keats, among others, studied from 1814-16 at the medical school, opened in 1769.

Hogarth's House (Hogarth Lane, W4): Hogarth's home from 1749-64. It was faithfully restored after the Second World War, and works by Hogarth are displayed.

Horse Guards (Whitehall, SW1): Built by W.Kent in 1753, it reminds one of the

Green Park, souvenirs

Horse Guards

Italian Renaissance. Today it is used for offices.

Houses of Parliament (Parliament Square, SW1): Edward the Confessor 1003–66) ordered the Palace of Westminster to be built; William the Conqueror 1027–87) had it enlarged, and Westminster Hall was added under William Rufus in 1097. Westminster Hall survived a fire, along with St.Stephen's Chapel (14C) and the crypt (1512). In 1567, Parliament moved into what had until 1529 been the royal palace: the House of Lords (the upper chamber) met in a room at the S. end, and the House of Commons (the lower chamber) met in St.Stephen's Chapel. In 1605, Guy Fawkes and some other Catholic conspirators attempted to blow up the Parliament building in the Gunpowder Plot. Since then, before the opening of

Parliament each year, men in historical costumes have searched the rooms in the basement for hidden explosives.

Another great fire broke out in 1834, but Westminster Hall, the crypt and some other sections of the building survived the conflagration. Consequently, from 1840–88, Sir Charles Barry built the present, neo-Gothic palace which blends with Westminster Abbey. Its façade decorated with turrets, battlements and detailed ornaments, with pairs of low corner towers as well as two similar but widely separated central towers, dominates the bank of the Thames. Standing back and to the N. is the bell tower housing Big Ben; in the centre a spire rises above the central hall, and to the S. is the Victoria Tower (completed 1858), which is a larger version of the towers of the façade. The building was faithfully restored after being bombed in

Houses of Parliament, ceiling of chamber

which appeared in 1755, are on display.

Keats's House (Keats Grove, Hampstead, NW3): The Romantic poet John Keats (1795–1821) wrote some of his most important poems in this house, built in 1815. Personal mementoes are on display.

Kensington Palace (Kensington Gardens, W8): This unusually plain brick building, surrounded by gardens designed by W.Kent, was purchased by William III in 1689, and subsequently altered and decorated first by Christopher Wren and later by Kent. It was the private residence of the Royal Family who today still use the rooms which are not open to the public. The state rooms include ones decorated by Wren with carvings by Gibbons; a large suite with paintings; and decor by Kent who was partly assisted by C.Campbell. The Victorian rooms contain mementoes of the Great Exhibition of 1851. In *King William's Gallery* there are paintings with townscapes of London (18/19C). There are also rooms with original furniture and mementoes of various sovereigns.

Kenwood House (Hampstead, NW3): Originally built in the early 18C, Kenwood was altered by R.Adam in 1764–73 and later enlarged. Its garden and the lake with false bridge merge with the adjoining heath. The interior is in the style of Adam throughout (pictures by Zucchi and A.Kaufmann). The library is one of Adam's finest works. At both ends side rooms are screened off by Corinthian columns supporting the entablature. The extensive *picture collection* (Iveagh Bequest) includes Rembrandt's 'self-portait in old age', Vermeer's 'Guitar Player', some Gainsboroughs, and works of the Dutch and English schools.

Lambeth Palace (Lambeth Road, SE1): The charmingly situated London res-

the Second World War. The sittings of the House of Commons and of the House of Lords are open to visitors and tickets may be obtained at St.Stephen's Gate. The various magnificent rooms of the palace (guided tours on Saturdays) can only be visited when the Houses are not sitting.

Imperial Institute Tower (Prince Consort Road, SW7): Only the tall, copper-covered campanile, built of pale stone, survives from the Imperial Institute, which was built by T.E.Collcutt in 1887 on the occasion of Queen Victoria's Golden Jubilee.

Johnson's House (Gough Square, EC4): The writer Samuel Johnson (1709–84) lived and worked in this 17C house. Personal mementoes and a first edition of his 'Dictionary of the English Language',

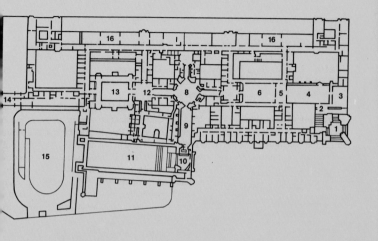

London, Houses of Parliament 1 Victoria Tower with visitors' entrance and Royal Entrance **2** Norman Porch with splendid stained-glass windows, ceiling carved with coats-of-arms, busts of Wellington and other premiers and carvings by Pugin. The Royal Staircase leads to **3** the Robing Room, where the lords robe themselves; it has a splendid wooden ceiling, a marble chimney-piece, carvings by Pugin, frescos by W. Dyce of the legend of King Arthur, portraits and emblems of peers and panels depicting scenes from the reigns of various monarchs. Queen Victoria's throne (1856) is situated in front of a splendid background incorporating royal coats-of-arms. **4** Royal Gallery with magnificent coffered ceiling, stained-glass windows with coats-of-arms, including the royal one. Two huge paintings by Maclise (the death of Nelson and the meeting of Wellington and Blücher after Waterloo); portraits of other peers **5** Prince's Chamber, with 16C portraits of Henry VIII and his wives, as well as other Tudor lords, and bronze relifs by Theed depicting scenes from Tudor history. The chimney-piece is by Pugin, and the statue of Queen Victoria by J.Gibson **6** Chamber of the House of Lords has additional red benches, a splendid coffered ceiling and panelled walls. The statues which stand between the stained-glass windows with peers' coats-of-arms (1360–1900) and the wall paintings of historical and allegorical scenes depict the barons at the signing of the Magna Carta in 1215. The wall behind the throne is splendidly decorated with coats-of-arms, statues and Gothic ornamentation. The Lord Chancellor sits on the Woolsack. **7** Peers' Lobby and Corridor, a Gothic room with a fine floor **8** Central Lobby with splendid ceiling, mosaic of the 4 national patron saints, statues of peers and great 19C statesmen **9** St. Stephen's Hall. Reconstruction of the original Gothic hall by Barry (1834). The glass windows bear coats-of-arms, and there are mosaics from the old St. Stephen's Chapel. There are also statues of peers and important statesmen **10** St. Stephen's Porch **11** Westminster Hall, with an oak ceiling, where Thomas More, Guy Fawkes and Charles II were all sentenced, and where dead peers lie in state. Underneath are the splendid Gothic crypt of St. Stephen and the baptistery **12** Commons Corridor and Lobby, Gothic rooms with statues of 20C statesmen **13** House of Commons, rebuilt after World War 2 by Sir G.Scott, with traditional green benches, whose elegance gives a good impression of the original furnishings; in the centre is the Speaker's Chair, which comes from Australia, with the front benches on either side. The red line which separates the Government and Opposition benches may not be crossed during a sitting. The two Dispatch Boxes, which are from New Zealand, contain the Old and New Testaments and the wording of the oath of the House of Commons **14** Clock Tower, with a bell known as 'Big Ben' after Sir Benjamin Hall, who was Commissioner of Works when it was hung in 1859; its chime is world famous as the time signal of the BBC **15** New Palace Yard **16** libraries for the Peers and Commons

dence of the Archbishop of Canterbury has managed to retain the appearance of a medieval castle despite rebuilding and restoration. The oldest section is the crypt (*c.* 1200), which has marble pillars. The chapel, with its modern glass windows, dates from 1230. The other buildings are 15&16C. The Anglican bishops' conference is held every ten years in the hall built in 1600-63. There is also a fine library.

Lancaster House (Stable Yard, SW1): This Victorian building, begun by Wyatt in 1825 and completed by Barry in 1840, has a massive projecting central section consisting of an arcaded ground floor surmounted by a colonnaded portico. The building is today mainly used for state receptions and banquets and its rooms are magnificently decorated.

Leighton House (Holland Park Road, W14): Begun by G.Aitchison in 1865 for the painter Lord Leighton, it contains a tiled *Arab Hall* with a mosaic frieze by W.Crane. Leighton's studio survives, and his own works and those of some of his contemporaries (e.g. W.de Morgan) are on view.

Mansion House (EC4): The Renaissance Mansion House was built in 1739-53 by G.Dance the elder. Its portico has Corinthian columns and a pediment decorated with a frieze. The building is the official seat of the Lord Mayor of the City of London and visits can be arranged by applying in writing. The Egyptian Hall and the Long Parlour, with its fine stuccoed ceiling, are both interesting.

Marlborough House (The Mall, SW1): A red brick house built by Wren in 1709 for the great general John Churchill, Duke of Marlborough (1650-1722). Inside there are splendid furnishings and notable wall paintings by L.Laguerre, which glorify the Duke's military feats.

Mayflower Inn (Rotherhithe Stree SE16): This charmingly situated inn named after the 'Mayflower' which too the Pilgrim Fathers to America in 162

Middlesex Guildhall (Broad Sanctuar SW1): During the Second World War th Allied courts of justice held sessions in th early-20C court building.

Old Bailey (EC4): The Central Crimin Courts stand on the site of the infamou Newgate Prison. All the major crimin trials held in London take place here. Bu in 1902-07 in Renaissance style, it is thre storeys high, with pilasters and a balu trade on its front. The visitor can atten public hearings if he awaits admission the gates. A statue of Justice crowns th dome of the tower which is designed on th model of St.Paul's.

Telecom Tower (Maple Street, W1): Th 585 ft. telecommunications tower wa completed in 1966.

Queen Elizabeth's Hunting Lodg (Rangers Road, E4): This 16C Tude building was formerly used for huntin Today, plants and animals from the are may be seen here.

Royal Albert Hall (Kensington Gor SW7): H. Scott completed his oval galle ied hall in 1871. Beneath the glass an metal dome there is a terracotta frie: depicting man's relationship with the ar and sciences at various different period It is used for events of all kinds.

Royal Courts of Justice (Strand, WC2 Built in 1868-82 in a recreation of 13 Gothic, it has three towers and a façade c the Strand. There is a large central ha

Royal Exchange (EC3): Sir Thom:

Houses of Parliament, St.James's Pa

Johnson's House (home of the author Samuel Johnson)

Gresham, a rich merchant and financier, founded the exchange in 1566. It was burned down in 1666 and 1838. The present classical structure was built by W.Tite in 1844. Note the Corinthian *portico* with eight columns. Its pediment has a relief by Sir R.Westmacott (allegories of commerce). The paintings of scenes from British history are also of note. In front of the building are a statue of Wellington and a war memorial.

Royal Festival Hall (South Bank, SE1): A concert hall built in 1951–65 and part of the South Bank complex which comprises two further concert halls, the National Film Theatre, the National Theatre (3 auditoriums), and the Hayward Gallery.

Royal Opera House (Covent Garden, WC2): Built by E.M.Barry (1858).

St. Bartholomew's Hospital (West Smithfield, EC1): This hospital was founded in 1123, along with the parish church of St.Bartholomew the Great and an Augustinian priory which was dissolved in 1539; Henry VIII gave it to the City of London in 1546 (see a stained-glass window in the large hall designed by Gibbs in the 18C). Gibbs also drew up the plans for rebuilding the hospital. The hospital church of St.Bartholomew the Less was altered in the 18&19C. Two wall paintings by W.Hogarth, and portaits of doctors, may also be seen.

St. James's Palace (The Mall, SW1): This palace, which was built by Henry VIII in 1532 on the site of a leper hospital dating from the 12C, forms a charming ensemble with Clarence House and Lancaster House. For a time it was the king's residence, and foreign diplomats are today still accredited to the 'Court of St.James'. The *Gatehouse,* and also the *Chapel Royal* (16C, later altered) with its finely painted, coffered ceiling and the good pews, still survive from the Tudor building. Numerous royal weddings have been held here. It now contains Grace and Favour apartments and houses the Gentlemen and Yeomen-at-Arms.

Somerset House (Strand, WC2): Sir W.Chambers designed the present building in *c.* 1775 on the site of an earlier 16C one. The façade faces the Thames and there was a water-gate in the basement before the Victoria Embankment was built. It will shortly become the home of the Courtauld Institute. King's College is housed in the E. wing, which, like the W. wing, was built in the 19C.

Staple Inn (Holborn, WC1): This building, formerly an inn for wool-staplers, dates back to the 14C and has been comprehensively restored in the 20C. Its half-timbered façade, one of the finest in London, is late-16C and has overhanging gables.

Stock Exchange (Throgmorton Street, EC2): The Stock Exchange building is of granite and dates from 1854.

The Temple (EC4): This district, which is charmingly situated amidst parks and is predominantly Georgian, today contains solicitors' offices and two of the four great Inns of Court, namely Middle Temple and Inner Temple, and also the Temple Church. The district originally belonged to the Order of the Knights Templar and later came into the possession of the Crown. Edward III established a school for lawyers here in the 15C. Despite bomb damage, the Middle Temple Hall dating from 1576 has retained parts of its original wood panelling, while the remainder has been faithfully restored. The Inner

Kensington Palace

Temple Hall, with a 14C crypt, had to be completely rebuilt after the Second World War.

Tower of London (Tower Hill, EC3): Legend has it that Julius Caesar founded the Tower. However, history tells us that William the Conqueror had the oldest part, the White Tower, built because he required a fortified residence and a site from which to observe shipping traffic. William II, his successor, completed the building. In the 12&13C the complex was fortified and extended, and took on what is substantially its present appearance. Another legend relates that the fortress, which has frequently been besieged but never occupied, will continue to stand for as long as the ravens live in its walls. Consequently these black-coloured birds are lovingly tended, and the Tower is one of the best-preserved medieval buildings in the country. It has in the course of its history been a royal palace (until the 15C), a prison (the inscriptions carved into the walls by various prisoners bear witness to this), and a place of execution. The most prominent victims were Sir Thomas More, Anne Boleyn and Catherine Howard (the two last-named were wives of Henry VIII), and Lady Jane Grey. Elizabeth I was held prisoner here until she was proclaimed Queen, and spies were shot at the Tower in the Second World War. It also contains the Norman *Chapel of St. John the Evangelist* (1080), which is the oldest church in London, and the 12C *Royal Chapel of St. Peter ad Vincula,* where persons executed in the Tower were interred. This chapel was restored in 1512 after a fire. Today the historic Tower is mainly a museum. Uniforms and medals of the Royal Fusiliers' Regiment are to be seen in the *regimental Museum of the Royal Fusiliers,* while in the *White Tower* an extensive *collection of weapons and armour* is on show. This has been built up from Henry VIII's arsenal and illustrates the development of weapons and uniforms in Eu-

rope until the First World War. Finally, the strictly guarded *crown jewels,* the nation's greatest treasures, are housed in the *Jewel House.* Of these, the following are outstanding: The St. Edward's Crown, which dates from 1660 and is the British coronation crown. The Imperial State Crown, which was made for Queen Victoria's coronation and includes not only the ruby which Edward the Black Prince received as a gift from Pedro the Cruel of Castile, but also one of the two 'Stars of Africa' (the other one decorates the royal sceptre) which were cut from the Cullinan diamond (the largest ever found): today this crown is worn at the opening of Parliament and other important events.

There are also: The Indian Imperial Crown; and the Crown of Queen Elizabeth (the crown of George VI's consort), which has the Koh-i-noor diamond.

MONUMENTS AND BRIDGES

Admiralty Arch (The Mall, WC2): A triumphal arch built for Queen Victoria,

Tower of London

standing between Trafalgar Square and The Mall.

Albert Bridge (Battersea/Chelsea): The oldest surviving suspension bridge in London, built by R.W.Ordish in 1873.

Albert Memorial (Kensington Gardens, W8): This splendid monument was designed by G.G.Scott to commemorate the Prince Consort (1861). It is approached by flights of steps on all sides and at the four corners there are marble allegories of the continents. Reliefs of famous artists and scientists cover the tall, classical pedestal, and at the corners are statues symbolizing trade and industry. A statue of Albert with the catalogue of the Great Exhibition is seated under a Gothic tabernacle, which is supported by clusters of columns, and has corner turrets, a tall cen-

London, Tower 1 entrance **2** Middle Tower (14C) **3** moats **4** casemate **5** Queen's Stair (steps to Thames) **6** Byward Tower (13C, with portcullis, guard room and 14C wall paintings) **7** Traitor's Gate, the entrance through which traitors were led **8** St. Thomas's Tower (13C) with Becket Chapel **9** Cradle Tower **10** Well Tower **11** Develin Tower **12** Brass Mount **13** Legge's Mount **14** Bell Tower (12C), in which Thomas More and Princess Elizabeth were among those imprisoned **15** Bloody Tower, dungeon and possible site of the murder of the princes in 1483 **16** Wakefield Tower (13C) with vaulted interior **17** Lanthorn Tower **18** Salt Tower (13C) with numerous inscriptions by prisoners **19** Broad Arrow Tower **20** Constable Tower **21** Martin Tower (13C, later altered); this is where Colonel Blood tried to steal the crown jewels in 1671, possibly on the orders of an impoverished King Charles II **22** Brick Tower **23** Bowyer Tower with torture chamber **24** Flint Tower **25** Devereux Tower **26** Beauchamp Tower (13C), where important prisoners used to be kept, as the inscriptions show **27** Queen's House, an impressive 16C half-timbered building, which is now the Governor's residence and is not open to the public. Adjacent on the N. side is the Yeoman Gaoler's House **28** New Armouries (17C) with 18&19C weapons, and collections of weapons and armour from Africa, Asia and Japan. **29** hospital **30** Royal Fusiliers' Museum **31** Waterloo Barracks (19C), former barracks of the Royal Fusiliers **32** Jewel House (crown jewels) **33** Chapel of St. Peter ad Vincula **34** scaffold formerly used for executions **35** Tower Green **36** Wardrobe Tower, on the line of the old Roman city wall **37** White Tower: archives, Napoleon's and Wellington's swords, hand-weapons, swords, a Tournament Gallery (exhibits drawn from throughout British history), mortars and cannons **38** Chapel of St.John (1066–1100), with original decorations on the capitals, crypt and lower crypt **39** Tower Wharf, from which important salutes are fired

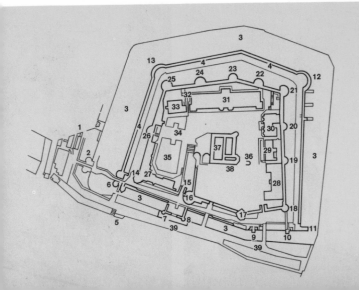

tral spire, and gables decorated with friezes.

Boadicea (Victoria Embankment): A statue of the warrior queen on her chariot (1902, Thornicroft).

The Cenotaph (Whitehall, SW1): This 'Empty Tomb', which was unveiled in 1920, is built of marble and bears military insignia and the inscription 'To the Glorious Dead'. It was designed by Sir E.Lutyens and today commemorates the fallen of both World Wars.

Statue of Charles I (Charing Cross, WC2): An equestrian statue of the Stuart king beheaded by Cromwell in 1649.

Statue of Charles II (Chelsea Hospital, SW3): A bronze statue by Grinling Gibbons of the founder of the Chelsea Royal Hospital.

Cleopatra's Needle (Victoria Embankment, SW1): This granite obelisk, made in Heliopolis for Thothmes VI in the 15C

BC, was brought to London in 1877 as a gift from the Egyptian viceroy. It has counterparts in New York and Paris.

Eros's Fountain (Piccadilly Circus, W1): A fountain cast by Sir A.Gilbert, topped by the figure of an angel, known as Eros. It is dedicated to the Earl of Shaftesbury.

Hammersmith Bridge (W6): This suspension bridge built by Sir J.Bazalguette in 1887 is a unique piece of engineering. It is borne by massive iron piers with large scrolls at their feet and crowned by pavilions. It is still a major arterial route into London, although it is at present undergoing structural repairs.

London Bridge (King William Street, EC3): The existing modern concrete bridge was built in 1973. The 12C bridge, which was immortalized in the song 'London Bridge is falling down', had to give way in the 19C to a new one which was more suitable for traffic and this, having in turn been acquired by an American, is today in Lake Havasu, Arizona.

Albert Memorial

Statue of Peter Pan, Kensington Gardens

Machine Gun Corps Memorial (Hyde Park Corner, SW1): A figure of King David by T.D.Wood.

Marble Arch (W1): This triumphal arch was built by Nash and is based on the Arch of Constantine in Rome. Originally in front of Buckingham Palace, it was moved to its present site in 1851. Nearby, a small memorial tablet marks the site of Tyburn Tree, which was London's place of execution from 1196 to 1783.

The Monument (Fish Street Hill, EC3): This obelisk was built in 1671-7 and is attributed to Christopher Wren. It is crowned by a ball of flames and commemorates the Great Fire of 1666, which began in nearby Pudding Lane. Latin inscriptions tell the story, and King Charles II is depicted in a relief by C.G.Cibbers. Inside, a spiral staircase leads up to the observation platform.

Nelson's Column (Trafalgar Square, SW1): The centre of this magnificently laid-out square, with its fountains, is W.Railton's Corinthian column crowned by a statue of the victor of Trafalgar (1805). Its base is covered in reliefs depicting Nelson's naval victories. There are four couchant bronze lions by Sir Edwin Landseer (1868) at the corners of the pedestal.

Peter Pan (Kensington Gardens, W2): A statue by Sir G.Frampton.

Statue of Richard I (Parliament Square): An equestrian statue of Richard the Lionheart (1157-99).

Roosevelt Memorial (Grosvenor Square, W1): This statue of the American President (1882-1945) by Sir W.Reid was unveiled near the American Embassy in 1948.

Royal Artillery War Memorial (Hyde Park Corner, SW1): A monument in the form of a cannon, sculpted by Jagger, for the artillerymen who fell in the First World War.

Shakespeare Monument (Leicester

View of Tower Bridge

Square): The statue of the great poet and dramatist surveys the town from its tall obelisk.

Temple Bar Memorial (Fleet Street): A column crowned by a gryphon marks the border between the City of London and the City of Westminster. It stands on the site of Wren's entrance gate to the Temple. The gate has been moved to Hertfordshire.

Tower Bridge (E1): Opened in 1894, its massive neo-Gothic towers make it one of London's landmarks. The two iron bascules can be raised to allow large ships to pass through.

Victoria Monument (The Mall): Sir Thomas Brock's monument of 1911 shows the queen surrounded by allegorical figures.

Wellington Arch (Hyde Park Corner, SW1): A triumphal arch built by Decimus Burton in 1825, crowned by a quadriga. Next to it is the **Wellington Monument,** an equestrian statue of the Duke with four British soldiers from various regiments.

Whittington Memorial (Highgate Hill, N19): A memorial to Sir Richard Whittington, the famous Lord Mayor of London.

Statue of King William III (St.James's Square, W1): An equestrian statue completed in 1807, the work of J.Bacon the younger.

Statue of the Duke of York (The Mall): A column with a statue (1834) of the Duke of York, later King William IV.

STREETS, SQUARES AND PARKS

Bedford Park (W4): London's first garden suburb. It is 19C and has buildings by N.Shaw and E.Godwin.

Tower Bridge

Belgrave Square (Hyde Park Corner, SW1): The early-19C Regency houses in what is London's most distinguished square mainly contain foreign embassies.

Bond Street (W1): London's most sophisticated and most expensive shopping street.

Brompton Road (W1): Harrod's, the famous department store, offers the visitor a 'different world'.

Burlington Arcade (Piccadilly, W1): An exclusive glass-roofed shopping arcade opened in 1819.

Downing Street (Westminster, SW1): Since the 18C, the current Prime Minister has lived in No. 10 Downing Street. The house is always guarded by a 'bobby'.

and the street was built by Sir George Downing in the 17C. It may sometimes be closed for security reasons.

Eaton Square (SW1): Note the memorial plaques to the famous figures who have lived in the 19C Georgian houses of this square.

Fleet Street: The offices of almost all the national daily newspapers are in this street.

Hyde Park (SW1): This park, which had been owned by Westminster Abbey, was converted by Henry VIII into a hunting park in 1536. In 1635 Charles I opened it to the public. In 1730 Queen Caroline commissioned R.Westbourne to build *The Serpentine,* an artificial lake. The bridge leading across to Kensington Gardens was constructed by G.Rennie in 1826. Since

1872, *Speaker's Corner* has been the place where anyone can speak publicly on any subject except the King or Queen. Decimus Burton built the entrance archway, while the frieze, which is a copy of the Elgin Marbles from Athens (British Museum), is by J.Henning and his sons.

Kensington Gardens: These gardens, which adjoin Hyde Park, were originally part of Kensington Palace and were opened to the public in the late 19C. They include the *Orangery of Queen Anne* (1704&5, Wren) and the *statue of Peter Pan.*

Lombard Street (EC3): London's banking centre. The old shields bearing the coats-of-arms of various banks are interesting features of the 19&20C buildings.

The Mall (SW1): This avenue was laid out

Bedford Park

Hyde Park, statue of Achilles

in the 17C and leads from Admiralty Arch to Buckingham Palace. It is flanked by Carlton House, Marlborough House, St. James's Palace, St.James's Park, and Lancaster House.

Piccadilly Circus (W1): A traffic bottleneck on which three major routes converge. It is also the gateway to Soho, the nightlife district. Eros (see above) stands at the centre of Piccadilly Circus.

Regent's Park (NW1): Laid out by Nash in the 19C, it has an artificial lake, sports grounds and a zoo (in the N.). Around its edge is the Outer Circle of neoclassical terraces.

St. James's Park (The Mall, SW1): A charming Nash park with an artificial lake.

Whitehall (SW1): These beautiful old buildings house most of the ministries.

MUSEUMS

Battle of Britain Museum (Aerodrome Road, NW9): A memorial with exhibits relating to the Battle of Britain.

Bethnal Green Museum (Cambridge Heath, E2): Established here in 1872, this museum displays dolls and toys as well as applied art.

British Museum (Great Russell Street, WC1): This was founded in 1753; its basis being the collections of Sir Hans Sloane, Robert and Edward Harley, and Sir Robert Cotton. In 1823 – 57, R. and S.Smirke built the present museum, a

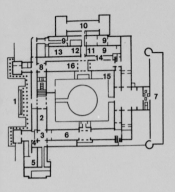

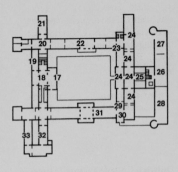

London, British Museum, Ground Floor 1 entrance hall **2** Grenville Library **3** Manuscript Room (with original Magna Carta) **4** Bible Room (first English Bible, 1525) **5** Reading Room **6** King's Library **7** King Edward VII Gallery with oriental exhibits **8** Assyrian Transept **9** Greek exhibits **10** Elgin Marbles **11** Roman exhibits **12** Assyrian exhibits **13** Nimrud Gallery **14** Nineveh Gallery **15** Palestinian antiquities **16** Egyptian sculptures

First Floor 17 Man's early history **18** prehistoric and Roman Britain **19** Greek and Roman terracotta **20** Greek and Roman tools and objects **21** coins and medals **22** Greek and Roman vessels **23** Hittite, Syrian, Persian and Arabic exhibits **24** Egyptian Gallery with mummies, vessels, papyri, burial objects, sculptures etc. **25** Coptic exhibits **26** prints and drrawings **27** oriental exhibits **28** Sumerian and Babylonian exhibits **29** history of writing **30** Asian exhibits **31** folklore section **32** Asian exhibits, including European medieval art **33** Iron-Age finds. There is a detailed plan in the entrance hall.

classical three-winged structure with a colonnaded front of massive Ionic columns and a central pediment decorated by a frieze. The collections include valuable exhibits from ancient civilizations such as Assyria, Babylon, Egypt, Greece, the Roman Empire, Asia, and Europe, and are among the finest and most extensive in the world. The valuable collection of works in the *British Library* comprises European and Asian books and manuscripts and is one of the best in Europe.

British Museum of Natural History (Cromwell Road, SW7): Devoted to the evolution and development of animals, plants and minerals from earliest times until today. The building was completed by A.Waterhouse in the Byzantine style in 1880. The Whale Hall contains an enormous blue whale.

Broomfield House Museum (Broomfield Park, N13): A museum of natural and local history, it is housed in a late-17C building with a ceiling and a wall painting by G.Lanscroon (18C).

The Clockmaker's Company Museum (Guildhall, EC2): A highly interesting collection of clocks (over 700 exhibits) from very early examples until the present.

Commonwealth Institute (Kensington High Street, W8): A survey of the history of the Commonwealth countries, with fine exhibits, film shows and a library.

Courtauld Institute Galleries (Woburn Square, WC1): The Courtauld Institute of Arts was founded in 1932 by Viscount Lee of Fareham and Samuel Courtauld, who bequeathed their art collections to the

University of London. Other endowments were added. The Courtauld collection consists mainly of the Impressionists and their followers. The Lee Collection includes paintings by Bellini, Botticelli, Goya, van Dyck, Rubens, Tintoretto and Gainsborough. The Gambier-Perry collection comprises 14&15C Italian paintings as well as glass and ceramics, some of which are also from the early 16C. The Fry Collection has 20C works. The Institute will be moving to Somerset House (see above) in the near future.

Dulwich College Picture Gallery (College Road, SE2): Sir John Soane built the first public gallery in London, opened in 1814. The pictures include works by Dutch, English, French, Italian and Spanish artists.

Fenton House (Hampstead, NW3): This red brick house (1693) displays the sparse decoration typical of the Dutch-influenced William-and-Mary style. The house stands amidst a sober walled garden with iron gates by Tijou (1707). Inside there is an outstanding collection of early keyboard instruments and English porcelain.

Foundling Hospital Museum (Brunswick Square, WC1): Thomas Coram established a home for foundlings here in 1739. The hospital of the Coram Foundation for Children has been moved to Berkhampstead. Today the building houses works by well-known artists such as Hogarth (portrait of the founder), Gainsborough, Reynolds and Ramsay, who all presented these works to the foundation; also note an organ donated by Handel and a manuscript of 'Messiah'.

Geffrye Museum (Kingsland Road, E2): Typical English domestic interiors (16–20C) arranged in what were almshouses built around 1713.

Geological Museum (Exhibition Road, SW7): A splendid collection of precious stones, and also minerals and fossils. Exhibitions showing the history of the Earth, with a simulated earthquake and volcanic eruption and a rotating globe.

Kensington Gardens, Moore sculpture

Goldsmith's Hall (Foster Lane, EC3): This museum, which can be visited by arrangement, has some old silver plate and the finest collection of modern jewellery and silver in the country.

Guildhall Art Gallery (Guildhall, EC2): The gallery was opened in 1886, although the building that houses it dates from 1670. It is used for temporary exhibitions by groups of London artists.

Hayward Gallery (South Bank, SE1): Temporary art exhibitions under the patronage of the Arts Council of Great Britain.

Hermian Museum (London Road, SE23): An Art Nouveau building to plans by C.H.Townsend (1901) with exhibits devoted to ethnology and natural history; and a collection of musical instruments.

Imperial War Museum (Lambeth Road, SE1): Built in 1815, its exhibits are devoted to the history of both World Wars and the military undertakings of the Empire and the Commonwealth since 1914. There are works by famous British war artists. HMS Belfast (Pool of London), a cruiser fitted out as a museum, is associated with the Imperial War Museum.

Jewish Museum (Woburn House, WC1): Ritual objects and exhibits relating to the history of the Jews.

Jewel Tower (Old Palace Yard, SW1): Remains of the Palace of Westminster (1365&6), with exhibits from it.

London Dungeon (Tooley Street, SE1): This 'horror museum' displays realistic scenes depicting the methods of torture and execution common in England from

British Museum, wooden sarcophagus ▷

the Middle Ages up until the 17C, as well as some historically-documented atrocities.

Madame Tussaud's (Marylebone Road, NW1): The waxwork museum, established here in 1835 by a Frenchwoman, Madame Tussaud, who had escaped to England in 1802, displays wax models of the major figures of world history (Grand Hall), famous historical scenes (The Tableaux), heroes (Heroes Live), all the British monarchs since William the Conqueror (The Hall of Kings), a reconstruction of the Battle of Trafalgar, famous criminals, victims and instruments of torture (Chamber of Horrors). There is also The Arcade (maze, slot machines), The Battle of Britain and its heroes, and the Planetarium.

Mall Galleries (The Mall, SW1): Temporary art exhibitions.

London Transport Museum (Covent Garden, WC2): A collection of old locomotives, trams and other vehicles.

Museum of Leathercraft (Basinghall Street, EC2): All kinds of leather goods from Roman times until the present.

Museum of London (London Wall, EC1): Exhibits relating to the history of London from Roman times until the present.

Museum of the Chartered Insurance Institute (Aldermanbury, EC2): Exhibits on the history of insurance and fire-fighting.

Museum of Mankind (Burlington Gardens, W1): The focal point here is the history of primitive peoples.

National Army Museum (Royal Hospital Road, SW3): Opened in 1971, this museum illustrates the history of the British armed forces since the 15C, and also of the Indian army and other troops of the former Empire, until the countries in question became independent. There are also battle paintings and uniforms.

National Gallery (Trafalgar Square,

Madame Tussaud's, The Beatles, Ringo Starr (l). National Gallery (r)

WC2): This building, designed by W.Wilkins in 1834–8 with a large colonnaded portico, houses one of the most extensive picture collections in the world, with works by all the important European artists and schools up until the 19C.

National Portrait Gallery (St.Martin's Place, WC2): This extensive collection, to which photographs were added in the 20C, displays the portraits of important figures who have played a role in British history from the 16C onwards.

National Postal Museum (King Edward Street, EC1): One of the most interesting philatelic collections in the world, with stamps, documents and a large library. There is also a history of the British postal service.

Passmore Edwards Museum (Rumford Road, E15): An original building completed in *c.* 1900, with geological, archaeological and historical exhibits from Essex and the area around London, an aquarium, and a small zoo.

Percival David Foundation of Chinese Art (Gordon Square, WC1): Valuable Chinese porcelain and ceramics from various centuries.

Pharmaceutical Society's Museum (Bloomsbury Square, WC1): This museum, which can be visited by arrangement, has exhibits on the history of pharmacies from the 17C onwards.

Pollock's Toy Museum (Scala Street, W1): Dolls and toys from various countries and centuries, and a dolls' theatre.

Public Record Office (Chancery Lane, WC2): This neo-Gothic building was designed by Sir J.Penethorne in 1851–71; it was in 1892–5 that Sir John Taylor added the wing facing towards Chancery Lane. This archive extends back to the Norman Conquest of England and is reserved for scholars and researchers. Many of the documents are now housed in a new office which has been built at Kew. The Domesday Book, Shakespeare's will, and the log-book of Admiral Nelson's 'Victory',

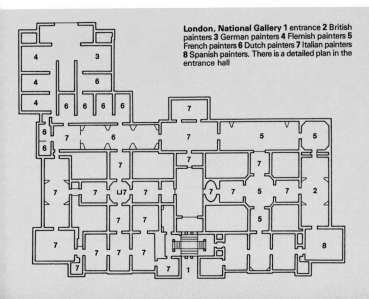

London, **National Gallery** 1 entrance 2 British painters 3 German painters 4 Flemish painters 5 French painters 6 Dutch painters 7 Italian painters 8 Spanish painters. There is a detailed plan in the entrance hall

Pollock's Toy Museum

are on display in the museum, along with other documents.

Queen's Gallery (Buckingham Palace, SW1): Exhibitions with items from the Royal collection.

Royal Academy (Piccadilly, W1): Exhibitions are held all year in the rooms of the Academy (founded in 1768).

Royal College of Music (Prince Consort Road, SW1): The museum can be visited by arrangement and it contains an extensive collection of musical instruments, including Haydn's piano and Handel's spinet. There is also an extensive library.

Royal College of Surgeons (Lincoln's Inn Fields, WC2): The collection, which can be viewed by arrangement, was begun by John Hunter the physician (1728–93), and illustrates his experiments.

Royal Fusiliers' Museum (EC3): (see under Tower of London).

Royal Geographical Society (Kensington Gore, SW1): The headquarters of the Royal Geographical Society, which was founded in 1830, contains a library and an extensive collection of maps.

Royal Mews (Buckingham Palace, SW1): The finest item in this handsome collection of state carriages is the Gold State Coach (1762) with paintings by the Florentine artist Cipriani. This coach has been used in all the coronation processions held since 1820.

Science Museum (South Kensington,

SW1): Devoted to the history of the development of science and technology, with numerous models, from Galileo's telescope through Stephenson's 'Rocket' to space satellites.

Soane Museum (Lincoln's Inn Fields, WC2): Sir John Soane built this house for himself in 1812 and it now contains his valuable and original collection of objets d'art and antiquities, and also the paintings which he himself assembled. Of particular interest is Hogarth's cycle, 'The Rake's Progress'.

South London Art Gallery (Peckham Road, SE5): This gallery which can be visited by arrangement displays Victorian pictures and works by 20C British artists.

Tate Gallery (Millbank, SW1): Sir Henry Tate established this gallery, which is housed in a classical building designed by S.R.J.Smith, with subsequent additions. Tate exhibited his own collection here, but nowadays only a part of the collections can be displayed. These collections cover all the major British painters (British Collection), and also foreign ones in the Modern Collection.

Victoria and Albert Museum (Cromwell Road, SW7): This museum provides an extensive survey of the fine and applied arts of Europe and the Near and Far East. Note in particular the collection of works by the landscape painter John Constable (1776–1837).

Wallace Collection (Manchester Square, W1): This, the finest private collection ever donated to a nation, was assembled in France during the 18&19C by two Marquises of Hertford. Their descendant, Sir Richard Wallace, brought a large part of it to England in 1871, and his widow bequeathed it to the State in 1897. The paint-

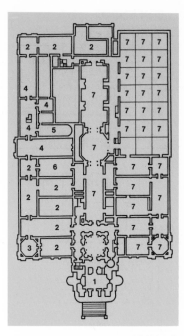

London, Tate Gallery 1 entrance **2** British collection **3** William Hogarth (1697–1764) **4** William Turner (1775–1851) **5** John Constable (1776–1837) **6** William Blake (1757–1827) **7** Modern Collection. There is a detailed plan in the entrance hall

ings include works by Rembrandt, Rubens, van Dyck, Hals, Watteau, Boucher, Fragonard, Velázquez, Titian, Murillo, Gainsborough, Romney, Reynolds and other famous artists. The furniture (mainly 18C) is the work of the greatest French craftsmen of the period. There are also: porcelain, ceramics (mainly from Italy), 16–18C gold and bronze items, European and Oriental weapons, and other fine pieces.

Wellcome Institute for the History of Medicine (Euston Road, NW3): Exhibits from all over the world on the history of medicine from the ancient civilizations until today; an extensive library.

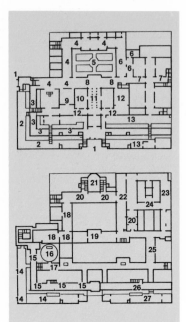

Tate Gallery

London, Victoria and Albert Museum, Ground Floor 1 entrance **2** English furniture and art (17&18C) **3** 17&18C European art **4** Italian Renaissance **5** quadrangle **6** European Renaissance **7** carpets and tapestries **8** Gothic **9** Indian art **10** Islamic art **11** early medieval art **12** Asian art **13** English and continental sculpture **First Floor 14** English art (18&19C) **15** ceramics, porcelain, faience **16** musical instruments **17** wrought iron **18** prints **19** library **20** gold and jewellery **21** lecture theatre **22** metalwork **23** textiles **24** works by John Constable **25** glass **26** Far Eastern Art **27** ceramics. There is a detailed plan in the entrance hall

Wellington Museum (Apsley House, Hyde Park Corner, W1): This late-18C house was extended by Benjamin Wyatt after the Duke of Wellington moved into it in 1817. The museum which it houses displays memorabilia, valuable paintings and porcelain. Behind the house is a statue of Achilles.

William Morris Gallery (Forest Road, E17): This original Georgian house displays works by William Morris, the craftsman and writer (1834–96).

EVENTS

Changing the Guard: The Changing of the Guard is performed outside Buckingham Palace at 10.30 every morning by the Foot Guards, whose bearskin hats make them unmistakable. A band escorts the new guard to the palace and, after the ceremony, it escorts the old guard back to the barracks.

Ceremony of the Keys: The head of the Yeoman Warders, who wear splendid 15C costumes and who are better known by their nickname of 'Beefeaters' (derived from 'Buffetier du Roi'), locks the gates of

he Tower in a formal ceremony held at ten
o'clock every evening.

Lord Mayor's Show: On the second
Saturday in November, the day after being
ceremoniously installed in his office, the
new Lord Mayor of the City of London
passes from the Guildhall to the Law
Courts in a magnificent and gloriously
colourful procession.

Mounting the Guard: The mounted Life
Guards (white plume and red coat), and the
Blues and Royals (red plume and blue
coat), change the guard outside the Horse
Guards every day at 11.00 a.m. (10.00 a.m.
on Sundays).

Opening of Parliament: At the beginning of November each year, the Queen
travels to the Houses of Parliament in a
magnificent procession to open the new
session of Parliament in the House of
Lords.

Quit Rent Ceremony: In a public
ceremony held in the Law Courts on 26
October, a representative of the city
presents an officer of the Queen with a
hatchet, a sword, six horseshoes and some
horseshoe nails as a formal quit rent for
some lands in Shropshire.

Royal Tournament: A splendidly colourful display by the armed services held in
Earl's Court each July.

Trooping the Colour: A splendid parade
by the regiments of the Household Division held on the second Sunday in June,
on the Queen's official birthday. It moves
from Buckingham Palace via The Mall to
Horse Guards Parade, where the actual
trooping of the colour takes place.

**Suburbs and environs — Greater
London**
Barking: *Eastbury House,* a 16C Tudor
House in a modern suburb. *Valence House,*
now a local history museum.

Battersea: Battersea, on the S. bank of the
Thames, is heavily industrialized; one of
its most outstanding buildings is
G.G.Scott's fine *Power Station* (1932-4),
which is to be turned into a museum of industry. The new Covent Garden fruit and
vegetable market (1975) is also of interest.
To the W., *Battersea Park* has a collection
of sculptures (e.g. Henry Moore's 'Three
Women', 1947&8). The *Georgian Parish
Church* (Battersea Church Road) has good
17C monuments. Nearby, *Old Battersea
House* (1699) has pre-Raphaelite paintings
and a collection of pottery by William de
Morgan.

Beddington Park: *Church of St.Mary the
Virgin,* a 15C church with a Norman font
and fine tombstones.

Brentford: *National Piano Museum* with
an interesting collection of instruments.

Deptford: Henry VII established docks
here in 1485 and it became an important
dockyard. Peter the Great worked in the
dockyard in 1698 and he lived in John Evelyn's house, which no longer exists. *Albury
Street* near St.Paul's has one of the finest
surviving early-18C terraces. In *St.
Nicholas's parish church* (Deptford Green),
rebuilt after the Second World War, there
is a fine carved reredos by Grinling Gibbons. In 1712-30, Thomas Archer built
St.Paul's (Deptford High Street), the finest
example of his work in London. It has
stairs to the N. and S., a semicircular W.
portico crowned by a round tower, and an
apse at the E. end. In the interior, which
is spanned by a flat panelled stucco ceiling, there are gigantic Corinthian columns
separating the nave from the aisles, which
are galleried.

Downe: Charles Darwin (1809-82) lived
and worked in *Downe House* (18C).
Mementoes of him are on display.

East Ham: *St.Mary Magdalene,* a Norman church, later altered, with 17C
monuments.

Eltham: Today this village to the SE of London forms part of its suburbs. Parts of three fine buildings have survived: *Well Hall* (Well Hall Road), the remains of an early-16C fortified country house, with a number of brick buildings dating fom 1568. *Eltham Lodge* (Off Court Road), the only building known to have been completed by H.May (1663–5), is a typical example of a Restoration house and has a wonderful staircase. Today it is a golf clubhouse. *Eltham Palace:* Edward IV's great hall (1470–80) still survives from what was the Plantagenets' favourite castle. It has an exquisitely ornamented hammer-beam roof.

Enfield: *St. Andrew's,* a 13&14C parish church with fine monuments. *Forty Hall:* This charming house was built in 1632 for Sir Nicholas Rayton, the Lord Mayor of London, and is today a museum. Charming *old houses,* especially in *Gentlemen's Row.*

Fulham: Today the site of the old market is covered with housing. Nearby, the *church* has fine *monuments;* the one to M.Legh (d. 1605) with a seated figure of the dead woman holding her two babies, is outstanding. Attractive *almshouses* by Seddon (1869). Of the great houses which once lined the river, Hurlingham House and *Fulham Palace* have both survived, the latter being the Bishop of London's residence. The core of the palace dates back to the 16C, and the building has been altered several times since. There are fine diamond-shaped mosaics in the courtyard (1500–20). There is an oriel window above the picturesque entrance hall. Plans have been made for the house and the collections in it to be opened to the public.

Greenwich: This small fishing village developed into an important town in the 15C. At that time a royal palace was built here. It was later extended and was a favourite residence of Henry VIII, who was born here, as were Queen Mary I and Queen Elizabeth I. In the 17C the medieval and Tudor buildings were replaced by the Queen's House and the Naval Hospital. In the course of its development, Greenwich maintained a greater independence from London than did any other district. Roads were built in the 17&18C. In addition to

Ham House (London)

he hospital, two other important buildings y Christopher Wren have survived: the *Morden College* (founded in 1695), a group f almshouses which are regarded as an utstanding example of Wren's domestic rchitecture. The central section of the *Royal Observatory* was built for the Astronomer Royal in 1675&6. An extensive ollection of scientific instruments is on isplay here. The most interesting houses i Greenwich stand on or near Croom's Iill. Apart from some attractive terraces f Georgian houses, note the following: the *Presbytery,* a well-preserved house dating om 1630, *The Grange* (17&18C) and a *Mansion* dating from 1700. To the E. of the Iospital is *Vanbrugh's Castle,* which Sir ohn Vanbrugh, the architect, built for imself in medieval style in 1717–26. *The Paragon* (Blackheath) is an attractive 18C rraced crescent. The *Town Hall* (1939) is good example of a modern, Dutch-ifluenced brick building. The parish hurch of *St.Alfrege* was built by Hawksoor and James in 1711–14. The tower ates from 1730. The extensive interior is anned by a stucco ceiling. The *Queen's*

House (now the *National Maritime Museum*) was built by Inigo Jones in 1616–37 and is a milestone of English architecture, marking the introduction of the Palladian. Inside, the hall is a precise cube. The spiral main staircase is also known as the Tulip Staircase after the form of its banisters. The *museum* is devoted to the history of British seafaring. The *Royal Naval Hospital* (now the *Royal Naval College*): Part of the Hospital was built by J.Webb in 1664 after the Tudor buildings had been pulled down. In the late 17C Mary, the wife of William of Orange had it completed as a home for navy pensioners; the counterpart to Chelsea Royal Hospital. Christopher Wren, who designed both the Chelsea and Greenwich Hospitals, incorporated Webb's existing building in his plans. He began work on this impressive group of buildings in 1698, with the assistance of Hawksmoor and Vanbrugh. The Hospital comprises two widely-separated wings by the river and, behind them, two further wings set closer together. The picture is rounded off by two domed pavilions. The Painted Hall (1703) with a large ceiling

Hampton Court (London), gardens

fresco by J.Thornhill in honour of William and Mary is one of the most lavish pieces of baroque in England. The chapel was rebuilt by S. and W.Newton in Greek style in 1779–89 after a fire, and is a typical example of its period. *The Ranger's House* was built in the early 18C and enlarged by the Earl of Chesterfield in 1750. It contains a suite of three ballrooms in the S. section, a gallery and a magnificent staircase. Today there is also a collection of portraits to be seen, with works by W.Larkin and others.

Ham House: In the late 17C the Duke of Lauderdale, a favourite of Charles II, ordered a number of prominent artists to enlarge a house dating from 1610. The result is a baroque gem. Today the house, which is used by the Victoria and Albert Museum, contains Flemish, Dutch and Italian paintings, a good collection of miniatures, sumptuous garments, tapestries and furniture.

Hampton Court: Cardinal Thomas Wolsey (1475 – 1530) began building this charmingly situated palace for himself in 1514 but he subsequently presented it to Henry VIII in order to regain his favour. The king had it enlarged in 1531–6, when the Great Hall, with its splendid hammerbeam roof, and other buildings were added. He embellished the chapel, built the tennis court, and had the astronomical clock in the Clock Court made in 1540. The W. front is an impressive piece of Tudor architecture. William and Mary commissioned Wren to work on the palace in 1689. He rebuilt the E. section, created the Fountain Court and the Cartoon Gallery, and refurnished the chapel, while Grinling Gibbons, the wood carver, was also active and he fitted out the state rooms, where pictures by Thornhill and Laguerre, and also works by Gibbons, Cibber and Nost, may today be admired. The exquisite wrought-iron work on the building from this period are by the French artist Tijou. There are also splendid wall hangings, clocks and furniture to be seen inside, while, outside, a walk through the fine gardens and a visit to the 'Maze' are well worth the effort.

Harefield: *Church of St.Mary* with splendid 17C monuments, some of them by

Hampton Court (London), Tudor gatehouse

Grinling Gibbons and J.Bacon the Younger; that to the Countess of Derby, who founded the adjoining almshouses, is outstanding.

Harlington: *St.Peter and Paul,* a 12–15C church.

Harrow: *Church of St.Mary,* 11–15C elements and fine monuments, including one by Flaxman (1815) to John Lyon, the founder of the nearby school.

Hendon: *Hendon Hall* was formerly the home of David Garrick, the celebrated Shakespearean actor and dramatist (1717–79).

Hillingdon: *Church of St. John the Baptist,* 14C, rebuilt by Scott in the 19C; with beautiful monuments.

Islington: Islington developed rapidly owing to its vicinity to the City, but later fell into decay. Today it is a fashionable residential area and there are numerous 18C and early-19C houses and terraces, including *Coolebrooke Row* (18C), elegant *Canonbury Square* (by H.Leroux, *c.* 1800), and, nearby, the fine *Canonbury House* (1770). There is also a very unusual house (1842–5), with Tudor stucco, by R.C.Carpenter in *Lonsdale Square. Canonbury Tower:* The tower and the adjacent buildings are all that remain of the old monastery which Sir John Spencer, the Lord Mayor of London, enlarged for use as a house in the late 16C. Inside there are rooms with Elizabethan panelling and fine stucco ceilings.

Kew: The parish church and the handsome houses around it are 18C. In 1759 Princess Augusta commissioned Capability Brown to lay out a *Botanical Garden.* It was opened to the public in 1841 and is today the *Royal Botanic Gardens,* with over 45,000 plants. Important scientific experiments are also carried out. There is also a collection of various types of wood, an interesting herbarium, and an extensive specialist library. In 1761, W.Chambers built the Pagoda. He also designed the other pavilions and small temples in the gardens. The glass Palm House is by Decimus Burton (1844–8). The 17C Dutch House, with its original decoration, was a favourite residence of George III, whereas Queen Victoria liked the Queen's Cottage built in the late 18C.

Kew (London), Botanic Gardens

Kingston upon Thames: Several Saxon kings were crowned on the *Coronation Stone* outside the modern, 20C Town Hall.

Osterley Park House: Sir Thomas Gresham (1519–79), the founder of the Royal Exchange, built a house here in the 16C. The existing building, with an Ionic portico approached by a flight of steps, corner towers and a balustrade, is by Robert Adam and dates from 1761–80, Adam was also responsible for the elegant stucco inside. In addition, most of the furniture still survives, and it includes some fine neoclassical pieces. There are also numerous paintings and splendid wall hangings and Gobelins from the 18C.

Paddington: Except for the small church on Paddington Green, the former terminus of the first London bus service and now dominated by the Westway motorway, no trace survives today of the 18C village that once occupied this extensive site. The road, the railway (Paddington Station, built by I.K.Brunel in 1850, was the terminus of the Great Western Railway) and the canal all favoured the development of the area.

Large stuccoed houses were built in Victorian times, as at *Little Venice* in Blomfield Road by the canal. Formerly occupied by the members of fashionable society, many of the houses in the area—though not in Little Venice itself—have either fallen into disrepair or else been replaced by multi storeyed buildings. Numerous *churches* were built in the 19C and two of them are masterpieces. *St.Augustine's* (Kilburn Park Road) is a red brick church built by J.L.Pearson in 1870–80 with a 245 ft tower. Inside, the double aisles support a gallery, and the transepts have ribbed vaults. The choir and ambulatory are separated from the nave by a large rood screen. There are also a number of paintings including, in the N. transept, Italian Renaissance paintings by Crivelli, Filippo Lippi, Titian and others. *St.Mary Magdalene* (Woodchester Street): This church of patterned brick and stone was built by G.E.Street in 1868–78. It has a graceful tower and a polygonal apse. Inside, it has a tall clerestory and a panelled ceiling. The crypt has numerous carvings by Comper.

Richmond upon Thames (London), Richmond Park

Petersham: A Georgian village with attractive 17&18C houses and a church with 13, 18&19C parts.

Richmond upon Thames: Little survives of the *palace* in which Elizabeth I died in 1603. There are fine 18C *houses* along Maids of Honour Row where the queen's maids of honour once lived. *Richmond Park,* laid out by Charles I as a deer park in the 17C, has fine old trees, lakes and a number of houses; it is one of the largest and most beautiful parks in the country.

Roehampton: Until recently, Roehampton retained the atmosphere of a village. Most of its Georgian villas and houses have been converted into public buildings. Roehampton Lane is now a major through road and is dominated by the *Roehampton Estate* (1955–60). These modern blocks of flats tower over Richmond Park and, as laid down by Le Corbusier, they are surrounded by gardens. Some of the old houses have survived, including *Manresa House* (1750, by Chambers). The Palladian former *Jesuit college*, with fine stucco ceilings and a chapel, is now used as a school. *Mount Clare,* a Palladian villa (1772–80), with a flight of steps up to a Doric portico. *Devonshire House* (now Garnett College), a red brick house built by Bettingham in *c.* 1770, with a fine garden and a cottage. *Roehampton House,* built by Archer in 1710–12, later enlarged by Lutyens, today houses the Queen Mary Hospital. Three more Georgian houses are used by the Froebel Institute.

Syon House: The origins of Syon House go back to 1415 but it was rebuilt by Inigo Jones in the 17C, while the interior is by Robert Adam. The contents include some splendid old furniture and a collection of paintings. Capability Brown laid out the garden.

Twickenham: There are numerous attractive 17&18C houses in this area. The poet Alexander Pope (1688–1744) died and was buried here and the writer Horace Walpole (1717–97) began building a neo-Gothic house on Strawberry Hill in 1748.

Wimbledon Common: Wimbledon is best known for the tennis championships. Caesar's Camp, on the common itself, is probably an Iron Age fort.

Woolwich: Henry VIII established a naval dockyard here, and Woolwich remained a military base for a long time. It includes the *Royal Dockyard,* the large Arsenal (closed since 1963) part of which was built by Vanbrugh, the *Royal Military Academy* built by Wyatt in 1805–8, and the *Royal Artillery Barracks* whose front is 1,000 ft. in length. Two major new projects are the *Thames Barrage* (1972–84), built to protect London from floods, and the new town of *Thamesmead* (begun in 1972), which is being built on drained marshland with the intention of housing 50,000 people. *The Rotunda,* a pavilion with a 'Chinese' roof, was built by Nash in 1814 in St. James's Park by way of a premature celebration of the Allies' victory over Napoleon, and was re-erected in Woolwich in 1819. It now contains some sections of the *Royal Ar-*

Syon House (London)

tillery Museum, whose other exhibits are housed in the Royal Military Academy.

Londonderry/Derry
Londonderry/Northern Ireland   p.326□D 9

This important port and industrial city, which stands at the point where the river Foyle flows into Lough Foyle, is the second largest city in Northern Ireland, with some 55,000 inhabitants.

History: The Celtic settlement of Derry was built around an early monastery founded by St.Columba in *c.* 546. There were frequent Viking raids in the 9&10C. In 1613 King James I proclaimed the city of Derry to be a part of the Corporation of London, and it was given the name of 'London-Derry'. The well-preserved fortifications also date from this period, and they withstood a siege by James II in 1688. A panel dating from 1633 in St.Columb's Cathedral has an inscription declaring that if stones could talk, they would praise London which caused this church and city to be built.

St.Columb's Cathedral: This Protestant cathedral was built in 1628–33 in the late Gothic style known as 'Planter's Gothic', but it also has Renaissance elements. In 1885–7 a *choir* was added to the single-aisled church. The *chapterhouse* has mementoes from the city's history.

Walls: The heart of the old town, standing on the hill above the Foyle, is surrounded by walls financed by the City of London in the 17C. There are four fine old gates: *Butcher's Gate, Ferryquay Gate, Shipquay Gate* and *Bishop's Gate,* which is the finest of the four. Also note the *ramparts* (to the N.), the *Double Bastion* with its old cannon ('Roaring Meg', 1642) and the *Royal Bastion* with the Walker Monu-

ment to George Walker, who defended the city in 1688.

Also worth seeing: The Catholic *St. Columba's church* was built in neo-Gothic style in 1873. A church dating from 1164 had stood on the site but it was destroyed in 1566. Nearby is St.Columba's stone. Not far from the central square, the *Diamond,* with an imposing *war memorial* (1926), is the classical *Court House* of 1813, and the neo-Gothic *Guildhall* of 1912, with its fine *council chamber* (ornamental window) and the *city museum. Magee University College* on the river Foyle is a neo-Gothic building dating from 1865.

Loughrea
Galway/Ireland   p.326□C 12

This small town on the Lough of the same name contains the ruins of a *Carmelite monastery* founded in *c.* 1300. A museum of medieval religious art has been established inside an old 15C *town gate,* near the cathedral. The neo-Gothic *St.Brendan's Cathedral,* built in *c.* 1900, with its fine pieces of contemporary Irish religious art (glass), is also worth seeing.

Environs: Athenry (about 9 m. NW): This town, whose Gaelic name of Ath-an-Riogh means King's Ford, has some interesting remains: *Athenry Castle* with a keep and outer walls (Gothic gateway) dates from the 13C. Some parts of the *town wall* (five towers and the town gate) dating from *c.* 1312 have also survived. The ruined church (1241) of the *Dominican Friary* has numerous 13–15C monuments. The Protestant *parish church* was built on the site of the 13C St.Mary's church.
Turoe Stone (about 4 m. NE): This famous stone is decorated with abstract ornament and dates from the early Celtic La Tène Iron Age (*c.* 300 BC).

Louth

Lincolnshire/England   p.328 □ K 12

Church of St.James: Rebuilt in Perpendicular style in the 15C, and restored by T.Fowler in the 19C. The *steeple* (completed in 1509; about 320 ft. high) is well worth seeing and is one of the finest in England. The interior has some good carved wood.

Also worth seeing: The ruins of a *Cistercian abbey* founded in 1139 (Louth Park). *Cromwell House* dating from 1600. *Mansion House* dating from the end of the 18C. *Thorpe Hall* (1584) rebuilt in the 18C; fine Renaissance terraces. Old *warehouses* at the end of the Louth Navigation Canal which enters the sea at Grimsby. The *old town centre* with fine houses.

Environs: Addlethorpe (about 17 m. SE): The 15C church of *St.Nicholas.* Inside there are some good old pieces of glass and some fine carving.

Alford (about 11 m. SE): The 14C church of *St.Wilfrid,* extensively restored by Sir Gilbert Scott in 1869; the S. porch is worth seeing.

Bag Enderby (about 9 m. S.): The church of *St.Margaret* (mainly 14C Gothic, with 15C additions; a fine Gothic font with a Pietà).

Burgh-le-Marsh (about 17 m. SE): With a *windmill museum* housed in a windmill which is still in operation.

Gunby Hall (about 15 m. SE): Built in *c.* 1700; inside, a good staircase, some fine panelling and paintings, including works by Reynolds.

Horncastle (about 12 m. SW): Horncastle occupies the site of the Roman *Banovallum* (remains of walls, among other items), with a well-preserved old *town centre;* in the church of *St.Mary* the monuments of the Dymoke family are worth seeing.

Ingoldmells (about 17 m. SE): The church of *St.Peter and St.Paul,* with a fine

late Gothic porch; inside it has an interesting 16C tomb.

Old Bolingbroke (about 16 m. S.): The birthplace of Henry IV (1367–1413); the remains of the *castle* of the Earls of Lincoln; there is also a notable *parish church.*

Saltfleetby All Saints (about 7 m. NE): Contains the church of *All Saints* (originally Romanesque, subsequently altered): an early Gothic tower with a 15C spire. The furnishings include a beautiful Renaissance pulpit.

Scrivelsby Court (about 14 m. SW): Formerly a seat of the Dymoke family, which held the hereditary office of the 'Champion of England'. Up until 1821, it was the duty of this champion to ride to the Coronation ceremony and issue a challenge to any rival to the throne of England. The *Lion Gate* and some other buildings survive.

Somersby (about 9 m. S.): With a manor built in 1722 to plans by Sir John Vanbrugh.

Spilsby (about 16 m. SE): The birthplace of John Franklin the explorer (see his statue in the market place). Inside the church of *St.James* are some notable 14–17C monuments to the Willoughby family.

Theddlethorpe (about 9 m. E.): The late–14C church of *All Saints,* with earlier parts. Beautiful Gothic windows and remains of old stained glass, and there is also a late Gothic reredos.

Ludlow

Salop/England   p.328 □ H 14

This little town at the confluence of the Teme and the Corve developed in the 12C around a Norman fortress. It has never suffered any major damage and many old houses survive.

Church of St.Laurence: This large parish church was begun in 1199 and completed in the 14C. It was restored by Sir Gilbert Scott and Sir Arthur Blomfield in the 19C, but numerous old furnishings have survived. The 15C *stained-glass window* in the E. wall is especially worth seeing, as is the large 14C *Jesse window* in the Lady Chapel. Note the *misericords*, where the carving has by no means been restricted to clerical motifs, probably because it was often hidden by the seats. Like the choir stalls, the misericords are 14C.

Ludlow Castle: This was begun by Roger de Lacy in 1085 as a border fortress against the Welsh, and in the 13&14C it was enlarged into an extensive castle. In the early 14C the castle was owned by Roger Mortimer, who helped his lover, Queen Isabella, to murder her husband, Edward II (1327). It was taken by Parliamentary troops in 1646, and from the 18C on it fell into disrepair. The round Norman *chapel* dedicated to St.Mary Magdalene, and some 13&14C Gothic rooms, have survived. The oldest surviving section of the castle is a Norman *watch-tower* about 65 ft. high. *Mortimer's Tower* dates from the 13C. Hugh de Mortimer, an opponent of Henry II, was held prisoner here.

In the NW of the castle is the room in which Prince Arthur, the elder brother of Henry VIII, died in 1502, only a year after his marriage to Catherine of Aragon. His heart was buried in St. Laurence's church.

Also worth seeing: The *Reader's House* is a fine example of a Tudor house with a Jacobean porch. It dates back to an old Church House used by the 'Palmers' Guild' as a place of assembly in the 14C. The 15C *Feathers Hotel* has plaster ceilings, carved panelling and well-executed wall paintings. The *Geological Museum* has an enormous collection of fossils and rocks from Salop and the surrounding counties.

Environs: Croft Castle (10 m. SW): This was the seat of the Crofts of the Domesday Book until 1957 and, with its four corner towers of reddish stone, the present castle was built in *c.* 1400. It was rebuilt in the mid 18C, except for the corner towers. Fine 17&18C decoration.
Stokesay (9 m. NW): The *Church of St. John the Baptist* dates back to the Nor-

Ludlow, Castle, watch tower

mans, but was rebuilt in the 17C after being destroyed in the Civil War. *Stokesay Castle* is one of the finest examples of a small fortified house with a rampart and moat. It belonged to the Saye family in the 12C, and in 1281 it was acquired by Laurence de Ludlow, remaining in the possession of his family until 1497. From 1627 to 1869 it was the property of the Lords Craven, and since then it has been owned by the Allcrofts. Oldest sections: two towers (1115 and 1291) and Hall (1284).

Luton
Bedfordshire/England   p.332□K 14

This industrial town at the S. end of Bedfordshire produces clothing and hats.

Church of St. Mary: This cruciform church dating back to the 13C is especially impressive given its industrial surroundings. The tower of this Gothic church was built in the 14C, and was enlarged again in the 15C. The interior is impressive for its pure style and for several good items.

The oldest of these is a 13C *font*, while the most beautiful is a large octagonal 14C *font*, made of stone and donated by Philippa of Hainault. The *Wenlock Chapel* was built in 1461. It has a fine wooden choir screen and a double triumphal arch. The *monument* to William Wenlock, who died in 1392, was moved here from the church after the chapel had been completed. Finally, the small *Barnard Chapel* was built on the S. side of the sanctuary in 1492.

Museum and Art Gallery: This is in a Victorian house and contains collections relating to local history, art, local crafts, and fashion. There is a separate collection devoted to the history of straw plaiting.

Environs: Flamstead (4 m. S.): The *Church of St.Leonard* is Norman and was built in the mid 12C. Its late Norman arcades rest on finely carved capitals. The restored 12&15C frescos show Christ Triumphant, the Trinity, and scenes from the Passion. There are carvings by William Stanton and John Flaxman.

Ludlow, Castle, round chapel

Luton Hoo (2 m. S.): The house, which stands in a large park laid out by Capability Brown, was built by Robert Adam in 1767–74 and completed by Smirke in 1816. It was almost completely destroyed by a fire in 1843, and not rebuilt until 1903–7. Today it contains the *Wernher collection* of paintings, tapestries, porcelain, medieval bronzes and ivories, and precious gold pieces from various centuries (items include 18C Chelsea porcelain figures and a late-15C reliquary). The former chapel was converted into a large *gallery,* which contains works by Rembrandt and Titian and also the famous St. Michael by Bartolomé Bermejo (1470).

Lyme Regis
Dorset/England　　　　　　　p.332☐G/H 16

This romantic little fishing town dreams away its existence in a most beautiful Regency atmosphere. The Duke of Monmouth landed at the old stone jetty called 'The Cobb' in 1685, and it was here that

Lyme Regis, The Cobb

Louisa Musgrove fell in Jane Austen's 'Persuasion' (1818). James Whistler and Paul Nash painted in Lyme Regis, while in 1811 the 12-year-old Mary Anning found the first petrified ichthyosaurus here.

Church of St. Michael: Only a portion of the nave survives from what was originally a Norman church. This now forms the W. porch. The present church was built around 1500, and its walls are adorned with monuments. The *pulpit* is a good piece of work, dating from 1613; a splendid 16C Flemish *tapestry* commemorates the marriage of Prince Arthur to Catherine of Aragon.

Philpot Museum: Contains exhibits on geology and local history.

Environs: Forde Abbey (12 m. N.): The abbey was founded by Cistercians from Waverley in 1138. In 1528, Thomas Chard, its last abbot, began to enlarge it extensively but Henry VIII dissolved the monastery in 1539. In 1649, Cromwell's prosecutor general, Sir Edmund Prideaux, purchased the building and expanded it still further. Parts of the original monastery do survive, including the 12C chapterhouse (which Thomas Chard turned into a chapel), the dormitory and the undercroft below it (the latter two are both 13C). The entrance tower with its traceried oriel, the Abbot's Hall and the cloister are late Gothic and were built by Thomas Chard. The most precious decorations are the Mortlake tapestries, based on Raphael cartoons, which were woven in Brussels on the orders of Charles I.

Macclesfield
Cheshire/England   p.328□H 12

Macclesfield was the centre of the English silk industry in the 18&19C.

Church of St. Michael: Although the church was rebuilt in 1739 and again in 1898–1901, it has remained of interest for its *tombs and tomb figures*, the earliest of which date from the 15C. One of the most beautiful is probably that of Thomas, Earl Rivers of Rock Savage. This baroque monument was made in 1696 and has a marble baldacchino, in curtain form borne by Corinthian columns, over the figure of the Earl. The title and honours of the Earl and his two wives are listed on a marble plaque.

West Park Museum: This museum, built in 1898, contains a collection of Egyptian antiquities, Victorian paintings and exhibits concerning local history.

Environs: Lyme Park (9 m. NE): The focal point of the estate—which belonged to the Legh family 1397 - 1947 — is an Elizabethan *house*. This was greatly altered by Giacomo Leoni in 1720; only the *gallery* has remained unaltered since 1541. Furnishings include good woodcarving, tapestries and Chippendale chairs. The house is surrounded by interesting *gardens* and a large *park*.

Maidenhead
Berkshire/England   p.332□K 15

This old stage-post on the Thames was formerly London's most popular summer resort. The *railway bridge*, completed in 1838, has arches with a span of 132 ft.; these are the largest brick-built arches in the world.

Henry Reitlinger Bequest: This typical Edwardian house contains an interesting collection of European, oriental and continental ceramics.

Environs: Shottesbrook (5 m. SW): The *church of St. John the Baptist* is early Gothic and has a cruciform ground plan with a central tower. The N. transept has two 14C tombs including that of Sir William Trussell, the church's founder. There are some interesting remnants of 14C stained glass; the font is also 14C.
Dorney Court (*c.* 2.5 m. E.): The *church of St. James* dates back to Norman times.

It acquired the Tudor-style W. tower during the Renaissance and its entrance hall in 1661. Some of the church stalls are 16C and the pulpit was completed in 1650. Traces of medieval frescos show that the church was once painted. The font is 12C. The alabaster tomb of Sir William Garrard and his wife dates from 1607.

Maidstone
Kent/England   p.332☐L 15

Originally a Roman and then a Saxon settlement, it is mentioned in the Domesday Book. The most famous son of this still flourishing town is the critic and essayist William Hazlitt (1778–1830).

All Saints Church: Built of ragstone in the 14C in Decorated and Perpendicular style, it has a Jacobean font, a few good 19C monuments and wonderful 18C stained-glass windows. A memorial plaque next to the tower door recalls Laurence Washington, great uncle of George Washington, whose tomb is in the graveyard.

Maidstone, All Saints' Church

Archbishop's Palace: (Next to All Saints Church.) Dating from the 14C, it belonged to the Archbishops of Canterbury up until the time of Henry VIII. The wings are Tudor; of particular interest is the wood-panelled Banqueting Hall.

St. Peter's Chapel: A former pilgrim's chapel from the 13C.

Chillington Manor: This Tudor house has an exhibition devoted to the history of Kent; items include a model of the Roman *Villa of Lullingstone*. The *Royal West Kent Regimental Museum* is also housed here.

Tyrwitt Drake Museum of Carriages: England's largest coach and vehicle museum; it is housed in a 14C Tithe Barn.

Also worth seeing: The town has several beautiful parks, such as *Mote Park* (with a large lake and *Mote House* from the 18C). The best modern buildings are *County Hall* and the 12-storey *Kent County Council Library*.

Environs: Allington Castle (c. 2 m. NE) The castle, which occupies a beautiful location, dates from the 13C and belonged to the Wyatt family up until Sir James Wyatt's ill-fated rebellion against Queen Mary I. It is now a *Carmelite monastery*. The chapel has a few fine sculptures and the castle itself has a good collection of religious pictures and icons.
Aylesford (3 m. NW): 13C *monastery* with a cloister of a later date. Interesting sculptures and ceramics.
Boughton Monchelsea Place (3 m. S.) A *Tudor House* of 1570 with some beautiful tapestries.
Kit's Coty House (3 m. N.): Remains of the most interesting Neolithic burial mound in Kent; the burial chambers were cut deep into the hillside.
Leeds Castle (6.5 m. SE): One of the most beautiful castles in the world, it sits pic-

resquely in the middle of a lake; 12C in origin.

oose (2 m. S.): *Wool House,* a 16C half-mbered farmhouse.

ld Soar Manor (9 m. W.): Remains of medieval *manor house.*

tham (*c.* 2 m. S.): *Stoneacre,* a typical te-15C house in a delightful setting.

Maldon
ssex/England p.332☐L 15

his little harbour on the River Black-ater existed as early as the 12C. Today it impressive for its picturesque old houses, ke the *Blue Boar Hotel* which is 15C.

ll Saints Church: Dating back to the 3C, it was extensively altered in later cen-uries. Of interest are its triangular *tower,* hich has a hexagonal spire, and the *crypt.* he *S. aisle* is 14C; the Gothic *nave* was ebuilt in brick in 1728. There are various 7C *tombs* .

A stained-glass window of 1928 is dedi-cated to George Washington's great-grandfather, who is buried in the churchyard.

Beeleigh Abbey: Built for Premon-stratensian monks in 1180. After its disso-lution the complex went into private ownership, new buildings were erected and the monastery church was pulled down. Still preserved are the *chapterhouse* and the vaulted cellar roof of the *dormitory;* both date from *c.* 1250 and have beautiful Pur-beck marble columns. The vaulted cellar roof has a chimney system which was ex-tended in the 15C. The window glass of the two buildings is 15C.

Moot Hall: A brick building of 1435, it is also called *D'Arcy Tower* after its builder. The house's tower is interesting and looks as if it were built for defensive purposes. The 19C *entrance hall* is adorned with columns.

Plume Library: Founded in 1704 by Dr. Plume, archdeacon of Rochester, in the re-mains of St.Peter's Church. The tower of

Maidstone, All Saints, W. window

Fresco

the former church now forms the library entrance.

Environs: Bradwell-on-Sea (20 m. E.): The church of *St. Peter's-on-the-Wall*, founded by St.Cedd, Bishop of Essex, is one of the oldest churches in England. It was built on the ruins of the Roman camp of *Othona* and used stone from the camp. The sanctuary no longer exists, but the nave, portal and W. window have survived unaltered through the centuries.
Tolleshunt (*c.* 9 m. NE): The church of *St.Nicholas* dates from the 15C, has a battlemented W. tower and was partly rebuilt in the 19C. Of interest is the collection of memorials in the N. chapel. *Beckingham Hall* is of interest for the unusual brick walls surrounding the 16C half-timbered house. At each corner the walls have little towers and the large gatehouse is also adorned with towers. The panelling from the Great Hall dates from 1546 and is now to be found in the Victoria and Albert Museum in London.

Mallow
Cork/Ireland   p.330☐B 14

This small agricultural town of some 5,500 inhabitants on the river Blackwater has beautiful *town houses* from the 18–19C, when it was popular as a spa and health resort. *Mallow Castle* of 1600 has polygonal corner towers on the N. side.

Environs: Ballybeg Abbey (*c.* 6 m. N.): The ruins of this *Augustinian monastery* with beautiful W. windows date from 1229.
Buttevant (*c.* 7.5 m. N.): The *Franciscan monastery was built in 1251; ruins of the church*, with beautiful windows in the S. chancel, have survived.
Castletownroche (*c.* 8 m. E.): Remains of the Augustinian monastery *Bridgetown*

Abbey (13C) and the medieval fortress *Ca tle Widenham.*
Dromaneen Castle: The ruins (*c.* 160 lie about 2.5 m. W. on the river Blackwat and include a *fortified house* with towe
Fermoy (*c.* 18 m. E.): A garrison tow founded by John Anderson, a Scotsma in 1789. The *church* dates from 1802 an attractive *Castle Hyde* is 18C. To the N is the extensive *megalithic tomb of La bacallee;* there are other traces of prehistor tombs to the S. at *Carntighernagh.*
Island (*c.* 8.5 m. S.): Halfway to Cork the well-preserved *megalithic tomb* (Galle Grave) of Island from the 2C BC.
Kanturk Castle (*c.* 12.5 m. NW): T ruins of the fortress dating from 1601 sho an interesting mixture of Irish late Goth and Tudor style (rectangular with massi square towers).
Liscarroll (*c.* 12.5 m. NW): Remains an extensive 13C *castle* including roun corner towers and gate towers (in the S. ar N.).

Malmesbury
Wiltshire/England   p.332☐H

A small town on the upper reaches of th Avon. Today the town reveals little of t former importance of its Benedictine A bey, which was one of the earliest abbe to be founded, as well as being one of t largest in the county during the Midd Ages. Established as early as 680, Kir Athelstan was buried here in 940. The f mous document 'Gesta Regum Anglorur was written within its walls by the chron cler William of Malmesbury, mon teacher and later abbot of the monaster He was buried here in 1143. The mona tery library was once renowned throug out Europe; a small reflection of this is th beautifully illustrated *Bible*, made b Flemish artists for the library in 140 (This can now be seen in the treasur chamber over the church portal.) The ab

Malmesbury, Abbey Church, lunette

ey produced an early pioneer of flight, when Elmer of Malmesbury attempted to ly from the church tower using home-made wings.

Abbey Church: The large abbey church vas mainly built 1115–1239. Its ground plan is typical of a large abbey church, having transepts, a central tower, chancel, nave and aisles and a tower at the W. façade. All of this was destroyed following the Reformation and only the *nave* remained of the Norman building, which was purchased by a rich merchant, who donated it to the community as parish church. Thus the *S. portal* of around 1165, with its 8 archivolts and splendid ornamentation, was preserved; this is surpassed only by the *ympanum* with Christ in Glory. In each of the lunettes on either side there are six postles seated opposite each other with an

angel flying over their heads. These sculptures form, without doubt, the peak of Norman art in England.

Man, Isle of

p.328□F 11

This popular holiday island with an area of 227 sq. miles and 56,000 inhabitants lies in the Irish Sea between Ireland, England and Scotland. The island was already occupied in the Mesolithic period (around 2000 BC) by a pre-Celtic hunting and fishing people. In the following period Celtic tribes settled here, as discoveries of Iron Age groups of dwellings show. St.Patrick is supposed to have converted the island's inhabitants to Christianity in the 5C. There later followed invasions by the Vikings and Normans (or English). Today the island is a 'Free State under the English Crown' with its own parliament. The Celtic Manx language is now barely spoken on the island.

Douglas (pop. 20,000): The island's capital with the seat of parliament (Legislative Building) is a popular holiday resort.
The *Manx Museum* (Finch Rd.) offers a survey from the island's earliest history up to the present day. Collections from prehistoric and early Celtic times, the Viking period and traditional furnishings; note the medieval *Manx Crosses*.

Castletown: The medieval capital of the island lies to the SE. The massive Viking castle, *Castle Rushen* (13C), with well-preserved walls and towers, contains some interesting items such as a sun-dial and Celtic crosses.
The *Nautical Museum* contains the yacht 'Peggy' (1791), as well as model ships and ship's instruments. There is also a museum of magic and witchcraft.

Environs: Ballasalla (*c.* 2 m. N.): Ruins

Manchester, Cathedral, N. window

of the Cistercian house of *Rushen Abbey*, founded in 1134 (dissolved 1540). Nearby is the well-known *King William's College* (1668) with a pretty chapel.

Peel (pop. 3,000): On an island by this fishing harbour on the W. coast stand the imposing 13C remains of *Peel Castle*. This well-preserved castle is built of sandstone and still retains walls and towers. Inside the walls is the interesting 13C *Cathedral of St.Germanus* with a Gothic choir and the even older *St.Patrick's Chapel* (9 or 10C).

Environs: St.John's (2.5 m. SE): This nearby village has a Bronze Age *burial mound* (cairn). Every year on 5 July the island's laws are read out in Manx on the Tynwald Hill.

Port Erin: This little harbour has an interesting marine biology station with a *marine aquarium*. Nearby, at *Mull Hill* (*c.* 2 m. S.) are 6 megalithic burial chambers (tritaphs), known as *Mull Circle*. Also worth seeing is the nearby *Manx Village Folk Museum* with reconstructions of ancient huts and workshops (smithy, weaving).

Ramsey (pop. 4,600): Near this small harbour lies the interesting 13C *Kirk Maughold*, which has a series of Celtic and other crosses in the churchyard.

Manchester
Greater Manchester/England   p.328□H 12

Founded by the Romans *(Mancunium)* at a major crossroads, but it was not until the 17C that it rose to be the centre of the local textile industry. In the course of the Industrial Revolution in the 18C it developed into the heart of the English cotton industry and the methods of the then unfettered capitalism were notorious.

Cathedral (Victoria Street): The town'

former parish church, dedicated to St. Mary, St.Denys and St.George, has been a cathedral since 1847. A sandstone church built in the 15C in Perpendicular style, it was rebuilt after bomb damage in World War 2. It has four aisles (240 ft. long and unusually wide at about 122 ft.), and a square *tower* (1868, *c.* 142 ft. high). Inside, the choir has richly decorated *stalls* (remarkable canopies and misericords) and a fine *roof.* In the nave, note the *pulpit* , also richly carved, as well as *St.John's Chapel,* the *Lady Chapel* and the *Manchester Regimental Chapel.* The ornate screens separating these chapels from the nave are their main feature of interest.

Chetham's Hospital and Library

(Long Millgate): Built in the 15C as a school for poor boys, altered in 1654; the *library* (over 80,000 volumes) contains a valuable collection of books from the 16–18C. The library is the oldest public foundation of its kind in England.

City Art Gallery

(Morley Street): Housed in a building erected in 1825–9 by Charles Barry, the architect of the Houses of Parliament in London, which has been used as a museum since 1882. Of particular interest are the *picture gallery* (extensive collection of English masters from the 16C to the present day, including the pre-Raphaelites, with 17C Flemish painters and French Impressionists) and the *sculpture collection,* the high points of which are works by Henry Moore and Jacob Epstein.

Free Trade Hall

(Peter Street): Built 1843, altered 1856, faithfully rebuilt in 1951, following bomb damage in World War 2, using the old fabric. The hall is the home of the 'Hallé Orchestra' one of England's major symphony orchestras. The large *concert hall* inside holds over 2,500 people (131 ft. long, *c.* 85 ft. wide and about 65 ft. high).

John Ryland's University Library

(Deansgate): This resulted from the amalgamation of the John Ryland's Library and the University Library; housed in a neo-Gothic building of 1899. The world-famous collections contain valuable

Manchester, Cathedral, choir stalls

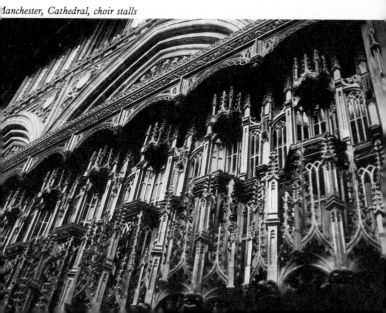

manuscripts (including a Gospel of St.John from the 1 or 2C) and many *first and early impressions* (including one of the three Gutenberg Bibles).

Town Hall (Albert Square): The Town Hall was built in neo-Gothic style to plans by Alfred Waterhouse in 1868–77; the clock tower is over 300 ft. high. Of the 300-odd rooms the most interesting are the *Mayor's offices* and the *Great Hall,* with 12 wall paintings by Ford Madox Brown (scenes from the city's history).

University (Oxford Road): Built in 1870 in the neo-Gothic style of the Victorian period (French in inspiration). It houses the *Manchester Museum,* with collections devoted to, amongst others, the natural sciences, archaeology (Egyptology and numismatics departments) and folklore. The *Whitworth Art Gallery* (S. of the Manchester Museum) contains an extensive collection of English watercolours and drawings from the 18–20C (particularly Turner and the pre-Raphaelites) and masterpieces of modern European painting (Cézanne, Van Gogh, Gauguin, Klee, Picasso). Also of interest are prints and wood-cuts from all over the world and a collection of textiles (clothing and wall hangings).

Also worth seeing: *St. Ann's Church,* 18C, remarkable wood inside. *Royal Exchange* (Cross Street), 1869, the former exchange, now containing a theatre. *Liverpool Road Station,* built in 1830, the world's oldest surviving passenger station. *Portico Library,* opened in 1806, with valuable old volumes.

Environs: Blackstone Edge (*c.* 12 m. NE): The best preserved section of a *Roman road* is to be found here (Manchester–Ilkley Roman road).

Bram Hall (*c.* 10 m. S.): 15C *half-timbered house* with 14C chapel.

Didsbury (*c.* 4.5 m. S.): The *Fletcher Mos. Museum* in a 19C house contains items connected with the town's history (old photographs etc.).

Eccles (*c.* 4 m. W.): The *Monks Hall Museum,* housed since 1961 in a Tudor building, contains a collection of early machine tools.

Foxdenton Hall (*c.* 5 m. E.): A *Stuart house,* restored 1965.

Harpurhey (*c.* 2.5 m. NE): *Queen's Park Art Gallery* with a collection of 19C paintings and sculptures; also houses a *Military Museum.*

Heaton Hall (*c.* 5 m. NW): *House* built in 1772; of interest inside is the *Etruscan Room* (beautiful wall and ceiling paintings) and 18C furniture.

Middleton (*c.* 4 m. N.): With *St.Leonard Church* (rebuilt in the 15C, enlarged in the 16C; beautiful tower of 1709; interesting window, 1520).

Oldham (*c.* 7.5 m. NE): Interesting *Art Gallery,* English watercolours and drawings from the 19&20C, as well as a bust of Churchill (1946) by Jacob Epstein.

Platt Hall (*c.* 3 m. S.): Built around 1760 housing the *Gallery of English Costume* (exhibits from the 17C to the present day).

Radcliffe (*c.* 6 m. NW): Interesting little *museum* devoted to the history of the town (adjoining picture gallery).

Salford (*c.* 4 m. W.): With *Peel Park Museum* and an *Art Gallery* (contains the most extensive collection of paintings by L. S. Lowry in England).

Stalybridge (*c.* 7.5 m. E.): The *Astley Cheetham Art Gallery* contains a collection of paintings from the Middle Ages and the Renaissance, as well as works by English masters of the 18&19C; also archaeological items.

Stand (*c.* 4.5 m. NW): With *All Saint Church,* built in neo-Gothic style by Charles Barry in 1825.

Wythenshawe Hall (*c.* 6 m. S.): 16C *half-timbered house;* contains paintings and furniture from the 17C and objects from the

Oriental Department of the Manchester City Art Gallery.

Margam Abbey
West Glamorgan/Wales   p.332☐G 15

Lying on the coast, halfway between Bridgend and Swansea (c. 10 m. NW of Bridgend), are the remains of the old Cistercian monastery *Margam Abbey* (founded 1147), which occupied the site of an earlier Celtic monastery. The late Norman *nave* (262 ft. long) is still partly preserved (now serving as the parish church). Beautiful Norman features, such as the interesting *portal* with capitals, massive pillars inside, 3 round windows over the portal; also many fragments and parts of walls, remains of columns, arches, the 13C *chapterhouse* (12-sided exterior, round interior with central pillar) and various old *tombs* (Mansel family).

Abbey Museum: The churchyard contains a unique collection of *Celtic crosses* and stone monuments from early Christian times: the *Stone of Bodvoc* is one of the oldest Celtic stone monuments (around 550). The undecorated stone is adorned from top to bottom with a Latin inscription: Bodvoci hic iacit filius Catotigirni pronepos Eternali Vedomavi ('The Stone of Bodvoc: Here lies the son of C., grandson of E.V.'). On the *Stone of Pumpeius Carantorius* is an Ogham inscription. *Thomas's Cross* (8 or 9C) with an inscribed cross and name. The *High Cross of Enniaun* (c. 9C with lavish ornamentation, mostly braided. The *Cross of Grutne* (around 1000), a sandstone High Cross (as most are) with a Latin inscription to the founder; also the *Wheel Cross of Cynfelyn* from around 900. The collection here is, along with the National Museum in Cardiff, the best testament to early Christian-Celtic burial practices.

Market Harborough
Leicestershire/England   p.328☐I 13

The principal town in S. Leicestershire has been a market town since 1203 (cattle market every Tuesday). The surrounding area is a centre of fox-hunting. Note *St. Dionysius,* a 13–15C church with richly decorated Gothic windows and an impressive tower, also the *Grammar School,* in the market place, which stands on columns and dates from 1614, and the old *inns* (the inn sign of 'The Three Swans', a splendid piece of 18C wrought iron, is particularly beautiful).

Environs: Claybrooke (c. 15.5 m. W.): *St.Peter's Church* (mostly 14C, choir original, nave altered to late Gothic; beautiful pointed windows, remains of medieval stained glass).

Foxton (c. 3 m. NW): With the *Foxton Locks,* a system of locks on the Grand Union Canal, built as early as 1808 (10 separate locks rise 75 ft. over a distance of half a mile).

Langton Hall (c. 5 m. N.): Old *house;* inside is a richly furnished drawing room (Venetian lace on the walls) and a valuable collection of Chinese furniture.

Lutterworth (c. 12 m. W.): Late Gothic *church* with beautiful wall paintings; John Wycliffe was parish priest here in 1374–84 (he was one of the 'Pre-Reformers', who campaigned against impropriety within the Catholic Church. He was the first to translate the Bible into English).

Stanford Hall (c. 11 m. SW): The ancestral home of the Cave family since 1340; present building begun in 1680, the stables were completed in 1745. Inside there is an interesting collection of 17C paintings, period furniture and costumes from the 16C onwards, also old kitchen implements. Of particular interest is the *Vehicle Museum* with a model of a flying machine built by the English pioneer Pilcher (1898).

Maynooth

Kildare/Ireland   p.326☐D 12

This little town (some 15 m. W. of Dublin) is now mainly known for its seminary *St.Patrick's College*, where most Irish Catholic priests are trained. It was opened in 1521 and, after being temporarily closed, was refounded in 1795. The *college buildings* date from the 18C (Stoyte House) and the 19C (St. Mary's and St. Patrick's Houses). The *College Museum* exhibits interesting works of art and antiques (14–17C). Nearby *Maynooth Castle* was built by Gerald FitzGerald around 1203. A massive *keep* (13C), the *Great Hall* and *Gate Tower* survive.

Environs: Carton House (*c.* 2 m. NE): A Georgian *stately home* from around 1735, incorporating older elements.
Celbridge (*c.* 5.5 m. SE): *Castletown House* (to the N.) was built around 1722 by the Italian Alessandro Galilei for William Conolly. It is one of the finest Georgian buildings in Ireland and is now the seat of the Georgian Society. Nearby is the 137 ft. memorial obelisk *Conolly's Folly* of 1740. Also of interest is the nearby *Ardrass Church* (to the SW), a small medieval stone oratory with a stone roof, S. portal and 2 E. windows.
Leixlip (*c.* 4 m. E.): Interesting medieval *W. tower* of the Protestant church (tower house) and *Leixlip Castle*, originally 14C, but greatly altered in the 18C.
Lucan (*c.* 5.5 m. E.): Beautiful *Lucan House* (1776) with fine interior.

Melrose

Borders/Scotland   p.324☐H 9

This little town at the foot of the Eildon Hills retains a few old *houses* and a *market cross* (1642), but is best known for the ruins of its abbey. According to Fontane, the German writer, these ruins are 'not only of Scottish ruins, but of all the ruins I have seen... altogether the most beautiful and captivating'. Walter Scott described them and made the abbey the subject of a novel and Turner drew them. The reality of the abbey is somewhat less romantic.

Melrose Abbey: The abbey was founded in 1136 by that great founder of monasteries, David I. For it he summoned Cistercian monks from Rievaulx in Yorkshire and thereby established a successor to the 7C Celtic monastery 2.5 m. to the E. But the new one was not to be spared damage. In 1322 it was pillaged by the soldiers of Edward II, and devasted by those of Richard II in 1385. On returning to Scottish hands again in 1385, the rebuilding was begun in late Gothic style. The building costs were in keeping with the wealth and importance of the abbey: The church alone was over 300 ft. long and a good 130 ft wide at the transepts. The buildings of the abbey as a whole covered an area of over 107,600 sq. ft. The entire late Gothic complex was destroyed simply because Henry VIII was unable to obtain Mary Stuart as a daughter-in-law! The main survivor of this destruction was the E. part of the *church*. The *choir*, the two *transepts* and parts of the *S. aisle* are also preserved, as are parts of the *tower*. The ruins are still impressive today thanks to the extraordinary *masonry*. The completeness of the Gothic tracery, the extremely finely carved capitals and the imaginativeness of the sculptures are outstanding. The mason with his trowel, the cook with his spoon and a gargoyle in the shape of a pig blowing the bagpipes are all realistically carved and are eloquent witnesses of the mastery of the stonemasons, who probably came from France.

There are also some remains of the *mo-*

Melrose, Melrose Abbey, transept

astery buildings. Of the *cloister,* which adjoined the N. aisle, parts of the arcades can still be seen. Excavations of the chapterhouse (2,530 sq. ft.) have revealed that it had a tiled floor. The extent of the W. parts is due to the fact that in the 15C over 200 lay brothers belonged to the abbey. The abbey's history is described in a *museum.*

Environs: Abbotsford House: This house was purchased by Sir Walter Scott in 1811, who also lived here for the last 20 years of his life. In 1817–24 he converted it to his own plans, using parts of historic buildings (doors from an Edinburgh prison), or copying details of other ones (cloister of Melrose Abbey). For the interior too he eagerly copied historic examples (the beamed ceiling in the library is a copy of the one in Roslin Chapel). His *study* and *collection of weapons* are preserved in their original state, as is his *library* with some 10,000 volumes.

Dryburgh Abbey (3 m. SE): The abbey's romantic setting in a loop of the Tweed made such an impression on Sir Walter Scott, that he even had himself buried here. This is actually the least romantic of the Borders' four large abbeys, although it does provide the best impression of monastic life and architecture in the 12&13C. The abbey was founded in 1150 by Hugh de Morville for Premonstratensian monks on a site where a small monastery had stood since the 6C. The complex was destroyed by the English in 1322, 1385 and finally in 1544.

In contrast to the other monasteries, there are in Dryburgh more remains of the monastery buildings and fewer of the church. The remains of the *transept* and *choir* reveal, in their lower parts, Romanesque influence. The other features are Gothic. The *portal* at the W. end is 15C. The *tomb of Sir Walter Scott,* designed by Chantrey, was placed in the N. transept. S. of the church, the monastery buildings lie on terraces leading down to the river. Of interest are the *barrel vaults* of the chapterhouse and a few living quarters.

Jedburgh Abbey (12 m. S.): This abbey was founded by David I, who offered the site to Augustinians from Beauvais in 1138. Malcolm IV died here in 1195, and Alex-

Melrose Abbey 1 nave **2** choir **3** S. transept **4** tower **5** N. transept **6** chapterhouse **7** cloister

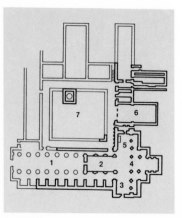

Melrose, Melrose Abbey

nder III was married here in 1285. The bbey was destroyed by the English in 544. There remains little of the abbey, but nore than usual of the church. The walls f the *nave* still reach the original height f the roof and have impressive arcades, nd Romanesque and Gothic windows. Much of the *tower*, dating from 1504–8, ias also survived. The lower parts of the *hoir* and *aisles* are still Romanesque, but he higher up the walls go, the more Gothic hey become. Dating from the 13C are the nain nave, with its 9 arches, and a new E. nd to the choir. The *W. front* is outstand- ng. It is the only one of its time which is lmost wholly intact and it is also the best xample of the transition from Roman- sque to Gothic. The few foundations of he monastery buildings are 14C.

Melton Mowbray

eicestershire/England   p.328☐I 13

Church of St. Mary: Principally a 3&14C Gothic building with Early Eng-

lish remnants. Cruciform ground plan, *tower* over crossing *c.* 100 ft. high (lower part 13C high Gothic, upper part from 1500); transepts with 2 aisles each. Note the clerestory.

Also worth seeing: *Carnegie Museum* (Thorpe End); various 18C *houses*.

Environs: Burrough Hill (*c.* 5 m. S.): Iron Age *hill fort*. The ramparts and the main entrance (SE corner) survive, along with various other features.

Edmondthorpe (*c.* 6 m. E.): *St.Michael's Church* (Decorated), tower not completed until the 15C; inside there are some beau- tiful 17&18C tombs.

Market Overton (*c.* 8.5 m. E.): Excava- tions have revealed remains of a *Roman set- tlement* (ramparts; finds include many coins, now in the museum at Oakham).

Stapleford Park (*c.* 4.5 m.E.): A *house* rebuilt in the 17C (fascinating collection of paintings, period furniture and tapes- tries); in the grounds is the church of *St. Mary Magdalene*, rebuilt in neo-Gothic style in 1783; the choir contains an interest-

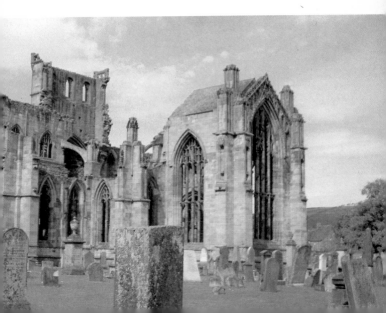

Melrose Abbey, ruined nave of church

ing marble sculpture (1732) by M.Rysbrack.

Teigh (c. 6.5 m. E.): *Holy Trinity Church* was rebuilt in Gothic style in 1782, original 14C tower (beautiful 18C furnishings).

Thistleton (c. 10 m. E.): *Church,* still with a beautiful round arch from a pre-Romanesque building of the 10C.

Whissendine (c. 5 m. SE): With *St. Andrew's Church,* Gothic, 14&15C; a richly decorated ceiling and the 16C screen in the S. transept.

Middlesbrough
Cleveland / England   p.328☐I 10

Middlesbrough owes its development, from a tiny village with 25 inhabitants to a town with a current population of some 150,000, to the iron ore discovered nearby in the early 19C. Together with its immediate neighbours, Ormesby, Thornaby, Stockton and Billingham, it forms the conurbation of 'Teesside' with a population of some 400,000.

Features of interest: *St.Hilda's Church* (Market Place), the town's parish church, built around 1830; *Old Town Hall* of 1846; *Custom House* of 1840; *Transporter Bridge* of 1911, the largest structure of its kind in the world; *Captain Cook Birthplace Museum* (in the Marton district, S. part of town), opened to commemorate the 250th anniversary of the birth of the great voyager and discoverer of Australia, James Cook (1728–79); containing mementoes and documents relating to his voyages of discovery; *Dorman Museum* (Linthorpe Road) with local natural history and archaeological collections.

Abbotsford House (Melrose)

Environs: Billingham (*c.* 1 m. N.): Of the original Saxon building of *St. Cuthbert's Church* only the 10C tower survives. The nave was rebuilt in the 12C. Inside is an interesting 17C font cover; pulpit of 1939.

Great Ayton (*c.* 5 m. S.): With the *Captain Cook Schoolroom Museum,* containing mementoes of the great navigator.

Guisborough (*c.* 6 m. SE): Remains of an *Augustinian monastery* founded by the Norman Robert de Brus in 1119 (Only the 13C E. end, with a richly decorated window, survives from the church; together with the 12C porter's lodge and a dovecote). Next to the priory ruins is the *Church of St. Nicholas,* built in the 15C, restored early 20C. Inside are remains of the old stained-glass windows and a 16C group of figures, which came here after the dissolution of the monastery.

Hartlepool (*c.* 7.5 m. N.): *St. Hilda's Church,* which takes its name from Hilda, who became the abbess of a Saxon nunnery here in 649, is mostly 12&13C, with a battlemented tower. Inside there is a beautiful font (1728). Also of interest is a section of the 13C *town walls* (in the E. of the town, near the sea) and the *Gray Museum* (local history; the *Art Gallery* contains works by English painters).

Kirkleatham (*c.* 5 m. E.): *St. Cuthbert's Church* rebuilt in 1763 at the same time as the patron of the church changed; the mausoleum of 1740 is by James Gibbs, also interesting works by the famous sculptors Peter Scheemakers and Henry Cheere.

Norton (*c.* 6 m. NW): The Saxon church of *St. Mary* (round arches on the tower and windows date back to this period); inside, stained-glass windows by C.E. Kempe, 1896; also note a 15C figure of a knight.

Ormesby: *Ormesby Hall* was built in the mid 18C and inside it has beautiful contemporary stucco.

Stockton (*c.* 1 m. W.): Market town since 1310. *St. Thomas's Church* (High Street) was completed in 1712, probably to plans by Sir Christopher Wren; inside is an interesting three-decker Georgian pulpit and choir screens made of oak from Cook's ship 'Endeavour'. Also of interest is the *Town Hall* of 1735 and (S. of the town) *Preston Hall* with an interesting museum (weapons and armour, also an original piece of the Stockton-Darlington railway).

Yarm (*c.* 7.5 m. SW): A once important stage-post on the road to the N.; interesting *Town Hall* (1710) and 14C *bridge* over the river Tees.

Minster/Isle of Sheppey
Kent/England   p.332□L 15

Abbey Church of St. Mary and St. Sexburgha:
This monastery near the coast is probably the oldest in England. It still serves as a good example of Saxon architecture. There are also two interesting 14C tombs here: those of Sir Robert Shurland and Lady Joan Northwode.

Monmouth
Gwent/Wales   p.332□H 14

This charming little town (pop. *c.* 7,000) at the confluence of the rivers Wye and Monnow probably stands on the site of the Roman fort of *Blestium* (no remains). The town developed around the 12C *castle* (few walls preserved) and in 1536 became the county town of Monmouthshire. Of interest is the well-preserved fortified gateway (town gate) on the bridge over the Monnow, the last surviving 13C structure of its kind in Britain.

St. Mary's Church: This church dates back to a Norman foundation of the 12C; however, only a Norman *half-column* with remnants of walls in the W. part of the nave and walls in the N. aisle (14C) survive from the original church. The rest is Victorian neo-Gothic (19C).

Also worth seeing: The Norman *Church of St. Thomas* (near the old Monnow bridge) has a beautiful arch between the nave and the choir from the original building. The *Naval Temple* was set up in 1800 in memory of Nelson's victory over the French at the Battle of the Nile (1798). Housed in the same building is a *Nelson Museum,* and also a local history collection. The founder was an admirer of Nelson, Lady Llangattock, mother of Charles S. Rolls (of Rolls-Royce fame), the town's most famous son, who in 1910 was the first to fly across the Channel and back, non-stop. The imposing *statue* in front of *Shire Hall* (18C) is dedicated to him.

Environs: Abbey Dore (*c.* 20 m. NW): In the valley of the river Dore lies the beautiful *church* of Abbey Dore. This dates back to a Cistercian abbey of 1147. The church has interesting capitals and sculptures; it was restored in 1634.

Grosmont (*c.* 15 m. NW): This town, with its small but highly interesting *ruined castle,* is a Norman foundation of around 1100. Of interest are the deep castle moat, remains of paving in the castle courtyard and a Gothic chimney (14C). The *parish church of St. Nicholas,* dating from the same time, still has original elements in the nave (*c.* 1240; Early English). The church was restored in 1868, with some alterations.

Skenfrith (*c.* 7.5 m. NW): Interesting *ruined castle,* which was founded around 1075 by the Norman conquerors of Wales; the remains still visible today date from around 1200, however. With the neighbouring castles of Grosmont and White Castle (see Abergavenny) it made up the

'Three Castles'of the Welsh Trilateral. The castle had four corner towers and was surrounded by a moat and the river Monnow. The *gatehouse* (few remains) leads into the *castle ward,* in the SW corner of which stands the circular *keep.* This was three-storeyed and the entrance on the middle floor was reached by ladders. Also of interest are the *postern* leading to the river, the circular *dungeons* and store rooms in the cellars of the corner towers, as well as remains of later *buildings* by the SW wall of the ward.

The adjacent old *church* (towards the village) was built in Early English Style, with Norman influence, around 1200. It is dedicated to the legendary Celtic St. Bridget (5C), whose symbols (acorn and oak leaves) appear on the lectern and in the sanctuary. From the early period date the tower, nave and choir. Also of interest are the stone altar of 1207, the E. window, with fragments of windows from the 15C, the stone basin to the right of the altar (13C), a sarcophagus in the N. aisle (16C) and pews from the 16–19C.

Morwenstow
Cornwall/England   p.330☐F 16

This tiny hamlet at the northernmost tip of Cornwall, directly above the Atlantic cliffs, was for over 40 years during the last century the home of Robert Stephen Hawker, who so well combined his religious duties as vicar with his poetical gifts.

Church of St.John: This Norman church still has superb original features. The Norman *portal* and the *N. arcade* are absolute masterpieces. Apart from chevron ornament, the arches on round columns have the most diverse forms of heads as decorations and, looking out from the arch spandrels, as if carved only yesterday, are hippopotami, antelopes and sheep heads. Whales and dolphins, dragons and mermaids, birds and humans—all giving stony testament to the fact that this is a church. The *barrel vault* and the *W. tower* (16C) are well suited to the superb Norman masonry.

Monmouth, bridge and gateway

Morwenstow, Celtic font

Environs: Kilkhampton (5 m. SE): The *Church of St. James* has a nave and two aisles and dates from Norman times. The nave and aisles each have a barrel vault of oak beams. The height of the W. tower is accentuated by the long, low nave. The S. portal is also Norman, the rest is Gothic. The finest item is the organ (1698), which was originally installed in Westminster Abbey. The ends of the pews (15&16C) are lavishly carved.

Stoke (9 m. N.): The church of *St.Nectan* is dedicated to a Welsh missionary. The Gothic tower, a good 130 ft. high, built directly above the cliffs, stands out like an exclamation mark in the landscape. The church was begun in the 14C and has a partly painted barrel vault, as well as an unusually beautiful traceried 15C choir screen. The Norman font is also particularly beautiful. Baptized heads look down from its four corners upon the raised, hope-filled heads of the unbaptized.

Much Wenlock
Salop/England   p.328☐H 13

This small town at the NE end of Wenlock Edge still makes a distinctly medieval impression.

Church of the Holy Trinity: This was founded in Anglo-Saxon times and enlarged around 1150. At that time it was mainly devoted to the cult of St.Milburga, granddaughter of King Penda of Mercia. At the saint's tomb in the church miracles are supposed to have occurred, which made the extension of the church possible. Penny Brookes, a pioneer of the modern Olympic Games, is also buried in the early Gothic church.

Wenlock Priory: This was founded as a nunnery by St.Milburga around 680. In 896 it was destroyed by the Danes; around 1050 Lady Godiva turned it into a semi nary. Shortly afterwards it was destroyed by the Normans, and Roger de Montgomery, Earl of Shropshire, re-founded the monastery around 1080 as a Cluniac priory, which was subordinate to the French mother house at La Charité-sur-Loire, to which it was obliged to pay tributes. The present ruins date from the 2nd half of the 11C and are transitional between the Norman and Early English styles. While the ruins of the *chapterhouse* are pure Norman, the *church* itself is Early English with Norman arches.

Environs: Bridgnorth (5 m. N.): This picturesque town is divided into an upper and lower town by the river Severn, the right bank of which is some 195 ft higher than the left bank. The *Church of St.Leonard* actually dates back to Norman times (traces on the S. tower), but it was almost completely rebuilt in neo-Gothic style from 1861 onwards. Only the 17C dragon-beam ceiling over the nave was retained. An interesting feature is the large number of old cast-iron memorial plaques. The *Church of St. Mary Magdalene* is a classical building, begun by Thomas Telford in 1792. The apse was added by Arthur Blomfield in 1876.

Coalbrookdale (c. 7.5 m. NE): The *Museum of Ironfounding* is devoted to the history of iron production and processing. Other sights include the smelting furnace which produced the iron for the Iron bridge.

Ironbridge (6 m. NE): The bridge over the Severn was England's first iron bridge. It was designed by T.F. Pritchard in 1774 and built in 1777-9. The bridge marks the start of industrial architecture and the use of iron on its own for construction.

Morville (3 m. SE): The church of *St. Gregory* is a small Norman church with a chancel arch from around 1110. Of particular interest are the font and the wrought iron decorations on the S. door, both 12C.

also an early-14C stained-glass window in the sanctuary.

Mull (I)
Strathclyde/Scotland   p.324☐E 7

The second largest island of the Inner Hebrides (over 250 m. of coastline) is of volcanic origin and, despite its size, still has barely more than 2,000 inhabitants.

Aros Castle: The ruins of this castle, lying right on the coast, was once the ancestral home of the Lords of the Isles. It was built as early as the 1st half of the 14C and was of strategic importance. The neighbouring coastal fortresses were each built so that they were in sight of one another and could communicate visually. In 1608 Lord Ochiltree arrived here to bring the rebellious Hebridean chieftains to reason. He managed this task using 'diplomatic' means, by inviting the chieftains on to his ship, capturing them and taking them to Edinburgh.

Duart Castle: The ancestral seat of the Clan MacLean dates back to the 13C and once served to control the traffic in the Firth of Lorn. The MacLeans obtained their seat back in 1390 through direct royal decree. In 1691 the Duke of Argyll had the castle set ablaze, and following the defeat at Culloden the castle and its lands were confiscated by the English Crown. In 1912 Sir Fitzroy MacLean bought back the dilapidated complex and restored it. It now houses an interesting collection of Scottish antiquities.

Moy Castle: The MacLaines of Loch Buie, relatives of the MacLeans of Duart, lived here until the late 18C and were mortal enemies of their kinsmen in Duart Castle. The castle, with casemates hewn out of the rock, has a prime example of a *bottle dungeon,* a bottle-shaped oubliette, the special refinement of which was its permanently flooded floor, the only dry spot being a little ledge cut out of the rock, upon which the prisoner could sit, but not lie.

Tobermory: The most beautiful Hebrid-

Much Wenlock, ruins of abbey

ean town, Tobermory was developed in the 18C as a fishing harbour. The houses, picturesquely placed around the bay, still largely retain their original form. At one time there were more than 10,000 inhabitants but there now remain only about 600. The little *Local Museum* offers an insight into the history of the island.

Mullingar
Westmeath/Ireland   p.326☐D 12

The county town (pop. *c.* 6,000) of Westmeath, set in a beautiful landscape of lakes and fields, has a modern *Church of Christ the King* (1936).

Environs: Ballymore (*c.* 9 m. W.): In front of the village lies the Celtic, preChristian royal seat *Hill of Ushnagh* with remains of tombs, houses and earth forts.
Ballynacarrigy (*c.* 7.5 m. NW): To the W. are the remains of the Cistercian monastery of *Abbeyshrule* from around 1200; the choir, tower and a cross survive.
Belvedere House (*c.* 5.5 m. S.): At Lough Ennell stands the beautiful *house* of the Earl of Belvedere, dating from 1742; fine rococo interior.
Bunbrosna (*c.* 8 m. NW): To the N. are the remains of the Franciscan *Multyfarnham Friary* with a ruined church and tower (15C).
Castlepollard (*c.* 10.5 m. N.): Nearby is *Tullynally Castle* (17C) with neo-Gothic alterations (1806); set in beautiful parkland.
Crookedwood (*c.* 5.5 m. N.): *Taghmon Church* (14C), with nave, choir and fourstoreyed fortified tower is a remnant from an old monastery.
Delvin (*c.* 12 m. NE): Ruins of *Delvin Castle* (12&13C, badly-preserved).
Fore Abbey (*c.* 13 m. NE): The church ruins date back to an early Christian monastery founded by St. Feichin (*c.* 630). *St. Feichin's Church* (13C) survives with elements from the 7C. Nearby are remains of a *Benedictine Abbey* with church, cloister and fortifications with towers (13–15C).

Much Wenlock, Church of the Holy Trinity

The font is Norman, while the choir stalls were not completed until the 17C.

Bunbury (*c.* 11 m. NW): The *Church of St. Boniface* originated as a collegiate church in the 14 and early 15C and has a W. tower. It contains numerous tombs, including an alabaster monument to Sir G. Beeston and Sir R. Egerton. Screens and doors are 16C, while everything else dates from the restoration after the last war.

Whitchurch (*c.* 13 m. SW): This small town was founded by the Romans, who called it *Mediolanum.* In the 12C the Normans built a white church, after which the town was called Blancminster. The name survived long after the disappearance of the white church and the *Church of St. Alkmund* is the fourth church to be built on the site. The third collapsed in 1711, making way for the new building by William Smith of Warwick (1713–15). He tried to achieve a Grecian style, which is in fact only realized in the imposing W. tower. The interior has massive columns and a gallery but fails to make a harmonious impression. The church is of importance owing to the tombs surviving from predecessors, including that of the 1st Earl of Shrewsbury (1388–1453), who appears as Old John Talbot in Shakespeare's 'King Henry VI'. The 17C font is adorned with a Tudor rose.

Nantwich

Cheshire/England   p.328□H 13

This small town was popular with the Romans for its brine springs. Nearly all its buildings were destroyed by a fire in 1583, following which it was rebuilt in Elizabethan style.

Church of St. Mary: This church, with cruciform ground plan and octagonal tower, is early Gothic with high Gothic parts. Although restored in the 19C, some fine features survive. Note the 14C *choir stalls,* the canopies of which are as remarkable as the beautiful misericords. Superb stone *pulpit* (14C).

Church's Mansion: This half-timbered house dates from the early 16C and survived the great fire. It is an excellent example of a merchant's house of the period. Some of the furnishings are still Elizabethan; the oak panelling is outstanding.

Environs: Acton (*c.* 2 m. NW): The *Church of St. Mary* is 13&14C, the upper part of the tower was rebuilt in 1757. Of interest are the various tombs, including a 14C tomb with the figure of a knight and a tomb with 2 figures from around 1650.

Navan/An Uaimh
Meath/Ireland   p.326□D 11

The capital of County Meath ('middle'), with about 4,000 inhabitants, lies at the confluence of the Boyne and Blackwater rivers. The town has scant traces of an Anglo-Norman *castle* (walls) and a Catholic *cathedral* of 1836 with a figure of Christ by E.Smith (*c.* 1792).

Environs: Athlumney Castle (or Dowdall Castle, *c.* 2 m. SE): The ruins, with a four-storey tower, date from the 15C. Adjacent is a 17C Tudor-style *house* with a beautiful gable.

Donaghmore (*c.* 1 m. N.): The monastery ruins are supposed to date back to a foundation by St.Patrick. An interesting round tower with a restored conical roof (11 or 12C), Romanesque portal and a group of figures is preserved. The neighbouring *church* dates from the 15C (memorial plaques). Nearby (to the E.) is the four-storey *Dunmoe Castle* (15C).

Slane (*c.* 8 m. NE): It was here that St. Patrick lit the first Easter bonfire in 433 to signify the successful conversion of the Irish. *Slane Friary,* a Franciscan house built around 1522 (on the site of older buildings) has a monastery church with a W. tower and an equally old priests' college (S.tower). *Slane Castle* is a beautiful neo-Gothic castle, built by J.Wyatt in 1785 on the site of a ruined castle.

Nenagh
Tipperary/Ireland   p.326□C 12

This agricultural centre with about 4,500 inhabitants has a ruined Norman *castle* from 1207 — a gatehouse with flanking towers and an interesting round keep with restored battlements (1860) survive. The refuge tower has a diameter of about 50 ft.

with walls 16 ft. thick, and is one of the finest towers of its kind in Ireland. Remains of a 13C Franciscan monastery are to be found in the old cemetery (Abbey Street).

Environs: *Lough Derg* ('Red Lake'), which stretches for some 23 m. along the Shannon, lies W. of Nenagh.

Inis Cealtra (or 'Holy Island', *c.* 18.5 m. W.): An island in Lough Derg with the remains of a *monastery* founded by St Caimin in the 7C. Of interest are the ruins of 4 chapels, the well-preserved, 82 ft. high round tower, a *pilgrimage spring,* 2 Celtic *crosses* (Cross of Cathasach) and the *graveyard* with old Irish funerary inscriptions.

Killaloe (9 m. SW): This village at the S. end of Lough Derg has a well-preserved (now Protestant) *parish church* dating from 1200 (St.Flannan's Cathedral). Note the Romanesque door (S. portal) with pilasters and sculptures (foliage, animal and human heads). Next to it is the stone shaft of a cross (10C) with bilingual inscriptions in Runes and Ogham. In the churchyard is the 12C Romanesque *St.Flannan's Oratory* with a steep stone roof. The *Oratory of St.Molua* (12C) in the Catholic churchyard, also with a stone roof, was moved from an island in the Shannon that was submerged. It was reconstructed here in its original form. Near the village is the Protestant *Bishop's Palace* (19C) and (*c.* 1 m. N.) *Beal Boru,* a massive prehistoric earthwork fortification.

Portumna (*c.* 15 m. N., at the N. end of Lough Derg): The Dominican *Portumna Abbey* was built around 1426 and its remains include the church of St.Mary (13C windows in the N. and S. walls), the cloister and the abbey buildings. At the S. end of the village are the ruins of *Portumna Castle* (1618), which was destroyed by fire in 1826. The castle, with a rectangular ground plan and 4 corner towers, has a beautiful view over Lough Derg. Nearby (to the N.) is the well preserved *Derry*

Killaloe (Nenagh)

hiveny Castle of 1643 with beautiful corner towers.
Tuamgraney (near Scarriff, on the W. shore of Lough Derg, *c.* 18.5 m. W.): 10C *village church*, 12C additions.

Newark-on-Trent
Nottinghamshire/England   p.328☐K 13

Church of St.Mary Magdalene: Begun in 1167 (from which time dates the still uncompleted *crypt*); the lower part of the *c.* 270 ft. high *tower* is Early English, the rest is Decorated. Nave, aisles, transepts and choir are Perpendicular and date from the late 15C. Of particular interest inside is the splendid *E. window* with remnants of medieval stained glass. Also of interest are the *choir screen*, the *choir stalls* of 1500 and *wall paintings* ('Dance of Death').

Museum and Art Gallery (Appleton Gate): The town museum is housed in the former Grammar School of 1529. The displays cover archaeology and local history (remains of a Roman cavalry helmet, Anglo-Saxon funeral urns and 17C coins).

Also worth seeing: The *castle,* built by the Normans in 1125, was greatly altered in succeeding years (King John died here in 1216; still standing, among other features, is the Romanesque gatehouse). *Beaumont Cross* (Carter Gate) of 1290, at the crossing of two old roads (Newark lies on the 'Foss Way', the longest Roman road in England). *Queen's Sconce* (in the S. of the town), remains of the defensive works from the Civil War.

Environs: Brant Broughton (*c.* 7 m. E.): *St.Helen's Church* (14C; late Gothic clerestory, Decorated tower; choir rebuilt during restoration in 1876).

Hawton (*c.* 3 m. S.): *All Saints' Church* has a splendid early-14C choir; of particular interest inside are the superb Easter sepulchre and the richly decorated sedilia (clerics' seats incorporated in the wall) on the S. side of the choir.

Kelham (*c.* 2.5 m. NW): The church of *St.Wilfrid* contains the interesting tomb of Lord Lexington (d. 1723). Also note the 19C neo-Gothic *Kelham Hall*.

Southwell (*c.* 6 m. W.) The interesting *Minster* dates from 1108, when an Anglo-Saxon church was rebuilt (fragments in the N. transept above the portal), and it is now a cathedral; beautiful Romanesque W. portal, magnificent Early English choir. Interesting features inside include the large E. window (with some old glass from a Templar chapel in Paris); also the remarkable 13C chapterhouse (its high Gothic decoration is unique in England). S. of the cathedral are the remains of the former *palace* of the archbishops of York, built in 1360.

Thurgarton (*c.* 7.5 m. SW): With the

former monastery church of *St.Peter* (remains of an Augustinian monastery from around 1140).

Newbury
Berkshire/England   p.332☐I 15

This town on the old Kennet-Avon Canal stands on land, which was settled in prehistoric times. It first began to flourish when John Winchcombe, alias Jack of Newbury, stimulated the local cloth trade with his own factory. By around 1520 he had set up over 200 looms with over 1,000 employees, making him England's first real industrial manufacturer. He proved his sense of patriotism when he led 150 of his men at the Battle of Flodden Field in 1513. During the Civil War there were two battles near the town. Lord Falkland fell in the first in 1643 (monument S. of the town), the second took place at the gatehouse of Donnington Castle.

Borough Museum: The county museum is housed in the Jacobean *Cloth Hall*. It is devoted to local archaeology and natural history, as well as mementoes of the Civil War, and offers a broad view of the methods of the clothing industry in the 17C.

Environs: Sandleford Priory (*c.* 2 m. S.): The former *Augustinian priory* was rebuilt in the 18C by Adam and Wyatt, with Capability Brown laying out the *garden*. It is now a school.

Wickham (9 m. NW): The church of *St.Swithin* has a tower made of cob (pebbles and mortar), built back in Anglo-Saxon times. The furnishings are by Benjamin Ferry and were completed in 1849. The papier-maché elephants which adorn the roof of the aisle were exhibited at the Paris World Exhibition of 1862.

Newbury, Borough Museum

MUSEUM

Newcastle upon Tyne
Tyne and Wear/England   p.328□l 10

Settled by the Romans as *Pons Aelii,* which was on Hadrian's Wall and called *Monkchester* by the Anglo-Saxons, the present city was founded by the Normans in the 11C. Most of the streets of the inner city were laid out in the early 19C by Richard Grainger to plans by John Dobson).

St.Nicholas's Cathedral (Collingwood St.):Built in Gothic style in the 14&15C; parish church of the city up to 1882 (one of the largest in England), since when it has been a bishop's seat. There is a battlemented *tower* (called the 'Scottish Crown'; the first of its kind in England) rising nearly 200 ft. and built in 1442. Of interest within are the *font cover,* a *lectern* (both from around 1500) and *sculptures* from the 15&16C and the present day (works by Flaxman, Baily, Theed).

Castle (St. Nicholas Street): The first, Norman castle was built by Robert Curthose (son of William the Conqueror). A new one was built in 1172-7 under Henry II (from which time the *keep* still dates). The *Black Gate* of 1247, originally the main gate of the castle, now houses the world's only Bagpipe Museum.

High Level Bridge (over the river Tyne): The city's emblem, built in 1846-9 by Robert Stephenson (son of the builder of the 'Rocket'). A pioneering technical achievement for its age, it is a two-level cast-iron road and rail bridge on brick pillars, about 160 ft. high.

University (Victoria Road): Founded in 1963, it contains a series of interesting *museums:*
Department of Mining Engineering, with a large collection of exhibits relating to mining; also worth seeing are paintings by T.H. Hair devoted to regional coal mines around 1830-40.
Greek Museum (Percy Building), with an interesting collection of Greek and Etruscan works (particularly ceramics, jewellery and weapons).
Hatton Gallery, with an extensive collection of works by European painters of the 14-18C, also paintings and drawings by modern English artists.
Museum of Antiquaries of the University and Society of Antiquities, one of the oldest collection of antiquities in the country (founded 1813) with objects from prehistoric (particularly Bronze Age), Roman (including some from Hadrian's Wall) and Anglo-Saxon sites. There is a highly informative model of Hadrian's Wall and a full-size reconstruction of a temple of Mithras.

Hancock Museum (N. of the university): Natural history museum, going back to the collections of Marmaduke Tunstall of Wycliffe, who died in 1790. Of particular interest are the ethnological department (including objects from the Pacific region

Newcastle uopn Tyne, Cathedral

and Africa; some from Cook's voyages) and the collection of ancient Egyptian mummies (a remarkable death mask of a young woman from Thebes, amongst others).

Laing Art Gallery and Museum (on the corner of Dobson Street/New Bridge Street): Picture gallery with oil paintings by English masters since the 18C; the watercolour collection offers a survey of the development of this technique in England. There is a major work by Sir Edward Burne-Jones, 'Laus Veneris'. Also of interest is the collection of old engravings and etchings. The adjacent *Higham Place Gallery* is used for temporary exhibitions.

Museum of Science and Engineering (Exhibition Park): Specialist museum on the history of mining, shipbuilding and mechanical engineering in NE England. Of particular interest are George Stephenson's locomotive of 1830 (built for the coal pits of Killingeorth) and the world's first turbine-engined ship ('Turbinia', built by Charles Parsons, 1894).

Also worth seeing: *All Saints' Church* (Sandhill), built in classical style in the late 18C (inside is a beautiful memorial plaque of 1429).—*Plummer Tower* (Croft Street), a remnant of the city's medieval fortifications (altered in classical style in the 18C; small *museum* inside). *Central Station*, the city's main station, built by J.Dobson in 1850. *Guildhall* (Sandhill) 16C, converted in 1796. *Theatre Royal* (Grey St.), 1830. *John G. Joicey Museum* (City Road), housed in the 17C *Holy Jesus Hospital*, with collections relating to the city's history.

Environs: Belsay (*c.* 12 m. NW): Beautiful Georgian *house*, incorporating a 14C *tower.*

Bolam (*c.* 15 m. NW): *St.Andrew's Church* (Romanesque, Anglo-Saxon W. tower; inside is a mutilated stone figure of a cross-legged knight).

Bothal (*c.* 12 m. N.): *St.Andrew's Church* from the 13&14C (containing remains of medieval stained glass and 16C alabaster figures).

Newcastle upon Tyne, Tyne Bridge

Causey Arch (*c.* 6 m. SW): The world's oldest *railway bridge,* built in 1727.

Cullercoats (*c.* 7.5 m. NE): *St. George's Church* (beautiful, tall tower), built by John Loughborough Pearson in 1884.

Ebchester (*c.* 11 m. SW): This village lies on the site of the Roman fort of *Vindomora* (Roman altar preserved).

Gibside Chapel (*c.* 7.5 m. SW): Georgian *Mausoleum* in the form of a Greek temple, built by James Pame in 1760 (church since 1812).

Heddon-on-the-Wall (*c.* 7.5 m. W.): With a good section of *Hadrian's Wall* (W. of the village).

Jarrow (*c.* 5 m. E.): *St.Paul's Church* was consecrated in 683 as the church of the monastery in which the historian the Venerable Bede died in 735 (there is still a glass window dating back to that time; the ruins themselves date from the 11C). There are interesting finds in the *Hall Museum* (1785).

Kirkwhelpington (*c.* 17.5 m. NW): *St. Bartholomew's Church* (12&13C; 14C, destruction of transepts and aisles; 18C, rebuilding of choir; beautiful stucco inside).

Morpeth (*c.* 12 m. N.): *St.Mary's Church* has a 'Jesse Window' at the E. end dating from the time of its building.

Ovingham (*c.* 10 m. W.): The church of *St.Mary the Virgin* (Romanesque W. tower, Gothic chancel and N. transept; beautiful lancet windows; interesting remnants of 14C stained glass).

Seaton Delaval (*c.* 8 m. NE): With the originally Anglo-Saxon church of *St.Mary* (13C W. tower and choir; of interest within are the font from the same period and the 16C pulpit). Behind the church is the splendid baroque house, *Seaton Delaval Hall* (a major work by Sir John Vanbrugh; restored in 1959 - 62). It contains fine period furniture and paintings by English masters such as Reynolds.

South Shields (*c.* 7.5 m. E.): Excavations of the Roman fort of *Arbeia* at the the E. end of Hadrian's Wall (interesting *museum*) and a *town museum* with a model of the first lifeboat, built by W. Woodhave in 1789.

Tynemouth (*c.* 6 m. NE): Remains of a *monastery* founded in the 7C (11&12C ruined church, 14C gatehouse).

Wallington (*c.* 17.5 m. NW): *House,* built in 1688 and altered in the 18&19C (contains interesting rococo stucco, as well as interesting collections of period furniture and porcelain).

New Lanark
Strathclyde/Scotland   p.324□G 9

The accumulation of cotton mills and workers' houses in the Clyde valley towards the end of the 18C is a special kind of monument to the Industrial Revolution in Britain. *Lanark Mills* was Scotland's first mechanical cotton mill, in which a water-powered spinning-machine built by Richard Arkwright was working in 1785. Towards the end of the 18C Scotland's largest cotton mill stood here, and it was as explosive socially as it was perfect technically. It was in this environment that Robert Owen, Britain's first practical socialist, found the ideal site for his activities. He saw to it that every working family had at least two living rooms and that the workers received free medical care and pension funds. With a co-operatively run shop he was able to offer the workers low prices, and in 1816 he finally built Britain's first primary school for workers' children—at a time when child labour was considered perfectly normal. He achieved all these social endeavours, not from the position of a worker, but from that of an employer. Instead of pure exploitation he attempted to offer his workers a decent living. His model estate on the Clyde was so famous at the start of the 19C that from 1815–25 alone it received over 20,000 visitors, including Tsar Nicholas. In 1825 Owen finally changed from employer to socialist, sold his factory and devoted himself to the trade union movement. An extensive restoration programme is currently trying to preserve the estate as an example of that period of industrial and social history.

Environs: Biggar (*c.* 12.5 m. SE): The *Gladstone Court Street Museum* has a complete reconstruction of a Victorian shopping street.

Craignethan Castle (*c.* 7 m. NW): This was once the ancestral home of the Hamilton clan. The castle dates from the 15&16C; in 1579 it was destroyed by the Protestants. A tower house with wall decorations, a tower and remains of outbuildings survive.

Newport/Casnewydd
Gwent/Wales   p.332□H 15

This industrial port with some 130,000 inhabitants lies at the mouth of the river Usk on the Bristol Channel.

St. Woolos' Cathedral: The principal church of the diocese of Monmouth has an unusual ground plan. The interior, with a nave and two aisles, is 12C Norman, with an ornamented *sanctuary* and beautiful Norman *portals* with sculpted *columns* (reputedly from Roman Caerleon nearby). Also of interest are the *font,* a few *tombs* and *sculptures; St.Mary's Chapel* between the nave and the massive square W. *tower* (15C).

Castle: A ruin, although the exterior is in quite good condition; it was founded by the Normans (Robert Fitz-Hamon, 1172); in the 13–15C the E. front in particular was rebuilt on several occasions. There is a *central tower* with a chapel on an upper storey and a water gate (formerly for entrance by boat). The *Bridge Tower* has Decorated windows.

Museum/Art Gallery (Dock Street): This has an interesting collection of Roman finds from the Roman forts of Caerleon and Caerwent; also local works and sculptures.

Also worth seeing: The *Transporter Bridge* (model in the museum) was built across the river Usk in 1906 as an electric 'ferry bridge' (unaffected by tides and storms). The only similar structure is at Middlesbrough.

Environs: Caerleon (*c.* 2.5 m. N.): Interesting remains of the former *Roman camp.* The fort was laid out under the name of *Isca* around AD 75 and was the largest legionary camp in Wales; until the 4C it was the headquarters of the II Legio Augusta. 10 cohorts (*c.* 5,000 soldiers) were stationed here along with civilian followers; there was a town with taverns, shops and an *amphitheatre* outside the fort. This was built around the same time as the Colosseum in Rome (*c.* AD 80), was equipped with grass pitches and a sand arena for gladiator combats and held around 5,000 spectators (sparse remains survive). Of the barracks, the foundation walls of 4 buildings give an impression of the ground plan; also remains of the enclosing rampart, a latrine with drainage in the W., as well as fireplaces and watch towers (remains of 5 ft. thick walls). Of the town there remains nothing other than a few *tombstones.* According to legend this was the home of King Arthur's famous Round Table. The historian Giraldus Cambrensis described the remains of the Roman settlement as 'splendid'. The *museum* (on the site of Roman officers' living quarters) houses an interesting collection of finds, including surgical instruments, dice, playing pebbles, earthenware, furnishings and a model of a legionary in full armour. Opposite the museum is *St. Cadoc's Church,* built in Gothic neo-Perpendicular style in 1867.

Dunbrody Abbey (New Ross)

New Ross
Wexford/Ireland   p.330☐D 13

This small town and former port at the N. end of the Barrow estuary dates back to a Norman trading settlement founded in about 1200. Remains of the early Gothic *St.Mary's Church* from the 13C with 15C alterations are to be seen in the present cemetery. The interesting *Tholsel* (Town Hall) was built in 1749 and rebuilt in 1806 (octagonal dome). The Catholic *central church* with a beautiful pietà by Hogan is 19C.

Environs: Craiguenamanagh (c. 9 m. N.): This old Cistercian *monastery* was founded around 1207 and was one of the largest in Ireland. The church was built around 1230, but fell into disrepair and was greatly altered when restored in the 19C (portal to cloister or baptistery survives).
Dunbrody Abbey (c. 9 m. S.): One of Ireland's most beautiful *Cistercian abbeys,* it was founded around 1175, dissolved in 1539 (at the Dissolution) and badly damaged during the peasant uprising in 1798. The nearly 200 ft. long cruciform *church* is dominated by a massive 15C central tower. Of interest are the Gothic windows and the filigree on the W. door. Next to the monastery church are remains of the former monastery buildings (to the E. chapterhouse and library, to the S. refectory and kitchens).

Dunganstown (c. 3 m. S.): Site of the *cottage* of the ancestors of U.S. President John F. Kennedy. Following his assassination a *memorial park* was laid out in 1968 with over 6,000 species of plants.

St.Mullins (c. 6 m. N.): Remains of the

Northampton, Church of St. Peter

medieval monastery of *St. Moling* (Round Tower, cross etc.).

Ullard (*c.* 12 m. N.): Here lie the interesting remains of a 12C *church* (16C rebuilding) with Romanesque elements. On a stone slab (originally part of a portal) are reliefs of the church's patron saints; also a beautiful granite cross (behind the church) with incised Biblical scenes.

Newry
County Down / N. Ireland   p.326□E 11

This little harbour on the long Newry estuary lies on a site of age-old strategic importance. Scarcely any traces of the *castle* of 1180 survive. The tower of *St. Patrick's Church,* one of Ireland's first Protestant churches (1578), dates from a medieval

church. Also attractive Georgian and 19C *buildings,* including the Court-House.

Environs: Derrymore House (*c.* 1776): This house is the seat of an Irish earl, with the historically important *Treaty Room* (county assembly of 1921).

Greencastle (*c.* 17 m. SE): A 13C *coastal castle* occupying a strategically important site (destroyed by Cromwell, 1652).

Killevy (*c.* 3 m. SW): E. of Slieve Gullion (mountain, 1,880 ft.) are two early medieval ruined *churches* with beautiful W. portals and E. windows. On the mountain peak are remains of prehistoric *tombs* (passage tomb). Further prehistoric traces to the W. of Slieve Gullion and to the S. near Killeen.

Moiry Castle (*c.* 6 m. S.): SW of Killeen lie the ruins of this *border fortress* (*c.* 1600), with a square tower.

Narrow Water Castle (*c.* 4.5 m. SE): The ruins lie on a rocky island at the mouth of the river Newry. They consist of a tall rectangular tower with a rampart (*c.* 1560), and traces of a look-out fort of 1212.

Rostrevor (*c.* 9 m. SE): On Slievemartin (good views, 1,595 ft.) lies the *round granite stone of Cloughmore* (*c.* 30 tons). Legend has it that the giant Finn MacCoul hurled it at his enemy Benandonner.

Newtownards
County Down / N. Ireland   p.326□E 10

This little town to the N. of Strangford Lough has beautiful 17&18C buildings (*Market House, Town Hall* with dome). In Court Street are the ruins of the *Dominican priory* of 1244 with church and tower (17C).

Environs: Bangor (*c.* 5 m. N.): This seaside resort is N. Ireland's third-largest town with some 41,000 inhabitants. It is also the site of what was once one of the largest and most important early Christian *monasteries* (scarcely any traces), which was founded by St.Congall around 555. This was a base for the conversion of the British Isles and parts of Central Europe (e.g. St.Gallus, founder of St.Gallens, Switzerland).

Greyabbey (*c.* 6 m. SE): An interesting ruined monastery (1193) in the N. part of the Ards peninsula. There is a cruciform, single-aisled monastery church with beautiful Gothic choir windows and W. portal, also remains of the chapterhouse and refectory. Just to the N. are the interesting *Mount Stewart Gardens,* which the Marquess of Londonderry had laid out from 1921 onwards. The buildings date from the 18&19C.

Kirkistown Castle (*c.* 17.5 m. SE): This was built as a sturdy *tower house* by the earls Savage around 1622. Nearby are the ruins of the *Derry Churches,* two 8 – 12C churches, built on Celtic remnants.

Nendrum (*c.* 7.5 m. S.): Interesting ruins of an early Celtic *monastery* (St.Mochua) of the 5 or 6C were discovered here, with remains of a concentric series of cells, chapel and Round Tower. The 12C elements date back to a medieval Benedictine monastery; nearby, the remains of the 15&16C *Nendrum Castle.*

Portaferry (*c.* 15 m. SE): This town at the mouth of Strangford Lough has a 16C *castle. Portaferry House* (with a beautiful ascent) dates from 1790; *Court House* of 1800.

Northampton
Northamptonshire/England   p.328☐ I 14

The county town of Northamptonshire no longer shows its true age, a great fire having reduced almost the whole town to ashes in 1675 (over 600 houses). The settlement on the N. bank of the Nene dates back to Saxon times. Simon de Senlis seized the Saxon fortress for the Normans, who

Northampton, Church of St.Peter

turned it into an important stronghold. The court which condemned Thomas à Becket took place here in 1164. In 1460 one of the decisive battles in the Wars of the Roses was fought outside the town walls, resulting in the capture of Henry VI. Charles II had the castle and fortifications razed as the town had sided with Parliament during the Civil War.

Church of the Holy Sepulchre: This is one of only four round churches in England and was built between 1100 and 1115. The 8 Norman *columns* bear 14C arches, but date themselves from the original phase of building. The church was modelled on the Church of the Holy Sepulchre in Jerusalem, at the instigation of Simon de Senlis. The present *nave* was built in the 13&14C as an extension of the Norman choir, the present *choir* was built in 1860-4 under Sir Giles Gilbert Scott.

Church of St.Peter: The town's second church from Norman times was built around 1160 and is one of the most beautiful late Norman churches in England. The *portal* in the W. façade is as richly embellished as the *capitals* inside. The massive *arches* are impressive, particularly that of the W. tower. The *shaft of a cross* inside dates back to Saxon times.

All Saints' Church: This large church in the town centre dates back to medieval times, but was completely gutted by fire in 1675 and thereafter rebuilt. Of the old church there remain only the *crypt* beneath the sanctuary and the lower part of the *tower*, which acquired its new dome in 1704. The *portico* with Ionic columns on the W. façade contains a statue of Charles II, by John Hunt (1712). The interior also has Ionic columns. *Font* and *pulpit* dates from about 1680.

Town Hall: This was built from 1861-4 by Edward William Godwin in Venetian Gothic style. The two-storey building has a campanile and a turreted gable and is adorned with numerous sculptures and statues of English kings and patron saints. The wing added by Matthew Holding in 1889 - 92 is also adorned with such sculptures.

Museum and Art Gallery: The museum, housed in the Town Hall, contains an interesting archaeological collection, with exhibits reaching back to the early Iron Age. There is also a geological collection, as well as a survey of the development of techniques and fashion in shoemaking (including the wedding shoes of Queen Victoria).

Environs: Althorp (7.5 m. NW): This house, dating back to medieval times, became the seat of the Spencer family in 1508, who altered it in 1573 and 1733. It acquired its present form through Henry Holland in 1787. Its picture gallery was begun by Robert Spencer, 2nd Earl of Sunderland (1640-1702) with works by Dutch and Italian masters. There is now a famous collection of paintings and furniture to be seen. Of particular note are the portraits by van Dyck, Lely, Kneller, Reynolds (18 by him alone) and Gainsborough.

Castle Ashby (8 m. E.): This Elizabethan *house* was begun in 1574 and was the ancestral home of the Compton family, members of whom became Marquesses of Northampton. The house, completed in 1635, acquired a S. wing designed by Inigo Jones. The interior dates from between 1600 and 1635 and includes fine stucco, panelling, stairs and fireplaces. Exquisite furniture and tapestries render the house as interesting as the collection of paintings, with works by Dutch, Italian and English artists. The *gardens* were landscaped by Capability Brown.

Church Stowe (c. 12 m. W.): The *Church of St.Michael* still has a Saxon W. tower and a Norman entrance. Although extensively rebuilt and altered, the interior still contains a few unusual monuments, above all a 13C figure of a cross-legged knight. There is an outstanding marble figure carved around 1620 by Nicholas Stone for the tomb of Lady Carey. Another interesting monument is that of Dr. Turner, President of Corpus Christi College, Oxford, who died in 1714; there are two life-size figures by Thomas Stayner, one standing on a celestial, the other on an earthly globe.

Earls Barton (c. 8 m. NE): *All Saints' Church* with its famous W. tower is one of the most interesting of Saxon buildings. The 10C tower was for a time part of the defences of the neighbouring Norman castle. The tower is adorned with a series of arches and two rows of zigzag fillets. No models for this kind of decoration have yet been found. Also dating from Saxon times is the lower part of the original W. entrance. A sanctuary and a small nave were built on to the tower in Norman times. In the 14&15C the church was extended and in the 15C the tower acquired its crenellations.

North Elmham
Norfolk/England   p.328□ L 13

Although it is no longer apparent, this small town was the seat of a bishopric founded in 673 and from 956 to 1075 it was the only bishopric in East Anglia. Later, the seat moved to Thetford and finally to Norwich. At the start of the 11C the Saxons built a *cathedral* here, the remains of which, behind the parish church, are visible, as are the foundations of the bishop's palace.

St. Mary's Church: This dates back to 1093 and was built as an atonement church. Although the church was later greatly altered, there is still a Norman *window* on the S. side. Also of interest is the partly painted *choir screen* and fragments of the 14C *stained glass*.

Environs: East Dereham (6 m. S.): The cruciform church of *St. Nicholas* has a beautiful tower over the crossing and a free-standing, unfinished 16C bell tower. The church was founded by St. Withburga, who is buried next to the bell tower. The present church is mainly Gothic, although there are Norman fragments. The ceilings in the N. and S. side chapels are finely painted. The font, embellished with the symbols of the Seven Sacraments, dates from 1468. The stained glass is 19C. The church contains the tomb of the poet William Cowper, whose monument is by John Flaxman (1802).

Elsing (6 m. SE): *St. Mary's Church* was built by Sir Hugh Hastings around 1330. The single-aisled church has an octagonal font with a painted cover. A superb brass commemorating the church's founder, who died in 1347, is the most interesting detail.

Tittleshall (8 m. W.): *St. Mary's Church* is partly early Gothic, partly Gothic. The church is of interest due to the numerous monuments to the Coke family, all of which are by excellent artists. Nicholas

Northampton, Church of St. Peter, arch

Stone made Sir Edward Coke's (1634), and his wife's, (Bridget Paston, 1598), Louis Roubiliac made the 1st Earl of Leicester's (1760) and Joseph Nollekens made a certain Mrs. Coke's (1800).

Norwich
Norfolk/England   p.328☐L 13

The county town of Norfolk was founded by the Saxons. Despite being destroyed by the Danes under Sweyn Forkbeard, by the start of the 10C it was again so important that the name Northwic was stamped on the coins of King Athelstan (925–40). In the 11C it was the seat of the Earl of East Anglia and in 1094 Norwich became a bishop's seat. From 1294 to 1320 the two and a half miles of *town walls* were built —these were the equal of London's.

Over the centuries there was occasional unrest, but the city was never really destroyed, which explains its maze of alleys. It was not until the last war that a few buildings were lost, but these losses were minor compared with those due to modernization. The castle, cathedral and many of the 32 pre-Reformation churches are well-preserved.

Cathedral: The bishop's seat of East Anglia can look back on a long history. It was founded in 630 by Felix of Burgundy in Dunwich. The seat finally came to Norwich, via North Elmham and Thetford, through Bishop Herbert de Losinga in 1094. Two years later Losinga began the building of the cathedral and by the time of his death in 1110 the choir, transepts, the E. part of the nave and the lower part of the tower had been completed. His successor, Bishop Eborard, completed the great nave in 1145. There was a major setback in 1272 when the townsfolk rose up against the bishop and set fire to the cathedral. In the mid 14C Bishop Percy built a new clerestory in the choir, and a century

later Bishop Alnwick altered the W. façade and completed the cloister. In the 2nd half of the 15C the nave and choir acquired their stone vaulting and the tower received its present spire. The cathedral suffered quite badly during the Reformation, but some items were saved during the restoration that followed.

The impressive exterior of the 440 ft. long church with its 345 ft. high *spire* (only Salisbury's is higher) is distinguished by its enormous ridged *roof,* the mighty Norman lower part of the tower and the Norman *arcades* on the E. side of the S. transept. The contrast between the large Gothic *windows* in the W. façade and the flanking Norman *towers* has a charm of its own.

The cathedral interior, with the exception of the roof, offers a rare example of a largely unaltered Norman church. The massive Norman *columns* of the nave's 14 bays, together with the light colour of the stone, create a lightness which is rare in Norman buildings. Equally unusual is the fact that the arches of the *triforium* are the same size as those of the *main arcades,* and that the *clerestory* still has its Norman windows. The *aisles* are also still entirely Norman. Only the *Prior's Door,* which leads from the easternmost bay to the cloister, is Gothic. The 15C vaulting of the nave is also Gothic.

Most unusual are the superb *bosses,* which depict scenes from the Old and New Testaments and only reveal their true beauty when seen through binoculars. On the E. side of the N. transept is the apse-like *St. Andrew's Chapel,* the stained-glass windows of which still date from the 15C. The Madonna is by John Skelton. The *choir* incorporates the three easternmost bays of the nave, and the screen is 15C. The extension of the choir E. of the crossing is another unique feature of this church, inspired by French models. Of particular interest is the position of the former *Bishop's Throne* behind the altar. This ar-

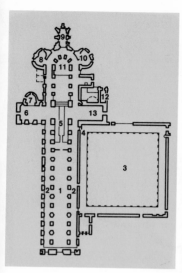

Norwich Cathedral 1 nave **2** aisles **3** cloister **4** Prior's Door **5** choir **6** N. transept **7** St.Andrew's Chapel **8** Jesus Chapel **9** St.Saviour's Chapel **10** St.Luke's Chapel **11** altar **12** sacristy **13** S. transept

Norwich Cathedral

rangement was only usual up until around the end of the 10C. The throne itself dates from the 8C and may have been brought from Dunwich by Bishop Losinga. At the E. end of the two choir aisles are almost circular *side chapels*. On the NE side is the *Jesus Chapel*, on the SE side *St. Luke's Chapel*, with the two *altarpieces*, donated to the cathedral by Bishop Despenser in 1380. These are very rare examples of the East Anglian School and have only survived because they were not in the cathedral during the Reformation. Rediscovered in 1847, they were returned to their original home in 1957. Both altarpieces depict the Crucifixion and the Resurrection. The E. end of the cathedral is formed by *St. Saviour's Chapel*, which was built in 1930–2 as a war memorial chapel. The two early Gothic arches at the entrance are relics of the *Lady Chapel*,

which was built around 1250 by Bishop Walter de Suffield and later demolished. The *cloister*, built in its present form in 1297–1425, is in keeping with the cathedral's rank. It is the only two-storeyed cloister in England. It has superb traceried windows and the bosses of its vaults are embellished with beautifully carved contemporary scenes.

Church of St. Peter Mancroft: This splendid Gothic church was begun in 1430 and completed in 1455. It has a superbly proportioned and embellished *W. tower,* the upper part of which was extended in 1881–95. A complete peal with 5,040 changes was rung from this tower for the first time in 1751. The interior is conceived as a straight hall without triumphal arch. The sense of space thereby created is enhanced by the light *arcade arches* and

Norwich, Cathedral, cloister

the generously proportioned *clerestory*. The double hammerbeam roof is covered by decorative vaulting. The large *E. window still contains its original 15C glass. The church has numerous monuments,* including that to Sir Thomas Browne, author of 'Religio Medici'. There is a *statue* of this famous writer in front of the church—he lived in Norwich in 1637–82. Valuable 13&14C manuscripts are preserved in the *sacristy.*

St. Peter Hungate Church Museum: The former parish church was rebuilt by John and Margaret Paston in 1460. It has a cruciform *hammerbeam ceiling.* Much of the 15&16C *glass* has survived. The church now serves as a *museum for church art* and contains superb medieval carving, church vestments, bells and valuable manuscripts going back to the 13C, some of which are beautifully illuminated. One of the museum's treasures is the *Wycliffe Bible* of 1388.

Castle Museum: This Norman castle built directly after the Conquest impresses with its massive, intact *keep,* which Henry I (1100–35) had built. The Norman *blind arcades* on its outer walls are to be found on no other castle of the period. The *city museum* has been housed in the castle since 1894 and is dedicated to archaeology, history, arts and crafts. The history of the city's development is very well documented.

Bridewell Museum: The vaulted lower storey of this house was built as early as 1325, the house itself, however, was not built until 1370 by William Appleyard, the first mayor of Norwich. The museum is given over to craft and local industry. The exhibits range from agricultural equipment, boat building and fishing techniques to weaving and bell founding.

Stranger's Hall: This museum is in an old merchant's house, the lower storey of which dates from the 13C, the upper part being built in the 15C. In 1921 L.G. Bolingbroke donated the house and its collection of furniture and domestic furnishings to the city. Today the individual rooms of the house are furnished in the style of various periods (early Tudor to late Victorian). The range extends from fine 15C tapestries in the large hall to 19C kitchen implements.

Environs: Caistor St.Edmund (*c*. 4 m. S.): Here stood the *Venta Icenorum* of the Romans, which was fortified in the 2C. The Saxons utterly destroyed the town, so that now only remains of the N. wall are to be seen. The ground plan of the settlement can nevertheless still be followed in the undergrowth. The Gothic *parish church* contains a fine font (1410) and a fresco of St.Christopher.
   Ranworth (7.5 m. NE): The Gothic church of *St.Helen,* has one of the most beautiful rood screens in the county, extending across the full width of the nave and aisles with 26 panel paintings of saints, an unusual portrait collection dating from 1470.
Wymondham (17 km. SW): The church of *St.Mary* is one of the most interesting churches in the county, has a tower at both the E. and W. ends. It was originally part of a priory (founded 1107); but in 1349 the nave and the N. aisle were made available to the parish, the choir remaining exclusively reserved for the priory. Since the priory and the parish could not agree on a communal tower, the priory built the octagonal tower at the E. end around 1400 and the parish built their W. tower around 1450. At this time the choir and nave were

cleanly divided by a roof-high wall. Following the dissolution of the monastery the stones of the choir and the monastery buildings were used by the parish in order to build the S. aisle in 1543–60. It retains beautiful Norman arcades, a harmoniously integrated Gothic clerestory and a splendid hammerbeam roof adorned with angels and bosses. Even the modern altar decoration, made by Sir Ninian Comper (1935) fits in well.

Nottingham
Nottinghamshire/England   p.328☐I 13

A Danish foundation in the heart of England; taken over by the Normans in the 11C, it has held market rights since 1155 (the famous 'Goose Fair' takes place annually during the first weekend of October). Home of Robin Hood (Sherwood Forest lay to the N.) The Civil War started here in 1642.

St. Mary's Church (Stoney Street): Largely 15C Perpendicular; note the massive battlemented *tower* over the crossing. It has interesting 19C *glass* (from the workshops of Ward-Hughes and Clayton-Bell, among others).

St.Peter's Church (St.Peter's Gate): The original building dated back to the late 11C. Practically none of it survives; the oldest part of the present church is the S. arcade in the nave from 1200 and the bulk of it is late-14C or early-15C Perpendicular, choir rebuilt in 1877/8.

Castle: Nothing remains of the original Norman fort (built under William the Conqueror in 1068 and destroyed by Parliamentary troops in 1651 during the Civil War); rebuilt for the Duke of Newcastle in the Italianate style of the 17C. Rebuilt again in 1831, having been destroyed by fire, it has been a *museum* since

1878. In front of the castle are *statues* of Robin Hood and his men.

Museums:

Castle Museum (City Museum and Art Gallery): On the ground floor are collections devoted to local history, exhibitions of ceramics, silver and glass (including 18C pottery from Nottingham), old vehicles of the 17&18C; on the first floor is a picture gallery (works by English artists since the Middle Ages, such as Reynolds and Gainsborough and by local painters R.P. Bonington and the Sandby brothers). Also of interest is the *Sherwood Foresters' Regimental Museum.*

Castle Gate Costume Museum (Castle Gate): Exhibition of splendid lace and Renaissance embroidery in 18&19C rooms with, in part, original furnishings. Also interesting 17C Nottinghamshire wall hangings.

Folklore Museum (Brewhouse Yard): Exhibits concerning everyday life in Nottinghamshire in recent centuries.

Also worth seeing: *Church of St.Nicholas* (Maid Marian Way), 17C with Gothic windows in the tower. *Council House* (Old Market Square), 1929. *'Ye Old Trip To Jerusalem'* (Castle Road) and *'The Salutation'* (St.Nicholas Street), probably the oldest inns in England (12&13C).

Environs: Holme Pierrepoint (*c.* 4.5 m.

E.): *St. Edmund's Church* (late-17C 'Gothick'); beautiful late Gothic font inside, also monuments by John Flaxman (19C) among others.

Mansfield (*c.* 14 m. N.): This town has an interesting *museum* (150 watercolours by A.S. Buxton depicting old Mansfield).

Newstead Abbey (*c.* 8.5 m. N.): Originally an *abbey* founded in the 12C, it passed to the Byron family in 1540. They turned it into a *house;* and it is now a museum containing, among other things, mementoes, letters and manuscripts of the Lord Byron, 1788–1824.

Papplewick (*c.* 6 m. N.): The enchanting church of *St.James* is, apart from the 14C tower, late-18C 'Gothick'; beautiful gallery, 13C brasses.

Ratcliffe-on-Soar (*c.* 6 m. S.): Church of the *Holy Trinity* with a beautiful Gothic tower; of interest inside are the 16C alabaster figures of the Sacheverell family.

Sandiacre (*c.* 5.5 m. SW): The church of *St.Giles* is Romanesque with Gothic alterations; the choir has richly decorated windows.

Strelley (*c.* 3 m. W.): *All Saints' Church,* 14C with a particularly beautiful choir; inside are the tombs of the Strelley family from the 14–16C.

Thrumpton Hall (*c.* 5.5 m. S.): *House,* with beautiful period furniture and mementoes of Lord Byron.

Wollaton (*c.* 2.5 m. W.): Splendid *house,* built in 1580–8. It now contains the *Natural History Museum of Nottingham* and an *Industrial Museum,* in the stables.

Oakham
Leicestershire/England   p.328□K 13

All Saints' Church: Principally 14C Gothic; *clerestorey* and beautiful late Gothic *windows were* added in the 15C in Perpendicular style. The tower is also 14C. Of interest inside are the capitals and the richly decorated *pointed arches* of the arcades. The interesting *church treasure* includes a 13C Bible.

Castle: Originally a fortified mansion, it was captured in the 11C by the Normans under William the Conqueror. Of particular interest is the late Romanesque *Great Hall* (*c.* 68 ft. long and 50 ft. wide), which contains a unique collection of decorated horseshoes (through the centuries these were traditionally demanded by the lords of the castle as a toll from nobles travelling through their domain).

Rutland County Museum: Housed in a former school dating from 1795 (with a remarkable wooden ceiling), it contains exhibits relating to local history and the history of Rutlandshire — formerly the smallest county in England, which became part of Leicestershire in 1974. Exhibits include Anglo-Saxon jewellery and finds

from Market Overton (see Melton Mowbray).

Also worth seeing: Next to the church is the original building of *Oakham School* , which was founded in 1587. In the market place there are old *foot stocks* formerly used for law-breakers.

Environs: Barrowden (*c.* 7.5 m. SE): 13C *St.Peter's Church* has a beautiful late-Gothic E. window.
Brooke (*c.* 2.5 m. S.): *St.Peter's Church,* originally Romanesque, was rebuilt in the 16C; inside there is a beautiful tomb of 1619).
Burley-on-the-Hill (*c.* 2 m. NE): *Holy Cross Church*, originally Romanesque, was restored in 1870. Inside there is a beautiful marble tomb figure by F. Chantrey (1820).
Egleton (*c.* 1 m. SE): *St.Edmund's Church* has a lovely Romanesque S. portal.
Empingham (*c.* 5 m. SE): *St. Peter's Church* has a beautiful 14C W. front; the early Gothic interior contains remnants of old wall paintings and stained glass.
Exton (*c.* 5 m. NE): The *Church of Sts.Peter and Paul* is of interest for its monuments which date from the 14–18C and include the work of Grinling Gibbons and Nollekens.

Hallaton (*c.* 8.5 m. SW): The 13C *Church of St.Michael* with Romanesque remains in the porch; on the N. side is a small extra tower. Of interest inside is the chancel; beneath the N. aisle is a small crypt.

Langham (*c.* 2 m. NW): With the *Church of SS Peter and Paul* (13/14C; of interest inside are the modern glass works of the 20C by N. Comper).

Lyddington (*c.* 6 m. S.): *St. Andrew's Church* from the 14/15C; inside are remains of old wall paintings and glass works; also of interest is *Bede House.*

North Luffenham (*c.* 5.5 m. SE): With the *Church of St.John the Baptist* (13/14C; inside are remains of old wall paintings, beautiful old glass works in the chancel).

Stoke Dry (*c.* 6 m. S.): *St.Andrew's Church* (originally Romanesque; of interest inside are the tombs of the Digby family from the 14–17C and only recently discovered wall paintings, dating in part from the 13C).

Withcote (*c.* 5 m. SW): With a 16C *church* belonging to a manor (beautiful contemporary glass works inside).

Oban

Scottish Highlands   p.324□F 7

This little town on the Firth of Lorn is now a popular holiday resort due to the numerous facilities it offers. Annual highlights are the West Highland Yachting Week in August and the Argyll Gathering in September.

St.Columba's Cathedral: This granite building was built to plans by Sir Giles Scott. The cathedral, which does not stand on historical soil, nor have a long history, is the spiritual centre for Catholics in the W. Highlands and the Hebrides. The liturgy is quite often conducted in Gaelic.

McCaig's Folly: These wall remains, up to 50 ft. high, on a hill overlooking the town testify to the attempt by a banker to build, from 1897 onwards, a large *museum* with a 164 ft high *observation tower.* His intention was to create a Scottish imitation of the Colosseum in Rome. As he died before the building's completion and as it was not continued by his heirs, the building has remained a ruin to this day.

Environs: An Cala Gardens (7.5 m. SW): These gardens on the W. point of the island of *Seil* are the best example of the pleasant coastal climate. Growing in a water garden and a rock garden are roses and azaleas, cherry and almond trees.

Ardchattan Priory (4.5 m. N.): This was the 3rd Valliscaulian foundation, following the priories of Beauly and Pluscarden, originating around 1230. Of interest are a few well preserved tomb slabs, as well as the fact that it was here that Robert the Bruce held possibly the last parliament assembly to be conducted in Gaelic.

Dunstaffnage Castle (2.5 m. N.): The ruin of this castle, dating from the 13C, stands on a rocky promontory jutting into Loch Etive. It was founded by Alexander II, who required it as operational base for a campaign. In 1470 it came into the posession of the Campbells. In 1685 and 1810 it was gutted by fire, in 1715 and 1745 it was garrisoned by the Hanoverians and in 1940 it was gutted once and for all. Still impressive today is the curtain wall, 13 ft. thick and 65 ft. high. The tower at the NW corner is the oldest preserved part.

Lismore Island (6 m. NW): This 10 mile-long island, 415 ft. at its highest point, was Christianized around 560 by St.Moluag, an Irish-Scottish monk. In the 13C Lismore was seat of the diocese of Argyll.

Omagh

Tyrone/N. Ireland   p.326□D 10

Capital of County Tyrone, it has a beautiful Catholic *parish church* (19C) with 2 towers and a marble altar; inside is the *Black Bell of Drumragh* (9C). Also of interest is the classical *Court House* (19C).

Environs: Clogher (*c.* 18.5 m. SE): This town is supposed to have been one of Ireland's first bishop's seats (St.Macartan, 5C). The neo-Gothic-classical style *cathedral* (*c.* 1745) has medieval elements; in the graveyard are 3 *crosses* (9/10C). In the environs (to the NW) are remains of prehistoric burial sites at *Knockmany* and *Sess Kilgreen*.

Orkney Islands
Scotland   p.322☐H 3

This archipelago to the NW of Scotland consists of no less than 67 islands. Although the islands are about the same latitude as Stockholm and lie quite unprotected in the middle of the North Sea, they were settled as long as 5000 years ago. In the Neolithic age grain was already being cultivated here and in the Bronze Age there was a relative population boom — around 500BC there were probably as many people living on the Orkneys as there are today.

Little came of the Romans' advance; that of the Vikings had a more lasting effect. In the 8C the Orkneys together with the Shetlands became a Norwegian earldom which, under Earl Thorfinn the Mighty, covered not only a great part of Scotland, but also the Hebrides and parts of Ireland. The islands belonged to Norway up until 1468 and Norn, a W. Scandinavian dialect related to old Norse, was spoken well into the 18C. Christianization began in 995. In the 12C it had its own bishop attached to the archdiocese of Lund. The see was not occupied by a Scot until 1418. Danish rights over the island (inherited from Norwegian rule) were dissolved in 1611.

Kirkwall: The capital of the islands lies on Mainland on the site of the Vikings main port. It was they who at the start of the 12C began one of Scotland's most important sacred buildings, the *Cathedral of St.Magnus.* Today it is the only really unaltered pre-Reformation episcopal church. Modelled on Durham Cathedral, the building was begun around 1137 and from this time date the mighty round pillars and the round arches of the arcades and triforium, as well as the decoration of the blind arcades which have a staggered arch arrangement. A century later chapels were added to the transepts and the original semicircular apse was replaced by an early Gothic chancel (pointed arches in the upper storey and foliate capitals with animal grotesques). The columned portals on the W. front were begun in the 13C and completed 200 years later without a change in style. The Reformation, however, meant that even here none of the interior furnishings survived. Only a few baroque tomb stones indicate the cathedral was also used as a burial place. A plaque commemorates the 833 men who died when the battleship 'Royal Oak' was sunk by a German submarine in the bay of Scapa Flow on 14 October 1939. *Bishop's Palace:* The oldest architectural fabric of this dates from the 12C. The most dominant part is a massive tower with numerous embrasures and a parapet, which was built *c.* 1550. It provides an impressive view into the hall below where the Norwegian King Haakon IV died in 1263 following the Battle of Largs. *Earl's Palace:* At about the same time as the Bishop's Palace reached its greatest size the Orkney's worst tyrant, Earl Patrick, also desired a palace. 1600–7 his subjects were forced, without food, drink or pay, to build one of the finest palaces of the period in Scotland. Even the ruins convey an impression of the life-style of this Scottish Renaissance prince.

Orphir: The ruins of Scotland's only

round *church,* the oldest church in the Orkneys, date from about 1120, when it was built in imitation of the Church of the Holy Sepulchre in Jerusalem. The circular nave had a diameter of 20 ft. The semicircular apse, which is some 6 ft. 6 in. wide and has a small Romanesque window has survived. The barrel vaulting reaches a height of 13 ft.

Skara Brae: In the winter of 1850 a storm blew away a dune on the W. coast of Mainland. What remained looked like an enormous heap of rubble, but was in fact the remains of 7 self-contained, interconnecting *prehistoric huts.* The roofed houses and alleys were covered with a mixture of earth and refuse as protection against the elements. The people's skill is reflected not only in the regular construction of the buildings, but also in the fine stone tools, necklaces of animal teeth and beads, and ivory needles. The furnishings are also fine and include beds and cupboards made of stone slabs; there áre also gutters for sewerage.

Birsay: Earl Thorfinn resided here until about 1065. Apart from remains of the *Earl's Palace* and an 11C *cathedral,* remains of early 7C buildings from the time of the Irish missionaries have also been discovered. It has also been shown that there was a Celtic monastery here up until the 9C.
Next to the little monastery church there is a Pict graveyard, in which the famous *Birsay Stone* was uncovered.

Broch of Gurness: This round *fort* (or broch) has a double ring of walls and dates from the Stone Age. The outer walls were originally about 40 ft. high. There was a large hearth, a cellar and its own spring. The Vikings were the last to use the broch.

Maes Howe: The largest burial mound in the Orkneys, it is the most impressive

chambered cairn in the whole of Britain with a ground diameter of 114 ft. and a height of 26 ft. A passage 36 ft. long, but only just over 4 ft. high, forms the entrance to the chamber, which was used as a kind of wall journal by the Vikings who thus left the world with one of the largest collection of runes. The burial chamber dates from the Megalithic era between 1800 and 1600 BC. Exactly how the stone slabs, weighing up to 3 tons, were so precisely hewn, transported and installed in their place has yet to be conclusively shown.

Egilsay: The *church* dedicated to St. Magnus probably dates from 1135–40. It makes quite an impression from a distance with its unusual round tower, the diameter of which narrows from the ground (10 ft.) to the top by just over 3 ft. within a height of 49 ft. The little church has a Romanesque portal and several small Romanesque windows; the chancel is concluded with a barrel vault.

Oxford
Oxfordshire/England   p.332☐I 14/15

The 'oxen ford' is first mentioned in an Anglo-Saxon chronicle of 912, although the settlement was probably already some 200 years old by then. By the mid 11C its importance had grown to such an extent that by 1071 the Normans had built a castle to oversee and protect the settlement. *St. George's Tower* has survived from the castle.
The university, which dates back to the 12C, developed from the monastery school of *St.Frideswide's Priory.* It received its first official privilege in 1214 from the papal legate Pandulf. In the 90 years after 1249 the first 7 colleges were founded, making the university strong enough to compete with Paris. Its great rise during the Renaissance was followed by the set-back

of the Reformation. The iconoclastic Calvinism under Edward VI emptied the university and the Test Act of 1672 turned it into an Anglican university, ensuring that up until 1871 all its members recognized the principles of Calvinism. It was not until 1920 that the University became a modern university which no longer required Greek as a necessary part of the education, admitted women and accepted a Government grant; thus ended its 700-year-old independence. But for all this 'modernity' Oxford remains what it has been for centuries, surely the most interesting and beautiful university city in the world.

Cathedral (also Christ Church's chapel): This goes back to the church of the convent founded by St.Frideswide at the start of the 8C. Ethelred II turned it into a seminary for secular priests in 1004 and in 1122 it became an Augustinian priory. The oldest parts of the present building date back to the restoration efforts of 1141–80 by Robert of Cricklade. Cardinal Wolsey had the 3 W. bays of the nave pulled down

Oxford, Cathedral, ceiling

Oxford, All Souls College

Christ Church, Tom Tower

of St. Catherine also has the original 14C glass in its windows. Here too are the most beautiful *tombs,* namely those of Prior Sutton (1316), Lady Furnival (1353) and Sir George Nowers (1425). S. of the nave adjoins what remains of the Gothic *cloister,* in the E. part of which is the Norman portal of the chapterhouse.

Church of St. Mary the Virgin: This predominantly Gothic church dates in its present form from the 15C, only the lower part of the N. tower dates back to the 13C; the baroque *S. porch* was built in 1637 by Nicholas Stone. Of interest within are the 15C *choir stalls,* the *pulpit* and numerous *tombs.* The church has served as university church since the 14C.

Church of St. Peter in the East: Dating back to Norman times, it has a *crypt* (below the sanctuary) with an impressive vault. Crypt, sanctuary and S. portal were probably built *c.* 1150. A few 15C stained-glass windows have survived. The church now serves as St. Edmund Hall's *library* .

when he was building Christ Church in the first half of the 16C. In 1870 Sir Gilbert Scott replaced the great *E. window* with the present combination of smaller windows and arcades, and altered the *W. front.* The 13C *tower* (163 ft. high) was fortunately spared any restoration attempts. Inside the alternately round and octagonal *columns* and the superb *vaulting* are most impressive. The *organ screen* and the *pulpit* are Jacobean. The front of the S. transept dates in its present form from Scott, who also installed the *gallery,* which provides a splendid view of the whole interior. The *E. window* in the *Chapel of St. Lucy* is a particular masterpiece and still has the original glass dating from *c.* 1330. The vaulting of the chancel and the windows of its clerestory date from *c.* 1490. Between the N. aisles of the chancel stands the *burial shrine* of St. Frideswide. The early Gothic *Chapel*

All Souls College: Founded in 1438 by Henry Chichele, Archbishop of Canterbury, its Gothic chapel, with carved *oak ceiling* and superb stone *retable,* is particularly interesting. The retable had been walled up for more than 200 years and was only restored in 1872–9. Parts of the 15C stained-glass windows have also survived. The college *library* was founded by Christopher Codrington.

Christ Church: This, the university's largest college (also called Cardinal College) was founded by Wolsey in 1525. Its chapel received the throne of the Bishop of Oxford in 1546, and the head of the college is dean of both college and chapter. Hanging in *Tom Tower,* built on top of Wolsey's gateway by Wren in 1681, is Great Tom, the 7 ton bell cast in 1680, which originally hung in Osney Abbey. Ever-

Magdalen College

evening at 9.05 the bell chimes 101 times in memory of the college's founder members.

Magdalen College: Founded in 1458 by William of Waynflete, Bishop of Winchester, it began taking students in 1470. The finest part architecturally is the splendid Perpendicular tower, built 1492–1506. Together with *Magdalen Bridge,* built by John Gwynn 1772–9, the tower has become a symbol of Oxford. The Gothic *chapel,* which was completed by 1483, was extensively rebuilt in the 19C. The *cloister* was built at the time of foundation, but it too had to be extensively rebuilt in 1822. The grotesque *figures* on the buttresses are called 'hieroglyphs' and date from *c.* 1510. The *hall* is impressive with its splendid panelling, a musicians' gallery over a Jacobean screen and a fine oak ceiling. The *library* is famous for its valuable manuscripts and early printed books.

Merton College: Founded in 1264 by Walter de Merton, it is the oldest of the colleges. The *gate tower* dates from 1418 and the *main front* was rebuilt by Sir Henry Savile in 1581. The *oak door* to the hall still has its 13C iron fittings. The *Treasury,* the college archive, is the oldest part; it dates from 1274 and has a steep stone roof. *Mob Quad* was built in 1309 and has what is probably the most interesting medieval *library* in England; during 1371–8 it was fitted out as the country's first Renaissance library, with books on shelves instead of in presses. The early Gothic *chapel* was begun in 1270 and acquired its interesting *tower* around 1450. In the 14C the chapel received transepts, but the nave was never built. Of particular interest is the tracery of the great *E. window* and the superb late 13C painted glass, much of which is still original.

New College: Founded in 1379 by William of Wykeham, Bishop of Winchester; in 1380 the foundation stone was laid for this the first college to be planned as one integral unit. Just 7 years later the complex, which surrounds a courtyard was completed, and the result was one of the earliest and best examples of Perpendicular. In 1675 another storey was added to the front quadrangle and new windows were added but this did not greatly alter the general impression of the complex. More serious were the interferences with the *chapel,* which was rebuilt by Gilbert Scott in 1879. He not only renewed the roof, but also raised it, thereby ruining the proportions of the interior. Only in the antechapel has the original 14C stained glass survived albeit with the exception of the large W. window, which was altered in 1777 to a design by Reynolds. The window glass in the chapel itself dates from 1740 and 1774. The renovated *choir stalls* still have their original miserichords. Adjoining the W. side of the chapel is the *cloister* with beautiful wooden vaulting. This was completed around 1400, as was the *bell tower.* Also of interest are the *gardens,* laid out before 1708; on one side they are bordered by the old *city walls,* which were built under Henry III.

University College: Claiming to have been founded by Alfred the Great, the college celebrated its millenary in 1872; however, it was first actually endowed in 1249 by William of Durham. Its buildings are in the main 17C Gothic. The *chapel,* consecrated in 1666, contains stained-glass windows by A. Van Linge from the time of construction.

Bodleian Library: One of the oldest and most important libraries in the world. The oldest part, dating from 1488, contained the library (some 300 manuscripts) of Duke Humphrey, the youngest brother of Henry V. Following the destruction of the Reformation, Sir Thomas Bodley made a new start from 1598. He brought in his own unusual collection and saved all that he could of the old.

Radcliffe Camera: The court doctor John Radcliffe left 40,000 pounds for a new library in Oxford, but disagreements meant that it was 1737 before James Gibbs began work on the classical rotunda. The architect, who had been educated in Rome, completed this (probably his most successful work) by 1748. The exterior of the building is graced with pairs of Corinthian *half-columns*; the ambulatory above these has a *parapet* with urns. The *dome* has a lantern and rests upon an *octagon* accentuated by striking buttresses. The *spiral staircase* inside is also by Gibbs.

Sheldonian Theatre: Paid for by Sir Gilbert Sheldon, Archbishop of Canterbury, who commissioned Sir Christopher Wren to erect a building for the university's public performances. It was built 1664-8 in imitation of the Theatre of Marcellus in Rome. The *ceiling fresco* inside depicts the triumph of Truth and the Arts and was created by Robert Streater in 1669.

Ashmolean Museum: The first public museum in the country, it opened in 1683. The present buildings were completed in 1845 to a design by Charles Cockerell. The museum is named after the astrologer Elias Ashmole and contains paintings by the greatest painters, as well as works of art of all kinds from the 16&17C, a collection of musical instruments, a coin collection and antique exhibits from Egypt, Crete and the Aegean.

Museum of the History of Science: The superb collection of early astronom ical, optical and mathematical instruments has no equal of its kind in the world. The museum buildings are a fine example of 17C Oxford architecture. Originally they housed the Ashmolean collection until the latter moved to its new buildings in 1845. Exhibits range from astronomical instruments of the Middle Ages to instruments of atomic physics.

Rotunda: Housed in this building of 1963 is what is probably the largest *Puppet Museum* in the world. The collection of doll's houses together with the complete contents mainly date from 1700–1850.

University Museum: Housed in a complex begun in 1854 and completed by 1914, it contains the university's zoological, mineralogical and geological collections.

Environs: Iffley (3 m. S.): The *Church of St. Mary* is one of the best-preserved Norman churches. Built *c.* 1170, it has a small square tower, a particularly fine W. front with one round and 3 arched windows and a stepped portal, all of which have excellent zig-zag ornamentation. The S. portal and some arches inside have also survived in their original style.
Stanton Harcourt (*c.* 12 m. W.): The cruciform *Church of St. Michael* dates from Norman times; the lower part of the cen-

Radcliffe Camera

tral tower is Early English, the upper part, like most of the church, is Gothic. The church is of interest above all for its numerous tombs which date from the 14C and are mostly of the Harcourt family—a particularly fine figure of a lord from this family was made by R.W. Sievier in 1832.

Paisley
Strathclyde/Scotland   p.324□G 8

This industrial town in SW Scotland is the world's greatest producer of thread and is famous for its cotton and silk shawls, which were originally no more than copies of cloths sent home by Scots serving in India. The most important sight here is the abbey, which likes to be referred to as the 'Cradle of the Stewart Kings'.

Paisley Abbey: The priory of Pasletum was founded by Walter FitzAlan in 1171 with 13 Cluniac monks from Wenlock. In 1219 the priory became an abbey, which was destroyed less than 100 years later by the English (1307). Not until after 1450 was it rebuilt in the form now apparent from its ruins. Most of it does not, however, date from this time, for after the Reformation the church alone was restored 4 times and also rebuilt in parts. The present *tower* replaced the first one, which collapsed in the 15C, destroying the chancel in the process. The only original elements remaining of the old church are the lower parts of the *W. front* and the *S. wall* of the nave. The roof of the nave had to be rebuilt in 1780, the first major restorations were begun in 1897 by Rowand Anderson and

McGregor Chalmers and were complete by Sir Robert Lorimer in 1928. The *W. fa çade* of the church has a deeply set Earl English portal, flanked by 2 blind arche with 3 traceried windows above. Of pa ticular interest in the nave are the *galle ies,* supported by stone consoles, whic formed a complete circuit at clerestor height. The wide, round arches of the *tr forium* are particularly beautiful. To th left of the W. portal is a *memorial stone t* John Hamilton, the last abbot of the a bey, who was executed in 1571 for su posed complicity in the murder of Darnle The S. transept is occupied by *St.Mirren Chapel.* The chapel built in 1499 is su posed to occupy the site where the Celti saint is thought to have built his firs chapel in the 7C. Buried in the chapel Princess Marjory, daughter of Robert th Bruce. Her son was Robert II, the firs Stewart King. S. of the church are a fe remains of the abbey buildings, parts c which were incorporated into the Palace Paisley in the 17C, which was used as tow house by the Hamiltons and later the Dui donalds.

Art Gallery and Museum: Founded i 1870, the museum not only has excelle local history and archaeological exhibit but also a superb survey of the shawls an plaids produced in Paisley (of which there are over 500 examples).

Environs: Crookston (c. 2 m. E.): *Crookston Castle,* early-15C, now ruined, is surrounded by a rampart and moat and stands on the foundations of a 12C castle. The tower house was built by Sir John Stewart, who was killed at Orléans in 1429.
Kilbarchan (5 m. W.): The 18C *Weaver's Cottage* is maintained in its original state.

Pembroke
Dyfed/Wales   p.330☐F 15

This small industrial town and port, with a population of some 15,000, lies on the Pembroke river. This flows into Milford Haven, a ria running deep inland which forms the largest and best natural harbour in Wales.

History: The Normans founded the present castle here as early as 1081. Around 1093 the SW of Wales around Pembroke (Pembrokeshire) was seized from the Welsh and incorporated into the English kingdom and as a result the area is very English in character and Welsh is little spoken. At one point Pembroke was held by the Tudors, the future Henry VII was born here.

Pembroke Castle: The Norman fortress of 1097 was largely extended to its present form in the 13C. The impressive and well-preserved castle—it was only taken once, by Oliver Cromwell in 1650—were naturally protected by the river Pembroke and what were once marshes. A strongly fortified *gatehouse* leads into the spacious *outer ward* (splendid gateway). The walls of the *inner ward* in the NW enclose the *Great Hall* (with chapel), from which a stairway leads to the *water gate* (Wogan cave), and the imposing *keep.* This tower had 4 storeys and was about 78 ft high. (diameter about

52 ft., walls 6–19 ft. thick). The entrance was on the first floor and the main room on the third floor. A spiral staircase can be climbed to the vaulted stone roof. There are 2 wall passages, the floors no longer survive. Nearby is the *Prison Tower* and various other towers from the massive curtain wall. Also of interest is the *Henry VII Tower* on the outer ward wall, where Henry VII was born.

Also worth seeing: The *church* at *Monkton* was part of the Benedictine priory founded in 1098, negligible remains of which survive. The church itself has a long, narrow, barrel-vaulted nave and was restored following its destruction. In the S. of the town parts of the *town walls* (13C) still stand, including the former *W. gate* (Main St.).

Environs: Angle (c. 9 m. W.): Angle has an old *castle* with a ruined, four-storeyed keep, moat and medieval dovecote. Nearby are old *blockhouses* from the time of Henry VIII (16C) and a *cemetery church* of 1447 (rebuilt). Nearby to the W. lies the Ne-

Paisley, Paisley Abbey, W. portal

olithic burial chamber of *Devil's Quoit*. The 13 ft. long cap stone still rests upon one support stone; the others have fallen.

Bosherston (4 m. S.): Near Sampson Farm there are interesting remains of prehistoric *menhirs* (standing stones).

Carew (*c.* 4 NE): Situated on the river Carew, which at this point is still tidal, the village has a beautiful ruined medieval *castle*, which was extended around 1300, from which time the W. front with high walls, 2 massive round towers, the Great Hall and a flight of steps. The 16C N. side, with tall, mullioned windows, is Elizabethan. Near the gate of the castle there is an interesting, 13 ft. high *Celtic Cross* (erected around 1000) with beautiful decoration and an inscription (Cross of Margiteut, son of Etguin). *Carew Church* is an impressive Early English building (14&15C) with a tower and chantry in the graveyard (interesting old tombs). The neighbouring *parsonage* probably dates from the late 15C.

Hodgeston (*c.* 5 m. SE): Here there is a beautiful Decorated 14C *church* with an old sedilia and font.

Lamphey (Welsh: Llantyfai, 2.5 m. SE): The interesting ruins of one of the 7 palaces of the Bishop of St.David's, which dates from the 13 – 16C. Bishop Henry Gower (1328–47) in particular added to the existing old hall (2 storeys) and the residential buildings (in the W.) a new hall (in the SE) and surrounded the whole complex with a wall. This included the NW gatehouse, which is still in good condition. The entrance to the living quarters was (as in a medieval keep) on the upper floor. The bishop's bed chamber lay at the S. wall of the upper floor. The chapel (added in the 16C) has a beautiful Perpendicular E. window; also of interest is the arcaded gallery of the new hall and the vault of the lower floor.

Pembroke Dock (*c.* 2 m. NW): Here on Milford Haven (with a closed naval dockyard) is an interesting *Motor Museum* . The Dock is very much a product of the Victorian era. At *Burton*, on the other side of the river (*c.* 3 m. NW), the world's first iron-clad battleship, 'H.M.S. Warrior', lies at anchor.

St. Govan's Chapel (5 m. S.): This ancient chapel, shrouded in many legends, lies in a cleft in the cliffs of the steep S coast. Its name is traced back to, among others, the hero Gawain, one of the knights of King Arthur's Round Table. The 13C chapel has a stone altar, bench and font and an adjoining cliff cell; behind this is a now exhausted old healing spring (once an object of pilgrimage).

Stackpole (3 m. S.): The church of *St. James and St. Elidyr* is probably pre Norman but the oldest surviving part of the building is the 13C tower at the N. end of the N. transept. Also of interest are the 13&14C effigies in the sanctuary and in the Lord's Chapel.

Thorn Island (*c.* 6 m. W.): This little island in Milford Haven, with a *fort* from the Napoleonic Wars, lies in West Angle Bay.

Penrith
Cumbria/England   p.328☐H

St. Andrew's Church: This was originally Norman (from which time the tower dates, reputedly built by Warwick the Kingmaker); altered in neoclassical style in about 1720. Inside are remains of the 15C *stained glass*, also of interest are the *pulpit, font* and *lights* from the 17&18C. In the adjoining graveyard is the 10C 'Giant' Grave', traditional burial place of the giant 'Owen Cesarius'.

Castle: Built in the 14&15C, it was particularly favoured as a residence by Richard III (1483–5). During the Civil War it was captured by Parliamentary troops after bitter struggle; now a ruin.

Also worth seeing: *Hutton Hall* with

medieval tower. *Gloucester Arms Inn,* where Richard III lived (his coat-of-arms is displayed in a room).

Environs: Appleby (*c.* 13 m. SE): The castle here was rebuilt in the 17C but the keep is still Norman. Also of interest is the *Moothall* (assembly hall, 16C).

Bolton (*c.* 8 m. SE): *All Saints' Church* Norman (note the N. and S. portals with beautiful Norman capitals; over the N. portal is a primitive relief with two jousting knights; inside is an interesting choir screen (19C).

Brougham (immediately SE of the town): With the church of *St.Nimian* (originally Anglo-Saxon, altered in Norman times and in the 17C); nearby are *St.Wilfred's Chapel* and *Brougham Castle* (keep and main gate survive). Close by are the remains of the Roman fort *Brocavum.*

Crosby Ravensworth (*c.* 11 m. SE): With an *archaeological zone* (Iron Age and Roman-British remains; surviving features include the earthworks and foundations of round, oval and angular dwellings).

Great Salkeld (*c.* 5 m. NE): Church of *St.Cuthbert,* Norman, in the 14C a strong tower was added as protection against raids by the Scots. Beautiful, Norman S. portal.

Greystoke (*c.* 5 m. W.): *St. Andrew's Church* is now mainly 15C; interesting E. window with 15C stained glass.

King Arthur's Round Table (immediately S. of the town): *Circular ramparts* from the late Neolithic (formerly 2 entrances; in the middle were once 2 upright stones). To the W. is a similar complex called *Mayburgh.*

Kirkoswald (*c.* 7.5 m. NE): Church of *St. Oswald* (variety of styles; 16C choir); nearby is the tower, built as late as 1897, and a few old sarcophagus lids. Also of interest are the remains of an old *border fort.*

Little Salkeld (*c.* 6 m. NE): Old *water mill,* authentically restored (original drive mechanism and millstones preserved).

Long Meg and her Daughters (*c.* 7.5 m.

NE): Bronze Age *stone circle* (also caled 'Druid's Circle): Of the original 59 monoliths 27 are still standing; 'Long Meg' herself stands on the SW side and is about 13 ft. high.

Lowther Castle (*c.* 4 m. S.): Ruins of the former ancestral seat of the Lowther family.

Ormside (*c.* 14 m. SE): Norman church of *St. James* (W. tower fortified against Scottish raids; 16C choir ceiling). The *'Ormside Cup'* (Anglo-Saxon enamel and gold), discovered in the graveyard in 1823, is now housed in the Yorkshire Museum.

Temple Sowerby Manor (*c.* 6 m. SE): 16C *manor house,* altered in the 18C; the *park* is also of interest.

Perth
Tayside/Scotland p.324□G 7

This industrial city has more to offer in terms of history than art. Lying at the end of the Firth of Tay, it was the capital of Scotland up until 1437, when James I of Scotland was murdered in the city's Dominican monastery, whereupon his widow removed the court to Edinburgh. James VI was kidnapped here in 1600, Charles I and Charles II resided here from time to time, Cromwell took it in 1651 and the Jacobites in 1715, and it was from here that Prince Charles Edward Stuart attempted to gain a footing in 1745 before the English finally reassumed power.

St.John's Kirk: This is Perth's only surviving medieval building. The *choir* dates from 1450 and the *nave* was built around 1490, around the same time as the *tower.* Here, on the 11 May 1559, John Knox pronounced his sermon on 'the cleansing of the Church from idolatry', which was to have such grave consequences. This was the starting signal for the iconoclasm of the Reformers, the removal of the altars, the plundering of the monasteries and even for the destruction of the buildings themselves.

Scone Abbey: This 12C Augustinian abbey to the N. of Perth is rich in historical associations. Until 1559 the abbey's church was the coronation church of the Scottish kings. Kenneth MacAlpine defeated the Picts here in 843, thereby clearing the way for a Scottish kingdom. He is supposed to have brought here the famous Stone of Scone, the Scottish coronation stone. The stone, probably a portable altar of a Celtic missionary, became the booty of Edward I of England as early as 1297—Edward brought it back to London as a symbol of his victory over the Scots. Even though England's struggle against the Scots was to continue, the English never returned this symbol of their earlier victory. Even the Scottish Nationalists failed to alter this state of affairs, when in 1950 they stole the stone from under the coronation seat in Westminster Abbey. Scotland Yard arranged its return when it was rediscovered in Arbroath. This historical site is now occupied by the

Perth, St. John's Kirk

family chapel of the Earl of Mansfield. His neo-Gothic country seat, designed by William Atkinson, was built in 1802–12. Behind its rather uninviting walls there is a valuable collection of French applied arts including an inlaid desk made for Marie Antoinette in 1770. 18C Parisian lacquer as well as a valuable collection of clocks and porcelain, make the palace worth visiting.

In Scone's park the Douglas Fir was grown for the first time in Europe. It was named after David Douglas, a gardener of the Earl of Mansfield.

Environs: Abernethy (4.5 m. SE): This village was once the capital of the Pictish kingdom. The early-12C, 75 ft. high *round tower* was added to the church, following Irish example, as a means of defence.
Dunkeld (*c.* 9 m. NW): This small town is historically closely connected with Scone Abbey. In 843 Kenneth MacAlpine had made it joint capital of Scotland with Scone, it was a bishop's seat from the 9C. The late Gothic *cathedral,* destroyed by the Reformers, was begun in 1318 and consecrated in 1464. The great NW tower was completed in 1501. Note the tracery in the nave, wall paintings on the ground floor of the tower, as well as memorial slabs in the nave and in the churchyard. The town still has good examples of late-17C *Little Houses.*
Newburgh (6 m. SE): Right on the shore of the firth stands *Mugdrum House,* built in 1786, with *Mugdrum Cross.* The cross may be well over 1,000 years old and was erected as a sanctuary.

Peterborough
Cambridgeshire/England   p.328☐K 1

This industrial city on the Nene was formerly known as Medeshamstede which grew up around a Benedictine monastery (see below).

Cathedral: Dates back to the Benedictine monastery founded by King Penda of Mercia in 656. The monastery's first church was destroyed by the Danes in 870 and the 10C Anglo-Saxon building which replaced it burned down in 1116. A year later the present building was begun, and the result is one of the most beautiful and impressive Romanesque buildings in England. The first builder was Abbot Jean de Seez. In 1155 William de Waterville took over construction of the church, which by that time had extended to the transepts. By 1177 the church, together with the central tower, but with the exception of the 2 W. bays, was complete. The latter were added by Abbot Benedict from 1177 onwards and he also completed the aisles, vaulted the whole building and by 1199 had installed most of the wooden ceiling. By 1210 under Abbot Acharius the extensive *W. front* with its 3 portals (nearly 100 ft. high) and blind-arcaded corner towers was begun. In the 14C the massive Norman central tower was replaced by a smaller and more slender one. In the following century the Norman windows made way for larger ones. By 1509 the *retro-choir* was completed with a fan vault. 2 years after the monastery's dissolution in 1539, the church became a cathedral.

Inside, the splendid Norman nave has a unique painted *wooden ceiling* dating from 1220. Its numerous lozenges are painted with figures of saints, church fathers and apostles. In the NW corner of the nave stands the 13C marble *font*. In 1888, foundations of the Anglo-Saxon church and the tombstone of two early bishops were uncovered in the S. transept. The transept ceiling is the only wooden ceiling to have survived from Norman times. The oldest part of the church is the *sanctuary*, the wooden roof of which is Gothic however. The N. chancel aisle has the *tomb slab* of Abbot Benedict, who died in 1192, as well as the tomb of Catherine of Aragon, which was destroyed by the Puritans. In the S.

chancel aisle stands the *Monks' Stone,* dating from before 900 and commemorating monks who died under the Danes in 870. The numerous *effigies* of abbots from the 12&13C make the cathedral unique in England. In 1587 Mary Queen of Scots was buried in the cathedral, although her son, James I, had her transferred to Westminster in 1612. Little remains of the once extensive monastery buildings; neither the Bishop's Palace nor the cloister survived the Dissolution of the Monasteries.

City Museum and Art Gallery: The museum has a unique collection of articles made during the Napoleonic Wars by French soldiers imprisoned in Norman Cross. The archaeological collection contains Roman and Anglo-Saxon exhibits; another collection is devoted to the area's natural history and geology.

Peterborough Cathedral 1 font (13C) **2** nave **3** choir **4** N. transept **5** tombstone of Abbot Benedict **6** tomb of Catharine of Aragon **7** altar **8** Monk's Stone **9** former tomb of Mary Queen of Scots **10** S. transept **11** sacristy **12** former cloister

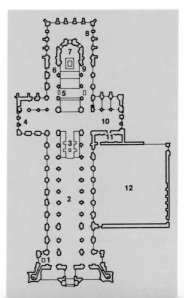

Environs: Barnack: (*c.* 12.5 m. NW): The Saxon church of *St. John the Baptist* was probably built at the start of the 11C. Inside there are a seated Christ from the early 11C and an early Gothic font with foliate decorations from the 13C. The oldest tombs date from the 15C.

Burghley House (*c.* 14 m. NW): This house, begun in 1552 by Sir William Cecil, is one of the most beautiful examples of domestic buildings from the time of Elizabeth I. The recently knighted Royal Minister built on to an existing mansion and then extended the new building to two storeys by 1563. Having become Elizabeth I's Chancellor of the Exchequer and acquired the title of Lord Burghley, he had the house completed in its present form by 1587. Although little remains of the original interior furnishings, the Romanesque staircase, built in emulation of one in the Louvre in Paris, wood carvings by Grinling Gibbons and wall paintings by Verrio are worth seeing. Today the house contains an extensive *painting collection* with works principally by Italian and British painters; there are also portraits by Holbein and Van Dyke. Furnishings include valuable furniture and tapestries.

Castor (5 m. W.): This little town dates back to Roman times. The church of *St. Kyneburgha* is the only church in the county dedicated to the eldest daughter of King Penda of Mercia, who founded a small convent in Castor and became its abbess. According to an inscription over the portal, the Norman church was dedicated to her in 1224. The church is of interest above all for its 14C frescos.

Elton Hall (*c.* 9 m. SW): This Jacobean house was built for Sir Thomas Proby 1662–89. Today it houses a *painting collection,* including works by Constable, Reynolds and Frans Hals. The *library* contains old Bibles and prayer books, including a prayer book belonging to Henry VIII with inscriptions by the king and Mary Tudor.

Longthorpe Tower (*c.* 2 m. W.): This 13C

fortified *mansion* has beautiful stone vaulting in the two lower storeys. In 1945 fine 14C frescos showing domestic scenes were discovered on the first floor.

March (*c.* 11 m. E.): The church of *St. Wendreda* was built in the 15C in a mixture of Decorated and Perpendicular styles. It has a fine spire and a beautiful double hammerbeam roof decorated with angels

Orton Longueville (*c.* 2 m. SW): The church of the *Holy Trinity* is 13C with 14C extensions. In the 17C an aisle was added. The church contains fragments of its original window glass and a 16C fresco of St. Christopher. The font is 15C. Of interest are a 13C sculpture of a knight, as well as sculpture of a seated woman by Sir Francis Chantrey.

Pickering
North Yorkshire/England   p.328☐K 1

Church of St. Peter and St. Paul: The town's parish church dates from Norman times and the round arches of the nave and the lower part of the tower have survived from this time; the rest of the tower is Early English, the clerestorey Perpendicular. Inside, above the arcades of the nave, there are interesting 15C *wall paintings* of biblical stories and scenes from the lives of the saints. (These were discovered in 1852, but whitewashed soon after and not uncovered again until 1880, when they were restored.) The church is frequently visited by American tourists because it contains a memorial to the British-American alliance of World War 1 and there are numerous memorial plaques, including one for Walter Hines Page, to bear witness to this.

Castle (in the N. of the town): Founded in the 11C, from which time there are a few

Pickering, Church of St. Peter and St. Paul, wall painting, St. Edmund

remains; the rest is 14C. The whole has survived in remarkably good condition. There is a complete *surrounding wall* and *3 towers* (one named Fair Rosamund after a companion of Henry II, who visited the castle). Earlier subdivisions into an outer and an inner ward and *keep* are still visible. Pickering Castle was a popular residence with the English kings, although not for Richard II who was imprisoned here for a time following his dethronement in 1399.

Environs: Cawthorne Roman camps (a few miles N. of the town): A hillside complex of 4 *Roman military camps* from *c.* AD 100. Further N., towards Wheeldale Moor, is part of a *Roman road* (one of the best examples of its kind in England).
Ebberston (*c.* 7.5 m. E.): *Ebberston Hall,* was built in 1718 in Palladian style. W. of the town is *King Alfrid's Cave,* where the Northumbrian king is said to have died from wounds sustained in the battle of 'Bloody Field' in 707.
Lastingham (*c.* 7.5 m. NW): The *church* was built in the 11–12C on top of an earlier building from the 7C in which St.Cedd, Bishop of the East Angles and founder of a monastery in Lastingham, was thought to have been buried in 654. The *crypt* , which is entered from the nave, lies below the chancel to the E. Built 1078–88, it is still in its original state and consists of a small nave, 2 aisles, and an apse; it has an old altar and remains of old crosses.
Middleton (*c.* 2 m. W.): The beautiful Norman *church* has interesting Saxon architectural fragments and a few Celtic crosses.
Thornton Dale (*c.* 2 m. E.): Beautiful 14C *market cross.*

Plymouth
Devon/England   p.330☐F 17

No other port in England played so impor-

tant a part in making Britain an important seafaring nation. Catherine of Aragon disembarked here in 1501. In 1580 Sir Francis Drake returned here on the completion of his circumnavigation of the world which had taken nearly three years. On 31 July 1588 the Spanish Armada of 130 ships gathered off the coast of Plymouth. In 1768 James Cook set sail in 'Endeavour' to discover Australia, and in 1919 an American seaplane berthed here following the first flight across the Atlantic. As the city was also one of Britain's most important modern naval bases, it was extensively destroyed by bombs in 1941. In 1966 Elizabeth II knighted the 65-year-old Francis Chichester with the sword of Sir Francis Drake, after he had sailed around the world in his little yacht in just 117 days.

Church of St.Andrew: Drake celebrated his glorious homecoming in this church, in which the Pilgrim Fathers later took leave of their homeland. The nave of the 15C church was gutted in 1941 and rebuilt in 1957. Its new beautiful *stained-glass windows* were made by John Piper and Patrick Reyntiens. Buried in the *sanctuary* are Sir Martin Frobisher (1594) and Admiral Blake (1657). A *memorial plaque* commemorates William Cookworthy, who, independently of Böttger, re-invented porcelain in England and established the first English factory in 1768.

Citadel: Built by Charles II in 1666 more to intimidate the townsfolk than to protect the town against attack.

City Museum and Art Gallery: Houses paintings by Reynolds, Old Master drawings, Plymouth and Bristol porcelain , Italian bronzes and the cup presented to Drake by Elizabeth I after his world circumnavigation.

Environs: Antony House (2.5 m. W.): This Queen Anne house was built 1711–21 in a park by Humphry Repton. The columned portico on the S. side was added in the 19C. Inside, the house still contains its original panelling, exquisite furnishings and a collection of family portraits of the Carew family.

Buckland Abbey (6 m. N.): This Cistercian monastery of 1278 was converted by Sir Richard Grenville (1542–91) into a country house and bought by Sir Francis Drake in 1581. The house now serves as a *museum,* in which the development of sailing ships up to the advent of the steam ship is documented; Drake memorabilia.

Cotehele House (8 m. E.): This Tudor granite mansion was built at various stages between 1485 and 1627 around 2 inner courtyards. For centuries it was the ancestral home of the Earls of Mount Edgecumbe. The hall is arranged as it probably would have appeared in the 15C.

Saltram House (3 m. E.): This country seat was built by John Parker from 1750. The dining room is by Robert Adam (1768); ceiling medallions by Antonio Zucchi. Sir Joshua Reynolds was a frequent guest and 14 portraits by him hang in the house. 9 others were painted by the American Gilbert Stewart, who was responsible for the best portraits of the first American presidents. Reynolds had his own portrait painted by Angelica Kauffmann in 1767, which hangs on the staircase. Also of interest is the chinoiserie, the fully working kitchen of 1799 and the porcelain collection.

Pontefract
West Yorkshire/England   p.328□I 12

One of the oldest boroughs in England. A military camp in Roman times, it was fortified by the Danes in the early Middle Ages because of its strategic position. Further extensions are Norman and date from the 11C after the Conquest. Pontefract is famous for its liquorice production, which

is thought to have begun with monks in the 13C, but which may possibly have started with the Romans.

St.Giles's Church (Market Place): The town's parish church since the Civil War, it was first mentioned in a document belonging to Henry I (1100–35), although it was probably founded well before then. It has been rebuilt and enlarged many times, particularly in the 17C. The *tower* dates from 1795 (lower part square, upper part octagonal). Inside, the *arcade* of 5 arches is 14C; the *chancel* was converted in the 19C. Fine Holy Communion vessels date from the 15–16C.

All Saints Church (South Baileygate): The town's oldest church dates from the time of Henry III when it was built as successor to a pre-Norman church. It was destroyed during the siege of Pontefract in the Civil War, since which time it has remained a ruin; only the outer walls of the nave and aisles (15C) and of the chancel (14C) still stand. The main part of the church was restored in 1967.

Castle: In a strategic location controlling an important N.-S., E.-W. crossroads, the castle was always the focus of attention. Built after the Norman Conquest of England in 1066 it was later extended into one of the largest Norman fortresses. Destroyed in 1649 at Cromwell's command, it has been a ruin ever since. Parts to have survived include the great round tower (trefoil cross section), parts of other towers (Piper Tower, Gascoigne Tower, Treasurer's Tower, N. Queen's Tower and King's Tower, and E.Constable Tower), parts of individual rooms ('King Richard's Chamber') and parts of the administrative buildings. Soldiers who fell during the Civil War are reputed to be buried in St. Clement's Chapel (14C). A small *museum* in the former gatehouse has excavation finds both from the castle and the town.

Old Town Hall (Market Place): Built in 1785. Inside there is the model for Nelson's Death in Trafalgar Square. Nearby is *Butter Cross,* an arcaded hall of 1734.

Also of interest: *Friarwood Valley Gardens* (Southgate/Mill Hill Rd.), where the monks of the 'Black Bothers' settled in 1221. Right next to this, by the hospital, is a *hermitage* of 1368.

Environs: Ackworth (*c.* 2.5 m. S.): St. Cuthbert (see Durham) was said to be buried in the village *church* until his remains were transferred to Durham (15C tower, otherwise completely rebuilt).
Darrington (*c.* 3 m. SE): Beautiful old *church;* 18C dovecote in the churchyard.
Heath Hall (*c.* 2.5 m. W.): Built in 1707 and extended by John Carr, who later became mayor of York; splendid ceilings.
Ledsham (*c.* 3.5 m. N.): The ancient, but well preserved *All Saints Church* was founded by Saxons, altered by the Normans and altered again in late Gothic style. There are fine old windows and tombs from the 17–18C).
Nostell Priory (*c.* 4.5 m. SW): *Mansion,* built in 1733 on the site of an Augustinian priory founded in 1110; of particular interest is the beautiful Chippendale furniture.
Sandal Magna (*c.* 7 m. SW): Recently excavated remains of a 13C *castle.* The church of *St. Helen* has a partly Norman tower over the crossing; the rest is 14C. Inside there are 2 beautiful Jacobean chairs.
Temple Newsam House (*c.* 3 m. N.): The predecessor of this house is reputed to have belonged to the Knights Templar 1155–1308; it was rebuilt in Tudor style in the 16C and extended in 1622. Lord Darnley, the second husband of Mary Queen of Scots, was born here. Of particular interest are the interior furnishings. The entrance hall has a fine Victorian oak staircase. The New Library has 19C Victorian furniture. The Blue Drawing Room has Chinese wall coverings. The Terrace Room has a fine collection of snuff boxes. The Blue Damask Room is named after its wall hangings. The Long Gallery has a series of portraits of people associated with the house.
Wakefield (*c.* 6 m. W.): Mentioned as 'Wachefield' in the Domesday Book, it was at its most important in the 15–16C, when it was a textile town. Especially worth seeing is the cathedral of *All Saints.* Begun in Norman times, it was rebuilt in 1329; the clerestory was added in 1470. The W. tower, which is 260 ft. high and dates from the 15C, was rebuilt in 1861. The 20C saw the lengthening of the chancel. *St.Mary's Chapel* stands on a 14C bridge over the River Calder; the chapel dates from the 14C and has beautiful Gothic windows. The *City Museum* has a good natural history collection. The *City Art Gallery* boasts of sculptures by Henry Moore.
Whitkirk (*c.* 6 m. NW): *St.Mary's Church* is 15C in Perpendicular style; there are fine tombs inside).

Port Laoise
Laois/Ireland   p.326□D 12

Port Laoise, formerly called *Maryborough,* is the county town of Laoise in the province of Leinster. It has a beautiful Protestant *parish church* (with obelisk tower) and a 19C *court building.*

Environs: Abbeyleix (*c.* 10 m. S.): This town was the seat of the Counts of Vesci (documented since 1215). The *mansion* was built in 1773 to designs of Wyatt in Georgian style on the site of the remains of a Cistercian Abbey of 1183. The *park* has the tomb of the last king of Leix.
Portarlington (*c.* 9 m. NE): This charm-

Portsmouth, Lord Nelson's flagship, 'H.M.S. Victory'

ing little town, which was founded by the Huguenots in 1667, has beautiful Georgian houses and doors. The town's name goes back to the former feudal lord, Lord Arlington (1641).

Timahoe (*c.* 11 m. SE): The 12C *Round Tower.* has a Romanesque portal carved with historical scenes. Nearby are the ruins of a 17C *castle* and 15C *church.*

Portsmouth

Hampshire/England   p.332□I 16

In spite of its extraordinary natural facilities, Portsmouth is not a particularly old city. Henry VII (1485-1509) was the first to discover its advantages and he set up the first dry dock and made the sleepy little town a Royal Garrison. While the merchantmen and the Elizabethan discoverers found their home in Plymouth, Portsmouth became the port of the Navy, the admirals and the docks. Charles II (1660 -85) employed the Dutchman Bernard de Gomme, who was the best fortress architect of his time, and had the city and harbour converted into a castle. In recognition of the fact that he who controls Portsmouth, controls the Channel and thereby England, the towers (*Round Tower,* around 1415, and *Square Tower,* around 1495) and castles (*Southsea Castle,* 1538-40, and *Cumberland Fort,* 1746-86) were built.

Charles Dickens was born here in 1812 and, 1882-90 the doctor Arthur Conan Doyle practised in the suburb of Southsea, writing the first Sherlock Holmes novel, 'A Study in Scarlet', here.

Cathedral: Dedicated to St.Thomas, this bishop's church of the diocese established in 1927 dates back to a Norman church built 1188-96, of which the *sanctuary* and the *transepts* have survived. The nave itself and the tower were rebuilt at the end of the 17C. A new nave has been in the pro-

Portchester (Portsmouth), Roman walls

cess of being built since 1935. The *S. chancel aisle* is dedicated to the heroes of the Royal Navy, in remembrance of which is a model of the 'Mary Rose'. On the NE wall of the *chancel* an impressive fresco dating from *c.* 1250 depicts the Last Judgement.

Museums: The *Royal Naval Museum* is opposite Lord Nelson's flagship 'H.M.S. Victory', which was raised and restored in 1921. Displayed in the museum are Nelson memorabilia and exhibits illustrating the sailor's life in the 18C. The Battle of Trafalgar is depicted in a 46 ft. panorama by W.L. Wyllie. Numerous model ships complete the collection. In *Southsea Castle,* founded by Henry VIII in 1546 as a defence against the French, exhibits of local history and of the city's military history are displayed. *Cumberland House* houses the

regional natural history museum. The *Dickens Birthplace Museum,* the house in which the writer was born, displays Dickens memorabilia.

Environs: Portchester (6 m. N.): On a spit of land at the N. end of Portsmouth's enormous natural harbour lies the Roman fortress *Portus Adurni* with its massive square of walls. Dating from the 3C, these are nearly 20 ft. high and have 20 bastions; they are the only Roman walls in the whole of N. Europe which are preserved in such proportions and at their full height. The walls were so splendid that nearly 800 years later the Normans made use of them practically unaltered. Only on the W. and E. sides were new gates built; in the NW corner a massive square defence tower was built. Under Henry I (1100–35) these were extended into a Royal Castle. In 1133 Au-

gustinian monks were allowed to settle in the SE corner and build a monastery. Of the monastery itself and its cloister there remain only foundations, but the monastery church is excellently preserved and has an interesting Norman columned portal and a good font. In 1396–99 Richard II extended the castle, which became the assembly point for Henry V's campaign against the French.

Titchfield Abbey (12.5 m. NW): This *Premonstratensian monastery* was founded by the Bishop of Winchester in 1232. In 1445 Henry VI and Margaret of Anjou were married in the monastery church, which was completed in 1238; in 1542 Thomas Wriothesley, Lord Chancellor to Henry VIII, built his palace here. He turned the church's main nave into his gatehouse, the refectory into the Great Hall and the cloister into an inner court. The complex fell into decay from the 18C onwards. Today the pavement tiles of the abbey, dating from around 1300, are of particular interest.

Presteigne
Powys/Wales   p.328☐H 14

This little town on the English border has attractive old *half-timbered houses*. It is called Llanandras (= St.Andrew) in Welsh, after its old parish church.

St.Andrew's Church: This church has some Norman features (dating from *c.* 1100) but was much altered in 1375 in Decorated Style. There are interesting *interior arcades* and a Perpendicular W. window. It has a nave and two aisles of different widths; the N. aisle is the oldest part with remains of Norman arches; 2 W. columns between the N. aisle and the nave are in Norman Transitional style. *Statue of St. Andrew* (outside, over the W. window, *c.* 1100), a Flemish *tapestry* with Christ's Entry into Jerusalem (16C), *font* (14C) and *tombstone* with cross from 1240 (restored).

Environs: Knighton (*c.* 5.5 m. N.): This little town is the town on 'Offa's Dyke': This *border rampart* (Welsh: Clawdd Offa) between the Midlands and Wales was built around 784 at the behest of King Offa of Mercia/Midlands (757–96). No Welshman was allowed to cross the earth rampart and moat (the total length from N. to S. was *c.* 140 miles interrupted by patches of woodland). Between Knighton and Presteigne there are still parts of the rampart which are visible (such as at *Discoed, c.* 2 m. W. of Presteigne).
New Radnor (*c.* 6 m. SW): Remains of a 13C *castle*.
Old Radnor (*c.* 4.5 m. SW): *Old Radnor Church,* is an interesting church in late Decorated to Perpendicular Style (15–16C)

with a W. tower, which is visible for miles. Of importance is the 6–7C font, which had earlier been used for pagan rituals; there are also a fine choir screen, old church pews, an oak ceiling and an organ case from the 16C (late Gothic).

Preston
Lancashire/England   p.328☐H 11

Richard Arkwright, who was born in Preston in 1732, did much to mechanize cotton production with his invention of the water frame in 1768. (see Bolton Museum of Textile Machinery). The town is also famous for its fair ('Preston Gild'; not due again until 1992), which takes place only once every 20 years.

Harris Museum and Art Gallery: Extensive collections cover the archaeology, natural history and social history of the region; also an interesting ceramics collection. The painting gallery has interesting works by 19&20C artists.

Environs: Blackburn (*c.* 9 m. E.): The *Lewis Textile Museum* documents the history of cotton production. The *Town Museum* has interesting antiquities (Greek and Roman coins, Egyptian objects) whilst the adjoining art gallery has over 1200 Japanese prints and beautiful English water colours. Also of interest is the (still uncompleted) *cathedral.*
Halsall (*c.* 17.5 m. SW): The interesting church of *St. Cuthbert* is 14C and has an octagonal 15C tower; of interest in the chancel is the portal with original oak door.
Houghton Tower (*c.* 6 m. SE): Converted in 1565 and restored in the 19C; of interest inside is the old 17C wall panelling and mementoes of the visit of James I in 1617.
Ormskirk (*c.* 17 m. SW): The Perpendicular church of *St. Peter and St. Paul* has a tower of 1540; inside there are interesting

tomb monuments to the Earls of Derby.

Ribchester (*c.* 7.5 m. NE): Excavations of the Roman fort *Bremetennacum,* which defended the intersection of two Roman roads (Manchester–Carlisle and , Ilkley–Fylde near Blackpool), have shown it to have been laid out by Agricola, father-in-law of the famous Roman historian Tacitus. Of interest, among other things, is an excavated granary and a well system. The adjoining *Museum of Roman Antiquities* has the finds from the excavations, including the tombstone of a soldier, as well as coins and ceramics, a copy of a bronze parade helmet (the original is in the British Museum), and the model of the fort.

Samlesbury Hall (*c.* 5 m. NE): 14C mansion; of interest inside are a collection of watercolours and beautiful cupboards.

Scarisbrick (*c.* 15.5 m. SW): Beautiful Gothic *Scarisbrick Hall.*

Southport (*c.* 15.5 m. SW): The parish church of *St. Cuthbert* was rebuilt in 1730; the tower was not built until later. The church was enlarged in the 19C. Of interest inside are the 18C font and the carved wooden altar wings from the same time. Also of interest is the *Atkinson Art Gallery* (temporary exhibitions of English painters

Ribchester, Roman excavations

of the 18–20C) and the Botanic Gardens Museum (of particular interest is the collection of 18C dolls).

Ramsgate
Kent/England   p.332□M 15

This port owes much of its significance to the fact that King George IV once spent a holiday here. It is now a popular seaside resort.

St. Augustine's Abbey and Church: This Roman Catholic abbey was consecrated in 1851.

St. George: This parish church was built in 1827 in the contemporary Gothic style.

St. Lawrence: This church dates back to the 13C.

Also worth seeing: The *Model Village* near St. Augustine's church is an attractive Tudor-style miniature village. *Pegwell Bay* has a replica of the 'Hugen', a Viking ship at anchor, which was brought from Denmark in 1949 to mark the anniversary of the Danish invasion of 449. A *Celtic cross* marks the spot where St. Augustine landed in 597 with 40 monks to spread Christianity among the Celts.

Environs: Birchington (5 m. E.): The *Powell Collection Museum* contains a dis-

play of African and Indian animal species and also of works of art from Africa, Asia and the Pacific.

Broadstairs (2 m. NE): *Bleak House* is a small Regency building where Dickens wrote 'David Copperfield'.

Minster (Isle of Thanet 4 m. W.): *St. Mary* is a fine cruciform church of Norman origin. *Minster Abbey*, the oldest building in the area, was founded in the 7C, later extended and is now occupied by Benedictines. The tomb of St. Mildred of Kent was discovered in 1929.

Richborough (4 m. SW): This was the initial landing-point of the Roman legions, and there are still remnants of *Fort Rutupiae*, including ditches. The *museum* of the excavations includes an extensive collection of coins.

Sandwich (4 m. SW): Before the bay receded, this was one of the Cinque Ports; today it is a sleepy coastal town. The most significant of its three churches is *St. Clement*, which is Norman in origin, as the tower and the attractive porch show; the church was enlarged in the 14&15C.

Reading
Berkshire/England   p.332□I 15

This is the county town of Berkshire, and

s situated at the confluence of the Kennet nd the Thames; in medieval times it was a centre of the textile industry. Its good poition made it the object of Danish attacks n 871 and 1006, but these did not affect ts prosperity. In 1121 Henry I founded a Cluniac abbey there, and its church was consecrated by Thomas à Becket, against he wishes of Henry II. It was eventually given a charter by Henry VIII in 1542, and oday it is an important industrial town, nd its old centre is marked by the *Church of St.Lawrence*, although this church has ecently been completely rebuilt.

Abbey: Very little remains of what was once the third largest abbey in the whole of England; there is only a *memorial stone* o indicate the tomb of King Henry I, who was buried here in 1135, and a small *plaque* reveals that in about 1240 a monk composed the canon 'Sumer is icomen in', the oldest surviving piece of music for several voices. The abbey was dissolved in 1539, and Hugh Faringdon, the last abbott, was hanged in front of his own gatehouse. Later the old gatehouse was used as a school.

Museum and Art Gallery: This is devoted to local history and prehistory; the most interesting exhibits are those from the Roman site at *Silchester*, which offer a fascinating picture of the day-to-day life of a Roman town.

Museum of English Rural Life: This museum was founded in 1951; it belongs to the university and serves as an information centre on all areas of rural life. The exhibits contain details of every conceivable aspect of life in a farmhouse, and include records, photographs, charts and a specialized library.

Museum of Greek Archaeology: This too belongs to the university and is largely devoted to a collection of Greek ceramics and ancient Egyptian relics.

Environs: Basildon Park (*c.* 6 m. NW): This is an attractive Georgian *manor house*, which was built by Carr of York for Viscount Fane in 1767.

Checkendon (7 m. N.): The *Church of St.Peter and St.Paul* dates back to Norman times, and still contains 12C frescos depicting Christ and the Apostles. Its W. tower is 16C.

Henley-on-Thames (9 m. NE): This is a small, idyllic town on the Thames, with an 18C *bridge* and a number of old Georgian *houses*.

Mapledurham House (3 m. NW): This is a picturesquely situated Elizabethan country house which is mainly known for its literary connections: it is the setting for John Galsworthy's celebrated 'Forsyte Saga' and Kenneth Grahame's 'Wind in the Willows'. It was also the location of Alexander Pope's romance with Martha and Theresa Blount.

Rotherfield Greys (6 m. N.): The *Church of All Saints* was built in 1100. Its portal was originally in the N. wall, and its round Norman arch is still visible on the wall's exterior. It was extended in 1260 by Walter de Grey, the Archbishop of York, who built *Grey's Court* nearby. The church was rebuilt and further extended in the 19C. William Knolly's monument to his parents (1605) is most interesting.

Reigate
Surrey/England   p.322☐K 15

This town is situated at the foot of the North Downs, and has existed since Norman times. There are still some remnants of its castle, which was destroyed by the Parliamentarians in 1648.

Church of St.Mary Magdalene: This large parish church dates back to Norman times, although the columns in the nave are later (around 1200). Lord Howard of

Richmond, Richmond Castle

Effingham (1536–1624), who led the fight against the Spanish Armada in 1588, is buried in the church; there is a large *monument* by Joseph Rose, who carved the figures and the architectural background in 1730. The two figures are life-size, and represent Truth and Justice.

Environs: Bletchingley (3 m. E.): The *Church of St. Mary the Virgin* was built around 1090 on the site of an earlier Saxon building. There are still Romanesque arches in the tower and the sanctuary, although the other arches are from the 13&15C. The church was extensively rebuilt in the 19C. The pulpit is 17C, and Richard Crutcher's tomb from 1707 is particularly fine. *Pendell Court* is a fine Jacobean gabled house (1636).
Walton-on-the-Hill (2 m. NW): The *Church of St. Peter* has a fine lead font

which dates back to Norman times. It is decorated with rounded arches, in which are sitting individual figures.

Richmond
North Yorkshire/England   p.328□I 10/11

St. Mary (access from Station Road): The town's parish church, which was thoroughly restored in 1860. There are two fine Norman *pillars* at the W. end, and the choir houses the carved *stalls* from Easby Abbey, with interesting misericords. The memorial chapel to the dead of the Green Howards Regiment, (stationed *c.* 3 m. S. in Catterick), is situated here.

Castle: This was built in 1071, after the Norman conquest, by Alan Rufus, who received the title 'Earl of Richmond' from

Richmond, Grey Friars' Tower

William the Conqueror, and with it lordship over the whole surrounding area; it stands on the steep cliffs over the River Swale, and became the centre of the later town of Richmond. It was subsequently enlarged: in 1146 the 115 ft. high keep, with its 10 ft. thick walls, was erected. It offers a panoramic view over the town.

Georgian Theatre (Friar's Wynd): This was built in 1788, and was not used for theatre after the mid 19C until its restoration and reopening in 1962. It is the only theatre of its kind in Great Britain which has been preserved in more or less its original form.

Also worth seeing: *Trinity Church*, in the market place, is known for its bells, which only ring at 11 a.m. on Shrove Tuesday, to remind the housewives to cook their pancakes. *Grey Friars' Tower* (N. of the market place) is Perpendicular in style; it is all that remains of the monastery church of the 'Grey Brothers', the Grey Friars who lived in Richmond from 1158 until the monastery's dissolution in the 16C, before the church was ever completed. *Green Howards Museum* contains mementoes of the regiment, which was stationed near Richmond (see St.Mary's Church). There are some remnants of the old *town walls*.

Environs: Easby Abbey (*c.* 1 m. SE): This is the ruins of a monastery built in 1155 for the Premonstratensian monks of Richmond. The remains of the monastery church include the E. end of the choir, part of the transept and some of the pillars in the nave; the S. side of the site includes the remains of the refectory, and the hospice is to the N.

Right by the site of the old monastery is the previous parish church of *St. Agatha*, which is somewhat older than the monastery itself. It has some fine 13C frescos and a Norman font.

Ellerton Priory and **Marrick Priory** (*c.* 8 m. W.): The ruins of these two 13C priories lie on opposite banks of the Swale in the upper reaches of its valley.

Rievaulx
North Yorkshire/England   p.328☐i 11

Rievaulx Abbey: This was founded in 1131 by Lord Helmsley, and was the first large Cistercian monastery in England; it was dissolved in the 16C, when the Church of England split from Rome. Recent excavation work has safeguarded the remains of the structure, which is among the most impressive in England. Parts of the church have been preserved, as well as the actual monastery.

Church: Because of its situation it is oriented N-S rather than W-E; the nave,

choir and transept have been preserved, as well as some of the supporting pillars from the side aisles. Some of the remnants are from an older Norman building, but otherwise the church is basically 13C Early English in style. The cloisters were originally to the W. of the nave, with the Early English refectory adjacent on the other side. To the S. are the ruins of another monastery building.

Environs: Byland Abbey (*c.* 9 m. SW): This was founded in 1171 by Cistercian monks from Furness (Cumbria), and was once the largest of the order's churches in England. The *church* is interesting: it has green and yellow glazed tiles and a fine rose-window in the W. front. Its small *museum* houses a highly-decorated capital from the church.

Gilling (*c.* 9 m. S.): Originally a 13C *castle*, which has now been converted into a school; it has an Elizabethan-style banqueting-hall.

Helmsley (*c.* 3 m. E.): The *church* is interesting—it was restored in 1867, but still

Rievaulx, Rievaulx Abbey

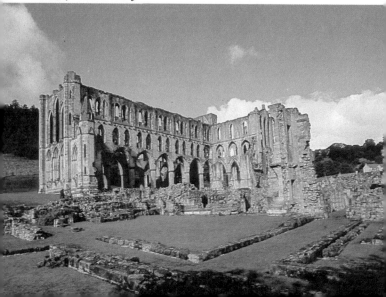

has its original Norman portal, and fine arches in the choir from the same period —and so is the *castle*, in Duncambe Park, which was built in 1186 – 1227 and defended by towers in the 14C. It was destroyed in the 17C, during the Civil War. The double ditches have survived, along with the huge keep and W. tower.

Hovingham Spa (c. 9 m. SE): There was a settlement here as early as Roman times (excavations have revealed a hypocaust system, hot baths and mosaic floors). The *church* has a Saxon tower and Norman sections. *Hovingham Hall*, a house which dates from 1760, is also interesting.

Kirkdale (c. 6 m. E.): The small church of *St. Gregory* is interesting, with a Saxon sundial and an old inscription above a piece of 11C restoration (from the priests Brand and Hawarth in the time of Earl Tosti).

Mount Grace Priory (c. 16 m. NW): Well-preserved remains of a Carthusian priory dating from 1398.

Newburgh Priory (c. 12 m. SW): The remains of an Augustinian priory founded in 1145, which was dissolved under Henry VIII in the 16C.

Nunnington (c. 7 m. SE): Has a 17C *manor house* (W. wing, 1580) and a *church* which is largely medieval, with interesting furnishings.

Stonegrave (c. 6 m. SE): An attractive small *church*, with a partially Saxon tower and a fine old cross inside.

Thirsk (c. 12 m. W.): The 15C late Gothic church of *St. Mary* is one of the finest Perpendicular churches in North Yorkshire; the manor house of *Thirsk Hall* was rebuilt in 1770 by John Carr of York.

Ripon
North Yorkshire/England   p.328□I 11

Probably England's second-oldest town; it was incorporated into the kingdom of Alfred the Great (871–99) in 886. Until 1604 the city guard was drilled by the 'Wakeman'. Every evening at 9 p.m. a horn is blown and a bell rung, a tradition dating back to 1598, although its roots are doubtless far older. The original 16C horn is on display in the Town Hall.

Cathedral of St. Peter and St. Wilfrid (Minster Road): The original church was begun in 669 by Bishop Wilfrid (the Saxon crypt is from this period), destroyed by the Saxon king Eadred, then rebuilt and destroyed again by the Normans (it is mentioned in the Domesday Book); the church we see today was begun in the 11C, and completed under Archbishop Roger de Pont l'Eveque (1154 – 81). During the course of the following centuries it was altered and extended, and restoration work was begun in 1829 (including work by Gilbert Scott) and has continued unbroken from 1956 to the present day. Since 1836, when the new diocese was formed, it has been the seat of the Bishop of Ripon. During the course of its long period of construction it incorporated every

Ripon, St. Peter and St. Wilfrid

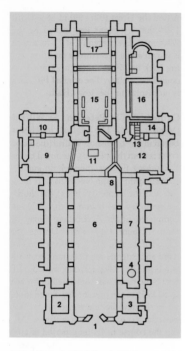

Ripon Cathedral 1 W. façade **2** NW tower **3** SW tower **4** font **5** N. aisle **6** nave **7** S. aisle **8** entrance to the Saxon crypt (St. Wilfred's crypt) **9** N. transept **10** N. transept aisle **11** crossing with tower **12** S. transept **13** entrance to Norman crypt **14** S. transept aisle **15** choir **16** chapterhouse **17** altar

architectural style from Saxon to late Perpendicular.

Exterior: The W. façade is Early English, and the main portal is from 1673; the W. tower and the tower over the crossing are both some 131 ft. high. The one above the crossing is a mixture of styles: the N. and W. sides are late Romanesque Transitional, the S. and E. sides Perpendicular. Its spire was destroyed by lightning in the 17C.

Interior: The ground plan comprises a nave and two aisles, with transepts and two aisles in the choir. Its total length is some 295 ft., its width some 95 ft., and its height around 98 ft.; making it England's fourth largest church. The nave pre-dates the aisles, and there are some isolated Transitional fragments; the W. end and the towers in particular have some fine Early English work, although they are predominantly Perpendicular. There is a simple triforium below the clerestory. The *roof* of the nave was restored after the model of the cathedral at York. The N. aisle contains the remains of a 17C *stained-glass window*, and the S. aisle a 14C *sarcophagus* by the font with some attractive reliefs: a man with a lion, in the tradition of the Irish eagle which brought a tame lion from Palestine. There is an ancient triangular *basin* in the S. wall, under which is a trapdoor which leads down to the Saxon *crypt*. At the W. end of the N. aisle is the diocesan *consistorium* (the lower section of the railings are allegedly from St. Wilfrid's shrine). The transept has a fine Perpendicular *oak ceiling*, and the N. section is original Transitional Norman. The *pulpit* is 15C. At the N. end is the 15C Markenfield family *tomb*. The aisle of the N. transept was for a long time the Markenfield funerary chapel and is also known as the *Markenfield Chapel*). The S. and W. sides of the S. transept are in the original Transitional Norman style, but the E. side is Perpendicular. The aisle of the S. transept (*Mallory Chapel*) contains Mallory family tombs: the tomb of Sir John Mallory of Studley, a Royalist in the Civil War, is on the E. side.

The entrance to the *choir* is through a late-15C choir screen. The stylistic difference is pronounced: the first three arches on the N. side of the choir are Transitional Norman, the opposite arches are Perpendicular and the others are Decorated. The glass of the large E. *window* is not original (it depicts the foundation of the new bishopric in the 19C). There is a memorial to those who fell in World War I on the *altar*; the *choir stalls* were largely rebuilt in the 15C. The S. aisle of the choir leads through to the *chapterhouse*; there is an old

Norman chapel nearby with an ancient stoup and fine vaulting; also the *Lady Chapel*, which is entered from the S. transept and has served as a *library* since 1624. Its finest items include a psalter from 1418, a 13C Bible and a number of incunabula. Cathedral *crypts*: *Saxon crypt* (entered from the S. aisle): the oldest section of the entire church, dating from the 7C; a barrel-vaulted space *c.* 12 ft. long, 8 ft. wide and 10 ft. high, laid out in the form of a 'confessio'. The *Norman crypt* (entered from the S. transept) is *c.* 80 ft. long and 20 ft. high, and was part of the church built by Archbishop Roger, the predecessor to the cathedral itself. It was used as a charnel-house until 1865, and is now *All Souls' Chapel*.

Wakeman's House (Market Place): This 13C house was the office of the last 'Wakeman' and first mayor of the city. The interior furnishings are 16C, and it houses a small *local museum*.

Also worth seeing: *St.Anne's Chapel* (S. of the cathedral) was built in the 15C as a home for the needy; it was destroyed in 1869, but there is a roofless chapel dating from 1100 still standing; the interior contains an altar, a basin and a font. *St.Agnes's Lodge* (adjacent) is a late-15C building with 17C additions (no access to the interior). *Thorpe Prebend House* (attached to St. Anne's Chapel) is 17C; the interior contains fine panelling and a staircase. The *Hospital of St.Mary Magdalene* (Magdalen's Road) was built under Archbishop Thurstan (1114–41) as a hospital for lepers; since its rebuilding in the 17&19C, it has become a home for needy women. *St. Wilfrid's R.C. church* (Coltsgate) has an interesting pyramidal roof. The *Bishop's Palace* (NW of the cathedral) was built in 1838–41 in neo-Tudor style, and was the former residence of the Bishops of Ripon.

Environs: Aldborough (*c.* 7 m. SE): The *Aldborough Roman Site Museum* is interesting: it houses the finds from the Roman settlement of *Isurium Brigantum* (ceramics, coins, inscriptions, etc.). The remains of the Roman fortifications are still standing. The church of *St.Andrew* is also notable (14C, with a 15C tower), and houses a statue of the god Mercury (presumably the church was built on the site of an ancient temple of Mercury).

Boroughbridge (*c.* 6 m. SE): To the W. of the village are the three *Devil's Arrows*, monoliths which were placed there during the Bronze Age (some 2000 BC). They are up to 23 ft. in height, with a circumference of over 16 ft. Their surfaces have been substantially eroded by the weather.

Markenfield Hall (*c.* 3 m. S.): This is a 14C *manor house*, with a fine banqueting hall with impressive windows, and an old kitchen.

Newby Hall (*c.* 3 m. SE): A *manor house* of 1705, which was extended by Robert Adam in 1770–76. The interior includes some interesting Gobelins and a collection of classical statues.

Rochester, Rochester Castle

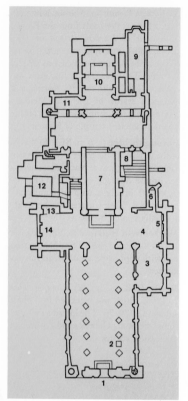

Rochester Cathedral 1 W. façade with portal
2 font **3** Lady Chapel **4** S. transept **5** tomb of Sir
Richard Watts and plaque to Charles Dickens **6**
sacristy **7** choir **8** entrance to the crypt **9** chapterhouse **10** presbytery **11** St. John's Chapel **12**
Gundulf's Tower **13** Jesus Chapel **14** N. transept

Rochester
Kent/England   p.332□L15

There was a Celtic settlement at this ford
over the Medway even before the Romans
developed the town whose street plan can
still be recognized today. It became a
bishopric in 604, the second-oldest in England. William the Conqueror made it an
important nexus, and today it is a port and
trading centre.

Cathedral: King Ethelbert commissioned a church here in 604; there is a mark
on the floor of the nave by the small W.
door. The cathedral we see today was built
in the 12&13C, when a Benedictine monastery was also founded here. The building was severely damaged in the Civil War
and restored in the 19C, and contains elements of Norman, Perpendicular and
Early English styles. The Norman *W. front*
has a fine *portal*, and the figures of Henry
I and Queen Matilda in the tympanum are
among the finest in England. The nave has
six Norman arches, and the *triforium*
opens on to the nave and the aisles. The
monument to Sir Richard Watts is in the
S. transept, and there is a memorial to
Charles Dickens, who lived in the town for
some years. The N. transept used to house
the tomb of the Scottish pilgrim William
of Perth (12C) who was killed in the neighbourhood. The *crypt* has heavy rib vaulting and the collection of bishops' tombs is

Rochester, Cathedral

among the finest in England. The *Wheel of Fortune*, a 13C wall painting opposite the modern bishop's throne is also interesting, as are the *Prior's Gate* and S. front. Near the cathedral are the ruins of the old *monastery building*, with three of the original gateways still standing.

St.Nicholas: This 15C church was rebuilt in the 17C; it now houses the diocesan offices and only the central area serves as a church.

Castle: This was built shortly after the Norman invasion and its massive keep, one of the best-preserved in England, overlooks the city. Some remnants of the walls are still standing.

Corn Exchange: A 19C building whose façade has a highly decorated clock and the coat-of-arms of Admiral Sir Cloudesley Shovel, a benefactor of the city.

Eastgate House: A late Tudor building which houses a museum of local history and the Dickens Centre.

George Inn: Built in the 16C on the site of an old church, with cellar vaulting reminiscent of the 13C; it was a post house in the 18C.

Guildhall (High Street): A red brick building of 1607 with Doric columns, with a fully equipped model sailing ship on the roof as a weathervane.

King's School: Dates from the time of Henry VIII.

Restoration House (Maidstone Road): Built in 1587, it takes its name from the fact that Charles II rested here in 1600 on the way to his coronation.

Royal Victoria and Bull: This was built around 1600 and rebuilt in Victorian times; Charles Dickens lived here, and wrote about it in the *Pickwick Papers* and *Great Expectations*.

The 'Six Poor Travellers' (High Street): An 18C gabled house; in the 16C Richard Watts bequeathed money for it to offer ac-

commodation and sustenance to six poor travellers, a tradition that continued until the middle of this century.

Environs: Chatham (1 m. S.): A flourishing harbour founded by Henry VIII on the site of an old Saxon settlement, with the *Military Museum* of the Corps of Royal Engineers.
Cliffe (5 m. N.): *St. Helen's Church* was built in the 13&14C and has splendid wall paintings.
Cobham (3 m. NW): *Cobham Hall*, a fine 16C house, was extended by James Wyatt, among others, in the 18C, and is now a girls' school.
Luddesdown (4 m. W.): The manor house of *Luddesdown Court* is supposedly the oldest in the area.
Sittingbourne (11 m. E.): *Court Hall Museum* has an interesting exhibition of local history.

Rockingham
Northamptonshire/England   p.328☐K 13

This small town, to the N. of the industrial centre of Corby, is a picturesque spot, with a number of old stone houses still standing.

Church of St. Leonard: This church is Gothic in origin, but was extensively restored in the 19C. There are a number of interesting *tombs* dating from the 16–19C. The most remarkable is the tomb of the 1st Earl of Rockingham, who died in 1724, which was carved by Peter Scheemaker. The Jacobean *pulpit* is also interesting, as is the *font* (1669).

Rockingham Castle: This was built for William the Conqueror and belonged to the Crown until the reign of Elizabeth I, who gave it to Edward Watson. The large *gatehouse* and its round towers are Norman;

the *Great Hall* was built under Edward I, and the house itself took its present form in around 1550. The castle, which now houses an exceptional collection of furniture and paintings, was a favourite residence of Charles Dickens.

Environs: Deene (5 m. E.): The *Church of St. Peter* dates back to the 13C, although only the W. tower still stands from the original building. Sir Digby Wyatt restored it extensively, finishing in 1868. It has a number of monuments, of which the most interesting are those to members of the Brudenell family. *Deene Park* has been the seat of the Brudenell family since 1514. It is a Tudor house, and is of especial interest in that it has remained almost unaltered. The *park* is also interesting, with rare trees and shrubs.
Fotheringhay (*c.* 9 m. E.): This is where Mary Queen of Scots, was tried and executed in 1587. The *Church of St. Mary and All Saints* is an impressive Perpendicular building with a fine W. tower which was originally a collegiate church in the early 15C. The nave and aisles are from this period, but the rest of the building is more recent. The old *inn* is attractive, and is also 15C.
Kirby Hall (4 m. NE): This building was commissioned by Sir Humphrey Stafford and begun by the architect Thomas Thorpe in 1570. Five years later Sir Christopher Hatton acquired the shell of the building and completed it. Alterations were made under Inigo Jones in 1638–40, but in 1809 the Hatton family left the house and it fell into disrepair. Only the SW wing has been restored, but although the rest of the house is in ruins, it is nevertheless of great architectural interest, since it contains details which at the time of its construction were only paralleled in France. There is no other building in England with such a combination of early Renaissance and Elizabethan styles.
Lowick (12 m. SE): The *Church of St. Peter*

is interesting because of the early-14C stained glass which is still in the windows. Its massive tower with its octagonal upper storey dates from the 15C, the same period as the oldest of the monuments.

Weldon (4 m. SE): The *Church of St.Mary the Virgin* is a rare example of an inland church which has been converted into a lighthouse. For this purpose the Gothic spire was removed in the 18C, and a 17 ft. high octagonal glass lantern was added. Its light served to guide travellers in Rockingham forest.

Roscommon
Roscommon/Ireland   p.326□C 11

This is the main town of the county of the same name, with some 1,600 inhabitants and the remains of *Roscommon Castle* from 1269. The castle has been destroyed and rebuilt many times and was for a long time in the hands of the O'Conors until its eventual destruction by Cromwell in 1652. The castle plan is preserved, with its powerful corner towers, sections of the walls and a fine E. gate flanked by towers. The Dominican *Roscommon Abbey* was founded by King Felim O'Conor in 1253. The *church* is still standing, and its interesting points include the tomb of the founder (from around 1300) in a niche N. of the choir, and the carved, decorated gable above it, which is 15C.

Environs: Athleague (*c.* 5 m. SW.): Near the village is a rounded *ritual stone* from the Celtic La Tène period.

Ballymoe (*c.* 12 m. NW): To the NE are the remains of the O'Conor's *Ballintober Castle* (1300, restored in 1677, and occupied until the 19C); there are also remains of *Glinsk Castle* (early 17C, to the S.).

Castlerea (*c.* 19 m. NW): This is the seat of the former royal house of O'Conor (Don), *Clonalis House*, a Victorian house. Nearby is *Emlach Cross*, an 11C high cross with fine decoration.

Tulsk (*c.* 10 m. N.): Near the village is the Celtic royal palace of *Rathcroghan*, with earthworks, gravestones and traces of megalithic tombs.

Roscommon Abbey

Roscrea
Tipperary/Ireland   p.326□C 12

This attractive small town has some 3,500 inhabitants and dates back to a monastery founded by the Celtic saint St.Cronan in the 7C. The W. wall of the 12C Romanesque *Church of St. Cronan* is still standing, with a finely-carved portal (with St. Cronan in the middle). The *round tower* opposite it is also 12C, although it has lost its roof. The 12C *Celtic cross* is also interesting; it depicts the Crucifixion and the patron saint. The portal of the *Catholic church* (Abbey Street) is the remains of a Franciscan monastery dating from 1490. The bell tower and sections of the choir and nave are also from the original structure. The ruins of *Roscrea Castle* (Castle Street) are from a Norman fortress of 1280 with 16&17C additions.

Environs: Birr (*c.* 12 m. NW): This small town's geographical position has led to its being described as the 'navel of Ireland'. It was built during the 18&19C and is at-tractively and regularly laid out in Georgian style. The *Protestant church* dates from 1810, the *Catholic church* from 1817 and Lord Rosse's *Ionic temple* from 1828. *Birr Castle* is an attractive 17C building with 19C neo-Gothic additions. The extensive *park* is also interesting, with ancient trees and the remains of what was at the time the largest *telescope* in the world; it belonged to the Earl of Rosse, who was an astronomer, and dates from 1845.

Mona Incha (2 m. E.): Once an island monastery, although the lake around it has now been drained, it was founded in the 12C. The *church* has a fine 12C portal, and 13C windows framed by capitals. The lower section of the *cross* is 9C, the upper section is 12C.

Roslin
Lothian/Scotland   p.324□H 8

This old mining town to the south of Edinburgh owes its fame to a combination of

Birr (Roscrea), Birr Castle

two factors: firstly, because it was known as a centre for stonemasonry in the Middle Ages, and secondly, because no less a writer than Walter Scott made it so popular with his 'Lay of the Last Minstrel' that by 1800 there was already a daily stage-coach service from Edinburgh just to bring tourists to the real-life location of the ballad.

Roslin Chapel: Founded by William Sinclair, the third and last Earl of Orkney in 1446, it later became the collegiate church of St.Matthew. At the time of its founder's death in 1484, only the five-bayed *choir*, the *ambulatory* and the *retro-choir* were complete, and that should have been the extent of the structure. The 69 ft. long chapel was the Sinclair family's mausoleum. In 1688 it was damaged by rebellious townspeople from Edinburgh, but it was carefully restored in 1862 by order of the Earl of Rosslyn.

Architecturally speaking, the chapel is barely worthy of mention: it is Gothic, with a square-ended choir and barrel vaulting, but the structure pales into insignificance in comparison with the ornamentation. There is literally nothing which is not covered and re-covered with the finest *masonry*—capitals and consoles, architraves and vaulting, even the tracery is worked over with decoration. As well as the splendid *ornamentation*, the allegorical *carvings* are especially fascinating; Virtues and Sins, Angels and Demons, religious figures and grotesques are almost brought to life. The most vivid example is the *Dance of Death* on the vault ribs of the retro-choir, which is not only the first sculptural treatment of the subject in Great Britain, but also one of the most fully-realized. The celebrated *Prentice Pillar*, or apprentice's pillar, has winged dragons darting round its base chasing stylized garlands. This splendid pillar was supposed to have been carved by an apprentice during his master's absence. When the master saw his apprentice's work, he is said to have killed him in a fit of jealous rage. The three heads at the end of the nave are said to be those of the protagonists: the master, the apprentice and his grief-stricken mother.

Roslin Castle: This castle is built on a cliff above the valley of the North Esk; it was begun by William Sinclair, who died in 1330. Its keep is late 14C, and it was enlarged by the third Earl of Orkney, who founded Roslin Chapel. It was destroyed by the English in 1544, but was extensively rebuilt in 1580. The surviving 14C elements include some remnants of the walls, the cellars, the dungeon and some cliff caves. There is an interesting *escape*, which came out below the level of the water in the moat.

Rothesay Castle
Strathclyde/Scotland   p.324□F 8

This castle is situated on the E. side of the island of Bute, and dates back to the early 13C. The ground plan is unique in Scotland: a circular inner courtyard entered through a huge surrounding curtain wall with four round towers. The whole structure is encircled by a deep moat and the entrance was protected by the unusual Great Tower, built by King James V around 1530. In 1240 the Norsemen tore a section of the curtain wall down and stormed the fortress, and in 1263 the Norwegian King Haakon took it. It was finally destroyed by Cromwell's troops.
Bute Museum houses an interesting exhibition of local history.

Royal Tunbridge Wells
Kent/England   p.332□L 15

In 1606 Lord North discovered the natural, iron-rich springs, and 30 years later the building of the town began; it is attractively situated, surrounded by wooded hills, and is one of England's best known spas.

The town has rows of fine Georgian and Victorian houses, particularly the *Pantiles*, whose original pantile paving is all but lost. *Calverey House*, which is now a hotel, is also of interest; it used to be a residence of Queen Victoria. The title of 'Royal' is a legacy of her visits. There is also an interesting walk to the bizarrely-formed sandstone rocks at *Runstall*.

Holy Trinity: This church, which was consecrated in 1829, is by Decimus Burton, who was the best-known architect of his time.

St. Charles the Martyr: This is a small, elegant church with a highly-ornamented ceiling dating from 1696; it is dedicated to King Charles I, who was executed by Parliament in 1649. A plaque points out the seat on which Princess Victoria used to to sit.

Chiddingstone (Royal Tunbridge Wells)

Museum and Art Gallery: This has a fine collection of local historical exhibits, and of toys and needlework; there is also a natural history section.

Environs: Chiddingstone (5 m. W.): The *Church of St. Mary* is 14C, with some fine old masonry, a Jacobean font and pulpit. *Chiddingstone Castle* is an 18C Gothic castle which houses Tudor and Stuart manuscripts and documents, and also has Egyptian and Japanese collections.
Hever (7 m. W.): *St. Peter's Church* is typical of the 14C, and has Sir Thomas Boleyn's tomb (Anne Boleyn's father). *Hever Castle* is 13C but was rebuilt in the 15C; it has Italianate gardens, and was Anne Boleyn's childhood home. It was restored this century by William Waldorf Astor.
Holtye (8 m. W.): A *Roman road*, covered with slag from the nearby iron workings.
Owl House (4 m. SE): A 16C *half-timbered house*; only the rose garden is open.
Penshurst (3 m. NW): *Penshurst Place*, the birthplace of the poet, soldier and statesman Sir Philip Sidney (1554 – 86), dates from the Middle Ages; there is a splendid 14C *great hall*, and the Sidney coat-of-arms and portraits are interesting, as is the *toy museum* in the former stables. The village contains some attractive houses.
Rotherfield (6 m. S.): *St. Denys' Church* is 13C, with a shingled bell tower and two-storeyed porch; there are interesting original wall paintings and a fine E. window.
Scotney Castle (5 m. SE): Attractively situated 13C ruins.
Sissinghurst (15 m. E.): This village became wealthy through the weaving trade; it is typical of Kent, with whitewashed, shingled houses. *Sissinghurst Castle* is the remains of a 15&16C castle surrounded by a wonderful garden laid out in Elizabethan style by Sir Harold Nicolson and Victoria Sackville-West in 1930. The finest section is the *White Garden* with the *Priest's*

House. Sissinghurst Court is an attractive 16C house with a garden.

Tonbridge (2 m. N.): Remains of a Norman *castle*; Early English parish church of *St.Peter and St.Paul.*

Withyham (7 m. SW): The 14C *Church of St.Michael and All Angels* was rebuilt in the 17C, and houses the Sackville family tombs; Thomas Sackville's (d. 1677) is by the celebrated mason Caius G.Cibber.

Rye
East Sussex/England   p.332☐L 16

This picturesque town was formerly one of the Cinque Ports, and in the course of its history has been captured and razed many times, as in 1377 by the French. When the harbour began to recede, trade and business in the town declined with it, and it is now a popular tourist resort. It has, however, maintained its charming medieval character.

Parish church of St.Mary: Originally built in the 12C, it has since been rebuilt and extended many times and is now a mixture of Norman, Early English, Decorated and modern. The great clock was completed in 1560 in Winchelsea and is reputed to be the oldest of its kind in England. On the clock face, on either side of a memorial plaque, are the *Quarter Boys*, which strike the quarter hours. The mahogany *altar* is 18C, and so is the *chandelier* in the choir. The *font* and part of the splendid *window* are 19C.

Ypres Tower: This is a huge square tower with 3 semicircular corner towers and a smaller, free-standing castellated tower from the 19C. It was originally part of a 13C fortress, and was taken over in the 16C by the authorities and served for a long time as a prison. It assumed its present form in 1928 and has since housed a *museum* of the history of the Cinque Ports. The surrounding *Canon Garden* was once the site of the cannons defending the harbour fort, but it is now a *viewing platform*.

Also worth seeing: *Marmaid Street* is the

Owl House, Royal Tunbridge Wells

most impressive of the town's many cobbled streets; the *Marmaid Inn* was formerly an important smugglers' meet and still maintains its 15–17C aspect. The *House Opposite* is from the same period, and is so called because many people mistook it for the Marmaid Inn and were directed across the street by the locals. *Lamb House* (West Street) was the home of the writer Henry James during his retirement, in 1898–1916, and later that of the English storyteller E.F.Benson, who was mayor in 1934–7. *Land Gate* is the only 13C town gate still standing. The former *Augustinian monastery* is now one of the town's numerous potteries.

Environs: Camber (1 m. S.): This resort is the site of the ruins of *Camber Castle*, which was built under Henry VIII against the possibility of a French invasion.

Dungeness (6 m. SE): In 1792 the English architect James Wyatt (1746–1813) built a *lighthouse* here, which is still standing. There is now a power station on the site.

East Guildford (1 m. NE): *St. Mary's Church* is a small, attractive brick church without a tower, dating from the 15C. Its furnishings are 19C.

Great Dixter (9 m. NW): Here there is a 15C *manor house* which was restored in 1910; it has a large hall, and is surrounded by beautiful gardens.

Winchelsea (3 m. S.): The old port was destroyed by the sea and the present town dates from the 13C. There are *3 town gates* still standing from this period, as well as the *Court Hall*, which now houses a museum of local history, and numerous *vaults*. The *Church of St. Thomas the Martyr*, built next to the ruins of the old church's choir, has the tombs of two Cinque Port admirals and magnificent glass windows by Douglas Strachan (1930).

Scotney Castle

Scotney Castle, moat

Saffron Walden
Essex / England   p.332□L 14

This peaceful little town dates back to the *Waledana* of Roman times. There are still *earth fortification systems* E. and W. of the town from Saxon times. A *castle* was built in Norman times, the *keep* of which survives. The town acquired its present name from the processing of saffron, which was the principle activity here from the days of Edward II to around 1800. There are still numerous half-timbered and brick houses from the 15&16C. There are also early examples of stuccoed houses.

Church of St.Mary the Virgin: This actually dates back to Norman times, but it was completely rebuilt in the 15&16C. Its massive, steepled *W. tower* was given its octagonal spire in 1831. The roof had to be restored recently. Apart from numerous other *monuments* and *memorial slabs,* the church also contains the tomb of Lord Audley, Chancellor to Henry VIII. The *stained glass* is 19C.

Audley End House: The *Benedictine Abbey* to the W. of the town was dissolved by Henry VIII and bestowed on Lord Audley, who built a Tudor house here. In 1603 it became the property of Howard of Walden, who was made Earl of Suffolk by James I. He began building an enormous Jacobean house with two large inner courts. Following the Restoration, Charles II confiscated the house and it was not returned to the Howards until 1701. Around 1720 Sir John Vanbrugh was commissioned to alter the house in contemporary style. He had about half of it torn down, while the exterior of the rest was preserved, sparing the beautiful *balustrade* and turrets. Much was altered inside, but on the whole to its advantage. The house now contains a valuable *collection of paintings* and all the *interior furnishings* are original.

Museum: This stands in the grounds of the ruined 12C Norman castle and, besides various exhibits relating to local history, it contains a fine Anglo-Saxon sword.

Environs: Finchingfield (*c.* 19 m. SE): This village is one of the most picturesque in the whole county. It owes its charm to numerous beautiful old houses, such as the *Guildhall* of *c.* 1500, a *windmill* and the *church* with its Norman tower. Just over 1 m. N. of the village lies *Spains Hall,* a beautiful 16C brick house with a two-storeyed entrance hall.

Hadstock (8 m. N.): The church of *St.*

St. Albans, Cathedral

Botolph may have been built by Canute in 1020 to commemorate his victory over Edmund Ironside in nearby Ashdon. The old structure has survived better than almost any other church of its period. Even the oak porch still dates from Saxon times and may be the oldest church porch in the country. The present sanctuary was not added until 1884 by William Butterfield.

Newport (4.5 m. SW): This little village still has several old houses, such as *Monks Barn* with half-timbering and brickwork from the 15C and beautifully stuccoed 17C houses. The church of *St. Mary the Virgin* was built in the 13&14C. Its W. tower was rebuilt in 1858. Superb pieces of furnishing include a 13C font, a painted portable altar, also 13C, and 14C stained-glass windows.

Strethall (3 m. NW): The church of *St. Mary the Virgin* is a small church from Anglo-Saxon times. The sanctuary and W. tower are 15C, but the triumphal arch survives from the old church and was built in the 11C.

Thaxted (15.5 m. SE): This town, which flourished in the Middle Ages due to its wool trade, still has old half-timbered houses. The *Guildhall* dates from 1475. The church of *St. John the Baptist* bears witness to the prosperity of the townsfolk in the 15C. Nearly all the furnishings date from that time. Of interest are the font cover, the choir screen, remains of the original stained glass, and a richly embellished wooden roof. Three windows were restored by C.E. Kempe.

Wendens Ambo (2.5 m. SW): The church of *St. Mary the Virgin* still dates from Norman times. The tower has small spires and the sanctuary was built around 1300. The pulpit dates from the 15C. Of interest are fragments of frescos painted in about 1330 of the life of St. Margaret.

St. Albans
Hertfordshire/England   p.332□K 15

This city on the river Ver has one of the richest histories in England. It was Roman *Verulamium,* capital of the province of Britannia. Verulamium was founded in AD 43 on the site of a settlement which dated from the 1C BC. Just two years later it became a municipium and continued as such until 410. The city owes its present name to a Roman soldier, who was martyred in 303 for offering refuge to the priest who had converted him. In honour of the first martyr to die on English soil, King Offa of Mercia founded the Benedictine abbey of St. Albans in 739. Because of the high esteem in which the saint was held by the faithful, the abbey developed into one of the most important in England. From 1154 to 1396 its abbot was also Archabbot of England, thereby making it the premier abbey of the whole country. In 1455 and 1461 major battles in the Wars of the Roses were fought outside the city's gates. Only the great church survived the monastery's dissolution and was taken over by the community as a parish church.

Cathedral: The oldest parts of the present church stand on the site of the earlier building of King Offa. In 1077 Paul of Caen began work and the first phase of 7 bays ended in 1116. A second stage followed in the 13C, when the present transepts, the presbytery and the W. bays of the nave were added. In 1856 Sir Gilbert Scott began the restoration work, which was completed by Sir Edmund Beckett. In 1877 St. Albans became a bishop's seat, making the church a cathedral. An interesting feature of the enormously striking *nave* (nearly 300 ft. long) is the junction of the

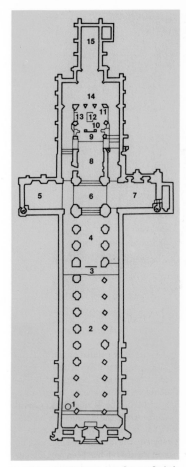

St. Albans Cathedral 1 font **2** nave **3** choir screen **4** choir **5** N. transept **6** crossing **7** S. transept **8** presbytery **9** altar screen **10** St. Albans' Chapel **11** memorial to Humphrey Duke of Gloucester **12** marble shrine of St. Alban **13** Watching Loft **14** retro-choir **15** Lady Chapel

Norman part and the early Gothic part completed in 1323. Three bays before the crossing is the stone *rood-screen* dividing the nave of the faithful from the monastic choir, which extends through the crossing into the presbytery. The Norman *columns*

St. Albans, Cathedral, altar

Nave and choir

of the nave were painted on the W. and S. sides. Important remains of these paintings have been revealed. They are by Walter of Colchester and may have been painted around 1220. The W. sides depict Christ's Passion, while the S. sides are adorned with saints. The *ceiling paintings* in the presbytery date from the late 15C. after this part of the church had been rebuilt under Abbot John de Hertford around 1450 the stone *altar-screen* was built under Abbot William de Wallingford in the 2nd half of the 15C. The *Martyrdom of St.Alban* in the S. choir aisle was made around 1530 and was originally in the N. transept.

The two *transpts* are the best-preserved part of the Norman church. On the E. side of the S. transept there is a *blind triforium*, the Norman arches of which are born by round columns with Norman bases and capitals. The *columns* themselves have sur-

vived from the Saxon church of King Offa. The *S. wall* also contains old fabric, because Lord Grimthorpe used the Norman portal and Norman arches of an old connecting passage during rebuilding. The area between the presbytery and retro-choir is known as *St.Albans Chapel.* Here stands the *marble shrine* to St.Alban, which was reconstructed from over 2, 000 broken pieces in 1872. The carved oak *Watching Loft* on the N. side originated around 1400, the *monument* to Humphrey Duke of Gloucester was completed after 1447. Lastly, the *Lady Chapel* was built by Abbot Hugh de Eversden around 1315. From the Reformation to 1870 it was used by the school and was not restored until thereafter.

Church of St.Michael: This was begun in 948. Sanctuary and nave still date entirely from the 10C and provide a good impression of Anglo-Saxon architecture. The two transepts were added in the 12C. Of interest are the superb Jacobean *pulpit* and fragments of medieval paintings, with a Last Judgement.

Clock Tower: This was built as the town's centre in 1403–12. It is one of the very few towers of its kind to have survived the centuries in England.

Roman Theatre: Relatively little is preserved of the capital of the Roman province of Britannia, but the remains of the theatre, built around 140 and extended around 300, are impressive. The finds from Verulamium are displayed in the *Roman Museum*. The outstanding feature of the collection is a mosaic pavement, which was discovered in 1959. It dates from the 2C and shows a lion bringing down a deer.

Environs: Hatfield (*c.* 7 m. E.): This old market town on the Great North Road still has beautiful Elizabethan and Jacobean houses. The church of *St.Etheldreda* actually dates from Norman times, but nothing from that time remains as the whole church was rebuilt by David Brandon at the end of the last century. The E. end and the transepts were incorporated, but the old fabric was not preserved. Of interest, however, is a small armoured statue from around 1200 and the elaborate tomb of Robert Cecil, first Duke of Salisbury, who died in 1612. His white marble effigy is born by kneeling maidens. The tomb is by Maximilian Colt, who also made the monument to Elizabeth I in Westminster. In order to ensure that it fulfilled its client's expectations, the artist had to make a model in 1609, which was then executed in marble in 1612 following the duke's death. *Hatfield House* was originally built by 1497 as the residence of Bishop Morton of Ely. Henry VIII made it a royal residence. James I exchanged it for Robert

Cecil's Theobalds Manor. The remains of this building still stand in the W. park. In 1607 Robert Lyminge was commissioned to build a new Elizabethan style house and this was completed in 1611. Still owned by the Cecil family, it is over 100 yards long and 160 ft. deep, its ground plan is in the form of an E. and there are rectangular towers at each corner. The lavish interior is crowned by the staircase, adorned with superb carvings and various sculptures, but there are also splendid tapestries and early-17C stained-glass windows, along with valuable paintings and furniture.

Hemel Hempstead (6 m. W.): The cruciform church of *St.Mary* dates back to Norman times and has a good central tower. Of interest is the ribbed vault in the sanctuary, which dates from the mid 12C. The church was restored by G.F. Bodley in the 19C, from which time the stained glass also dates.

St. Andrews
Fife/Scotland   p.324□H 8

Legend has it that the Greek monk Regulus ran aground here in the 4C. As he brought with him the relics of St.Andrew, the site became a place of pilgrimage for Celtic Christians, who built St. Rule's Church as a reliquary church for their saint. This later became by far the largest church ever built in Scotland. Due to the spiritual importance of the town, Scotland's oldest university was founded here in 1410. The Reformers wrecked havoc in St.Andrews and the historic town suffered a severe decline.

St.Rule's Church: This, the first large church, was built from 1127–44 in the town, which had been a bishop's seat since 908. Its 100 ft. high, square *tower* is still the city's emblem. The sanctuary and choir are discernible, but the nave has disappeared completely.

St. Andrews, ruined castle

Cathedral: The building of the great cathedral was begun in 1161 by the monk and former Abbot of Kelso, Bishop Arnold. The *W. façade* took its present form in 1273–9. The *choir* was completed in 1238. The cathedral was consecrated in 1318 in the presence of King Robert the Bruce. Following a fire and a thorough rebuilding the church enjoyed its heyday from 1440 onwards. The last great event was the betrothal of King James V to Marie de Lorraine in 1538. Of its former splendour there remains only the 60 ft. high *E. façade* (12C), a corner with a stairway in the *transept* (blind arcades) and the *S. wall* of the nave. Particularly interesting here is that the 4 W. windows have round arches, while the adjoining 6 E. windows are Gothic. Also preserved are a few Gothic *arches,* but of the monastery buildings themselves only the foundations remain.

The *museum* displays Celtic tombstones and a sarcophagus with Celtic ornamentation and scenes from the life of King David (9C).

Castle: The bishop's fortress on a cliff in the N. of the city was built round 1200. Its ownership changed several times before William Lamberton took it over in 1314 and extended it further. During succeeding years the English and Scots often fought over the castle, destroyed it, rebuilt it and destroyed it again. From 1425 the castle served as residence to James I, then Cardinal David Beaton (1539–46), who in the March before his death watched the burning of the Reformer George Wishart for heresy from the castle walls. Just two months later he was himself hung from a window of his castle by friends of the executed Reformer. After the turmoil of

St. Andrews, ruined cathedral

the Reformation the City Council decided in 1654 to extend the harbour using material from the castle. Today the *entrance gate* and the four-storeyed Renaissance *S. tower* survive. Probably the most interesting part of the castle are the tunnels made during the great siege of 1546–7, with which the besiegers attempted to blow up the castle. The besieged occupants for their part bored into these tunnels, thus foiling the enterprise. The *Mine* and *Counter Mine* are preserved and open to the public.

Also worth seeing: *St. Mary's College,* founded by Cardinal Beaton in 1537, is part of the university. It still has a white-thorn tree which is supposed to have been planted by Mary Queen of Scots. The old *Town Hall* contains the executioner's Axe along with other exhibits. *Holy Trinity*

Church was begun in 1412, its tower dates from the 16C. There are remains of the choir stalls of 1505 and the tomb of Archbishop Sharp, murdered in 1679. The 15C *University Church* contains the oldest tabernacle in Scotland.

Environs: Anstruther (*c.* 6 m. S.): This village not only has the oldest *parsonage* in Scotland (from 1590 and still inhabited) but also the interesting *Scottish Fisheries Museum*.

Balmerino Abbey (7.5 m. NW): Founded in 1226 by William the Lion's widow, who brought Cistercian monks here from Melrose. The English destroyed the complex in 1547, but the ruins of the late Gothic chapterhouse and its vaulting are still worth seeing.

Leuchars (3 m. NW): The *sanctuary* and *apse* from a 12C Norman church were integrated into a modern building. The old apse is the one of the best examples of Norman craftsmanship in Scotland.

St. David's/Tyddewi
Dyfed/Wales   p.330☐E 14

This little town in the extreme SW of Wales has been the 'Holy City' of the Welsh since the Middle Ages. The national saint, St.David, who evangelized S. Wales, lived and died here in the 6C.

St.David's Cathedral: Nothing remains of the monastery founded by St.David in the 6C. The present cathedral dates back to c. 1180, during the time of the Norman Bishop Peter de Leia. Externally the dark purple sandstone building is in transitional and Decorated styles. The mighty *crossing tower* of 1250 makes an austere and even sombre impression. The *W. front* acquired its final appearance in 19C restoration. Internally the Norman *nave* has survived, along with a great variety of Gothic forms. Worth noting are: the alternation of round and octagonal pillars; the beautiful *pilaster arches* and archivolts; the Decorated *side windows* (c. 1340); and the 15C *wooden roof* of Irish oak. The *S. gatehouse* , with a Tree of Jesse and Christ's genealogy on the portal dates from c. 1340. There are 2 pre-Norman *fonts* and *recumbent effigies* of bishops in the S. aisle. The *tomb* of Bishop Henry Gower (c. 1350) can be found in front of the fine 14C *choir screen* . The crossing is occupied by the *choir* with its remarkable 15C *choir stalls* (lovely misericords) and the *Bishop's Throne* (re-

stored). 4 splendid transitional *arches* divide the choir ambulatory from the *presbytery* and *sanctuary*. The lancet windows have been partially restored.

The S. choir ambulatory leads to the *Holy Trinity Chapel* with a beautiful Perpendicular ribbed vault. Preserved here in *St. David's Shrine* are the relics of the saint. The *Lady Chapel* (c. 1295), the vaulting of which collapsed in 1775, was restored in its old style. The *transepts* are partly original and partly rebuilt in early Gothic style after the collapse of the tower (1220). In the N., the *Chapel of St. Nicholas* has an interesting crucifix; in the N. transept, the *Chapel of St. Thomas,* built by Bishop Gower in c. 1340, has a beautiful 13C double font. Recognizable on the N. side of the cathedral are the remains of *St.Mary's College* (founded c. 1365), which has a slender *square tower* and a Perpendicular *chapel*

Bishop's Palace (near the cathedral): The ruins of the medieval Bishop's Palace are imposing. The original building, erected by that enthusiastic builder Bishop Henry Gower as a fortress-like residence in c.

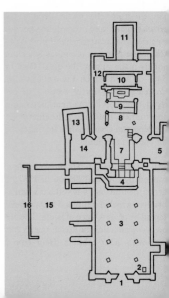

St.David's Cathedral **1** W. façade **2** font **3** nave **4** choir screen **5** S. transept **6** chapterhouse **7** choir **8** presbytery **9** sanctuary **10** Holy Trinity Chapel **11** Lady Chapel **12** St.Nicholas's Chapel **13** St.Thomas's Chapel **14** N. transept **15** cloister **16** former St.Mary's College

342, has an *arcade and parapet* running round the top. Grouped around the *inner court* are the *Great Hall* to the SW, the *chapel* to the NW (with picturesque little towers), the *kitchen* and other buildings. The NE *gateway* has a semi-octagonal arch. After the transference of the residency to Abergwili near Camarthen in 1540 the palace fell into decay. The remains of the 13C walls enclosing the whole cathedral complex are still recognizable.

Environs: Chapel of St.Non (*c.* 1 m. W.): The Chapel of St.Non, mother of St. David, stands on the cliffs. Remains of the early medieval *chapel* and a walled *healing spring* have survived.

Ramsey Island (*c.* 3 m. W.): This little island just off the coast has the sparse remains of an old *Benedictine abbey*. The island is a nature reserve with rare plants and insects.

St.David's Head (*c.* 2.5 m. NW): This promontory has a prehistoric rampart known as *Warrior's Dyke* and the remains of stone rings; caves in the cliff have a beautiful view over the sea.

St. Michael's Mount
Cornwall/England   p.330□E 17

This little circular granite island in Mount's bay off Penzance can be reached on foot along a narrow causeway for 3 hours at low tide; at other times it can only be visited by boat. The island is some 212 ft. high

The mount was known to the Romans as *Ictis*, whence the tin mined in Cornwall was shipped. The first Christians may have settled on the island by the 5C. However, the first documented evidence comes from the 11C, when Edward the Confessor had a church built here (1047) which was subject to the Benedictine Abbey of Mont St.Michel in Normandy. In the 12C this became an independent *Benedictine monastery*. After the dissolution of the monasteries, the mount finally came into the possession of the St.Aubyn family. In 1875 the family developed it into their permanent residence, fortunately without destroying any of the surviving buildings. Thus the former *refectory* is still graced

St.David's, St.David's Cathedral

Tower, roof

with a stucco frieze of 1641 depicting hunting scenes, and the former *Lady Chapel* has preserved its white vaulting ornaments (only Chippendale furniture has been added).

Environs: Chysauster (*c.* 4 m. NW): The *prehistoric Iron Age village* consists of 8 houses in pairs on a village street. Rooms were arranged around an oval inner court and each house had a garden bounded by stones at the back. The houses were roofed with straw and may have been inhabited into Roman times.

Helston (12.5 m. E.): This little town was once one of the 'Stannary Towns', to which Richard I granted considerable independence, because of their tin mining. In 1901 Marconi produced the first wireless link across the Atlantic from the cliffs of Poldhu Point to the S. This pioneering achievement is described in the *museum* , which also has items relating to local history.

Penzance (2.5 m. W.): The centre of the Cornish Riviera. Apart from a few old fishermen's houses, Penzance has an *Egyptian house* dating from *c.* 1830. Built by John Foulston, under whose direction the Egyptian library in Plymouth was also set up just 10 years earlier, it has papyrus bundles arranged as columns, caryatids with palm-frond capitals bearing lions and unicorns, unusual windows and is green, brown and yellow in colour. Thus the house is a unique example of Egyptian architecture seen from an English point of view. The *Natural History and Antiquarian Museum* has items of local interest, including Bronze and Iron Age finds.

St. Ives (9 m. N.): The adopted home of Ben Nicholson, Barbara Hepworth and Bernard Leach still exudes the attraction of an artists' colony. *Trewyn Studio* has been set up as a museum devoted to Barbara Hepworth; *Zennor Folk Museum* has exhibits of local interest, including those concerned with the development of mining in Cornwall e.g. a model of a tin mine.

St. Osyth
Essex / England   p.332 □ L 1

A little village near the NE shore of th Colne estuary, where Osyth, Queen of th East Saxons, was murdered by the Danes Miracles were said to have occurred at he tomb, which consequently attracted pil grims and led to the foundation of a mon astery.

St. Osyth's Priory: Of the old monaster there remains the *chapel* and a 13C *tower* The great *gatehouse* acquired its presen form in the 15C; it now houses an art col lection, which includes painting an ceramics.

Church of St. Peter and St. Paul: Th parish church next to the monastery com plex also dates back to the 13C, but it ac quired most of its present form in the 16C when nave and aisles were built in brick The *hammer beam ceiling* dates from tha time. The oldest monuments date from th 2nd half of the 16C.

Salisbury
Wiltshire / England   p.332 □ I 1

There is barely another town so carefully laid out as *New Sarum* on the Avon, whic replaced *Old Sarum* (2 m. N.) in the 13C Bishop Richard Poore transferred his se in 1220, because its proximity to the Roya Garrison had led to constant friction. Th townsfolk moved with him down into th Avon valley and, within 40 years had per formed the unsurpassed feat of buildin the cathedral, which is one of the mos stylistically pure in England.

Cathedral: Begun in 1220 on a wid

St. Osyth, St. Osyth's Prior

Salisbury, Cathedral, cloister

meadow in a meander of the Avon, it is built throughout in Early English Gothic. As early as 1258 Bishop Giles de Bridport consecrated the building, which was complete but for its tower. The slenderest and most graceful crossing tower in England was completed by 1334. With a height of 400 ft. it is the highest church tower in the country.

The building has a double transept and the rectangular conclusion to the choir has the Lady Chapel. The *W. façade*, framed by corner towers, has 5 levels of niches; like those of Wells Cathedral, these niches contain figures of saints. The relatively narrow *nave* is divided into 10 bays by bundles of columns of Purbeck marble. Incorporated into the great, triple *lancet windows* on the W. wall are remains of glass from the 13–15C. A window in the S. aisle dates from the 14C and depicts the Tree of Jesse.

The *clock* in the N. aisle dates from 138[and is one of the oldest in Europe. Th[great W. transepts correspond to the con[struction of the main nave, the Gothi[arches in the crossing had to be built in a[the end of the 15C under Bisho[Beauchamp, because the original arche[threatened to collapse under the weight o[the tower and the tower began to lean. Th[lack of feeling with which Wyatt cleare[the cathedral in 1788–9 is particularl[noticeable in the choir and in the E. aisle[That which was lost could not even b[saved by the restoration endeavours of S[Gilbert Scott. Thus the vault paintings o[1870 must be seen as an attempt to repro[duce the original state in the 13C. Th[*choir stalls* and the *bishop's throne* were als[restored under Scott. Of interest in the N[choir transept is the *memorial slab* of 137[for Bishop Wyvill (the castle tower, in th[

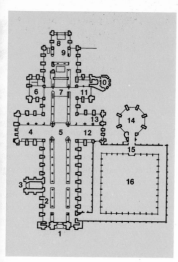

Salisbury Cathedral 1 W. portal **2** clock mechanism, 1386 **3** N. portal **4** NW transept **5** crossing with tower **6** NE transept **7** presbytery **8** Lady Chapel **9** shrine of St. Osmund **10** sacristy **11** SE transept **12** SW transept **13** War Memorial Chapel **14** chapterhouse **15** library **16** cloister

Salisbury, Cathedral

middle of which he is depicted, symbolizes the wealth of the bishop, who, as a lord of the manor, also had great secular power). The *Lady Chapel* forms the rectangular E. conclusion, which was also the first part to be built. In its windows there are still remains of 14&16C glass. The *Shrine of St. Osmund* commemorates the Bishop of Old Sarum, who died in 1099. Distributed throughout the entire cathedral there are a wealth of *monuments* from each century since the cathedral was built. Adjoining the W. side of the nave is the great *cloister*, which was begun by Bishop de la Wyle in 1271, although there was never a monastery at the cathedral. The E. side was built over in 1446 and has contained the *library* since 1756, whose most valuable possessions include an Anglo-Saxon liturgy and one of the 4 copies of the Magna Carta. Adjoining to the E. is the octagonal *chapter-*

house, which was built from 1260–84 in emulation of Westminster Abbey's. Its slender central pillar opens into a fine fan vault, which appears to float above the tracery windows in the walls.

Salisbury and South Wiltshire Museum: This has an excellent archaeological collection with finds from and models of Stonehenge, a Roman mosaic, finds from Old Sarum, medieval objects from the city and a collection of English glass and ceramics.

Environs: Old Sarum (*c.* 2 m. N.): Even before the Romans there was a castle fortified with a moat and rampart on a hill to the N. of Salisbury, which the Romans named *Sorviodunum.* The Saxons as well as the Normans used the site as a fortress, which acquired new importance when the

Bishop of Sherborne came here in 1078. Under St.Osmund the building of a Norman *cathedral* began and this was consecrated by 1092. When the building of a new cathedral was begun in the valley in 1220, the old church on the hill was gradually torn down as the stones were used to build the new one. Castle and town declined. Most of what could be excavated in the 19C dates from Norman times. No traces of the Romans could be found. The foundations of the old cathedral and of the castle were positively identified and can still be clearly seen today.

Wilton (4 m. W.): In the former capital of Wiltshire the kingdoms of Kent and Wessex were unified by King Egbert in 838. The *Church of St.Mary and St.Nicholas* was designed by Thomas Wyatt in 1843 as an attempt to revive early Christian architectural forms. With its campanile and numerous round arches it is reminiscent of an Italian Romanesque cathedral. Inside too a revival was attempted with twisted columns, mosaics and stained glass from the 12–16C which was collected from the most diverse sources. *Wilton House* goes

Wilton (Salisbury), Wilton House

back to a former Benedictine abbey, given by Henry VIII to his brother-in-law General William Herbert following the monastery's dissolution. The Tudor house which he built burned down in 1647 leaving just a tower; by 1653 it was rebuilt as a simple classical mansion by Inigo Jones and John Webb. James Wyatt's attempted Gothification was done away with in the 20C. The *Palladian Bridge* in the park was built by the 9th Earl of Pembroke in 1736–7. The 7 state rooms inside emanate the finest baroque splendour. The showpiece, however, is the *Double Cube Room* (30 x 30 x 60 ft.), whose white walls with their gilded embellishments of garlands of flowers and fruit provide the suitable setting for the Van Dyck paintings, which date from 1632–5. Apart from numerous other old masters the house also contains 55 gouaches of the Spanish Riding School by Baron D'Eisenberg, 1755. The splendid furnishings are completed by superb furniture.

Scarborough
North Yorkshire/England   p.328☐K 11

A Roman signal station in the 4C AD, it became part of Henry II's realm in *c.* 1160 as *Scardeburg*. Since the end of the 17C it has been a spa and seaside resort (England's oldest) amongst which it is recognized as Queen.

St.Martin-on-the-Hill (Albion Rd): Built in 1863 to plans by G.F.Bodley. In 1879 the nave was extended with the addition of a bay and the narthex, and in 1902 the Lady Chapel was added. Inside there is interesting art from Bodley's Pre-Raphaelite circle (including wall paintings and stained glass by Burne-Jones and the choir ceiling by Webb and Morris).

St.Mary's Church (below the castle):

Founded in the 12–13C, it was considerably damaged in the 17C during the Civil War (particularly the choir). When it was rebuilt in 1669 the former crossing tower became the E. tower. Still preserved from the original building is an *arcade* with beautiful pillars and the *chapels* in the S. aisle. Modern stained glass dates from 1958. Also of interest inside are the *sculptures* (including a work by the French sculptor Roubilliac from the 17C). The *churchyard* has the tomb of Anne Brontë (see Bradford).

Castle: The castle hill (*c.* 330 ft. above sea level) has been settled since the Bronze Age. Excavations have been carried out since 1921 and finds date from the 5C BC). The Roman levels have revealed a signal station. Dating from the Middle Ages are the remains of the walls of 3 chapels, one of which is pre-Norman. Still preserved of the 12C *castle* (built by William LeGros, Earl of Aumale) are the *curtain walls* (up to 13 ft. thick, with a moat and further rampart; entrance originally only through a strongly fortified gate on the W. side of

the complex) and the *keep* (completed 1158; originally about 100 ft. high, four-storeyed with underground dungeon; destroyed during a siege in the Civil War, 1644–5). Remains of further towers within the outer walls are still discernible. S. of the keep are the ruins of *Mosdale Hall* (known after John Mosdale, who was made Life-Governor in 1397), formerly a royal stopping place. On the E. side (overlooking the sea) are the remains of the *Roman signal station:* built *c.* AD 370 together with 4 others along this stretch of coast to relay reports of enemies (particularly Picts) approaching from the N. The building was originally square with a small tower (model of the complex in the Archaeology Museum).

Scarborough Museum of Regional Archaeology (Vernon Rd): Housed in a circular edifice built in 1829 by the 'Philosophical Society' of Scarborough for a natural history collection. The two wings were added around 1860. The collections are chronologically ordered; one wing contains the pre- and early history department,

Scarborough, St.Mary's Church

the other the medieval (objects from later times are in the main building). Of particular interest in the pre- and early history dept. are the *excavation finds from Starr Carr* (near Seamer, SW of Scarborough), a Mesolithic settlement which was well preserved by a peat bog and excavated 1949–51, a *Bronze Age oak sarcophagus* and *finds of the signal station* on castle hill.

Wood End Museum (The Crescent): A natural history museum housed in a former summer house of the Sitwell family; the collections display objects related to the geology and the flora and fauna of the region. The library has a valuable collection of old manuscripts and books.

Also worth seeing: *St.Peter's R.C. Church* (Castle Rd.), a modern building of interest for its stained-glass windows with figures of saints (Augustine, Andrew, Patrick as well as more recent saints e.g. St.Vincent de Paul and St.Philip Neri). *Art Gallery* (The Crescent) has an interesting collection of paintings and temporary exhibitions. *St. Thomas's Museum* (East

Scarborough, King Richard III Café

Sandgate): Scarborough's local museum has been housed in the former 'Fishermen's Church' of St.Thomas since 1970. *King Richard III Café* (Sandside), where Richard III stayed (1483–85), has been used as a restaurant since 1964 and still contains its old furnishings.

Environs: Filey (*c.* 7.5 m. SE): Of interest is the church of *St.Oswald* (nave and aisles date from the 12C; choir and transepts were rebuilt in the 13C). Unusually the choir is at a lower level than the rest of the interior; the tower has a 'weather fish' as opposed to the normal weather cock.
Hackness (*c.* 2.5 m. W.): Norman *church* (nave and choir from 1050). At the E. end of the S. aisle there are remains of an 8C cross.
Hunmanby (*c.* 9 m. SE): Norman *church* with original tower, chancel arch and N. arcade of the nave; also of interest is the 19C Early English style *gate* to Hunmanby hall.
Reighton (*c.* 12.5 m. SE): The town has a remarkable 12C *church* , which was built over an earlier Anglo-Saxon building; constant restorations since 1890. Inside, the highly decorated font dates from Norman times and is in the form of a Roman altar.
Scalby (*c.* 1. m. NW): Mentioned in the Domesday Book as *Scallebi,* its *church* dates from 1150 (old sun dial on the portal) and was formerly part of Burlington Priory.
Speeton (*c.* 13.5 m. SE): The little church was originally Anglo-Saxon and then converted by the Normans.

Selby
North Yorkshire/England   p.328☐J 11

Abbey Church: Last remains of a monastery built under William the Conqueror (1066–87) to pacify the North. Founded

Scarborough, Castle

Selby, Abbey Church, Norman portal

by Benedict of Auxerre, the church was begun *c.* 1097 under Hugh de Lacy, 2nd abbot of the monastery; it was completed with the choir *c.* 1340. The roof and tower were rebuilt in their original form in 1909 after being destroyed by fire in 1906 but it is still one of the most impressive former monastery churches in England. The monastery was dissolved in the Reformation and the church is now the town's parish church. Of particular interest are the 2 Norman *portals*. There is a cruciform groundplan and the nave, which is some *c.* 325 ft. long, clearly shows the building's development from Norman to Early English (particularly in the *triforium*). The *choir* is in Decorated style and has an ornate *E. window*. Also of interest is a beautiful coloured Jesse window from the 14C and the *coat-of-arms* of the Washington family.

Environs: Hemingbrough (*c.* 4 m. E.): The beautiful church of *St. Mary* dates from 12–15C and has a cruciform groundplan with a massive crossing tower. Inside: a remarkable wooden ceiling, interesting stalls and a pulpit of 1717.
Monk Fryston (*c.* 6 m. SW): The church of *St. Wilfrid* has a remarkable Anglo-Saxon W. tower; the rest of the church is Early English and Decorated. Inside: beautiful early Gothic font and old windows with paintings.
Sherburn in Elmet (*c.* 6 m. W.): *All Saints Church* was originally Norman. The arcades of the nave have survived from the original construction; the rest is Gothic. Inside there is a beautiful 15C cross.
Snaith (*c.* 6 m. S.): The old monastery church of *St.Lawrence* was founded in Norman times and converted in the 13–15C. Of interest is the battlemented W. tower.

Chartwell (Sevenoaks), Churchill's former home

Inside there are beautiful tombs from the 15C and later (including a sculpture by Sir Francis Chantrey).

Settle
North Yorkshire/England   p.328☐H 11

This little town in Ribblesdale has *c.* 2,500 inhabitants and some good 17&18C buildings. It lies in an area of great geological interest—there are a series of caves which were inhabited as early as prehistoric times. The town has a private *Museum of Speleology* whose exhibits include the remains of prehistoric men and animals.

The most important cave is *Victoria Cave* (*c.* 2 m. N. and *c.* 1,600 ft. above sea level): Excavations have revealed that the cave was inhabited by hyenas towards the end of the last Ice Age (finds of bones of their prey); after the change in climate *c.* 8000 BC it was inhabited by humans of the Middle Stone Age (finds of stone tools and implements). It was then uninhabited for a few thousand years until AD 450, when it became a refuge of romanized Britons during the Anglo-Saxon invasion.

Environs: Giggleswick (directly W. of Settle): The church of *St.Alkeda* was built in Perpendicular Style. Inside there are many 17C items, especially the pulpit and lectern); also of interest is a picture, in rather poor condition, of Sir Richard Tempest, a patron of the church who died in 1488 and was said to have had himself buried with the head of his favourite horse. In the village a modern *chapel* dates from the early 20C.

Kikby Malham (*c.* 5 m. SE): The Perpen-

Ightham Mote (Sevenoaks)

dicular church of *St.Michael* has a beautiful Romanesque font and church stalls from the 17–18C.

Stainforth (*c.* 2.5 m. N.): The *stone bridge* over the River Ribble dates from *c.* 1670.

Sevenoaks
Kent/England   p.332☐K 15

This beautifully located town, now a popular residential area for commuters, developed from a 12C settlement. The parish church of *St.Nicholas*, built in the 13–15C and restored in the 19C, contains a few sculptures which are possibly Saxon. *Sevenoaks School,* founded in the 15C, is one of the oldest in England.

Environs: Chartwell (6 m. SW): Former country home of Sir Winston Churchill (1874–1965), to whose memory it is now devoted.

Combe Bank (5 m. W.): This 18C *mansion* is now a girls' school.

Ightham (*c.* 3.75 m. SE): *St.Peter's Church* from the 15C has Norman foundations and 2 tombs from the 14C and 17C. To the SW are the remains of *Iron and Stone Age settlements*. Ightham Mote, a moated medieval country house was converted in the 16C. (14C entrance hall, 16C Tudor Chapel and beautiful Jacobean staircase).

Knole (1.5 m. E.): One of the greatest private houses in England. It dates from the 15C and once belonged to the Archbishops of Canterbury; later it was owned by the writer Thomas Sackville. The fine interior furnishings date from the 17–18C; interesting fireplace resembling an altar.

Quebec House (6 m. W.): 16–17C house

of General James Wolfe, conqueror of Quebec.
Sundridge Old Hall (4.5 m. W.): Medieval mansion of 1458 with original stone hearth in the enormous hall (not open to the public).
Westerham (6 m. SW): Birthplace of General Wolfe; *Squerryes Court* (1681) has Dutch paintings and Wolfe memorabilia. The town has statues of Wolfe and Churchill.

Shaftesbury
Dorset/England   p.332□H 16

Picturesquely situated on a sandstone hill, Shaftesbury is one of the oldest towns in England. There are, however, few ruins; although the buried town on its 650 ft. high hill had no less than 12 churches and a large abbey, only scant foundations testify to its former importance. Founded by Alfred the Great in 880 as an abbey for Benedictine nuns for his daughter Ethelgiva, the tomb of the canonized first abbess and of King Edward (martyred in 978) made the abbey church a place of pilgrimage, bringing the greatest wealth to the abbey itself. Around the turn of the 10–11C the abbey together with that of Glastonbury owned more land than the English crown.

Museums:

The *Abbey Ruins Museum* evokes a lively picture of the abbey and town in the Middle Ages. Cut stones, decorated paving tiles and other finds from the abbey are exhibited. A model of the abbey church and the town shows their probable appearance in the 16C.
The *Local History Museum* includes archaeological exhibits from the region.

Environs: Stourhead (c. 20 m. NW): Colin Campbell built this splendid *mansion*

Shaftesbury, abbey, tomb

for the London banker Hoare in 1721–4. It contains good pictures by various artists, as well as furniture and other furnishings by the younger Chippendale. However, the *gardens* on the other side of the house are the main atttraction. Laid out *c.* 1740, they are among the most beautiful examples of the English style of garden. The lively lay out of temples, statues, bridges and grottoes surround a lake amid the most remarkable landscaping, resulting in a complete harmony between nature and horticultural skill. Here, among other things, is the 14C Gothic *Bristol Cross*.
Wardour Castle (5 m. NE): Built by Lord Lovell in 1392 around a hexagonal inner court. It was acquired by the Arundell family in 1547. Hotly fought over in the Civil War, it was so badly damaged that it had to be abandoned. Since the ruins blended so romantically with the land-

scape, the owners did not rebuild the castle, but in the 18C integrated them into the park and had a new castle built in Palladian style by James Paine in 1769–76. This 3-storey building with its two 2-storey wings acquired a splendid staircase with a Corinthian columned gallery and richly embellished dome. The staircase was designed by the architect Robert Adam.

Sheffield
South Yorkshire/England   p.328☐I 12

Cathedral Church of St. Peter and St. Paul (Church St.: The city's parish church until 1913, it was originally built in the 12C and rebuilt in Perpendicular style in 1435. It was partly rebuilt in 1963–6 following bomb damage in the Second World War. Inside, the superbly coloured *stained glass* is of interest (depictions of the city's early history in the chapterhouse); there are also 16C *monuments* (in particular those of the Earls of Shrewsbury).

Cutlers' Hall (Church St.: Built in neoclassical style in 1832, it belongs to the 'Cutlers' Company', the cutlers' guild, which was founded by decree in 1624— their annual feast is still a major event in N. England. (Sheffield is the centre for high quality steel in Britain). Of principle interest inside, apart from the marble *main hall*, is the Regency *banqueting hall*. The building contains a unique *silverware collection* (with the hallmark 'Sheffield Assay Office', used since 1773).

Museums:
Abbeydale Industrial Hamlet (Abbeydale Rd., in the S. of the city): Industrial Museum on the site of an 18C works producing scythes. Among other things, the original water-powered iron hammers dating from 1785 have survived.
City Museum and Mappin Art Gallery (Weston Park): Of principle interest in the museum is a unique collection of crockery and cutlery produced in Sheffield over the past 5 centuries; there are also examples of 'Sheffield Plate' produced here since the 18C. Interesting natural history

Sheffield, St. Peter and St. Paul

16C tomb

department. The art gallery contains interesting paintings (from the Middle Ages to the 19C).

Graves Art Gallery (in the Central Library, Surrey St.): European painting and art from Asia and Africa.

Also of interest: *City Hall* (Barker's Pool) of 1932. The *Town Hall* in Surrey St. has a tower some 200 ft. high with a statue of Vulcan as symbol of the local industry. The W. tower and foundation walls are all that remains of *Beauchief Abbey,* a monastery founded in 1175. *Shepherd Wheel* (Forge Dam) is an 18C cutlery works. The *York and Lancaster Regimental Museum* documents the regiment's history since 1758.

Environs: Carl Wark (*c.* 6 m. SW): Remains of an *Iron Age hill fort.*
Ecclesfield (*c.* 1.5 m. N.): The church of *St.Mary* is late Gothic; of interest inside are the stalls and some medieval glass.
North Lees Hall (*c.* 7.5 m. W.): *Manor house* built in 1410 and restored in 1959 (beautiful staircase inside).

Rotherham (*c.* 6 m. NE): Late Gothic *All Saints Church* was restored by Sir Gilbert Scott in the 19C. Inside there are beautiful choir stalls and a Renaissance pulpit of 1604. Also of interest are the *Chantry Chapel of Our Lady* (1383) and the *town museum* (in a house of 1780; exhibits include porcelain, ceramics, glass and Roman finds).

Templeborough (*c.* 4.5 m. NE): This town occupies the site of a *Roman fort* (excavation finds in the museum in Clifton Park).

Wentworth (*c.* 3 m. N.): Of the original church of the *Holy Trinity* only the choir and N. chapel have survived; the rest is 19C neo-Gothic to plans by J. L. Pearson.

Sherborne
Dorset/England   p.332☐H 16

This little town is of special importance for two reasons. Firstly, it was a crystallization point for medieval monastic culture in

Sherborne, Abbey, memorial

Fan vaulting

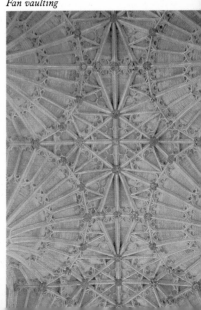

southern England and secondly, it is probably the most beautiful medieval town centrein Dorset. There was already a bishop's see here in 705 and this was transferred to Old Sarum (Salisbury) in 1075. By that time there had already been 27 bishops, including the legendary scholar Aldhelm, who may have taught Boniface at school. In 909 the cathedral became the abbey church of a Benedictine monastery, the most famous part of which was to become its school.

Sherborne Abbey: Begun as a cathedral in 705 and completely rebuilt after 1122. Of the Norman church the *S.portal* and the *crossing* have survived. *Nave* and *choir* were rebuilt in the early 15C. The late Norman S. portal, built around 1170, is a wide, round arch with chevron decoration on pairs of columns with demon capitals. No less splendid than the old parts are the newer ones. The superb fan vaulting in the nave and choir dates from *c.* 1450 and is English Gothic at its best; of its type it is only exceeded by the vaulting of King's College Chapel, Cambridge, built a few decades later. The *choir stalls* with splendidly carved misericords date from the mid 15C, while the numerous *tombs* date back to the 13C. A *memorial slab* in the N. transept marks what is probably the burial place of Thomas Wyatt. The largest tomb, arranged with baroque splendour, is dedicated to John Nost, Earl of Bristol, who died in 1698.

Old Castle: Built on the orders of Bishop Roger in 1107–39 and ahead of its time with concentrically arranged *ramparts*. In 1592 Elizabeth I permitted Sir Walter Raleigh use of the castle. In 1599 she actually gave it to him, although this did not hinder her from taking it away in 1603 when he fell from favour. It was bombarded in the Civil War and extensively damaged by Parliamentary soldiers in 1645.

Sherborne Castle: While still in posession of of the old castle Sir Walter Raleigh built his new summer residence from 1594 onwards. Sir John Digby took it over in 1617, added 4 more wings with balustrades and corner towers and crowned the whole with a battery of chimneys, thereby creating his family's ancestral home. Today the castle contains furniture and paintings from the 17&18C, as well as books, charters and documents going back to the 16C.

Environs: Bradford Abbas (3 m. SW): The church of *St.Mary the Virgin* was built in the 15C and has an impressive W. tower. The W. front has 11 tabernacles, two of which have figures. The stone choir screen was completed in the 15C; the pulpit is 17C.

Trent: (3 m. W.): The church of *St.Andrew* dates from the 13C; the S. tower, vaulting and the Gothic choir screen are 14C. The most beautiful of the tombs dates from the 14C and has an effigy of a knight. Richly carved pew ends have survived from the 16C and what is probably a Dutch pulpit was made *c.* 1600; a few stained-glass windows also date from that time.

Shetland Islands
Scotland   p.322☐1 2

This archipelago consists of more than 100 individual islands, of which less than 20 are now inhabited. Their history is very like that of the Orkney Islands; they were settled in early times, the first immigrants probably reaching the islands between 2500 and 2000 BC. To date about 70 Neolithic settlements have been found.

Jarlshof: Looking at Jarlshof, on the S. tip of Mainland, you can get a clear idea of the pattern of settlement of the island as a

Sherborne, St.Mary the Virgin

whole. For over 3000 years, from the New Stone Age onwards, people have built houses on this spot, consequently it is now one of the most important *prehistoric excavation sites* in Britain. The name of the settlement originated as a fictitious Old Norse name in 1816, when Sir Walter Scott so described the ruins of a mansion (dating from *c.* 1600) in his Shetland novel 'The Pirate'. When the New Stone Age settlement was discovered around the turn of the century it naturally acquired the name invented by Scott.

Remains of 3 prehistoric villages and 2 settlements from later periods were revealed in an area of just 10,000 sq m. The earliest level dates from the Bronze Age and corresponds in lay out to that of Skara Brae in the Orkney Islands. Dating from the Iron Age are a broch and several wheel houses. In the early 9C the Vikings extended the settlement considerably. They had proper stables and barns, a smithy and possibly even a small temple. In the 13C the building of a farmstead began; its greatest size was attained under Earl Patrick and it was the ruins of these buildings which inspired Sir Walter Scott.

Broch of Mousa: This refuge castle on the little island of Mousa to the E. of Sandwick may have originated in the 1C BC; it is the best preserved broch in Scotland. With a diameter of about 50 ft. it has survived to a height of over 40 ft. In the 3C AD the circular *inner court* was converted into a *wheel house*. The 6 *galleries* inside are interlinked by a narrow *stairway* just 3 ft. wide.

Lerwick: The capital of the Shetlands owes its status to its excellent *natural harbour*, which enabled the Norwegian King Haakon to assemble his fleet against the Scots here in 1263. Now the harbour is principally used to supply the oil rigs in the North Sea. Of interest is the *Shetland Museum*, a regional museum with good historical and local collections.

Environs: The *Broch of Clickhimin* (less than 1.5 m. S.) is not as well preserved as that of Mousa, but there are still various Bronze Age houses.

In *Scalloway* (*c.* 3 m. W.) the old ruins of a medieval *keep* belonging to the tyrant Earl Patrick have survived. The four-storey building has particularly impressive cellar vaulting.

Shrewsbury
Salop/England   p.328□H 13

Scrobesbyrig was the Anglo-Saxon name for the settlement in a loop of the Severn which had existed since the 5C. Towards the end of the 8C it was captured by Offa, King of Mercia; the Saxons and then the Normans became lords of the settlement. Somewhat more peaceful times were enjoyed under Roger de Montgomery in the 11C. During the struggle for Wales (1277 –83) Edward I ruled from here. The town again became a headquarters under Charles I in 1642, falling to Parliament 3 years later.

Church of St.Mary: The town's largest church was founded as a collegiate church in 970. However, little has survived of this first pre-Norman building; the present building is mainly Early English, only the seats in the choir are Norman. The church's greatest treasure is the *stained-glass*, with a fine tree of Jesse at the E. end. Sir John de Charlton and his wife Lady Hawis had these superb windows made in the 14C (they were originally in the church of St.Chad). Just as impressive are the windows with scenes from the life of St. Bernard (by the Master of St.Severin in Cologne *c.* 1500 and brought from Altenburg Abbey). *Trinity Chapel* is 15C and has 16C windows from St.Jacques in Liège. Also of interest are the 14C *portrait of a knight* and 14C *alabaster reliefs*.

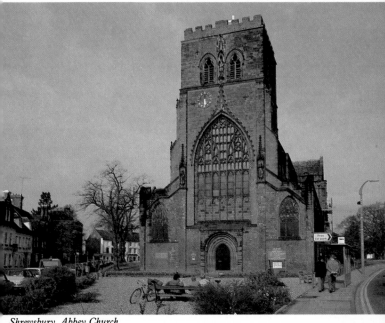

Shrewsbury, Abbey Church

Abbey Church: The monastery dedicated to St. Peter and St. Paul was founded by Roger de Montgomery in 1083. This red sandstone church has an imposing early Gothic *tower* (the lower part of which is Norman) with a fine large Gothic *window;* the *statue* above the window is reputed to be of Edward III. The nave is Norman, with the exception of the 2 westernmost bays which were built at the same time as the upper part of the tower. The *pulpit* dates from 1888 and is by James Pearson. The *stained-glass windows* are also 19C. The church contains numerous *tombs* and *monuments* dating back to *c.* 1300. Opposite the N. gate are remains of an *altar* dedicated to St. Winifrid, dug up in an allotment in 1933.

Castle: Founded by Roger de Montgomery in 1070 on the neck of land en-closed by the meander of the river, it was extended by Edward I. In 1138 it was seized by the Norman Stephan de Blois, who immediately hanged the entire garrison. In 1283 Edward I had David, last King of Wales, hanged here. The castle now contains the town's *council chamber.*

Rowley's Mansion: This house, built in 1618, now houses the *Viroconium Museum* which has a superb collection of Roman finds from the settlement of Viroconium (present-day Wroxeter). The collection is completed by prehistoric and geological finds from the area.

Environs: Haughmond Abbey (*c.* 4.5 m. NE): Founded for Augustinian monks by William FitzAlan in 1135. Of the 12C church little has survived; however, the ruins of the 12C *chapterhouse* and *refectory,*

Shrewsbury, Castle

as well as the 14C *hospital* are most impressive.

Wroxeter (*c.* 6 m. SE): The remains of Roman *Viroconium* are all that is left of the capital of Britannia Secunda. Founded before AD 70 it was abandoned *c.* 400. Still easily recognizable are the *forum* and the public *baths.* Roman stones were used in the building of the *village church,* which has a Saxon nave and a 12C pulpit. The most important finds, including a silver mirror from the 2C produced in a Roman workshop, can be seen in Rowley's Mansion in Shrewsbury.

Skipton

North Yorkshire/England   p.328☐I 11

Holy Trinity Church: Built in the 14C

in Perpendicular style with a simple W. tower. Of interest inside are the beautiful *roof* of the nave dating from the time of Richard III (1483–5), the 16C *choir wall,* the 13C *sedilia* (seats for the clergy, let into the S. wall of the choir) and a remarkable 17C *font cover.* The church is the burial place of the Clifford family, who were the Earls of Cumberland and their splendid *sarcophagi* can be seen on either side of the sanctuary.

Castle: Originally built in Norman times under William de Romillé, it has been the home of the Clifford family since 1309. As the last bastion of the Royalists in the North during the Civil War, it was surrendered to Parliamentary troops and destroyed. It was rebuilt and extended shortly afterwards. Of particular interest are the Tudor *main gate* with 4 towers and the 15C inner court. Noteworthy inside are the *banqueting hall*, which is over 50 ft. long, the old *kitchen* with a massive oven, the *dungeon* and the *Shell Room*, the walls of which are clad with coral and shells).

Craven Museum (in the Public Library): Mainly collections devoted to local history, natural history and the prehistory of the Craven District (including finds from El-bolton Cave, an Iron Age sword and tools used in lead mining from the nearby mines).

Also worth seeing: *High Corn Mill* (at Mill Bridge over Spring Canal), a 13C corn mill.

Skye (I)
Scottish Highlands   p.324☐E 6

The largest island of the Inner Hebrides is called Eilean á Cheo, the 'Misty Isle' in Gaelic, due to the Cuillin Hills in the S. of the island, which rise directly out of the sea to a height of 3225 ft. and cause the air passing over them to deposit its moisture on the island. Regardless of the mist and rain these hills have become one of the most popular climbing areas in Britain.

Dunvegan: The *castle* on Loch Dunvegan is the ancestral seat of the clan MacLeod of MacLeod who, in 1577, asphyxiated 395 members of the neighbouring clan Mac-Donald to death in a cave filled with smoke. The castle stands on a rock surrounded by water and until the 19C it could only be reached by boat or via an underground passage. The foundation walls are some 10 ft. thick and date from the 14C, as does the gruesome bottle-neck dungeon into which prisoners were thrown to a depth of 16 ft. Those who did not break their necks faced drowning through flooding of the dungeon.

Skipton, Holy Trinity, font

Sligo
Sligo/Ireland   p.326☐C 10

This port and county town (population 14,000) on the NW coast of Ireland (Sligo Bay) was founded *c.* 1250 by the Norman Maurice FitzGerald. The *castle* which he built was completely destroyed in later battles.

Dominican Monastery: Founded by FitzGerald *c.* 1252. The beautiful *monastery church* with choir (13C), pointed-arch windows (15C), altar decorated with sculptures, tower and 16C transept has survived. In the N. of the nave the tomb of Cormac O'Craian of 1506 is of interest. The 15C cloister with beautiful arches, columns and a pulpit is in a good state of preservation and is one of the finest in Ireland.

Also worth seeing: The Protestant parish church of *St. John* (in the W.) was built 1730–1812 (neo-Gothic rebuilding). The Catholic *cathedral* was built in Italian Romanesque style *c.* 1870. The *museum* (County Library) has historical exhibits and a collection commemorating the famous poet W.B. Yeats (1865–1939), who for a time lived in and around Sligo and described the delightful countryside, particularly around neighbouring Lough Gill. (Yeats was awarded the Nobel Prize for Literature in 1923.)

Environs: Ballysadare (*c.* 6 m. SW): Remains of a *monastery* founded in the 7C by St. Fechin; 13C *church ruins.*

Carrowmore (*c.* 2.5 m. SW): Here is the largest collection of *megalithic tombs* in Ireland, with vast graves, burial chambers, dolmen and stone circles. Unfortunately most of the tombs have been plundered and damaged.

Cliffony (*c.* 9 m. N.): A *mansion* belonging to the Mountbatten family, built around 1842. Nearby (to the W.) is the interesting *burial ground* (Court Cairn) of

Carrowmore (Sligo), megalithic grave

Creevykeel which dates from the 3C BC.

Deerpark (2.5 m. E.): The *prehistoric burial site* on the N. side of Lough Gill is called *Magheraghanrush.*

Dromahair (*c.* 11 m. SE): Scanty traces of a *castle* which appears in many legends. The beautiful Queen Devorgilla fled here with Dermot, King of Leinster in 1152. The latter, having been spurned by the Irish Kings, appealed to the Anglo-Normans under Henry II for help and thus began the start of the Norman invasion. The *Old Hall* (at the end of the village) is a fortified mansion of 1626. Nearby are the interesting ruins of *Creevelea Abbey,* the last Franciscan foundation in Ireland which dates from 1508 (fine burial sites).

Drumcliff (*c.* 7 m. N.): The Celtic St. Colmcille founded the first monastery here *c.* 572; a 12C round tower has survived. The village graveyard has the grave of the famous poet W.B. Yeats on whose tomb are the words, 'Cast a cold eye on life on death. Horseman pass by'. Nearby is the interesting, carved *High Cross of Drumcliff* (11C) with beautiful carvings. Behind Drumcliff looms the limestone mass of *Ben Bulben* (1,715 ft.), mentioned in many old Irish sagas (e.g. Dermod and Grainne).

Inishmurray Island (*c.* 9 m. NW): This little uninhabited Atlantic island has interesting *early Christian ruins* , e.g. little churches, beehive huts (clochans) and a circular stone wall formerly used as fortification. The monastic settlement was founded in the 6C by St. Molaise (or Laisren).

Knocknarea (2.5 m. W.): THe whole area around Sligo, particularly the Knocknarea peninsula in the W., is rich in prehistoric (megalithic) and early Celtic sites. On the highest point (1085 ft., superb view) lies the legendary *barrow* of the Celtic Queen Maeve *(Maeve's Cairn).* The earth rampart contains a (still unexcavated) megalithic passage grave.

Park's Castle (*c.* 7 m. E.): 17C *castle* with

urrets in a fine state of preservation (to the NE of Lough Gill).

Southampton
Hampshire/England   p.332☐I 16

This large port at the mouth of the Itchen was important to both the Romans and the Saxons. In Roman times it was known as *Clausentum,* and in Saxon times as *Hamwih.* The Normans fortified the town and the harbour with rampart and moat and saw its protected position behind the Isle of Wight as an ideal place for the assembling of ships. In 1338 a large fleet of French, Spanish and Italian ships plundered the town; however, a century later the port was handling most of England's trade with the Mediterranean. In more recent times it became the port for the great ocean liners. The 'Mayflower' departed here in 1620; the 'Titanic' left on its disastrous voyage on 10 April 1912. In the thirties came the great flying boats and in the sixties the Hovercraft.

Town Fortifications: Large parts of the Norman fortification system have survived, particularly on the W. side. The walls, up to 33 ft. high, were strengthened with towers and had 7 gatehouses. The *W. Gate,* built in the 14C, led directly to the W. wharf, which was then the port's main wharf. The *N. Gate* was the most important in the Middle Ages, for here duty was collected on all goods coming into or going out of the town. The oldest part of this structure, a semicircular arch, was built *c.* 1175. The *Guildhall* above it (*c.* 1400) was originally the assembly room of the merchants' guild. It now houses a small local history *museum.* God's House Gate at the SE corner of the fortifications was built as a fortress tower in the early 15C and now serves as the *Archaeological Museum,* in which exhibits from prehistoric, Roman, Saxon and medieval times are displayed.

Wool House: Built in the 14C as a warehouse for wool and used as a gaol for French prisoners in the 18C, it now houses the *Maritime Museum.* The original Spanish chestnut roof has survived.

Knocknarea (Sligo), megalithic grave

Art Gallery: Principally devoted to modern English painting, the gallery also has the 'Perseus Cycle' by Burne-Jones. An interesting collection of contemporary ceramics is also displayed.

Environs: Netley Abbey (3 m. SE): Founded as a Cistercian abbey in 1239 by Henry III, the first monks came from Beaulieu. The complex was once large, covering an area *c.* 500 x 325 ft. (the church alone was over 230 ft. long), but declined after the dissolution of the monasteries. Visible today are parts of the walls of the church, the cloister, the chapterhouse and the farm buildings.
Romsey (10.5 m. NW): The *Abbey Church of St. Mary and St. Ethelfleda* belongs to a Benedictine convent founded in 907, the first abbess of which was St. Ethelfleda, daughter of King Edward the Elder (899–925). The abbey church, going back to an early Saxon building of 967, dates principally from *c.* 1130. With a length of 280 ft. and a width of more than 130 ft. (at the transept), it is not only one of the most beautiful, but also one of the largest virtually unaltered Norman churches in England. The building is most impressive in the choir, especially the clerestorey and triforium. The E. corner of the S. choir aisle has a Saxon crucifix; another crucifix by the S. portal is probably 11C. Paintings in the N. aisle and transept date from *c.* 1500 and depict the Resurrection with saints.

Southend-on-Sea
Essex/England   p.332□L 15

This town on the N. bank of the Thames estuary has a promenade some two miles long but no great history.

Prittlewell Priory Museum: The museum building incorporates the remains of a former *Cluniac priory*, founded *c.* 1110. The *refectory*, the *Prior's Room* with its 14C ceiling and some *cellars* have survived. The museum's collections, housed in a new building of the 19C, include exhibits concerned with the archaeology, history

Southampton, St. Michael, window

Tomb

and natural history of the S. part of Essex. The Bronze Age and Roman period are particularly well represented.

Beecroft Art Gallery: The painting collection covers European painting from the 17C onwards; there is also a collection of the work of local artists.

Environs: Laindon (12.5 m. W.): The little church of *St. Nicholas* dates from the 14&15C and has beautiful woodcarving in the S. entrance. Added to the W. end is a single-storey priest's house (17). The finest item inside is a 13C font.

South Uist (I)
Scotland   p.324☐D 6

This island in the Outer Hebrides forms a single unit with the islands of *Benbecula* and *North Uist,* with which it is interconnected by bridges and dams. The islands are a centre for Gaelic culture and language. Prince Charles Edward Stuart hid on South Uist for 3 weeks following his de-

feat at Culloden in 1746, until Flora Mac-Donald helped him escape to Skye.

Daliburgh: S. of the village is a *wheel house* from *c.* 200 BC. This round building has a diameter of *c.* 32 ft. and is sunk *c.* 6.5 ft. into the ground; the walls rise about 6.5 ft. *c.* above the ground. The circular living room has a diameter of *c.* 20 ft. and is made up of a ring of 10 chambers in the segments. Pillars supported a roof of wood and reeds.

Howmore: The nature reserve of Loch Druidebeg (N. of the village) is one of the most important breeding grounds for the greylag goose. The tall figure of *Our Lady of the Isles* at the N. edge of the reserve was made in 1957.

Southwold
Suffolk/England   p.328☐M 14

This little town near the mouth of the Blyth was devastated by fire in 1659. To-

Southampton, Wool House, timber roof

Tudor House

Crowland (Spalding), abbey ruins

Figures among the ruins

day it has beautiful brick houses from the 2nd half of the 17C and colourfully painted houses of a later date.

Church of St. Edmund: This Gothic church has a large *W. tower*, a *S. entrance* of two storeys and surprisingly large *windows*. The large *choir screen*, which takes in the whole breadth of the church, dates from the early 16C, as does the panelled *ceiling* and roofed *choir stalls*, which are decorated with beautiful carvings. The 7 sacraments are depicted on the *font*, the cover of which dates from 1930.

Museum: Housed in a 17C house (one of the oldest in the area), it displays collections of local and natural history.

Environs: Blythburgh (4.5 m. SW): The church of the *Holy Trinity* dates prin-

cipally from the 15C and has an attractive W. tower. Dating from the same time are the font, the fine choir stalls and the carved sides of the pews which are decorated with the Seven Deadly Sins.

Heveningham Hall (c. 13.5 m. SW): This is one of the most interesting Palladian houses in England and was designed by Sir Robert Taylor in 1779 for Sir Gerald Vanneck. The interior furnishing is by James Wyatt, the walls and vaulted ceiling were painted by Biago Rebecca. The gardens were laid out by Capability Brown. Heveningham Hall is still owned by the Vanneck family.

Wenhaston (6 m. W.): The church of *St. Peter* dates back to Norman times, but was later extensively altered. Of interest inside is a large painting on wood which dates from c. 1500 and depicts the Last Judgement.

Crowland (Spalding), Triangular Bridge

Spalding
Lincolnshire/England   p.328☐K 13

Church of St. Mary and St. Nicholas:
Begun at the end of the 13C in Decorated
Style. The late Gothic hammer beam roof
is decorated with angels and there is fine
Victorian *stained glass.*

Ayscoughfee Hall: Originally a late
Gothic mansion, it was renovated in the
18C by its owner Maurice Johnson,
founder of the 'Spalding Gentlemen's Society'. Today it contains a *Local Museum*
(with an interesting collection of native
birds).

**Spalding Gentlemen's Society Mu-
seum:** Museum of the oldest scientific and
literary association in England (founded in
1712; members included Isaac Newton).
The *library* contains valuable volumes of
a scientific, historical and archaeological
nature.

Also worth seeing: *'Ye Olde White Horse
Inn',* probably the oldest house which is
still inhabited in Spalding. The *May car-
nival* consists of a tulip parade (Spalding
is one of England's flower-growing
centres). Fine *Georgian houses* on the banks
of the River Welland in the centre of the
town.

Environs: Bourne (*c.* 10 m. W.): Home
of 'Hereward the Wake', the last Saxon
chief to offer resistance to the Normans. Of
particular interest is the former abbey
church of *St. Peter and St. Paul* (Romanesque nave arcades, rest early Gothic) and
Red Hall, a brick building of 1620.

Crowland (*c.* 7.5 m. S.): Remains of an *abbey* founded in 716 by King Ethelbald. The N. aisle of the abbey church is now the village parish church; the richly decorated W. front has survived. The 14C *Triangular Bridge* in the middle of the village has three arches and now stands on dry land.

Fleet (*c.* 9 m. E.): The church of *St.Mary Magdalene* is 14C; beautiful pointed arches in the nave, splendid W. window and detached tower.

Gedney (*c.* 10 m. E.): The church of *St. Mary Magdalene* has an unfinished tower, whose lower part is early Gothic; inside are remains of medieval stained glass.

Holbeach (*c.* 7.5 m. E.): Gothic *All Saints Church*, has not been altered since 1380 (N. porch flanked by turrets).

Long Sutton (*c.* 11 m. E.): The church of *St.Mary* has a detached early Gothic tower; inside there are Romanesque round arches and an interesting old desk; beautiful 15C porch.

Moulton (*c.* 3.5 m. E.): *All Saints Church* has a late Gothic tower; the nave has beautiful leaf capitals and a richly decorated 18C font.

Tydd St. Mary (*c.* 12.5 m. SE): The church of *St.Mary* is 14C; inside there are remains of a former building. Richly decorated choir windows; beautiful 15C font.

Whaplode (*c.* 5 m. E.): The church of *St. Mary* has interesting tombs, some of which date back to the 13C; the nave is partly Romanesque.

Stafford
Staffordshire/England   p.328☐H 13

Izaak Walton (1593–1683) was born here. Before the Industrial Revolution Stafford was a little country town and some of its former character can still be discerned here and there.

Church of St. Mary: This large parish church has a *central tower*, an Early English *nave* and early Gothic *transepts*. A *bust* of Izaak Walton commemorates the writer's baptism in the church's Norman font.

Stafford, Church of St.Mary

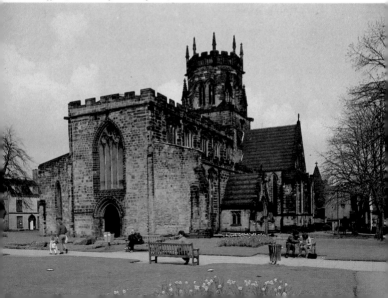

Church of St.Chad: This large church, dating back to Norman times, has a superb *chancel arch*. The Norman *arches* in the nave are impressive in their simplicity. The Norman *font* is also very fine.

Museum and Art Gallery: Exhibits concerned with local history, the development of local industry and the art of the area.

Also worth seeing: *William Salt Library* in an 18C house with a valuable collection of books and manuscripts.—*High House*, from 1555, where Charles I and Prince Rupert met in 1642. *Chetwynd House* (now the Post Office), where the Duke of Cumberland stayed in 1745.

Environs: Blithfield (6 m. E.): The *Museum of Childhood and Costume* is housed in an Elizabethan mansion, which was the ancestral home of the Bagot family for over 600 years. The museum's showpieces are 2 Victorian doll's houses and various antique dolls. Doll's furniture and clothes and books about dolls complete the collection.

Sandon (3.5 m. N.): The church of *All Saints*, dating back to the 11C, was rebuilt in 1310; tower and a side chapel were added around 1450. The font is Norman; the pulpit and frescos are 17C. There are several tombs of the Erdeswick family.

Shugborough (3.5 m. E.): The core of this *ancestral seat* of the Earls of Lichfield was built by William Anson, father of Admiral Lord Anson (1697–1762). The admiral had the Chinese House built in 1747 to the designs of one of his officers in Canton. Thomas Anson, the admiral's elder brother, commissioned James Stuart to build the two wings and a gallery for sculpture. Together with the architect he also laid out the classical *gardens*. When the Prince Regent was expected in 1803 James Wyatt added a spacious reception room to the W. front. The large relief in this room is the work of Peter Sheemakers. Today the house contains a collection of 18C French furniture and the *Staffordshire County Museum*.

St. Chad, Norman font

Main portal

Stamford

Lincolnshire/England   p.328☐K 13

A Danish foundation of the 7C, which developed into a flourishing town in the Middle Ages (due principally to its wool trade). Today the little town is of interest for its appearance which has remained practically unchanged since the 17–18C, particularly the medieval churches and the squares and streets surrounding them.

Churches: *All Saints:* 13–15C Gothic; beautiful Perpendicular tower and spire. *St. George's:* 13–15C Gothic. *St. John's:* Built *c.* 1450, it has fine oak and glass. *St. Leonard's Priory:* A Benedictine monastery founded from Durham in 1082; of the original building there remain 5 bays of the nave and the W. front. *St. Martin's:* This late Gothic building of 1480 has 2 interesting tombs. *St. Mary's:* 15C church with a 13–14C tower.

Also worth seeing: *Burghley Hospital,* with a beautiful 12C front. Remains of the 13C *castle. The George Hotel* is the town's most beautiful, and probably oldest, inn which has been in business since 1568. Remains of the old *town fortifications* date from the 13–15C. *Stamford Museum* has medieval ceramics and clothes belonging to Daniel Lambert, a famous fat man who died in 1809. The *squares* and *streets* adjoining the churches are also very beautiful, with fine medieval and Georgian buildings.

Environs: Clipsham (*c.* 7.5 m. NW): St.Mary's church dates from the 12–14C; inside there are remarkable Romanesque capitals and an old font.
Deeping St. James (*c.* 7.5 m. E.): The church of *St. James* once belonged to a monastery founded in 1139. The arcades of the nave and the font are Romanesque; the rest was repeatedly altered up to the 18C.
Essendine (*c.* 3 m. N.): The church of *St.Mary*, which consists solely of nave and choir, is in part Romanesque in part; interesting S. portal.
Great Casterton (*c.* 2.5 m. NW): The

Stafford, Church of St.Mary, nave

church of St. Peter and St. Paul is 13C and has a beautiful Romanesque font and the remains of medieval wall paintings.

Ketton (*c.* 3 m. SW): The church of *St. Mary* dates from 12-14C; the chancel was rebuilt in the 19C; fine glass by Sir Ninian Comper.

Little Bytham (*c.* 6 m. N.): The church of *St. Medard* has remains of a Saxon building in the nave. There is an interesting portal in the chancel which is inset with a medallion.

Little Casterton (*c.* 2 m. N.): The church of *All Saints* is 12C and has a W. bell tower; remnants of 14C wall paintings inside. Also of interest is *Tolethorpe Hall.*

Ryhall (*c.* 2.5 m. N.): The Church of *St. John the Evangelist* is 12C; 14C sedilia in the choir. In the wall of the N. aisle there are the remains of a 7C hermitage.

Tickencote (*c.* 2.5 m. W.): *St. Peter's Church* has the original 12C chancel and a fine richly decorated chancel arch.

Tixover (*c.* 5 m. SW): Fine, mainly Romanesque *church* with old stone seats in the chancel; a beautiful arch dates from 1140.

Stirling
Central Scotland   p.324☐G 8

This town overlooking the meanders of the Forth was called by the Welsh *Place of Striving*. Around the castle hill there are no less than 15 different battlegrounds. Whoever held Stirling also held the way to the Highlands and could consider himself Lord of Scotland. The history of the town and castle is correspondingly closely connected with the House of Stuart, whose residence it was many times from the early 12C onwards. Alexander I died in Stirling in 1124, in 1297 William Wallace defeated the English under Edward I here and recaptured the castle for the Scots. The English returned just 7 years later before they were again crushed by Robert the Bruce at the Battle of Bannockburn in 1314. James II was born in the castle in 1430, as was James V in 1512. In 1651 General Monck captured the castle for Cromwell. The Jacobite advance faltered here in 1715 and in 1746 Prince Charles Edward Stuart failed to capture the castle.

Stirling, Stirling Castle

Stirling Castle: The grey castle towers 245 ft. over the town. Most of it was built under James III (Great Hall, 1475–1503), James V (the palace itself, 1534–42) and James VI (castle chapel, 1594). Apart from bits of the fortifications, the *Great Hall* is the oldest part of the castle. James III had it built as a throne room and banqueting hall for parliamentary assemblies and public ceremonies. Furnishings for the Gothic hall, with a musicians gallery and hammer-beam roof, were suitably costly. In the 18C, when the castle was converted into a garrison, the Great Hall had to be used as barracks; attempts are now underway to restore it to its former splendour.

James VI had the *castle chapel* rebuilt for the christening of his eldest son. The early Renaissance building was originally furnished with a beamed ceiling decorated with flower ornamentation, while the walls were adorned with heraldic paintings. W. of the chapel is the *Nether Green* garden, laid out in 1532.

The core of the castle is formed by the *palace*, laid out by James V around a square inner court, a unique example of the French-influenced Scottish early Renaissance. Between the windows the façade has niches in which half-dressed or naked mythical and allegorical figures stand on richly decorated columns, which are themselves carried consoles in the form of devils and demons. Armed warriors stand guard on the parapet. The royal chambers were on the first floor as in Linlithgow Palace. The king had the N. wing and the queen in the S. wing. The *Stirling Heads*, carved oak medallions, which once adorned the wooden ceiling of the royal audience chamber at the NE corner of the palace, testify to the meticulous furnishings. 31 of the 60 or so medallions were saved from being burned by the soldiers. They depict the kings of Scotland and also various symbolic figures, the significance of which has still not been entirely clarified.

Church of the Holy Rude: This 15C church, the town's parish church for over 500 years, is one of the few medieval churches in Scotland to have survived the furious destruction of the Reformation. In 1543, when she was 9 months old, Mary Queen of Scots was anointed queen in its Gothic choir. In 1567 her son James VI was crowned here, the sermon being preached by none other than the Reformer John Knox. 1656-1935 the church was divided into a W. and an E. parish church; this was changed when it was restored 1936-40.

Also worth seeing: The *Old Town* is characterized by several *Little Houses* from the 16–18C and by its Victorian buildings. Next to the church of the Holy Rude lies *Mar's Wark*, the fortified town residence of the Earl of Mar. This Renaissance palace, built 1570-2, was never quite completed, although James VI lived here for a time until his own palace was completed; it was destroyed by the Jacobites in 1746. The town house of the Earl of Stirling, built in 1630, is known as *Argyll's Lodging* after a later occupant. It was built by William Alexander of Menstrie, founder of Nova Scotia, the Scottish colony in North America. At *Mercat Cross* in Broad St.Archbishop Hamilton was sentenced to death and hung in 1571. The *Old Stone Bridge* to the N. of the town centre was the only bridge over the Forth for over 400 years, although it was an even older bridge some 300 ft. upstream, which gave its name to the battle of 1297. On the top of a hill *c.* 1.5 m. N. stands the *Wallace Monument* which commemorates the battle. A tower 220 ft. high provides an excellent view over the Forth valley and the scene of so much bloody conflict.

Environs: Bannockburn (3 m. S.): Here

Stirling, Stirling Castle, exterior wall with allegorical figures

Stirling, Stirling Castle, approach

Robert the Bruce regained independence for Scotland in 1314. The course of the battle is detailed in a National Trust information centre.

Menstrie Castle (5 m. NE): A 3-storey 16C structure built in natural ashlars of uniform size; stepped gables and typically Scottish corner turrets on consoles.

William Alexander, the founder of Nova Scotia, was born in the superbly restored castle. A Nova Scotia exhibition in the castle is run by the National Trust.

Stoke-on-Trent
Staffordshire/England   p.328☐H 13

This industrial town is the centre of the English pottery industry.

City Museum and Art Gallery: The museum has a unique collection of local pottery and porcelain along with examples from Europe, the Near and Far East, North America and South America.

Keele Hall: Within the University of Keele (founded in 1962); it houses a collection of over 5 million aerial photographs taken 1939–46.

Environs: Alton Towers (*c.* 8.5 m. E.): There was a settlement here in the Iron Age. Later it became the ancestral seat of the Earls of Shrewsbury and was provided with a large park by the 15th Earl, Charles Talbot. In 1814–27 he had an area of farmland and uncultivated land converted at enormous expense into a picturesque park with a Roman *columned hall,* a Chinese *temple,* a Gothic *summer-house* and a Swiss *mountain hut.* His successor extended the park, calling his part 'Her Ladyship's Garden'. All these enterprises meant that there was no money left for the upkeep of the neo-Gothic mansion, which today stands as an empty shell on the hill. A monument to the creator of the park bears the motto: 'He made the desert smile'.

Barlaston (4.5 m. S.): One of the most important men in the pottery industry was Josiah Wedgwood who in 1769 founded Etruria between Newcastle and Hanley (erroneously believing that the classical vases which he copied came from Etruria). The growth of the firm is documented from its beginning up to the present day in the *Wedgwood Museum.* Designs are illustrated by the finished products which range over the last 200 years and provide a fascinating insight into the development of public taste. The exhibition's most valuable piece is one of the 6 vases made by Wedgwood himself on the first day of the firm's existence.

Little Moreton Hall (9 m. N.): Built 1559–80, it is one of the county's most picturesque *half-timbered houses.* With its crooked walls, decorated gables and quaint

Stonehenge, view

windows, it is reminiscent of a fairy-tale cottage. Both inside and out the wood is richly carved.

Stonehenge
Wiltshire/England   p.332☐H 15

The standing stones in the middle of Salisbury Plain form what is probably Europe's most important Bronze Age temple. Its origins lie in the 3C BC, at the end of the Neolithic Age. The complex may have been completed *c.* 1500 BC. The first to be built was the moat and rampart *ring*, with a few smaller stones marking the entrance. Then, *c.* 2100 BC came an *inner ring* of 60 smaller, uncut blue basalt stones, which possibly came from the Presely Mountains in Wales, nearly 200 m. away.

In the following century the *outer ring*, with a diameter of 100 ft. was built. This consisted of 30 stones in pairs linked together by covering stones. More than half of these still stand today; 6 of the covering slabs are also still in their original positions. These lintels or capping stones are exactly dressed as segments to fit the curve of the circle and have holes carved in the underside, which lock on to the corresponding tenons of the monoliths. The lintels were raised with alternately placed levers with wood layed cross-wise underneath. The large *horseshoe* with its 5 trilithons may have been built shortly afterwards. 3 of these still have their lintels. The horseshoe was originally bordered by 19 monoliths, all of which came from the Marlborough Downs. In the last building phase *c.* 1500 BC the blue basalt stones were rearranged into their present shape. At the same time the monolith known today as the *'Altar Stone'* was placed in the middle.

Stonehenge may have served a double purpose. On the one hand it was an enormous burial complex with nearly 400 tombs thought to be of the Wessex culture. On the other hand the complex served the priests as a permanent stone calendar. On the day of the mid-summer solstice the sun rises exactly over the Heel Stone, marking the axis of the procession route running down to the Avon. For the mid-winter solstice there is a corresponding stone arch, through the middle of which the sun sinks as it begins its course for the winter half year.

Stranraer
Dumfries and Galloway Region/Scotland
p.326☐F 10

This town on Loch Ryan goes back to Roman times. The bay of Stranraer is very favourably situated and was therefore frequently used as an anchorage by the Romans, who named it *Rerigonus Sinus*.

Stranraer Castle: This little castle, begun in the mid-15C, stands in the middle of the town and was the residence of John Graham of Claverhouse, the great scourge of the Covenanters. In the 17C it was converted and used for a time as a prison. Tradition has it that the castle was built on bales of wool to prevent the stones sinking into the marshy ground.

Environs: Glenluce Abbey (11 m. E.): This Cistercian abbey was founded in 1192 by Roland, Lord of Galloway. The first monks came from Dundrennan. The ruins of the abbey are extraordinarily well preserved in places, such as the S. aisle and the S. transept of the church. Of particular interest is the almost intact chapterhouse of 1470, whose vaulting has

Stonehenge, silhouette

survived well. Still easily discernible is the plumbing, together with the mechanism for supplying the complex with water. Also preserved is a series of good clay pots, which may have been made in the region of Bordeaux.

Lochnaw Castle: The former family home of Clan Agnew, dating from 1426. For over 300 years the clan held the position of Sheriff of Galloway. The picturesque building is set in a beautiful rhododendron park.

The ruins of *Kennedy Castle* (built in 1607 and destroyed in 1715) are also of interest. Here too there is a splendid rhododendron park; the park's pinetum may be the oldest in Scotland.

Logan (12.5 m. S.): Its *Botanic Garden* is famous and has subtropical plants from all over the world. Near the coast there is a sea fish pond, built 1788–1800.

Stratford-upon-Avon
Warwickshire/England   p.328□I 14

This market town, founded by Richard I in 1196, is the birthplace of England's greatest writer. William Shakespeare was born here in 1564 and died here on 23 April 1616. The stream of visitors began shortly after his death, and the town attracts some 300,000 visitors to the Avon every year.

Holy Trinity Church: The church where Shakespeare was christened and buried. It dates from the 13&14C. The *central tower* (originally wooden) and the *transepts* were built in the 13C; the *nave* and the *aisles* are early 14C. The sanctuary was rebuilt towards the end of the 15C and the old wooden tower was replaced in 1763 by William Hiorn. The choir stalls were made towards the end of the 15C. Remnants of Early English have survived. On the N. side of the sanctuary are the tombs of Shakespeare, his wife and his daughter. A monument to him was erected on the N. wall with an arch and two black marble Corinthian columns. Next to the font, where the poet was baptized on 26 April 1564, copies of the parish registers are displayed.

Shakespeare's Birthplace: The early 16C building was divided into two residences during the poet's lifetime. The W. half was a shop, while the E. half was an inn for many years. Today the W. side has been restored to its probable 16C appearance. The room in which he was born on the first floor is still furnished with a few of the original pieces. The adjacent *mu-*

Stratford-upon-Avon, Anne Hathaway's Cottage

seum contains manuscripts, books, etc. relating to the Bard.

Royal Shakespeare Theatre: The original building was built in 1877–9 and staged all Shakespeare's plays before it burned down in 1926. In 1932 it reopened and is now used as a summer festival theatre. The building also contains a *library* with over 10,000 volumes of Shakespeariana, as well as a *Picture Gallery and Museum* (on the first floor) which includes costumes, designs for stage sets and mementoes of Shakespearian productions from 1879 to the present day.

Also worth seeing: *Anne Hathaway's Cottage* dates from the 15C and was the family home of Shakespeare's wife. The *Guild Chapel* dates back to 1269. Sir Hugh Clopton rebuilt the nave in 1495. A wall-painting of the Last Judgement on the chancel arch was painted *c.* 1500. The Guildhall for the brotherhood of the Holy Cross was built next to the chapel in 1416–8. The young Shakespeare may have seen his first play performed by travelling theatre people in the hall on the ground floor. He went to the elementary school on the first floor. *New Place* (built by Sir Hugh Clopton in 1483) was the largest house in the town. Shakespeare bought it in 1597 and lived here after his return from London until his death. Unfortunately there remain only the foundations of the house. The *Shakespeare statue* is by Lord Gower, who donated it to the town in 1888. It depicts Hamlet, Lady Macbeth, Falstaff and Prince Hal as symbols of wisdom, tragedy, comedy and history.

Environs: Compton Wynyates: This ex-

Stratford-upon-Avon

tensive mansion with its walls of red brick and white sandstone is one of the most beautiful houses in England. Back in the early 13C there was a country seat of the Compton family here. In 1481 Edmund Compton started building the present house. The 4-winged complex was completed around 1515 by Sir William Compton. The house is remarkable for the variety of its rooms, its half or completely hidden stairs and the chapel, which was rebuilt after the Reformation and has ceiling paintings from around 1665.

Sudbury	
Suffolk/England	p.332☐L 14

This little town on the Stour still has many old half-timbered houses; *Old Moot Hall* and *Salter's Hall* are 15C. Thomas Gainsborough was born here in 1727 and his birthplace has been preserved as a *museum,* containing numerous of his works and memorabilia. His *statue* in the market square is by Mackennal (1913).

Church of St. Gregory: The town's parish church, which is Gothic and has a W. tower, was built by Simon de Sudbury, Archbishop of Canterbury, who was murdered by Wat Tyler in 1387. His head is preserved in the church. Of interest are the *wooden font cover* and the *misericords* of the choir stalls.

Environs: Acton (4.5 m. NE): *All Saints Church* was built *c.* 1300 and contains one of the oldest and most beautiful tomb slabs in England. Made for Robert de Bures, who died in 1302, the monument is adorned with a life-size figure of a knight.

Brent Eleigh (8 m. NE): The early Gothic church of *St. Mary* has a 14C W. portal; 17C pulpit and font cover, and fine 14C frescos, which were discovered and exposed in 1961.

Clare (10 m. W.): Here an *Augustinian priory*, stood. Built in 1248, it was the birthplace of Lionel, Duke of Clarence, son of Edward III. The sometimes ancient houses of the town, which date back to the 15C are very beautiful. The church of *Peter and St. Paul* dates mainly from the 14&15C, although the W. tower is much older. The fine font is Gothic; wooden furnishings are 17C. The original window glass was unfortunately destroyed by William Dowsing.

Lavenham (10 m. NE): This picturesque old town was a centre for the wool trade in the 15C and numerous half-timbered houses date from that time. The most beautiful old buildings are the old *Wool Hall* (c. 1500), the *Tudor Shops, De Vere House*, the old *Primary School, Mullet House* and *Shiling Old Grange*. The church of *St. Peter and St. Paul* in its present form dates mainly from the 15C. It has a large W. tower, a beautiful clerestory and side chapels with large windows. The choir screen dates from the 15C, as do the choir stalls with their superbly carved misericords. Also of interest are the Spring Chantry and the Oxford Chantry from 1523. The splendid monuments date back to the 15C. The beautiful half-timbered *Guildhall* in the marketplace was built in 1530; originally it belonged to the Corpus Christi brotherhood.

Long Melford (4.5 m. N.): This town has a high street some 2.5 miles long in which there are a few superb old buildings, such as *Melford Hall* (1554), *Holy Trinity Hospital* (1573) and *Kentwell Hall* (1564). The late Gothic church of the *Holy Trinity* has a Lady Chapel with three gables; the W. tower was rebuilt by G.F. Bodley in 1901. The most valuable part of the interior decoration is the superb stained-glass of the aisle windows. (Most of the stained glass was in fact destroyed in the 16&17C, but what remains gives a good idea of their original beauty.) The Clopton Chantry in the N. aisle contains interesting memorial

Lavenham (Sudbury), Guildhall

plaques and monuments. In the nave there is a seat which came from Granada Cathedral and is embellished with the arms of Ferdinand and Isabella. *Melford Hall,* a mansion built by Sir William Cordell 1554–78, has been owned by the Hyde-Parker family since the 18C. It now houses the *Hyde Parker Collection,* which includes valuable furniture, old paintings and a collection of Chinese porcelain.

Sunderland

Tyne and Wear/England   p.328□I 10

Holy Trinity Church: Built in classical style in 1719, the apse was added in 1735. The interior is defined by splendid Corinthian columns. Among other interesting features is the *monument* of 1838 to the neoclassical sculptor Francis Chantrey R.A.

Museum and Art Gallery (Mowbray Park): The highlight of the archaeology

and history department is the collection of Saxon *glass* (mostly from Monkwearmouth); also of interest are old Sunderland *ceramics* and a *collection of model ships.* The art gallery consists mainly of works by English artists.

Also of interest: *St. Michael's Church* from the 18C.

Environs: Beamish (*c.* 12 m. W.): The *North of England Open-Air Museum* is devoted to the social and industrial history of N. England; exhibits include houses, railway stations and colliery buildings.

Easington (*c.* 8 m. S.): The church of *St. Mary the Virgin,* although originally Norman, was later altered; of interest inside are the choir stalls and 2 13C monuments.

Hylton Castle (W. of the town): This castle has a massive tower and was built in the 14C to resist the attacks of the Scots, (It is reputedly haunted by the so-called 'Cauld Lad', the ghost of a stable boy who drowned in the castle well in 1609.)

Long Melford (Sudbury), Melford Hall

Sunderland, Church of the Holy Trinity

Monkwearmouth (N. of the River Wear): Remains of a *monastery* founded in 674 by Bishop Benedict (the Venerable Bede joined the monastery in 680). This, together with its sister monastery in Jarrow (founded in 684) determined the spiritual life of England at the time. The church was restored in 1866, but of its original 7C fabric there remains the W. tower with a porch which has the oldest medieval vault in England. On the outside of the tower there is a relief with a standing figure, which is in poor condition.

Penshaw Monument (*c.* 5 m. W.): *Monument* to the 1st Earl of Durham (1792–1840), built in 1844 in the form of a Doric temple.

Pittington (*c.* 7.5 m. SW): The 12C church of *St. Lawrence* has beautiful Romanesque round arches on richly em-

bellished columns on the N. inner wall; also of interest are the wall paintings from the time of construction).

Roker (*c.* 2.5 m. N.): *St. Andrew's Church* was built in 1906–7 by E.S. Prior. Above the choir there is a Gothic tower. Of particular interest inside are the splendid furnishings (carpets and altar covers by Morris, wall hangings by Burne-Jones, altar cross and lectern by Ernest Grimson).

Seaham (*c.* 5 m. S.): *St. Mary's Church* has a pre-Norman nave, 13C choir and W. tower. The font is early 13C, the pulpit 16C.

Washington Old Hall (*c.* 6 m. W.): Ancestral home of the Washington family 1183–1613; the mansion of 1610 still contains building fabric from the Middle Ages. Inside: beautiful period furniture and memorabilia of George Washington.

1st President of the USA (the Washington coat-of-arms, 3 stars and 2 stripes, became part of the US flag).

Swansea/Abertawe

W. Glamorgan/Wales   p.332□G 15

This city at the mouth (aber) of the Tawe in Swansea Bay is the location of important industries (tin plate, copper and zinc processing); Swansea also has an enormous export harbour which deals with the shipping of coal. Its population has grown from 6000 in 1800 to over 170,000 today, making it Wales' second-largest city after Cardiff. Swansea was badly damaged by German bombing raids in World War 2.

Swansea Castle: The Norman castle of 1099 was rebuilt by Bishop Gower of St. David's. However, a few original remains have survived (turretted tower, parapet with arcades on Castle St.

Also worth seeing: The *Glynn Vivian Museum* contains paintings by English and Welsh artists and a beautiful porcelain collection. The *Guildhall* (1934) contains the interesting 'British Empire Panels' (17 painted wooden panels with colonial scenes from 1924). The *Industrial Museum* contains old looms, a reconstructed factory and old vehicles.

Environs: A worthwhile excursion from Swansea is the round-trip through the delightful scenery (bluffs, cliffs, dunes, caves) of the *Gower Peninsula* . To the SW, of Swansea, the peninsula is *c.* 14 m. long and 7.5 m. wide and has sites of prehistoric interest.:
Oxwich (*c.* 9 m. SW): This coastal village has an interesting village church, *St.Illtyd* which dates from the 12–14C and has an old Celtic font. *Oxwich Castle* is a 15C mansion.

Penmaen (*c.* 6 m. SW): Near the village is the Neolithic burial chamber, *Park Cwm*, a barrow some 75 ft. long with 4 side chambers and a porch. Of the Cotswold type, it is one of the best preserved in the country.
Penrice Castle (*c.* 7.5 m. SW): These picturesque ruins are situated in a beautiful park and date from the 13–14C.
Port Eynon (*c.* 10 m. SW): To the W. of this coastal village are the *Paviland Caves*, where skeletons of prehistoric man were dicovered.
Reynoldstown (*c.* 11 m. SW): Near the village is the megalithic tomb *Arthur's Stone*. The barrow's enormous covering stone, which is linked with the legendary King Arthur, weighs about 25 tons and is supported by 9 smaller stones. Nearby are the sparse remains of 13C *Weobley Castle* (in the village of Llanrhidian).
Rhossili (*c.* 11 m. SW): A cliff top village with a magnificent view over the sea; the *church* has a late-Norman gateway with a sun-dial.
The Mumbles (*c.* 5 m. S.): This popular resort with the impressive cliffs of the Mumbles Head is dominated by the ruins of *Oystermouth Castle*. Of the former Norman castle (*c.* 1094), which was destroyed and rebuilt many times, the picturesque gatehouse, the banqueting hall and the chapel have survived.

Swindon

Wiltshire/England   p.332□J 15

This old market town on the NE border of Wiltshire became a modern industrial town when the Great Western Railway set up their locomotive and carriage works here.

Great Western Railway Museum: Set up in 1962, it contains splendid locomotives and carriages of historical interest, including such famous vehicles as the 'City of Truro', which reached an average speed of 70 m.p.h. between Exeter and Bristol in 1904. There is also a reproduction of the 'North Star', which was the first passenger train and operated between Paddington and Maidenhead in 1838. Apart from many model trains, there are exhibits of everything which has anything to do with the railway or railway equipment. A special room is devoted to the great engineer and builder of bridges, Isambard Kingdom Brunel.

Museum and Art Gallery: Part of the museum houses coins, geological exhibits and other items of a natural scientific nature, musical instruments and even, curiously, a collection of pot lids. Another part of the museum displays works by 20C artists such as Henry Moore, Ben Nicholson and Graham Sutherland.

Environs: Aldbourne (8 m. SE): *St. Michael's Church*, which dates back to the 12C, was later enlarged and acquired its W.

Swindon, Great Western Railway Museum

tower in the 15C. The S. is Norman; the 2-storey entrance hall is Gothic. Inside: the roof dates from the 15C, the pulpit is Jacobean and the octagonal font is 17C.

Ashdown House (*c.* 4.5 m. SE): The first Lord Craven built this large *hunting lodge* in the late 17C, dedicating it to Elizabeth of Bohemia. The house has 4 storeys and a dome and is surrounded by beautiful gardens. The enormous staircase takes up over a quarter of the inside of the building.

Cricklade (6 m. NW): The church of *St. Sampson* was built in the 16C and has a central tower with 4 spires. The church foundations are Saxon; the church was extended for the first time by the Normans. *Saxon Burh* is a system of fortifications from the time of King Alfred, who realized that only solid bastions could protect his soldiers in the event of war. For this reason he (and his son Edward the Elder after him) built fortifications in many places S. of the Thames.

Faringdon (9 m. NE): *All Saints Church* is a large cruciform church with a low crossing tower, which lost its spire in the Civil War. The church, which was begun in the 12C, in the main dates from the 13C; it has, however, been repeatedly restored in later centuries. The N. portal, built around 1170, is Norman; the S. portal is early Gothic and dates from the late 13C. The font is also 13C. The church contains numerous monuments to members of the Unton and Pye families.

Littlecote (12.5 m. SE): This Tudor mansion was begun in 1490 and completed in 1520. It has a generously proportioned hall and a long gallery. Panelling, stucco and furnishings date from the time of construction. The Great Hall displays weapons from the time of Cromwell.

Lydiard Tregoze (3 m. W.): The church of *St. Mary* is mainly Gothic, although some alterations were carried out in 1633. The pulpit dates from the early 17C. However, the church is of interest above all for the tombs of the he St. John family, whose splendid monuments date back to the 16C and are adorned with sculpted figures of the family in various poses; one monument has a painted family tree. *Lydiard Mansion,* the ancestral home of the St.Johns dates back to the 15C (alterations in the Georgian style in 1749).

Purton (4.5 m. NW): *St.Mary's Church* has two towers; the central crossing tower has a spire, the W. tower is flat-topped. This Norman church was greatly altered in the 14&15C. Of interest are a few frescos, including a depiction of the Death of the Virgin Mary from the 14C. Fragments of the medieval stained glass have also survived.

Uffington (c. 5.5 m. E.): This place is of more than regional importance because of the *White Horse,* an enormous figure of a horse, carved in a chalk hillside, which dates from 600-100 BC. Nearby is *Uffington Castle,* an Iron Age hill-fort. The town itself has an interesting 13C *church* in Early English style with an octagonal tower and lancet windows.

Swords
Dublin/Ireland   p.326□E 12

This former bishop's seat is *c.* 6 m. N. of Dublin and has remarkable medieval

ruins: A Round Tower and remnants of buildings are evidence of a former *abbey* founded by St. Columba. Of the 13C *Bishop's Castle* a gatehouse, chapel and 14C defensive tower have survived.

Environs: Doulagh (c. 3 m. SE): A Dublin suburb with the little church of *St. Doulagh* , which has a stone roof from the 9C, 12C additions in the chancel and a 15C tower. The oldest part of the church, *The Hermit's Cell,* on the W. side is reputed to contain the tomb of the church's founder St.Doulagh (c. 600).

Lusk (c. 6 m. N.): This pretty village has a 5-storey *Round Tower* from the 12C, which is in an excellent state of preservation. It is a remnant of a monastery founded in the 5-6C. Such towers, with conical tops—also called 'Irish minarets' —were used in the 9-12C, principally as a place of refuge from attacks and pillaging. Nearby there are further remains of other towers. The *church,* which was rebuilt in the 19C, contains beautiful tombs.

Malahide (c. 3 m. E.): Originally a Norman *castle* belonging to the Earl of Talbot, it was enlarged in the 18C. Nearby are ruins of a 15-16C *abbey.*

Skerries (c. 12.5 m. E.): Remains of 15C *Baldongan Church.*

T

Tara

Meath/Ireland   p.326☐E 12

Next to this village is the highly significant prehistoric and early Celtic religious and residential settlement of *Teamhair na Riogh* (kings' city). The earliest *burial chambers* and *burial mounds* date back to the 2nd millennium BC. During the heathen Celtic period, from *c.* 400 BC to AD 400,

the Irish kings were chosen and crowned on the mound *Rath na Riogh* (royal enclosure). All that stands today are the circular *bank-ditches* and *earthworks*. The once huge *Halls of Tara*, which had doors set with precious stones, wooden columns and gold and bronze furnishings, have disappeared without trace.

In the centre of Rath na Riogh are the interior walls of *Cormac's House* (Gaelic: Teach Cormaic), with the old coronation

Tara, Teamhair na Riogh 1 Rath Laoghaire (former royal court of Laoghaire) **2** Rath na Riogh (court of the Irish kings) **3** Cormac's House (Teach Cormaic) **4** Lia Fail (coronation stone) **5** statue of St. Patrick **6** Royal Seat (Forradh) **7** Mound of the Hostages (prehistoric passage grave from *c.* 1800 BC) **8** Rath of the Synods (surrounding walls) **9** St. Patrick's Church with Adamnan's Cross **10** Banquet Hall **11** Rath Grainne (earthwork)

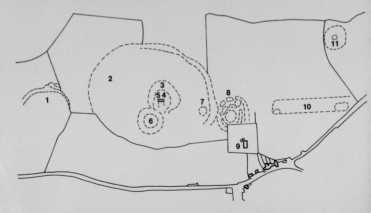

stone of *Lia Fail*. Nearby is a *statue of St. Patrick*, in memory of the saint's attempt to convert King Laoire (Laoghaire). Also inside the wall is the *Royal Seat* ('Forradh') and the *Mound of the Hostages*, a prehistoric burial chamber in the N. from *c.* 1800 BC. To the S. is the circular earthwork of Rath *Laoghaire*, the former royal enclosure of Laoghaire, and to the N. that of the *Rath of the Synods*, the parallel walls of the *Banquet Hall* and the circular earthwork of *Rath Grainne*. The pillar stump of *Adamnan's Cross* is interesting: it is situated near the graveyard chapel and has a depiction of a Celtic deity (Cornnunos). About half a mile S. are the remains of the prehistoric ring fort of *Rath Maeve*, defended by ramparts and ditches. In the early 19C the nationalist Daniel O'Connell held a mass meeting here.

Environs: Dunshaughlin (*c.* 4 m. SE): The remains of a medieval *church* with a fine gravestone.

Taunton
Somerset/England   p.332☐G16

The county town of Somerset and the home of cider, Taunton was founded in 705 by Ine, king of the West Saxons, as a border fortress against the Celts. In the early 12C the construction of the *castle* was begun; in 1497 the unsuccessful rebellion of Perkin Warbeck ended here; and in 1644 the Royalists tried in vain to take the city. In 1685 the Duke of Monmouth was crowned king in the market place, and in the same year Judge Jeffreys took bloody revenge for this act after the battle of Sedgemoor: over 500 supporters of the protestant pretender to the throne were hung in the aftermath.
Little survives of the once important Norman castle; today the county museum stands on its site.

Somerset County Museum: The interesting archaeological, natural and technical collections range from prehistoric exhibits, through a Roman mosaic from Low Ham to steam-driven aeroplane parts. The most valuable exhibit is probably the portrait of Charles I and his queen by van Dyck.

Environs: Bridgwater (11 m. NE): This small town on the lower reaches of the Parrett is the birthplace of Robert Blake (1598–1657), Oliver Cromwell's admiral. The *Church of St.Mary* is early Gothic and has a 200 ft. high tower which was built by Nicholas Wleys in 1366. Its pulpit is Gothic, and the choir screen, Jacobean in style, is particularly fine. The *Admiral Blake Museum* is housed in Blake's birthplace, and includes many mementoes of the admiral, and also of the Battle of Sedgemoor (1685) and the Duke of Monmouth (1649–85).

Tenby/Dinbych-y-psygod
Dyfed/Wales   p.330☐F 14/15

A charming and popular cliff-top resort on the W. side of Carmarthen Bay, it has some 5,000 inhabitants.

St.Mary's Church: This is an interesting 13&14C high Gothic church, which was decorated in the 15C with a finely-carved *oak ceiling*, a number of *sculptures* (of which there are still 75 originals in the chancel alone), and also numerous plant motifs and grotesques, including a mermaid. The ceiling depicting God the Father on his Throne is original, but most of the other pieces in the nave are copies. The church has a raised *sanctuary*, with steps leading up to it, and a *crypt*. The numerous medieval *sarcophagi* are also interesting, with effigies of the dead (e.g. Thomas ap Rees in the NE St.Nicholas's Chapel);

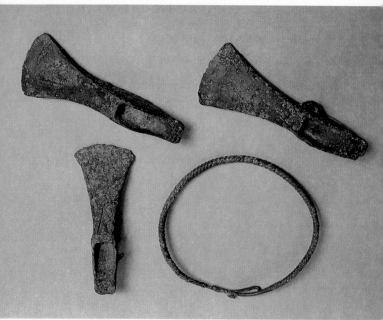

Taunton, Somerset County Museum, Bronze Age tools

in the SE St.Thomas's Chapel is a *plaque* to the celebrated mathematician Robert Recorde, who invented the 'equals' sign here in the 16C. Near the church are a few *arches*, the remains of an old *church school*.

Also worth seeing: Near the church (to the W.) are the remnants of the *town walls* with 15C bastions; the surviving town gate, *Five Arches*, is interesting. Between the church and the castle hill are the town's two oldest buildings: the *Tudor Merchant's House*, now a museum, and the nearby *Plantagenet House*, now a pub, both of which are 15C in origin. The castle hill is past the harbour in the E. of the peninsula; there is little left of the 13C *castle*. The small *Tenby Museum* below the castle has a shell collection, and also archaeological finds from the surrounding area (e.g. the bones of a mammoth).

Environs: Amroth (*c.* 9 m. NE): On the site of an old 12C castle, whose gateway still stands, is *Amroth Castle*, a 19C manor house. The old castle was apparently part of a chain of fortresses with which the Normans in SW Wales guarded against local uprisings.

Caldy Island (*c.*2 m. S.): This island was inhabited as early as Mesolithic times, to judge by the weapons and tools on display in Tenby Museum. In the 6C the first (Celtic) monks arrived; there is a 9C *stone* with an Ogham and some later Latin inscriptions, which is situated to the S. of the Old Priory Church. The Benedictines founded a new *monastery* here in the 12C (the Old Priory), and its well-preserved buildings date from the 12, 13&15C; restored 1897. There is a church, a gatehouse, a refectory, a prior's residence (which today serves as a guest house), and

Taunton, Somerset County Museum, Roman mosaic

other buildings. The Benedictines departed in 1536; in 1907 it was occupied by Anglicans and from 1929 by Trappists. There are 20 or so monks still living there, working the land and producing goods. The churches are the most interesting buildings to visit, especially the *new monastery church*, the old restored *monastery church of St.Illtyd* and the *village church of St.David*, which are both medieval.

Manorbier (*c.* 6 m. SW): This village on the S. has a strikingly well-preserved *castle* high over the bay. The first castle, built of wood and earth, was begun in the 11C but the present stone one is 13C. The castle's original near-impregnable position can still be appreciated: the inner ward is surrounded by a curtain wall with a gatehouse to the E., outside which are the (now much altered) living quarters, which are still occupied, the chapel, the Great Hall (manor house), and the sundials to the W.. This is where the celebrated Welsh historian Giraldus de Barri (Giraldus Cambrensis) was born in 1146. His 'Travels through Wales' (1188) are still informative today. Opposite the castle is the old parish church of *St.James*, an interesting 13C building with a sanctuary, tower and transept. The N. aisle was added in 1300, the N. transept was extended in the 14C, and the S. aisle was added. During the extensions, Early English arches were added. Nearby (to the SW) is the less than well-preserved megalithic stone burial chamber of *King's Quoit*, on the Priest's Nose promontory. The cap stone and two short support stones are still standing.

Penally (*c.* 3 m. S.): There is an attractive 13C *church* here with an old tomb and an interesting Celtic *high cross* in the churchyard.

St.Catherine (*c.* ½ m. E.): Just offshore by the castle is this small island with a 19C fort; it can be reached at low tide.

Tewkesbury

Gloucestershire/England p.332□H 14

This small town near the confluence of the Avon and the Severn has a number of 16&17C houses, and a whole row of 15C ones. *King John's Bridge* was built around 1200, and not widened until 1964. In 1471 Edward IV beat the Prince of Wales at Bloody Meadow, Just to the S.. The town's most important building is its abbey church.

Abbey Church of St.Mary the Virgin: This was begun in 1092 by Sir Robert Fitzhamon as the successor to a Benedictine monastery which was founded in 715. The *choir* was built in 1123, the *tower* and the *nave* completed by 1160. The *choir chapels* were added between 1330 and 1350. After the battle of 1471, the huge church, 330 ft. long and 130 ft. wide, was rebuilt and re-consecrated, since when it has remained largely unaltered. The Dissolution of the monasteries left it unscathed, since the local council bought it for some 400 pounds. The same authorities added the four *corner turrets* in 1660 to the 165 ft. high tower over the crossing.

The interior of the nave is dominated by its huge Romanesque columns. The *vaulting*, which was rebuilt in the 14C, has exceptionally fine bosses. The transepts are entirely Norman, except for the windows, which were restored in the 14C at the same time as the S. side of the aisle. The S. transept contains the *Lady Chapel*, which now houses Raphael's 'Madonna del Passeggio', which used to belong to Madame Pompadour. The Romanesque *chancel* has 14C windows, which are dedicated to the local Lords of the time. The various *chapels* are most interesting, especially the *Beauchamp Chantry* from 1422, the *Founder's Chantry* (for Lord Fitzhamon) from 1397, and the *Trinity Chantry* from 1378, whose early fan vaulting and kneeling figure of Edward le Despenser are particularly fine. The church contains numerous *tombs* and

Tenby, view

memorials, including that of the Duke of Clarence, who was murdered in 1478. Little is left of the huge abbey: only a 15C *gatehouse* to the S. and the *Abbey House*, which is also 15C.

Environs: Deerhurst (2 m. SW): The *Church of St. Mary* belonged to a Saxon monastery founded in 804; the lower section of the tower dates from this period, as does the remarkable and well-preserved font from around 800. The transitional Romanesque/Gothic nave incorporates a Saxon choir, which is 20 ft. long. The remains of the apse are visible from the outside. The E. wall of the tower has the celebrated triangular window; but the finest example of 14C stained glass is St. Catherine and her wheel in the S. aisle. She is kneeling beneath a magnificent structure with small stylized towers and flowers. The tomb of Sir John Cassey and his wife in the N. choir aisle is also interesting. Near the monastery church is *Odda's Chapel*, which was built in 1056 as a memorial chapel for Odda's brother Aelfric.

Thetford
Norfolk / England   p.328 □ L 13

This small town on the Little Ouse does not look at first glance as if it was the residence of the Kings of East Anglia and a bishopric from 1075 to 1094. Before the Reformation there were no less than 20 parish churches here, as well as numerous monasteries. There are still some remains of a *Cluniac priory*, an *Augustinian priory*, a *Franciscan monastery* and a *Benedictine convent*.

Ancient House Museum: This is in a 15C house and is dedicated to the natural and social history of the town and its environs. The exhibits date back to the early Stone Age, and include a display of weighing and measuring implements.

Castle Hill: This 100 ft. mound stands to the E. of the city and has the remnants of a Norman *tower* surrounded by Iron Age earthworks. The castle was destroyed in 1173.

Tewkesbury, Abbey Church of St. Mary the Virgin

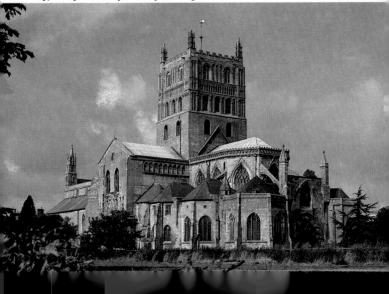

Thorney, St.Mary and St.Botolph

Window

Environs: East Harling (9 m. E.): The *Church of St.Peter and St.Paul* is 14C, and has a fine hammerbeam ceiling in the nave. The large E. window still contains sections of the original glass, and the octagonal font is Gothic. The church contains a number of 15&16C monument, notably those to the Harling and Lovell families.
Euston (4 m. S.): The *Church of St. Genevieve* was rebuilt in the 17C, and only the tower remains from an earlier date. The finely carved wooden pulpit is interesting, and the altar panels are attributed to Grinling Gibbons.
Grime's Graves (5 m. NW): This is the site of the interesting *flint quarries*, which provided one of the Stone Age's most important raw materials. There are some 400 pits, up to 50 ft. deep; they date from 2, 100 BC, and are remarkably well-preserved due to the process of filling up one used

mine with the debris from the next. Flint is still cut in nearby Brandon.

Thirlestane Castle
Borders/Scotland   p.324☐H 8

This is one of the best-preserved castles in Scotland, and it is situated near the small town of Lauder. Its basic structure dates from 1595, and it was extended in 1675 and 1841. Its *W. façade* is by Sir William Bruce and the oldest section is the central block, which is surrounded by four huge *round towers*. The 4th floor of the towers is in the form of a square Cap-House, with the corners resting on consoles. The corner-towers have symmetrically-arranged spiral staircases, which begin on the second floor. By the four corner towers are six further *round towers*, which add still further to the castle's romantic aura. Its interior has attractive stucco ceilings and 17–19C furnishings. Today it is the seat of the Lords of Lauderdale.

Thorney
Cambridgeshire/England   p.328☐K 13

The origins of this town go back to a monastery founded in the 7C, which was destroyed by the Danes in 870 and later rebuilt by the Normans, after which it continued in existence until its dissolution in 1539. Near the monastery is the site of Hereward the Wake's last stand against William the Conqueror. After the Dissolution of the monasteries, the town and much of its surrounding area passed to the Dukes of Bedford.

Church of St. Mary and St. Botolph: This church still contains sections of the old Norman monastery church, including the fine *W. façade* and the splendid *arcades* in the nave. The transept, the crossing tower and the sanctuary have unfortunately disappeared; the entire E. end of the present church was rebuilt by William Blore in Norman style in 1840.

Thorney Abbey: After the Dissolution of the monasteries in 1539, this building stood empty for 100 years, before being renovated in 1638. The *W. façade* is impressive, with two huge 12C *towers* with 15C octagonal additions. The *windows* above the portal were added in the 17C, while the *gallery*, which runs between the towers, has nine statues and dates from the Middle Ages.

Abbey House: This is late-16C and was a manor house of the Dukes of Bedford. It is undecorated on the outside, but the interior has fine *panelling* and a lavishly decorated *chimney-piece*.

Thorney, St. Mary and St. Botolph

Thurles
Tipperary/Ireland   p.330☐C 13

This is the rural centre of the county of Tipperary, which served as a fortress on the river Suir during the Middle Ages; in 1174, Strongbow's Normans were defeated here. There are remains of a 15C *bridge tower*, and of *Black Castle* (in the centre). The Catholic *cathedral* from 1860 has a fine 17C baroque tabernacle by Andrea Pozzo.

Environs: Holy Cross Abbey (*c.* 4 m. W.): The remains of this former site of pilgrimage are among the most beautiful pieces of late Gothic architecture in Ireland. The *Cistercian monastery* was founded in 1180 by the King of Munster and possessed a relic of the Holy Cross (hence the name). The buildings are arranged around a courtyard: to the N. is the 12C cruciform monastery church with 15C extensions including the choir and the highly decorated sedilia niches. The nave is interesting, with some sections of barrel vaulting and some of three-capped cross-ribbed vaulting, and the window tracery, especially in the sexipartite E. and W. windows and the window in the S. transept, is especially fine. The relic of the Cross (now in Blackrock, Cork) was probably kept in the sanctuary in the S. transept, which has arches, twisted columns and a ribbed ceiling. The N. transept has one of the few Irish frescos (a hunting scene), and fine sculptures, which are also in evidence on the pillars of the crossing. The huge central tower over the crossing is 15C. The remains of the cloisters, the dormitories (to the W.), the press house, the chapterhouse, the sacristy, the hospital and the abbot's house are still standing.

Kilcooly Abbey (*c.* 7 m. E.): The ruins of this Cistercian abbey date from the 13&16C; it was founded in 1182, and the church, which dates from 1200, was rebuilt in the 15C (choir, central tower). There are fine sculptures and tombs from the 15C.

Tintagel
Cornwall/England   p.330☐F 16

According to the chronicle 'Historia Regum Britanniae', which dates from 1136 and was written by Geoffrey of Monmouth, Tintagel was the residence of King Arthur, the legendary (Celtic or Roman?) commander who led the Celts to victory in 515 against the invading Angles and Saxons at Badon Hill. If the chronicle is to be believed, King Arthur died in his castle in 542, but no other facts about his life have since come to light.

Tintagel Castle: The ruins of the castle in which King Arthur is said to have lived are 12C, with additions from the following century. In the 16C, part of the structure fell into the sea, and in 1852 steps were taken to preserve the remnants. There are extensive earthworks which suggest that a

Tintagel, view from Tintagel Castle

Celtic *monastery* stood on the castle cliffs between 500 and 850. It is, however, not convincing evidence for any particular piece of the Arthurian legend.

Old Post Office: This is the town's only old house; it dates from the 14C and follows the ground plan of a medieval manor house. From 1844–92 it served as the local post office, and the National Trust have furnished one of the rooms as it was in Victorian times.

Tralee
Kerry/Ireland   p.330□A 13

This busy town is the capital of the county of Kerry, and has some 13,000 inhabitants; until 1583, it was the seat of the Earl of Desmond, but there are very few old remains. Every year in September it is the site of the election of the 'Rose of Tralee', a beauty contest with contestants from all over Ireland.

Environs: Ardfert (7 m. NW): This was a bishop's seat in the Middle Ages, and was originally founded by St.Brendan. The remains of *St.Brendan's Cathedral* are 13C, and include a fortress-style wall with battlements, Romanesque arcades and an old (12C) W. entrance, S. transept and chapel in the NE, with an effigy of a bishop in the choir. *Temple-na-Hoe:* A late Romanesque 12C church with attractive flower patterns. *Temple-na-Griffin* is 15C and has an interesting stone slab with a dragon and griffin. The *Franciscan Friary* (Ardfert Abbey) was founded in 1253 by Lord Fitz Maurice. The 13&14C church is still standing, and has fine windows, S. aisle and 15C transept. There is also a 15C corner-tower, a cloister and part of the 12&15C monastery building.
Ballyduff (*c.* 19 m. N.): The remains of a 15C abbey and the 12C *round tower* of

Rattoo, which is some 92 ft. high and in good condition, with a restored roof.

Traquair House
Borders/Scotland   p.324□H 9

This *house* dates back to the 10C and claims to be the oldest continuously inhabited manor house in Scotland; no less than 27 English and Scottish monarchs have allegedly lived or stayed here, including William the Lion (1209) and Mary Queen of Scots with Lord Darnley (1566). In the 17&18C its owners were Jacobites —see the relief on an *oak door* from 1601, which to depicts a Scottish unicorn boring in to the torn throat of an English lion. The *Bear Gate* is equally symbolic: it has not been opened since 1745, when the 5th Earl of Traquair swore after Charles Edward Stuart left the castle that the door would not be opened again until the Stuarts were back on the throne. The reasons for its still remaining shut, despite the last Stuart having died in 1807, must be left to the visitor's imagination.
The oldest section of the house is 12C, and was the old royal *hunting lodge;* today it forms the NE corner of the structure. The tall, square *main section* dates from 1642, and the two *wings* were later 17C additions. The furnishings are largely original, and there are some interesting memorabilia of Mary Queen of Scots and Prince Charles Edward Stuart. The 18C brewery is still in use, and the gardens are most attractive.

Environs: Bowhill Castle (12 m. SE): This is the seat of the Scotts of Buccleuch; it is a small Georgian villa dating from 1812, with a Victorian extension from 1825 which was supervised by Sir Charles Barry, the architect of London's Houses of Parliament. The most interesting aspect of the building is its fine *art collection*. The furnishings, tapestries, porcelain and hand-painted Chinese wallpaper are mostly 17C, and the paintings include works by Leonardo da Vinci, Guardi, Claude, Reynolds, Gainsborough and Canaletto.

Neidpath Castle (6 m. NW): This slender tower-house stands above the Tweed; it dates from the 13C, and originally belonged to the Frazer clan and later to the Hays of Tweeddale. Cromwell's cannons battered the castle into surrender, despite its 10 ft. thick walls. The 1st Duke of Queensbury bought it in 1686 and had it rebuilt.

Trim
Meath/Ireland   p.326□D 12

This small town is situated on the river Boyne, some 28 m. NW of Dublin, and has a number of medieval buildings in good condition.

Trim Castle (Castle Street): This riverside fortress was built by the Anglo-Norman Hugh de Lacy in 1173, and under King John a massive rectangular *keep*, ten *drum towers*, a *gatehouse* and *curtain walls* with outworks and a moat were added, making it one of Ireland's largest castles. It is known for this reason as *King John's Castle*.

Talbot Castle (Abbey Lane): This fortress (1415) has recently been modernized. Nearby are the 15C remains of *Nangle Castle*, and those of the *Yellow Steeple*, a fine 14C five-storey bell tower in the 13C *St. Mary's Abbey*.

Also worth seeing: *St. Patrick's Church* was rebuilt in the 19C, but its tower is 15C. It stands on the spot where St. Patrick founded Ireland's first monastery in the 5C. There are a few gates still standing from the old 13&14C *town walls* (Sheep

Gate, Navan Gate, Dublin Gate, Water Gate, Athboy Gate), and some sections of wall. The suburb of Newtown Trim (*c.* ½ m. E.) contains the fine cathedral of *St. Peter and St. Paul*, which is on the banks of the Boyne and dates from the 13C, with remains of the *Augustinian priory* which was founded in 1206 (church, priory garden, refectory and workhouses).

Environs: Athboy (*c.* 6 m. NW): The ramparts of the old Celtic meeting-place *Hill of Ward* (Tlachta), which has a pagan altar.

Bective (*c.* 4 m. NE): The remains of the Cistercian *Bective Abbey*, which was founded around 1150, with 15C cloister and additions.

Truro
Cornwall/England   p.330□E 17

Cornwall was without its own episcopal seat for a good 800 years, being technically subordinate to Devon, but in 1876 Truro was made the seat of the bishopric of Cornwall. Since this old 16C *Church of St. Mary* was too small to serve as a cathedral, a new building had to be erected as quickly as possible.

Cathedral: This is an Early English style cathedral which was built between 1880 and 1910 by J.L. Pearson. The old Gothic parish church survives in part in the S. choir aisle, but the new building is an anachronism and although one cannot deny the cohesion between the pointed arches and lancet windows, the choir and nave aisles and the transepts, the bareness of the interior is an unmistakable sign that, as far as buildings are concerned, the spirit of a past style cannot be captured: the exterior, with its spire over the crossing and twin-towered façade, is only unfulfilled promise without the corresponding interior furnishings. The towers, however, have noble names: the central tower is the Memorial tower to Queen Victoria; the left tower of the front is the Memorial Tower to Edward VII; and the right one is the Memorial Tower to Queen Alexandra.

County Museum and Art Gallery: The exhibits, which illustrate life in the county, range from the Bronze Age to the present day. There is also a celebrated *mineral collection,* and an interesting *painting collection,* with works by local painters, including the portrait of Anthony Payne, the Cornish giant, who Charles II had painted at his full height of 7 ft. 4 in.

Environs: Pendennis Castle: This round hill to the W. of Carrick Road, opposite St.Mawes Castle, served in exactly the same way, as a precaution against a French invasion. When, instead of the French, the Spaniards began to threaten the coast of Cornwall, Elizabeth I strengthened the castle with corner bastions, ramparts and moats to such an extent that in 1646, during the Civil War, Parliament had to besiege it for 5 months before the occupants were forced to surrender.

Perranporth (10 m. NW): The tiny *Church of St.Piran* is a chapel which was not uncovered from the dunes until 1835. It is dedicated to a follower of the Irish missionary St.Patrick, the patron saint of the Cornish hill people, and has a simple, square oratory which may date from the 6C; this would make it the oldest church in SW England.

St.Mawes Castle (13 m. S.): This castle stands on the SE promontory at the mouth of Carrick Roads and was built to counter invasion by the French. It was begun on the Roseland peninsula in 1540 and completed three years later. It was built as a defensive structure against attack from the sea, so when Cromwell's troops attacked

Truro, cathedral

it from the land in the Civil War, it took only a day to capture.

Tuam
Galway/Ireland   p.326□B 11

This old episcopal town is now the seat of the Catholic archbishop of Connaught; it was founded by St.Iarlath around 540.

Protestant Cathedral (High Street): This neo-Gothic building dates from 1861 and incorporated sections of a 12C Norman church. The old *choir* is 12C and has a splendid chancel arch, arcades and E. window. The baroque *choir stalls* date from 1740 and are from an Italian monastery. In the S. aisle is a 12C *Celtic cross* with the inscription in honour of the king who founded the old church, Turloch O'Conor and the abbot, Aedh O'Hession.

Other points of interest: The Celtic *market cross* has a 9 ft. 6 in. shaft and an overall height of 14 ft. 5 in.; it dates from the 12C. The reliefs on the plinth are interesting: they depict ornamental beasts, while those on the upper section have images of the saints. The *Catholic Cathedral* in Bishop Street is neo-Gothic and was built between 1627 and 1837.

Environs: Dunmore (*c.* 9 m. NE): *Dunmore Castle* was built in 1225; a mighty square tower is still standing, as well as a section of the walls. It is also the site of some remains from an *Augustinian monastery* from 1425, whose church has survived (nave, choir, choir tower and decorated W. portal).
Feartagar Castle (*c.* 5 m. NW): A well-preserved 16C *tower* with a staircase, vaulted ceiling and machicolation.
Kilbennan (*c.* 2 m. NW): Only the 12C *Round tower of Kilbennan* (*c.* 2 m. NW) still stands from the 6C early Celtic monastery of *St. Benen*, along with remains of a *Franciscan monastery* founded here in 1428, which has a fine gateway and windows.
Knockmoy Abbey (*c.* 7 m. SE): The ruins of the *Cistercian monastery church* date from the 12&13C; the most interesting piece is the medieval kings' fresco (from around 1400) on the N. side of the choir. The words of the three dead kings to the three living ones are: 'We have been as you are, you shall be as we are'.

Tullamore
Offaly/Ireland   p.326 □ D 12

This is the county town of Offaly; it has some 6,000 inhabitants and is situated on the *Grand Canal*, which was begun in 1765 and completed in the 19C. It was meant to run 165 miles from W. to E., and link the capital, Dublin, with the Shannon river system, but it was closed in 1959 and is now only used for restricted pleasure-trips. The town contains some fine buildings from the 18C (*Market House*) and 19C (*Court House, Canal Hotel*).

Environs: Durrow Abbey (*c.* 4 m. N.): The ruins date from an early Christian monastery founded by St. Columba around 555. It was frequently destroyed over the centuries, and the restored church dates from 1802. There is a fine 10C *high cross* close by, covered with scenes from the Bible (Isaac, Christ, David, Entombment). Nearby are some *gravestones* with old Gaelic inscriptions from the 11&12C.
Rahan (*c.* 6 m. W.): The interesting remains of an abbey founded in the 6C by St. Carthach. There are remains of three 12C Romanesque *churches* with fine chancel arches, ornamented windows and sculptured heads; rebuilt in the 15&16C and restored in the 18C.
Tihilly Church (*c.* 2 m. NW): These medieval church ruins are the remains of an early Christian monastery founded around 670 by St. Fintan. The *high cross* nearby is interesting.

Walsingham
Norfolk / England   p.328☐L 13

In the Middle Ages this little town was one of the most famous pilgrimage centres in England. The pilgrimage originated from a dream of the pious Richeldis de Favarques, who saw in her dream the house of the Holy Family. She had a chapel, the Shrine of Our Lady, built in memory of this. After the chapel had been taken over by Augustinian monks in 1153, it became a priory.

Walsingham Priory: The pilgrimage to the Shrine of Our Lady had become so popular in the 13C that the Augustinian monks built a large priory church. The heyday of the pilgrimage and priory was abruptly interrupted by the Reformation, and today only ruins of the priory and its church survive. Its most impressive section is the church's large *E. window* (14C). Some remains of the *refectory wall* are all that survives of the priory. The pilgrimage, which originated in the Middle Ages, was revived in 1921 and two churches were established for this purpose. An Anglican church was built in 1931 and enlarged in 1938, while for the Catholics the *Slipper Chapel,* 2 m. S., was installed and con-

secrated in a 14C building, also in 1938.

Environs: Binham Priory (4 m. NE): The present *parish church* of the village is the nave of the priory church begun in 1091. Its impressive W. front dates from 1226–44, and parts of the arcades date from *c.* 1230. The large window with its geometric tracery was probably added in the late 13C. The well-worked font is also Gothic, as are the choir stalls with their beautiful misericords. Ruins of the priory survive near the church.

Burnham Norton (9 m. NW): The *Church of St.Margaret* dates from the 13C and was enlarged in the 15C. Its round tower may well be Saxon and its choir screen dates from 1458. The pulpit is of especial interest, being decorated with images of the founders and church fathers. The font is Norman.

Holkam Hall (6 m. NW): This Palladian *mansion* with its H-shaped ground plan was built by William Kent in 1734–59 for Thomas Coke, Earl of Leicester. The principal rooms of this outstandingly decorated house still contain the original furnishings with painted stucco ceilings, sumptuous tapestries, and furniture of outstanding quality. The individual rooms were designed by William Kent, and their composition makes each of them a small work of art in its own right. However, the house is also worth seeing for its extensive *art collection* with fine works by artists such as Leonardo da Vinci, Rubens, Raphael, Veronese, van Dyck, Reynolds and Gainsborough.

North Creake (5 m. W.): The *Church of St.Mary* was built in *c.* 1300, and on its N. side is a battlemented Gothic tower, while the nave has a stuccoed timber ceiling, with a faded fresco above the triumphal arch.

South Creake (5 m. SW): The *Church of St. Mary* dates from the 13C and was rebuilt and expanded in the 14C. Its hammerbeam ceiling is worth seeing, being decorated with carved and painted angels. There is an interesting and unusual memorial depicting a priest recumbent between his parents.

Warwick

Warwickshire/England   p.328☐I 14

Founded in 914 on the N. bank of the Avon, it retains much of its medieval charm despite being almost completely destroyed by flames in 1694.

Church of St.Mary: This 12C collegiate church was almost entirely rebuilt after the fire of 1694 by Sir William Wilson. Part of the original Gothic design was retained, while other sections were built in Renaissance style. Two impressive features are the *sanctuary* dating from 1394, with its high vaulting, and the 12C Norman *crypt*. The *alabaster figures* holding hands with one another in the middle of the sanctuary depict Thomas Beauchamp, the Earl of Warwick who built the choir and died in 1369, and his wife.

The finest part of the church is the Perpendicular *Beauchamp Chapel*, built in 1443-64 on the S. side of the choir. Its choir stalls date from 1449, while the Last

Judgement above the W. door is from 1678. The N. wall of the chapel is decorated by the tomb of Robert Dudley, the Earl of Leicester who died in 1588, and of his wife Lettice. This Elizabethan monument betrays nothing of the fact that the childhood friend of Queen Elizabeth I lost his first wife in mysterious circumstances just at the time when he was thought to be the Queen's lover. The most sumptuous details in the chapel are to be found in the *stained-glass windows* executed in 1447 by John Prudde, the royal window-maker. All the technical resources of the period were employed in these masterpieces, and the result is one of the best examples of 15C stained glass.

Warwick Castle: This castle is among the few medieval fortresses in England still lived in today. Its exterior, with its *fortifications* which have survived intact, is a splendid example of a 14C fortress, and its interior reflects the 17&18C lifestyle. The castle, which stands on a hill above the Avon, was founded by Ethelfleda, the daughter of Alfred the Great (871-99), and was probably begun in *c.* 915. William the Conqueror (1028-87) ordered the Earl of Turchil to enlarge it. The fortifications which survive today are 14C. The castle was never captured, but in 1871 a fire destroyed large sections of the living apartments. Today it harbours an interesting *collection of weapons*, including a helmet belonging to Cromwell and the armour of Lord Brooke, who died near Lichfield in 1643. The principal rooms contain some fine *paintings*, including works by Rubens, van Dyck and Holbein. The famous Warwick vase—nearly 7 ft. tall, by a Roman artist from the reign of the Emperor Hadrian—used to be on display in a house in the park; now in the Burrell Collection, Glasgow.

Museums: The *Doll Museum* is in a mid-16C Elizabethan house and contains a large number of dolls of widely varying periods, materials and countries. The *County Museum* is housed in a market hall built in 1670 and displays exhibits from all periods.

Also worth seeing: The *Lord Leycester Hospital* was built in 1383, having been founded by a religious association, and in 1571 the Earl of Leicester converted it into an asylum for twelve poor brothers. Today the hospital refectory houses the *regimental museum* of the Queen's Own Hussars.

Environs: Kenilworth Castle: The castle was built in 1122 by Geoffrey de Clinton, Henry I's Treasurer. The outer wall dates from 1203–16, and in 1244 the castle passed to Simon de Montfort. From 1399–1563 the castle was a royal fortress, and after this the building was handed over to Robert Dudley, a favourite of Queen Elizabeth I. He enlarged it and the Queen was a frequent guest. The castle was restored from 1937 onwards. Today the oldest part is *Caesar's Tower,* which was built in 1160–70 and has walls 16 ft. thick. In the SE wing are the rooms where Queen Elizabeth I stayed in 1575 when she was Robert Dudley's guest.

Warwick, Warwick Castle

Waterford

Waterford/Ireland   p.330☐D 13

This bustling harbour, situated at the point where the Suir flows into the elongated bay of Waterford Harbour is today the fourth largest city in Ireland, with some 33,000 inhabitants.

History: Waterford was founded by Danish Vikings in 914. Strongbow, the Norman warlord, occupied the city in *c.* 1170; the English King Henry II annexed it in 1170 and proclaimed it a royal city. It enjoyed a heyday in the 18C, when it was

known the world over for its lead crystal (Waterford glass).

Reginald's Tower (Mall Street): The cylindrical *fortress tower* dating from the 11 or 12C is about 80 ft. tall and has walls 10 ft. thick. It takes its name from the Viking prince Reginald (Rognald). In the 15C it was used as a mint, and in the 19C (restored in 1819) as a prison. Today it houses a *local museum.*

French Church (near Reginald's Tower): The ruined church with its central tower is a former Franciscan monastery church dating from 1240. It was later used as a church by Huguenots (1695), hence its name.

Also worth seeing: Mall Street, the beautiful *City Hall* dating from 1788 and the

Waterford, Reginald's Tower

Royal Theatre built by J.Roberts in the same period. The City Hall has various exhibits relating to the town's history (archive, liberation flags of 'Young Ireland' dating from 1848). Nearby, in Catherine Street, are the *Court House*, built in 1849 on the site of an Augustinian monastery, and the 18C neoclassical *palace* of the Protestant bishops. The Protestant cathedral of *Christ Church* (or *Holy Trinity Church*) was built in *c.* 1770 above the ruins of a 12C Romanesque church. The crypt survives from this period, and there are some 15&16C monuments. After a fire in 1815, the church was rebuilt in *c.* 1891. The Catholic cathedral of *St.Patrick's Church* in Barronstrand Street is of somewhat ponderous design and is also by the architect J.Roberts (*c.* 1790). It was enlarged in 1830–81. The Georgian *Chamber of Commerce* (O'Connell Street) was built in 1795

and is J.Roberts's masterpiece, fine staircases. In the Dominican *St.Saviour's Priory* (Arundel Street), the 13C (bell) tower still survives. A few remains are all that are left of *St.John's* Benedictine monastery. The remains of the *city walls* with their separate towers, and the *Holy Ghost Hospital* with its 15C wood carvings, are also worth seeing.

Waterville
Kerry/Ireland   p.330☐A 14

This popular salmon fishing centre is on a narrow strip of land between the Atlantic to the W. and the attractive fresh water Lough Currane. The reputed *House of St.Finan* (8C), and also a 12C Romanesque *ruined church,* are to be found on *Church Island* in the lake.

Environs: Ballinskelligs (about 9 m. W.): The remains of a 13C *castle* and of an *abbey* (12 - 15C) founded by the Skellig monks.
Cahersiveen (about 11 m. W.): The remains of the prehistoric stone forts of *Cahergal* and *Leacanabuaile.* There are also the ruins of *Ballycarbery Castle,* a medieval fortress of the MacCarthys. Daniel O'Connel, the famous campaigner for Irish independence, was born here in 1775. In 1866, the first transatlantic cable, to Newfoundland, was laid, its starting point being the offshore island of *Valentia* in 1866.
Great Skellig Island (about 11 m. W.): This small Atlantic island was once an important centre for monks and pilgrims (St.Michael). A flight of 600 stone steps leads to the unique *ruined monastery,* which was occupied by hermits (5&6C). Six dry stone 'beehive huts' (clochans), two dry stone oratories, the surroundings of two holy springs, and the 10C St. Michael's Church, built of stone.
Staigue Fort (5 m. SE): Near Castle Cove is this famous prehistoric *stone fortress.* Cir-

cular in form, it is 100 ft. in diameter and its dry stone wall is up to 13 ft. thick. In the N., the wall still survives up to its original height of some 16 ft.; the entrance is to the S. There are also two chambers and a well-preserved staircase.

Wells

Somerset/England   p.332□H 15

This small city with its large cathedral has preserved its medieval character to a greater extent than almost any other small English town. The medieval quarter extends from *Vicar's Close*, a row of terraced houses completed in 1348, to the unbroken row of mid-15C house fronts in the market place. Virtually everything in Wells is connected with the church in some way.

Cathedral: This was founded by King Ine in 704 as the Church of St. Andrew. The bishopric moved to Wells in 909, but in 1090 Bishop John de Villula transferred it to Bath, which was strongly fortified at that time. It was only in 1244 that the bishop's seat finally returned to Wells, but with the limitation that, until the dissolution of their abbey in 1539, the monks of Bath shared the right to elect the bishop with the cathedral chapter of Wells. Bishop Reginald began building the present church in *c.* 1175. The transepts, the W. bays of the choir, and the E. bays of the nave, were the first to be built. The *choir* and *nave* were completed after the turn of the century, and Thomas Norrey built the superb *W. front*. In 1239 work on the cathedral had progressed far enough for it to be consecrated. The *chapterhouse* was completed by 1319, and the central *tower* by 1321. The two *W. towers* are by William de Wynford and were finished in 1403. The nave, choir and W. front are Early English, while the towers and chapterhouse are high Gothic.

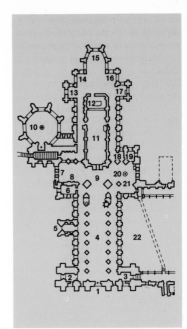

Wells Cathedral 1 W. front (with splendid sculpture gallery) **2,3** W. towers **4** nave **5** N. portal **6** sacristy **7** N. transept **8** lunar clock **9** crossing with tower **10** chapterhouse **11** choir **12** sanctuary **13** St.John the Evangelist's Chapel **14** St.Stephen's Chapel **15** Lady Chapel **16** St.John the Baptist's Chapel **17** St.Catherine's Chapel **18** St.Calixtus's Chapel **19** St.Martin's Chapel **20** font **21** S. transept **22** cloister

The two W. towers were not added in line with the nave, but to the N. and S. of it. The result of this was a W. front 160 ft. wide, which its builders turned into a *sculpture gallery* unparalleled anywhere in England. Over 400 figures, which are life-sized and in some cases larger than life, were installed in several galleries running across the front, one above another. This arrangement was based on the portal sculptures in Reims and Chartres. All the figures were originally painted in glowing colours and gave a thorough-going theatrical pageant of the world: kings and nobles, bishops and abbots, angels and apostles, with Christ towering above them in glory. Although only some 300 of them survive today, they are by some way the most splendid medieval collection of sculptures in England.

The interior is dominated by three enormous *ogee arches* beneath the square tower of the crossing. These were added at a later date in the cathedral's history when, in 1338, it turned out that the Early English walls of the nave, aisles and transepts were unable to bear the pressure exerted by the tower. The *nave,* some 195 ft. long, is Transitional with suggestions of the Early English, which make it appear considerably taller than its actual height of about 65 ft. Among the most beautiful features are the outstanding *crocket and storiated capitals.* Some of these capitals show complete scenes from everyday life. The *clock showing the phases of the moon,* with the sun and moon revolving around the Earth in circular orbits, was installed in the *triforium* of the N. transept in *c.* 1390. Four knights in combat appear every hour on the hour. The clock's original mechanism was not replaced by a new mechanism until 1835 (today the original is in the Science Museum in London). The 12C *font* has a Jacobean cover and an unusual position in the middle of the S. transept. The *choir* and *Lady Chapel* are entirely in the early Gothic style. The aisles adjoining the choir and nave, and also the transepts, contain some remains of the 14C glass. The *E. Jesse Window* dates from 1340, and stained-glass windows from Rouen have been installed in the SE transept. These were made shortly after 1500 and were brought here in 1812.

The cathedral has over 20 *tombs of bishops,* whose identity is known, and also numerous tombs of other prominent persons. There are also some 13C tombs of persons who have not yet been identified. An outstandingly well-proportioned early Gothic *staircase* leads from the N. transept up to the *chapterhouse* completed in 1315. This octagonal room has a central pillar from which 32 ribs radiate out, forming a uniquely beautiful fan vault.

Bishop's Palace: Bishop Jocelin began work on this in *c.* 1210. Bishop Ralph of Shrewsbury completed the palace by digging a large moat between himself and his faithful flock of believers. Unfortunately, only some ruins still survive from the *Great Hall* completed by Bishop Burnell in 1292, but the *chapel* built by the same bishop gives a slight impression of the Decorated style that was also employed in the Great Hall.

Church of St.Cuthbert: This 15C parish church has a Gothic *tower* and a particularly richly carved and painted *timber roof.*

Welshpool/Trefaldwyn
Powys/Wales   p.328□G 13

This small town of some 7,000 inhabitants in the E. part of mid-Wales contains the 14C *St. Mary's Church,* with a massive tower, an old roof and some fine tombs. By the entrance to the church is the *Maen Llog Setin,* probably a former Druid's altar (later an abbot's throne). *Powis Castle* dates from the 13&14C, has a fine park, and has been restored several times after being destroyed. Inside it contains furniture and collections from various periods. The *Powysland Museum* displays some interesting finds from the Roman period, and also some old Welsh objects.

Environs: Llanrhaeadr-ym-Mochnant (*c.* 16 m. NW): The *church* contains a 10C tombstone.
Meifod (*c.* 4 m. NW): The church of this village, an early seat of the princes of Powys, contains a Celtic *tombstone* with a cross (*c.* 11C).
Montgomery (5 m. S.): This ancient town

contains the beautiful 14C church of *St. Nicholas,* with a magnificent rood screen, a Norman font, old stalls with misericords, and medieval tombs. The remains of *Montgomery Castle* (11C), rebuilt by Baldwin in the 12C, are on the ridge of hills above the town. Nearby, half a mile to the E., are the remains of *Offa's Dyke,* the rampart which ran the length of the border between England and Wales.

Newtown (*c.* 12 m. S.): The house, with a museum, where Robert Owen, the pioneer socialist (1771–1858), was born. His *tomb* is in the graveyard by the Old Church.

Pennant Melangell (*c.* 34 m. NW): A Norman *church* with old memorials and a carved rood screen (14&15C).

Strata Marcella (*c.* 3 m. NE): The foundation walls are all that survive of the old Cistercian monastery.

Westport
Mayo/Ireland   p.326□B 11

This charming little town to the SE of the broad Clew Bay has some 3,000 inhabitants. The Marquis of Sligo founded it as recently as 1780. It was designed by the famous architect James Wyatt, and almost the whole town is Georgian. The Mall, and the main square, the *Octagon,* are among the most beautifully laid-out squares in Ireland. Near the Octagon is *Westport House* (1731–78,) the Georgian mansion that belonged to the Marquis of Sligo. The dining room by Wyatt, and the picture collection, with works by Reynolds (1723–92) and others, are worth seeing, and there is also a collection of silver and crystal (Waterford glass).

Environs: Achill Island (*c.* 19 m. NW): Some remnants of *Kildownet Castle* (15C) are to be found on this wild and romantic Atlantic island with its magnificent craggy coastline. The castle was occupied by the legendary pirate queen Grace O'Malley, who bitterly opposed the English in the 16C.

Ballintober Abbey (*c.* 7 m. SE): The interesting remains of the *Augustinian monastery* dating from 1216 are at the N. end

Westport, Westport House

Wexford, the town

of Lough Carra. The 13C cruciform Romanesque church survives. It has a tower over the crossing and a Gothic cloister (15C, restored in 1966), and also early Gothic E. windows and Romanesque capitals. The former sacristy, which served as a mausoleum for the Earls of Mayo in the 17C, is also worth seeing (depictions of Apostles, and a 17C Renaissance tomb). Despite being forbidden by the English, the Catholic mass continued to be celebrated here.

Castlebar (*c.* 11 m. NE): This, the county town (6,000 inhabitants) of Mayo, has an elegant main street *(The Mall)* and a *market square*. The town played a part in the French invasion of 1798 ('Castlebar Races').

Clare Island (*c.* 12 m. W.): Apart from the remains of the Cistercian *Clare Abbey* (*c.* 1500, with wall paintings in the choir), a 16C *ruined castle* of the pirate queen Grace O'Malley is also to be found here.

Croagh Patrick (about 2 m. W.): The mountain (2,500 ft.) is regarded as Ireland's 'holy mountain'. St. Patrick, the patron saint of Ireland who died in about 461, is said to have worked here for a time. On the peak there is a small *oratory* and a *statue of St. Patrick* (splendid view). A pilgrimage is held every year on the last Sunday in July. The route leads from the ruins of the 14C Augustinian *Murrisk Abbey* at the foot of the mountain (or from the neighbouring Croagh Patrick House) up to the mountain peak.

Moore Hall (*c.* 9 m. SE): This fine 18C Georgian house was built by John Moore, who was proclaimed 'President of the Republic of Connaught' in 1798.

Newport (*c.* 9 m. N.): Near this fishing village at the NE end of Clew Bay are the remains of the Dominican monastery of *Burrishoole Friary,* dating from 1486. The church, with its tower and transept, and also some friary buildings, survive.

West Wycombe
Buckinghamshire/England   p.332□K 15

This village to the W. of the town of High Wycombe has remained largely unaltered. There are numerous half-timbered and other houses dating from the 16, 17&18C.

Dashwood Mausoleum: Built in 1763 by order of Sir Francis Dashwood, the founder of the Hell-Fire Club, on a hill above the village. The hexagonal monument, which has no roof, is decorated with columns and vases. It was built by John Bastard.

West Wycombe Park: The Dashwood family built the original three-storeyed brick building in spacious grounds in 1698. From 1750 onwards this initial house was altered and enlarged by Sir Francis Dashwood in Palladian style. He built the two-storeyed *colonnade,* with its Corinthian and Tuscan columns. The *Ionic portico* on the W. side was designed by Nicholas Revett, while the *Tuscan portico* on the E. side is the work of John Donowell. Today the house contains ceilings painted by Borgnis, fine furniture, tapestries, and a picture collection. The *park* was laid out by Humphry Repton.

Environs: Bledlow (6 m. NW): The *Church of the Holy Spirit* was originally Norman. Arcades built around 1200, and also some good capitals, survive inside. The round font is also Norman and is decorated with tendril patterns. The old parts of the church also include the S. portal, probably built in the late 13C. There are some interesting remains of medieval

wall paintings of Adam and Eve and St. Christopher.

High Wycombe (4 m. SE): The *Chair and Local History Museum* is devoted to the town's main industry. There is an extensive collection of chairs and armchairs on display, as well as some exhibits relating to the history of chair manufacture.

Penn (7 m. SE): The 11C *Church of the Holy Trinity* contains one of the very few surviving Norman fonts to have been made of lead. Other items worth seeing are a painting on the triumphal arch of the Last Judgement, and the nave roof, which dates from 1380 and is regarded as the finest in the county.

Wexford
Wexford/Ireland   p.330□D 13

This is the small county town, with about 13,000 inhabitants, of the county of the same name, and was founded as *Vaesfjord* by the Vikings in the 9 or 10C. It was in *c.* 1169 that Wexford became the first Irish town to be occupied by the Anglo-Normans, who expanded it into a flourishing trading centre and port. The floodings of the river Slaney subsequently forced the port to move to the adjoining Rosslare Harbour. The long *quays* in Wexford Bay, the stone breakwater, *Ballast Bank,* and some remnants of the port, can still be seen.

St.Selskar's Church: The ruins of the church of *Selskar Abbey,* a former Augustinian priory, date from the 12C. This abbey was dedicated to St.Peter and St. Paul. The ruined *nave* and a 15C battlemented *tower* still survive.

Also worth seeing: In the town centre are the remains of the medieval *monastery church* of the Knights of St.John. The ruins of the medieval *St.Patrick's Church* and of the Franciscan *monastery church* are to be found in John Street. The remains of the old *town wall* with the 14C *Westgate Tower* are by the Protestant church near the graveyard. A notable 17C *house* with a gable and a monument to the peasants' uprising of 1798 are in the Bull Ring, so called after the Norman bull-fighting arena. The famous Music Festival is held in the small 18C *theatre* in October of each year.

Environs: Bargy Castle (5 m. S.): This castle is near Lady's Island Lake, and includes the ruins of a 13C *tower house* and a *ruined monastery.* Nearby is the interesting *windmill* of *Tacumshane* dating from 1846.

Clonmines (*c.* 12 m. SW): This town has a strongly fortified *church* resembling a castle.

Coolhull Castle (about 16 m. SW): The castle dates from the late 16C and is still in good condition.

Johnstown Castle (*c.* 4 m. SW): This imposing neo-Gothic castle was built in *c.* 1840 above the ruins of a medieval castle and today houses a *museum of landscape and agriculture.*

Kilmore Quay (*c.* 16 m. SW): This village on the S. coast is known for its well-preserved *fishermen's cottages* with their whitewashed walls and thatched roofs.

Rathmacknee Castle (*c.* 5 m. S.): This ruined castle dates from the 15&16C. A well-preserved battlemented tower and the wall around the castle ward are a good example of castle architecture at that time.

Slade (*c.* 16 m. SW): The well-preserved *Slade Castle* near the small fishing harbour at the entrance to Waterford Bay dates from the 15&16C. The castle has a captivatingly picturesque setting and battlemented tower walls.

Tintern Abbey (*c.* 12 m. SW): This former *Cistercian abbey* was founded in *c.* 1200 by the monks of the abbey of the same name in Monmouthshire, Wales. Most of the remains (the nave and central tower) are from the late 13C; later additions were made in the 18&19C.

Whitby
North Yorkshire/England   p.328☐K 10

In the course of its history, this little town, which today has some 13,000 inhabitants, has twice emerged from obscurity: the Synod held here in 664 decisively affected the direction Christianity took in England, and in 1768 Captain James Cook, who lived in Whitby for quite some time, sailed from here on his voyage to the Pacific.

Whitby Abbey (reached via Abbey Lane): The first monastery on this site was founded in the early Middle Ages (7 or 8C: excavation work has brought to light some remains of walls both of the monks' cells and of the Romanesque church). It was destroyed by the Danes in 867, and was rebuilt from 1067 onwards after the Norman Conquest. The monastery was dissolved in the 16C during the Reformation under Henry VIII. The sole significant remnant of the abbey is the *church:* built in the 13&14C, it was allowed to fall into disrepair after the dissolution. The nave fell down in *c.* 1763, and the crossing tower collapsed in 1830. The W. front was severely damaged by a shell in World War 1, but was faithfully rebuilt in 1921.
The *choir,* the *transepts,* part of the *N. aisle,* and the *W. front* are still standing. What remains is predominantly Early English (particularly fine at the E. end of the choir and in the N. transept), although there are some Decorated windows, and the W. front has a Perpendicular window. Not much survives of the *interior* of the church: In the nave are the pillar bases (one pillar, rebuilt in 1790, is still standing; the remains of the arcades have been collected in an open field N. of the church). The niche for the Communion vessels ('Aumbry') is in the N. wall of the E. aisle of the N. transept. A 15C *cross,* some 10 ft. tall, stands on a round base of five steps near the crumbling walls which surrounded the monastery.

S. of the church are the ruins of *Abbey House:* the S. side is Tudor and was built in *c.* 1580 using materials from the earlier monastery, and was rebuilt in the 17C. The banqueting hall, built in 1670, fell down in 1760.

St.Mary's Church (near Whitby Abbey, it is reached by the 199 steps of the so-called 'Jacob's Ladder'): Norman, built in *c.* 1150, enlarged and altered in the 17C. The first two storeys of the tower are 12C and the rest dates from the 13C, while the pointed windows were only added in the 15C. The Early English transepts were added in the 13C, and the galleries and pews, among other items, were installed in the 17&18C. A fine Romanesque *S. portal. Inside,* the S. transept has a Romanesque *altar slab* (discovered during excavation work in 1922, it is all that remains of at least four other altars in the church). On the S. wall of the same S. transept there is a piscina (a basin for washing out the Communion vessels). To the S. of the chancel arch we find a so-called 'hagioscope' or 'squint' (a hole in the wall through which the rituals performed at the altar could be observed from the outside too). In the churchyard stands the *Caedmon Memorial Cross,* a richly worked cross some 20 ft. tall in memory of Caedmon, a 7C monk who is the 'father of English sacred songs'. On a slab are the opening lines of his 'hymn of creation'.

Museum and Art Gallery (Pannett Park): The showpiece of the prehistoric collection is the fossil *Teleosaurus,* a crocodile found at Saltwick, SE of Whitby, in 1824. The *collection of model ships,* with its exhibits devoted to James Cook and William Scoresby, is also viewing. The *Roman stone* from the 4C AD, discovered near Ravenscar in 1774, is also on display.

Also worth seeing: *St. Hilda's Church* (Royal Crescent) with its interesting in-

terior in which oak is the dominant feature. The oak ceiling, the richly worked pulpit with its oak sounding board, and a carved oak reredos are particularly beautiful. There are also fine windows at the E. and W. ends. Near the bridge is the *Old Town Hall,* built in 1788. The 'Court Leet and Baron' held its sessions here until 1905. *Captain Cook's House* (Grape Lane), built in the late 17C; Cook spent his apprenticeship here. His *monument* is above the harbour; 'Resolution,' his famous ship, is depicted at the foot of the statue.

Environs: Danby Rigg (*c.* 12 m. W.): Excavations of a Bronze Age *burial ground.*
Goldsborough (*c.* 5 m. NW): The remains of a Roman *signalling station* from the 4C AD. This site had a ditch and a rampart with corner bastions. The finds include two skeletons and some late Roman coins.
High Bridestones and **Flat Howe** (about 4 m. SW): The former is a circular site with Bronze Age *menhirs* (some have fallen over, others have been completely destroyed), and the latter is a *Bronze Age burial mound.*
Hinderwell (*c.* 7 m. NW): A Communion chalice dated 1420 is used in the *church* here.
Hulleys (*c.* 17 m. SE): The remains of a *prehistoric settlement* and of a *Bronze Age burial mound* (near Cloughton Moor).
Lythe (*c.* 4 m. NW): The church of *St. Oswald the Martyr* was originally Norman but has 12C Early English additions. Recent restoration and excavation work has brought to light some 10C Saxon fragments, including tombstones, altar slabs, and parts of crosses.
Mulgrave Woods (*c.* 2 m. NW): This town has a fine *castle* built in the late 17C and enlarged in the 18&19C. Nearby are the remains of an old *fortress* (surviving features include parts of the main gate).
Ravenscar (about 7 m. SE): The town takes its name from the raven which is said to have been on a flag raised here by the

Danes after their invasion. A Roman *signalling station* was discovered near Ravenscar in 1774 (the finds from it are in the museum in Whitby).

Robin Hood's Bay (*c.* 5 m. SE): The church of *St.Stephen* was formerly dependent on the Abbey of Whitby and was rebuilt in 1822. A Roman font found in a field in 1898 can be seen in the new church of St.Stephen in Fyling.

Whitehaven
Cumbria / England   p.328 ☐ G 10

The buildings of this small, old port, which was of some importance in the Middle Ages, still display the influence of Sir Christopher Wren, the great English architect (1632–1723). *Lowther Street* is especially fine (Sir John and Sir James Lowther began laying out new roads in the town in 1690).

The church of *St.James* (18C; fine Georgian decoration and the tomb of the grandmother of George Washington, the first President of the USA); the ruined church of *St.Nicholas* (destroyed by fire in 1972; only the tower survives) and the town *museum*, devoted to the town's history, are the main points of interest.

Environs: Calder Bridge (*c.* 8 m. SE): The remains of a 12C *abbey* founded by Cistercian monks from Furness. It was refounded after being destroyed by the Scots in the 13C. The ruins of the church and of the chapterhouse survive.

Egremont (*c.* 6 m. SE): The *castle* was built in *c.* 1140 to secure Norman rule in this region. It was destroyed in the 16C.

Eskdale Mill (*c.* 17 m. SE): A rebuilt medieval *mill* adjoined by a small *museum* dealing with the history of milling.

Gosforth (*c.* 11 m. SE): In the graveyard is a 10C Anglo-Saxon *cross* with an inscription.

Ravenglass (*c.* 6 m. SE): *Muncaster Castle,* E. of the town, is worth seeing. It was founded in *c.* 1200, was restored in the 19C, and has been the seat of the Pennington family for about 600 years. Inside there is a rich art collection (period furniture, porcelain etc.; the pièce de résistance is a

Egremont (Whitehaven), ruined castle

glass bowl which is not on public display. Called 'Luck of the Muncasters', it was presented to the lord of the castle by Henry VI in 1461 as a reward for his help. Another interesting feature, to the SE, is the remains of the Roman settlement of *Glannaventa* (the items excavated include a villa and a bath). Still further to the SE is *Waberthwaite Church*, with the remains of an Anglo-Saxon cross in the graveyard.

St.Bees (*c.* 4 m. S.): With the church of *St.Mary and St.Bega*, initially founded in *c.* 650; the present one is Norman, having previously been destroyed by the Danes; inside are some 19C tombs.

Whithorn
Dumfries and Galloway/
Scotland   p.328 □ G 10

The history of this little town dates back to 397, when St.Ninian returned from a pilgrimage and study trip to Rome and introduced Christianity to Scotland. He built what is probably the first stone church in all Scotland. Its exterior walls were excavated in 1949 and were found to be covered with a layer of white gypsum. This white house was called *huit aern* in Anglo-Saxon; hence the town's name. The early Christians gave their chapel the Latin name of *Candida Casa*. This Christian cell became a major cultural and missionary centre. A collection of legends relating to the miraculous deeds of St.Ninian was established in the adjoining monastery in the 7C. After this his shrine became the goal of a popular early medieval pilgrimage. In 1160, the Premonstratensians began building a large priory to accommodate the flow of pilgrims. Nearly all the Scottish kings from Robert the Bruce to James V made the pilgrimage to this site. James IV even undertook the pilgrimage on foot. Finally, in 1581, the Reformers had the pilgrimage declared illegal.

Whithorn Priory: The 13C church has withstood the test of time, but some alterations were carried out in the 17&18C. Inside are two 13C tombs. An *early Christian burial ground* was discovered above a *Roman urnfield* to the W. of the church. The 16C gatehouse contains a *museum* with some significant early Christian crosses, including the *Latinus Stone* (*c.* 450), the earliest Christian monument in Scotland, and the 7C *St.Peter's Stone* which, curiously, bears some written characters of a kind usually found only in France.

Wicklow
Wicklow/Ireland   p.326 □ E 12

This small harbour (3,000 inhabitants) on the E. coast of Ireland about 25 m. S. of Dublin is the county town of the county of the same name. It was founded by the Vikings in the 9C and its name means 'Vikings' lighthouse'. The *Black Castle* was built by the Anglo-Normans in the 12C and completely rebuilt in the 16C. There

Whithorn, Whithorn Priory, portal

are also Norman remains on a cliff E. of the town. Fragments of the Romanesque portal of the medieval St.Patrick's Church have been incorporated in the 18C Protestant *parish church*. In the *parish garden* are the remains of a Franciscan monastery belonging to the medieval church.

Environs: Arklow (*c.* 12 m. S.): This fishing harbour was founded by Vikings in the 9C. The ruins of *Butler Castle* are 12C Norman, while the remnants of a *Dominican monastery* are 13C. The town has an attractive Catholic church dating from 1840 and a Protestant church of 1900. The River Avoca is spanned by a medieval *bridge* with 19 arches.

Rathdrum (*c.* 7 m. SW): *Avondale House* (1779) is the house where Charles Stewart Parnell, the famous 19C campaigner for Irish independence, was born. He was regarded as Ireland's new king without a crown.

Rathnew (*c.* 2 m. NW): Near this village is the fine *mansion of Clermont* (1731), built of red brick and with a rustic interior. About 1 m. to the NW of Rathnew are the extensive *Mount Usher Gardens* (open to the public), with rare plants from all over the world and a *coach museum*. Close by is the *Devil's Glen*, where there is a waterfall on the river Vartry.

Wight, Isle of
England   p.332☐J 16

This island, which is separated from the mainland by the Solent to the NW and by the Spithead to the NE, was a peninsula in the Stone Age. The Romans conquered it in 43 BC and named it *Vectis*; in 661 it became part of the kingdom of Wessex, and was converted to Christianity; during the 10C the Danes used it as their headquarters. William the Conqueror presented it to William Fitz-Osborn, and

it finally came into the possession of the Earls of Devon, from whom the Crown redeemed it in 1293. However, the island's heyday came in the 19C, when Queen Victoria established her summer residence here, making it the Mecca of the Victorians.

Bembridge: The *Ruskin Galleries* are the largest existing collection of John Ruskin's pictures, manuscripts and letters. However, only part of the collection is in Bembridge, the other part being in Brantwood in Lancashire. The *windmill* built around 1700 is the last one surviving in the island. Its wooden grinding machinery was in operation until 1913.

Carisbrooke: The *Church of St.Mary* is a former Benedictine priory church dating from the 12C. Its beautiful tower was built in 1474, and the sanctuary was torn down in the 16C by Sir Francis Walsingham, a secretary of Queen Elizabeth I. However, apart from the tower, the Norman aisle and arcades from the 12C have survived. The pulpit and font are 17C. The modern sculpture of the 'Madonna and Child' is by John Skelton (1969). *Carisbrooke Castle* was built in early Norman times on the site of a Roman fortress. The owner of the keep was William Fitz-Osborn, and the Gate House was built in the 14&15C. In 1588, when the Spanish Armada was threatening England, the exterior bulwarks, and the well which is over 160 ft. deep, were added. The fortress became renowned for its prominent prisoners: Parliament held Charles I prisoner here from November 1647 until September 1648. Prince Henry and Princess Elizabeth, his children, were also brought here as prisoners in 1650. The 15-year-old princess died only a month later, while the prince held out for three years. Some of the sections which can be visited today have been rebuilt, such as the Chapel of St. Nicholas. The *castle museum* contains an

Whithorn, Whithorn Priory

archaeological collection and some exhibits of local historical interest.

Godshill: The *Church of All Saints* is Gothic, having been built in the 14&15C. It is mainly of interest for a fresco, rare of its kind, depicting Christ hanging on a Cross decorated with leaves. A painting showing Daniel in the lions' den is attributed to the school of Rubens. The most interesting monument in the church is that dedicated to Sir John Leigh, who died in 1520.

Osborne House: This country house, a favourite of Queen Victoria's, was built in 1846–51 by her consort Prince Albert of Saxe-Coburg. Thomas Cubitt was the architect. It is Palladian in style, with a campanile, loggia and terraced garden. Probably nowhere else in the United King-

dom were so many purely Victorian items collected during the long reign of Queen Victoria as in this house. A year after Queen Victoria had died here, in her favourite house, King Edward presented it to the nation in memory of her.

Sandown: The *Museum of Isle of Wight Geology* deals with the geology of the island, where over 5,000 fossils have been found. The finest of these fossils, and also some diagrams and models, are used to illustrate the island's structure and development.

Winchester
Hampshire/England   p.332☐I 16

This city on the Itchen is one of the great

English historical sites. There was a tribal centre here before the Romans arrived, and the Romans themselves built *Venta Belgarum*, the fifth largest city in Britain. After the Romans had departed, the Saxons named it *Wintanceaster*, and in 519 they chose the city to be the capital of their kingdom of Wessex (West Saxons). It was in 634 that Bishop Birinus brought Christianity to the city. In 827, Egbert was crowned the first king of all England here and it flourished under Alfred the Great (871–99), with 897 being regarded as the official date of its foundation. London's increased importance did not make itself felt until the time of William the Conqueror, who declared both cities to be capitals and, like several of his successors, had himself crowned king in both of them. In the 13C, Winchester was still the second most important city in the kingdom after London. However, when it was taken by Cromwell in 1645, it began its irreversible decline into a small provincial city.

Cathedral: The history of the cathedral is closely related to that of the Anglo-Saxon and Norman royal city. The site of *Saxon Old Minster*, built by King Cenwalh in 634–48, has been located N. of the present cathedral. The relics of St.Swithun, who died in 862, were moved here in 971. This was the occasion for the church to be extended first towards the W. and later also towards the E. To the N. of the church, King Alfred had also founded an abbey, which was expanded by King Edward from 903 onwards. Today nothing survives of these two complexes. The present cathedral is the third church, having been begun by Bishop Walkelin in 1079. A Norman structure, it was consecrated in 1093. 100 years later, Bishop Godfrey de Lucy began making alterations in the Early English style, and also added the Lady Chapel. Decisive changes then followed under Bishop Edington (1346–66). He tried to convert the Norman nave into a Gothic nave, and also rebuild the W. front. This work was completed by Bishop William of Wykeham (1367–1404). The pointed arcades and the fan vaulting of the nave both date from this period. The entire cathedral was given new foundations in a dramatic rescue operation carried out in 1906–12, in order once and for all to prevent it from subsiding into the soft subsoil. The *exterior* of the cathedral is less impressive. Its W. façade is not as splendid as that of Wells, nor is its tower as impressive as that of Salisbury. On the other hand, a surprising feature is its unusual length of over 550 ft., making it the longest medieval church in Europe. The reason for this length is that the cathedral formerly served a dual purpose: the choir was used as a monastery church by the Benedictines, while the nave was employed as a cathedral for the faithful.

In contrast, the *interior* of the cathedral has a multitude of precious treasures despite the Gothic rebuilding. A particularly interesting feature is that the Norman pillars were not replaced in the Gothic alterations, but merely hewn anew. On the other hand, the *clerestory* was enlarged, whereas the triforium was reduced in size. Remains of the 14C glass survive in some of the windows. Easily the finest item in the nave is the Norman *font*. The work of Flemish artists, it was carved of black Tournai marble in the 12C and decorated with scenes from the life of St.Nicholas. No more than seven such fonts exist in England today. The *transepts*, especially the N. transept, offer the best impression of Bishop Walkelin's late-11C design. They are the most complete example of early Norman architecture in England. Of particular value are the 12&13C *wall paintings* with their scenes from the life and sufferings of Christ. They are to be found in the *Chapel of the Holy Sepulchre* under the N. side of the organ loft.

Winchester, cathedral

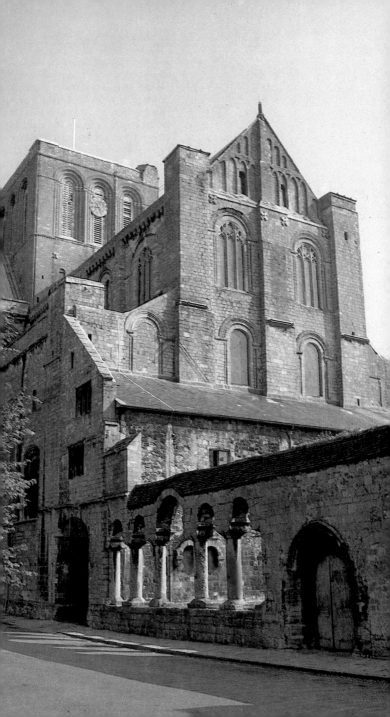

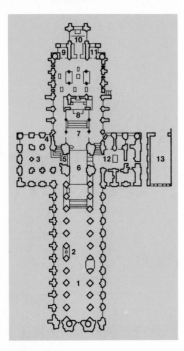

Winchester Cathedral 1 nave **2** font **3** N. transept **4** entrance to Norman crypt **5** Chapel of the Holy Sepulchre **6** choir (with original stalls from 1305–10) **7** sanctuary **8** high altar **9** Guardian Angels' Chapel **10** Lady Chapel **11** Langton's Chapel **12** S. transept **13** chapterhouse

The entrance to the S. aisle of the choir has a wonderful 12C *grille*. The *choir* itself still houses the original *choir stalls* of 1305–10, with their misericords richly carved with figures. These choir stalls are the oldest in England to have survived intact. The glass in the E. window dates from *c.* 1525. The choir contains an abundance of *monuments to bishops*, some of them quite outstanding pieces. The *crypt* underneath the N. transept is also entirely in the Norman style of the period when the church was founded. The chapterhouse was added to the S. aisle, and the room above it today houses the *library*, which was brought up

to date in 1668 and, in its own way, documents the cathedral's significance in the Middle Ages. One of the most precious manuscripts is the Aethelwold Benedictional, written in *c.* 980 (today it is in the British Museum in London). Bishop Henry of Blois ordered six monks to copy out the Vulgate in Winchester in the 12C. Its three folio volumes have initials with unique illuminations which depict complete stories and are attributed to the 'Master of the Leaping Figures.'

St.Cross Hospital: This hospital for thirteen poor brothers was endowed in 1136 by Bishop Henry of Blois, the half-brother of King Stephen. Cardinal Beaufort added another endowment for poor nobles in 1446. This is the oldest almshouse in England and the rules for those living in it are still those drawn up by the founders, although today it is an old people's home. The pensioners in the endowment of Henry of Blois wear a black coat with a silver cross on the left breast and a biretta, while those of Cardinal Beaufort's foundation wear a red coat and a cardinal's hat. By purchasing his entrance ticket, every visitor pays for and receives the alms formerly given to the passing pauper: 'a horn of beer and a crust of bread'. All the buildings of this endowment have tall round chimneys, and are maintained as they were when they were built, over the period stretching from 1136 to 1445. The oldest section of the complex is the *church,* built between 1136 and 1250. A *memorial panel* dating from 1410 opposite the altar commemorates one of the hospital supervisors. The wooden *lectern* dates from 1510 and is the only one dating from this period in the whole county. Some remains of the 15C *stained-glass windows* survive, as do fragments of medieval *wall paintings*.

Castle Hall: This is all that remains of the castle built by William the Conqueror and enlarged by Henry III prior to 1236. The

Cathedral, main portal

Clocktower

Early English hall has columns of Purbeck marble and is among the largest and most beautiful medieval rooms in England. Many sessions of Parliament, the court proceedings against Sir Walter Raleigh, and Judge Jeffrey's Bloody Assizes, were all held in this hall with its three aisles and timber roof. The *W. wall* is decorated by the *Round Table of King Arthur,* which was painted by order of Henry VIII on the occasion of a state banquet given for Emperor Charles V. The table top itself was probably made in 1340 for Edward III and his order of the 'Knights of the Round Table'.

Winchester College: This, the oldest public school in England, was founded by Bishop William of Wykeham in 1382 and it served as a model for all the country's great public schools. Henry VI was the first to follow its example when, 60 years

later, he founded Eton College. In the late 14C, after the school buildings and chapel had been completed, Winchester College was the most liberally furnished school in Europe. Its founder's motto still applies here today: 'Manners Makyth Man.'

Museums: The *City Museum* deals with local prehistory and history. The scope covered ranges from prehistoric pottery through Roman mosaics and Saxon coins to the original drawings for the palace which Charles II commissioned Christopher Wren to design.

The *Royal Greenjackets Museum* and the *Royal Hampshire Regimental Museum* are regimental museums.

The *Westgate Museum* is more directly concerned with the history of the city itself. There is an interesting and extensive collection of widely differing weights from various periods, including a set of weights from the time of Edward III.

Windermere
Cumbria/England   p.328☐H 11

Church of St.Martin (in Bowness): This, the parish church of Windermere, was built in Perpendicular style in 1483, the previous building having been destroyed by fire. The choir, sacristy and tower were not completed until the 19C. The main object of interest in the church is the splendid *E. window* of the choir. This window dates from between 1438 and 1480, while parts of it are 13C; it probably originated from the abbey church of Cartmel and it depicts a Madonna and Child, figures of Saints, abbots, and knights. There is also an old carved *font* in the nave and a neoclassical *monument* to a bishop by John Flaxman in the S. aisle. The *S. porch* has a fine old round arch above the inner portal.

Environs: Ambleside: (*c.* 5 m. NW):

Contains the 19C church of *St.Mary* (fine stained-glass windows inside), and a *toll-house*, over 200 years old, on a bridge across the River Rothay.

Brantwood (*c.* 8 m. W.): From 1872–1900 this was the home of John Ruskin, the 19C writer (1819–1900). Inside there are numerous works by him, and also some personal mementoes.

Coniston (*c.* 7 m. W.): The *John Ruskin Museum* has mementoes of the artist, his collection of minerals, and paintings and books by him.

Grasmere (*c.* 7 m. NW): *Dove Cottage* was the home of the poet William Wordsworth from 1799–1808. The *Wordsworth Museum* has many mementoes and manuscripts. The poet is buried in the cemetery of the church of St.Oswald.

Hawkshead (about 4 m. W.): The church of *St.Michael* is 15C, but there is known to have been an earlier, Norman church. The medieval gatehouse of *Hawkshead Hall,* and the *primary school* attended by William Wordsworth from 1778–83, are also worth seeing.

Hill Top (*c.* 2 m. SW): This is the former

Ambleside (Windermere), Bridge House

home of Beatrix Potter, the painter and authoress. Inside this 17C house are some beautiful old pieces of furniture and drawings by this artist.

Rydal Mount (*c.* 6 m. NW): This was the home of the poet William Wordsworth from 1813–50. Inside is a small *museum* (portraits, first editions, period furniture).

Troutbeck (*c.* 3 m. N.): *Townend* farmhouse, built in *c.* 1626, has are some fine wood-arvings, old furniture and documents.

Windsor

Berkshire/England   p.332□K 15

This town situated W. of London on the Thames is best known for its castle, the largest in the country and the main residence of the kings and queens of England for over 850 years.

Windsor Castle: This fortress on a limestone hill above the Thames was originally built of wood by by William the Con-

queror, whose aim was to secure the W. approaches to London. Henry II continued the work in stone, and Henry III and Edward III systematically enlarged it. When he held a banquet here after his marriage to Adeliza of Louvain in 1121, Henry I was inaugurating a long series of royal celebrations. Edward III was born here in 1312, and Henry VI in 1421. King David II of Scotland, King John of France, and King James I of Scotland were all held prisoner here. James I later managed to escape with Jane Beaufort, who was to become his wife. In 1348 Edward III (1327–77) founded the Order of the Knights of the Garter in the castle and had some new state rooms. These were largely rebuilt by Charles II (1660 – 85). St. George's Chapel was founded by Edward IV (1461-83). Finally, the enormous castle was, designed, in its present form, by Sir Jeffrey Wyatville, the architect employed by King George IV (1820–30).

St. George's Chapel is dedicated to St. George, the patron of the Order of the Garter. Work on the chapel was begun by

Windsor, Windsor Castle

Henry Janyns in 1478 by order of Edward IV, and it was completed by William Vertue in 1503–11. This outstanding Gothic work is of a quality that can be matched only by King's College Chapel in Cambridge and the Henry VII Chapel in Westminster Abbey. The corners of the nave, and both aisles of the choir, contain a number of 16C *memorial chapels*, which frequently also include tombs from that period. Thus the tomb of the Earl of Lincoln, who died in 1585, is to be found in the SE chapel, also known as *Lincoln Chapel*. In the NW corner is the tomb of George V, who died in 1936, and also that of Queen Mary (1953). The large W. window still contains parts of the *original glass* dating from *c*. 1500. Since 1785, the nave

Windsor Castle 1 Henry VIII's Gateway **2** Salisbury Tower **3** Garter Tower **4** Horseshoe Cloisters **5** Curfew Tower **6** Canon Residences **7** St. George's Chapel **8** Lower Ward **9** Albert Memorial Chapel **10** Dean's Cloister **11** Canon's Cloister **12** Deanery **13** Winchester Tower **14** Middle Ward **15** Round Tower **16** Norman Gateway **17** North Terrace **18** Home Park **19** George IV Tower **20** State Apartments with fine carving by Grinling Gibbons. The rooms include the Inner Entrance Hall with etchings by great masters; the China Museum with valuable porcelain; the Grand Staircase (1866) with a statue of George IV by Chantrey, and arms including a suit of armour of Henry VIII; the King's Dining Room with a ceiling fresco by Verrio; the King's Drawing Room with paintings by Rubens; the King's State Bed Chamber; the King's Dressing Room with a ceiling by Wyattville and some fine paintings; the King's Closet; the Queen's Drawing Room, with a painting by van Dyck from 1637 of King Charles I's five eldest children; the Queen's Ball Room; the Queen's Audience Chamber with a ceiling fresco by Verrio and late-18C Gobelins; the Queen's Presence Chamber, similar to the previous chamber; the Queen's Guard Chamber, with weapons and a knight's armour from the 16C, and busts of the Duke of Marlborough, Wellington and Churchill, the bullet which killed Nelson and the sword with which the Japanese commander surrendered to Lord Mountbatten in 1945; the Garter Throne Room, where the private meetings of the members of the Order of the Garter are held; St. George's Hall; the Great Reception Room, the finest and most expensively furnished of all; the Waterloo Chamber; the Grand Vestibule with weapons and ornaments of the crown and state of George IV and a statue of Queen Victoria **21** Cornwall Tower **22** Brunswick Tower **23** Prince of Wales Tower **24** private apartments **25** Chester Tower **26** East Terrace **27** Clarence Tower **28** Victoria Tower **29** Augusta Tower **30** South Terrace **31** York Tower **32** George IV's Gateway **33** Lancaster Tower **34** Visitor's Apartments **35** Edward III Tower **36** St. George's Gateway **37** Henry III Tower **38** Military Knights' Residences

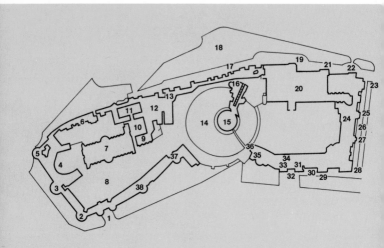

and choir have been separated by a *choir screen,* the work of Henry Emlyn. The choir has late-15C *choir stalls,* and the *banners* of the members of the Order of the Garter hang above their stalls. The choir contains numerous *tombs* of English kings. Edward VII (1910) and Queen Alexandra (1925) are buried S. of the altar, Edward IV in the N. aisle of the choir, and Henry VI and Henry VIII in the S. Charles I, George III, George IV, William IV, George VI, and numerous members of the Royal Family are buried in the *crypt.*

The chapel now known as the *Albert Memorial Chapel* was built by Henry VII as a burial chapel, but was not used for this purpose. In the Civil War the magnificent monument that it contained was destroyed and it was not until the reign of Queen Victoria that the chapel was given a new purpose when she built a *cenotaph* to the Prince Consort.

The *State Rooms* in the NE section of the castle are superbly furnished and contain some very valuable *paintings* from the Royal collection. Such artists as Rubens, van Dyck, Canaletto, Dürer, Holbein, Memling, Reynolds and others are represented here; furniture, carpets and tapestries are of the same high standard. *St. George's Hall,* which has been used as a banqueting hall for the Order of the Garter since 1348, has a particular feature: the *portraits* of the English kings from James I to George IV, painted by the leading artists of the times, adorn its walls.

The large *Waterloo Chamber* contains *portraits,* mostly by Lawrence, of the figures who played a decisive role in the fall of Napoleon.

Queen Mary's Dolls' House was designed by Sir Edwin Lutyens to a scale of 1 inch to 1 foot, and its building in 1922–3 involved over 1,500 craftsmen.

Windsor Great Park: The most important parts of the large park are the *Savill Garden* and the *Valley Gardens.* Valley Gardens contain the largest rhododendron collection in the world and beautiful azaleas, while the Savill Garden has rare plants from all over the world.

Windsor Guildhall Exhibition: The

Windsor Castle, St. George's Chapel

Eton College (Windsor)

Guildhall of the town of Windsor was designed by Sir Thomas Fitch in 1686 and completed in 1707. Today it is used as a *museum* and its exhibits include a collection of Royal portraits from the time of Elizabeth I onwards, followed by a series of scenes of life at Windsor Castle and some exhibits of local natural history. There are also special exhibitions, which are changed every year, dealing with particular topics from the history of Windsor Castle.

Environs: Eton College (1 m. N.): This is the most famous of all English schools, and was founded by Henry VI in 1540 as a collegiate church with a grammar school and almshouse attached. Today the school comprises buildings from different periods arranged around two large courtyards. The larger courtyard has a statue of Henry VI

(1719). On the N. side is the *Lower School,* built in *c.* 1500. Its wooden columns date from 1625. The *College Chapel* was begun in 1441 and was originally intended to be of cathedral-like proportions. Thus the chapel, completed by William Orchard in 1483, is nothing more than the choir, reduced in size, of the cathedral which was originally planned. It is decorated with frescos painted in 1479–88. These were discovered in 1847 underneath some more recent painting, and restored in 1927. They show a markedly Flemish influence and are among the most beautiful frescos of their kind in England. A gatehouse built in 1517 leads to the second courtyard, where the original *refectory* dating from 1450 and the *library* completed in 1729 are to be found.

Warfield (6 m. SW): The *Church of St. Michael* is mostly early Gothic, while the N. aisle is Transitional. The E. window has stained glass from the 14&19C, skilfully combined with beautiful tracery. The choir screen leading to the N. chapel dates from the 15C.

Wisbech

Cambridgeshire/England   p.328☐K 13

A river port on the Nene, it has two streets of houses along the banks of the river which form what are probably the most beautiful *Georgian ensembles* in England. The two roads were built by the Dutch, who were engaged in draining the Fens, a project which had been begun by the Romans before them. The character of the houses is unmistakably reminiscent of Holland.

Church of St.Peter and St.Paul: 12C, its size reflects the town's former importance. The free-standing N. tower and the second N. aisle, were added in the 15C; as were the stained-glass windows, although some of them were rebuilt in the 19C. Of the various *monuments,* that to Joseph Nollekens is probably the finest. The brass of Thomas de Braunstone, who died in 1401, is 7 ft. long and bears an inscription in Old French.

Peckover House: This is the finest house in the town and was built in 1722–6 for Sibalds Home. It contains some outstanding *rococo decoration* by the best wood-carvers and stucco artists of the day.

Museum: This deals with local history and includes the original manuscript of 'Great Expectations' by Charles Dickens.

Environs: Leverington Hall (2 m. NW): About half of this *country house* is Elizabethan; the rest dates from 1660–75. The staircase is particularly fine.

Walpole St.Peter (6 m. NE): The *Church of St.Peter* is one of the many outstanding Gothic churches in the Fens. Most of it was built in the 2nd half of the 14C. Inside there is fine Gothic tracery, some of which adorns the windows of the aisles and of the clerestory. The unusual tie-beam ceiling is decorated with good bosses. The font is 16C, while its cover dates from the early 17C. The choir screen, the choir stalls with their good misericords, and the pulpit, are all also early-17C. Finally, there are some fragments of the old stained-glass windows.

West Walton (3 m. N.): The *Church of St.Mary* was built in *c.* 1240. A curious feature is that the 13C tower stands nearly 65 ft. away from the church. Inside the church are fragments of medieval frescos, and a Gothic font.

Wolverhampton

West Midlands/England   p.328□H 13

This town is named after Wulfruna, the

sister of King Edgar II. She endowed its first collegiate church in 994.

Church of St.Peter: This large church was built in the 15C but some of its foundations are older. The tower and the N. transept were added in the 17C, while the W. front and the sanctuary were rebuilt in 1865. The stone *pulpit,* some of the internal walls, and the octagonal *font,* are all 15C. Parts of the *choir stalls* were brought from Lilleshall Abbey (now ruined) in 1544, and the W. gallery was built in 1610 for the grammar school pupils.

Of the *monuments,* that to Admiral Sir Richard Leveson of Lilleshall stands out, with its bronze statue.

In the churchyard is *Dane's Cross,* a carved column nearly 13 ft. tall, probably dating from the 9C.

Environs: Chillington Hall (7 m. NW): This has been the Giffard family seat since the 12C. Their house was rebuilt in Georgian style in the first half of the 18C, with the S. front being designed by Sir Francis Smith in 1724. The large hall and the main rooms were designed by Sir John Soane in 1785. The park and the artificial lake were laid out by Capability Brown.

Moseley Old Hall (2 m. N.): After losing the battle of Worcester in 1651, Charles II was sheltered in this house, the Elizabethan family seat of the Whitgreaves. His secret hiding-place is on display, as is his bed. The decorations of the house, mostly Elizabethan, are worth looking at.

Weston Park (12 m. NW): This *country house* built in 1671 was the family seat of the Earls of Bradford for 300 years. Today the house is worth visiting for its valuable tapestries and the paintings by Holbein, van Dyck, Gainsborough, Reynolds and others.

Wightwick Manor (2 m. NW): This *half-timbered building* dating from 1887–93 contains a notable art collection: Pre-Raphaelites predominate, and there are

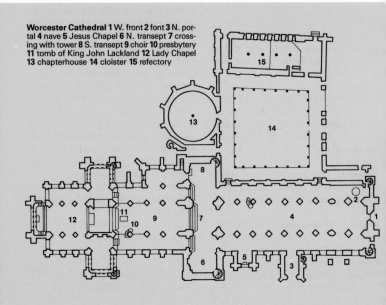

Worcester Cathedral 1 W. front **2** font **3** N. portal **4** nave **5** Jesus Chapel **6** N. transept **7** crossing with tower **8** S. transept **9** choir **10** presbytery **11** tomb of King John Lackland **12** Lady Chapel **13** chapterhouse **14** cloister **15** refectory

works by Ruskin, Burne-Jones, Millais and de Morgan.

Worcester
Hereford and Worcester/England p.328 □ H 14

This city on the lower reaches of the Severn was founded by the Anglo-Saxons, who gave the name of *Wigorna Ceaster* to the settlement which they founded in *c.* 680. Privileges were granted to the city by Richard I (1189) and Henry III (1227), and in 1621 James I elevated it to the status of a county borough. In 1651 Cromwell forced the young Charles II to flee from the city gates. Porcelain has been manufactured here since 1751, and the Royal Worcester Porcelain Company was established in 1862.

Cathedral: This cathedral, with its sturdy 14C tower, stands above the Severn like a fortress. Its history dates back to the late 7C. At that time a church dedicated to St.Peter was built. Bishop Oswald rebuilt it in the 2nd half of the 10C and made it an integral part of a Benedictine monastery. A Norman cathedral was completed in 1089 on the site of the Benedictine church. This cathedral was built under Bishop Wulfstan (1062–95), who was later canonized, and its crypt still survives, being the oldest part of the present cathedral. Miracles were reported at the tomb of Bishop Wulfstan, and a stream of paying pilgrims began to visit Worcester. Their contributions made it possible to start the present cathedral in the early 13C. Work on the Lady Chapel, and also on rebuilding the choir, began in 1224. The nave and transepts were built during the 14C. The

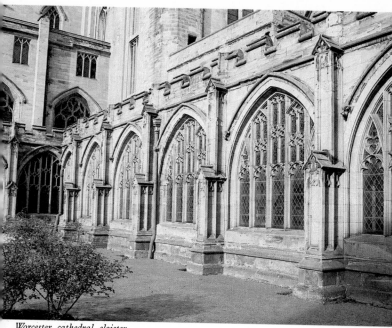

Worcester, cathedral, cloister

200 ft. central tower was completed in 1374.

The oldest and most impressive part of the cathedral is its *crypt* of 1084. It is the second largest apsidal crypt in England, only the crypt of Canterbury Cathedral being larger. Dedicated to St.Oswald, the King of Northumbria who fell in battle in 642, it is situated beneath the raised floor of the presbytery. The *choir* built in 1220–60 is one of the finest choirs in any English cathedral and is comparable to the choir of Beverly Minster. The Lady Chapel, the sanctuary, and the transepts of the choir, are an outstanding example of the transition from the Norman style to the early Gothic and the spandrels of the vault, with their various carvings, are particularly interesting. The pulpit is 16C; the choir stalls Victorian, the earlier 17C ones having been replaced. At the E. end of the presbytery is the tomb of King John Lackland (1199–1216). Although the tomb itself was probably not built until 1504, the marble effigy dates from as early as 1218. It was formerly painted and decorated with jewels.

The *nave* has nine bays, and an aisle on each side. It clearly shows the different periods at which the individual bays were built. The two westernmost bays, begun in 1160, are entirely late Norman, and only the arches, which taper to a point, hint at the Gothic. In the remaining bays, the manner in which the cathedral was built from N. to S. can be exactly retraced. The N. side is still in the early Gothic style, whereas the S. side shows some high Gothic elements. This can also be seen in the arcades of the triforium. The absence of uniformity in style is seen in the transepts more plainly than anywhere else.

Worcester, cathedral, chapterhouse

Here, Norman and Gothic elements are harmoniously juxtaposed, although the Norman dominates.
The *cloister*, rebuilt in 1375, survives from the former Benedictine abbey. It adjoins the S. aisle and it has fine bosses in its vault. S. of the cloister is the refectory dating from 1370. Its finest section is the cellar, where the vaulting is still wholly Norman. The *chapterhouse* is circular and dates from *c.* 1150. It is one of the earliest examples of a vault supported by a central column.

Commandery: Founded by St. Wulfstan, who originally built it as a hospice in 1085. From his death until 1540 it was the seat of an order of knights, and in 1541 Richard Morrison altered it in Renaissance style. Finally, it became the headquarters of the Royalists at the Battle of Worcester.

Guildhall: Built 1721 – 3 to plans by Thomas White, the main body is still in the Queen Anne style, but its façade is already early Georgian. A collection of weapons from the battle of Worcester is on display inside.

Dyson Perins Museum: This is housed in a Victorian former school (1843) and includes a unique collection of Worcester porcelain from 1751 onwards.

Worksop
Nottinghamshire/England   p.328□J 12

Priory Church of Our Lady and St. Cuthbert: The late Norman Transitional *nave*, and the richly decorated *W. front* with its twin towers, both originate from the priory church founded in 1103. The crossing tower and the choir were not completed until 1974 (the church is today the town's parish church). A particular feature inside is the *Lady Chapel*, with its fine 13C Gothic lancet windows.

Gatehouse (S. of the Priory Church): Built in the early 14C; the old *market cross* is outside the entrance. Inside, it still has the original, oak-beamed *roof*; the late Gothic *chapel* is also worth seeing.

Environs: Cresswell Crags (*c.* 5 m. SW): The *limestone caves* were inhabited from Palaeolithic times until the Middle Ages (bone and flint tools have been discovered).
East Markham (*c.* 11 m. SE): Contains the church of *St. John the Baptist* (late Gothic 15C). The remains of the old glass survive, and there is an interesting 19C window by Sir Ninian Comper.
Edwinstowe (*c.* 8 m. S.): Named after the Saxon King Edwin of Northumbria who is buried here. There is a *church* with a fine Gothic tower.
Egmanton (*c.* 11 m. SE): The church o

St.Mary was largely rebuilt by Sir Ninian Comper in 1898 (some remains of the Norman structure survive in the nave).

Laxton (*c.* 12 m. SE): The church of *St. Michael* is 12C; there are interesting 13C tombs inside.

Steetley (*c.* 2 m. W.): With the Romanesque chapel of *All Saints,* standing in an open field. Inside there are some fine Norman arches.

Thoresby Hall (*c.* 6 m. SE): Rebuilt in Victorian style in 1864 after the destruction of the previous building erected by John Carr.

Whitwell (*c.* 3 m. SE): Church of *St. Lawrence* (Norman, with Gothic choir and transept; the items inside include a fine Norman font).

Bramber (Worthing), castle ruins

Worthing
West Sussex/England   p.332☐K 16

This popular seaside resort was originally a fishing village. Princess Amelia, the daughter of George III, discovered it in 1798, and this was the beginning of its development as a seaside resort. The chief attraction is the *Museum* with the adjoining *Art Gallery.* Apart from archaeological finds from the times of the Romans and Saxons, the museum also has a prehistoric collection, 19C toys and dolls, a peep-show theatre, 18C costumes, and a Viking ship built in *c.* 900. The gallery has paintings mainly by English artists such as Holman Hunt, Callow and others, with a special collection of early watercolours.

Environs: Bramber (3 m. NE): Ruins of a *castle* destroyed during the Civil War; in the *House of Pipes* there is an impressive collection of pipes from a period of over 1500 years. *St.Mary's* is also worth seeing: this is a 15C half-timbered house with painted 17C panelling and an interesting collection of butterflies.

Broadwater: This NE part of Worthing has a Norman church, which was restored in the 19C and houses two monuments to the de la Warr family.

Chanctonbury (2 m. NW): A ring of birches planted in the 18C surrounds the remains of an *Iron Age fort* and of a *Roman temple.*

Cissbury Ring (1 m. N.): *Neolithic flint mines* and a 3C *fort.*

Highdown Hill (2 m. W.): In the Iron Age there was a *fort* here above a Bronze Age settlement. A *Roman bath* and a Saxon *graveyard* have also been unearthed during excavations.

Sompting (½ m. E.): The small *St.Mary's Church* is overlooked by a bell tower with a helm roof, the only one of its kind in England. In the 12C the Templars added three chapels to the N. and S. It was given

Sompting (Worthing), St. Mary's Church

Muchelney Abbey (Yeovil), fireplace

its present cruciform ground plan by the Knights of St.John, who added some further chapels.

Steyning (5 m. NE): *St.Andrew's Church,* with a Norman nave, 16C elements, and a 12C font.

Wrexham
Clwyd/Wales   p.328□H 13

This N. Welsh coalmining and industrial town has some 35,000 inhabitants and is English in character.

The only item of interest is the Perpendicular church of *St. Giles* (1472). This fine five-storeyed church is one of the 'seven wonders' of Wales (see its ornaments). The churchyard gate, built by Hugh Davies in 1720, is also of interest.

Environs: Gresford (*c.* 3 m. N.): This village has a fine Perpendicular *parish church* (1460). The tower is built in the Somerset style and contains an important peal of 12 bells.

Notable features inside are the font, the casement windows (the N. chapel has scenes from the life of the Virgin), the pews, and the monuments in the Trevor Chapel (all dating from around 1500). A fine churchyard with old yew trees, planted in *c.* 1714.

Holt (*c.* 4 m. NE): This border town on the Dee has a 13C ruined *castle* and an eight-arched *bridge*. The 14&15C medieval church of *St. Chad* is also worth seeing.

Yeovil

Somerest/England   p.332☐H 16

Church of St. John the Baptist: This large 14C parish church is unusual for having remained predominantly in one architectural style (Perpendicular). It has an impressive *W. tower*, a large *window*, a *transept* of fine proportions and a vaulted *crypt* beneath the sanctuary.

Borough of Yeovil Museum: Local historical exhibits range from prehistoric times to the present day. The firearms collection was donated by Henry Stiby; there is an interesting collection of manuscripts.

Environs: Cadbury Castle (*c.* 7 m. NE): Legend has it that this huge *Stone Age hill fort* became King Arthur's royal seat of Camelot. Excavations have revealed that up to the time of their destruction by the Romans the fortifications had been rebuilt and extended many times; altogether there are five defensive walls with moats.

Huish Episcopi (*c.* 14 m. NW): The *church* has one of the finest towers in Somerset; it dates from the 15C. The stained glass of 1899 is by Burne-Jones; Norman S. portal.

Ile Abbots (*c.* 11 m. NW): Splendid ornate Perpendicular church tower; the S. portal has exquisite tracery.

Ilminster (*c.* 11 m. W.): The *church* has a fine Perpendicular tower; within there are the tombs of Nicholas and Dorothy Wadham. The old *grammar school* was built in 1586.

Lytes Cary (*c.* 9 m. N.): This *manor house* was the seat of the Lyte family for over 500 years. It was begun in 1343 and completed in 1535. The most famous member of the Lyte family was Sir Henry Lyte, who published 'Niewe Herball' (1578), the definitive gardening book of its time.

Montacute House (*c.* 3 m. W.): One of the finest Elizabethan *country houses*, it was built 1588–1601 for Sir Edward Phelips, Speaker of the House of Commons under James I. It has an E-shaped groundplan, many-sectioned windows, Flemish gables and ornate chimneys. Across the gallery on the E. side, niches contain figures of nine great heroes, including Joshua, David, Hector, Alexander, Caesar, Arthur and Charlemagne. Symmetry is strongly in evidence in the garden borders, with their hedges, obelisks and pavilions and also in the house itself, where the huge-dining room and the servants' quarters have almost identical groundplans. The most spacious area is the long gallery on the second floor, which is nearly 200 ft. in length and extends the width of the house. The interior is full of valuable furniture and tapestries, the most valuable being that in the dining-room which depicts a knight in full armour on a magnificently arrayed horse (thought to have come from Tournai in about 1480). About 100 fascinating 16–17C portraits (by courtesy of the National Portrait Gallery) provide a further reason for a visit.

Mulcheney Abbey: (12 m. NW): This, the county's second oldest monastery, was already well established in the 10C. The 14C *Abbot's House*, which has some impressive frescos, still stands. The *parish church* nearby has 17C frescos on the barrel vaults.

York
North Yorkshire/England   p.328☐J 11

In 71BC the Romans made the local settlement into a garrison town known as *Eboracum*, which became the capital of the Roman province of Britannia. It was the residence of many Roman emperors, including Hadrian and Constantine the Great who was proclaimed emperor here. Later, as *Eoforwic*, it was the capital of the Saxon kingdom of Northumbria, and was converted to Christianity in the 7C. In 867 it was conquered by the Danes (who called it *Jorvik*) and, in 1069, by the Normans. In the ensuing years it became one of the main cultural centres of the North. The Archbishop of York bears the title Primate of England. York's unique buildings and fascinating medieval streets make it one of the most interesting towns in the whole of Britain.

Minster: The original building dates from the 7C, during the time of St. Paulinus, first Bishop of York. It was later extended, e.g. by Alkuin in the 8C, who later went to Charlemagne at Aachen, before being destroyed by the Normans in the siege of 1069. The next building was destroyed by fire in 1137. The building we see today was begun shortly after 1100 by Archbishop Walter de Gray and not completed until 1472. Despite the extended period of construction, the combination of styles is not unharmonious. The transept is 13C Early English, nave and chapterhouse are 14C Decorated, and the chancel and tower are 15C Perpendicular. Damaged again by fire in 1829 and 1840, although not structurally, it survived the air raids of the Second World War unharmed (windows were removed). A fire in 1984 damaged the S. transept which is now undergoing extensive restoration.

Groundplan and Exterior: The minster has a nave and two aisles, a long chancel and a transept, both of which are divided into three. The octagonal chapterhouse is attached to the N. transept. The whole structure is *c.* 575 ft. long and 245 ft. wide; over the intersection of nave and transept there is a massive *crossing tower*, some 213 ft. high and 98 ft. wide, whose four sides each have two late Gothic windows. The two W. towers are *c.* 213 ft. high, lack spires but have eight small turrets and a balustrade. The *W. front* has an elaborate Gothic portal, with the Temptation and Expulsion of Adam and Eve from Paradise in the tympanum, above which a magnificent window has stained glass from 1338. The E. front has the famous window (*c.* 85 ft. high, *c.* 10m wide), with the stained glass described at greater length below; beneath it are sculptured figures of Christ and the 12 apostles. The window in the *N. transept* has famous 12C stained glass and is known as the Five Sisters. Until the fire of 1984 the *S. façade* had a fine window with pointed arches and a rose-window.

Interior: The nave is some 278 ft. long, 114 ft, wide and 104 ft. high and has seven *columns* with foliate capitals which separate it from the aisles and support highly decorated pointed arches. The *crossing lantern* is supported by four huge pillars; the gallery can be reached from the S. transept. The lantern itself is intricately decorated. In the S. transept is *St. George's Chapel*, and in the N. *St. John's*, which has memorials to those from Yorkshire military divisions killed in action. Between the crossing and the chancel there is an ornate stone *screen* (organ above) which has 15 statues of English kings; from the late 15C, it is by William Hindley. Behind the chancel is the *Lady Chapel* with its remarkable E. window (see E. front), with over 200 lozenges depicting Biblical scenes (visions of the Kingdom of Heaven, scenes from the Old Testament up to the death of Absalom and images from Revelations). The crypt is predominantly transitional in style, and has remnants of the early cathedral building from the 8C. The Horn of Ulf is an interesting relic. Under the crypt a *pillar pedestal* is attributed to a Roman praetorium of late antiquity.

Interior Furnishings: The most valuable of the church decorations are the numerous stained-glass windows which, in addition to those already mentioned, include the *Cuthbert Window* in the N. transept. Also

of note are the numerous *tombs* of the Archbishops of York in the chancel, including Archbishop Scrope, who was beheaded for high treason by Henry IV (on the left of the Lady Chpel) and Archbishop Walter de Gray (N. aisle of S. transept).

The *chapterhouse* can be reached from the N. transept; it is octagonal, with fine early Decorated windows, six of which contain stained glass from Edward I's time.

Museum Gardens (access from Museum Street): These botanical gardens also have some interesting buildings. The ruins of the **Benedictine Abbey of St. Mary**, which was founded in Norman times, include the church, the guest-house, the gatehouse and the enclosing walls. Every three years, during 'York's Festival of Music and the Arts', a mystery play is performed in front of the ruins. The remnants of **St. Leonhard's Hospital** are 13C.

The **Multangular Tower** was originally the W. corner-tower of the Roman fortress from the 4CAD; the transition from the lower section's Roman brickwork to the

York Minster 1 W. front **2** crossing with tower **3** rood screen **4** S. transept **5** St. George's Chapel **6** entrance to gallery and tower **7** N. portal **8** tomb of Archbishop Walter de Grey **9** Zouche Chapel **10** All Saints' Chapel **11** Lady Chapel with the famous E. window **12** tomb of Archbishop Scrope **13** high altar **14** entrances to crypt **15** presbytery **16** choir **17** N. aisle **18** St. John's Chapel **19** 'Five Sisters' window **20** chapterhouse

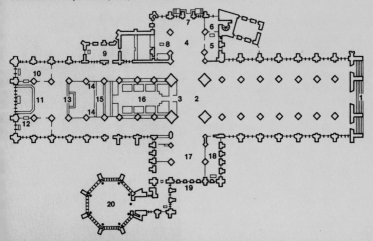

larger medieval upper section can be clearly seen.

Kings Manor (15-17C) is the former residence of the Abbot of St. Mary's. The Yorkshire Museum, in the manor gardens, is described under 'Other Museums'.

Assembly Rooms (Blake Street): Built in Georgian style in 1736. The *Egyptian Hall* (115 ft. long and 39 ft. wide) is interesting.

Clifford's Tower (access from Tower Street or Castle Gate): This is all that remains of the original Norman castle erected by William the Conqueror in 1068-9. The lower section of the former keep is 13C and the groundplan is unusual being quatrefoil (the only other example in England is a tower in Pontefract.) It was used as a prison until 1684, when it was destroyed by an explosion.

Treasurer's House (Minster Yard): This is the former residence of the cathedral treasurer and stands on the site of a previous Roman building (the pedestal of an old Roman pillar is still visible in the cellar). It was originally built in the 13C, but the building we see today dates from the 16-17C. After the Reformation it went into private ownership until shortly after 1930; it is now civic property. There are some fine furnishings dating from the time of its construction.

St. William's College (Minster Yard): The cathedral seminary since the 15C (during the Civil War it was used as a mint and printing press). The *front* of this half-timbered house is medieval; the *portal* in the inner courtyard is Georgian. The interior contains an interesting *staircase* from the 17C, and a fine open roof truss in the main room.

Medieval Guild Houses: Merchant Adventurer's Hall (Piccadilly): Built in

1357-68, it is the finest of York's surviving guild houses. It was used by York's merchants, who were mostly involved in the wool trade (the old scales on which wool was weighed have survived). The *Great Hall*, which is in fine condition, has an open roof truss, and today houses the *Guild Museum*. In the cellar the original oak beams are visible.

Guildhall (on the River Ouse): Built in 1448 and restored faithfully to its original condition in 1960 after being damaged by bombs in World War 2. In the 15C *Committee Room* the English paid a huge ransom to free King Charles I, who was imprisoned by the Scots.

Merchant Taylor's Hall (Aldwark): This is the tailor's guild house, which has been restored; it has fine 17C *glass* and an interesting musicians' *gallery*.

St. Anthony's Hall (Aldwark): Built in the 15C on the site of an 11C hospital; it now houses a *library* with old ecclesiastical documents.

York, Minster

City Walls and Gates: The first fortifications were erected after the Norman conquest in 1069, but most of the walls standing today are 14C in origin. Surrounding the inner city and with a circumference of *c.* 3 m., they are accessible to the public. The most important gates (clockwise from the N.) are:

Monk Bar: Built in 1480 in Decorated style over a still indentifiable Norman structure, this gate has the original portcullis, and a *balcony* for addressing the people (over the middle arch); particularly fine view of the cathedral.

Walmgate Bar: The most recent gate (near the Roman road), it is the only one still to have a watchtower. It still has huge old *oak door leaves*. During the Civil War this gate resisted the artillery of the Republican army.

Micklegate Bar: This was the main entrance to the town from the S. The lower section contains traces of Norman architecture, but the upper section dates from the 14C when it was a powerful fortress. The gate was restored in the 18–19C, when the portcullis was removed. Here, heads of executed criminals were displayed.

Bootham Bar: Built on the site of one of the Roman gates using fabric of the latter. The city's northernmost postern gate, it was the scene of decisive skirmishes against the Scots.

Other Churches of interest: The church of *All Saints* (Pavement) has a fine 15C *tower*. **Holy Trinity Church** (Goodram Gate) is 13C and has interesting 18C *pews*; it is to be found in York's oldest quarter of 14C houses. **Holy Trinity Church** (Micklegate) is part of an old Benedictine abbey and has Norman elements in the nave and aisles. Its *tower* was part of the adjacent church of St.Nicholas which was destroyed in the Civil War. **St. Deny's Church** (Walmgate) has a Norman *portal* and 12C *glass*. The **Church of St. Margaret** (N. of Walmgate) has a Norman *portal* (from the destroyed church of St.Nicholas). The **Church of St. Martin-cum-Gregory**

(Micklegate) has made use of Roman *materials* in the tower; fine 15C *window*. The **Church of St. Martin-le-Grand** (Coney Street) has a *tower* from 1437; the rest of the church has been rebuilt since its destruction in World War 2. **St. Mary's Church** (Castlegate) has the highest *tower* in the city (*c.* 167 ft., 14–15C Perpendicular), which is one of the distinctive features of the York skyline. The church has some fine old stained-glass *windows* and a *stone* with an inscription in Anglo-Saxon. **St. Mary's Church** (Bishophill Junior) has Saxon elements in the tower. **St. Michael's Church** (Low Ousegate) has an interesting *tower* and old stained-glass windows.

Castle Museum (access from Tower Street): Built as a women's prison in 1780, it now houses one of the most interesting local museums in England with three authentically reproduced shopping and industrial streets from old Yorkshire. The old debtor's prison, which is now part of the museum, has original 18C prison cells, a *manuscript collection* (1st floor) and a *military museum* (2nd floor). On the River Foss there is a reconstructed *mill* (early 19C).

Other museums: Yorkshire Museum (Museum Gardens): A natural history museum, which also has exhibitions of Roman and medieval art. The **City Art Gallery** (Museum Gardens) has both old masters and modern works, as well as a collection of Japanese and Chinese art. The **National Railway Museum** (Leeman Road) includes old trains, such as an 1822 model by Stephenson and Wood.

Also worth seeing: *Mansion House* (Lendal) dates from 1726 and was the official residence of the Mayor of York. The *Judge's Lodgings* (Lendal) is a fine Georgian building from 1720.
Some of the streets are interesting, especially the medieval ones, e.g. *The Pave-*

ment, Shambles (a side-street off the Pavement), the old *Butcher's Lane, Goodramgate* and *Micklesgate*, to the W. of the Ouse.

Environs: Beningbrough Hall (*c.* 8 m. NW): An 18C Georgian *manor house* with a particularly fine oak staircase.
Bishopthorpe Palace (*c.* 2 m. S.): The residence of the Archbishop of York since 1266; the 18C palace has a 13C chapel (permission to view required in advance in writing).
Skelton (*c.* 4 m. NW): This village has a fine 13C *church* which is attributed to one of the architects of York cathedral.
Sutton Park (*c.* 8m. N.): An 18C *mansion* with the original interior furnishings; superb porcelain collection.

Youghal
Cork / Ireland   p.330□C 14

The history of this small harbour and seaside resort is closely connected with two important men from the 16 – 17C, Sir Walter Raleigh, Queen Elizabeth I's favourite and 'soldier of fortune' and Richard Boyle, Earl of Cork. Raleigh was executed in 1618 after a lengthy imprisonment in the Tower of London; Richard Boyle moved from being a penniless immigrant in 1588 to become the richest landowner in Ireland.

St. Mary's Church (North Main Street): This Protestant church was built in the 13C on the site of a former religious building; it was extended in 1464 and restored *c.* 1850. The detached *bell tower* is interesting, as are the *W.* and *S. doors* of the cruciform church, the *E. window, oak ceiling, pulpit,* the fine lidded *font* and the episcopal *throne*. There are some interesting *tombs* in the S. transept, some of which are 13C; the most interesting is that of Richard

Ardmore (Youghal), monastery ruins

Boyle, Earl of Cork, which dates from 1620 and has a sculpture of the dead man lying at rest with little figures of his family.

Also worth seeing: Behind St. Mary's church are sections of the old 15–17C *fortifications*. Nearby is *Tynte's Castle*, which was much altered in the 15C. Opposite is the *Red House*, built by a Dutchman in 1706, and also in the High Street is the *Almshouse*, which was founded by Richard Boyle in 1634. The large *bell tower* in the High Street dates from 1777 and has served as a prison; it is now a *museum* of local history. Near St.Mary's is *New College House*, which dates from 1781 and has two fine towers built by Richard Boyle in *c.* 1641. Nearby is the attractive 16C Elizabethan house of *Myrtle Grove*, which was Sir Walter Raleigh's residence. This is said to be the place where the first potatoes and Virginia tobacco were cultivated in Europe.

Environs: Ardmore (*c.* 7m. E.): This coastal village includes remnants of one of the oldest *early Christian settlements* in Ireland. Before St.Patrick's time, St.Declan founded a *monastery* here, to the SE of the village. Among the elements still standing are the finest *round tower* in Ireland (some 100 ft. high) and a simple thick-walled *oratory*, with the reputed grave of St.Declan. *St.Declan's Cathedral* nearby dates from *c.* 1200 and was built on the site of an older structure. It has a late 11C Romanesque nave and a 13C Gothic chancel with three Ogham stones. The pointed arches in the chancel are interesting, and so are the interior walls, but most remarkable is the Romanesque arcading along the old W. front. The rather weathered reliefs depict biblical scenes (Fall of Man, Salome, the

Ardmore (Youghal), wall relief

three Magi). Little *St. Declan's Well* (with reliefs) lies on the coast road. Here too is also a small 12 – 14C *church* known as *Temple Disert*, which is the destination of the St.Declan pilgrimage, on 24 July each year.

List of towns and places of interest mentioned in the Environs sections. The entry in which they appear is indicated by the → symbol